FERTILITY IN DEVELOPING COUNTRIES

FERTILITY IN DEVELOPING COUNTRIES

An Economic Perspective
on Research and Policy
Issues

Edited and introduced by

Ghazi M. Farooq
and
George B. Simmons

Foreword by
Rafael M. Salas

St. Martin's Press   New York

ISBN 0-312-28752-6

Library of Congress Cataloging in Publication Data

Main entry under title:

Fertility in developing countries.
   Bibliography: p.
   Includes index.
   1. Fertility, Human – Developing countries – Addresses,
essays, lectures.   I. Farooq, Ghazi Mumtaz.
II. Simmons, George B., 1940–
HB1108.F46 1985   304.6'32'091724   83–40609
ISBN 0-312-28752-6

Contents

v

List of Figures

List of Tables

Foreword

The dynamics of population in the developing countries during the past 30 years has been unique, and has not only led to a re-examination of traditional explanations for demographic transition, but has also questioned the conventional thinking on the interrelationship between population and development. One of the recent consequences of this has been a closer interaction between the fields of economics and demography. While it is true that the ways in which an economy interrelates with the pattern of population change have always attracted economists, the present interest in the study of that interrelationship is directed towards its implications for policy and programmes in developing countries.

The demographic disequilibrium that we witness in developing countries is the result of net changes in the individual demographic processes of fertility, mortality and migration. While each one of these components is universally important, and while any one of them is more important than the other two in specific situations, fertility assumes the greatest significance in view of its implications for demographic growth, of the urgent need for its regulation so as to achieve health and development gains, and of the difficulties of identifying effective policies and programmes for fertility regulation.

In this context, the present volume is indeed a welcome addition to the literature on population policies in general, and on fertility dynamics in particular. The volume has achieved a delicate balance between theory and empirical analyses. While it presents multiple views on the subject-matter, it also makes an attempt to synthesise them. The case-studies (Costa Rica, India, Kenya, Mexico, Nigeria, Turkey and Yugoslavia) illustrate the great variations that exist in the socio-economic context of reproduction in developing regions, and their inclusion in the volume makes the comparative analysis extremely meaningful.

In the various contributions to the book, constant references are made to the relationship between fertility and such variables as the level of infant and child mortality, the distribution of income, the availability of alternative roles for women, and the ease of access to family-planning services. Thus, fertility emerges as a variable which both influences and is influenced by a wide range of economic and social factors.

Further aspects of the volume that are particularly noteworthy are the strong plea it makes for research to be directly relevant to policy-making and programme-formulation, and the emphasis given to the role of government and policy processes in the development of population programmes.

It is a pleasure to welcome this volume, and to congratulate the editors and the International Labour Office on making it available to a wide audience.

New York   RAFAEL M. SALAS
Executive Director
United Nations Fund for Population Activities

Preface

Population growth and its consequences have been a concern of economists since the inception of the modern science of political economy. Thomas Malthus, in *A First Essay on Population* (1798), argued that there was a conflict between population and the standard of living. David Ricardo and John Stuart Mill in the early and mid-1800s and, following them, others known for their contributions to the development of classical economic theory, also treated the relationship between population growth and economic growth as part of the main body of economic theory.

In modern times, population issues came to the forefront when the low population growth experienced by the developing countries prior to the Second World War was transformed into unprecedented rates of natural increase during the 1960s and 1970s. In many countries, large-scale family-planning programmes were instituted to help curb what were seen to be excessively rapid population growth rates. These programmes were viewed by both national governments and the international donor community as an adequate and ready-made solution to population problems. In most cases, these high expectations were not met. Family-planning programmes did not have nearly as much impact on population growth as was originally expected. It was, therefore, no surprise that at the first intergovernmental meeting on population, the 1974 United Nations World Population Conference in Bucharest, it was officially recognised that the solutions to population problems were to be found within the context of broad-based social and economic development.

Even when the population policy objective is limited to a reduction in fertility level, which appears to be the case in many Asian and some Latin American and African countries, a more comprehensive population and development programme, not simply a family-planning programme, may be required to achieve this goal. According to the recent United Nations Inquiry among governments on population and development (United Nations, 1980), 46 developing countries, including four-fifths of the total population of less-developed regions, wanted lower rates of natural increase. Empirical evidence obtained from a number of country studies conducted under the auspices of the ILO (International Labour Organi-

xix

sation) programme mentioned below, from the case-studies included in this volume, and from elsewhere, seem to indicate that often a decline in fertility is associated with an improvement in the roles and status of women, restrictions on child labour, reductions in child and infant mortality, and reductions in the incidence of poverty and inequality in income distribution. The evidence on each of these points is complex, but it seems clear that fertility reduction is part of a broad pattern of social change. As a result, the expansion of family-planning schemes without identifying the factors responsible for high fertility might very well turn out to be self-defeating. Moreover, the design and implementation of family-planning programmes may be greatly strengthened by an awareness of the context in which fertility and contraception decisions are taken. It is in this broad context that the present volume could be helpful particularly to researchers and data collectors in developing countries, who have the responsibility for conducting policy-relevant fertility research that can provide guidelines for the designing of policies and action programmes. The volume will also be of interest to students of population economics, and to government officials with policy-making responsibilities, especially economic planners.

The present study has a long history. In 1972, the United Nations Fund for Population Activities (UNFPA) began providing generous support to a programme of research and action on population and employment based in the ILO. From the start, this programme identified the determinants of fertility as a crucial issue if the impact of population growth on income, employment and inequality were to be better understood. Papers and monographs resulting from this programme cover a variety of aspects of population and employment, but fertility is a dominant theme; a number of publications (ILO, 1982) dealt with attitudes to fertility, aspects of household economics, community-level factors, the interactions between work and fertility, and a range of other relevant issues. The origins of the present volume lay in a desire to distil some general conclusions from this research. Though this remains one objective, the volume also brings together new material and draws upon new ideas emerging from current economic–demographic research in academic circles as well as in the ILO. At the same time, technical cooperation in the field of population and development has gained substantially in importance. Many of the contributors from the ILO, including one of the editors, are deeply involved in these activities. This helps reinforce the policy focus of the present work.

The volume contains an examination of the more important theories of fertility, with an attempt at a particularly thorough treatment of general problems associated with economic models of fertility. This examination is then used as a basis for suggesting elements of an improved framework for the study of fertility. To this end, a number of methodological and measurement problems involved in the analysis of fertility differentials and behaviour are identified. The idea, to reiterate, is to show how research strategies can be devised so that the results of research are immediately useful as inputs to the formulation of effective policies and action programmes in the field of population or in related areas of social concern such as education and employment.

The first part of the book, consisting of four chapters, provides a survey of major theories of fertility and their limitations, suggests ways of making such theories more policy-relevant and theoretically adequate, and looks at the implications of fertility research for policy and action. The second part, consisting of six chapters, discusses methodological issues, including the definition (and measurement) of fertility and key explanatory variables, and empirical questions such as time-series versus cross-section and pooling techniques, aggregation and specification problems, simulation/econometric approaches, and the use of anthropological techniques and theories to supplement economic approaches. The final part, consisting of seven chapters, includes a set of six empirical case-studies based on survey and/or national population census data from Kenya, Nigeria, India, Turkey, Yugoslavia, Mexico and Costa Rica, respectively. The last chapter deals with the effects of income redistribution on fertility, using cross-sectional data for a sample of developing countries. It might be mentioned that many of the case-studies were undertaken prior to the preparation of the Part I and Part II chapters. Hence, the reader should recognise that while the case-studies present important empirical findings and methodological insights, they do not consistently illustrate the empirical or theoretical methods that we recommend in Part I. Thus, the state of rapid evolution in the field of fertility research is reflected in this volume.

The various chapters reflect the views of their respective authors, although there has been an extensive exchange of ideas during their preparation. The usual disclaimer is warranted here: studies included in the volume represent the views of their authors and not necessarily those of the ILO and other contributors. Since the country case-studies deal with the same theme, some repetition is unavoidable but, by the same token, the diversity in the analytical approaches employed by the authors is highlighted.

Given its rather ambitious scope, the book has been under preparation for a long time. The editors give special thanks to the contributors for the care they have taken in preparing their papers. We are also very grateful for the comments and assistance provided at various stages of preparation of the volume, in alphabetical order, by Richard Anker, Charles Calhoun,

Enyinna Chuta, Deborah DeGraff, Kailas Doctor, Janet Farooq, Jason Finkle, Rolph Van Der Hoeven, Eric Jensen, Ashok Madan, Gerry Rodgers, René Wéry and a score of other colleagues. We should also like to thank Lucie de Vries and Nancy Wolfe who did a major part of the typing, and Jane Mackie-Mason, Murali Vemuri and Nancy Biller for research and editorial assistance. Finally, we express our gratitude to UNFPA for providing generous financial support for the programme under which this book was prepared. The editorship is named alphabetically since the two editors of this book shared the work and responsibilities *equally*.

We do not regard this volume as the final word in the rapidly changing, and often disputed, field of fertility research. Rather, it is one step in an ongoing programme, a review and reassessment of the issues, which may advance the debate. If this volume raises the interest of readers in critically analysing the determinants of fertility, and increases their ability to do so, then it will have well served its purpose.

GHAZI M. FAROOQ
GEORGE B. SIMMONS

Notes on the Contributors

The contributors to this volume represent a wide variety of countries and backgrounds and are all well known in the field of population and development economics. They have all done research on the problems of more than one developing country, and each has to his/her credit a number of important publications in areas varying from fertility, family planning and role of women to employment, income distribution, poverty and development.

The following is a list of the contributors with their affiliations:

The editors

Ghazi M. Farooq, International Labour Office, Geneva

George B. Simmons, Center of Population Planning, University of Michigan

The other contributors

Richard Anker, International Labour Office, Geneva

Mark Browning, Department of Economics, University of Illinois

Lee E. Edlefsen, Department of Economics, University of Washington

Gerardo González, United Nations Latin America Demographic Center, Santiago

Samuel S. Lieberman, Population Council, New York

Miroslav Macura, Population Division, United Nations, New York

Richard T. Monteverde, Harvard University

Christine Oppong, International Labour Office, Geneva

Gerry B. Rodgers, International Labour Office, Geneva

M. T. R. Sarma, Consultant with the International Labour Office, Regional Office in Bangkok

Boone A. Turchi, Department of Economics and the Carolina Population Center, University of North Carolina

Andras Uthoff, Regional Employment Programme for Latin America and the Caribbean, ILO, Santiago

René Wéry, International Labour Office, Geneva

C. R. Winegarden, Department of Economics, University of Toledo

PART I: OVERVIEW

As I have pointed out elsewhere, short of nuclear war itself, it
[population] is the gravest issue that the world faces over the
decades immediately ahead . . . it inevitably is: a central determinant of humanity's future, and one requiring far more attention than it is currently receiving.

> Statement by Robert S. McNamara in his Address to the
> Board of Governors of the World Bank, Belgrade, 1979
> (quoted in Roth and Little, 1981).

1 Introduction

GEORGE B. SIMMONS and GHAZI M. FAROOQ

During the last 30 years, most countries have experienced gains in almost all measures of human welfare. Life expectancy has improved, per capita incomes have increased, and literacy and education have been extended to a larger proportion of the population. While widespread, these gains have not been evenly distributed, nor can it be assumed that they will continue. To assure their continuation, policy-makers need to understand the broader social and economic forces that underlie current trends. Changes in population have been strongly associated with the recent period of economic and social transformation. This volume is intended to improve our understanding of one important aspect of population growth – fertility.

Economists have had a long-standing interest in the relationship between population growth and economic transformation. The macro-economic analysis undertaken almost 200 years ago by Malthus, Ricardo and J. S. Mill treated population growth as a central element in the process of economic change. The central role awarded to population is continued in the work of many contemporary economists working on development problems. Population growth and fertility are recognised to have direct and indirect effects on most measures of well-being, and changes in the human condition influence fertility. For example, population growth affects the denominator of per capita income and also has a relatively direct, although delayed, effect on the size of the labour force, and thus on employment goals. Perhaps more importantly, it indirectly influences almost all aspects of the social environment within which national development planners work to promote increased levels of well-being.

The relationships between population growth and social and economic change are exceedingly complex, and many of the factors involved are poorly understood. Research in the areas can be justified just in terms of the widespread scholarly interest in a subject area so closely tied to the conditions of life for the people of the world. It is also clear, however, that anticipating and adjusting for population growth is essential if policy goals are to be met (Anker and Farooq, 1978; Farooq, 1981). As the experience of Third World countries has shown, rapid population growth has many social and economic consequences.

3

These consequences relate to the whole range of economic and social conditions in both developed and developing countries. Whether they are positive or negative, they will be of concern to policy-makers. Educational systems, health, food and housing needs, the quantity and quality of the labour force, the nature of markets for consumers and producers – these are all influenced by population growth. With an improved understanding of the forces that shape population growth and its relationship to social transformation, policy-makers will be better positioned to anticipate changes and influence the outcomes.

THIS VOLUME

This volume has three major objectives. The first is to present a review, with emphasis on economic research, of the current state of knowledge, both theoretical and empirical, of the determinants of fertility. This chapter serves as a general introduction to the subject, and the following three chapters deal in more detail with the current state of theories of fertility, related empirical findings, research problems of an empirical nature and the application of research methods and findings to policy-making. On the basis of our review, we suggest some of the new directions that we think will be important during the coming years.

A second purpose of the volume is to examine some of the chief methodological issues in the empirical study of fertility. Since fertility is obviously a complex subject and is, in many respects, more complicated than other areas of economic research, the appropriate methods of research need special attention. These methodological issues seem particularly important at this time when there is an expanded level of fertility analysis made possible by the existence and availability of fertility data collected through the World Fertility Survey and other programmes.

The third objective of this study is to present some new empirical studies of fertility, most of which have been sponsored by the International Labour Office (ILO) as a part of its Population and Employment Research Programmes which are funded by the United Nations Fund for Population Activities (UNFPA). We believe that these studies shed new light on fertility issues, and illustrate some of the methods that can be effectively utilised in the study of fertility.

Fertility-related research has long been the subject of partisan debate. The subject undoubtedly warrants extensive scientific attention, given its close relationship to many other aspects of economic and social development. We recognise, however, that there will be many grounds for a policy concern with fertility, and that policy formulation depends both on scientific inputs concerning the way in which given activities might affect national policy goals, and on normative decisions concerning what those goals should be in the first place. Fertility research is relevant whether a country has a pro- or anti-natalist policy, or whether its primary concern is anticipating the labour supply and employment implications of past fertility.

PATTERNS OF POPULATION GROWTH

World population has grown at unprecedentedly high rates during the past several decades, and much of the growth has been in developing countries. As Table 1.1 shows, between 1950 and 1980 the population of the world grew at an average annual rate of approximately 2 per cent. This aggregate percentage masks the considerable diversity that exists among and within different regions: the well-off 'developed' countries have a rate of population growth much lower than that of poorer nations. Wealthy countries tend to grow at less than 1 per cent per year and poor countries at more than 2 per cent per year. Moreover, among the poorer nations, population growth rates vary between $1\frac{1}{2}$ per cent to more than $3\frac{1}{2}$ per cent per year.

Rates of natural increase[1] vary from one country and time period to another, depending on the combination of fertility and mortality levels. Table 1.2 shows birth and death rates for various regions of the world during 1975–80. Prior to this century, mortality rates were generally much higher than they are today, and the fertility rates of populations tended to be correspondingly high. In our time, this equilibrium has been altered, largely due to a dramatic decline in mortality. Explanations of this decline range from the success of public health measures in controlling infectious disease, to the general improvement of economic conditions (Preston, 1980). In any event, it is a universal phenomenon that mortality has declined, and that the decline has been dramatic in many of the developing countries. Fertility remained at high levels, and the result has been a high rate of natural increase in much of the Third World.

The recent gradual, but significant, decline in world fertility levels has not been shared by all countries or regions. Instead, the decline tends to be concentrated in certain areas of the larger countries of Asia, and, to some extent, among countries of Latin America. For example crude birth rates in Asia, where the statistics are dominated by China and India, tend to be

TABLE 1.1 *Total population size and average annual rates of growth, by major regions, 1950–80*

Region	Mid-year Population (millions)		Average annual rate of growth (per cent)					
	1950	1980	1950–5	1955–60	1960–5	1965–70	1970–5	1975–80
World	2524	4432	1.76	1.94	1.99	1.95	1.91	1.72
More developed	831	1131	1.28	1.27	1.19	0.87	0.84	0.71
Less developed	1692	3300	1.99	2.25	2.33	2.38	2.32	2.08
Africa	220	469	2.12	2.34	2.48	2.59	2.73	2.90
South Asia	716	1403	1.85	2.19	2.40	2.44	2.36	2.22
East Asia	673	1174	1.84	2.00	1.94	2.01	1.96	1.38
Japan	83	116	1.43	0.93	0.99	1.07	1.33	0.88
China	556	994	1.98	2.09	2.02	2.11	2.02	1.40
Latin America	164	363	2.73	2.75	2.80	2.66	2.54	2.45
North America	166	247	1.80	1.78	1.49	1.12	0.86	0.95
Europe	391	483	0.79	0.83	0.91	0.64	0.63	0.40
Oceania	12	22	2.25	2.18	2.08	1.97	1.85	1.47
Australia and New Zealand	10	17	2.33	2.18	1.99	1.85	1.68	1.21
Soviet Union	180	265	1.71	1.77	1.49	0.91	0.95	0.93

SOURCE United Nations, 1982.

TABLE 1.2 *Vital rates for major world regions, 1975–80*

Region	Births per 1000 population 1975–80	Deaths per 1000 population 1975–80
World	28.5	11.4
More developed	15.8	9.4
Less developed	33.0	12.1
Africa	46.0	17.2
South Asia	37.1	14.8
East Asia	21.0	7.3
Japan	15.1	6.3
China	21.3	7.4
Latin America	33.6	8.9
North America	16.3	9.1
Europe	14.4	10.5
Oceania	21.8	9.0
Australia and New Zealand	16.8	7.9
Soviet Union	18.3	9.0

SOURCE United Nations, 1982.

less than 30 per year, while in Latin America they range from the 20s to the 40s. In western and eastern Africa, crude birth rates remain at levels near 50 per thousand population. There are also extensive variations in fertility levels over time and among regions or social and economic groups within individual countries.

These regional variations in fertility are likely to persist for some time, thus continuing the major differences in the population growth patterns among these regions. All the United Nations projections (UN, 1982) show high rates of population growth during the last quarter of the century. Even the lowest projection suggests that world population will be only slightly less than six thousand million persons in the year 2000, as compared with four thousand million in 1975. The high projections suggest a world population of six and a half thousand million by the year 2000, and the range of estimates increases consistently for later years.

REASONS FOR INTEREST IN FERTILITY RESEARCH

Fertility is inextricably bound up with many aspects of economic and social behaviour. Consequently, an understanding of fertility behaviour may yield information on a wide range of social and economic phenomena, such as labour force participation, income distribution, and educational aspirations for children. Fertility and population growth are such major elements in the process of development that they would excite keen scholarly interest even if the policy implications of fertility were obscure.

However, an ability to specify the magnitude of changes in fertility, and the causes of those changes, is required background information for the development of policy in many areas. Examples abound. For the projection of expenditure on primary education, the analyst must know the number of children who may be enrolled, and such projections make use of data concerning fertility and levels of child survival. Labour force projections of an intermediate or long-run nature also require knowledge of fertility patterns. Even more obviously, knowledge about fertility is required for the design of policies that are likely to have direct or indirect effects on fertility. It is equally important to the extent that policy-makers wish to manipulate demographic variables to affect levels of economic development or to achieve other desired outcomes.

These concerns are especially strongly felt where high levels of fertility are perceived to represent an obstacle to development. As the Planning Commission of the Government of Pakistan observed: 'A vicious circle is set in motion in which high fertility and socio-economic stagnation breed upon each others.' (Pakistan, Government of, 1978.) Solutions to this type of problem are likely to be built on a thorough understanding of the relationship between economic development and fertility patterns.

The results obtained from the recent UN Inquiry among Governments on Population and Development are instructive (United Nations, 1980). Governments of fewer than half of the developing countries (46 out of 116), as compared with three-quarters of the developed countries (32 out of 42), felt that the advantages of their current natural increase rates outweighed the disadvantages. The difference between the perceptions of developed countries and developing countries was, however, all the more remarkable when seen in terms of the proportions of populations covered. Only 17 per cent of the population of the developing countries, compared with 85 per cent of the population of the developed countries, had governments which were of the view that the advantages of natural increase rates outweighed the disadvantages. Whereas none of the industrialised countries wanted lower natural increase rates, this was stated to be the objective of

46 of the developing countries, representing four-fifths of the total population of less developed regions. Fourteen developed and 58 developing countries were reported to have taken actions to modify fertility. In order to lower the rates of natural increase, governments in 32 developing countries (representing 78 per cent of the total population of less-developed regions) considered 'full intervention appropriate', and in 8 developing countries 'some support appropriate'.

As is evident from Tables 1.3 and 1.4, a breakdown by region shows substantial differences in the perception and policies of governments with respect to the population growth rates. The proportion of countries dissatisfied with their current rates is highest among the countries covered by the Economic and Social Commission for Asia and the Pacific (ESCAP) – 16 out of 30 countries, including 90 per cent of the total population of the region, viewed their rates as too high, and considered full intervention appropriate. On the other extreme, none of the 12 countries in the area of the Economic Commission of Western Asia (ECWA) wanted to lower the rates, and five countries (accounting for about one-quarter of the total population in the area) wished to increase population growth rates.

The case, therefore, seems clear for a strong policy interest in fertility, its determinants and its consequences. The case may be most strongly felt in those countries that wish to reduce fertility, but knowledge about fertility may also be important in those places where the government feels no need for fertility control or where, as in some Middle Eastern and European countries, there is a desire to raise fertility levels. Because fertility affects so many social and economic objectives, an understanding of its dynamics and its determinants is an almost universal requirement for planning.

Policy-makers' interest in the nature and content of fertility-related research depends on their ranking of policy objectives and their perception of how an understanding of fertility will help them achieve their policy goals. For example, the projection of fertility requires the understanding of a set of relationships different than for the formulation of fertility policy. Moreover, since fertility projection involves the estimation of changes in fertility over time, it may be important to study fertility in its time context rather than examining it from the point of view of cross-sectional differences in fertility among the households or regions involved.

The importance of and difficulties involved in integrating demographic variables into overall social and economic planning are highlighted in a recent paper by Farooq (1981). As summarised in the report of the UNFPA conference on Population and Development Planning (1979a, p. 24), there are still many problems:

TABLE 1.3 *Governments' perceptions of the effect of natural increase on development, its acceptability and the desirability of intervention to change rates, by areas of responsibility of regional commissions[a] and level of development, July 1978*

Government perceptions of the effect of natural increase as a constraint on development, and the desirability of intervention

	Rates too low — *Higher rates desirable*			Rates neither too low nor too high — *Neither higher nor lower rates desirable — No intervention appropriate*			Rates too high — *Lower rates desirable*		Total
	Effect of constraints						*Effect of constraints*		
	Predominant (A) — Full intervention appropriate (1)	Significant (B) — Some support appropriate (2)	Minor (C) (3)	No constraints (4)	Minor (C) (5)		Significant (B) — Some support appropriate (6)	Predominant (A) — Full intervention appropriate (7)	(Total)
ECA[a] area									
Eastern Africa	1	–	–	1	7		1	5	15
Middle Africa	4	–	2	–	3		–	–	9
Northern Africa	1	–	–	1	1		–	3	6
Southern Africa	–	–	–	–	–		–	4	4
Western Africa	2	–	1	2	8		2	1	16
Total	8	–	3	4	19		3	13	50
ECWA[a] area									
Western South Asia[b]	4	1	1	1	5		–	–	12
ECLA[a] area									
Caribbean	–	–	–	1	–		1	6	8
Middle America	–	–	–	–	2		3	2	7
Temperate South America	2	–	–	–	1		–	–	3
Tropical South America	1	1	–	2	4		1	–	9
Total	3	1	–	3	7		5	8	27

								Total
ECE[a] area								
Eastern Europe[c]	2	–	3	1	–	–	–	6
Northern Europe[c]	–	3	4	–	–	–	–	7
Southern Europe[c]	–	2	3	3	–	–	1	9
Western Europe[c]	4	2	1	1	–	–	1	9
Cyprus, Israel and Turkey	1	–	–	–	–	1	1	3
Northern America[c]	–	–	1	1	–	–	–	2
USSR[c]	–	–	–	–	–	–	3	3
Total	7	7	12	6	–	1	6	39
ESCAP[a] area								
China	–	–	–	–	–	1	–	1
Japan[c]	–	–	–	1	–	–	–	1
Other East Asia	2	–	–	–	–	1	–	3
Eastern South Asia	2	–	1	2	–	4	–	9
Middle South Asia	–	–	1	1	–	6	1	9
Australia and New Zealand[c]	–	1	–	1	–	–	–	2
Melanesia	–	–	–	–	–	1	–	1
Micronesia-Polynesia	1	–	–	–	–	3	–	4
Total	5	1	2	5	–	16	1	30
More developed regions	8	8	12	9	–	–	5	42
Less developed regions	19	1	10	33	8	38	7	116
Total	27	9	22	42	8	38	12	158

11

[a] For countries in each area, see annex table 38 in the source. ECA refers to the Economic Commission for Africa, ECWA to the Economic Commission for Western Asia, ECLA to the Economic Commission for Latin America, ECE to the Economic Commission for Europe, and ESCAP to the Economic Commission for Asia and the Pacific.

[b] Excluding Cyprus, Israel and Turkey.

[c] More developed regions.

SOURCE   United Nations, 1980, Table 13.

TABLE 1.4 *Percentage of the population by category of view of the consequences of current rates of natural increase, areas of responsibility of regional commisions and level of development*

	Higher rates desirable	Neither higher nor lower rates desirable	Lower rates desirable	Total
ECA area	7	60	33	100
ECWA area	24	76	0	100
ECLA area	11	56	33	100
ECE area	40	56	4	100
ESCAP area	1	9	90	100
More developed regions	37	63	0	100
Less developed regions	3	17	80	100
Total	13	30	57	100

SOURCE United Nations, 1980, Table 10.

a lack of adequate demographic information; the poor use habitually made of this information in formulating plans; the lacunae still apparent in an understanding of the complex inter-relationships between population and policies, the content of which penetrates into all spheres of development planning; and lastly, the internationally accepted normative framework regulating the instruments used to achieve such policies.

Population growth and fertility have been researched, subjected to theoretical speculation and targeted by various kinds of social and economic policy for 20 years or more. Despite all this attention, there exists relatively little consensus on the underlying determinants of fertility behaviour or the policy measures that may affect population growth.

A variety of government and private interventions to influence population growth have been attempted. During the past 15 years, population programmes have received considerable funding. But these outward indications of action are not based on any widespread agreement on the fundamental issues involved. There is little indication that a consensus is emerging on the magnitude of the problem constituted by high fertility, nor is there agreement about what will be most effective in accomplishing policy objectives, or even on what kind of framework should be used for the study of fertility.

The level of disagreement that still exists concerning fertility and its determinants can be illustrated by reference to the heated discussions that have ensued during the past 10 years over alternative policy interventions in the area. In some measure, this controversy is part of a larger debate about the best means of achieving goals of material well-being and social justice for people living in the Third World. Some believe that no form of intervention is likely to bring about fertility reduction unless there is immediate progress toward the goal of general development and toward a fundamental revolution in living conditions. This school of thought is often associated with the slogan raised at the 1974 Bucharest World Population Conference: 'Development is the best contraceptive.' Others argue that specific interventions aimed toward regulating fertility can and will have a large impact on population change even before the onset of substantial development in other areas. The debate is not about the larger social goal of increasing the standard of living for people of the Third World, but about the means by which this goal can be achieved, and specifically, whether population-related interventions have a useful role.

Even among those who support efforts to reduce fertility, there is disagreement about the most effective approach. An example is provided by the sharp differences of opinion between supporters of family planning and sceptics about the observable impact of family-planning programmes. Bogue and Tsui (1979), for example, claim that programmes have been a major factor in the recent declines in fertility experienced by a number of developing countries. Demeny (1979a, 1979b) argues that the observed reductions in fertility are more logically attributable to fundamental social and economic forces.

Differences of opinion about appropriate policy interventions are often based on varying perceptions of the underlying determinants of fertility. Some argue that fertility is basically a rational process and that individuals or couples will adjust their fertility to their own personal goals. Others argue that the basic determinants of fertility lie in social structure and that, generally, control of fertility lies beyond the realm of individual initiative. Research may shed light on the importance of different factors influencing fertility.

AN ECONOMIC APPROACH TO THE STUDY OF FERTILITY

There are several reasons for thinking that economic analysis may have a particularly important role in the study of fertility. One reason is that many surveys indicate that people in both developed and developing countries think of childbearing as having major economic consequences for their families. There is also evidence that economic consequences exert a considerable influence on couples' reproductive decisions. Thus, in terms of the subjective self-assessments of individuals making fertility decisions, the trade-offs between children and other personal objectives of a material nature – that is, economic calculations – are of considerable importance. Tables 1.5 and 1.6, drawn from the work of the Value of Children Project (Fawcett *et al.*, 1974), illustrate the general proposition. A significant proportion of parents from all of the countries covered by the project report that the cost of having children or the conflict between childrearing and other objectives is seen as a disadvantage of having children. Parents also often report that children can play a positive economic role for the family in terms of work contributions or old-age security and other parental objectives. Thus, desired fertility is, for many parents, a balance between the costs and benefits of having children.

Parental recognition of the economic gains and losses associated with fertility would be of little interest if parents could not exercise significant control over fertility. But there are many indications that fertility behaviour is purposive – that is, people adjust their fertility to the larger goals in their lives. Coale (1973) has observed that such behaviour was a precondition of the demographic transition: people had to have distinct ideas about the number of children they wanted, and needed to feel that they had some measure of control, before fertility could begin to decrease. Similarly, Tabbarah (1971) has argued that the high fertility of many African societies is deliberate. Couples plan to have large families because such behaviour is consistent with other goals.

One bit of evidence for the idea that fertility is in some degree purposive comes from the literature on attitude–behaviour consistency. A large number of studies have now been done (Knodel and Prachuabmoh, 1973; Kar, 1978; L. C. Coombs, 1979b; McClelland, 1979, Hermalin *et al.*, 1979; Hendershot and Placek, 1981) that illustrate the relatively high correlation between survey responses to questions about the number of children people want to have, and their subsequent behaviour.

There is also evidence that this consistent and goal-oriented behaviour is natural in the sense that it corresponds to people's own sense of priorities, providing some face validity to the notion that fertility is rational, at least in part, and that economic methods can therefore contribute to research in this area (Blandy, 1974). Perhaps because, in a wide range of countries and settings, fertility behaviour is in significant measure an outcome of a process of choice, economic approaches to the study of fertility have

TABLE 1.5 *Advantages of having children: percentage of respondents who mentioned at least one advantage under each of specified major code categories, by socio-economic (SES) group and country*

SES group and country	Happiness, love, companionship	Personal development of parent	Childrearing satisfactions	Economic benefits security	Benefits to family unit	Kin-group benefits	Social, religious influences	General intrinsic value of children	Other advantages
URBAN MIDDLE									
Republic of Korea	69	39	54	12	25	15	5	5	1
Japan	61	29	37	7	28	3	4	1	a
United States (Hawaii)									
Japanese	74	48	47	15	51	21	4	17	7
Caucasian	73	66	61	14	40	23	8	15	5
Philippines	79	34	17	80	26	8	5	6	a
Thailand	67	35	8	20	42	23	5	1	7
URBAN LOW									
Republic of Korea	72	39	42	25	30	23	2	1	1
Japan	69	21	36	9	35	4	1	2	a
United States (Hawaii)									
Japanese	84	55	43	22	33	18	1	17	1
Caucasian	66	54	55	13	34	17	1	18	5
Filipino	86	22	13	76	20	21	a	3	2
Philippines	83	29	21	84	17	16	8	6	a
Thailand	35	6	3	80	6	18	4	1	4
RURAL									
Republic of Korea	56	22	42	45	4	32	11	6	2
Japan	63	17	46	19	14	11	1	3	a
United States (Hawaii)									
Filipino	90	19	5	96	6	12	a	4	a
Philippines	68	17	20	91	13	6	4	6	a
Thailand	25	3	3	76	4	37	13	1	0

a Less than 1 per cent

SOURCE Fawcett *et al.*, 1974.

TABLE 1.6 Disadvantages of having children: percentage of respondents who mentioned at least one disadvantage under each of specified major code categories, by socio-economic group and country

SES group and country	Financial costs	Emotional costs	Physical demands on parents	Restrictions on alternative activities	Marital problems	Kin-group costs, problems of inheritance	Societal costs, overpopulation	Other disadvantages
URBAN MIDDLE								
Republic of Korea	41	56	15	51	24	a	a	3
Japan	42	38	6	57	12	a	a	a
United States (Hawaii)								
Japanese	31	50	12	70	7	1	a	5
Caucasian	49	66	12	79	15	a	1	5
Philippines	60	82	15	37	2	a	a	1
Thailand	44	56	15	19	a	1	a	2
URBAN LOW								
Republic of Korea	69	60	8	25	6	a	1	2
Japan	40	49	9	54	2	a	a	a
United States (Hawaii)								
Japanese	42	45	16	82	9	3	4	3
Caucasian	43	51	3	63	8	a	2	6
Filipino	68	74	23	50	1	a	a	3
Philippines	56	75	12	33	3	a	1	1
Thailand	61	38	9	18	a	a	a	8
RURAL								
Republic of Korea	46	63	7	21	4	a	a	2
Japan	43	45	5	33	3	1	1	2
United States (Hawaii)								
Filipino	90	82	30	57	a	a	2	1
Philippines	57	74	12	23	a	a	a	a
Thailand	54	36	31	21	1	1	a	2

a Less than 1 per cent

SOURCE: Fawcett et al., 1984.

yielded levels of explanation quite comparable with those yielded by other disciplines such as sociology, where fertility has been a strong traditional focus. Cross-disciplinary comparisons are difficult, especially because economists have just begun to come to grips with the questions raised by fertility research, but we expect that economic research will lead to an improved understanding of many aspects of fertility, particularly from the point of view of providing action guidelines.

A quite different ground for thinking that economics is important in the study of fertility is that if societies are to make general choices related to economic development, many of the professionals who are involved in trying to define those choices will be economists. It is important for them to understand the role of fertility within the context of the larger choices that society faces.

One should not assume that rational or utilitarian models of fertility are found only in the field of economics, or that the study of the economics of fertility is restricted to economists. Hass (1974) has presented a model of fertility decision-making that is based on a non-economic approach to decisions. Nag *et al.* (1978, 1980, 1981) has contributed to an understanding of the role of economic factors through his analysis of ethnographic studies from the Third World. In Chapter 10 of this volume, Oppong presents an anthropological view of the economics of fertility behaviour.

It should also be noted that there are some aspects of fertility that do not fit the simplest notions of rational or goal-oriented behaviour. Conflict between sexual needs and family-size desires or poor communication between husbands and wives may lead to behaviour inconsistent with the ideals of rational behaviour. There may also be psychological processes that lead to fertility patterns not easily described within a rational framework (Hoffman, 1974; Horner, 1972; Hoffman and Hoffman, 1973). Alternative approaches to understanding fertility decisions (or non-decisions) are reviewed by Burch (1981).

It may also be argued that rationality at the societal level is perhaps more important than rationality at the level of the individual or couple. With the exception of studies relating to government decisions, sociology as a discipline may have more to say about this level of societal rationality than has economics.

It is important to define the dimensions of the role of economics in the study of fertility. At both the micro and the macro level, it is useful to think of fertility as mediated by a set of variables defining exposure to intercourse, the probability of conception, and the probability of successful gestation and parturition. These intermediate variables constitute a mechanical framework, which, by definition, must stand between fertility and any kind of social or economic explanation: all elements of choice or social behaviour work through the intermediate variables to influence fertility. This kind of relationship is illustrated in Figure 1.1.

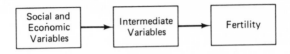

FIGURE 1.1   *A simple view of the determinants of fertility*

The role of the economist or, for that matter, of any social scientist studying fertility, is to explain how the various intermediate variables are affected by social or economic circumstance. At the micro level of the family or the household, the physician or biologist may study processes in which intercourse, conception and pregnancy lead to an increase in family size, but it is the role of the social scientist to explain how social conditions influence the magnitude of these intermediate variables that, in turn, affect fertility. At the social level, the demographer may define how the distribution of characteristics such as age or marital status affect fertility, but social explanation is required to show how these distributions change under the influence of various social and economic forces.

The research tools of the economics profession may help to tease apart the complex set of relationships which link fertility with other social phenomena. Theoretical frameworks have been developed for describing complicated systems of interdependence among variables, and empirical methods have been worked out for the estimation of some of the parameters. Where direct methods fail, economists have developed simulation approaches that help to unravel particularly complex or distant relationships.

A basic ground for economists' interest in fertility is that the impacts of fertility behaviour extend far beyond the individual families within which children are born. The children born today will be the parents, the labour-force members and the political leaders of the next generation. Since many of the consequences are of a public nature, understanding the processes by which they originate is in the public interest. This relationship between the fertility behaviour of the individual family and its social consequences implies the need to develop a research framework that will provide an appropriate information base for action strategies. This framework should identify variables that can be influenced by policy or programmes, and should show how these variables work their way through the social and economic system and the intermediate variables to affect fertility. Thus, not only is there a need for economic research concerning fertility, but it is important that the research be so defined as to indicate the way in which public policy may affect or be affected by the levels of fertility.

Economics can help to achieve the objectives of policy-oriented fertility research, through both theory and empirical work. Economic theory proceeds by developing a set of formal postulates and related relationships as a basis for deductive generalisations about the economic aspects of human behaviour. With respect to fertility, the economic theorist's role is to identify the most appropriate set of assumptions about the nature of human behaviour in the area of fertility, and to show how those assumptions work their way through the economic system to affect decisions and behaviour concerning fertility.

Complementing the economists's theoretical approach to fertility is a set of well-developed tools that permit the economist to confront theory with data to test its predictive power. Given the complexity of the task and the early stage of development of economic theories of fertility, it is not always possible to design decisive tests, but, cumulatively, the empirical research on fertility is beginning to suggest some important avenues for further development of theory. Empirical research in the economics of fertility can also establish relationships that can be used for the purposes of prediction and control. It is one thing to argue, on the basis of theory alone, that as the cost of raising children increases people will choose smaller families, and it is quite another to be able to predict within some reasonable bounds how much of a reduction in fertility will result from a change in those costs.

Theory and data-based research are, of course, complementary. Theory depends on an adequate set of empirical generalisations, and empirical research depends on a well-specified theoretical framework. Increases in one kind of understanding help to bring about further improvements in the other. In the process, the possible contribution which research makes to our understanding of fertility should be greatly enhanced.

NOTE

1. This volume does not deal with migration. There are, however, many sending and receiving countries for which migration is of particular economic or social importance (see, for example, Birks and Sinclair, 1980; Böhning, 1981). Middle Eastern countries, for example, tend to be characterised by fairly large rates of in- or out-migration, depending on their endowments of natural resources. The economic and social systems of these countries are greatly affected by these migration trends.

2 Theories of Fertility

GEORGE B. SIMMONS

This chapter focuses on theories of fertility. In our view, the theory is important both because of its essential role as a part of the scientific process and because it provides a framework within which policies and programmes are formulated. This dual role provides an essential tension which is the source of much controversy about theories in the area of fertility or other parts of the social sciences. It is rare that social scientists are able to formulate and test theories in such a way as to leave all observers persuaded as to the correctness of a given position and the corollary implications for policy. The much more common situation, nowhere better illustrated than in the area of fertility studies, is that several or many theories co-exist, with none being fully dominant. This situation encourages extended debate about the policy alternatives, where both alternative value structures and alternative theoretical perspectives vie with empirical evidence in the complex process of deciding research priorities and policy options. This reality heightens our need for an understanding of the role of theory and of the specific theoretical alternatives which have been proposed in the literature.

The emphasis here is on the major theories of fertility that can be called economic theories. These are theories that treat fertility at either the level of the individual/household or at the level of the larger social unit as determined, at least in part, by a process, conscious or unconscious (latent or manifest), involving the allocation of scarce resources. The first section deals with some of the characteristics of theories. The actual review begins with the views of Malthus and Marx, which have done much to set the tone for the modern debate about population. We then discuss in turn (i) a set of theories that treat fertility as largely determined at an aggregative or societal level, (ii) a second set that focus on micro or household behaviour, and (iii) a set of writings that show the beginnings of some new approaches.

20

ABOUT THEORY

A theory is

> a deductively connected set of empirical generalisations. These general-
> isations, no matter how well established they may be, are always hypo-
> thetical. A theory, accordingly, is often referred to as a hypothetico-
> deductive system, because it states deductive connections among
> hypotheses. The premises of a theory are empirical hypotheses that
> explain the generalisations they imply.   (Brodbeck, 1968, p. 457.)

The term 'theory' has taken on a broad set of meanings, especially as
used in the literature on the economics of fertility. A theory must have
the characteristics included in Brodbeck's definition, but even a definition
of this sort leaves a great deal of room for variation. Theories can be
stated verbally or mathematically. They can be based on a familiar set of
empirical generalisations such as those of the theory of neoclassical consumer behaviour as used by the new home-economics school in its writings
on fertility behaviour, or on a less familiar set of generalisations about
family obligations as used by Caldwell. Theories can be designed to provide specific hypotheses about the magnitude and form of key relationships, as in Becker's early writing on the income–fertility relationship. All
statements about the relationship between fertility and other aspects of
the human condition do not, however, meet the definition of theory. To
qualify as a theory, the set of statements should be based on logic, and
should have implications which can be tested by appropriate empirical
tests.

There is a general consensus that a theory should be logical in terms of
the relationships that exist among its component statements. In fact,
however, there is great variation among theories in the degree of detail
and tightness with which the generalisations that make up the theory are
related to each other. In some cases, the linkages between the axioms of a
theory and the theorems that are subject to refutation are very tight –
based on careful definitions, with mathematically-exact formulations and
precise verbal statements. More commonly, there are logical gaps or
elements of fuzziness in the connection among the constituent statements
of a theory. Thus, in practice if not in principle, there are great variations
among theories in the degree of rigour of their formulation.

Even with regard to the principles of the matter, there is less agreement
on the extent to which the empirical generalisations making up a theory
should be subject to empirical verification. All agree that the theorems

derived from a theory should be testable; that is, it should be possible to show that they are inconsistent with the data. However, many social scientists feel that the axioms of the theory do not necessarily have to meet this test. Friedman's argument, shared by many economists, is that the generalisations derived from a theory are the basis for testing, not the assumptions. Thus, unrealistic assumptions that form the basis of many economic theories, such as the assumption that economic decision-makers have perfect knowledge of alternatives, do not, by this view, destroy the potential validity of the theory. The theory's validity is rather to be determined by empirical tests about the theorems derived from the assumptions. Other economists argue that all of the empirical generalisations that make up a theory should be subject to verification, but there is agreement on the point that a theory must have some logically-dervied propositions that can be refuted.

Theories differ in their scope. Some theories, such as Newton's theory of gravity, have generated a wide range of testable propositions. Most theories in the social sciences are less ambitious. In fact, in the literature on fertility there is a tendency to trade off the number of specific testable implications against the range of a theory. Some of the broadest statements about fertility are theories only in the loosest sense of being a set of deductively-connected generalisations. Freedman's sociological framework for the study of fertility and Easterlin's microlevel socio-economic framework both fall within this category. They are important because they help establish the agenda of research questions that students of demography should address, but without considerable additional specification they do not provide any specific refutable theorems.

At the other extreme from the broad framework type of theories are the more limited investigations of relatively simple relationships. An investigation may, for example, suggest that there is a relationship between a couple's fertility and the previous experience of mortality among its earlier births. This generalisation can be taken as a simple theory since, properly formulated, it is possible to refute, but it represents the simplest form that a theory can take. Often, such statements are part of a larger set of empirical generalisations that may or may not be explicit in the theoretical statement. In this discussion, we shall label these statements as 'hypotheses', and discuss them separately from the more elaborate, multi-statement theories of which they are often a part. Thus, a theory of fertility should be a set of postulates and statements of relationships among well-defined variables that, taken together, can explain the major forces affecting fertility. It must be recognised, however, that any theory applies to a domain limited in some respects (e.g. developed versus developing countries or individual versus aggregate behaviour) and, even within its domain, will involve a large degree of abstraction. Thus, no theory of fertility will provide specific predictions on the details of any form of behaviour covering all societies and individuals.

The complex assumptions and data-manipulations necessary to operationalise a theory further increase the complexity of matching the hypotheses of a theoretical structure with the realities of the world. The construction of measurement instruments corresponding to the theoretical variables in a theory involves assumptions that are never fully met in practice. A theory of fertility, for example, may involve resource scarcity, and the researcher may assume that this theoretical variable is approximated by the income of the family, a variable which is very difficult to assess (or even to define), particularly in Third World countries. The operationalisation of a theory can never be perfect; rather, it always involves some degree of uncertainty, and a resulting need for researchers to tread cautiously in attempting to establish the connection between theory and empirical observation.

Since theories are inevitably less than perfect in their ability to explain any given behaviour, and since more than one theory can be used to explain any given empirical observation, it is necessary to have some rules for choosing among the alternative theories. Among economists, the most popular rule in the abstract arsenal of methodologists is probably *predictive power*. But the predictive power of alternative theories may in many cases be difficult to compare. In those fairly rare instances where one possible theory explains most of the variation in a wide set of observations, and an alternative theory explains little, it is accepted that the theory with the best predictive power should be preferred. But where there are overlapping claims, as for example when two different theories can explain the relationship between fertility and female labour-force participation, neither theory dominates. Thus, while this volume emphasises empirical strength, it is also necessary to mention some other criteria used by economists for choosing among theories.

One important approach to choosing between or among theories for which predictive power can be neither assessed nor reasonably compared, is examining the plausibility of the postulates on which the theory is based. Is it reasonable, for example, to assume that economic decision-makers are perfectly informed about the consequences of their actions? Such questions may provide insight as to the overall likelihood that a theory will be a reasonable basis for understanding a phenomenon, especially where direct tests of hypotheses generated by the theory are indecisive. Two related additional criteria often used by economists are *elegance* and *simplicity*. If a theory requires few assumptions, and predicts as well as an alternative theory that requires many assumptions, it will be preferred. More generally, if a theory seems to offer a more complete or plausible explanation than an alternative, it will be preferred.

There is an enormous diversity among theories of fertility. Our focus is upon theories that are economic in nature, but we recognise that there are important alternative theories that derive from the medical or biological sciences, or from other social sciences such as sociology or psychology. As difficult as it is to compare theories within a discipline, the complexity increases when comparisons are attempted across the widely divergent disciplines that have generated research in the area of fertility. Medical researchers may focus on aspects of fertility that are of little interest to economists, such as post-partum amenorrhoea. Economists tend to be more concerned with matters of choice. Therefore, even if the knowledge of the biological condition surrounding fertility is able to explain a high proportion of the observed variation in fertility, economists may not consider the findings very relevant unless they can be built into a larger model of individual or societal choice.

Within the domain of a given discipline, theories are constructed with widely divergent purposes. Some theories may be directed toward the explanation of the aggregate fertility experience of different communities or regions. Others may be oriented toward explaining the fertility of couples or individual men or women. Some theories may be designed to explain adaptation in fertility behaviour over time, while others concentrate more on explaining differentials at a given point in time.

TWO NINETEENTH-CENTURY PARADIGMS - MALTHUS AND MARX

The theories of fertility most closely debated during the nineteenth century are, in many respects, simpler than those being discussed today. The nineteenth-century theories lack detail, and, needless to say, they reflect little knowledge of the changes in technology and social organisation that have taken place during the past century. Nonetheless, they have had a persistent influence on how we think about the relationship between population growth and resource scarcity, and about the specific question of fertility.

Malthus

Malthus argued that there is a positive relationship between family-size and income. Given the strong and stable passion between the sexes, and given that sex can legitimately take place only within marriage, the major determinant of fertility is the age of marriage. When the economic condition of young unmarried individuals is favourable, they marry relatively early, and the natural result is high fertility. When economic conditions are less advantageous, the age of marriage rises and fertility declines. This relationship is strongly affected by existing social institutions, especially those influencing the ability to marry. If each couple is responsible for assuring that there are sufficient means to provide for its offspring, then marriages and thus fertility will be limited by the extent of the resources that the couple commands. But, Malthus argued, when political interventions are introduced to shield the couple from the rigours imposed by scarcity, marriages will take place at younger ages and fertility will rise, bringing with it a train of 'misery' as people are forced to face the consequences of sharing a limited pool of resources among a larger body of claimants. Malthus emphasises that fertility and mortality are interdependent elements that interact with population size and the basic set of resources available to determine the general level of prosperity. He presents both a theory of fertility and, more generally, a theory of economic behaviour. The statements about fertility that are embedded in the larger theory are extremely simple: (i) the passion between sexes is constant: (ii) marriage is a precondition for childbearing; and (iii) discouragement of early and improvident marriage through economic and other sanctions affects the level of fertility. While Malthus did speculate in his later editions about the possible deliberate variation of fertility within marriage, he considered such a possibility as relatively unimportant and morally wrong. The theory of fertility within marriage used by Malthus is thus biological in nature. Malthus assumes that married couples do not control the number of children they have. This orientation contrasts with that of the recent authors in micro-economics, who emphasise the choices that people make within marriage. In many respects, Malthus' theory of fertility is the weakest link in his grand design. For, contrary to his theory, fertility within marriage is in almost all times and places subject to some degree of choice, and has in many countries declined more or less continuously from his time to ours (Flew, 1973; Davis, 1955; Petersen, 1979).

The overall theory of Malthus is a 'macro-theory' in that it attempts to explain the relationship between poverty and population growth through a set of statements that, taken together, embody a relatively complete set of social interdependencies. In Malthus' theory, one cannot predict fertility or population growth through an examination of the family in isolation. The position of the family and, therefore, its fertility behaviour, will depend on its class status, and on scarcities that, while they have an impact on the family, are essentially derived from the resource position of the larger society. Malthus thought that property would inevitably be unevenly distributed – the law of property was, in his opinion, very close to a natural law. He believed that poverty flows neither from this uneven division of wealth nor from the form of government; the main source of poverty is the confrontation between population growth and scarce resources. The redistribution of landlords' income derived from rents, to labourers whose income would otherwise be restricted to subsistence wages, would only hasten the day of complete immiseration. The only hope was for a voluntary delay of marriage and thus a reduction in fertility. Marriage would, in turn, be delayed or reduced only if poverty were strongly discouraged by social sanctions and normative prescriptions. The low regard that Malthus held for this prospect may be the reason why economics was tagged the 'dismal' science.

History has given little support to the central propositions of Malthus' theory. Not only have his hypotheses about fertility not been borne out, but his notions of an environment characterised by fixed land and unchanging technology have been dramatically overturned, and his ideas of the rigidity of class structure have been, in large measure, eroded. Despite the weaknesses of the theory's elements, Malthus has had immense influence, because he was able to build a theory integrating fertility, mortality and population growth with economic conditions more completely than any of his predecessors. His work is being favourably re-examined, not because his overall conclusions are seen as correct, but because many of the elements in his work, the method of his analysis and his extensive use of data anticipate the ideas of more contemporary authors (Petersen, 1980). The central Malthusian themes of resource scarcity and the importance of a negative feedback from population to economic well-being have been widely echoed (and criticised) by present-day authors. Similarly, there are many people who believe that existing social institutions and programmes encourage excessive fertility among the poor. While the mechanisms advanced by contemporary authors to explain fertility are different, the overall analysis is still very close to Malthus' original diagnosis of the causes of poverty. Thus, even in the contemporary world, the influence of Malthus' theories of fertility is widespread.

Marx

Marx did not develop a very complete theory of fertility. It is possible, however, to derive some idea of Marxist theory of population growth and fertility from his reactions to contemporaries or near contemporaries, including Malthus, who made population growth a part of their own thinking, from an examination of his theory of historical development, and from the writing of his followers. It must be emphasised that, even more than in the case of Malthus, any Marxist theory of fertility is part of a larger system of social thought (Meek, 1971).

Marxist thinkers argue that fertility is not so much the product of the 'natural' laws emphasised by Malthus as it is of the social laws that characterise a given society at a given time. There is no immutable law of population, but a separate and distinct law for each time and situation. Such population laws as exist will have the same basis as other laws that exist contemporaneously; they will result from the class structure of the society, the existing technology of production, and the material resources available.

Marxists argue that the level of fertility is a function of the existing class structure and the roles assigned to different classes within the society. Within the capitalist system there is a need to keep the cost of labour low so that control and high profits can be maintained by the capitalist class. Therefore, the capitalist system encourages the formation of a 'reserve army' of the unemployed, and a major function of high fertility in such a society is to increase the size of this army. Marx implicitly and Engels explicitly (Meek, 1971, pp. 75, 119) argued that in a communist system, there would be no need to create this type of proletariat. Capital and land would be controlled by the state, which represents the people, and each individual would enjoy the full gains from his or her own labour – exploitation resulting from private ownership would be abolished. In a communist society, children would not be born out of the compulsion inherent in the capitalist or pre-capitalist system. For Marx, fertility is a reflection of social and political conditions. For him and his followers, it is a derivative concept, while for Malthus, fertility is the independent force responsible for the existence of poverty. Causality is thus reversed in these two perspectives.

Other contrasts between the analytical systems developed by Marx and Malthus help to explain the differences between the beliefs about the relationship between population growth and the standard of living. Malthus argued that major resource limitations were an inevitable fact of life, and that the size of the population would be inversely related to the standard of living, since more people would share a total product that could not increase proportionally. Given these limited resources, value ultimately derives from the scarce resources. Marx, in contrast, saw value as deriving from labour. The more people, the more potential labour, and the better off the society.

While Malthus saw the class structure as a divinely-inspired mechanism for preserving social order, Marx saw it as a form of social organisation inherently characterised by internal conflict and, in its capitalist form, the source of oppression for a large part of the population. Thus, Marx saw as inevitable the class struggle to transfer the power from the exploiting capitalist and land-owning classes to the wealth-producing labouring classes. Malthus tended to be a technological pessimist, as exemplified by his assumption that the production of food could grow at best arithmetically, while population has the potential for growing geometrically. Marx, writing later, was convinced that technological change would be a continuous force for change. Malthus believed resource scarcity to be unrelieved, or nearly so, by technological change, whereas for Marx, technology was seen as one of the dynamic elements in the economic system. In the Marxian world-view, fertility is the mechanism by which the labour force replaces itself, but it is by no means the source of poverty. Because this is the case, fertility control cannot lead to improvements in well-being, except as part of some larger pattern of social change.

Whether or not fertility has an independent role with respect to improving the standard of living has been much debated. Within the context of explaining the persistence of low levels of per capita income in developing countries, some Marxists now recognise that existing high levels of fertility may be dysfunctional. In most cases, this admission is heavily qualified by an emphasis on other factors that are more immediate sources of poverty, and by the accusation that high fertility is a legacy of capitalist and pre-capitalist exploitation and colonialism, and will inevitably be brought under control after the revolution. The emphasis in Marxist literature is on the secondary importance of fertility as a social force. Nonetheless, Marxist scholars and policy-makers have increasingly given attention to fertility as one element in a larger social system (J. Robinson, 1979; Guzevatyi, 1975).

What, then, are the distinctive features of a Marxist theory of fertility? The major characteristic of such theories is a concern with social class as an-explanatory variable. A second characteristic is the definition of fertility as a part of the larger economic and social system. Associated wih these two points, Marxist theories of fertility see little independent role to be played by cultural or biological factors.

In many ways, Marxist theory overlaps with other contemporary theories of fertility in its explanatory variables and in some aspects of its framework for explanation. A major difference involves the policy implications drawn from empirical evidence concerning the determinants of fertility. The subject of policy will be addressed in Chapter 4.

Malthus and Marx were both concerned with the influence of social organisations defined at the broadest level. Neither demonstrated a great concern with variables such as the level of infant mortality or the role of women. These were, at best, intervening variables that could help to transmit the effects of larger social forces. One of the characteristics of contemporary theorising is that even authors working with macro-data have tended to develop their theoretical models in such a way as to leave room for a more highly differentiated causal structure.

Neo-Malthusian Theory

Neo-Malthusians share with Malthus a belief that there are inherent limitations on the resources that a nation or a family can marshall for its economic well-being. Further, given these constraints, any rational family will want to limit the number of children it has to the number that is consistent with maintaining a reasonable standard of living in the face of these constraints (Enke, 1960). Within this framework, children can be a source of poverty if they dilute a fixed or relatively inelastic income. The neo-Malthusians differ from Malthus in believing that contraception (and not only delayed marriage) is a possible way to reconcile a family life with limited resources. The solution they advocate is the dissemination of contraceptive knowledge and the public provision of contraceptive services, for if the means are available to limit family-size and if children are indeed a potentially immiserating life event, then no rational couple would want more than a minimum number.

The neo-Malthusian model does not deal explicitly with all of the features of the standard household model of economic behaviour. There is little attempt to define a utility function, much less the role that children would play in such a function. There is only limited discussion of the virtues of alternative definitions of the resource constraint. Each family (couple) is assumed to be an isolated entity that derives relatively little direct economic benefit from its children. Parents shoulder the full burden of providing resources for their children; they are given help neither by the extended family (including older children) nor by the wider community. The basic assumption is that children are an expensive source of pleasure, and while there may be reasons to invest some resources in childbearing, there is rapidly diminishing utility associated with increasing family-size.

While the neo-Malthusians represent themselves as describing the economics of childbearing for a typical family, and the models of Enke and others are couched in micro-terms, their theories are more normative descriptions of forces that operate at the level of the society than a description of the behaviour of individuals.

The Malthusian framework stresses the *role of marriage*, while the neo-Malthusian perspective concentrates on *contraception*. Neither deals extensively with structural factors such as the distribution of resources or the political system. In both frameworks, moreover, the emphasis is on the extent to which population (or fertility) affects the standard of living, and only to a slight extent on the way that the standard of living affects population change.

As emphasised in the previous paragraph, the neo-Malthusian perspective is a theory more of poverty than of fertility. The prescription of contraceptive use, the best known characteristic of this perspective, is based on very simple notions of fertility. Basically, couples are assumed to have more children than they want simply because of ignorance and/or lack of access to contraceptives. It should be noted, however, that neo-Malthusians are not the only advocates of making contraception or fertility control available. Even Marxists and structuralists generally, who are often viewed as opponents of the Malthusian position, see a role for contraception, but the role in their eyes is as a supporting element in a social and economic policy rather than as the centrepiece of a population policy. The key empirical question which arises from consideration of these positions is the extent to which the supply of contraceptive information and services is by itself likely to influence fertility, and the extent to which other social and economic changes are likely to be prerequisites for fertility change.

THE DEMOGRAPHIC TRANSITION THEORY AND OTHER AGGREGATIVE APPROACHES TO FERTILITY

The work of Malthus and Marx is aggregative or macro-economic in orientation because the key outcomes central to the theory are aggregative in nature. There are a number of contemporary theories which share this orientation to aggregate demographic behaviour.

The Theory of the Demographic Transition

Malthus and Marx set out their ideas on the determinants of fertility before the dramatic declines in birth and death rates had taken place or were fully understood. Contemporary authors are well aware that one of the significant facts of the modern period in the industrial countries has been the reduction of both fertility and mortality to their present low levels. The theory of the demographic transition is a set of generalisations that describes this process of change. The theory begins with the observation that in pre-modern populations, fertility and mortality were generally very high by modern standards, and in contemporary industrial countries, fertility and mortality are both low. In between, in the words of Demeny, 'is the demographic transition' (Demeny, 1974; Notestein, 1944; Coale, 1973). Stated so simply, the demographic transition can scarcely be called a theory. At this level, it is a tautological framework within which aspects of historical population change can be organised.

Much of the writing about the transition has provided a more elaborate rationale for the profound changes that take place between the pre-modern patterns of high fertility and mortality and the contemporary demographic patterns. The phases of the transition have been labelled, the changes have been linked with socio-economic developments, and the resulting set of statements have been used to make and test predictions. In its more elaborate form, the demographic transition writing has taken on many of the attributes of a theory as we have defined it.

The more elaborate version of the theory begins with the assumption that mortality is linked to either (i) living conditions, in that the economic and social changes that have characterised the modern period brought about a fall in death rates, or (ii) a set of poorly understood exogenous forces that reduced the force of mortality. Under either assumption, decreasing mortality is responsible for a significant increase in the rate of population growth. This increase puts pressure on the families in the system, increasing the likelihood that they will reduce fertility. In most versions of the demographic transition theory, there is also a recognition that the same modernising socio-economic changes that work to influence mortality affect fertility as well. The precise mechanism is not clear, but presumably the shift to urban patterns of life with the associated higher costs of raising children, the higher level of education of the parents, the higher educational expectations for children, and greater opportunities outside the home all combine to encourage a reduction in fertility. In this theory, the combination of the contemporary shifts in socio-economic environment and the prior reductions in mortality push the society towards lower levels of fertility. In addition, some discussions have stressed the possible role of societal norms concerning fertility and related aspects of human behaviour such as child-care and child-education. The theory is macro since the forces that affect both mortality and the socio-economic environment are defined outside of the family, and the theory implies that the key variables should be defined at a high level of aggregation.

Criticism of the demographic transition theory has taken a number of forms. One important criticism is that the theory is incomplete because it focuses exclusively on fertility reduction as a response to the population pressures resulting from mortality reduction. Little attention is given to alternative responses such as internal or international migration or economic development (Davis, 1963; Easterlin, 1972). Another criticism arises from the observation that, frequently, fertility rates decline before mortality is significantly reduced or before the usual forces of modernisation set in (Coale, 1973; Petersen, 1960; Leasure, 1963; Beaver, 1975). Although it provides a framework for the analysis of a number of aspects of fertility change, the demographic transition is often presented in such broad terms that it is difficult to subject it to rigorous tests. Like the Malthusian theory of poverty, the demographic transition theory can always be defended against outside criticism by simply admonishing the sceptics to be patient and to wait for the predictions to be verified. It may be true that both fertility and mortality have fallen in a number of countries, but the demographic transition theory is often used as a more complete model of the process of fertility change than can be tested by a simple statement of outcomes. To receive empirical support for the theory in its complex form, there must not only be a fall in mortality and fertility, but the fall should follow the time pattern and have the relationship with socio-economic development suggested in the theory. Thus, the empirical research that demonstrates these relationships to be weak undercuts the generalisability of the basic framework. Recent work on the diffusion of fertility limiting knowledge and behaviour may help to extend the theory (Retherford, 1979).

Theories of Post-transition Fluctuations in Fertility

The theories discussed in the previous subsection deal with the fertility transition. Typically, in developed countries, even after fertility has fallen to low levels, there is a persistent pattern of fluctuations that are of great economic and social significance. Easterlin (1972) and Lee (1974, 1976a) have developed a set of far-reaching models to explain the long-term patterns of fertility change in societies like the United States.

Like the Malthusian and the demographic transition theories, these models are characterised by an attempt to integrate into the analysis a broad range of economic and social changes. Beginning with the assumptions that (i) couples exercise control over their fertility, (ii) they have more children when they feel prosperous, and (iii) their feelings of well-being are a function of the size of the cohort into which they are born, as mediated by educational and employment opportunities, the Easterlin model provides a dynamic set of relationships that defines the variations of fertility and cohort prosperity over time, and their interrelationship.

This theory has a great many attractive features for explaining the pattern of economic and demographic change in contemporary industrial countries. It is less easily applied to the fertility of developing countries or the fertility change that takes place during the transition. However, even in the Third World, there are increasing numbers of countries where significant fertility reductions have been achieved during the past 20 years. In such countries, the past drop in fertility, along with future fluctuations, may lead to varying cohort-size, with important implications for fertility.

Alternative Macro-economic Approaches

One new approach to the study of aggregate fertility patterns involves the application of hypotheses dervied from the micro-economic literature on fertility. The grand theories of Marx, Malthus and the Demographic Transition have left out questions related to age-structure, and have omitted or greatly reduced the influence of the intermediate variables. They ignore a number of specific hypotheses (often derived from studies of household behaviour) about the determinants of national demographic change. For example, it is likely that at the national level, the labour-force behaviour of the female population will be closely related to fertility behaviour. Labour-force participation, in turn, may be affected by national patterns of education. Winegarden (1980 and Chapter 17 in this volume), Anker (1977) and Lieberman and Monteverde (Chapter 14 in this volume), among others, have designed macro-economic models to bridge the gap between the grand macro-models, with their crippling lack of specificity, and the more theoretically grounded micro-economic models, with their lack of applicability to the entire system.

These models are usually based on a set of hypotheses drawn from a variety of sources. Fertility is hypothesised to be a function of mortality levels, of per capita income, of female labour-force participation, or education levels. Early contributions involved little effort to specify an appropriate functional form or to model the relationships involved beyond the fertility function. Later applications have involved complex multiple-equation simulation models involving a detailed specification of these relationships (see, for example, Chapter 9 in this volume).

Such models have often had as their primary purpose the establishment of a framework for simulation or for empirical estimations. They usually involve a combination of hypotheses and empirical data drawn from diverse sources. The advantage of such models is that they permit a detailed examination of system dynamics (including the determinants of fertility) at a level of aggregation where either the complexity of the relationships involved or the lack of adequate data precludes direct observation. The hybrid nature of such models and their complexity also made the interpretation of results very difficult (Arthur and McNicoll, 1975; Rodgers *et al.*, 1976; Hirschman, 1981).

MICRO-ECONOMIC THEORIES OF FERTILITY BEHAVIOUR

In this section, we move to a discussion of theories that are oriented primarily towards explaining household differences in fertility. Among theories of fertility, the micro/macro contrast is a matter of emphasis rather than of kind. While both types of theory involve implications for each level of social aggregation, their orientation is different. Micro-theories may be acceptable if they adequately model differentials within a society, without defining the forces that determine the overall level of fertility. Macro-theories, on the other hand, should be able to describe the level and pattern of change in a society as a whole, even if they are not able to explain the observed variations in the household fertility. A complete theory should be able to reconcile the micro and macro perspectives.

The traditional domain of micro-economics has been the market-related choices made by individuals or households and firms. It would probably not have occurred to theorists such as Marshall that economic theory could furnish important insights into the determinants of human fertility. During the last three decades, however, economists have extended their inquiry into areas as seemingly remote from the market as marriage, criminal behaviour and fertility. In this section, we describe some of the recent developments in the area of micro-economic theory. The models that fall in this class are presented in mathematical form in the appendix to this chapter. (Model 0 presents the basic approach.)

The primary justification for the application of a micro-economic framework to fertility is that fertility decisions are made in a manner that is, to some degree, analogous to more usual economic choices. Fertility involves the use of resources and has implications for other aspects of human behaviour such as labour/leisure or saving/consumption choices that have long been considered part of economic behaviour. On the other hand, fertility has special characteristics that differentiate it strongly from the usual market choices. In particular, the production of children involves marketed commodities only indirectly, and traditionally many elements in the family-building process, such as the sexual relationship between the parents or the bonds of loyalty among family-members, fall within the traditional domain of fields such as psychology or sociology. Moreover, the time-span of fertility and family-building decisions is longer than that of most market phenomena, and the very assumption that 'choices' are made may not be appropriate for all populations or time periods.

Theories of household fertility behaviour within an economic tradition tend to be presented in the language of the micro-economic theory of consumption. Individuals or couples are assumed to possess a utility function, to face environmental constraints that can be defined in economic terms as 'prices' or 'costs', and to maximise their utility subject to these well-defined budget constraints. But the models differ enormously in terms of the rigour with which they are presented, the variables that are included as arguments, the treatment of time, and the populations whose fertility they are intended to explain. In this section, we shall review the various models that have been developed. Before undertaking this examination, however, it is worth noting some of the central issues that any models developed in this area must confront.

Firstly, virtually all economic models of household consumption behaviour assume the existence of a utility function – a well-ordered and consistent set of preferences concerning alternative states of the world. The definition of the utility function is particularly difficult in the area of fertility behaviour, because children generate a wide variety of benefits and costs for their parents and others. Some of these benefits take the form of consumption utilities comparable to utility gained from the consumption of marketed commodities. Other benefits take the form of increasing the income of the family, and thus have the characteristics of gains from investment rather than consumption. Even among the consumption utilities, some benefits have close market parallels, while others do not. The satisfaction derived from close affectional ties or kinship roles is likely to be less easily available from market sources. Since child-rearing involves a perspective that is much longer than the market period of conventional economic theory, there is also a question of how the behaviour of potential parents is affected by time. Should models of fertility make any attempt to incorporate the possibility of learning or other time-behaviour? Further complicating the definition of the utility function is the fundamental fact that fertility behaviour necessarily involves at least two individuals and may, in many cases, be influenced by many more, for example, the extended family. Micro-economic theory usually deals with this problem by assuming a single utility function with all of the desired mathematical properties, but this solution may not be adequate.

A second central issue is that the constraints are difficult to define in the case of fertility. Beginning with the recognition that fertility behaviour is not normally a market activity, the various constraints are defined more as trade-offs within the household or as perceived costs than they are in the form of objective 'prices' determined in an impersonal market, as with normal consumer goods. Some of the costs of children are objectively defined in market terms, such as hospital costs associated with delivery. Other costs may be defined outside the market, but can be measured in fairly objective terms, such as food for an additional child in a self-sufficient peasant household. Still other costs are psychological, such as the disruption that an additional child may bring to a house. Even the nature of the relevant income constraint is difficult. Should it include the earnings or potential earnings of both parents, or should it include earnings from children already living in the family? Certainly, surveys of parents in developing countries indicate that the income contributions of children are valued.

A third issue is how the analysis should deal with the basic biological elements of fertility. Should the model assume that there are no limitations? Should it assume that they can be treated as 'supply' factors, while all of the other variables measure 'demand'? How should one deal with the uncertainties of timing, sex and health that are inherent in the biological nature of fertility?

Such questions will have to be answered by any model, either through the incorporation of appropriate definitions and relationships within the model, or by a process of abstraction in which a given factor is excluded on the assumption that it is not central to the analysis. In the following discussion, we shall review various micro-economic approaches to fertility, trying to keep in mind how each approach deals with these central questions.

Many economists have developed micro-economic models of fertility. For our purposes, we shall somewhat unfairly lump these into three sets: the new home-economics school, the social-determinants school and the others. These different schools have co-existed now for more than 20 years, thus it is difficult to use a chronological decision rule as to which should be discussed first. Because it derives most directly from the central trends in the economics literature, we shall discuss the new home-economics school first.

The New Home-economics Approach

The 'new home-economics' approach to the micro-economics of fertility has grown out of the work of scholars associated with the University of Chicago and the National Bureau of Economic Research in the United States. We begin with this work, because it is the most highly developed and influential approach to the micro-economic study of fertility, and because it comes closest to the definition of 'theory' and the use of theory in science as discusssed in the early part of this chapter. The central characteristic of work in this tradition is a concentration on the definition of the appropriate price and income parameters of the family and the manner in which fertility will vary as these constraints are altered. Authors within this tradition have deliberately chosen to ignore the role of preferences, i.e. the utility function, as a source of predictable variation in observed fertility (T. P. Schultz, 1976a, p. 95).

The point of departure for much of the literature on the economics of fertility is Becker's 1960 article on the subject (Becker, 1960). (See Model 1 of the appendix for a formal presentation.) Becker's central argument is relatively simple: fertility decisions are economic in that they involve a search for an optimum number of children in the face of economic limitations. Therefore, the central problems are to articulate the basic elements in this choice phenomenon, to derive relevant hypotheses from the theory, and to subject them to the same kind of empirical testing to which hypotheses derived from other economic theories are exposed. Becker systematically addressed each of these problems.

The theory which he sketched suggests that parents have three arguments in their joint utility function: the number of children that they have, the quality of those children, and the quantity of other goods which they consume. They face a lifetime income constraint, and their problem is to maximise utility given that income constraint. In Becker's theory, the quantity and the quality of children are closely interrelated; the product of these two variables and the price of children is the total expenditure on children. To draw any conclusions about the number of children a family would have under different circumstances, it is necessary to make some assumptions about the trade-off between quantity and quality. Becker assumed that both the quality and quantity of children are normal goods in the economic sense; that is, as parents gain more income they want both more children and higher quality children. This assumption, combined with the assumption that income and childbearing are not interdependent, allowed Becker to derive a testable hypothesis about the relationship between income and the quantity of children: the higher the income, the more children a family will have.

This hypothesis has been the subject of a great deal of interest on the part of economists and other social scientists, in large part because it is inconsistent with commonly-held expectations about the relationship between fertility and income. In general, evidence from both the time-series (e.g. the demographic transition) and the cross-section (e.g. the numerous studies of fertility which show that families with high status have smaller numbers of children than do low status families) suggests that income and fertility should be negatively related. Much of Becker's original article is devoted to a discussion of the reasons for empirical findings which contradict his hypothesis. He argues that access to contraception (a 'supply' factor, as opposed to the 'demand' variables that are the central feature of his model) is directly related to income, and that the reason poor people have more children than rich people is not that they want them but that they do not know or have access to the means to prevent them.

Becker's first article on fertility, while incomplete and inadequate in many respects, was one of the earliest applications of the tools of main-stream, modern micro-economics to fertility. The article and Becker's continuing interest in the subject did much to legitimise the study of this subject in the field of economics. His focus on the strong counter-intuitive hypothesis about the relationship between income and fertility attracted both economists and non-economists to the economics of fertility, and the inadequacies of the article and its underlying reasoning gave both groups a very full work agenda.

While any theory must simplify and abstract from its subject, Becker's original approach was excessively simple. The theory says little about the opportunity costs associated with childbearing. Becker himself (1965) and other economists such as Mincer (1963) soon remedied that gap by build-ing the opportunity cost of the wife's time into the theory. The demand orientation of the model is also a limitation, especially for applications to fertility experience of developing countries, but this orientation in the Becker model constitutes a precedent followed by most economists working within the new home-economics framework. Other problems with the original theory include: the vague definition of income, the very general specification of the utility function, and the static time-frame within which the theory was stated. Nor does the model deal with learning, the stochastic component of fertility, or externalities (Turchi, 1975a).

Because Becker did not present his illustrations as full-blown tests of the hypothesis derived from this theory, it may be unfair to place too much weight on his empirical results. However at best his first article provides only casual observations concerning the empirical income/fertility relationship.

The pursuit of theoretical and empirical questions inspired by Becker's theory has more or less continued over the past 20 years. There have been a number of landmarks along the way. The first of further refinements was Mincer's (1963) recognition of the economic importance of the close connection between the labour-force participation of women and their levels of fertility. Later articles by Becker (1965, 1974) stressed the same theme, by incorporating the time constraints of the family into the model. (See Model 2 in the appendix.)

In subsequent papers, the basic model was further elaborated. Willis (1973) developed an elegant and theoretically-complete model of the demand for children. Other scholars have contributed by introducing new elements such as uncertainty and educational aspirations (Michael and Willis, 1975; DeTray, 1973; Becker and Lewis, 1973; other contributions in T. W. Schultz, 1974). The most recent presentations of the new household-economic models assume an intermediate activity approach to link resource constraints with the utility function. They also tend to expand the budget constraint to include the parents' time as well as their money income. Several important findings follow.

Firstly, Becker's original deduction that the number of children born to a family should be positively associated with family income does not hold true for the more complex models which recognise the time costs of raising children. In these models, the time of the mother (in most formulations) can be used either for producing income or for raising children. An increase in the wife's working income would thus have two offsetting effects: firstly, a positive income effect, and secondly, a negative price effect. This result lends sophistication to the model, but has left the theoretical prediction of the marginal effects of income change greatly qualified. If one assumes that one spouse (usually the wife) has primary responsibility for the time inputs to childbearing, the theory emphasises that the fertility effects of an increase in family income will be positive if the extra income comes from the spouse with relatively little child-care responsibility, and indeterminate in the case of the spouse who spends a great deal of time with the children. Empirical findings from developed-country settings have tended to confirm the hypothesis that the opportunity cost of the wife's time in childbearing is negatively associated with fertility, and that the husband's wage or income has either no net association or a weak positive association with fertility. As will be discussed in the next chapter, the conclusions are much less clear for the less-developed countries.

Secondly, those writers in the new home-economics tradition who have attempted to apply the theory to fertility in developing countries have emphasised that it is surviving children that enter the utility function of parents. Thus parents may want to adjust their fertility to offset the child-deaths they have experienced or that they anticipate. The writing of T. P. Schulz (1969a, 1976b, 1978a) has been particularly important in clarifying the potential importance of child-mortality for fertility.

The new home-economics approach thus provides a theoretical justification for two of the most commonly explored hypotheses in the empirical literature on fertility: women's status should be negatively related and child-mortality positively related to fertility. Beyond these two, home-economics models differ in their emphasis. Some, such as the work of Evenson (1978) and colleagues on fertility and time use, derive specific propositions about wage rates, fertility and the way parents use their time. Rosenzweig (1977) (see also Rosenzweig and Evenson, 1977) stresses the economic utility of children as sources of family income. The formal theoretical models are often difficult to estimate directly, since consensus on the empirical definition of many of the key variables, e.g. the opportunity cost of the mother's time, are lacking; and the explicit descriptions of justifiable theoretical propositions become more complex with the addition of variables to the system. Despite (or perhaps because of) the intricacies involved in extending the model, and despite the finding that estimated empirical relationships are often inconsistent with these major hypotheses, this research tradition has become something of a growth industry in itself.

There are a number of limitations on the applicability of the new home-economics class of models. Firstly, these models are still static. In most versions of the model, couples are assumed to have stable utility functions and to know at a very early stage, perhaps even before marriage, the set of opportunities that will be available to them, including their future income and occupation. Even when variables which may have long-run implications are built into the model, they are seldom given an explicit time-dimension. Thus, in contrast with the models of the demographic transition or the thinking of Easterlin or Liebenstein (to be discussed in the next section), all of which focus to a large extent on the way the subjective benefits and costs of childbearing change during the process of modernisation, the new home-economics model emphasises the impact of externally-determined changes in income or costs on a stable utility function. Secondly, the long time-horizon of fertility decisions creates a set of problems that is partially theoretical and partially empirical. For example, the definition of income is more difficult when the period of measurement is a lifetime than when it is a market period. This problem is in part theoretical, because there are a number of alternative definitions, and the one which is chosen depends in large measure on theoretical considerations. Thirdly, uncertain events related to fertility are built only imperfectly into the model; contraceptive failure, the fact that the sex of children is a random event, the mortality experience of both parents and children. Finally, the nature of husband/wife interaction is not well understood. Becker (1974, 1981) has discussed the logic of using a single utility function for the analysis of fertility decisions involving at least two people, but the new home-economics model incorporates little of the bargaining that many sociologists and psychologists believe to be inherent in decisions about and within marriage. In general, the distribution of the gains from childbearing within the family has been neglected by researchers.

The importance of externalities, although given considerable prominence in the policy-oriented literature, has not been incorporated into the new home-economic models. Policy-makers have long been concerned with the gap between the private and social assessment of the benefits and costs of population growth. To the extent that costs (or benefits) have their impact outside the decision unit, there may be a systematic bias toward higher (or lower) fertility than would have existed if the full incidence was within the family. There has been considerable speculation about this possibility (Demeny, 1971; Hardin, 1968; Kahan, 1974), but little attempt to measure the strength of such effects empirically. These effects are not incorporated into the new home-economics model.

The new home-economics model is, in its most highly refined form, still relatively ill-suited for the analysis of fertility problems in developing countries. T. P. Schultz (1976a, 1981), Rosenzweig (1977) and others have explored many of the possible applications of the theory in a developing-country context, but some of the most salient concerns of the basic model, i.e. the income–fertility relationships and the effect of women's participation in the labour-force, do not transfer easily to the developing-country context. This does not mean that this literature is irrelevant to the concerns of the developing countries. For the moment, however, given the limited range of questions that can be addressed within the new home-economics theoretical structure, the framework does not provide an adequate basis for the derivation of hypotheses for empirical testing. As a result, much of the empirical work in the study of the economics of fertility is based on the study and testing of hypotheses that are specified in an *ad hoc* fashion rather than derived formally from a complete theory.

Much research is currently oriented to expanding the domain of the new home-economics household models of fertility. Many economists working in this tradition believe that fertility is part of a large simultaneous system of relationships dealing not only with fertility but also with marriage, career decisions and migration. Furthermore, this model assumes that people make these decisions simultaneously at some point early in the life-cycle and that the decisions hold throughout the individuals' lives. This set of assumptions has important implications for empirical work in the area of fertility economics. It implies that the best approach to the study of fertility is one that examines the full range of these relationships simultaneously, and that the variables used in any hypothesis testing should be designed to apply to the individual's full lifetime and not to the moment at which a particular event takes place (e.g. at birth or at conception). Naturally, people working within the framework provided by this model recognise that there will be deviations from the ideal programme, in the form of unanticipated life events, but that such deviations will take the form of statistical error rather than of phenomena that should be studied directly. In this sense, the new home-economics models differ substantially from the models of some of the other schools of fertility research, which deal with variables characterising the environment of each decision as phenomena of interest in and of themselves. Thus, the new home-economics model gains a certain elegance and statistical manipulability at the expense of realism. A loss in realism may be worth paying if there is no alternative, but some economists claim that there are more realistic alternatives to the new home-economics model which provide at least equivalent degrees of explanation.

The Social-determinants School of Thought

In the new home-economics tradition, the burden of explanation is put on income, relative prices, or the variables which are assumed to work through these (T. P. Schultz, 1976a, 1977, 1981). There are a number of authors who have suggested that families differ fundamentally in the value they place on children, i.e. that their utility functions differ. These authors also suggest that biological constraints on fertility are important contributors to this variation. They argue that micro-economic models should treat preferences and the biological basis of reproduction as explanatory variables. Thus, Leibenstein, Easterlin and Turchi, among others, would all argue that empirical economic models should use variables like religion and education as control variables. They develop theoretical structures to support this position.

Leibenstein's contributions (1957, 1969, 1974, 1977) to the literature on the economics of fertility can be grouped in two parts. In his early writing, he concentrated on the fertility decision and the way it changed during the development process. His more recent work provides a critique and alternative to the new home-economics approach.

Leibenstein (1957) attempts to provide a reconciliation of the micro and the macro perspectives. His central questions are: 'How does the experience of parents change during the process of development?' and 'How does development transform the various forces which affect fertility?' Clearly, as societies modernise agricultural methods or industrialise to raise per capita incomes, there will be dramatic alterations in the roles of children and in the relationships between children and parents. Leibenstein argues that the best way to understand this change in basic human relationships is to focus on the decisions made by parents who move or do not move from parity 'n' to parity '$n + 1$' as the society changes. He suggests that there are three elements in the benefit/cost calculations parents make when they decide about additional children. Firstly, parents derive direct utility from the experience of having and raising children. In a sense, children are a consumption activity for parents. Secondly, there are both direct and indirect costs to having children. Direct costs include the cost of providing food and shelter to the additional child; indirect costs might include the lost wages from a parent who remains at home to look after the children. Thirdly, there are direct economic gains in the form of wages, old-age security or labour input, which children, as they mature, can provide to their parents. Leibenstein argues that while the basic consumption utility of an additional child (say a fourth child) remains constant during the process of economic development, the cost of raising that (fourth) child increases, and the economic returns associated with the child decrease. Thus, the relative gains associated with having the '$(n + 1)$ th' child are reduced, and the benefit/cost calculation of the parents is shifted away from childbearing. This result is consistent with the theory of the demographic transition, but it is presented with more explicit linkages between the behaviour of the individual or the couple and the changes taking place in the society.

In his later papers, written in response to various developments in the literature, Leibenstein (1969, 1974) has significantly elaborated on his ideas, and differentiated them from those of the neo-Malthusians and those of the new home-economics school. In fact, he has in some sense thrown the gauntlet down to the mainstream practitioners of micro-economic theory, contending that the basic structure of accepted micro-theory is inadequate, and that stronger and more general conclusions could be drawn by reformulating the axioms of the theory. For example, he argues that it is not helpful or necessary to argue that couples maximise a global utility function. Rather, they are concerned with a more limited set of goals. Drawing from his general theory, he refers to this more limited focus as the principle of 'limited rationality'. As applied to fertility, the most important of Leibenstein's new contributions may be his insistence that marginal decisions to increase family-size are of economic interest only after parents have had a certain number of children. He argues that the early decisions in a family-building experience may be largely arational and unplanned, and that it exceeds the competence of the profession of economics to try to deal with all aspects of family formation. (The Leibenstein model is formalised as Model 4 in the appendix.)

The Leibenstein theory is presented in largely informal terms. In contrast with the new home-economics model, there is no attempt to explicitly derive a demand function (or its equivalent in the language of the 'limited rationality') from a utility function and a well-defined budget constraint. The various forces affecting parental decisions are also discussed in general rather than specific terms, and Leibestein neither provides evidence to support the theory nor presents it in a form which is easily testable. In commenting on the Leibenstein framework, Keeley (1975) suggests that there may be no testable implication of the model. Certainly, arguments such as the suggestion that the negative income–fertility relationship is explained by local discontinuities in the utility function are greatly dependent on what seem to be *ad hoc* and empirically untestable assumptions. of course, the same case can be made about any argument that depends on variations in a largely unobservable utility function, which is one of the reasons that the new home-economics school has emphasised the importance of observable variations in 'prices' and 'income'. Perhaps because of his reliance on explanatory variables derived from his special version of micro-economic theory, Leibenstein's contributions, despite the attraction of a theory which gives tastes a central role and which makes the trade-offs parents face more personal than they are in the new home-economics model, have gained few active adherents.

Easterlin (1969, 1975, 1978, 1980) has developed a micro-economic theory of fertility which extends the framework of the new home-economics model and complements his own macro-theoretical perspective. (This framework has been used as a basis for the recent National Academy of Sciences' review of the determinants of fertility (Bulatao and Lee, 1984).) His point of departure is the assumption that a simple economic approach provides an insufficient basis for understanding fertility behaviour, especially in the developing countries. He has argued (Easterlin, 1969, 1978) that a full integration of economic and sociological approaches will yield insights superior to those that can be gained through the exclusive use of either model.

The Easterlein model begins with a recognition that there are a number of factors involved in fertility decisions which are difficult to model in the basic economic framework; biological factors, differences in tastes, and the fact that people have a need for sex unrelated to childbearing. Within the model, specific relationships are worked out to describe the demand for children and the supply of children. The result is a specification that is very different from that of the new home-economics school, but closer to its spirit than to the work of Leibenstein.

In the Easterlin model, an analysis quite similar to that in the original Becker article is developed to explain the economics of fertility decisions. Parents have a utility function in which the number of children and other goods consumed by the parents are arguments. Parents face a budget constraint, and children are assumed to have a price. (Easterlin does not follow Becker in making the distinction between the quality and quantity of children.) Based on this information, one can estimate the number of children parents might choose if they were unconstrained in their choices – that is, if biological constraints or cultural practices did not limit their fertility in any way. However, Easterlin does not stop his analysis with an examination of 'demand'. Central to his concern is the integration of the 'biological' constraints on fertility ('supply') and the choice constraints families face.

On the 'supply' side, Easterlin argues that a combination of biological and cultural factors determines the natural fertility of the population and defines the upper limit to family-size. Populations have different levels of 'natural' fertility, depending on such factors as the frequency of intercourse, the length of breastfeeding, the existence of fecundity impairments from causes such as venereal disease or the practice of temporary abstinence, as in parts of India where the wife returns to the home of her parents after the birth of a child, or in other developing countries where the male household members may be away from home as seasonal workers for months at a time.

We have enclosed the terms 'supply' and 'demand' in quotation marks to indicate the special use of these terms in this literature. Usually, economists think of supply and demand as distinct sets of forces which are equilibrated through the market. Here, the reference is to two different but not entirely distinct sets of forces, both of which presumably operate within the individual (or by conventional but debatably inappropriate extension the couple, the family or the household). A problem arises because a number of the forces which affect fertility can easily be conceptualised as working through either supply or demand, or both. The effect of child-mortality is the most obvious, but the role of contraception is another. Thus the use of these terms at best lacks the precise meaning it has in some other situations, and at worst can be misleading. Whether the average family in the society reaches this limit depends on the availability and the use of contraception or deliberate individually-decided efforts to limit fertility. Since contraception involves costs, the decision-maker finds himself or herself trading off the possible gains to be had from family limitation against the costs of contraception. Thus, the 'sociology' or 'supply' side of the Easterlin model concerns the biological and cultural mechanisms which affect the ability of the family to achieve a desired number of children. The assumption is that these mechanisms are beyond the control of the family; they are constraints in the environment of the family rather than decision variables.

Easterlin used these two concepts of 'supply' and 'demand' to explore a number of different equilibrium solutions for the individual family, and for the society as it moves from a situation of 'excess demand' to one of restricted fertility. Thus, his model is quite consistent with the new home-economics models in terms of the 'demand' side, but extends the work of the Chicago school by introducing the wider range of questions associated with the 'supply' side as well. (The Easterlin model is discussed as Model 5 in the appendix.)

The Easterlin model has shortcomings, some of which it shares with the new home-economics model: it is not dynamic, and it has problems of variable definition. The model, like those of Leibenstein and most of the new home-economics school as well, ignores sex preferences, uncertainty and irreversibility as elements in the family-building process. A major problem with the model is that, as a general framework, it offers few specific testable propositions. It does suggest that biological factors and variables related to preferences will be relevant to the explanation of fertility differentials, but it does not provide explicit guidelines as to how they should be incorporated into an empirical science of fertility. Moreover, some of the variables which enter through the 'supply' side may be relevant to a study of the demand side of fertility as well. For example, natural fertility and contraceptive technology are both affected by fertility attitudes, which are given prominence on the 'demand' side. Without a clear distinction between the two classes of factors that affect fertility, the model may fail to precisely or uniquely identify the influence of individual variables on observed fertility.

In addition to Leibenstein and Easterlin, a number of other economists have studied fertility from a perspective consistent with the social-determinants approach discussed above. In contrast, much of this additional work is basically empirical in its orientation. Shared by all of these authors, however, is an emphasis on the role of preferences in explaining fertility differentials. Preferences, as defined by economists, are usually considered to be unobservable. This is true whether we are defining preferences as in the utility function of the new home-economics school or the special characteristics of the preference function used by Leibenstein. One of the central problems in the theoretical assertion that preferences are important is finding a way of measuring preferences so as to test the degree of association which exists between preferences and observed fertility behaviour.

Economists have used a number of different strategies for trying to operationalise the notion of preferences. Turchi (1975b) has suggested that preferences might be measured by such social characteristics as rural/urban origin, education or religious affiliation, arguing that there should be differentials in the fertility behaviour of persons of different social backgrounds, even when income and price effects are controlled for, as measured in conventional home-economics models.

In his formal model builidng, Turchi, like those writing in the new home-economics framework, uses an allocative, utility-maximising framework. In contrast with the new home-economics school, he permits the socio-economic background variables to enter both the theoretical and the empirical models through a number of mechanisms. Firstly, he makes the price of children (which in the original Becker model is the same to all couples) a function of family income. Secondly, the production function for children is taken to be a function of socio-demographic background. Finally, background characteristics are allowed to enter the estimation equations directly as a measure of differences in preferences. Thus, while the Turchi framework is consistent with that of the new home-economics school in many respects, it extends it considerably without sacrificing the formal properties as does the Easterlin model. Turchi also uses his model to derive a set of equations to be estimated.

There are limitations to the Turchi model which restrict its applicability to the study of fertility in developing countries. As the model is basically designed to explain fertility differentials in the US, there is no consideration of the biological constraints in the formal model. The model also shares with most of the models discussed above the problem that it is a static lifetime maximisation approach. Thus, there is little possibility of adaptive behaviour within the framework.

Mueller (1972) has suggested that preferences can, to some degree, be measured directly through the use of survey instruments. She asked respondents a series of questions, which was then used as a basis for constructing indices of their perceptions of the benefits and the costs of children. She has also used social characteristics in the same manner as Turchi, to construct indicators of social groups. She found that parents' perceptions of the costs and benefits of children are important in predicting fertility, and also that there is an important predictive impact of social group status that goes beyond what might be expected from the theory as constructed by economists working within the tradition of the new home-economics. Similar findings have been made in India (Anker, 1977; Anker and Anker, 1982).

Some social scientists have gone further in attempting to measure preferences directly. The Value of Children Project (Fawcett, 1974), for example, asked respondents in a wide variety of cultural settings about the gains and losses which they associated with different family-sizes. Researchers involved in the study found that their respondents were able to describe a large number of roles that children played in the lives of the family and were able, in some sense, to articulate major elements in the preference structure as it relates to choices between fertility and alternative uses of time and other resources.

A complication with the use of preferences as explanations of fertility behaviour arises in the identification of the causal structure which is involved. Many economists, even those associated with the new home-economics school, might agree that preferences would yield empirically reliable predictions of fertility. Many of these same economists would argue that these preferences were themselves a reflection of the basic economic circumstances in which the family finds itself. Thus they would argue that instead of being independent causal structures, preferences are intermediate structures translating the effects of exogenous forces such as the value of the wife's time or the resource base of the family into fertility behaviour. In this interpretation, preferences, instead of having an independent causal relationship to fertility, are links in a more complex process which may be better studied by abstracting from their very existence (T. P. Schultz, 1981, p. 151).

Summary of Micro-economic Approaches to the Study of Fertility

During recent years, there has been a vast expansion in the number of studies of household fertility behaviour undertaken by economists. This range of studies has confirmed that there is a significant degree of association between fertility and many other predictive variables of interest to economists, whatever school of thinking they are associated with. In general, however, the level of empirical explanation using economic models has not been high, and even where significant levels of statistical association are reported, there is an open and largely unresolved question as to whether the micro-economic models address questions related to the fundamental changes in society, or whether they only mirror minor variations within a larger societal pattern. Thus, there is, at this stage, certainly no reason for thinking that the results of empirical research within the micro-economic tradition give us an adequate basis for predicting fertility change during periods of rapid social change. They may give us guidance for how some social-change programmes operate within a relatively stable social environment, and they may suggest hypotheses about variables operating at the level of the society, but there is every reason to believe that there will be a continuing need for research which is conducted both at the societal and at the individual level. There is also a need for the development of new theoretical structures which might shed further light on how these two levels of social behaviour are interrelated. These approaches are the subject of the next section.

NEW THEORETICAL APPROACHES

Despite the complexity and the sheer magnitude of the work that has gone into developing an adequate theory of fertility, there is little consensus on a single theory which dominates all others. Empirical tests, some of which will be reviewed in the next two chapters, have not by most measures led to sufficient support for any particular line of theorising. Perhaps more important, among both economists and other social scientists there is a feeling that present theories do not capture, even in a heuristic manner, the most important elements in the process which determines fertility at either the household or the societal level. As a result, there is continuing theoretical ferment in the economics of fertility. Given the amount of work that has been done in this area previously, it is not to be expected that the new work would represent entirely new approaches, but cumulatively substantial shifts seem inherent in some recent writing. Two kinds of innovation can be discussed here. Firstly, there has been a new interest in the question of how social institutions affect the decisions made at the level of the couple. In other words, there is a new concern with reconciling the macro-economic with the micro-economic approaches. Secondly, and not independent from the first point, there is a new concern

Overview

with the causal framework within which the theory is expected to operate.

A number of groups have suggested the need to examine social structures other than the extremes of the nuclear family or the society at large. A focus on intermediate structures may yield insights into the relationship between economic conditions and fertility. Structuralists such as McNicoll (1975, 1978, 1980) argue that the micro theories of fertility, while interesting and perhaps worthy of further investigation, are not complete in and of themselves. One alternative is to examine the general characteristics of a society and its relationship to fertility. This approach concentrates neither on the macro-economic characteristics of the society such as per capita income, nor on the attributes of individual families. Rather it focuses on the structures which connect families, i.e. social classes, lineage groups, political and administrative structures, etc. The micro behaviour in this analysis is not self-contained, but is explicitly related to other structures such as the local political system.

The purpose of the structuralist analysis as applied in the field of population studies is to better understand the full set of interrelationships between population and development and, as a by-product of that analysis, to make clear the full determinants of fertility.

> [D] emographic change over the course of development cannot properly be isolated from the overall style of the development process. Demographic behavior, just as economic behavior, is governed in important respects by underlying patterns of social and administrative organization. (McNicoll, 1978.)

Two elements in this general approach seem of special importance. Firstly, the analysis pays specific attention to the possibility that there may be an explicit interdependence between population change and other aspects of development. Demographic behaviour is not only determined by the economic environment, but may itself affect that environment, and the social scientist must take into account both kinds of interdependence in order to permit adequate predictions or explanation. This dynamic perspective would seem to imply that the researcher must build a distinct time perspective or historical viewpoint into the research. Secondly, and perhaps more important, the focus of analysis should not be restricted to the family, as is often the case in micro-economic theories of fertility, but should include other social units as well.

The empirical orientation suggested by the structuralist perspective contrasts sharply with that of the micro-economic perspectives reviewed in the previous section. Thus far, this school has emphasised case-studies of particular countries or regions. Arthur and McNicoll (1978) have reviewed the special characteristics of Bangladesh society which encourages continuing high fertility despite the social costs of high population growth. McNicoll (1980) has, in another paper, provided examples of social institutions in Bali and parts of China that encourage social control of fertility. The acknowledged weakness of this empirical orientation is its inability to generate falsifiable hypotheses relating to a particular region before the data for the region are collected and used. On the other hand, the method yields major insights into the dynamic interrelationships between population and development. Other complementary approaches may eventually lead to generalisability of the results from structuralist research. This research approach draws on techniques from outside the usual range of tools used by economists. In any case, given the low levels of explanation and the static nature of the results from the micro-economics approach, there is much to be gained by exploring alternative approaches. One particularly interesting application of this general approach has been the suggestion that a central dimension characterising different social and economic systems is the degree of inherent economic security. Some systems provide less protection for their members than others; and, as a result, to the extent that a large family reduces risk, there may be a strong pro-natalist force in societies with inadequate provisions for mutual economic security (Cain, 1980).

The special contribution of the structuralist approach may be to focus attention on the need for a reconciliation of the macro and micro perspectives. Much of the research on Third World societies taken as national units has suggested that rapid rates of population growth may make it more difficult to obtain desired gains from development. While there may be some aspects of development that are unaffected by population growth or are even improved by it, and while rapid population growth may be desirable in some circumstances, in many Third World situations its effects are likely to be detrimental. On the other hand, the basic emphasis in the literature on the economics of the family gives quite a different perspective, for in this literature it is assumed that families make decisions that are in their own self-interest, and if they have a large number of children it is because they want them. The reconciliation of negative gains at the level of the society, with positive gains for the family, is one of the central analytical challenges for theorists and their empirically-oriented counterparts.

One explanatory model which is often advanced draws on game theory (Hardin, 1968; Kahan, 1974). The so-called 'prisoner's dilemma' is used to illustrate that the outcomes to individuals and the society can depend in a very sensitive manner on whether there is cooperation among individuals; i.e. whether there is a functioning community with interdependence among its constituent units, or whether individuals act on their own. In the following matrix, individuals *A* and *B* receive the pay-offs indicated in the four cells, depending upon the conditions spelled out in the headings.

	A cooperates and reduces fertility	*A* refuses to cooperate and has high fertility
B cooperates and reduces fertility	8, 8	10, 4
B refuses to cooperate and has high fertility	4, 10	5, 5

If both individuals involved in this simple interaction attempt to cooperate, each receives higher benefits or gains than he would if both refuse to cooperate. The dilemma arises because if one of the two cooperates and the other refuses, the one cooperating will lose both absolutely and in comparison with the other. Conversely, the non-cooperator will gain on both counts. Thus, in the absence of any system of assuring joint compliance, there is a strong incentive to 'go it on your own'.

How is this theory relevant to fertility? The basic idea is that if a community can reduce its fertility, all of the members may gain through a higher standard of living, but there is no easy mechanism to ensure this outcome. In the absence of an enforced agreement, the individual is better off by maintaining high fertility. Thus, independent of what B chooses, A's pay-off is larger if column 2 is chosen.

The model clearly has some weaknesses when it is applied to Third World nations taken as a whole. Usually, the élite, even in the Third World, seem to have lower fertility than their less advantaged counterparts, and it is difficult to see that they are harmed, at least in a relative sense, by their lower fertility. On the other hand, the model may be a more reasonable explanation of one of the barriers to fertility-decline in a village-size community where there is more homogeneity of background and where there are likely to be direct opportunities for individuals to make decisions about the degree of cooperation they will show to each other.

The structuralist approach is closely related to the contemporary Marxist (neo-Marxist) approach to the study of fertility. Marxists are particularly concerned with explaining how demographic patterns within any given time-period or social environment relate to the dominating economic and political institutions. Thus, they have a strong concern with the pattern of change over time. They also tend to focus on social class and its relationship to fertility. Mamdani (1972), in a well known critique of Wyon and Gordon's (1971) study of a North Indian community, has attempted to explain fertility differentials in terms of class interests. The modern Marxist perspective is somewhat narrower than the structuralist perspective, in that it is not concerned with intermediate organisational structures except as they can be given a dialectical interpretation.

Complementing the structuralist (or the related Marxist) approaches is the recent emphasis on community-level variables in the study of fertility, which has grown largely out of the empirical literature on fertility. Communities, taken as aggregate structures (village, extended family or clan, region, etc.) between the nuclear family and the nation, may play at least two kinds of roles in determining fertility (McNicoll, 1975; Caldwell, 1976; Anker, 1977). Firstly, there is a strong extra-familial but local influence on the way preferences are defined. An important implication of this influence is that an examination of the immediate environment of the individual may give some clue to his or her preference structure. Secondly, both in terms of preferences and other constraints on fertility such as the availability of contraception, the community environment provides ways of approaching the individual that may not be obvious when research deals with the individual family in isolation. From a policy point of view, this suggests, for example, that one may choose to work through the leadership of a village rather than directly approaching individuals. The possibility of measuring variables at the level of the community provides the opportunity for defining both preference-related variables and environmental constraints on the basis of information drawn neither from the family nor from impersonal aggregate statistics. It is hoped that this possibility will open economic theory in this area to a wider range of fertility determinants, and to new ways of thinking about the aggregation of family behaviour.

Thus far, economists have paid little attention to the question of who is the decision-maker in the area of fertility. Husbands and wives may have conflicting interests. Either one of them or some other family member, such as the husband's mother, may be the primary decision-maker in the area of fertility. Alternatively, there may be a process of bargaining or joint decision-making. The Caldwells' work suggests that this question needs a thorough examinination. Once a clearer idea is developed of who makes decisions, the implications for economic analysis can be examined. Economic models of bargaining or learning, some of which are not based on optimisation, may then be explored in the hopes that these models could give better predictions of fertility decisions than those derived from the theories we have examined thus far. Theories built within this framework are likely to emphasise sequential rather than lifetime decisions. A second implication is that external effects more generally will have to be built into economic theories of fertility. This re-examination of the family may also provide a linkage with some of the structuralist concerns described above. The couple's decision framework may be greatly influenced both by the extended family and by the wider community (Thadani, 1978).

Another new emphasis which seems to be emerging in recent literature is a recognition that the appropriate framework for analysis may be not the full lifetime of the couple, but each year as it occurs. The basic new home-economics framework assumes that the couple makes a lifetime decision about fertility and related matters such as the work involvement of the wife. But, for many purposes, it may be that the couple will make decisions on a year-to-year or a child-by-child basis. The fertility decision for this year may take the form of deciding, on the basis of the current endowment of children and of other resources, whether to go on to have additional children, stop, or undertake some sort of intermediate step (e.g. use contraceptives with some risk of pregnancy). Similar decisions will be taken each time-period, rather than taken singly at the beginning of a marriage. Within this framework, adaptations to uncertain events such as the death of a child, the loss of a job or the sex composition of the family may be more easily dealt with than in the case of the lifetime decision framework.

CONCLUSION

During the last 30 years, there has been a steady expansion of interest among economists in the study of demographic phenomena and, in particular, fertility. No single dominant model has emerged from this work. Largely independent traditions of research tend to exist for households and aggregate populations. At the household level there has been, however, a convergence in the terms of the language that is now used to describe the elements in the theory. Economists view fertility as a rational process where the actors (the couples, men and women at risk of conception) go through some sort of weighing of the costs and benefits of different family-sizes or of having additional children. Parents are seen as having a choice, conscious or unconscious, over their family-size. According to this approach, the behaviour of these actors can be predicted by understanding the criteria that the parents use for making choices, and the environmental constraints which limit their ability to attain the optimum number of children.

We introduced this chapter with a discussion of theories and the role that they play in the progress of an empirically-based science. The rest of this chapter has been devoted to a review of the theoretical literature on the economics of fertility. This review suggests that while there has been a great deal of theorising about fertility, on the whole this process does not correspond very closely to the ideal scientific process described in the introduction to the chapter. Instead of a process where theories and their testable implications are worked out and then compared with existing data, and rejected or further refined for additional rounds of testing, we find that the field is characterised by a wide range of co-existing but partially-contradictory theories, with few if any characteristics which would permit a decisive test.

The current state of economic theories suggests that the scientific process is still at a very early stage of development. We have recognised a range of empirical regularities characterising fertility behaviour in different settings. While there has been some consensus developed about the broadest characteristics of a micro-economics of fertility, we still have a variety of abstract 'stories' to tell about these relationships. Often, different stories can be used to explain the same observations, and no one has yet managed to formulate a story that incorporates enough of the facts to convince all, or even a large percentage, of the professional and policy-making audience.

APPENDIX: THE FORMAL STRUCTURE OF MICRO-ECONOMIC MODELS OF FERTILITY BEHAVIOUR
Eric Jensen

In this appendix, the analytical core of several economic models of fertility is examined. An economic model is defined as one in which scarce resources are allocated according to some decision rule. The result is a class of models which includes, but is not limited to, utility-maximisation subject to a budget constraint. The first model presented below may be thought of as the 'basic' micro-economic model of fertility – prices are exogenous, preferences are well-behaved and constant over time, and income is measured in purely monetary units. The models which follow this basic one deviate from it in one or more of these assumptions. For example, the 'new home-economics' models make prices endogenous and time a component of the budget constraint. Leibenstein allows for increasing marginal utilities, thus focusing attention on the preference function rather than the budget constraint, and Easterlin goes one step further and allows preferences to change over time.

Model 0: The Basic Model

The simplest model is one in which parents derive utility from number of children, N, and all other 'goods', Z. They attempt to maximise over their lifetimes a utility function whose arguments are N and Z, subject to a lifetime (or permanent) income constraint. That is, they

$$
\begin{aligned}
&\text{maximize} \quad U = U(N, Z) \\
&\text{subject to} \quad p_N N + p_Z Z = I,
\end{aligned}
\tag{1}
$$

where p_N and p_Z represent the price of N and Z, and I is lifetime income.[1] In the standard analytical model of consumer theory, people's choices are described by the maximisation of a utility function subject to the price and income constraints of the budget equation. In order to model fertility within this framework, it is necessary to treat the number of children born as the result of a single decision; thus, parents are assumed to know all that will happen to them over their lifetimes, or in other words, to maximise a lifetime utility function. It is then possible to perform comparative-static analysis, which compares the change in the optimal level of consumption for any good as prices and income change, of the fertility decision as if it were any other consumption decision. Comparative static conclusions about behaviour can be drawn from inspection of the first-order conditions and differentiation of the budget constraint. The first-order conditions, which are the first derivatives of the maximisation problem with respect to the goods (and the budget constraint), describe optimal choices given the constraints faced by the family, while differentiation of the budget constraint shows how this behaviour will change as the constraint changes. From the first-order conditions, we have

$$
\frac{\partial U(N^*, Z^*)}{\partial N} = \lambda p_N \quad \text{and} \quad \frac{\partial U(N^*, Z^*)}{\partial Z} = \lambda p_Z \quad \text{or}
\tag{2}
$$

$$\frac{\partial U(N^*, Z^*)/\partial N}{\partial U(N^*, Z^*)/\partial Z} = \frac{p_N}{p_Z}, \tag{3}$$

where λ is the Lagrange multiplier (or the marginal utility of money).

The second expression says that parents will choose $N^*(p_N, p_Z, I)$ and $Z^*(p_N, p_Z, I)$ such that the marginal rate of substitution, which is the ratio of marginal utilities provided by consuming N and Z at the optimal levels N^* and Z^*, equals the price ratio. As either price changes, the quantities N^* and Z^* demanded will change as well (when income is held constant). It is possible to examine how a given price change affects demand, but this is beyond the scope of this appendix (see Henderson and Quandt, 1980, pp. 31-6; or Varian, 1978, pp. 95-9).

N^* and Z^* will also change as income changes. The effect of a small change in income can be analysed by differentiating the budget constraint with respect to income. The derivatives $\partial N/\partial I$ and $\partial Z/\partial I$ are interpreted as the increase in demand accompanying the increase in income. Differentiating the budget constraint with respect to income yields

$$1 = \frac{Np_N}{I} \eta_N + \frac{Zp_Z}{I} \eta_Z, \tag{4}$$

where the η_{X_i} represent income elasticities $\partial X_i/\partial I \cdot I/X_i$. The income elasticities, weighted by the proportion of income spent on each good, sum to one, since all of the change in income must be spent.

In order for these implications to be of any practical interest, they must be empirically falsifiable. It is intuitively clear upon examination of (3) that without knowledge of what $U(N, Z)$ is, one cannot know what values $\partial U(N, Z)/\partial N$ or $\partial U(N, Z)/\partial Z$ take, and so what the optimal consumption levels N^* and Z^* are for prices p_N and p_Z. A functional form must be imposed upon the utility function, from which the relevant demand functions can be derived. In fact, having demand functions, which express optimal consumption as functions of prices and income, is a much stronger result than merely being able to solve for N^* and Z^* at given values of p_N, p_Z and I. A common way to proceed is to assume, for example, that the utility function is Cobb–Douglas (log-linear). The utility function is then written as

$$U(N, Z) = N^a Z^b \quad \text{or}$$
$$\ln U(N, Z) = a \ln N + b \ln Z, \tag{5}$$

where ln represents the natural logarithm. Maximizing (5) subject to the budget constraint, and solving the resulting first-order conditions for N and Z, yields demand functions for N and Z in terms of prices and income, that is, the desired consumption of N and Z given income, I, and prices, p_N and p_Z. By substituting a/N for $\partial U/\partial N$, b/Z for $\partial U/\partial Z$ in (3) and using $p_N N = I - p_Z Z$ (from the budget constraint), one can derive the following demand functions:

$$N(p_N, p_Z, I) = \frac{aI}{(a + b)p_N}, \tag{6a}$$

$$Z(p_N, p_Z, I) = \frac{bI}{(a + b)p_Z}. \tag{6b}$$

Suppose one wants to estimate these functions. Assuming that prices and income and quantities consumed are known, it is possible to regress, say, N on I/p_N to obtain an estimate of $a/(a + b)$, call it $\hat{a}(\hat{a} + \hat{b})$. An empirical estimate of ϵ_{NN}, the own-price elasticity of $N(p_N/N \cdot \partial N/\partial p_N)$, which is a measure of how responsive N is to a change in its price, is then

$$\epsilon_{NN} = \frac{p_N}{N} \frac{\partial N(p_N, p_Z, I)}{\partial p_N} = -\frac{\hat{a}}{\hat{a} + \hat{b}} \frac{I}{p_N N}. \tag{7}$$

Observed values of I, N and p_N make up the remainder of expression (7).

Note that demand functions are defined for unchanging preferences, so that regressions based on cross-sectional data do not yield estimates of the same parameters as those discussed above, since preferences vary across people. Such regressions are helpful, however, in obtaining an estimate of the 'average' values of these parameters. They make it possible to compare the differential effects for the population studied on consumption of two goods, given a change in their prices, for example.

While some haziness in the definitions of variables is natural in theoretical models, the transition to estimation points up the severe problems one would encounter in attempting to actually obtain values for an expression like (7). Using the observed values of I, N and p_N sounds simple, but in fact this procedure raises several questions. The theoretical answers which have been developed are described below.

Model 1: The Becker Model

Firstly, Becker's (1960) model was developed around the idea that parents care about the quality as well as the quantity of children. The model can be specified as

$$\text{max.} \quad U = U(N, Q, Z)$$
$$\text{s.t.} \quad p_N N + p_Q Q + p_Z Z = I, \tag{8}$$

where Q represents 'quality' per child.

While, intuitively, this specification seems more realistic than our earlier version, this small modification actually weakens the empirical usefulness of the model. Compare the following equation, obtained by differentiating the budget constraint of (8) with respect to income, with equation (4):

$$1 = \frac{N p_N}{I} \eta_N + \frac{Q p_Q}{I} \eta_Q + \frac{Z p_Z}{I} \eta_Z. \tag{9}$$

In (4), which is based on the assumption that child quality is not an argument in the utility function (i.e. does not matter to the parents), part of a change in income would be allocated to N and the other part to Z - clear income elasticities would result. However if the theory assumes that parents derive utility from the quality as well as from the quantity of their children, as in (8), the effect of a change in income on N is less clear. Since the portion of income allocated to Z and the income elasticity of Z have not changed as a result of specifying the source of satisfaction from children in greater detail, it must be the case that the observable effect of a change in income on N (the income elasticity η_N from (4)) is not the true effect of income on the number of children demanded - some part of what we actually observe is the quality response. Thus, we are left with one equation in which two unknowns - η_N and η_Q - determine the observed income elasticity, and so an unfalsifiable hypothesis, unless, of course, η_Q is known. Alternatively, one may assume a value or sign for η_Q and derive conditional conclusions. For example, DeTray (1973) has employed a set of variables describing the parents, in an attempt to estimate a production function for quality, in order to treat Q as if it were known. Quality is assumed to be measured by average educational expenditure per child within United States counties. The estimated income elasticities of expenditures for husband's and wife's income are conditional estimates of η_Q if expenditures are assumed representative of child quality.

Model 2: The Simple New Home-economics Model

The idea of the 'new home-economics' (see Becker, 1965) is to include non-monetary costs and resources, specifically time, into the decision-making process. In this simple model, quality is not assumed to be a concern to parents. Defining 'full income' as

$$wT + Y = F, \tag{10}$$

where w represents the wage rate, T the total time available (e.g. 16 hours per day per person) and Y non-labour income, we have a measure which reflects the dual constraints facing parents – money, which is obtained from market labour, and time, which is used in non-market activities as well as in market labour. Multiplying hours spent on children (or other home-produced goods) by some prevailing wage rate, the parents' decisions are more accurately represented, since by employing this formulation we include both monetary and time costs incurred by the parents in their consumption decision. It is possible, following Willis (1973), to explicitly develop the mechanisms through which the money and time costs of inputs to children are translated into the price of N. A full presentation of these results is inappropriate here. The assumption will be made that these 'home production functions' are sufficiently inelastic that an increase in the cost of any input to N yields an increase in p_N.

Theoretical work by Mincer (1962) on wage functions, together with empirical work such as Gronau's (1974) or Heckman's (1974, 1976) on self-selection bias, demonstrate that the 'shadow wage' – the wage of non-employed persons – can be estimated. Since the wage of employed persons is (we hope) observable, knowledge of the time spent on various child-related activities, together with information on expenditures for purchased goods, is enough to estimate prices which reflect the opportunity cost of different activities.

The inclusion of shadow prices into the model introduces a new set of theoretical problems. To concentrate on these problems, the presentation here is restricted to the simplest model consistent with the new constraint defined by (10), where quality is not an argument of the utility function; that is,

$$\begin{aligned} \text{max.} \quad & U = U(N, Z) \\ \text{s.t.} \quad & wT + Y = F = p_N N + p_Z Z. \end{aligned} \tag{11}$$

The demand functions are the same as those of Model 0, except that money income, I, is replaced as an argument by full income, F, e.g. $N = N(p_N, p_Z, F)$. Because prices depend on the wage rate, the effect of income on fertility is again unclear. To see this, differentiate the budget constraint with respect to full income:

$$1 = N \frac{\partial p_N}{\partial F} + \frac{N p_N}{F} \eta_N + Z \frac{\partial p_Z}{\partial F} + \frac{Z p_Z}{F} \eta_Z. \tag{12}$$

If full income changes because of a change in the wage rate of a parent who supplies time inputs to children, both prices and income change. Because, for example, an increase in wages yields both a higher price for 'goods' such as N which require parents' time and (assuming a positively-sloped labour-supply curve) higher income, the total effect which a wage change has on demand for N (or Z) is unclear. The positive sign of $\partial p_N / \partial F$ (the price increase) may or may not dominate the income effect, η_N, associated with an increase in the wage rate. Thus, the effect on N^* of an increase in the wage rate is unclear.

Model 3: Becker–Lewis

Becker and Lewis (1973) have analysed a model which incorporates child-quality as both an argument of the utility function and a full-income budget constraint:

$$\begin{aligned} &\text{max.} \quad U = U(N, Q, Z) \\ &\text{s.t.} \quad pNQ + p_Z Z = F \end{aligned} \tag{13}$$

where p represents the price of a unit of NQ, that is, of a child of given quality. Unsurprisingly, the result is a quite complicated model. For the sake of concreteness, we again impose the Cobb-Douglas form on the utility function, and so solve the following problem:

$$\begin{aligned} &\text{max.} \quad U(N, Q, Z) = N^a Q^b Z^c \quad \text{or} \\ &\text{max.} \quad \ln U(N, Q, Z) = a \ln N + b \ln Q + c \ln Z \\ &\text{s.t.} \quad pNQ + p_Z Z = F. \end{aligned} \tag{14}$$

The first-order conditions include the following:

$$\frac{a}{N} = \frac{\partial U(N, Q, Z)}{\partial N} = \lambda Q p,$$

$$\frac{b}{Q} = \frac{\partial U(N, Q, Z)}{\partial Q} = \lambda N p, \tag{15}$$

$$\frac{c}{Z} = \frac{\partial U(N, Q, Z)}{\partial Z} = \lambda p_Z.$$

The shadow prices of N, Q and Z (that is, the prices on which the parents base their decisions, which may not be observable or even derivable by the researcher) can be written as $\pi_N = Qp$, $\pi_Q = Np$ and $\pi_Z = p_Z$. That Qp is the shadow price of N and Np the shadow price of Q is implied by (15), because at the utility-maximising solution, the marginal utility of a good (such as N and Q) must equal the shadow price of that good times λ, the marginal utility of money. Thus, the budget constraint is non-linear in N and Q. π_N increases as Q increases, and π_Q increases as N increases, yielding a curve which is convex to the origin. These comments are illustrated in Figure 2.1.

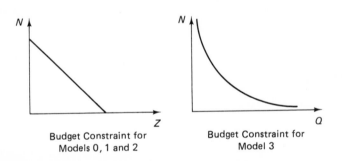

Budget Constraint for　　　　　Budget Constraint for
Models 0, 1 and 2　　　　　　　　Model 3

FIGURE 2.1

One can examine the comparative-static implications of a change in full income by differentiating the budget constraint with respect to full income. Compare the result to equation (4):

$$1 = NQ \frac{\partial p}{\partial F} + \frac{N\pi_N}{F} \eta_N + \frac{Q\pi_Q}{F} \eta_Q + Z \frac{\partial \pi_Z}{\partial F} + \frac{Z\pi_Z}{F} \eta_Z. \tag{16}$$

Clearly, even if a change in F comes from changes in non-labour income, so that price changes are zero (i.e. $\partial \pi_i / \partial F = 0$), we are faced with our earlier child-quality result: namely, that the effect of any exogenous change in income on fertility is ambiguous, since the increase can change both N^* and Q^*, and π_N and π_Q change as Q and N change. The situation is made worse when the income change is the result of a change in the wage rate, since, in addition to the above indirect effects, π_N and π_Q also vary directly because of changing costs. Proceeding to estimation, the endogeneity of prices presents further problems. The demand function for number of children is

$$N(p, p_Z, F, Q) = \frac{a}{(c+a)} \frac{F}{pQ(p, p_Z, F, N)} \tag{17}$$

and for quality is

$$Q(p, p_Z, F, N) = \frac{b}{(c+b)} \frac{F}{pN(p, p_Z, F, Q)} \tag{18}$$

Once again, we have solved the first-order conditions jointly for N and Q to obtain these functions, using the budget constraint to substitute for Zp_Z. The two equations must be simultaneously estimated, since the demand for quality depends on number, and the demand for number depends on quality. As shown above, the return on the effort involved in formulating and estimating a simultaneous empirical model is small at best. The model, even if it were estimable (in particular, if it were identified), yields no testable theoretical implications.

Model 4: The Leibenstein Model

It is possible to construct a testable model consistent with Leibenstein's theory. Defining $\bar{Z}$ as the SIG-determined consumption standard (see text for a more complete description), the problem faced by the family can be written as:

$$\begin{aligned} \text{max.} \quad & U = U(N, Z, \bar{Z}) \\ \text{s.t.} \quad & p_N N + p_Z Z = \text{I.} \end{aligned} \tag{19}$$

This utility function, in contrast to the earlier ones, is defined over a somewhat shorter time-period than those of the previous models. The exact period under consideration is left by Leibenstein to the researcher's discretion. He refers to 'direct' and 'indirect' (or opportunity) costs in childraising, arising through foregone activities (generally on the part of the mother), so that p_N should probably vary with income. Thus, differentiating the budget constraint will yield a result identical to that obtained in Model 2, except that Leibenstein does not employ the notion of full income:

$$1 = N \frac{\partial p_N}{\partial I} + \frac{N p_N}{I} \eta_N + Z \frac{\partial p_Z}{\partial I} + \frac{Z p_Z}{I} \eta_Z. \tag{20}$$

Lacking an explicit notion such as full income, the exact meaning of the terms $\partial p_N / \partial I$ and $\partial p_Z / \partial I$ is unclear. (Recall that in the new home-economics framework, these derivatives were based on changes in the underlying home-production functions.)

Suppose that the parents receive positive utility from consumption of Z which exceeds $\overline{Z}$, and negative utility if Z falls short of $\overline{Z}$. Then it is possible to specify the following log-linear utility function:

$$U(N, Z, \overline{Z}) = N^a (Z/\overline{Z})^b \quad \text{or}$$
$$\ln U(N, Z, \overline{Z}) = a \ln N + b \ln (Z/\overline{Z}), \tag{21}$$

which, when maximised subject to the budget constraint of (19), yields first-order conditions

$$\frac{a}{N} = \lambda p_N, \quad \frac{b}{Z} = \lambda p_Z, \quad p_N N + p_Z Z = I. \tag{22}$$

There is no first-order condition associated with $\overline{Z}$, since this is not subject to choice. The resulting demand functions are similar to those of Model 0 (equation (6)) (and of Model 2, except for the definition of income):

$$N^*(p_N, p_Z, I) = \frac{aI}{(a+b)p_N}$$

and

$$Z^*(p_N, p_Z, I) = \frac{bI}{(a+b)p_Z} \tag{23}$$

This presentation seems to capture the basic thrust of Leibenstein's model, but in his description he also mentions a number of issues which cannot be easily formalised. Without this greater elaboration the model is not empirically differentiable from Model 2.

Model 5: The Easterlin et al. Model

Easterlin (1978) and Easterlin, Pollak and Wachter (1980) have modified Model 2 so that it takes into account two relevant parameters – the cost of fertility control and the biological limit on fertility. Letting α represent the disutility attached to fertility regulation (an indicator of the non-monetary costs), where $0 < \alpha \leq 1$, p_B represent the variable cost per birth averted, p_I be the cost expended in finding out about fertility regulation, and Y be the level of natural fertility, Model 2 can be rewritten as

$$\begin{aligned} \max. \quad & U(N, \alpha Z) \\ \text{s.t.} \quad & p_N N + p_Z Z + p_I + p_B (Y - N) = I, \quad N^* \leq Y. \end{aligned} \tag{24}$$

If the demand for children, $N(p_N, p_Z, p_I, p_B, I, \alpha)$, is at least as big as Y, the demand functions are simple:

$$N^*(p_N, p_Z, p_I, p_B, I) = Y, \quad Z^*(p_N, p_Z, p_I, p_B, I) = \frac{I - p_N N}{p_Z}; \tag{25}$$

that is, all the income that is left over after supporting the children is spent on Z. If $N^* < Y$, the demand functions are again analogous to those of Model 2. Maximising the logarithm of a utility function such as

$$U(N, \alpha Z) = N^a (\alpha Z)^b, \tag{26}$$

subject to the constraints of (24), yields demand functions such as

$$N^*(p_N, p_Z, p_I, p_B, I) = \frac{a(I - p_I - p_B Y)}{(b + a)(p_N - p_B)} \tag{27}$$

Comparison of equations (25) and (27) with equation (6a) shows that (6a) is likely either to understate the demand for children or to overstate the importance of economic variables when natural fecundity is a binding constraint, and, because it does not include all of the relevant prices, that (6a) is likely to be incorrect even if fecundity is not a binding constraint.

NOTE

1. Formally, the problem is one of constrained maximisation. This type of problem is solved by setting up the Lagrangian function

$$L = U(N, Z) + \lambda(I - p_N N - p_Z Z) \tag{1a}$$

and differentiating it with respect to N, Z and λ, the Lagrangian multiplier. From these three equations (or, in general, the $n + 1$ equations, where n is the number of arguments of the utility function which parents are able to choose), it is possible to eliminate λ and solve for the quantities of N and Z which maximise utility. See Chiang, 1974, pp. 373–403, or any basic calculus text, for further reference.

3 Research on the Determinants of Fertility

GEORGE B. SIMMONS

In Chapter 2 we emphasised the necessary interaction between theory-building and empirical research. Theories are meaningful only if under some imaginable circumstances they could be proven wrong, and in an ideal world there would be a constant interplay between the two parts of the scientific process. In that chapter, however, we gave little emphasis to the history of empirical research and to the findings that have accumulated during the past two decades. The first part of this chapter provides a review of this literature. The purpose of this review is to examine briefly the empirical findings concerning the extent to which a variety of explanatory variables, including biological variables, infant and child mortality, the role of women, education, and access to resources, have been shown to directly or indirectly explain observed variations in fertility. Many of these variables are used in the case-studies in Part III of this volume. The second part of the chapter presents an overview of some of the major difficulties with doing empirical research on fertility.

It needs to be emphasised that there is no very exact correspondence beween empirical findings and particular theories. More than one theory may suggest the importance of a given variable, and a given empirical variable may be used as a proxy for more than one theoretical concept. In reviewing each of the variables discussed in this chapter, we seek to examine the theoretical reasons for using each variable in empirical research, and the general experience with the variable.

FINDINGS FROM EMPIRICAL RESEARCH ON FERTILITY

Explanations of fertility can be sought at many levels: the level of the biology of a single birth or in terms of the general social and economic characteristics of an entire population. In this chapter, we shall proceed from the most immediate biological determinants of fertility to the general social and economic background variables. In general, we shall follow, moving from right to left, the framework provided in Figure 3.1. The variables are organised to be consistent with economic theories, but the general pattern should be familiar to other social scientists working in the study of fertility. As a result, some variables which might be considered important in a sociological model, such as norms (R. Freedman, 1975), have been played down. Other variables have been grouped in ways that would discomfit authors working from a political or administrative perspective: for example, the policy and programme box does not distinguish policy formulation from programme implementation (R. Simmons *et al.*, 1975, and 1983). For the sake of simplicity, the framework, as presented here, does not include all of the possible causal arrows, and especially ignores all of the feedback mechanisms, some of which are likely to be important.

This diagram allows for either a micro (family) or a macro (societal) perspective, but the interpretation of the variables is different in the two cases. The diagram is drawn for a given point in time. The current fertility of a family or society is assumed to be determined in part by its past fertility experience.

The diagram can be divided into four sections, moving from left to right. The dependent variable is fertility. There are three levels of independent variables represented in the diagram. The immediate explanation of fertility is in terms of the proximate or intermediate variables. These variables are, in turn, explained by a set of variables measuring the characteristics of decision-making households and their immediate environment. Finally, there are a set of environmental variables which influence the attributes of the household. Fertility is influenced by all three sets of independent variables, but a strategy decision is required of the researcher as to which level, if any, should be given special emphasis.

The diagram is very general, and any given application would want to eliminate or elaborate on variables or variable groups. Many demographers might want to stress the connections between the intermediate variables and fertility, for example, to the exclusion of the other variables in the system. The structuralists cited in Chapter 2 might ignore most of the variables not related to the environment. The variable mix would also vary according to whether the research emphasised the individual or the community as the focus of analysis, and to how the fertility variable is measured and the period to which it refers.

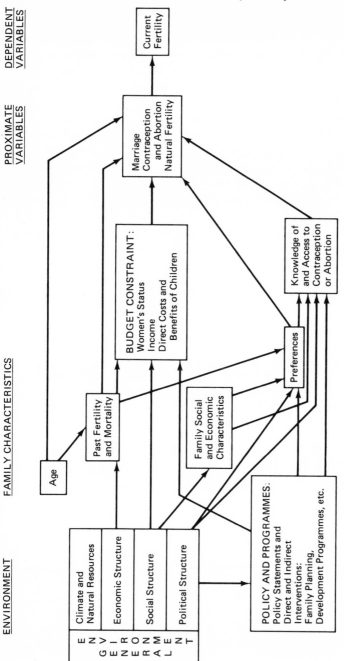

FIGURE 3.1   *The determinants of fertility in developing countries*

Proximate or Intermediate Variables Influencing Fertility

Economics is concerned with broad levels of social explanation related to
scarcity. Biological variables receive little emphasis unless they enter into
the theoretical model as explanatory or conditioning variables. However,
even within a framework which emphasises the role of choice, recognition
should be given to the role that biological factors play in mediating the
effects of more basic determinants of fertility. A complex set of biological
conditions and interactions must exist for a birth to take place: two
sexually-mature and currently-fecund individuals must interact sexually,
contact between sperm and ovum must occur in an appropriate biological
environment, and a uterine environment favourable to fetal development
must exist. Certainly, the process is more complex than most market transactions. Many aspects of fertility are governed by factors such as age or
health status, which are not to any significant degree under the control
of the individual. For example, sterility associated with menopause or
involuntary abortion (miscarriage) are seldom elements of choice in
fertility. Consequently, while it may be fully appropriate to recognise
choice as one element in a theory of fertility, the biological framework
within which that choice is thought to operate should be well specified.

Thus, in any discussion of fertility it is useful to begin with a recognition
of the role of intermediate variables. Davis and Blake (1956), in a frequently cited article, provide a taxonomy of mutually-exclusive intermediate variables which mediate between fertility and explanatory variables
of a behavioural form. They suggest that there are three categories of
variables that are necessary for successful reproduction: (i) variables which
define the probability of sexual intercourse, such as age at marriage, (ii)
variables which define the probability of a conception resulting from sexual
intercourse, such as the use of contraception or the pattern of primary or
secondary sterility; and (iii) variables which define the probability of a
conception resulting in a live birth, such as spontaneous or induced abortion. Since a live birth cannot take place without sexual intercourse, conception and a successful pregnancy and parturition, any study of fertility
behaviour should include some consideration of the way these variables
are to be treated. Moreover, this imperative exists whether research is
conducted at the micro or the macro level.

Often, the intermediate variables are used by researchers to define the
sample population of interest. In studies of individuals or households, for
example, it may be possible to focus on the women who are fecund by
studying the fertility behaviour of women aged 15 to 45. Or research may
concentrate on the reproductive behaviour of currently married women,

thus ignoring the fertility of women who are single, divorced or widowed, and the question of what determines marriage patterns in the first place. Studies of societal fertility levels also deal with the problem of intermediate variable influences by carefully defining the dependent variable. Thus, instead of using the crude birth rate as a measure of fertility, with the possible result that observed variations can be attributed to changes in age structure, marriage patterns or marital fertility, researchers may concentrate on areal or temporal variations in age-specific marital fertility rates. Chapter 5 in this volume describes the possible measures of fertility available to researchers.

Bongaarts (1978, 1982) has presented a useful classification of the intermediate variables and their influence on fertility in high- and low-fertility situations. His classification has four major categories: (i) the proportion of the population married or in sexual unions, (ii) the proportion of the married population contracepting and the effectiveness of contraception, (iii) the extent to which a population uses induced abortion. and (iv) the average length of breastfeeding in the population, To distinguish this classification from that of Davis and Blake, Bongaarts calls these the 'proximate' variables.

Marital status

In explaining historical patterns or the cross-sectional variation in fertility across countries or among regions and groups within a country, the proportion of the population ever married, the age of marriage, or the age at entry into sexual unions and the probability of widowhood and remarriage are often more powerful determinants of overall fertility than the level of marital fertility itself. The relatively low level of fertility in western Europe during the eighteenth or ninteenth century is better explained by the relatively high proportion of women who never married, and by the relatively late age of marriage, than by the levels of marital fertility *per se* (Kumar, 1971). The female mean age of marriage was in the mid-twenties for most western European countries, compared to the middle or late teens as is the case in many of the present-day developing countries. While the age at marriage is generally low in the Third World, it varies from one country to another, and it has changed significantly during recent decades. The general rule is that the higher the age at marriage, the lower will be fertility, but it should also be noted that there are some populations, for example in parts of rural India, where women marry so young on average that the mean age of marriage would have to increase by several years to have a significant effect on fertility. Marital disruption may be a factor in

Overview

reducing fertility in other places. The determinants of the age of marriage and marital stability are not well understood.

The decisions as to whether and when to marry are, in many of their aspects, a form of economic behaviour (Population Information Program, 1979). In pre-modern European populations, for example, marriages were often supposed to take place only after the couple marrying could provide themselves and their children with an income at a prescribed level. This often had major demographic effects. Among the population of nineteenth-century Ireland, economic difficulties associated with the potato famine led enough couples to delay marriage that fertility fell rapidly. More recently, the government of China has made a systematic attempt to raise the age of marriage in order to reduce fertility. Thus, the age of marriage can be used to deliberately control fertility at either the individual or the societal level. Indirectly, the age at marriage is likely to be associated with the level of education, female employment and other variables, but the causality may work in either direction, and the strength of the relationships must vary from one situation to another.

Two other intermediate variables of particular interest to economists are the use of contraception and induced abortion. These variables involve choices made by the individual couples involved and/or the societies in which they live. Often, their choices are economic in that they involve an attempt to limit or space births in a way that is perceived as involving a better allocation of resources.

Contraception

Contraception is central to the whole question of fertility control. By definition, some form of contraception or abortion must be used if married couples wish to reduce their fertility. It is notable, however, that contraception can take many forms, some of which are associated with sexual activity and may require high motivation to be used effectively (e.g. coitus interruptus or the condom), and some of which are independent of sexual activity and are generally more effective (e.g. hormonal contraceptives or intrauterine devices). From the perspective of economic research on fertility, it may be advisable to include contraception, sterilisation and deliberate abstinence from sexual relations all under 'contraception'. While there are many advantages to modern contraception (and some disadvantages as well), more traditional methods can also be effective in reducing the level of fertility. In the absence of modern contraceptives, for example, European and North American populations were able to reduce their marital fertility to relatively low levels.

Contraceptives can be obtained from a wide variety of sources: without any outside assistance in the case of withdrawal; from private commercial channels in the case of condoms; from private physicians, or from volunteer agencies or government clinics in the case of other forms of contraception. Since some form of contraception is likely to play a major role in the reduction of marital fertility, it is not surprising to find a strong inverse correlation between contraceptive prevalence and current fertility. Analytically much more difficult is the question of the independent role of government-sponsored efforts to promote contraceptive use. This topic will be discussed later in this chapter.

So central is contraceptive practice to the explanation of deliberate attempts to control fertility, that it is often treated as a dependent variable in economic research on fertility. Researchers have been quite successful in using research techniques to estimate the level of contraceptive use.

Abortion

Abortion is another intermediate variable which has a large potential effect on fertility. There are populations where more pregnancies are aborted than result in live births. As in the case of contraception, government programmes and legislative activities play an important role in determining the extent to which abortion is used. Abortion has become quite common in a number of industrial countries. However, it is more difficult to study abortion than to study contraception. Abortion statistics are often inadequate, and in many cases the fact that abortion is illegal and subject to public disapproval leads to resistance on the part of survey respondents to discuss it.

Intermediate variables other than age at marriage, contraception or abortion, are grouped by Bongaarts under the general heading of natural fertility variables (1978). Although Bongaarts regards the natural fertility variables as less significant than the other proximate variables in particular situations, especially where there is universal early marriage and little deliberate control of fertility within marriage, they may be important determinants of the sometimes large variations in fertility. Every society has cultural practices which influence fertility. Examples are provided by Lesthaeghe (1980). Prolonged breastfeeding can considerably extend birth intervals (as is illustrated in the Nigerian case-study presented in Chapter 12). Health conditions may be associated with sterility. Variations in the frequency of intercourse may lead to differences in fertility from one region to another, or from one couple to another. However, apart from encouraging breastfeeding, which should have a mild effect on reducing fertility, and encouraging good health practices, which may raise fertility, natural fertility variables have less policy significance than variables relating to exposure or to control of fertility within marriage.[1]

From a research point of view, economists have adopted a number of strategies for dealing with the intermediate variables. Often, they are ignored on the grounds that what is really important is the set of explanatory variables which relate to couples' decisions. In this strategy, the intermediate variables are part of a 'black box', the contents of which can be ignored as long as one knows what goes into the box and what comes out. A second and perhaps the most common strategy is to selectively ignore the intermediate variables by restricting research to the marital fertility of individuals, so that within the scope of the research the possible influence of some intermediate variables is dampened. This strategy permits an examination of contraception or abortion, but ignores the determinants of the age and duration of marriage. Finally, it is possible to develop models explicitly recognising the complete mechanisms through which fertility is affected by economic influences.

Variables Corresponding to the Characteristics of Families and their Immediate Environment

While there is consensus that all variations in fertility must be mediated by the particular set of intermediate variables described above, no such agreement exists about the next set of variables within the framework presented in Figure 3.1. Researchers from different social science disciplines would list quite different variables for emphasis. In this subsection, we shall examine research findings concerning a numbr of variables emphasised by economists in their research.

Age

Age is one of the most important of the variables which characterise individual participants in the fertility process. Similarly, age structure is one of the major determinants of a society's fertility patterns. At both the individual and the societal level, age is closely related to the intermediate variables. The age of the potential parent plays an important role in fertility outcomes because fertility is, in most senses, a cumulative process closely related to the life-cycle of each parent and of the family unit. Thus, age is closely associated with marriage, with divorce or widowhood, with menarche, with the frequency of intercourse, with the probability of conception, and with menopause. Age is also related to many of the economic variables. Income, for example, is likely to increase over much of the life-cycle.

Empirical research confirms the importance of age as a determinant of fertility. In the case-studies by Anker and Farooq (Chapters 11 and 12), for example, age is the dominant variable in regressions done for all women in reproductive ages. In fact, age is so closely related to fertility that many authors suggest researchers should analyse the determinants of fertility within age groups. Farooq, in Chapter 12, and Macura, in Chapter 15, demonstrate that different factors determine fertility among younger and older women.

Mortality

Mortality affects fertility through a number of mechanisms. Firstly, it affects the number of couples of reproductive age through its general influence on the age and sex structure of the population. Correspondingly, at the individual level, the number of children a couple is likely to have will be influenced by the probability of the full reproductive life of the couple remaining unbroken by the death of one of the spouses. Secondly, infant and child mortality have been hypothesised to affect fertility through both biological and behavioural mechanisms. Finally, the level of mortality may influence the environment in which fertility decisions are taken at both the family and the society levels. For example, policy-makers in countries with a recent experience of high mortality may be reluctant to adopt a fertility-control policy, or the existence of high mortality may lead to the development of institutions that encourage early marriage.

The demographic component of mortality's effect on the number of potential parents or the average length of a couple's reproductive life can be analysed using straightforward demographic techniques. Behavioural adjustments are more complicated, and have not received extensive attention. Historical evidence from European populations suggests that marriages were often delayed until inheritances were assured; consequently, the age at marriage fluctuated inversely with mortality. However, the question of the way that inheritances or other mortality-related social institutions in the Third World influence marriage patterns has not received extensive attention.

While mortality as it affects the number of potential parents may have a large influence on fertility, the major focus in the literature has been on the way in which infant and child mortality influences the behaviour of parents within marriage. A central concept in 'demographic transition' literature is the idea that mortality-decline precedes fertility-decline. Many authors have extended this observation to the conclusion that a 'reduction in mortality is considered a necessary, although insufficient condition for a reduction in fertility' (Frederiksen, 1969, p. 838; see also Zachariah, 1973). The conclusion has been further encouraged by the observation that among countries in the contemporary world, those that have high mortality tend to have high fertility as well (World Health Organisation, 1974).

As a result of these relationships at the level of the society, a search has been initiated for corroborating household-level relationships. Based on the assumption of specified sets of family objectives, a number of scholars[2] have used a non-empirical deductive methodology to explore the fertility which would be associated with different levels of child mortality. Heer and Smith (1968) have been able to demonstrate that, in the face of high mortality, parents who want to assure that a targeted number of their children survive to adulthood, will have to give birth to more children than they might otherwise want. This research, however suggestive, is not empirical, and the conclusions that are reached depend heavily on the exact assumptions that are made. For example, a reduction in the probability of child survival which parents are assumed to use in their calculations will change family-size considerably. Empirical investigations are thus required to test the hypothesis that mortality is a determinant of fertility and to determine the magnitude of any such effect. Several of the case-studies in this volume provide illustrations of research on this question.

Empirical household-level studies on the relationship between infant and child mortality and fertility have increased considerably in recent years. Several distinguishable aspects of the relationship between infant mortality and fertility are addressed in these studies. For example, it has been recognised (Chowdhury *et al.*, 1976) that there may be a purely biological effect of some importance: the death of the infant of a lactating mother frequently has the important effect of shortening the period of post-partum amenorrhea and thereby reducing the interval to the next conception. While there is nearly universal agreement concerning the direction of this effect, there is some difference of opinion about its quantitative importance. More central to the theme of this volume is the importance of the other possible responses to the experience of infant and child mortality. These other responses, which collectively can be termed the 'behavioural response', include the conscious or unconscious efforts on the part of parents to alter their fertility behaviour so as to make up for the past death of an infant, attempts to raise fertility in anticipation of the experience of child mortality within a family, and efforts to maintain high fertility within a family because of social norms that encourage fertility as a response of the community to the experience of mortality (Rutstein, 1974; Heer and Wu, 1975). The behavioural response to mortality should be larger and more influential than the biological response. These two effects together may create a situation in which high infant and child mortality lead to fertility in excess of that required to replace lost children (Hassan, 1973). In other words, in some situations population growth could be expected to be greater with high mortality than with low mortality, other things being equal.

A theoretical basis for the behavioural response to mortality is found in the theories of the new home-economics, which would suggest that since family-size desires are probably established in terms of 'surviving children', parents adjust their fertility to offset the deaths of children. Parents may also adjust to anticipate mortality. In the theoretical literature, the suggestion is often made (Easterlin *et al.*, 1980; T. P. Schultz, 1978a) that parents want 'surviving' children, 'C'. These in turn will be a function of the total number of children born, 'N', and the probability of survival to adulthood, 's'. Thus, $C = sN$, and parents can be expected to adjust their fertility behaviour to their expectations about mortality. The theory suggests that rational parents will have higher fertility to offset possible child-deaths. There is still considerable question, however, as to exactly how the relationship should work. How long do children have to survive to satisfy family needs? One year? To maturity? To the age where they contribute to family income? To the death of the parents? Also, if the parents try to anticipate mortality, what degree of certainty do they require before family-size is considered complete? There may also be an offsetting 'price' effect, since the waste associated with child mortality makes it more expensive to raise children with a high level of education.

The empirical evidence for an association between fertility and mortality is mixed. At the aggregate level, some studies report a strong association at about the levels to be expected with full replacement behaviour (see T. P. Schultz, 1978), but others, such as Chapter 17 by Winegarden in this volume, report smaller effects.

At the household level, the results are even more mixed. There seems to be a great deal of variation in the nature of the relationship between one sample and another (T. P. Schultz, 1978a). A number of studies have found some replacement effect, but it is consistently less than would be necessary to increase population growth. Taylor, one of the best known advocates of the idea that high infant mortality leads to high fertility, and colleagues (Taylor *et al.*, 1976) have concluded that, 'although an association between infant and child mortality and fertility levels has been widely accepted, little direct evidence has been available either to support the assumptions or to define possible mediums of interaction'. The empirical findings provide little hope that the moderate reductions in infant mortality, by themselves, will lead to a rapid reduction in fertility. Preston (1978, p. 12) observes that while a replacement effect is evident (in some of the research contained in his volume), 'in no population are as many as 50 per cent of the child deaths replaced by additional births, once proper statistical controls are instituted'. He also presents a classification of the various mechanisms by which fertility and mortality may be interrelated, and suggests that while the replacement effect is the largest, there may be an additional insurance effect. Overall, however, 'only a small fraction of mortality variation at the family level seems to translate into fertility variation' (Preston, 1978, p. 15).

Most of the literature on the relationship between fertility and mortality hypothesises that exogenous changes in mortality cause changes in fertility. There is, however, a growing awareness that high fertility may lead to increased mortality (Kunstadter, 1978; Scrimshaw, 1978; T. P. Schultz, 1978a; G. B. Simmons *et al.*, 1982; Rosenzweig and T. P. Schultz, 1982). Thus, policy-makers must be exceedingly careful to examine the causal implications of measures of association. Deliberate replacement is likely to be less important, to the extent that high fertility leads to infant and child mortality because children are unwanted.

While the relationship between mortality and fertility is of interest in its own right, there is a special concern with the implications of this relationship for policy. If there is a strong association between infant-child mortality and fertility, it may be possible to undertake special health or nutrition programmes which simultaneously reduce fertility and indirectly contribute to a reduced fertility. An assessment of this policy option will depend upon the effects of the programme on each policy objective. An assessment of the implications of such programmes for fertility reduction alone is complicated because, to be complete, the analysis needs to go beyond the fertility–mortality relationship narrowly defined. In particular, the technology of mortality reduction, the administrative and political feasibility of its applications, and the costs involved, will all need to be examined before one can consider attempts to influence infant or child mortality as a policy intervention for the purpose of fertility reduction.

Recent research on the control of infant mortality does not provide grounds for administrators to be sanguine about the possibility of further reductions in infant mortality. In many countries where mortality has already been reduced, further progress may depend on economic and social changes as they bring in improvements in the standard of living of people on a sustained basis. In one part of the Philippines, it was found that reductions in infant mortality below seventy per thousand are not likely with only medical or health interventions (Williamson, 1982).

Gwatkin (1980) has more generally cautioned us to expect the rate of progress of mortality declines to be reduced in the future.

The budget constraint

The parameters in the family budget constraint for marketed commodities can be easily defined as the total income of the family and the prices of goods the family may want to purchase. Since fertility does not involve market behaviour in the usual sense, and since the time-periods involved in family-building are large, the budget constraint is more complicated in economic models of fertility. The budget should take into account both time and money income, and prices should measure the costs and benefits of children generally, not just those that work through the market.

Economists have long argued that the presence of children in the family involves economic costs and benefits for parents, and that variations in these may be a major determinant of variations in fertility. The costs of children are not easy to measure, since there is no market transaction involved. The same is true of many of the benefits in a non-monetised economy. Thus much of the debate has revolved around the question of how child-related gains and losses should be measured. The most commonly cited measure relates to the opportunity cost of the mother's participation in childrearing. If women devote themselves to the family, then they cannot be involved, or as fully involved, in the marketplace. Another measure of child costs is given by direct outlays on food, shelter, etc. A third is the extent to which the child represents a productive economic asset from the perspective of family decision-makers.

The status of women

Many authors have cited the status of women as a key determinant of fertility, and have suggested that changes in women's status may be the central element in successful efforts to reduce fertility (Germain, 1975; United Nations, 1975). The literature linking women's status and fertility is voluminous, and an assessment of the policy implications must be undertaken with care because there are many possible relationships, and they seem to vary according to time and place. It should also be noted that women's status can influence fertility through the age at marriage, fertility choices within marriage or natural fertility. Level of educational attainment, participation within the work-force, decision-making authority within the family unit and health status, are all treated as measures of women's status which may influence fertility. While each has its own special contribution and limitations, the two indices of women's status which dominate the literature are education and employment.

Fertility differentials in both developed and developing countries indicate a negative relationship between the level of education attained by women and their fertility (Goldstein, 1972; Husain, 1970; Jordan, 1976; Rodríguez and Cleland, 1980; A. Jain, 1981). This relationship tends to be strongest when factors such as husband's education, woman's employment and type of education, and place of residence are uncontrolled; and it seems to be strongest at younger ages. Fertility differentials by education diminish greatly for older women, suggesting that, at least in Africa, births may be caught-up in later years of marriage (Ware, 1975). As a result, there is little agreement in the literature as to the strength or even the direction of the net effect. Because of the preponderance of intervening factors upon which the existence of a negative relationship depends, it has been proposed (United Nations, 1975) that women's education 'may just be the most visible or quantifiable element in a cluster of independent forces affecting fertility'.

In addition to these intervening factors, the extent to which education influences fertility depends both upon the level and type of education and upon whether or not that education leads to economic activity (McGreevy and Birdsall, 1974; Cochrane, 1978). The inverse relationship between fertility and education is strongest for the highest levels of educational attainment, suggesting that education may have little or no effect on fertility until a threshold level (e.g. high school) has been attained (Encarnacion, 1974). Anker in Chapter 11 and Farooq in Chapter 12 demonstrate the curvilinear relationship between education and fertility in African household-level data. Adding to the complexity of this relationship is the important influence of economic and urbanisation variables. It is difficult, at least, to cite education as the crucial determinant of fertility reductions among the more highly educated women, because those women with the highest educational attainment in the less-developed countries are generally also the most 'modern' (Jordan, 1976). The evidence that education for women is a necessary or sufficient condition for lowered fertility is weak (Cochrane, 1978; Graff, 1979). To the extent that an inverse relationship exists, it does not appear to be 'education *per se* which influences a woman to have a smaller family, but rather the association of education . . . with other social and environmental factors which ultimately result in decreased fertility' (Piepmeier and Adkins, 1973). Moreover, Timur (1977) has observed that it is likely that the only countries for which the inverse relationship may be at all consistent are those where fertility has just begun to decline.[3]

Cochrane (1978) has assessed the implications of education on each of the intermediate variables. In general, the strongest negative effects are on the proportion marrying and the age of marriage, and on the use of contraception. Education may have positive effects on fecundity, and it has mixed effects on the demand for children. The overall effect will depend upon the full set of influences and, within a given setting, women's education may have different effects on each of the intermediate variables.

The net result of these theoretical and empirical studies is to suggest caution. Certainly, the education of women may have important implications for fertility, and in some settings it may be a central variable for policy-makers; but each situation needs to be examined in its own right before specific interventions are designed.

The contemporary economic literature on fertility lays great stress on the possible conflict that may exist between a woman's role as mother and her role in the marketplace. In the new home-economics models discussed in Chapter 2, couples are expected to make decisions early in their married life which simultaneously determine fertility and labour-force participation (as well as other factors such as further human capital development, location, etc.). To the extent that a woman has the opportunity to work in the labour-force and that participation conflicts with raising children, the couple may elect to have fewer children. Opportunities to enter the labour-force may depend on a great many factors, but the woman's education is often thought to be a reasonable proxy for the opportunity cost of entering the labour-force (Standing, 1978, ch. 7).

The relationship between fertility and women's labour-force participation is even less clear (Kupinsky, 1977). While there is agreement that in developed countries a negative relationship often exists between employment and fertility, the causes of the relationship are not well understood. Moreover, even if the existence and interpretation of the relationship within the industrialised world were accepted by all, its relevance to developing countries would not be established, since efforts to examine the relationship in the developing countries context have yielded conflicting results. For national population samples, the World Fertility Survey results confirm the existence of a negative relationship between fertility and female employment (Rodríguez and Cleland, 1980). While a few studies provide evidence of a negative association, many others demonstrate a positive relationship or no relationship at all. For example, even in the urban areas of developing countries, women's employment has not been found to be consistently associated with fertility (McGreevy and Birdsall, 1974). Furthermore, in rural areas, women's participation in the workforce often appears to be positively associated with fertility. The complexity of the relationship is underscored by the observation that, in some cases, working women in rural environments of the developing countries have higher fertility than non-working women in urban areas. Occupational status is also cited as a crucial factor, but a strong inverse relationship exists only for women employed in higher-paying, professional jobs (Goldstein, 1972; and in the Nigerian case-study, Chapter 12). This relationship is complicated by the association of high-status employment with greater educational attainment and 'modern' life-style. As a result, a direct causal relationship between women's labour-force participation and fertility has not been adequately demonstrated. The fact that the relationship is often negative, and significant only for high status, also raises a question of how important it can be from a national perspective, since only a small fraction of the female population has or is likely to have access to high-status employment.

There have been several attempts to explain why a consistent inverse relationship between fertility and labour-force participation has not been found in developing countries. (For reviews of the theoretical and methodological issues see Safilios-Rothschild, 1977; Weller, 1977; Oppong and Haavio-Mannila, 1979.) Weller and others have hypothesised that only where the role of 'worker is incompatible with the mothering role will there be an inverse relationship' (Weller, 1968a, 1968b; Jaffe and Azumi, 1960). Women are seldom forced to choose between employment and a large family because the extended family is prevalent in many developing societies, and because children often take responsibility for each other at young ages. Furthermore, in the developing countries, work for both men and women is structured very differently than it is in an industrial society. The hours and environment of work are less formalised, thereby reducing the need for women to choose between employment and family formation. The role-incompatibility hypothesis has been questioned on the basis of recent research (Mason and Palan, 1981). A second complicating factor is that women often work in order to survive and not as a result of a choice among alternative life-styles. The harsh physical, economic and social conditions in many developing countries make the participation decision qualitatively different from what it is in developed-country settings (Cain, Khanam and Nahar, 1979; various contributions in Kupinsky, 1977).

In the cases where employed women in developing countries do have smaller families, cause and effect have not been identified. Fertility may influence work status or, as with women's education and fertility, the linkages may be indirect. The strength and direction of the relationship may depend on a number of socio-economic 'background' variables. Moreover, fertility itself may be a determinant of labour-force participation, in some cases a source of high status and in some cases a contributing cause of weak status. In such cases, the causality runs from fertility to status, and any measure of association is subject to misinterpretation. It should also be noted that this complex interdependency creates difficulties in estimation, and may invalidate estimations of a relationship based on the assumption that the causal relationship runs from labour-force participation to fertility. In Chapter 15, Macura demonstrates the use of simultaneous-equation estimation techniques in estimating separate equations for marital fertility and labour-force participation, in a country that has recently experienced the fertility transition. The causality question will be discussed further in the last part of this chapter and in Chapter 8. Any policy which attempts to reduce fertility by improving the status of women should be based on a reasonable presumption that the relationship between the two variables is negative, that the causality runs in the hypothesised direction, and that the magnitude of the relationship is significant. Research to date does not provide direct and conclusive evidence to support any generalisation about the strength and direction of this effect in different settings. Thus, as with education for women, one must assume that the relationship between fertility and female employment will depend upon local circumstances.

For policy purposes, one would want to know not only about the levels of association between women's status and fertility, but also something about the interventions that could be introduced to affect fertility. There are many indications that while it is possible to encourage female employment, such efforts are often socially and administratively complex (Dixon, 1982), and may be costly.

The direct costs and benefits of children Such costs and benefits to the family have been the subject of considerable speculation, but of little systematic quantitative work. Such research as has been done is reviewed by Nag (1981). This anomaly may arise for many reasons, not the least of which is the difficulty of both a conceptual and an empirical nature in collecting such data. On the conceptual side, it would be necessary to have a good definition of what constitutes a cost or a benefit, and to whom such gains or losses are accruing (Anker *et al.*, 1982). Caldwell (1980), among others, has stressed the importance of transfers among family members, but he has provided little empirical evidence for their influence. Mueller (1976) and Cabañero (1978) have argued the importance of these variables, and given some estimates of their magnitude. Mueller has also attempted to assess the importance of some indices of the perceived cost and benefits of children as predictors of fertility behaviour, and has shown that these variables are important predictors even in the presence of controls for various socio-economic variables. Rosenzweig and Evenson (1977) have used indirect measures of the returns that parents might expect from their children, as measured by prevailing wage rates, to predict fertility behaviour in a sample of rural households from India. Cain (1977) found that the economic gains associated with children were a significant reason for the persistence of high fertility.

Despite these effects, there has been much less effort to directly assess the benefits and costs of childrearing than there has been to measure the indirect opportunity costs implied by the wife's time or her involvement in the labour-force. It seems likely that research in this area will constitute one of the frontiers for the next decade. For such an effort to be successful, there will have to be a much greater involvement of economists in the collection of data, since present data sets seldom include the information which would be required for estimating the benefits and costs of children for the family.

Income This may be the most studied of the variables that economists have proposed to explain observed variations in fertility. Malthus argued that improvements in income above subsistence levels would lead to early marriage and socially-irresponsible parenthood. The demographic transition literature emphasises the transforming role of the increases in family income associated with development. In Chapter 2, the celebrated positive-income hypothesis of Becker was discussed at great length.

While the income variable is important in almost all economic treatments of fertility, even a cursory review indicates that 'income' means a variety of things to different researchers. In some macro-economic studies, income or income per capita is taken as a measure of modernisation. In micro-economic studies, income per family member or total family income are alternative measures of the resource constraints existing in the family. In the area of fertility, the exact role of income may be complex. Neither at the level of the individual family nor at the society level is income likely to act as a direct barrier to having children. Since the birth of children is not exclusively mediated by the market, families can make a variety of adjustments to accommodate differing numbers of children within a given budget. Moreover, while children may be a net claim on family income when they are young, as they mature they may become net contributors. Thus while the prevailing opinion among economists is that income should be an important determinant of fertility, its influence on fertility may be weaker and less predictable than its influence on market demand.

Economic theorists have suggested that income may have a number of different effects on fertility. Firstly, income has been used as a measure of social and economic development by authors concerned with the overall transformation of society. In this sense, income is a proxy for the level of communication in the country, the division of labour, the degree of mechanisation and, more generally, the extent to which the society has developed modern industrial patterns of organisation. Most social scientists, basing their judgement on the contrast between the poorer developing countries with high fertility and the industrial countries with low fertility, or the parallel history of change associated with the demographic transition in Europe, would hypothesise that a pattern of reduced fertility is part of the general process of transformation which accompanies development. Thus, increases in the level of income should be associated with decreases in fertility. In this application, income is used as a general measure of social organisation and technology. Economists, while sharing this general expectation, are less happy with the explanatory mechanisms that are offered. Thus they are more inclined than other social scientists to interpret the income/fertility relationships in terms of more standard interpretations of individual behaviour.

Empirical studies have reached very mixed conclusions concerning the relationship between income and fertility. At the macro-economic level, the relationship tends to be negative. That is, the richest countries in the world tend to have low fertility, and the poor countries, with their much lower levels of per capita income, are characterised by high fertility. The demographic transition literature suggests a negative relationship as well. All of the currently low-fertility countries at one point had high fertility, and the decline has been associated with very considerable improvements in the standard of living in the countries involved.

A contrasting picture emerges if one concentrates on the relationship between income and fertility within either set of countries. Among developed countries, for example, there may be a positive correlation between economic well-being and fertility in the short run. This relationship was anticipated by Malthus, and has been predicted for the modern United States by Easterlin and others.

The use of the income variable in aggregate studies of fertility contrasts sharply with its application in the literature on individual fertility. At the micro level, income is an indicator of the resource constraints confronting the family. Thus, income places limits on the ability of parents, or consumers more generally, to have the things they want. This basic limitation on the range of choice is what economics is all about. If children are pure consumption goods, and if the enjoyment of children does not restrict other familial choices, one would anticipate that the more income a family has, the more children it will want, just as more income is generally associated with a desire for more of other things.

The more that economists have reflected on this association, the more they have qualifed the conclusion. Four reasons for doubt stand out. Firstly, as Becker (1974) suggests, there is an open question as to whether the 'quality' of children is a separate issue. Secondly, in some circumstances, particularly in poor countries, children can be sources as well as users of income; that is, high levels of fertility in the family may increase the family's income because there will be more potential earners in the family. This possibility raises questions of causality that are not addressed in most empirical models. Thirdly, the inclusion of wife's income in the overall measure of family resources, and the possibility that wife's work may conflict with childrearing, complicates the relationship between income and fertility. Finally, the relationship between income and fertility depends on the definition of income which is used. At the micro level, then, economic theory has provided a number of hypotheses about the possible direction of the effect of income on fertility. In some cases, we would expect income to have an unambiguous positive effect, in others an unambiguous negative effect; and in others an indeterminate effect.

At the level of the household, empirical studies of the income–fertility relationship have yielded mixed results. There are a number of studies which have confirmed the existence of a pure and positive income effect, but there are at least as many examples of research which have yielded either no relationship or a negative relationship.

Micro-economics theorists have been particularly concerned with the level of income and alternative measures of the resource limitations constraining a family. Measures of average income for a community or a nation can mask important variations in the distribution of income among the members of the community. From a macro-economic perspective the concern with the level of income is complemented by an attempt to examine the effects of *income distribution* on fertility. Two major kinds of effects of income distribution have been proposed. Firstly, variations in the distribution of income will affect the absolute levels of income within a community. If income is concentrated in the hands of a few wealthy families, the rest of the community will have lower absolute living standards for any given national per capita income. As reviewed above, it has been argued that the absolute income affects the fertility of a family. If unequal income distribution leads to lower incomes for poor families (in a non-linear form), then these pure income effects will result in a reduction of their fertility. Thus absolute levels of living for the poor may explain fertility differentials. On the other hand, the poor in a country with a more equal distribution have a higher standard of living, they have a more central role in the economy, and they may feel that children play a different role in their lives than they would if they were more destitute.

A second interpretation of income distribution would hold that it is the relative income that matters and not the absolute level. The poorest segments feel worse off because of their relative deprivation, and this affects their fertility. By this interpretation, income distribution is part of the environment of family decision-making (see Figure 3.1).

A number of authors have suggested that a more equal distribution of income will lead to reductions in fertility. In countries where the poorest people receive a significant share of the benefits of economic activity, people are more likely to seek to reduce their fertility of their own accord than they would in countries where income is less evenly distributed. This proposition is derived from a small number of case-studies, represented by the suggestive work of Kocher (1973) and Rich (1973). Systematic empirical work is limited, and is thus far restricted to the examination of the cross-sectional characteristics of a large number of countries. This concept is still at a formative stage, and caution should be exercised in using preliminary findings as a basis for policy. For example, given the substantial differences among nations in the way income distribution is measured, measurement error has a potentially large effect on the estimation of relationships. When income distribution data for two countries such as Chad and Bulgaria are used in the same regression, it is possible that different procedures for the measurement of income distribution, or bias resulting from the exclusion of important variables such as the nature of the political régime, may distort or even reverse the estimated relationship between income distribution and fertility. Also, cross-sectional data used in this research include both developed and underdeveloped countries, and the same relationship may not hold within the set of developing countries. A related problem is that the cross-sectional result can not always be used to predict the impact of changes in income distribution that occur over time.

Despite these problems, most studies of income distribution indicate the existence of a modest negative association between fertility and the amount of inequality in the income distribution, and, therefore, reinforce the notion that improvements in income distribution should help to reduce fertility. However, the evidence does not speak to the question of causality, and, as in the case of infant mortality and women's status, there are grounds for doubting that equitable income distribution is necessarily a cause of fertility reduction. For example, in the comparison of Chad and Bulgaria, even if income distribution and fertility are adequately measured it may be that lower fertility and a more even income distribution in the latter are both due to the level of development in a broad sense, and to the nature of the political régime. A plausible hypothesis, supported by some evidence, suggests that a reduction in fertility may lead to improvements in income distribution, thereby reversing the causal direction (Chenery *et al.*, 1974; Ahluwalia, 1976; Kuznets, 1976). The few studies which have treated the relationship between income distribution and population as simultaneous have tended to find a linkage going from fertility or population growth to income distribution stronger than the reverse (Winegarden, 1978; Boulier, 1975; Birdsall, 1977; Repetto, 1979). Some of the issues involved in estimating these relationships are discussed by Winegarden in Chapter 17.

Moreover, the implementation of a programme of redistribution, while being a central goal of policy in many countries, is by no means a trivial objective. There are many examples of countries which preach a doctrine of redistribution but have realised few changes, or even attempts at change. Even where such redistribution programmes have been implemented, they have taken a variety of forms, some of which may have very different implications for fertility. Given the complexity of restructuring income distribution, experience suggests that if attempts at income distribution are to become a central instrument in the attempt to reduce fertility, such reduction may be delayed for years.

Research conducted thus far has suggested a number of possible relationships between fertility and income. These are reviewed by J. L. Simon (1974, 1977), T. W. Schultz (1974) and Fulop (1977a, 1977b). Their conclusions will not be assessed here, except to note that there is certainly not enough consensus to permit policy-makers the luxury of any *a priori* expectations concerning either the magnitude or the sign of the relationship. In this context, the income variable can be used as a prediction of fertility only after careful research has established the nature of the relationship in a particular country or region.

Preferences The third major element in the micro-economic approach to understanding behaviour is the utility function or the preference structure which defines the individual's sense of well-being as a function of the choices he makes among market goods. All economists would agree that preferences or tastes or utility functions are likely to differ from one individual to another. Some individuals may prefer a family-oriented existence; others may derive greater satisfaction from a life-style that emphasises travel or restaurant-dining. Such differences in tastes would be likely to have important implications for fertility behaviour, and thus one might expect the examination of preferences to have a key role in an empirical economics of fertility. In fact, the actual history has been much more complicated. Economists are divided on the question of tastes as on few other issues in the economics of fertility.

The Chicago National Bureau of Economic Research group takes the strong position that while tastes may have a theoretical impact on fertility, they are difficult or impossible to measure, and are likely to have at most a random effect on observed fertility differentials. Thus the empirical strategy of this school is to concentrate on price and income effects on fertility. T. P. Schulz (1981, p. 152) puts the case succinctly:

In the absence of a psychological theory that specifies relationships between observable characteristics of parents, except perhaps for their religion, and their tastes for children, this line of inquiry has not yet proved notably fruitful. Given the nonpecuniary context in which satisfactions are obtained from parenthood, and the highly subjective and intangible nature of certain tastes for parenthood, there is no obvious way presently at hand to integrate and empirically analyse the role of tastes within a theory of fertility.

Thus all individuals are assumed to share the same utility function embodying their preferences or preferences are distributed independently across observed individuals. Systematic differences among individuals in appraising specific goods are then attributed to systematic differences in their environmental constraints.

In contrast with the position of Schultz, economists such as Easterlin or Turchi have argued that tastes or preferences should be an explicit part of any empirical research on fertility. Easterlin and his colleagues state the position for explicitly treating tastes:

The Chicago-Columbia approach is most simply characterised by what it emphasises and de-emphasises. Particular emphasis is placed on cost factors and on the opportunity cost of a wife's time, little or no attention is given to taste factors and to the births production function . . .

Our main reservation about this line of work is that its de-emphasis of tastes and 'supply' factors severely limits its empirical relevance. For developed countries the model is of limited application because it ignores preference variables. This is most strikingly illustrated by the failure of the Chicago-Columbia approach to advance an explanation for the recent fertility swing in the United States. For less developed countries, fitting a 'demand' model to data for households whose fertility is largely uncontrolled leads to unwarranted inferences about 'demand' elasticities. Furthermore, the subordination of taste considerations lends itself to dubious conclusions about economic welfare and public policy. Minimizing the importance of tastes makes it easier to draw unambiguous inferences about the desirability of policies aimed at reducing 'unwanted' fertility, but the lack of attention to tastes make such inferences questionable. At the same time, the approach is unlikely to be helpful to those directing family planning programs, who must make choices between attempting to alter preferences (for example, by allocating resources to advertising the benefits of small families) and simply providing contraceptive information or cheaper services. Hence, we believe that both the analysis of fertility behavior and of the welfare effect of government programs requires a more balanced approach, one in which economic research on preferences and natural fertility takes equal place with the usual concerns of the Chicago–Columbia approach. (Easterlin *et al.*, 1980, p. 85-6.)

In practical research terms, preferences have usually been taken into account in empirical studies by using measures such as religion or ethnic affiliation as a control for other variables which measure more traditional economic concepts. Increasingly, however, economists may team up with other social scientists to obtain precise measures of preferences that may make a contribution to our understanding of fertility. Measures of preferences may take a number of forms. One approach may be to measure directly the differing commitments to children that families have. Scales might be developed by asking parents questions relating to the trade-off between children and other desired activities. Another approach may be to investigate the subjective assessments that parents make about the costs and benefits of having children. Mueller (1972) has provided an example of how such research might proceed. Other scales might be explored for assessing the role of sex-preferences in explaining fertility (L. C. Coombs, 1975). In any case, the examination of preferences is likely to be part of at least the social-determinants approach to the study of fertility. There is little consensus, however, on more exacting questions of how preferences should be measured or built into economic models of fertility.

The Environment

The third category of variable reflected in Figure 3.1 relates to the environment within which family decision-making is undertaken. There are two basic kinds of variables which fall under this heading. Firstly, there are the variables which relate to the political, social and economic status of the community as a whole. Under this heading would fall such variables as the nature of social institutions, the level of economic development and the nature of the political régime. The second category of variables relates to specific policies and programmes which are likely to have a direct or indirect influence on population or one of its components.

The general environment

Families do not live in isolation from their environment. They will be influenced by the nature of the community in which they live, and by the norms and expectations of their neighbours. Their economic circumstances – market prices, work opportunities, incomes, etc. – will depend upon the patterns of production and distribution associated with the economy as a whole. The political system will influence the relationships between the population and local government, public administration and many of the other variables in the system. It is likely to have a particularly strong impact on the decisions of the government in the area of population policies and programmes.

The 'community' can be defined at many levels. The village is the level at which the term may be most relevant for families living in rural parts of a country, but there may also be a sense in which community is defined by a larger region or by the nation as a whole, or even by ethnic affiliation.

The general environment is likely to influence fertility through other variables in the system, but it is seldom that economists build variables measuring such conditions into their models, especially the models of family-level fertility. That is, most micro-economic models take the characteristics of families to be exogenous variables, and do not concern themselves with the influence of the general environment. There are exceptions, as mentioned in the last section of Chapter 2. Most such studies do not involve statistical estimation, but concentrate on a description of the way in which the general environment influences fertility (McNicoll, 1980). Exceptions are Anker (1977) and Anker and Anker (1982), who find that even after controlling for the influence of individual characteristics, there is a statistically significant effect of community on fertility. Farooq, in Chapter 12 of this volume, shows that the fertility behaviour of rural and urban residents in Nigeria differs considerably. Lieberman and Monteverde (Chapter 14), by analysing both community and individual data, illustrate both the extra insights which are possible by distinguishing between these two levels of analysis and the specific contribution of environmental data. Sarma (Chapter 13) shows the influence of community variables in the determination of variations in fertility in India. Oppong, Macura and Winegarden, in their respective chapters, emphasise the same theme using macro data.

The connection between the general environment and the policy and programme environment has been more carefully studied, but largely by social scientists working in a different tradition. Ness and Ando (1984), for example, have shown the influence of variables relating to the political system on the establishment of programmes. Misra *et al.* (1982) show the importance of both organisational and environmental factors in the delivery of family-planning services in rural India.

The role of government policy or programmes

The independent or facilitative role of government in effecting changes in fertility is perhaps the most controversial area in the study of fertility. Governments can and have enacted programmes designed to facilitate contraceptive use, to encourage or discourage the use of abortion, or to change the age of marriage, and all of these activities will have some effect on fertility. They have also enacted many programmes (e.g. in the area of health or nutrition) that may have influenced the natural fertility variables. The controversy is not about the role of the intermediate variables themselves in affecting fertility. There is agreement that changes in the age of marriage or contraceptive practice will be central determinants of fertility. Difference of opinion is rather about the extent to which government programmes have an independent causal effect on these intermediate variables.

The definition of cause is difficult in any case. Here we can distinguish two questions. The first is whether the existence of a government-sponsored programme is 'necessary' (as opposed to 'necessary and sufficient') for the use of contraception. In the absence of a government programme, would individuals and groups find access to contraception through private channels? Does the existence of government encouragement speed the diffusion of contraceptive practice? Empirically stated, what proportion of the variation in contraceptive prevalence between times or among regions can be explained by the existence or the relative strength of government programmes designed to affect intermediate variables?

The second question deals with the extent to which programmes are exogenous variables within the system of social determinants which affect fertility. That is, are programmes themselves the results of forces which exist in society which generate government activities? For example, does the increase in income in society lead to a more widespread pattern of government intervention to facilitate contraception? Or, in terms of regional variations, does the existence of a set of social conditions lead to a greater likelihood that a family-planning clinic will be both well-staffed and well-managed? This question is relevant, of course, for most of the other variables which have been discussed in this review.

In reviewing the literature on the economic determinants of fertility, it is remarkable how often economists have managed to ignore completely the role that is potentially played by government. This neglect may arise from a number of factors. Economists have a tendency to search for explanations in terms of manipulable environmental variables which can be related directly to economic theory. Classical economic theory sees major determinants of demand, including perhaps the demand for children, as being the household income or the prices of the demanded commodities and their major substitutes. Thus, economists have tended to place great stress on the income effects, as we saw in the previous section. Contraception, to the extent that it is recognised as a force, is thought to be a facilitating factor, an endogenous variable in a complex system, that, while of interest, is less important than the exogenous variables which determine the values of the key dependent variables in the system. Thus the use of contraception may play a role in transmitting the effects of exogenous variables, but is not of great interest in and of itself. This view has the important implication that if one can properly specify the determinants of fertility in terms of the exogenous influences, the relationships among the endogenous variables in the system can be ignored. This may provide the intellectual basis for the tendency of many economists to ignore the intermediate variables and other variables such as preferences in their research.

The one case where it is very difficult to ignore such variables is in the evaluation of programmes designed to affect fertility in an upward or a downward direction. In such cases, economists and other researchers have generally treated variables such as access to contraception as key variables (G. B. Simmons, 1979; T. P. Schultz, 1974b; Srikantan, 1977; Kelly *et al.*, 1982; Stycos *et al.*, 1982; Phillips *et al.*, 1982; Stinson *et al.*, 1982). Most of these studies have demonstrated the existence of a relationship between programme variables and fertility, but there still remains a dispute about the causality which is in effect. Projects with an experimental design have the potential of unravelling some of the causal issues, but are often contaminated by implementation problems (see Cuca and Pierce, 1977; or Hilton and Lumsdaine, 1975).

Some researchers have treated programme variables as fully exogenous, thus testing the influence of programme variables as if it were independent of socio-economic conditions. Others have recognised that in many places the extent of the programme intervention is itself determined in part by the prevailing socio-economic conditions. Better staffing and facilities may be possible in urban rather than in rural clinics, for example. Whatever the exact model, such studies are in a fairly early stage of development and are as yet not well-integrated with many other economic studies of fertility.

There is, however, a perceived need among policy-makers for some research in this area (Miró and Potter, 1980b).

Among empirical studies, the greatest attention has been paid to international cross-sectional research although there are good reasons for thinking that in-country studies may be more relevant for many purposes. Among those finding a strong relationship between programmes and fertility are R. Freedman and Berelson (1976), Mauldin *et al.* (1978) and Tsui and Bogue (1978). Recent sceptics include Demeny (1979a, 1979b) and Hernandez (1981).

It should also be recognised that many government activities in addition to family-planning influence fertility. Herrin (1979) has documented the influence of a rural electrification programme on rural fertility in one province of the Phillipines. Barlow (1982) has assembled a set of case-studies illustrating the impact of development projects on demographic variables.

One way to approach the problem may be to systematically try to work out all possible causal chains, beginning at the link between the intermediate variables and fertility (perhaps as classified by Bongaarts, 1978) and proceeding back to the independent variables further removed from fertility. Thus a first step might be to see how different government programmes might influence variables relating to marriage. Does government housing policy influence the age at which young couples can set up housekeeping? Does the rural works programme oriented towards women encourage women to remain single or discourage remarriage after widowhood or divorce? The variables likely to influence contraception, fecundity or abortion could be examined in similar fashion. Considerable insight into the potential role of government policies and programmes would come out of this step by itself, but it could be pursued further to see how government activities affect variables further removed in the causal chain, as suggested in a very sketchy fashion in Figure 3.1. Any exercise of this kind will be based on the lessons learned from a broad-based analysis of the determinants of fertility. It is likely that it will underscore the idea that fertility is influenced by a range of government activities much wider than the family-planning effort. The relative importance of these different influences from a policy perspective turns on the results of further analysis.

Once this kind of examination is undertaken, and once some empirical estimations are made on the magnitudes of the effects involved, it may be possible to proceed to use the information generated for cost-effectiveness studies of how to influence fertility. Thus the general framework provided by this approach may give policy-makers a tool for making decisions about strategies for national population programmes. A key link, however, is the identification of possible relationships, and research to demonstrate their empirical importance. In this process, there is no reason to think that variables measuring government activity should be ignored. From a policy point of view, they are the most exogenous of variables.

Summary

Table 3.1 is provided as summary of the many findings reviewed in the previous pages. For each of the major variables which have been discussed in this chapter, the table gives a summary of key findings from the empirical literature. The first column indicates the general direction of the relationship when uncontrolled for competing influences. The second set of columns indicates the nature of the relationship when the variable is controlled for other possible influences. A column is provided to indicate whether or not the literature suggests that there is a question as to whether the causality always runs from the explanatory variable to fertility. The final column indicates the range of findings from the case-studies presented as Part III of this volume.

In general, the findings from the multivariate literature suggest that multivariate controls tend to reduce the influence of individual variables. Moreover, there are reasons to raise questions about the direction of causality in almost all of the variables. That is, in almost all cases, authors have raised questions such as whether fertility may not influence the level of the variable in question, or whether the variable in question is not an intervening variable for some more fundamental determinant of fertility.

PROBLEMS WITH EMPIRICAL RESEARCH ON THE ECONOMICS OF FERTILITY

The study of human fertility presents an especially difficult set of problems for economic research. While fertility behaviour has a large number of similarities with market-behaviour problems, it also differs in some important ways. The development of economic research in this area is complicated by the long time-periods involved, the lack of a formal market, and the awkward problem of reconciling individual and aggregate behaviour. Many of these problems have been illustrated in the empirical research in the first part of this chapter.

Two kinds of issues are particularly important. Firstly, research must be based on a specific statistical model. In most cases, this model will be

TABLE 3.1 *A summary of the effects of individual variables on fertility*

Variable name	Effects as reported in literature					Effect as reported in case-studies
	Uncontrolled effect	Controlled effect			Evidence of causal explanations for assistance	Direction
		Predominant diection	Range	General strength (strong/med/weak)		
Infant mortality	+	+	+	weak	yes	+/n.s.
Women's education	−	−	−/+	strong	yes	curvilinear
Women's labour-force participation	−	−	−/+	medium	yes	+/−
Per capita income	−	−	−/+	weak	yes	+/−
Income distribution	−	−	+/−	weak	yes	−
Preferences						
Number	++	+	+/−	weak	yes	
Sex	++	+	+	medium	yes	+
Family-planning services	−	−	−/+	medium	yes	−/+
General environment	−	−	−/+	medium	no	+
Population programme and policies	−	−	−/+	medium	yes	+

derived from the kind of theoretical considerations discussed in Chapter 2, but the specific model is of great importance, and within any given theoretical framework, a number of strategies are possible. Secondly, even after the statistical model explaining the relationships among the variables is specified, the exact measurement and definition of specific variables is an additional issue of concern.

The challenge is especially great for empirical research because the conceptual problems are compounded by the genuine difficulties of measurement. There is little tradition within economics of collecting and processing data for research purposes: economists generally use data generated through the efforts of national statistical systems, or through market surveys which are conducted by third-party organisations. Such experience with data collection that does exist is not concerned with areas such as fertility, which are at the edge of economics' traditional domain. This lack of orientation towards the collection of original data is particularly important because the research issues involved in the study of fertility are complex enough to require specifically tailored data. These measurement problems complicate the already delicate task of specifying the theoretical and econometric relationships that one expects among the variables. On the whole, then, there are many problems of empirical method and of finding an appropriate match between theory and empirical research (Turchi, 1975a, 1975b; see also Chapter 8 in this volume).

The following is a short overview of some of the chief problems involved in empirical research on the economics of fertility. Here our principal concern is summarising findings reported in more detail in later chapters of Part II of this volume, and discussing some topics that are not covered in those chapters.

Problems of Variable Definition and Measurements

In testing the implications of a theory, the goal is to gather empirical information which corresponds closely to the key concepts that are embodied in the theory. This counsel of perfection is seldom attained in the social sciences. In most instances, proxies or surrogate variables are used to measure influences that cannot be measured directly. While, in general, it has been easier to measure economic variables than the equivalent variables for psychological or sociological studies, the measurement tradition in economics has dealt with a relatively restricted range of market phenomena, for which commercial and other records have provided reasonable sources of information. In the case of the economics of fertility, there are not equivalent data sources for most of the key variables used in research. While in many developed countries there is adequate statistical information about both the overall size of the population and vital events, the explanatory variables are seldom easily available in fully appropriate form. Thus even in resource-rich societies, there are data inadequacies which affect our ability to test the implications of economic models. In the developing countries, the situation is much worse; not only are the phenomena in question much less likely to have been adequately measured, but the measurement of explanatory variables is also highly inadequate.

Dependent variables

In most economic models of fertility, a basic assumption is that couples make rational decisions about the number of children that they will want to have over their lifetimes. Research is then concerned with understanding what factors explain variations in the patterns of choice that people exhibit. In order to test levels of association, it is, of course, important to have an appropriate measure of the dependent variable. That measure will differ from aggregate or household studies.

At the aggregate level, researchers will want a measure of fertility which adequately distinguishes marital fertility from age structure or nuptuality effects. They will also be concerned with the distinction between period measures of fertility and cohort measures. Thus an important first step is to break down aggregate measures such as the crude birth rate into measures that are more precisely defined by the age and marital status of different risk groups. Inevitably, there will be some gaps in the data. For example, it will be true by definition that the fertility experience of younger cohorts will be very incomplete. Researchers who may be concerned with the way environmental constraints affect the lifetime fertility experience of a cohort will have no short-term means of obtaining an accurate measure of fertility which corresponds to the theoretical construct in question. Adjustments will have to be made using data relating to intentions or to the behaviour of other age-groups. Thus, aggregate attitudinal measures such as 'desired family-size' or period measures such as total fertility rate or the gross reproduction rate may be used as surrogates for the preferred measure of the completed fertility of women born during a given period.

There are problems of measuring fertility at the level of the household as well. While the problems of age or marital structure are more easily handled with individual-level data, other problems exist. Therefore, the scholars involved in the analysis of household data will have to make strategic decisions concerning how fertility should be measured. If the underlying theory deals with completed fertility, any measure based on the incomplete histories recorded in the survey will be inadequate in some respects. Even variables such as the number of children ever born, adjusted for age, are likely to suffer from this problem. While it is possible to make adjustments by asking parents about their intentions concerning future reproduction, both the incomplete control exercised by parents over their fertility and the possibility that they may change their minds is likely to make these statements of intention less than perfect predictors of behaviour. Many respondents do not seem to have such a preference, or they refuse to share it with interviewers, saying they 'don't know' or that the number of children is 'up to God'. Thus, for some studies of fertility, there may not be any empirical measure which corresponds to the underlying theoretical concepts; we are always dealing with measures that are flawed in one respect or another.

Fertility levels are not easy to measure. Substantial miscounting of events is not uncommon, so that even if empirical data exist which correspond reasonably well to the theoretical measures of fertility which are appropriate for a piece of research, undercounting may limit their application in research. Survey data are prone to understatement of past fertility levels, and further complication may result if misspecification of timing makes period estimation difficult. The World Fertility Survey and associated efforts are designed to correct this problem for national data, but even with reliable national estimates for one year, difficulties in estimating the pattern of change over time and the pattern of regional variation will remain.

Measurement error of fertility as the dependent variable has many implications for economic research on fertility. In studies that use regression techniques, a substantial error component in the variance of the dependent variable may result, which leads to lowered explanatory power but not to bias in the estimated regression coefficients. On the other hand, where the measurement error is associated with explanatory variables, the coefficients will be biased. For example, if older respondents or poor people misstate their fertility more than others, the level of explanation in estimated regression equations will be reduced, but if they overstate their age or income, there will be a positive bias in age and income coefficients.

Independent variables

In the first part of this chapter, we reviewed many independent variables which theorists and empirical researchers suggest have explanatory value for studies of fertility. One of the most commonly discussed variables is *income*, which seems a relatively straightforward concept when applied to market studies of consumption in a modern market economy. However, research on income and its association with variables like fertility is fraught with problems of definition and measurement. There are some general problems, such as trying to find a short-term measure of income which adequately indicates long-term income potential of the family. In the new home-economics models of fertility, it is assumed that fertility is a long-term pattern of behaviour in which parents make adjustments to environmental constraints that they perceive over their entire reproductive age-span. For testing this theory, the most appropriate income measure would be a measure of permanent income which illustrates the resource limitations that the family (or couple) believes it will encounter during its reproductive years or entire lifetime. Typically, micro studies of fertility have had available, at best, measures of income for a specific time-period, such as the calendar year when a survey was undertaken. Measure of life-time income or of future income expectations at the time a birth takes place are seldom available. As a result, the measured income may not cor-respond to levels experienced or anticipated earlier in the reproductive cycle, or to what might later be experienced by a couple with incomplete fertility. For some theoretical models, however, current income may be fully adequate. The size of family land-holdings and the education of the husband have been used as proxies for lifetime income, but since they also measure other dimensions of the family, it is not clear what interpretation should be placed on empirical results.

In survey data, there are many sources of error in the estimation of income. While income in kind, e.g. grain produced and consumed on a farm, is a very important element in the total resource constraint of a family living in a developing country, it is likely to be underestimated in income assessments. Not only are people often unaware of the exact amounts involved, but they may be afraid to reveal the size and source of their income to outsiders. There are other complications as well. To some extent, the problems of measurement and conceptualisation overlap. For example, in many developing countries, there is a pattern of extended family residence in which multiple sets of parents, usually related by descent from a common ancestor, share their incomes and some of the responsibilities for childrearing. In this case, there is an empirical question both in terms of gathering information concerning the income constraints that exist for the extended family, and in assessing the extent to which individual components of the family take on responsibility for various children. It may be impossible, in such cases, to assess the income appropriate for predicting the behaviour of a single couple. Thus, the notion of income as a constraint on the family deviates significantly from the notion of income as it is generally used in market analysis.

There are severe problems of both a measurement and a conceptual nature in the specification of other independent variables. In the literature, a number of different variables have been used to measure *the costs of childrearing*. One of the most common variables employed by researchers is the education of one or both of the parents. The use of this variable is based on a belief that time has a higher opportunity cost for parents who are better educated than for less-educated parents and, as a result, they will be reluctant to make the same investments of time in children. However, the same variables which are used in this case to measure the cost of childrearing may be used to measure some aspects of the utility function of the parents, or in some cases, as mentioned above, may even be used as proxies for the level of income. Thus, the variable 'education' can take on a wide range of interpretations, depending on which version of economic theory is being examined. This problem is illustrated further in the discussion of Chapter 10.

Another variable which measures the opportunity cost of children is the wife's participation in the labour-force. It is reasonable to suppose that a woman who has a job outside of the home may find that maintaining the job conflicts with having a family and may, as a result, reduce the size of her family. It is not clear, however, that female employment by itself will have this impact. In fact, as shown by some of the case-studies in Part III of this volume, frequently women in the rural areas exhibit patterns of employment which do not in any way impede the process of family formation, and are quite consistent with large families. In such instances, if a researcher uses female employment as a measure of the high opportunity cost of childrearing, the results may be quite contrary to the hypothesis. This result derives not from the fact that parents have more children when the costs are high, but because this measure of costs is inadequate. The use of proxy variables may be unavoidable, but it complicates enormously the application of ideas drawn from the economic theory of fertility to the empirical study of fertility behaviour in developing countries.

Even variables such as *mortality* present measurement problems. If very detailed information is not available at the micro level, it is difficult to distinguish between a situation where the death of a child leads parents to want to have another child, and situations where the birth of a second child causes the death of the earlier-born child. The two underlying hypotheses are diametrically opposed to one another: one assumes that the causality runs from fertility to mortality, and the other assumes the reverse. While each assumes a high degree of association between infant deaths and fertility, without detailed information on the timing of the events and on other related factors, researchers are left without any means of distinguishing between competing hypotheses. Similarly, at the aggregate level the measure of mortality used by researchers may lead to bias in the estimated coefficients. The use of crude birth rates in empirical work has the disadvantage that the existence of a high birth rate will itself lead to a situation of high death rate, because a large proportion of the population is in the vulnerable ages. Thus, the birth rate leads to high mortality, not the reverse as is commonly hypothesised. Difficulties in finding an adequate measure of mortality have the effect of confounding two kindred but theoretically-distinct relationships.

Problems with Econometric Specification

Empirical work on the economics of fertility is hampered not only by problems of variable measurement and definition, but by problems of econometric specification. In this section, several of these problems are discussed, along with some of the alternative approaches that have been employed. Many of these particular problems are discussed in greater detail in later chapters, particularly the chapters of Part II which deal specifically with methodological issues.

Most economists approach the empirical study of economic behaviour with the tools of regression analysis. In the simplest case, an equation will be derived from a set of theoretical propositions, and estimated using ordinary least squares. In this kind of specification, it is generally assumed that the major influences on the dependent variable are specified, and that the effects of all of these exogenous influences can be represented by their additive relationship with the dependent variable. We have already seen that there can be great difficulties in the measurement of particular variables. There can also be problems when the relationship among variables under examination is inconsistent with the assumptions of ordinary least squares. Some of these problems derive from an insufficiently close relationship between theory and the particular empirical specifications; others are a result of problems of the measurement of particular variables.

While it is important that there be a reasonable correspondence between theoretical and empirical specifications, a perfect correspondence is never achieved; there are many ways in which the two approaches can deviate. For example, in Chapter 2 it was observed that many of the theories or hypotheses about fertility variations in developing countries have been derived from neoclassical micro-economic literature. Ideally then, the hypotheses are suited for the testing of relationships specified at the level of the household, but data collected at this level are often unavailable, which may lead the researchers to search for alternative ways of testing the hypotheses. Thus, researchers have often used aggregated data to test some of the propositions drawn from the micro-economic literature. While it is possible that the population in question is sufficiently homogenous to warrant such treatment, such an estimation strategy will often lead to biased estimators of the relevant micro-level parameters. The kinds of bias that result, and their importance, are discussed in Chapter 7 on aggregation, but we shall draw the general conclusion that this type of testing procedure is frequently a highly inadequate substitute for the more direct testing of micro-economic hypotheses using micro-economic data. There are a number of courses of action which alleviate the problem. One is to be very cautious in defining only such hypotheses as are testable on the basis of the particular match of theory and data which is available. Another alternative is to be sure that the theoretical statement underlying the research adequately matches the empirical data sources which are available. This alternative implies that for micro hypotheses, the data set should be drawn from a source such as a household survey. Conversely, when the data set is aggregative in nature, researchers should use appropriate theoretical specification involving societal-level units of analysis.

There are also some specific statistical problems associated with the question of aggregation. While some researchers think that it is appropriate to use empirical data drawn from aggregate sources for the study of micro-economic hypotheses, others believe that there are severe limitations to what can be learned from this sort of data set. W. S. Robinson (1950) has argued that it is often possible to observe correlations among the aggregate data which are based more on measurement effects than on underlying relationships which exist in the data. In this volume, Edlefsen and Lieberman (Chapter 7) take issue with Robinson's general conclusion, and warn that the use of aggregate 'ecological' data can raise serious doubts about research conclusions.

Another type of inappropriate match between theory and estimation involves situations when simultaneous relationships may exist between or among some of the key variables in the system. For example, there are well-known hypotheses which suggest a causal relationship between fertility and the labour-force participation of women. The new home-economics literature suggests that the causal relationships may go in both directions. As a result, the researcher may greatly oversimplify the relationship between the two variables if he attempts to estimate only the effects of labour-force participation on fertility, and ignores the reverse effect. If the relationship exists in both directions but only one is acknowledged, biased and inconsistent estimators result. If, on the other hand, the researcher acknowledges the simultaneity but uses a hazily defined model, he is likely to face problems of identification. For example, if a first equation specifies that wife's labour-force participation, wife's education and husband's income are determinants of fertility, and a second equation posits that a wife's labour-force participation is a function of fertility together with wife's education and husband's income, it will not be possible to jointly estimate such a two equation system. Clearly, through division of the first equation by the coefficient of labour-force participation, it is possible to transform it into the second equation, or to transform the second into the first by dividing it by the coefficient of fertility.[4] With the estimation of a system of equations comes the need for a theoretical model sufficiently precise to distinguish between the separate processes embodied in the different equations. Thus, where appropriate, a variable indicating rural or urban residence might be added to the list of predictors of labour-force participation, and age and religion could be included as explanatory variables in the fertility regression. There are now two separate, estimable equations comprising the system. A further discussion of the problems in simultaneous equation models of fertility can be found in Chapter 8 by Turchi.

Missing variables constitute another problem. Theory specifies the existence of a particular variable(s) which is (are) not contained in the data set. As a result, any estimated coefficients will include both the influence of the specified variables and of the omitted variable(s), which, in general, yield biased and inconsistent estimators.

An additional but related problem is that there may be interaction among some of the chief variables in the system. The existence of interaction implies that an ordinary least squares estimation of relationships among the variables will generate biased and inconsistent estimates of the chief relationships specified in the system, since the absent non-linear terms are missing relevant variables. An example of interaction is that education may have different effects on fertility, depending on the age-groups of the women involved. Younger women, for whom education has been generally available, may have different responses to education than would the older cohorts, for whom a given level of education may have had quite distinct implications. Where identifiable, interactions can be dealt with by an adequate specification of the estimation equation, although that specification would no longer take the form of a linear additive regression model.[5]

In economics, the assumption is generally made that variables are perfectly measured, but that the relationships among variables are imperfectly modelled; the differences between actual and measured concepts are either non-existent or negligible relative to the error in the equation. Unfortunately, the variables of interest to a fertility researcher are unlikely to be so clearly defined or readily observable as market prices and quantities or government spending. Thus, another problem in the transition from theory to empirical estimation in fertility research is that a theoretically-important variable may be unobservable, either by nature or because of data-set limitations. Examples of the former are aptitude measures (IQ) or permanent income, and an example of the latter is response errors on surveys. Reporting errors transform an otherwise observable variable into an unobservable variable with the addition of a random error term. Usually assumed to have a mean of zero, these error components lead to biased and inconsistent estimates by distorting the variances and covariances of the affected variables, unless they are estimated and controlled for. Unfortunately, this means that the researcher is faced with the same underlying estimation problem as in the simultaneous equations case: if the error covariances are not restricted to zero, the number of parameters to be estimated increases as the factorial of the number of unobservable variables, rendering identification impossible in all but a few cases. If measurement error or inherent unobservability is judged likely to be present in the problem, a model is indicated in which the *a priori* assumption of zero-error covariance is justifiable. If measurement error in the dependent variable is uncorrelated with all other measurement errors, it may be ignored with no ill effects on the estimators.

One way to deal with the identification problem in observables is to have several observations on a given unit, i.e. a panel study. Assuming that reporting error is constant over time but varies across units, it is possible to identify a model with a larger number of non-zero-error variances and covariances. Nerlove's variance component technique is outlined in this volume by Browning (Chapter 6), and the reader is referred to Hausman and Taylor (1979) for further details.

A final empirical concern is what kind of data are appropriate for testing a given hypothesis. Very often, the research questions of concern are those of how behaviour will change over time, but the available data are cross-sections of either individual households or of aggregate units, such as regions or counties. In this case, it is tempting to use the cross-sectional data set, and to assume that people of different income levels or different socio-economic characteristics represent a cross-section of differences similar to those that would have been observed over time. That is, it is assumed that the behaviour of poor people in the cross-section can be compared with that of rich people in the same way that the behaviour of poor people in a given year of the time -series observation are related to the behaviour of the same people if they are measured to be richer a few years later. Thus, cross-sectional data sets are used to test propositions about changes in behaviour over time. This procedure can yield useful results, but its adequacy depends very much on a detailed knowledge of the behaviours involved. (See Chapter 10 for a discussion of the conditions under which cross-sectional data can be used to project future behaviour.) In a changing society, one is particularly likely to falsely label a 'vintage effect' – that is, a difference between young and old cohorts which is due to real differences apart from the age difference – as a life-cycle change which occurs as the young cohort ages. Where the procedure does not work, we are left with a need to reconcile often conflicting empirical generalisations based on different data sets. For example, it has been observed that over time, there is a negative relationship between income and fertility, but in the cross-section, there is often an observed positive effect between income and fertility. The data, then, do not give us an adequate way to estimate which of these effects is stronger, or how they should be disentangled. It is encumbent upon the researcher to bring theoretical knowledge to bear on the issue, which will disentangle these effects. Thus, for a given research issue, it is important to be aware that there are different implications for using time-series or cross-sectional data sets; in some instances, there may be strong advantages to combining cross-sectional and time-series data in the form of a pooled data set. However, as with all deviations from the simplest case, there are trade-offs involved. In this volume, these trade-offs are discussed by Browning in Chapter 6.

On the Limitations of the Economic Approach to Empirical Testing

The primary empirical tool of the economist is the use of the class of statistical tools and economic theory-building known as econometrics. Econometrics is developed around the analysis of statistical data and careful reasoning about the implications of a theoretical economic system. The strength of econometrics is its careful use of deductive reasoning and a corresponding emphasis on relatively sophisticated statistical methods.

The strengths of the approach, however, are also in part responsible for its shortcomings. The use of formal analytical methods and computations based on the computer encourages a narrow view of the research methods that are likely to be productive. It can be argued that the issues we are dealing with in this volume are so complex, and the state of our knowledge so incomplete, that there is a drastic need for more basic methods of data collection. Anthropological studies, detailed family profiles, historical analyses of the structural changes taking place in a society – all of these approaches are likely to generate the kind of knowledge base that may help us to better define hypotheses for testing with statistical data. Caldwell's (1976, 1980) hypothesis concerning resource allocations within the family, for example, was generated more on the basis of direct and intensive contact with the population being studied than by the use of econometric methods.[6] Alternative approaches to fertility research are also likely to get researchers out into the field and put them in contact with the people being researched. Quite independent of which methods of data collection and analysis are used, field contact itself may contribute to a greater understanding of a particular situation.

In Chapter 2, the relatively narrow range of variables that has been used by most of the micro-economic theories of fertility was discussed. The range of empirical variables is also quite restricted. In this situation, the direct involvement of economists in the data-collection stage may enhance both the explanatory power of statistical research and our understanding of how people make their reproductive decisions. Any comprehensive understanding will be based on the cumulative impact of many such episodes, with supplementation and systemisation from the econometric studies. Thus, while theoretical and econometric methods may be the dominant approaches used by economists to study fertility, the methods need supplementation from alternative approaches, many of which may be unfamiliar to economists.

Future research in the economics of population is likely to go in two different but complementary directions. On the one hand, the current efforts at building increasingly sophisticated theoretical and econometric models will proceed apace. On the other hand, these efforts are likely to be complemented by a more basic inquiry into the nature of fertility decisions within the family and community context. At its best, the exchange between these two traditions may lead to a productive period of research, leading economists to explore new variables and relationships and encouraging other researchers to make use of the rigour and generalisability which is sought by economic researchers.

NOTES

1. There is a vast literature on the role of the intermediate variables. An excellent source for current views and bibliographic references is the periodical *Population Reports*, published by the Population Information Program, The Johns Hopkins University, Hampton House, 624 North

Broadway, Baltimore MD 21205, USA. It provides regular updates on contraception, abortion, age at marriage, and other factors which affect fertility.

2. See Heer and Smith (1968). It should be noted that alternative assumptions lead to very different results. Venkatacharya (1978) is able to show that if parents have a strong sex-preference, then the insurance effect may be much smaller than is indicated by Heer and Smith.

3. Timur's classification is somewhat undercut by the inclusion of the Philippines and Indonesia among Stage I countries, but the analysis of the role of the family and the age at marriage suggests ways in which the role of education and fertility could be clarified (Timur, 1977).

4. Let L denote wife's labour-force participation, F fertility, E education, and Y husband's income. Then the system can be written as

$$L = \alpha_0 + \alpha_1 F + \alpha_2 E + \alpha_3 Y \quad \text{and} \tag{1}$$

$$F = \beta_0 + \beta_1 L + \beta_2 E + \beta_3 Y \tag{2}$$

But (2) can be rewritten as

$$-\beta_1 L = \beta_0 - F + \beta_2 E + \beta_3 Y \quad \text{or}$$

$$L = -(\beta_0/\beta_1) + (1/\beta_1)F - (\beta_2/\beta_1)E - (\beta_3/\beta_1)Y, \tag{2a}$$

which is clearly the same equation as (1), where $\alpha_0 = -\beta_0/\beta_1$, $\alpha_1 = 1/\beta_1$, $\alpha_2 = -\beta_2/\beta_1$ and $\alpha_3 = -\beta_3/\beta_1$.

5. It would be non-linear in the original explanatory variables; however, some interactive models, such as an equation using these variables in combination with their desired products as the explanatory variables, are estimable by OLS.

6. Diesing (1971) has argued the importance of such methods for the social sciences, and the dangers of using the limited statistical methodology.

4 Towards a Policy-relevant Framework

GEORGE B. SIMMONS and GHAZI M. FAROOQ

Previous chapters have outlined the basic thrust of recent research on the economics of fertility. We have examined a wide variety of economic models and empirical results, and some of the problems associated with economic thinking about the study of fertility. The first two sections of this chapter briefly restate the current status of the economics of fertility both as social science and in terms of its contribution to policy. The last section outlines some research strategies.

THE ECONOMICS OF FERTILITY AS SCIENCE

Economics, like other social sciences, has aspired to develop the characteristics of the natural sciences. Economists aspire to a close relationship between theory and empirical research. They assume that the theories can be used not just as general guidance, but as a very specific frame of reference for researchers as they examine 'facts' from the real world. They are disappointed when empirical research draws little guidance from theory, and are unsatisfied by theoretical statements that do not lead to easily testable empirical hypotheses. The reviews contained in the earlier chapters should make it clear that there is still a profusion of work to be done in the domains of both theory and empirical testing. Moreover, the correspondence between the theories and empirical research is not close. Most empirical research has been inspired by theory, but it is seldom that the empirical specification is derived specifically from a formal theory. Empirical studies are much more likely to be based on loosely connected sets of hypotheses about fertility behaviour than they are on tightly defined theoretical propositions derived from the main body of economic theory.

*General Tests of Economic Models of Fertility and Findings from the
Empirical Studies in this Volume*

The variable by variable examination, common in empirical studies, leaves
open the question of the extent to which theories involving complex
multiple-variable explanations are supported by the evidence. Demographic
transition models suggest, for example, that a fall in mortality *and* changes
in other modernisation variables will lead to a sustained decline in fertility.
Similarly, the new home-economics models suggest that a number of
variables – infant mortality, income, women's status – will have specified
effects on household fertility. Thus in trying to assess the value of a theory
as a guiding framework in the knowledge-cumulating process, unless one
can identify a decisive test of a theory revolving around one variable, it is
important to examine the full range of hypotheses generated by the theory,
and not just one specific relationship. The empirical support of some of the
major theories will be illustrated by a brief examination of the empirical
research in the seven chapters which make up Part III of this volume.

Chapter 11, by Anker, and Chapter 12, by Farooq, illustrate the
application of general socio-economic models of fertility to African
fertility data. In general, their model corresponds reasonably closely to
what we have called the social-determinants model in Chapter 2. They
demonstrate, in their respective chapters, that variables such as age,
education of wife and infant mortality are associated with variations in
the number of children ever born. Anker goes further, and demonstrates
that the exact nature of the association depends upon the way that variables are specified, and further that the socio-economic context, e.g. rural
versus urban residence or the ethnic affiliation of the family, are associated with fertility variations. Farooq also goes beyond the basic core
of models which are associated with the social-determinants school,
and explores some of the biological constraints, such as breastfeeding,
which influence fertility.

Sarma, in Chapter 13, adopts an approach to explaining variations in
household fertility somewhat closer to a new home-economics model.
Many of the variables are the same as those used by Anker and Farooq,
but Sarma deliberately attempts to concentrate on the exogenous variables
in the system, such as the education of the wife, the economic circumstances of the family, and the history of child mortality. He also focuses
more strongly on older women, thus reducing the overall influence of age.

Lieberman and Monteverde (Chapter 14) propose an analytical framework which contains features of social-determinants and structuralist
models. They demonstrate that separate models can be developed to

explain the variation among counties in Turkey and the variation among households. In their community-level analysis, they try to take into account the historical and geographical circumstances of different regions, and the extent to which these characteristics influence the demographic responses adopted by communities to deal with changing circumstances. One interesting feature of the model adopted is that migration is recognised as one possible demographic response. The micro model corresponds more closely to the new home-economics approach, with the interesting extension that community-level variables are added to provide a partial link to the aggregate model and to provide measures of the exogenous prices and other constraints on the behaviour of the household.

In Chapter 15, Macura examines the determinants of marital fertility and of female labour-force participation using a simultaneous-equations specification. His framework is generally derived from the new home-economics, but many of the specific variables included are justified on the basis of the specific circumstances of Yugoslavia rather than on the basis of purely theoretical considerations. The Macura and the Sarma chapters both illustrate the general power of the new home-economics framework, but they also illustrate how difficult it is to design a decisive test of the model. Most of their findings are consistent with the model, not all of the relationships are strong, and many of the important variables could have been part of any of the models reviewed in Chapter 2.

Two general comments can be applied to these chapters and to much of the empirical literature. Firstly, the inherent complexity of the relationships and the lack of appropriate data frequently make it difficult to assess causality. For example, the mortality and family-planning variables may be determined by fertility rather than be determinants of fertility. Secondly, a large proportion of the variance in fertility is often left unexplained, especially in research related to the least-developed countries, despite the inclusion of a large range of explanatory variables in the research, and the use of variables such as age that are in and of themselves strongly related to accumulative fertility.

Uthoff and González (Chapter 16) examine the relationships between fertility and female labour-force participation, but their focus is on aggregative behaviour, and they devote a great deal more attention to the mediating effects of variables such as age and marital structure than do most of the other authors of the chapters in Part III. By showing the important role of marital patterns in explaining the different patterns of fertility in Costa Rica and Mexico, they underscore the importance of assessing the general context in which individuals make their decisions.

Winegarden's research (Chapter 17) is also aggregative in nature. He uses a cross-section of data from different developing countries to estimate a model relating fertility, income distribution, school enrolment, mortality and family-planning. He makes the case that these variables are to some extent simultaneously determined, and that the distribution of income, measured by the income share of the poorest two-fifths of households, is in significant measure influenced by previous levels of fertility. Winegarden argues that the impact of income distribution in fertility depends upon the mortality conditions which prevail, but, on balance, the effect is slight. Mortality and family-planning are shown to be stronger determinants of fertility. The Winegarden chapter is a good example of a relatively complete model, but it does not correspond very closely to any of the major schools we have identified in Chapter 2.

In general, the chapters in Part III do not give decisive support to one or another approach to the study of fertility. While they are in general supportive of the notion that people do make choices with regard to the number of children they wish to have, most of the key variables which are demonstrated to be strongly associated with fertility have been incorporated into all of the models. Thus little basis is provided for choosing among the competing models. Clearly, there are many aspects of fertility which are not captured by any of these papers. The correspondence between theory and empirical results is impressive at a very general level, but it is also true that some of the empirical research, either in Part III of this volume or in the general literature, offers decisive tests of a specific version of the socio-economic theory of fertility. The papers also, with the possible exception of the chapter by Winegarden, illustrate the difficulty in identifying and measuring causal relationships, and linking the variables in the system to policy instruments.

General Observations Concerning the Economic Approach to Research

In the ideal world of scientific research, we would expect that knowledge would be cumulative. Present research should build on past efforts, and, over time, we would find ways of winnowing those grains of truth from the masses of straw and chaff that accumulate in any research process. The review of the literature which we have conducted in the earlier chapters suggests that we are, as of yet, in the very early stages in this process, and that our aspirations towards a pure scientific method in the area of the economics of fertility may be premature. The number of systematic truths which we have been able to glean from the complex realities in the Third World is, as of yet, relatively small, and given the limited number of robust and universal findings, it is difficult to be optimistic that the methods we have hitherto employed will be more productive in the future. It should be quickly added, however, that the same generalisation can be made about many of the attempts by social scientists to understand the broad process of change now taking place in the Third World.

To the editors of this volume, the above observations suggest the need for diversity in the form and manner of economic research related to fertility and of tolerance among economists engaged in fertility-related research of findings and methods which may not fall within the accepted range of economic reasearch activities. A conservative assessment of previous research accomplishments would suggest that the economics profession has a great deal to be modest about in terms of its research in the area of fertility. Many papers have indicated that there should be a negative relationship between women's employment and fertility, or that one should expect mortality and fertility to be positively related. Yet these predictions are not universally validated in developing countries and, perhaps more importantly, can be derived from the theoretical perspectives of a number of disciplines. The number of observations about expected empirical relationships in the developing countries that would not be derivable from a large number of disciplinary perspectives is indeed limited. Nor has economic research or econometric methodology allowed us to make estimates with sufficient precision to predict fertility accurately, nor is our theoretical basis for those predictions well differentiated from that of other disciplines. What, then, can be said in defence of economic theory and of economic studies of empirical relationships in this area?

The economic approach has the strong advantage of making explicit the nature of relationships which are often unclear in other forms of research. For example, through the use of theory, economists have established that there is a basic ambiguity in the predicted partial effects on fertility of the increase in family income which takes place when the wife enters the labour-force. Econometric methods have also brought a special sophistication to the study of many empirical relationships in the area of fertility. Thus it seems to us that there is more than ample justification for the research efforts that have been undertaken in the past, but it seems equally clear that we have no basis for resting on our laurels at this stage. We need to generate more imaginative theory. We need a better application of the sophisticated methods of econometrics to research questions. We need a more precise identification of data needs. All of these things must be done before we can expect economics to contribute at its full potential to the study of fertility.

Economists working on fertility should also be prepared to accept a somewhat more pragmatic approach to theorising in their work. We should recognise that while new theoretical approaches may eventually give us an integrated framework for examining the full set of propositions about fertility and economic behaviour, until that event occurs, we may want to concentrate on a simpler set of often *ad hoc* generalisations. For example, it may be impossible at this stage to specify a utility function and a budget constraint so that they faithfully mirror the complexities of reproductive decisions in Third World households and, simultaneously, can be used for the derivation of specific and estimatable demand functions. In the absence of such a specification, we may want to accept theories of fertility that involve multiple variables, each justified on its own terms.

We may also want to accept new empirical practices that might enhance an understanding of the economics of fertility, even if they do not make use of the full array of techniques used by the skilled econometrician. For example, case-studies either at the community level or at the family level may help to generate information about important relationships which cannot be easily studied using data from large-scale surveys. Small-scale studies of a few families – a method commonly employed by anthropologists – may tell us more about the flow of resources between generations than we can expect to learn from surveys which are characterised by brief and impersonal contacts with the population being studied. Even in the case of large-scale research studies, economists may need to devote a great deal more of their own time to data collection (Ryder, 1973).

There are many possible innovations in the theoretical and empirical tools used for the investigation of fertility. Certain trends seem fairly clear. Firstly, there is likely to be greater use of large-scale structural models for examining fertility relationships. This approach to modelling has the advantage that many relationships can be explored within a reasonably consistent framework, that causal relationships are emphasised and that policy variables can be built in more appropriately than in many other frameworks. Turchi discusses structural equation approaches and their advantages in Chapter 8.

Secondly, both theoretical and empirical researchers are likely to make creative use of the differences between fertility behaviour at the level of the family and that of larger social aggregates. On the empirical side, the increasing interest in community-level variables and in the complementarity of data gathered at different levels of aggregation should lead to a better understanding of the determinants of fertility at the levels of both the family and the community.

Thirdly, new research on fertility is likely to give increasing emphasis to sequential decision-making. Theoretical structures which emphasise such a decision-making framework are increasingly common, and new data sources may provide the data for testing theoretical propositions drawn from this framework. Browning discusses some of the econometric issues involved with the use of such data in Chapter 6. The use of panel data collected from repeat visits to the same households makes it possible to test hypotheses that cannot be legitimately addressed with cross-cultural data sets.

Finally, simulation models may provide a mechanism for linking fertility research with complex models of economic development. Such models have the advantage of permitting the examination of relationships which cannot be estimated directly and which are too complicated to be explored through mathematical theories. Such models may be an important link to policy, and may supplement other approaches to fertility research. Rodgers and Wéry explore the advantages and disadvantages of simulation models in Chapter 9.

It is our belief that all of the approaches discussed above will become more commonplace in the coming decade. Because we believe these techniques to be important, we have encouraged a set of colleagues to write the chapters making up Part II of this book. These chapters should provide researchers with an overview of the new techniques and their application to fertility research.

All of the new techniques discussed in Part II will facilitate advances in fertility research. These new techniques should also permit more effective exploration of causal hypotheses and, as a result, may encourage a more policy-relevant generation of fertility research studies. Effective policy research must be based on hypotheses about variables that are of interest to policy, either because they represent variables that policy-makers wish to influence, or because they represent variables that may be instruments in the effort to influence some other goals. Thus, to the extent that the new research techniques that are available for researchers permit the identification of causal mechanisms for influencing fertility, they will encourage the development of policies and programmes with a scientific basis. The effectiveness of policy research depends on more than improved techniques, however.

THE POLICY SIGNIFICANCE OF ECONOMIC RESEARCH ON FERTILITY

Research concerning the determinants of fertility needs no special justification, yet it is fair to say that much of the research about fertility in the

Third World has a basis in the policy orientation of researchers in those countries. In many countries, population research has been stimulated by a concern with the implications of rapid population growth. In other countries, while there is a less acute sense of the negative implications of fertility, there is still a recognition that the impact of fertility levels on the need for social services and social welfare investments merits close study. Projections and plans for the future are based on expectations about fertility, and these expectations need to be well founded in an empirical understanding of fertility and its determinants. Thus, there is a general interest in the policy implications of fertility behaviour.

The economic literature on fertility, although extensive, has concentrated its attention on a relatively narrow range of variables which are thought to affect fertility, e.g. income, infant mortality, women's status. Demeny (1976, p. 127) has commented that 'if interpreted as instrumental variables in a policy model', the short list of key explanatory variables given prominence in the literature has 'offered an almost grotesquely thin menu of choice for collective action'. Moreover, the relevance of many of these variables for government intervention is not well defined.

While the policy orientation among Third World researchers is well established, it is less clear how economic research undertaken thus far contributes to an understanding of the policy options available. Certainly, it is important that economists oriented toward policy recognise that, to be relevant for policy, research must give some indication of the programmes, the legislative changes or the other initiatives that may be undertaken by government which can be hoped to lead to a change in fertility. Much of the research on the economics of fertility that has been done to this point has focused on establishing the relationship between a given level of social development and fertility. Thus research has established a link between women's labour-force participation and fertility, without necessarily taking the further step of exploring in a connected fashion the programmatic initiatives that will need to be undertaken to change the pattern of women's employment. Hence, one of the goals of policy-related research should be to build in, more systematically, an understanding of the means policy-makers can use for bringing about changes which will indirectly lead to fertility change. In this case, there should be a research concern with the way in which female labour-force participation rates can be increased. The more general problem would be to provide the information required for a qualitative and quantitative assessment of available policy options, both direct and indirect (G. B. Simmons, 1979).

Policy-oriented research should be concerned with the instruments of policy as well as the objectives. This point is sufficiently important to require further elaboration. Imagine the sequence of events that must be involved if a government is to undertake an action that will result in an increase or a decrease in fertility. Assume, for example, that the government policy-makers have reviewed the literature on the economics of fertility, and have discovered that a reduction in infant mortality is thought by many researchers to be a necessary condition for a subsequent reduction in fertility. How would they go about making the programme and policy steps required to reduce fertility through this means? One cannot just wave a magic wand and have mortality go down. Presumably, there must be some information about the underlying causes of mortality and the mechanisms by which these conditions can be reduced through government action or encouragement. An administrative structure must be created to undertake the appropriate steps for the implementation of the programmes that are involved, and this in turn implies that efforts must be made to see that adequate financing is available and all of the required resources are in place. For example, suppose the government seeks to reduce infant mortality through a programme designed to immunise infants. The technology will need to be identified, finance will have to be secured and staff appointed. Eventually, the steps required to reach the village population and to provide the children with a viable vaccine will be complete. Child deaths will begin to be less frequent than they were previously. Now the question will be, what is the reaction of the parents and potential parents in the communities that are affected? Will they reduce their fertility? If they do reduce their fertility, what is the mechanism by which this reduction takes place, and does the existence of government programmes or policy affect the outcome in any way? All of these questions will have to be addressed in any assessment of a policy oriented towards reducing fertility through an immunisation programme which seeks to reduce infant mortality. The same kind of questions would have to be asked about the programmes designed to reduce mortality through sanitation, improved nutrition, or any other means.

The basic point is that if researchers want to contribute to the policy process, they have to recognise that variables such as infant mortality are not policy instruments in themselves, and that in order for research to be very helpful to the policy process, it must go one step further and build in a careful examination of all the steps from the decision or the potential decision to undertake the programme to the ultimate objective, which is to change fertility.

The problem is not strictly empirical. One of the reasons why the empirical literature has given little emphasis to the kind of policy research that we are describing here, is that this sort of research question is given little emphasis in the theoretical literature. Neither the economic models nor their competitors from other disciplines stress the full set of linkages with policy or programmes. Rather, they are concerned with the determinants of fertility in a world in which the government has little part. Moreover, it is often felt by many of these researchers that research which makes government programmes and actions an explicit focus is somehow tainted or less important than that which gives pride of place to more general socio-economic variables. This view seems to be changing somewhat, but the existing literature does not accord a very central role to policy or programmatic variables.

Taking into account the kinds of issues discussed above, we can outline the following guideline for policy-relevant research.

Firstly, the populations which are the subject of policy-related research should be representative of a sufficiently large class of individuals to be of policy significance. Thus, it may be of some interest to study a particular region or sector of the population, but if that community is known to have special characteristics which make it atypical of the kind of response one would expect generally, then it may not be a suitable subject for policy-related research. More generally, this suggests a need for appropriate sampling procedures.

Secondly, the research which is intended to have policy significance should concentrate on relationships of sufficient empirical strength to justify strong policy conclusions. It is not very helpful for policy-makers to know that variable X is significantly related to variable Y measuring fertility in a sample of 10,000 households when the relationship explains only a tiny portion of the variance in fertility.

Thirdly, the research framework should build in an explicit linkage between the policy variables of concern in governmental initiatives which can be undertaken.

Finally, there should be a concern for feasibility of programmatic intervention. Research findings which suggest possible effects which are of no practical significance for programmes are not likely to be of interest. Thus, feasibility should be an important criterion for policy-relevance of research findings.

Assuming, then, that we know some of the general characteristics of research which is judged to be policy-relevant while at the same time being empirically based and founded in generally-accepted theories of social behaviour, the question remains of what are the determinants of the utilisation which research findings enjoy. It has often been the experience of social scientists that their research findings are largely neglected, and we know of few examples of economic research on the determinants of fertility which have been used as a basis of policy. How do we encourage a stronger connection between policy-makers and researchers? How do we assure that the connection does not become too strong, i.e. that policy-makers dominate the process and content of research?

There is, of course, no easy answer to such questions. One of the first concerns should be that the research is significant in the sense discussed above. Research findings which have no programmatic significance are unlikely to be accepted as guidelines for action by policy-makers. A more important criterion for research being utilised by policy-makers may be the extent to which the policy-makers have been involved in identifying the fundamental research questions and in the process of implementing and assessing research findings. In this regard, the pattern established by the Economic and Social Commission for Asia and the Pacific of creating special research boards (with responsible programme administrators as members) for the guidance of many research projects may be particularly appropriate. More generally, efforts should be made to involve programme administrators and policy-makers in some aspects of the research process. To the extent that research is undertaken without regard to the concerns of these individuals, it is not likely to be understood or utilised by them in policy formulation.

It should also be stressed that research can be adversely affected if politicians or bureaucrats have excess control. People who have been responsible for past population policies may seek to steer researchers away from important research questions that might reflect adversely on their own contributions. They may also misguidedly interfere in the definition of research questions or procedures. Thus efforts must be made to assure a reasonable degree of independence for researchers.

To summarise, economic researchers concerned with fertility must be prepared to adopt a diverse range of theoretical models and empirical methods if they expect their research to be effective. If they restrict themselves to the narrow range of theory and methods defined by the neo-classical tradition, they are unlikely to be instrumental in the recognition and development of new approaches to understanding fertility behaviour or to the design of effective policies. In the same connection, it is also important that researchers expose themselves more to field conditions and to the influence of policy-makers. Only by interacting with the real world are we likely to develop more effective theories and a more complete understanding of the behaviours which we are trying to influence.

RESEARCH STRATEGIES AND THE EMPIRICAL STUDIES IN THIS VOLUME

The above observations, though rather general, have implications for how economists and other social scientists should pursue research in the area of fertility.

Firstly, there is no single set of determinants of fertility that is applicable to the world as a whole or, for that matter, to all parts of the Third World. While we may seek universal truths, the insights which will be most helpful to policy-makers and others with an interest in fertility may involve local relationships that are not easily generalisable. The distribution of income or the employment of women may be an important predictor of fertility in one country, and be of minor importance elsewhere. We have not yet accumulated enough understanding of fertility to ascertain when a given variable is likely to be most predictive. This observation would seem to suggest the need for more research in different places, and for greater flexibility in the way research is conceptualised and conducted. Basic models of fertility should be tested in a wide variety of settings, and the results should be used as the basis for exploring alternative approaches to further research and policy.

A related conclusion is that given the variety of relationships that exist in different countries, and given the very great variety of relationships that have been documented, there is a need for a wide range of theoretical and empirical explanations. At this stage, a philosophy supporting the bloom of a hundred research flowers seems highly appropriate. This need for creative exploration of different models should extend to the techniques of research as well.

While there is little doubt that the careful reasoning patterns of economic theory and econometrics are likely to yield great insights in the area of fertility, it is also true that these techniques need adequate ammunition or material to work with if they are going to be effective. This means that there will be a need for qualitative studies of household or governmental behaviour which can provide details of the mechanisms used by households in their fertility decisions or non-decisions, and equivalent information on the processes of action or decision of other social units. It also means that special efforts should be made to assure that more quantitative economic researchers get access to this kind of material as an input to their own modelling and empirical testing. The related problem of having economic researchers more involved in the data-collection process was stressed in Chapter 3.

Most of the discussion of this chapter has been oriented towards general questions of research philosophy and of the connection between research and policy. Implicit in the discussion of the earlier chapters is our feeling that there are significant substantive issues as well. What are the research questions which deserve greater stress in the literature? What methods are likely to provide insight into fertility patterns?

To some extent, our bias should be clear from the discussion. The models which have received the greatest attention from economists during recent years are the micro-economic models of the new home-economics school and the closely related Easterlin school. It is our impression that fertility research on the key variables in these traditions has reached a dead end or, at least, the pace of new insights from this literature has slowed to a trickle. There does not seem to be a great deal more to be learned if we insist on concentrating our energies on the relationships among household fertility, household income, infant mortality and women's labour-force participation.

Some of the approaches which we labelled structuralist in Chapter 2 seem more likely to provide insight, if for no other reason than that they involve variables which have received little empirical attention during the past decade. Several of the case-studies in this volume support the idea that community forces may be important determinants of household fertility behaviour.

We also believe that government policies and programmes, and the way they influence both individual and community behaviour, constitute a second and not unrelated area of research deserving priority. One of the features of our era is the involvement of governments in many aspects of people's lives, including their reproductive lives. Even if these involvements did not explain variations in fertility behaviour in previous generations, they are likely to be influential under present circumstances. Research on government should also be directed more broadly than just towards family-planning programmes. The social security system, food support and health programmes all affect the environment in which fertility decisions are taken. Government programmes which deal with labour-policy, physical infrastructure and education are likely to influence fertility even if that is not part of the goals of any given programme.

Research is required in the form of causal modelling. Many of the research efforts described in the literature review in Chapter 3 involve multivariate analysis of the influence of a variety of variables on fertility. But often, that research has assumed a very primitive view of the causal structures involved, ignoring the influence of feedbacks or other causal structures which are inconsistent with the basic hypotheses that have dominated the economic literature.

Economic researchers can profitably devote more attention to the proximate variables and the way they mediate the effects of social or economic variables. Economists have paid little attention to nuptuality, and, as we have argued earlier, neither ignoring contraception and abortion as in the new home-economics models nor treating them as 'supply'-side questions as in the Easterlin framework seems very adequate to us.

For many questions of central research, new methods of gathering data may be required. For example, the distribution of benefits from family-growth to different members of the family is a very important question. Its connection with classical issues in economics should be clear, yet it seems unlikely that any of the current methods are likely to yield much insight on this question. In-depth interviews aimed at understanding the flow of resources within the family may clarify why there seems to be a conflict between the findings of individual-level research on fertility and national level assessments of the consequences of population growth.

This list of research priorities is relatively short. Other issues are discussed specifically in the chapters which follow. It should be mentioned that there are several different reviews of the research priorities in the area of fertility, and interested readers are directed towards these sources for a broader list of priorities (McGreevy and Birdsall, 1974; T. P. Schultz, 1976a; Population Council, 1981; Bilsborrow, 1981; Miró and Potter, 1980a, 1980b).

The materials in this volume provide some examples of the research scope that we believe to be important in the study of fertility. The research presented uses a variety of data sources, analytical methods and theoretical models to explore the variations in fertility that can be observed among and within the developing countries.

The case-studies were, in general, carried out independently of each other by the respective authors. Hence, there is some repetition among the variables emphasised in the analyses of the determinants of fertility presented among the case-studies. There is also some commonality in the research techniques used to assess the determinants of fertility. These shared elements, however, are overshadowed by the diversity in settings, methods and findings. We feel that the case-studies included in the volume are an important contribution to the understanding of the use of different methodologies for policy research in the area of fertility behaviour.

PART II: METHODOLOGICAL PROBLEMS

The Government are very keen on amassing statistics. They collect them, add them, raise them to the nth power, take the cube root and prepare wonderful diagrams. But you must never forget that every one of those figures comes in the first instance from the village watchman, who just puts down what he damn pleases.

Sir Josiah Stamp
Inland Revenue Department (England) 1896–1919

5 The Definition of Fertility: Measurement Issues

GHAZI M. FAROOQ

INTRODUCTION

Most economic models of fertility behaviour are confronted by the problem of fertility measurement: how to make particular measures correspond to the theoretical notions inherent in the model. As a general rule, the researcher should develop a meaningful concept of human reproduction and an unbiased measurement of its variation *before* launching the actual modelling exercise. This conviction, though generally accepted, is seldom strictly followed. Economists, in particular, have been accused of using biased fertility indicators as dependent variables. It appears that in the development of the early new home-economics models, certain marginally-relevant exogenous variables were treated more meticulously than the measurement of variations in human reproduction behaviour *per se*.

The measurement difficulties arise because there is no unique standard of fertility measurement which is adaptable to all purposes, despite the fact that the fundamental notion of fertility is quite clear. Fertility relates to the actual number of live births which occur in a given population during a specific reference period.[1] In essence, the source of the problem is that due to the inherent peculiarities of the distribution of live births in a population, fertility may be measured in several ways (for details see the standard demography textbooks, e.g. Barclay, 1966; Shryock, Siegel and associates, 1973; and Palmore, 1975). Age and marriage factors greatly affect fertility patterns and have to be controlled for when the analysis of fertility behaviour requires measurement of reproduction *per se*. Empirically, the most serious problem is due to data limitations or errors which prevent the use of a measure which is theoretically correct for a particular fertility model.

In this chapter, the more important fertility measures which are or could be used in the behavioural analysis of fertility are outlined, and their relative merits and disadvantages discussed from the points of view of concept and data collection. The broad purpose is to show how fertility should be treated as a dependent variable in economic analyses of *fertility behaviour*. The discussion of macro and micro measures progresses from simple, relatively crude measures to more complex, refined ones requiring detailed or specialised types of data. Criteria used for the appraisal of a measure include how closely it approximates the true reproduction level and propensity of reproduction. These criteria need to be fulfilled if a researcher is interested in assessing the determinants of fertility behaviour.

A distinction is made between macro level or aggregative measurements, discussed in the second section, and micro-level measurements, discussed in the third section. Where possible, the *demand* and *supply* aspects of fertility measurements are differentiated. It is important to mention that the traditional economic approach to the micro analysis of fertility behaviour is couched in terms of demand analysis, i.e. parents' desires for children. But, whereas the Chicago school's economic demand models of fertility might have been fairly successful in their application to economically advanced, low-fertility populations, they are less so for less advanced, high-fertility populations. One explanation is that observed fertility in the developing countries does not necessarily reflect the actual demand for children. In many instances, *supply* (if taken as equivalent to either observed fertility or to the number of surviving children) and *demand* (if taken as equivalent to either desired number of children or to desired number of surviving children) are not in equilibrium, as is assumed in a typical economic model.[2]

MACRO MEASURES OF FERTILITY

Macro fertility measures refer to fertility rates/ratios for a population as a whole or for subgroups, determined by such characteristics as age, ethnicity, occupation, religion, education or residence (urban–rural or geographical areas). These measures can be divided into two broad groups: period or calendar fertility rates and cohort fertility rates. A distinction is made between measures yielding observed rates and measures of adjusted rates. More attention is devoted here to the indirect measures, because frequently in empirical research for developing countries, direct information on fertility is either not available or deficient. In addition, standard demography textbooks seldom include a discussion of indirect methods.

Period Fertility Rates

Period fertility measures refer to the fertility level of a given population over a specified period of time - one month, one year, or five years, for example. These measures, which are usually indicative of the period/current fertility level of the population, include: child–woman ratio, crude birth rate, general fertility rate, age-specific birth rates, birth order-specific fertility rates, total fertility rate and gross reproduction rate, as well as approximations and adjustments of these different measures.

Child–woman ratio

The child–woman ratio is defined as the ratio of the number of children under 5 (or 10) years of age per 1000 women of childbearing age (between ages 15 and 44 or 49), and serves as measure of the overall incidence of childbearing. It is the simplest measure of human reproduction and requires minimal data. Information on the age and sex distribution of the population is sufficient. Its usefulness lies in the fact that while many developing countries do not collect birth statistics through a vital statistics registration system, a national population register system or national demographic sample surveys, they have undertaken national population censuses at one time or another which provide some data on age–sex distribution. As a result, the child–woman ratio is often used for international comparative studies or for comparison among various groups in a given population for which the direct birth statistics are not available. However, this method is inefficient because age reporting, especially for ages 0–4, is frequently inaccurate, and, more importantly, the measure does not refer to actual number of births but the survivors of births during the 5-year period preceding the census. Hence, in a cross-sectional and time-series study using some administrative unit (e.g. district or province) as the unit of observation, child–woman ratio cannot be used if wide regional differentials in infant, child and adult mortality exist, as was found to be the case in Turkey (Farooq and Tuncer, 1974), or if the incidence of net interregional migration is high. The child–woman ratio as an index of fertility also shares the same limitation as that of the crude birth rate in that, as discussed below, both are greatly affected by the age–sex structure of the population. The use of this measure should be avoided whenever possible.

Average crude birth rate by reverse projection technique

This method is suggested in place of the child–woman ratio when suitable life-table values on survival rates are available at subnational level accounting for the regional differentials in infant–child mortality rates. By using the idea behind the estimation of annual crude birth rate (CBR), the reverse projection technique makes it possible to construct an *average* CBR, for a given region, over a specified time-period. The reported population below age 5 (or 10) is converted into the total number of live births which have occurred in the past 5 (or 10) years in the region by applying a relevant life-table mortality factor. The formula for computing average CBR for the period t to $t + 5$ is

$$\text{CBR}_{t,t+5} = \left(\frac{P_{t+5}^{(0-4)}}{_5L_0} \right) \Bigg/ \frac{1}{2} (P_t + P_{t+5})$$

where t refers to census year t, and $t + 5$ to census year $t + 5$, $P_{t+5}^{(0-4)}$ refers to population in age group 0-4 in census year $t + 5$, $_5L_0$ refers to the person-years lived between ages 0 and 5 in a life-table with radix 1.0, and P_t, P_{t+5} refer to the total population enumerated in census year t and census year $t + 5$, respectively.[3]

The expression in the first bracket gives the average number of annual live births during the 5-year period. The appropriate denominator is the mid-period total population. This method is a more relevant measure of intracountry fertility differences if information is available on area differentials in mortality. However, this measure is appropriate only if net internal migration is non-significant, or if migration statistics are available to make the required adjustments in regional birth rates for any inter-regional population movement that took place during the reference period. In analytical terms, this method shares the same limitations as CBR discussed below.

Crude birth rate (CBR)

When direct information is available on number of live births occurring during a specified period of time, CBR is the most convenient and direct summary measure of fertility. It is defined as the proportion of live births to person-years lived during the reference period. It is usually computed as the number of live births in a year per 1000 mid-year population, and shows the relative frequency of births. Although it is easily understandable as well as the most commonly available and used indicator of fertility, CBR suffers from a number of serious limitations. It averages the differentials among various groups or subgroups in the population. It is seriously affected by, *inter alia*, the sex–age structure of the population, because of the inclusion of groups not exposed to the risk of childbearing, the age structure of the women of childbearing ages, and the level and age pattern of nuptiality.[4] As a result, changes in CBR may reflect changes in factors other than the fertility itself. Hence, the value of CBR as a measure of fertility in the analytical treatment of fertility behaviour is limited, even though it does have a useful descriptive value, in that in combination with crude death rate, and given its additive nature, it provides an estimate of the nature increase rate. A good index of fertility should take into account age structure, marital composition, duration of marriage, and parity distribution.

If additional information is available on live births by age of woman and on sex-age distribution of a population, a number of conventional refined measures which correct for the limitations inherent in CBR can be used. These include, by degree of progressive complexity, *general fertility rate* (GFR), *age-specific birth rates* (ASBRs), *total fertility rate* (TFR), and *gross reproduction rate* (GRR). Formulae and data requirements for these measures are outlined below (for examples, see Shryock, Siegel and associates 1973; Palmore, 1975).

Formula	*Data requirements*
$$GFR = \frac{B}{Pf_{15-44}{}^*} \times 1000$$	Number of live births during the 12-months period and number of women aged 15 to 44 years
$$ASBR_i = \frac{B_i}{Pf_i} \times 1000$$	Live births by age of mother
$$TFR = 5 \times \sum_{i=15-19}^{i=45-49} \left(\frac{B_i}{Pf_i}\right)$$	Same as for $ASBR_i$
$$GRR = 5 \times \sum_{i=15-19}^{i=45-49} \left(\frac{Bf_i}{Pf_i}\right)$$	Female live births by age of mother

or (as an approximation)

$$= TFR \times \frac{\text{female live births}}{\text{total live births}}$$ Live births by age of mother and the sex-ratio at birth

---

*If there is relatively very little fertility reported among women in the ages 45 to 49 years, it is appropriate to exclude this group from the calculation, otherwise the age range should be extended to 15-49 years.

where B refers to total number of live births registered during the year, B_i to the live births occurring to women in the age group i (i is an interval of 5 years), and Bf_i to *female* live births occurring to women in the age group i. Pf_{15-44} refers to the female population 15 to 44 years of age, and Pf_i to the female population in age group i.

It can quickly be discerned that these measures represent the required analytical improvements over the child–woman ratio and CBR. Instead of relating live births to the total population, GFR relates live births to the actual population at risk – women in the childbearing years. The measure is, however, still affected by the age distribution of women within the childbearing ages. If additional data are available on live births by age of mothers, a better measure than GFR is ASBR, which also captures the degree of variation in birth occurrences across reproductive ages. ASBR schedules provide valid comparisons of fertility levels among different population groups because they are not affected by any difference among these groups in sex–age structures. Based on the summation of ASBRs and ASBRs which include only female births, TFR and GRR respectively represent the two summary cross-sectional period fertility rates which are independent of the effects of age–sex composition and mortality. TFR indicates the average number of live births that would be born, on average, to a cohort of women by the end of their reproductive period if the current ASBRs remain constant and there is no attrition in the cohort size due to death during the reproductive age-span. TFR can be viewed as an approximation of 'complete family-size'. GRR is the same as TFR except that instead of the total number of live births, it measures the total number of daughters a cohort of women will have. GRR is sometimes preferred as it gives the rate at which a population is reproducing itself, i.e. the extent to which daughters are born to replace the present 'generation' of mothers.

It is analytically desirable to study birth rates specific to *live birth order* and to see how women move from one parity to the other. For various obvious reasons, the probability of an additional birth occurrence is affected by the number of live births a woman has already had. Calculation of *birth order-specific fertility rates* is the same as for GFR except that one substitutes the number of live births of order i ($i = 1, 2, 3, \ldots, n$) for the total number of live births in the numerator, and the denominator remains as women 15 to 44 years of age. Birth order-specific fertility rates can also be calculated specific to age groups (for examples see Palmore, 1975; Shryock, Siegel and associates, 1973). Distribution of birth order-specific rates can be used to explain the dynamics of human reproduction in a society. Another related measure of fertility is the *parity progression ratio* (PPR), which can be defined for either a birth cohort or a marriage cohort. In each case, it is calculated as the proportion of females having at least $j+1$ live births out of those having at least j live births.[5] However, in the developing countries, information on live births by birth order (and age of mother) is difficult to obtain, and generally is not collected.

For international, interregional and intertemporal comparative analyses, if the only information available to the researcher is on crude birth rates, it is recommended that they be converted into GFR, TFR or GRR. It is easy to convert CBR into GFR if information from some alternate data source is available, or if a suitable indirect approximation can be made of the proportion of women 15–44 years in total population. Using the notations developed above, the appropriate formulae can be derived as follows:

$$\text{CBR} = \frac{B}{Pf_{15-44}} \times \frac{Pf_{15-44}}{P}, \tag{1}$$

where P refers to the total population,

$$\text{CBR} = \text{GFR} \times \frac{Pf_{15-44}}{P} \tag{2}$$

and, therefore,

$$\text{GFR*} = \text{CBR} \times \frac{P}{Pf_{15-44}} \tag{3}$$

(GFR* is the average rate per woman).

The researcher should, however, make an effort to transpose CBR into a theoretically less biased and more relevant measure, such as GRR. Anker's study (1978) contains an excellent example of calculating an approximate GRR by removing the age-distribution component from CBR.[6] In a *stable population*, there exists an almost perfect correlation between GRR and the total births population 15–44 ratio, i.e. $B/P_{15-44} \approx \frac{1}{29}$ GRR. Using this relationship, the following equation (using natural logarithms) is obtained:[7]

$$\ln \text{CBR} = 3.367 + \ln \text{GRR} + \ln \frac{P_{15-44}}{P}.$$

The relationship between CBR, GRR and P_{15-44}/P can be empirically estimated by the ordinary least squares method. In the Anker study, the GRR equation is estimated with 1960 data from 50 countries,[8] and is employed for obtaining GRR estimates for the 1968–70 period using country data on CBR and P_{15-44}/P.

One could also make use of *indirect* methods of fertility estimation when the required data are either not available or are defective. Some such methods have been developed by Brass (1975) and Coale (1977).[9] However, most of these methods, which are based on the assumption of stationarity of fertility and mortality schedules in a closed population - and, therefore, the stability of the population growth rate and age structure - are not applicable in situations where fertility and mortality levels and patterns are undergoing changes.

Adjusted Period Fertility Rates

In populations where fertility is almost completely confined to marital unions, as is the case in many developing countries, age-specific distributions of the proportion of women married and marital fertility rates determine the overall fertility level and its changes. Therefore, in addition to adjusting for sex-age composition, it is also useful to adjust fertility rates for the proportion of women married (or cohabiting) in each age-group. As an example, TFR, which is already a sex-age-adjusted measure, can be adjusted for marital status by using age-specific marital fertility rates (ASMFRs). However, it would be erroneous to base nuptial or marital status-adjusted TFR on the summation of ASMFRs, as the sum would be heavily weighted by the high birth rates in the earlier age groups where the number of married women is comparatively low.

An easy method for calculating marital TFR is to weight ASMFRs by proportions of women currently married in corresponding age-groups in the standard population (Shryock, Siegel and associates, 1973, p. 486). The formula is

$$\text{Marital TFR} = 5 \times \sum_{i=15-19}^{i=45-49} (\text{ASMFR}_i \times m_i),$$

where m_i refers to proportion of women currently married in age group i in the standard population.

Marital TFR might be considered as a better fertility index than TFR, since it restricts human reproduction measurement to the 'true' population at risk of childbearing. Two populations with the same ASFR schedules (and therefore same TFR) can have quite different fertility levels if they differ significantly in the average age at marriage as well as in the incidence of widowhood, divorce and separation. However, if one is studying human reproduction within a particular population where marriage patterns do not vary significantly, TFR may serve as an appropriate measure.

In cases where age data is not available but information on 'duration of marriage' exists, the fertility measure can be adjusted for duration of marriage and marital status. In this case, the adjustment by duration of marriage would be done in lieu of adjustment by age. Mathematically, the marital fertility level of a population is a joint function of the distribution of married women by number of years married and the duration-specific marital fertility rates. Hence, marital TFR can also be based on duration-specific marital birth rates.

In light of the above discussion, the more efficient fertility measures would be, in theory, those which allow for decomposition of overall fertility in marital fertility and nuptiality components. The Coale indices (1967, 1969) present an example of the more general process of using standardisation as a means of ensuring the comparability of different populations which differ simultaneously in two or more dimensions. The Coale standardisation controls for the general age-distribution by examining only the women in the childbearing years. In addition, it controls for the marital distribution by decomposing fertility into two separate indices, and assures that the basic index will lie between 0 and approximately 1 by dividing by the number of births that would be expected in a very high fertility population. In terms of data required, the Coale standardisation has the advantage of using data only on total births; it does not require data on births by age of mother. Where more detailed data is available, some of the other measures of fertility described earlier might be used and, if desired, they can be combined with age and marital distribution to create a variety of standardised indices (see Shryock, Siegel and associates, 1973). Construction of Coale's indices is explained below.

Using the marital fertility schedule of Hutterite women during 1921-30[10] – one of the highest recorded fertility schedules – as the standard, overall fertility of a given population is measured by the index I_f, defined as

$$I_f = \frac{B}{\Sigma Pf_i F_i},$$

where F_i refers to marital fertility rate for Hutterite women in age group i, B refers to total annual number of live births, and Pf_i to all women in age group i in the given population.

This index gives the ratio of total number of live births reported for the given population to the number of live births that *all* women, married or not, would have had if they had been subjected to the standard fertility schedule. I_f can be conveniently decomposed into an index of marital fertility, I_g, and an index of proportion married, I_m, as described below.

The index of marital fertility, I_g, otherwise analogous to I_f in construction, pertains to married women only. It represents the ratio of live births that married women actually had to the number of live births that they would have had under the Hutterite fertility schedule. Assuming that illegitimate live births are negligible, the formula, with all symbols already defined, is [11]

$$I_g = \frac{B}{\Sigma Pfm_i F_i} .$$

I_g will have a value of unity if the married women in the given population share the same fertility patterns as that of the Hutterite women. The difference between unity and the realised value of the index roughly gives an indication of the extent to which fertility limitation is practised by the population. Of course, this difference $(1 - I_g)$ might also partly be due to such Davis–Blake (Davis and Blake, 1956) intermediate variables as involuntary sterility and abortions, abstinence and foetal mortality from involuntary causes (e.g. still-births).

The index of proportion married, I_m, compares the number of live births *married* women would have if subjected to the Hutterite schedule to the number of live births *all* women would have under the same condition. The formula, with all notations already defined, is

$$I_m = \frac{\Sigma Pfm_i F_i}{\Sigma Pf_i F_i} .$$

Hence, by taking a form directly related to fertility, I_m represents a weighted index of the proportion of women currently married. It is a convenient summary of the nuptiality pattern within the childbearing period and its effect on overall fertility. I_m has a value of unity if all women aged 15–49 years are married.

Assuming illegitimate fertility to be negligible, it should be obvious from the formulae of the above three indices that:

$$I_f = I_g \times I_m .$$

The above indices are especially useful measures for international cross-sectional (if there is no difference in births out of wedlock) and intertemporal comparative fertility analyses when a wide diversity of nuptiality patterns and marital fertility exists among the concerned populations. Data requirements for the construction of these indices include the reporting of the total annual number of live births, the age distribution of all women and the number of currently married women.

Cohort Fertility

As mentioned in the subsection on period fertility rates, the cross-sectional period fertility rates TFR and GRR can be viewed as pertaining to a synthetic cohort. The researcher, however, might be interested in the analyses of fertility histories of actual cohorts.[12] This involves calculating fertility rates specific to a real birth or marriage cohort (i.e. the group of women born or married in the same calendar year), which permits separating out the effect of timing of births. Generally, cohort rates are calculated with reference to birth cohorts. Cohort fertility analyses are pertinent for various reasons, the most important of which are discussed below.

Firstly, childbearing during a particular year or age interval will depend partly upon how many children the individual women have produced up until that year, as well as the number of live births during the preceding year or age interval. Secondly, the influence of fertility-related social customs and norms may be more uniform for a given cohort than across different cohorts. With socio-economic advancement, tastes and preferences for children can be expected to vary more between successive generations than within a generation. Thirdly, the age patterns of bearing children and changes therein have important implications for current population growth rates. The period fertility rate of a population, at any given time, would usually be higher where cohorts display relatively early childbearing than where they are characterised by relatively late childbearing, even though average completed family-size is the same. Fourthly, with suitable cohort measures, the phenomenon of child-spacing or birth-intervals, which is important in its own right, can be studied. In theory, fertility decision-making can be viewed as encompassing a joint decision concerning both the number of children and the timing of births. Along with age at marriage, birth-spacing determines the age pattern of childbearing which, as discussed above, affects the level of current fertility.

The above reasons, however, do not mean that cohort fertility measures are better than period fertility ones – both are useful (Palmore, 1975). The use of either type of measure depends upon the purpose and scope of the intended study as well as on the availability of data. This point is particularly important, because most developing countries lack the data required for construction of cohort fertility rates. The relevant rates can be calculated only when the information is available *either* on yearly live births, by age of mothers, *or* on the cumulative number of children ever born, by age of mothers. The derivation of the measures is explained below.

With data on yearly number of live births, age-specific birth rates for each calendar year can be calculated. The *cumulative fertility rate* for a given cohort can then be estimated by summing the observed birth rates for women of this cohort in each successive year until the reporting year. The *completed fertility rate* for the cohort at the end of its fecund period is simply the summation of its annual birth rates from year t to $t - 35$, where t is the calendar year when women in the cohort are 49 years old, and $t - 35$ refers to the calendar year when they were 15 years old. Hence, for the birth cohort of 1931–49 years of age in 1980 – the completed fertility rate is the sum total of following annual rates:

$$\text{ASBR}_{15}^{1946} + \text{ASBR}_{16}^{1947} + \ldots + \text{ASBR}_{49}^{1980}.$$

Population census or survey questions on the number of children ever born yield direct information on the cumulative fertility of different birth cohorts. For example, in reporting year t,

$$\text{CEB}_{35-39}^{t} = \frac{\text{number of children ever born to married women 35–39 years}}{\text{number of married women 35–39 years}}$$

is the cumulative fertility rate of married women aged 35–39. Note that the reproduction history of this cohort could be constructed if similar information were available at 5-year intervals, for the preceding 20 years and the subsequent 10-year periods. CEB_{45-49} or CEB_{40-44} represents the *completed family size*, because very few births are observed past this age interval, and is equivalent to the *completed fertility rate* discussed above.[13] Conceptually, average CEB for the women at the end of their reproductive period is comparable to the TFR of the cohort.

It is apparent that the construction of complete reproductive histories by either of the *above two methods* requires collection of data spanning a 30–35 year period. In theory at least, it should be possible to generate the required information with a carefully designed one-shot inquiry. The inquiry would be composed of retrospective questions on the timing of each live birth for women belonging to different birth cohorts beyond the reproduction years. However, the older the birth cohort, the greater is the probability of reporting error on the timing of births and of underestimating births due to the memory or recall lapse with respect to deceased children.

Conclusion

In treatment of fertility as the dependent variable, it is important to take into account its inherent property as representing a dynamic process. Especially in macro fertility analyses, the importance of intermediate variables should be recognised explicitly. Economists frequently move directly from the set of social and economic explanatory variables to fertility in their framework for empirical estimations of fertility behaviour, ignoring the fact that intermediate variables, such as the nuptiality level and its age patterns, have a large impact upon the quantum of fertility. It is crucial to look at fertility in terms of age and marital status; the study of nuptiality patterns should be part of the analysis. The most appropriate fertility indicators are, as explained in the first two subsections, the ones based upon fertility rates specific to age and marriage.

MICRO MEASURES OF FERTILITY

The aggregate characteristics of a society, such as its social, economic and cultural systems including traditional sex-roles, religion, customs and traditions, broadly determine group fertility norms. The more a society is tradition-bound, the closer an individual's or couple's reproductive outcomes will be to the societal fertility norms. In such cases, macro fertility analyses should suffice and, theoretically, if carried out within a suitable framework, should reflect the dynamics of the fertility behaviour of a typical micro-unit. However, most developing countries are undergoing significant social and economic structural changes, and are experiencing a weakening of traditional societal values, customs and norms. It is safe to hypothesise that in the societies within which social changes and economic advancement are particularly rapid, households will be increasingly engaged in independent and conscious decision-making which deviates from traditional behaviour. If this hypothesis is correct, micro analyses of fertility behaviour become even more important for obtaining insights into human reproduction phenomena, as well as for delineating the scope of population and related socio-economic policies, their formulation and their implementation. Empirical sociological-economic analyses of fertility behaviour, such as the ones in the present volume, have shown that changes in fertility are strongly affected by personal socio-economic and biological characteristics, aspirations and preferences of couples.

In micro fertility analyses, it is useful to cover both the actual reproduction experience of women or couples *and* their preferences concerning the number of children, i.e. desired family-size (DFS). The study of DFS is important for, *inter alia*, the following reasons: (i) for the couples still in the childbearing age span, DFS is a more appropriate indicator of expected completed family-size; (ii) if actual fertility falls short of DFS due to certain biological constraints (i.e. prevalence of fecundity impairments), the level of DFS is an estimate of the potential future fertility level when physiological fecundity is improved by availability of better health services, better levels of nutrition, etc.; (iii) if actual fertility level is higher than DFS, the extent to which actual number of children born exceeds desired number of children defines the scope for fertility limitations practices, including contraception use; and (iv) perhaps most importantly, the identification of the determinants of DFS is relevant for designing appropriate policy measures through which the policy-makers may wish to alter individuals' attitudes and preferences towards the number of children wanted in order to cause structural changes in the aggregate fertility levels. The more relevant indicators of actual fertility and family-size preferences are discussed below.

Actual Fertility

Micro fertility behaviour can be studied in terms of the *cumulative* level of fertility performance for the couple until the time of enquiry, and/or in terms of the *current* fertility performance in a preceding number of years. The two approaches, along with their indicators and related applications in empirical analyses, are discussed in this section.

Cumulative fertility

The most commonly used micro fertility indicator is children ever born (CEB) or parity – the cumulative number of live births a woman has had. Unless otherwise specified, CEB refers only to married women. In a typical life-cycle model of fertility, CEB serves as a natural measure of the 'stock' of children. All the micro case-studies in the present volume make use of this measure for reproduction performance. It is easy to see that information collected on CEB by age of mother provides a measure of the cumulative fertility of women up to specific points in their childbearing age-span.

Comparatively, CEB is the easiest fertility indicator on which to collect data. Conceptually, it may provide an unbiased measure and is meaningful for determining the effects of different factors on fertility. Time-reference errors are not expected to occur, since timing questions are not involved.[14] However, underreporting can result from age misreporting and omission of children who died, especially those who died soon after birth. Misreporting and omission can occur because of memory lapses or for cultural reasons, and because some children have not been living with parents for a long period of time. This problem of underreporting is more serious for older women, particularly where illiteracy is high, where women have a large number of pregnancies and live births, and where infant mortality is high. Fortunately, these problems are now well recognised. Household surveys have become more sophisticated in the construction of efficient questions and in the handling of field work.

In explicit recognition of age-fecundity-duration of marriage–fertility interactions, Boulier and Rosenzweig (1978) argue that these must be accounted for, otherwise estimates of the effects of socio-economic variables on fertility are biased and ambiguous. They suggest the use of *duration ratio* (DRAT), which adjusts CEB for age at marriage and duration of marriage. The ratio is constructed by dividing the actual number of children born by the number of children a woman would have had, had she followed a natural fertility schedule (i.e. marital fertility with no fertility limitation practices) from the time of her marriage to the enquiry date.[15] Assuming that a woman is married once and is still married at the time of survey, DRAT is calculated as follows (Boulier and Rosenzweig, 1978, p. 488):

$$DRAT(a) = \frac{CEB\,(a)}{\int_{m}^{a} n(x)\,dx}$$

where a refers to the age of the woman at survey and m to her age at marriage, and $n(x)$ refers to natural fertility at age x.[16]

The advantage of DRAT over simple CEB as a fertility index is that it compares actual cumulative fertility with the expected fertility of a woman, controlling for age and duration of marriage following a standard regime of natural fertility. As a result, it controls for the biological effects of age and duration of marriage. However, the resultant DRAT values can be biased if the selection of $n(x)$ is inappropriate for the population under consideration and if there are substantial variations in fecundity among women. The measure also suffers the limitation that women who have been married for less than five years are excluded from the sample because newly-married women are not representative of the population in terms of the risk of becoming pregnant (Boulier and Rosenzweig, 1978, p. 488). Hence, care must be taken in the use of this measure.

In general, the major analytical problem with parity-based measures is that they do not take into account recent changes in fertility and changing determinants of fertility. With substantial and swift social and economic changes, such as have been experienced by some developing countries in recent years, net negative effects on fertility may be assumed. Parity, however, is irreversible. Many studies, such as those by T. P. Schultz (1974a), DeTray (1973), DaVanzo (1971) and Harman (1970), use a completed fertility indicator, CEB of women aged 35–39 or 35–49, as the dependent variable, and a set of social and economic factors which are dynamic in nature, being in a constant state of change, as independent variables. Because they control variables in this manner, such studies may not provide a fully-reliable analysis of the effects of socio-economic changes on fertility. At the risk of belabouring the obvious, since observations collected on most exogenous variables refer to the time of enquiry or thereabouts, there is a timing mismatch between the birth occurrence and the indicators of current socio-economic status. This problem can be expected to be most serious for variables such as labour-force participation, employment and occupational patterns, wage rates, family income, land ownership, child schooling, infant-child mortality, migration status or health.

Hence, in estimating an economic behavioural model of fertility, CEB of women aged 35–39 or 35–49 may not be appropriate as a dependent variable because the time-lag problem is most serious for this age-group. The recall error is likely to be more pronounced among women of this cohort than it is among younger age-cohorts. Also, if the society had only recently experienced a socio-economic transformation, the estimated coefficients of social and economic variables would be substantially underestimated. In fact, from the policy point of view, it is more important to assess correctly the effects of changing social and economic conditions on the fertility goals of the cohorts most exposed to these changes. Therefore, as shown in the Nigerian case-study (Chapter 12), the fertility decision model appears to apply best to the middle reproductive age-span of 25–34 years. For the early ages (15–24 years), reproduction experience is largely affected by age at marriage, biological maxima and the factors which influence child-spacing. Ideally, fertility equations should be estimated for at least three broad age groups, such as 15–24, 25–34 and 35+ years, and the variations among the different age equations should be carefully analysed.

Current fertility

Most demographic enquiries, as a matter of common practice, collect information on live births by age of mother during the 12-month period preceding the time of enquiry. This information is widely used for calculating annual level of fertility and changes therein, as well as age-specific fertility rates and the various other aggregative measures.

In light of the various limitations of CEB discussed above, live births during the past year could also be utilised as a measure of current fertility in micro fertility analyses.[17] In addition, this and such other period rates which pertain to reproduction experience of a woman during a given period of time are sensitive to any rapid adjustment in fertility behaviour. Hence, whereas CEB provides a measure of stock of children, the period rates help the researcher to explain differences in the rate of childbearing over the life-cycle. It should be obvious that use of both cumulative and suitable current fertility measures would be desirable for a more complete analysis of the problem.

The use of a 12-month reference period for measurement of current fertility, however, does not seem to be appropriate for an economic analysis of fertility. The waiting time to conception, and the length of the natural gestation period, make current economic factors less relevant to an explanation of current fertility, even in the absence of a lag in the response of couples to economic influences. In addition, experience shows that collection of these statistics in developing countries is seriously hindered by reporting problems. Some live births which occur before the reference period are included in the count, and others which occur within the period are omitted. Also, short-lived births are often not reported. The reference period is too short to yield a sufficiently large number of degrees of freedom, particularly if the sample-size is not very large.

For various reasons, *live births during the past 5-year period* may be a superior dependent variable. The period is long enough to avoid the limitations of the measure based on 12 months and short enough not to suffer significantly from recall error. According to Brass (1975, p. 16), data-collection for the purpose of this measure would be nearly as reliable as that for completed fertility. This measure would largely be devoid of the problem of a time lag between endogenous factors and the dependent variable, because both permanent and current socio-economic status indicators would be relevant. The 5-year reference period is suggested in preference to one of two or three years as, with the addition of a supplementary statistic on *order of birth*, it will be possible to undertake detailed analyses of the factors determining different birth orders, and the factors determining child-spacing. The benefits of such analyses are obvious, particularly in terms of their potential contribution to a more complete understanding of human reproduction phenomenon, and to formulation and implementation of effective population and related socio-economic policies and measures.

Family-size Preferences

In some developing countries, observed fertility may not reflect the actual demand for children. Attitudinal variables approximating family-size preferences may be theoretically superior to actual fertility measures in capturing the notion of the demand for children. Attitudinal questions regarding family-size preferences – ideal or desired number of children – have been included in KAP (knowledge, attitude and practice) and other fertility sample surveys, including WFS (World Fertility Surveys). However, as discussed below, these attitudinal variables may be more susceptible to errors of measurement than are the ones pertaining to actual fertility experience.

KAP-type surveys generally employ the concept of 'ideal family-size' for eliciting husband's, wife's or couple's preferences regarding family-size (for a survey of the use of this concept see Ware, 1974). Respondents are typically asked: 'What is the ideal number of children for a family like yours to have?' 'What do you think is the ideal (generally desirable) number of children for a woman in this area to have?' Such questions may be meaningless, since the responses to such questions, as pointed out in the Nigerian case-study (Chapter 12, p. 315), 'could very well apply to some hypothetical ideal family, which may not necessarily share the respondent family's social, economic, cultural and demographic milieu' (see also the references included on this in Chapter 12; and Knodel and Prachuabmoh, 1973).

Empirically, 'desired family-size' (DFS), which is defined as the number of existing children plus the number of additional children desired (ACD) by parents, is found to be a better measure of family-size preferences than is ideal family-size.[18] In many societies, however, the application of DFS is beset by the problem of non-numerical response which occurs when a significant proportion of respondents' answers to the question on additional number of children wanted are couched as 'up to God'.[19] Also, the DFS is not devoid of measurement error. It fails to reflect differential demographic pressure among those wanting no additional children, by assigning zero value to all cases of excess fertility, irrespective of its magnitude. Using longitudinal data from Thailand – 1969 and 1972 – Rodgers (1976) investigated the usefulness in behavioural fertility analysis of two attitudinal variables, ideal family-size and ACD. He found that the theoretical superiority of these two variables as direct measures of demand for children may be outweighed by errors in reporting and/or even imprecision in the concepts used. Although ACD is characterised by a smaller stochastic variation, and, as a result, was measured more accurately than ideal family-size, it had a large measurement error. The error variance was of the same order of magnitude as the true variance (Rodgers, 1976, p. 515). Demographic factors did not explain a reasonable proportion of the change in ACD over the 3-year period under study.[20] While conceptualisation of ACD was relatively clear at lower parities, it became vaguer at higher parities. In general, with each birth there was an increase in the family-size target.

As a theoretical construct, desired family-size (DFS) fails to reflect variations in the underlying preferences for children because it essentially restricts the response of a woman/couple to only *one* value. As expressed in the Nigerian study in Chapter 12, 'although a couple, at any given time, may have some idea of the number of children it would like to have, this number itself can change with the actual fertility experience, i.e. the number of pregnancies, birth parity order, relationships of parents with existing siblings and so on'. Those reporting similar values for DFS may have orderings over alternative family-sizes that are quite different. Matters become more complex when dealing with societies with a strong preference for children of one sex. For example, in societies such as those of Bangladesh, India, Pakistan and Muslim Middle Eastern countries, sons are more valued than daughters, for status and security reasons. Such sex biases have different implications for the subsequent fertility behaviour of families reporting the same value for ACD or DFS. The development of family-size preference scales based on 'unfolding theory' and conjoint measurement is an attempt to tackle these issues (C. H. Coombs, 1964; L. C. Coombs, 1975, 1979a; C. H. Coombs, L. C. Coombs and McClelland, 1975).

By interviewing with carefully phrased questions, and by properly structuring the answers, it is possible to obtain the respondent's rank order of family-size preferences. The basic idea is quite simple: given a set of alternatives, the specification of how the respondent ranks them allows the researcher to determine the underlying distribution of family-size preferences. As an example, if the permissible choice of number of children ranges from 0 to 3, then there are 24 possible orderings. Construction of the preference scale is provided in Figure 5.1. Family-size preferences are arranged on the real line, with four levels in this case. This range of levels can be divided by six 'mid-points' between each of the six pairs of levels, viz. 01, 02, 03, 12, 13 and 23. These mid-points, drawn for the purpose of scaling, are arbitrary, but allow comparisons among individuals with respect to the number of children they prefer. In this sense, the scales may be considered analogous to the concept of indifference curves in neo-classical micro-economics. Seven intervals are thus identified and labelled I-1 to I-7 in Figure 5.1, yielding what is referred to as 'I-scale' numbers.

The location of a respondent on the I-Scale is determined by her or his stated preference orders. For example, a woman with preference ordering 0123, according to the schema in Figure 5.1, will be placed in interval I-1, since she prefers zero children to all other choices, and has not crossed the mid-point 01.

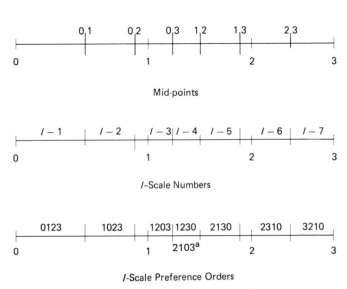

FIGURE 5.1   *Relation of preference orders to I-scale numbers*

SOURCE   Reproduced from L. C. Coombs, 1975, p. 15.

[a] There are two preference orders which correspond to the fourth interval on the scale. They reflect a difference in metric relations which is useful for some purposes.

A woman with preference order 1203 will be placed in the I-3 interval since she has psychologically crossed mid-point 01 (she prefers one child to zero) and mid-point 02 (she prefers two children to zero children), but has not crossed mid-point 03 (she prefers zero children to three children).

Thus the stated preference ordering corresponds uniquely to a single interval of the *I*-scale. A necessary and sufficient condition for placement of an individual on the *I*-scale is that the individual's preference ordering be single-peaked. (A preference function involving choices A, B and C is said to be single-peaked if $A > B > C$ implies neither $A > C > B$ nor $C > A > B$.)

The *I*-scale for sex preferences is derived in the same manner. Combined models of family-size preferences and sex composition are also possible (L. C. Coombs, 1975). Hence, if in view of the social and cultural characteristics of a society a feasible range of choices regarding number of children is included, the *I*-scale will represent a more appropriate attitudinal variable than the variables discussed earlier in this section. However, while applying this approach, its limitations should be kept in view. These are: (i) though it captures underlying preferences it, like the ideal family-size question, is based upon a series of hypothetical situations; (ii) it may represent an incomplete ordering of fertility attitudes. The existence of inadmissible orderings (i.e. violations of single-peakedness) implies that these observations must be ignored or handled in an *ad hoc* manner; (iii) there can also be some intensity differences among populations having the same ranking; and (iv) since it is essentially an ordinal measure, its statistical treatment as a dependent variable is difficult.

Conclusion

Micro fertility analyses, in order to be useful for understanding human reproduction as well as for formulating public policy, should attempt to cover both the actual fertility experience of women or couples and their preferences regarding family-size. The latter could be conceived as influencing actual fertility experience and vice versa. Namboodiri (1972), for example, argues that the determinants of actual fertility behaviour and family-size preferences are interrelated, and that 'a study of one, therefore, cannot be completely divorced from that of the other'.

Actually, fertility, when the data permits, should be considered from the point of view of both cumulative fertility for given cohorts and periodic or current fertility. CEB serves as a convenient indicator of 'stock' of children (in terms of surviving children) over the life-cycle, but its various limitations outlined in the subsection on cumulative fertility should be accounted for by the researcher in design of the study and interpretation of results. Births during the past 5-year period could serve as an efficient indicator of current fertility. Along with the information on order of birth, this variable would allow analyses of the factor determining birth orders and child-spacing.

For the study of family-size preferences, the conventional concept of ideal family-size is found to be deficient. A better attitudinal variable is desired family-size. However, since DFS may fail to fully reflect variations in the underlying preferences for children, it is suggested that, where feasible, the preference scales developed by L. C. Coombs and associates (*I*-scale) also be used. These scales measure demand for children as a distribution with different levels of preferences associated with each attainable family-size.

NOTES

1. Fertility is not to be equated with *fecundity*, which refers to the biological or physiological capacity of the population to bear children. There is no direct measurement for the level of fecundity.
2. The paradigm-setting study by Easterlin (1978) takes into account situations of demand–supply disequilibrium.
3. The analogous formula for computing average CBR for the period t to $t + 10$ is

$$\text{CBR}_{t,t+10} = \left(\frac{P_{t+10}^{(0-9)}}{10L_0} \right) \Big/ \frac{1}{2} (P_t + P_{t+10}).$$

    For details on the application of this method, see Farooq and Tuncer (1974) and Shorter (1968).
4. A change or difference in any one of these factors or a combination thereof can cause significant changes in CBRs. For detailed mathematical relationships, see United Nations Secretariat, 1979, pp. 54–5.
5. If the births of order $n+$ are grouped together, PPR of order $n - 1$ and above (assuming them to be of equal magnitude), say for a marriage cohort, can be computed as the ratio of average number of live births of order $n+$ to the average number of live births of order $n - 1$ and above per marriage (see Pressat, 1967; Ryder, 1969).
6. Some researchers argue that given the high correlation between CBR and GFR, GRR or other such fertility measures, CBR should serve as an adequate fertility proxy (for example, see Gregory and Campbell, 1976, p. 838). Anker's study (1978, p. 59) shows both theoretically and practically that it might be wrong to do so, as the disturbance term in a CBR equation will contain an age-distribution component besides the usual error component.

7. This equation is derived in the following manner:

$$CBR = \frac{B}{P_{15-44}} \times \frac{P_{15-44}}{P}$$

and, since $\dfrac{B}{P_{15-44}} \approx \dfrac{1}{29} GRR$,

$$CBR = \frac{1}{29} GRR \times \frac{P_{15-44}}{P}.$$

8. The estimated equation (Anker, 1978, p. 60) is:

$$\ln GRR = 3.133 + 0.976 \ln CBR - 1.129 \ln \frac{P_{15-44}}{P}, \qquad R^2 = 0.97.$$

9. For example, based on the assumption that fertility control always causes a proportionate reduction of fertility below the 'natural' fertility schedule in a fixed pattern by age, Coale (1977) developed a set of model marital fertility schedules as follows.

$$\gamma(a) = M\, n(a)\, e^{m\, v(a)},$$

where $\gamma(a)$ refers to marital fertility at age a, $n(a)$ refers to natural fertility schedule, which is determined empirically from a set of observed fertility schedules, $v(a)$ refers to typical pattern of the level of reduction in fertility at age a below the natural level (determined empirically from a set of observed schedules), M refers to the scale factor expressing the level of marital fertility at about age 20 relative to natural fertility, and m refers to the extent to which the fertility control affects the pattern of marital fertility in the population.

For a detailed discussion of this method, and application of 'M' and 'm' as the respective measures of marital fertility and the degree of fertility control, see Chapter 15 by Macura.

10. Age-specific marital fertility rates for Hutterite women were 0.300, 0.550, 0.502, 0.447, 0.406, 0.222, 0.061 for age-groups 15–19, 20–24, 25–29, 30–34, 35–39, 40–44, 45–49 years, respectively (Coale, 1967, p. 209).

11. In societies with a considerable number of births occurring outside marital unions, two separate indices, viz. index of legitimate fertility and index of illegitimate fertility, should be calculated. For formulae, see Coale, 1967.

12. Such analyses would be particularly relevant in cases where fertility and mortality patterns being not stationary (i.e. population is not 'stable'), the period fertility measures diverge from the actual cohort fertility rates.

13. If relevant data are available, a number of other cohort measures could be used. These include, for example, mean age of mother (= mean age of childbearing), median age of mother, mean and median intervals between live births, birth probabilities specific by age, parity, age-

parity, etc. For an expository account, refer to Shryock, Siegel and associates, 1973, pp. 489–93.

14. Actually, when complete information is available on fertility history, including the timing of individual births, the study of fertility behaviour could be made more comprehensive with an analysis of decision-making regarding not only the number but also the spacing/timing of births. Total number of CEB and child-spacing are also, to some extent at least, interrelated. But, unfortunately, the survey experience so far reveals that it is extremely difficult to obtain in developing countries reliable statistics on dates of birth occurrences, particularly for women with many births.

15. A keen reader will notice the conceptual similarities between this micro fertility index and the macro fertility indexes developed by Coale, discussed in the subsection on adjusted period fertility rates.

16. $n(x)$ schedules can be obtained, for example, from Coale and Trussell, 1974.

17. Note that because the dependent variable is essentially binary (having the value one if the birth is reported, zero otherwise), the ordinary least squares estimation of the standard errors may be biased by the heteroscedasticity problem. In addition, the disturbance term is bounded. The researcher using such binary dependent-variable regression estimation should exercise caution in making inferences on the basis of marginally-significant parameters (Anker and Knowles, 1978, p. 150). Actually, since the assumption of normal distribution of error terms is violated with binary dependent variables, the use of probit (and logit) transformation is frequently recommended (see Kmenta, 1971).

18. Desired family-size was observed to be by and large consistent with actual fertility experience in Nigeria (Farooq, Ekanem and Ojelade, 1977). See also R. Freedman, 1975, and Hermalin *et al.*, 1979.

19. For example, in Nigeria such response was recorded for two-fifths of the respondents (see Chapter 12).

20. Theoretically, over time the number of ACD should have a one-to-one correspondence with births and deaths – one more birth should reduce ACD by one and one child death should increase ACD by one. In the Thai case, the responsiveness was far from complete – for each additional child born, the number of ACD decreased by around a half for the total sample, more at lower parities and less at higher parities. The response to child deaths, though significant, was smaller still (Rodgers, 1976, pp. 515–16).

6 Time-series, Cross-sections and Pooling

MARK BROWNING

As governments have become more active in population policy, the demand for accurate knowledge concerning the determinants of fertility and of other demographic events has increased. This is especially so with regard to isolating the effects of variables which can be considered policy-relevant, such as family-planning or female education. Coincident with this development is a steady increase in the amount of data which can be utilised both to test various theories of fertility and/or to estimate more precisely the effects of different variables on fertility. This increasing amount of information is being collected in many formats: cross-national data, aggregate time-series data, regional data, survey data, panel data, etc.; each of which may contain different types of information concerning the determinants of fertility. Researchers must choose the data they wish to use, and an accompanying statistical methodology with which to analyse the data. This chapter discusses issues that are raised by the availability of cross-section, time-series data.

A cross-section, time-series fertility data set for T time-periods and N units allows a researcher numerous possible avenues of investigation: one could estimate between 1 and T cross-section regressions of fertility on its hypothesised determinants; one could estimate up to N time-series regressions; or one could pool the data using any of a variety of techniques. The choice of methodology depends upon the characteristics of the data set and the information desired about fertility, as well as any purely statistical concerns. In the first part of this chapter, the possible distinctions between cross-sections and time-series are discussed. The second part of the chapter discusses the issues which are raised in pooling cross-section, time-series data, and gives guidelines on the appropriateness of various statistical techniques that can be used to pool the data. An appendix formally describes the pooling techniques and provides some simplifying algorithms useful in their computation.

149

TIME-SERIES VERSUS CROSS-SECTIONS

Estimates of the parameters of an econometric model based on time-series data often differ substantially from estimates of the parameters of the same model based on cross-sectional data.[1] A common interpretation of this difference is that the time-series data reflect the short-term effects of the variables in question, while the cross-section data reveal the long-term effects. This presumes that the variable in question responds slowly to changes in the relevant explanatory variables; in this case levels of fertility change slowly in reaction to changes in income, education, or infant mortality, etc. Since short time-series data, such as annual data rather than data for different decades, tend to reflect only recent changes or cyclical changes, the relationships found in time-series data may reflect only short-run adjustments. Cross-section data, however, while not completely free of cyclical or momentary changes, tend to be dominated by variations which are longstanding in nature. Estimates derived from cross-section data are therefore said to reflect the long-run adjustments.

Econometrically, one could interpret a discrepancy between cross-section and time-series estimates as being due to misspecification, with the misspecification being that some relevant variables have been omitted from the analysis.[2] As is well known, this in general causes the coefficient estimates of the included variables to be biased. The size of the bias is a function of the following: the magnitude of the coefficient of the omitted variables, the correlations between the included and the omitted variables, and the relative amount of variation in the two types of variables. Algebraically, for the case of one included explanatory variable and one omitted explanatory variable,

$$\text{Bias}_I = B_O \times r_{OI} \times (SD_O / SD_I),$$

where Bias_I is the bias of the estimated coefficient on the included variable, B_O is the true coefficient on the omitted variable, r_{OI} is the simple correlation coefficient between the included and the omitted variable in the sample, and SD_O and SD_I are respectively the sample standard deviations of the omitted and included explanatory variables.[3] The correlation, the ratio of the standard deviations, or both could be different in the time-series data than in the cross-sectional data, causing the expected coefficient estimates to diverge.

For example, let us consider analysing the relationship between fertility (F) and income (I). In a cross-section, it is not uncommon to find the relationship to be an inverse one, while in a time-series, the relationship is at times found to be positive.[4] Let us presume that educational attainment (E) negatively affects F, and that for lack of data, it is missing from an analysis of fertility. In a cross-section, E and I are likely to have a strong positive correlation, and due to this, the estimated effect of I on F will contain a bias downwards because I will be partially a proxy for E. In a short time-series, the variations in I are likely to be dominated by cyclical fluctuations, and the correlation between I and E will be attenuated, so that the estimated effect of I on F in the time-series will be little affected by this missing-variable bias. The time-series yields the short-run effect, in the sense that I has fluctuated relatively independently of E, while the cross-section reveals the 'long run', in the sense that E has adjusted to the differences in I, and the level of F has adjusted to both.

Another example of the bias from omitted variables occurs when previous values of included variables are incorrectly left out of the equation. Staying with the F-I example, perhaps levels of F are determined by past as well as current levels of I. Differences in I across units (individuals, regions, countries, whatever) are likely to be fairly longstanding, so that current I is highly correlated with past levels of I. The estimated effect of current I based on cross-sectional evidence will thus incorporate the effect of longstanding differences in I across units. Over a short time-series, however, the variation in current I within a unit will not be as closely related to fluctuations in previous levels of I, and thus the estimated effect of current I will not be biased to the degree that the cross-section estimate will be. The time-series estimate is a better approximation of the effect of current I on F; but it yields little information about the effect of past I on F.

Two caveats must be placed on the interpretation that the cross-section estimates of the relationship between current F and current I are estimates of long-run behaviour. The first is that current I is not a perfect proxy for past levels of I or for other excluded variables, so that an error-in-variables problem arises and the 'long-run' estimate will be biased downward to some extent – depending upon how accurate a proxy current I is for the omitted variables. The second caveat is that the relationship between current I and the omitted variables must continue on into the future. That is, in the first example, the relationship of E to I must continue in future years or the estimate obtained from the cross-section will not be a useful predictor of the future long-run effect. This point is especially important for policy analysis, as one may be looking for politically feasible and effective policy interventions. For instance, perhaps the effect of female E on F over a cross-section has been found to be relatively large. Increases in female education may not be too expensive and may even be politically attractive, so female E could be viewed as an attractive policy tool for changing the fertility rate. However, if female E was a proxy for religion, culture, or caste, etc., these factors may not necessarily shift due to a change in female E, so that the effect in the future will be less than the cross-sectional evidence indicated. In this specific example, it is also important to remember that, demographically, the long run can be a generation or longer. Changes in female education may not begin to appreciably affect fertility for 10-15 years – the time it takes for the women affected to enter into the prime childbearing years.

Likewise, the longer the time-series, the more likely it is that the variation in the data is due to long-run shifts, rather than cyclical changes. For instance, if one has data over a number of decades, the differences in the level of I in different decades normally are going to be dominated by the secular change in I and not by the economy's relative position in the business cycle at those points in time. The long-run–short-run distinction, if present, is thus one of degree. It may be more profitable to view the distinction as between different possible biases in the two types of estimates, as the next example illustrates .

Using the missing-variables framework to analyse the possible differences between the time-series and cross-section estimates does not necessarily lead to a short-run–long-run distinction. Consider the Example 3.1.1 used by Edlefson and Lieberman in Chapter 7 of this volume.

$$Y_{it} = a_1 I_{it} + a_2 \overline{I}_t,$$

in which Y_{it} is individual fertility, I_{it} is individual income, and $\overline{I}_t$ is aggregate income. If one had data for only a cross-section, then only a_1 could be identified and estimated, because $\overline{I}_t$ does not vary across individuals at any point in time. And, as Edlefson and Lieberman point out, if one has the aggregate data only over time, one can only estimate the sum of the two coefficients, $a_1 + a_2$.

This example points out the need for time-series data in order to identify and estimate the effects of variables that vary solely over time, and analogously the need for cross-section data for estimating the effects of time-invariant variables. The example also shows that looking solely at cross-section data eliminates possible bias from missing variables that vary solely over time, and similarly using time-series data does the same for missing variables that vary solely over the cross-section.[5]

The above examples are essentially a reminder of the consequences of misspecifying a relationship by omitting relevant variables from an analysis, either because of lack of knowledge or because of lack of data. The issue that is pertinent here is that the consequences of this misspecification can be different in the two types of data because the characteristics of a time-series data set are generally different than those of a cross-section data set. The possible differences in estimates discussed above are due to the misspecification. They are not due to the determinants of F over time not being the same as the determinants of F across units.

One should note that these differences may or may not be large. Other econometric problems may also be present in a given data set, such as simultaneity or heteroscedasticity, which can overshadow any differences between cross-section and time-series information.[6]

POOLING CROSS-SECTION, TIME-SERIES DATA

The above discussion emphasises the different information that might be contained in each type of data. This section discusses the joint issues of whether and how to pool the two types of data.

In this discussion, I shall assume that a model of fertility has already been specified as fully as possible in terms of a linear model suitable for regression analysis. In the example utilised above,

$$F_{it} = \beta_0 + \beta_1 I_{it} + \beta_2 E_{it} + \epsilon_{it},$$

with F_{it}, I_{it}, E_{it} being fertility, income and education, respectively, in unit i, in period t; β_0, β_1, β_2 are the unknown coefficients that we hope to estimate, and ϵ_{it} an unobserved error term, with as yet unspecified characteristics.

One could calculate separate time-series regressions for each cross-sectional unit, one could calculate separate cross-sectional regressions for each time-period, or one could pool all or part of the data. The general reason for pooling is to increase the amount of data available. The need to increase the amount of data could arise because of an overall shortage of data, or from a shortage of data in either the cross-section or the time-series dimension. A typical case is that there is a reasonably ample number of units to analyse, but very few time-periods of data. In this case, pooling can allow the researchers to synthetically expand the time-horizon.

Before statistical analysis begins, a number of questions must be asked about the specification of the relationship. The answers to these questions will help one to decide which of the pooling techniques to use. The techniques are then described, and the conditions appropriate for each are given. An appendix describes the various techniques formally, and presents simplified algorithms for their computation.

The first question is whether the slope coefficients of the model, as it is specified, are the same in all the time-periods, or in all the cross-sectional units. In our example, is the effect of a change in I on F in each unit the same in a rural area as in an urban area? If one or more of the slopes are different, can this difference be modelled? If the effect of I on F does vary with the per cent urban, can this be specified and incorporated into the model?[7] From here on, it will be assumed that those systematic differences that could be incorporated into the model specification have been incorporated.

Secondly, is there likely to be a difference between the cross-sectional information contained in the sample and the time-series information? The first part of the chapter discusses why misspecification, perhaps unavoidable, could cause these differences to arise. If there is a difference, which information is desired?

Thirdly, are there unit-specific or time-specific effects which would shift the whole relationship by a constant amount? A unit-specific effect is something about a unit which causes the specified model to systematically underpredict or overpredict fertility in that unit, likewise for a time effect. Unit effects might occur because variables that affect fertility are missing from the analysis, due to lack of knowledge or of data. In our example, besides E and I, perhaps infant-mortality levels affect fertility, and these vary across time, or perhaps breastfeeding practices vary across units. A key question to ask is whether the unit-specific or time-specific effects are correlated with the included variables. In our example, if infant-mortality does cause unit effects to exist, is infant-mortality related to I or E?

The above questions are clearly not independent. In particular, a misspecification that leads to differences in the cross-section, time-series relationships can be generated by unit-specific and/or time-specific effects which are correlated with the included variables.

I shall now discuss the three common pooling techniques, and how answers to the above questions determine the appropriate technique to use. I shall also briefly mention a pooling technique recently proposed by Hausman and Taylor (1981), and one discussed by Mundlak (1978).

ESTIMATION WITH POOLED DATA

The three statistical techniques that will be discussed in detail are Ordinary Least Squares (OLS) on all or part of the data, Error Components-Generalised Least Squares (EC) and Ordinary Least Squares with Dummy Variables (OLSDV). The formal specifications of the statistical techniques have been placed in the appendix. The criteria to be used in evaluating each technique will be the bias and efficiency of each in a given situation.

These three techniques are differentiated by the way they combine the cross-section and the time-series variation in the data. While the previous section pointed out why the two types of information may yield dissimilar results, this section focuses on how that affects the choice of estimating technique.

As in our example, the formal regression model specifies fertility to be a linear function of the explanatory variables plus an unobserved error term (Appendix equation (1)). The error term arises from the effects of relevant variables which have not been included in the model, errors of measurement in the data, and any inherent randomness that governs the fertility process. Formally, arguments about the correct statistical techniques will be concerned with the properties of this error term, and its relationship with the included variables. The presentation in this section will begin with the specification in which OLS is the appropriate technique. The specification will then be changed to demonstrate the situations in which the other techniques are appropriate.

For OLS to be appropriate for pooling all the cases in a cross-section, time-series data set, the following must hold true. Firstly, the slopes of the relationship must be the same in each region and at each point in time, which implies that the time-series estimate must not be hypothesised to be different from the cross-section estimate. Secondly, it is assumed that the error term is independent of any of the included explanatory variables. The third assumption is that the error term in any one cross-sectional unit at a point in time is independent of the error term in any other cross-sectional unit or at any other point in time; and the fourth assumption is that the error term has the same variance at all points in the cross-section and over time.[8]

To demonstrate the second assumption, consider our example of F being explained by I and E, with a residual error term. If part of the error term is due to infant-mortality being excluded from the specified relationship, then for the second assumption to hold, infant-mortality must be uncorrelated with I and E, or we have our familiar omitted-variables bias. The third assumption states that the error term is not systematic in any way, so that there can be no region or time effects. The last assumption is that one expects the model to be no more inaccurate in any time-period or unit than it is in another time-period or unit.

If all of the above assumptions hold, and these are basically the assumptions of the standard linear model, then OLS is unbiased and efficient.

If the first assumption is dropped and replaced by the assumption that the slopes are different in each unit, then separate regressions must be calculated for each unit. It is possible to test whether all the slopes are significantly different, or whether a subset of the slopes are different.[9] If there is sufficient data, this test should normally be performed, as this assumption is basic to the whole strategy of pooling the data. If the null hypothesis of constant slopes in all units is rejected, then one must try to regroup the data into groups that do have similar coefficients, and one is left with a disaggregated analysis. Unfortunately, data limitations often keep the test from being performed, if there are more variables than time-periods; or the test is not very powerful, either due to limited cases, or due to limited variation in the data. Besides moving to a completely disaggregated approach, intermediate positions are possible, in which some of the coefficients are allowed to vary by unit, while others are held constant across units.

A common specification in pooling is that the error term contains unit-specific or time-specific components.[10] This violates the third assumption above, as it causes error terms in the same unit or in the same time-period to be correlated. The consequences of this specification depend on whether the unit or time component is correlated with the included explanatory variables.[11] Let us consider only unit-specific effects, and first analyse the case in which the unit-specific effects are uncorrelated with the explanatory variables.

Given this error-term specification, the resulting OLS coefficient estimates will still be unbiased. However, OLS will no longer be efficient. OLS weights all the variation in the data, both within units and across units, equally in calculating the coefficient estimates. The unit-specific component of the error term causes the information in the across-unit variation to be less reliable than the information contained in the within-unit variation. The equal weighting given to the relatively unreliable information causes the OLS estimate to be less reliable.

One solution is to apply the Ordinary Least Squares with Dummy Variables (OLSDV) technique, which calculates separate intercept terms for each cross-sectional unit, essentially estimating the unit-specific component of the error term. In this case, OLSDV is unbiased but it too is inefficient. Whereas OLS gave the unreliable across-unit variation too much weight, OLSDV completely ignores it, as estimating the intercept terms eliminates the cross-section variation.[12]

The Error Components (EC) technique is a middle ground between OLS and OLSDV.[13] The EC technique utilises a weighted average of the within-unit and the across-unit variations in calculating the coefficient estimates. The weights are determined by the relative reliability of the two sources of information. For example, if the unit-specific component was relatively large, this causes the across-unit variation to be relatively unreliable, and thus this variation would be given a relatively low weight. Given our current specification of the model, EC yields unbiased and efficient estimates.

The above finding that all three of the methods are unbiased, with EC yielding the most reliable estimates, depends crucially on the assumption that the unit-specific (or time-specific) component of the error term is uncorrelated with the included explanatory variables. How likely is it that this is, in fact, the case, and what are the consequences if this assumption does not hold?

The unit-specific effects arise because the specification of the relationship is incomplete, either because of lack of theoretical insight or because of lack of data. The question becomes that of whether or not the omitted variables bear a relationship to the included variables. Since the included variables in an analysis of fertility are usually ones which are central to a society, such as education, income, religion, urbanisation, etc., it is quite likely that any missing variables will be related to these included variables. The researcher should be alert to this possibility and, where possible, test to see if the correlations are present.[14]

The consequence of this correlation is that both OLS and EC will produce biased estimates of the coefficients, as they are in part based on the cross-unit variation in the data, within which the correlation between the included variables and the unit-specific component of the error term is contained. Since OLSDV ignores the cross-unit variation in the data, it remains unbiased.

For clarity, let me again list the conditions for the above to be true. This case assumes that the error term is composed of a component specific to each unit, and a residual component that is random across units and time-periods. It further assumes that the unit-specific component is correlated with the included explanatory variables, although the residual component is uncorrelated with the included variables. In our continuing example, this could arise if F were determined not only by I and E but also by the incidence of infant breastfeeding, which was not included in the model. The incidence of infant breastfeeding, if unchanging over time, would be the source of the unit-specific component of the error term. If infant breastfeeding were correlated with E and/or I, then the EC or OLS procedures would yield biased estimates of the effect of I and E. OLSDV would yield unbiased estimates, because it considers only the time-series variation and, in this example, the incidence of breastfeeding does not vary over time. If breastfeeding practices did vary over time, one would have to argue that it was correlated cross-sectionally, but not over the time-series, otherwise OLSDV would also be biased.

The benefit of using OLSDV in the case above is that it is unbiased, but this property is not without cost. To achieve it, one ignores the cross-sectional information in the sample and in fertility research the relative variation in fertility generally is concentrated across units, rather than within units. Thus the estimates derived may tend to be subject to a wide margin of error. The EC estimates, since they take into account the cross-sectional variation, will be more stable. The point is that the appropriate technique to utilise depends on one's judgement as to how biased the EC estimates may be, versus how limited is the information that OLSDV bases its estimates on.

Another problem with using the OLSDV method is that it does not allow the estimation of coefficients of time-invariant variables. Thus if one had panel data on adults, and one wanted to estimate the effect of primary school education, this would not be possible with OLSDV, as this variable would, in almost all individuals, not vary over time. Thus if one is forced to choose between OLSDV and EC, for some variables it may be a choice between estimating and not estimating.

A pooling method recently proposed by Hausman and Taylor (1981) allows one, in certain circumstances, to estimate consistently the coefficients of time-invariant variables, even if some of the variables in the regression are correlated with the unit-specific component of the error term. They divide up the explanatory variables into four groups. Group one consists of variables that vary across units and over time, and are not correlated with the unit-specific component of the error term. Group two consists of like varibles, except that they are correlated with the unit-specific component of the error term. Group three consists of time-invariant variables which are uncorrelated with the unit-specific component of the error term; while group four consists of like variables, except that they are correlated with the unit-specific component of the error term.

To be able to apply the Hausman–Taylor methodology, the number of variables in group one must be at least as large as the number of variables in group four. If this condition is satisfied, then the essence of the method is to use the cross-sectional variation of the variables in groups one and three to produce instruments for the cross-sectional components of the variables in groups two and four. If there are exactly as many variables in group one as in group four, one then calculates a standard instrumental variable estimate of the coefficients. If there are more variables in group one than in group four, then the above can be improved upon essentially by combining the instrumental variables technique with the EC technique (this is described in the appendix).

The crux of this method requires that the analyst be able to specify which variables fall into which groups, with particular care that he does not include variables in group one or three that belong in groups two or four, as this would cause this method to be inconsistent.[15] Since the commonly-specified explanatory variables such as income, education, infant-mortality, etc., are not likely to be candidates for inclusion in group one, this method may be of only limited usefulness to fertility researchers.

Mundlak (1978) describes a technique to help overcome the possibility that the OLSDV estimator, although unbiased, may be subject to a large variance. The proposed method is based on minimising the mean squared error of the coefficient estimates. It is similar to the EC technique, in that it is calculated by taking a matrix weighted average of the OLSDV estimate and the estimate based on the cross-sectional variation, but unlike the EC technique, the weights take into account the fact that the cross-sectional estimates are biased. The properties of this estimator in small samples are not currently known, given that one has to estimate the relative error components and bias, though the presumption is that even in reasonably-sized samples, it outperforms the OLSDV estimate in terms of mean squared error. This technique is consistent in large samples but biased in small samples, since it, in part, relies on the cross-sectional variation in the data.

How does the cross-section, time-series distinction discussed in the first section of the chapter fit in with this discussion? Essentially, that discussion translates into whether the individual effects are correlated with the included variables, with the individual effects being the result of missing variables. The OLSDV estimate is simply the time-series estimate, while the other methods combine the time-series and cross-section information. If one believes that there is no distinction between time-series and cross-section, then one can utilise estimates based on both types of information.

To sum up, the methodology one chooses depends to an extent on how one believes the world is structured, and how well one's specification fits that world. If one has confidence that one's model specification has captured all the systematic variation in the data, then time-series information and cross-section information are interchangeable, and OLS would be the appropriate technique to utilise, though one should test to see if the data support this belief. If one specifies a model in which unobservable unit-specific effects remain, then a number of possibilities exist. If the effects are independent of the included variables, then the EC technique is appropriate, and again this model specification can be tested against the data. If the effects are not independent, which I believe is the most likely case in fertility analysis, then a number of paths are open. If there is a relatively large amount of time-series variation in the data, then utilising OLSDV is a reasonable way to proceed. If one can specify confidently some of the variables to be uncorrelated with the unit-specific effects, then the Hausman-Taylor avenue is a possible fruitful route to follow. Otherwise, one is forced to a solution, such as the one proposed by Mundlak, which combines the biased, but probably low-variance, cross-section estimate and the unbiased, but probably large-variance, time-series estimate (OLSDV).

As a practical strategy, it is generally worthwhile to calculate the OLSDV and the 'between' regressions (the EC and OLS results are matrix weighted averages of these; for the 'between' regression, see fifth section of the appendix). If the results of these differ significantly, it indicates that the types of data are not consistent, or put another way, the EC assumptions do not hold. If this occurs, perhaps a respecification of the relationship is in order, rather than a change of estimating technique.

APPENDIX: THE FORMAL MODEL SPECIFICATION

We are interested in estimating a model of the form

$$Y_{it} = \beta_0 + \beta_1 X_{it}^1 + \ldots + \beta_K X_{it}^K + u_{it}, \tag{1}$$

in which Y_{it} is a measure of fertility in cross-sectional unit i, during period t (N units and T periods in total); $X_{it}^1, \ldots, X_{it}^K$ are the K explanatory variables; $\beta_0, \ldots, \beta_K$ are, respectively, the constant term and the K slope coefficients, all of which are unknown; and u_{it}, is an unknown error term. Combining all the terms in matrix notation,

$$Y = X\beta + u, \tag{2}$$

where

$$Y = \begin{bmatrix} Y_{11} \\ Y_{12} \\ \cdot \\ \cdot \\ \cdot \\ Y_{1T} \\ Y_{21} \\ \cdot \\ \cdot \\ \cdot \\ Y_{NT} \end{bmatrix}, \quad X = \begin{bmatrix} 1 & X_{11}^1 & \dots & X_{11}^K \\ 1 & X_{12}^1 & \dots & X_{12}^K \\ \cdot & \cdot & & \cdot \\ \cdot & \cdot & & \cdot \\ \cdot & \cdot & & \cdot \\ 1 & X_{1T}^1 & \dots & X_{1T}^K \\ 1 & X_{21}^1 & \dots & X_{21}^K \\ \cdot & \cdot & & \cdot \\ \cdot & \cdot & & \cdot \\ \cdot & \cdot & & \cdot \\ 1 & X_{NT}^1 & \dots & X_{NT}^K \end{bmatrix}, \quad \beta = \begin{bmatrix} \beta_0 \\ \beta_1 \\ \cdot \\ \cdot \\ \beta_K \end{bmatrix}, \quad u = \begin{bmatrix} u_{11} \\ u_{12} \\ \cdot \\ \cdot \\ \cdot \\ u_{1T} \\ u_{21} \\ \cdot \\ \cdot \\ \cdot \\ u_{NT} \end{bmatrix}.$$

The Ordinary Least Squares (OLS) Specification

For our purposes, the following set of assumptions concerning the error term are needed to justify the use of OLS. The first and foremost is that the error term is independent of the included explanatory variables,

$$E(u \mid X) = E(u) = 0, \tag{3}$$

with $E(\ )$ being the expectation operator. This assumption assures that OLS will yield unbiased estimates. It is further assumed that the different u_{it} are mutually uncorrelated, and that each u_{it} has the same variance, $-\sigma^2$:

$$E(uu') = \sigma^2 I_{NT}, \tag{4}$$

with I_{NT} being the identity matrix of order NT. This assumption assures that OLS will yield efficient estimates.

The well-known OLS estimate b, in matrix notation, is

$$b = (X'X)^{-1} X'Y, \tag{5}$$

which has an expected value

$$E(b) = \beta \tag{6}$$

and variance

$$\mathrm{Var}(b) = \sigma^2 (X'X)^{-1}. \tag{7}$$

The Error-components Specification and the OLSDV Method

In the full error-components specification, the error term now contains components which are specific to time (γ_t) and unit (λ_i) as well as purely random components (μ_{it}):

$$u_{it} = \gamma_t + \lambda_i + \mu_{it}. \tag{8}$$

The γ_t, λ_i and μ_{it} are assumed to be fully independent, and

$$
\begin{aligned}
E(u_{it}u_{js}) &= \sigma_\gamma^2 + \sigma_\lambda^2 + \sigma_\mu^2 = \sigma^2 & i = j, \quad s = t, \\
&= \sigma_\gamma^2 & i \neq j, \quad s = t, \\
&= \sigma_\lambda^2 & i = j, \quad s \neq t, \\
&= 0 & i \neq j, \quad s \neq t.
\end{aligned}
\tag{9}
$$

Variants of the model assume that only the λ_i or the γ_t exist, with a subsequent dropping of the σ_γ^2 or σ_λ^2, respectively.

In matrix notation,

$$E(uu') = \Omega = \sigma_\gamma^2 B + \sigma_\lambda^2 A + \sigma_\mu^2 I_{NT}, \tag{10}$$

in which

$$
A = \begin{bmatrix} J_T & O_T & \cdots & & O_T \\ O_T & J_T & O_T & \cdot & O_T \\ \cdot & \cdot & \cdot & \cdot & \cdot \\ \cdot & \cdot & \cdot & \cdot & \cdot \\ \cdot & \cdot & \cdot & J_T & O_T \\ O_T & \cdot & \cdot & \cdot & J_T \end{bmatrix}, \quad
B = \begin{bmatrix} I_T & I_T & \cdots & & I_T \\ I_T & I_T & \cdots & & \\ \cdot & \cdot & \cdots & & \cdot \\ \cdot & \cdot & \cdots & & \cdot \\ \cdot & \cdot & & I_T & I_T \\ I_T & I_T & \cdots & & I_T \end{bmatrix},
$$

with J_T being a $T \times T$ matrix in which all elements are ones, O_T being a $T \times T$ matrix in which all elements are zeroes, and I_T the $T \times T$ identity matrix; the dimensions of Ω, A, B and I_{NT} and $NT \times NT$.

Given the above error structure, there are three common techniques used to estimate the relationship. The first would be to estimate via the OLS methodology described in the previous section. If one assumed that the error terms for various components are independent of the explanatory variables (i.e. if equation (3) still holds), then OLS is unbiased, although equation (7) is no longer a correct derivation of the variance of the OLS estimates. Also, if equation (3) is not a correct assumption, then OLS is biased.

One common approach to the problem is to estimate the individual γ_t and/or λ_i, and this is the so-called OLSDV method. If one has no computational restrictions, one specifies $N - 1$ additional explanatory variables for estimating the λ_i: $Z_{it}^2, \ldots, Z_{it}^N$, with

$$
\begin{aligned}
Z_{it}^n &= 1, \quad i = n \\
Z_{it}^n &= 0, \quad i \neq n.
\end{aligned} \tag{11}
$$

One also specifies $T - 1$ explanatory variables for estimating the γ_t: $W_{it}^2, \ldots, W_{it}^T$, with

$$
\begin{aligned}
W_{it}^j &= 1, \quad t = j, \\
W_{it}^j &= 0, \quad t \neq j.[16]
\end{aligned} \tag{12}
$$

One then calculates a simple OLS regression of Y on X and the Z_{it} and W_{it} (the so-called Dummy Variables - hence OLSDV).

The OLSDV regression with all the Z_{it} and W_{it} can be computationally burdensome, as it involves estimating $K + N + T - 1$ variable coefficients.

A procedure which involves a transformation of the data and then a K-variable OLS regression is described below.

The most common case is one in which only λ_i is specified, that is, only a cross-sectional component to the error term is assumed, but no time-series component. Instead of estimating coefficients for all the Z_{it}, one first transforms the data. Calculating the deviations around the unit means,

$$Y_{it}^* = Y_{it} - \bar{Y}_i \tag{13}$$

and

$$X_{it}^{*k} = X_{it}^K - \bar{X}_i^k, \quad \text{for all } k, k = 1 \ldots K$$

with $\bar{Y}_i$ and $\bar{X}_i^k$ as the unit means

$$\bar{Y}_i = (\sum_{t=1}^T Y_{it})/T,$$

$$\bar{X}_i^k = (\sum_{t=1}^T X_{it}^k)/T.$$

One then calculates an OLS regression of Y^* on the X^*, omitting a constant term. The coefficients calculated in this way will be exactly the same as if one estimated the full model. However, one will have to adjust the coefficient standard errors to take into account all the coefficients which have been implicitly estimated. This is done by multiplying the standard errors by the factor $(\sqrt{NT - K})/(\sqrt{NT - N - K})$.

A strictly analogous procedure would apply if one was specifying the existence of only the time-specific component. One would calculate the deviations from the time-period means, and calculate an ordinary least squares regression on the transformed data. The coefficient standard errors would be adjusted by the factor $(\sqrt{NT - K})/(\sqrt{NT - T - K})$.

If both time and cross-sectional effects are included, then the following transformation must be performed:

$$Y_{it}^{**} = Y_{it} - \bar{Y}_i - \bar{Y}_t + \bar{Y},$$

$$X_{it}^{**k} = X_{it}^k - \bar{X}_i^k - \bar{X}_t^k + \bar{X}^k, \quad \text{for all } k, k = 1 \ldots K \tag{14}$$

with $\bar{X}_t^k$, $\bar{Y}_t$ being the time-period means, and $\bar{X}^k$, $\bar{Y}$ being the overall means of the variables. Again, one just calculates an OLS regression using the transformed data. The standard errors in this case must be transformed by the factor $(\sqrt{NT - K})/(\sqrt{NT - N - T - K + 1})$.

The OLSDV method is unbiased as long as the X_{it}^k are independent of the μ_{it}, even if the X_{it}^k are correlated with the γ_t or the λ_i. This is because the transformations above eliminate any time-invariant or cross-sectionally-invariant variables from the data.

The Error Components Method

The third method is a generalised least squares approach based on the error component structure (EC). In matrix notation, theis estimate is

$$b^* = (X'\Omega^{-1}X)X'\Omega^{-1}y, \tag{15}$$

with Ω being defined in equation (10). This method also can be computationally burdensome if applied directly, because it requires the inversion of the $NT \times NT$ matrix Ω. As in the OLSDV case, it is possible to transform the data, and then calculate a simple $(K + 1)$-variable OLS regression.[17]

The transformation is as follows. Define p, f, s_1, s_2, s_3, s_4, such that

$$p = \sigma_\lambda^2/(\sigma_\lambda^2 + \sigma_\gamma^2 + \sigma_\mu^2),$$
$$f = \sigma_\gamma^2/(\sigma_\lambda^2 + \sigma_\gamma^2 + \sigma_\mu^2),$$
$$s_1 = 1/\sqrt{1 - p - f + pT + fN},$$
$$s_2 = 1/\sqrt{1 - p - f + fN},$$
$$s_3 = 1/\sqrt{1 - p - f + pT},$$
$$s_4 = 1/\sqrt{1 - p - f}.$$

Then calculate $\overline{Y}_{it}$, and the $\overline{X}_{it}^k$:

$$\overline{Y}_{it} = Y_{it}^* s_4 + \overline{Y}_i^*(s_3 - s_4) + \overline{Y}_t(s_2 - s_4) + \overline{Y}(s_1 - s_2 - s_3 + s_4),$$
$$\overline{X}_{it}^k = X_{it}^{k*} s_4 + \overline{X}_i^{k*}(s_3 - s_4) + \overline{X}_t^{k*}(s_2 - s_4) + \overline{X}^k(s_1 - s_2 - s_3 + s_4),$$
$$\text{for all } k, k = 1 \ldots K \tag{16}$$

One then simply calculates a simple OLS regression of $\overline{y}_{it}$ on the $\overline{X}_{it}^k$, including a constant. To obtain the correct value for the constant term, one must either apply the above transformation to the column of ones used to estimate the constant term, or multiply the constant term by s_1.

Since the variances of the error components (σ_λ^2, σ_γ^2 and σ_μ^2) are generally not known, these also must be estimated. Wallace and Hussain (1969) propose the following method. The first step is to estimate an OLS regression on the pooled data to obtain the OLS estimates of the coefficient vector, b. One then calculates the OLS residuals e_{it} as follows.

$$e_{it} = Y_{it} - b_0 - \sum_{k=1}^{K} b_k X_{it}^k.$$

The e_{it} are then used to form estimates of the variances as follows:

$$\hat{\sigma}_\mu^2 = \frac{1}{(N-1)(T-1)} \sum_{i=1}^{N} \sum_{t=1}^{T} (e_{it} - \bar{e}_i - \bar{e}_t)^2,$$

$$\hat{\sigma}_\lambda^2 = \frac{\sum_{i=1}^{N} (\bar{e}_i)^2}{N} - \frac{\hat{\sigma}_\mu^2}{T},$$

$$\hat{\sigma}_\gamma^2 = \frac{\sum_{t=1}^{T} (\bar{e}_t)^2}{T} - \frac{\hat{\sigma}_\mu^2}{N}, \tag{17}$$

with

$$\bar{e}_i = (\sum_{t=1}^{T} e_{it})/T$$

$$\bar{e}_t = (\sum_{i=1}^{N} e_{it})/N.$$

A similar method is proposed by Amemiya (1971), except that the initial coefficient estimates are from an OLSDV regression rather than an OLS regression. Other methods for calculating the variance estimates are described in Maddala and Mount (1973), and they present evidence that none is clearly superior to any of the others. The method proposed above does allow estimates of the variance components to be negative, in which case the estimates should be set to zero.

The Hausman–Taylor Methodology

As described in the text, this methodology requires one to divide the variables into four groups. The first group, the $X_{1\,it}^k$, vary over time and are uncorrelated with the unit-specific component of the error term. The second group, the X^l_{2it}, vary over time but are correlated with the error component. The third group, the Z^j_{1i}, do not vary over time and are uncorrelated with the unit-specific component of the error term. The last group, the Z^m_{2i}, do not vary over time but are correlated with the error component. It is necessary that the number of variables in group one be greater than or equal to the number in group four, or this methodology is inappropriate, and one must be content with OLSDV.

The first step in the procedure is to create instruments for variables in groups two and four, since these variables are correlated with the error term. To obtain these for the L X^l_{2it}, one calculates $\hat{X}^l_{2it} = X^l_{2it} - \bar{X}^l_{2i} + \hat{\bar{X}}^l_{2i}$, for all L variables in group one. $\bar{X}^l_{2i}$ is the group mean of X^l_{2it}, and $\hat{\bar{X}}^l_{2i}$ is the predicted value of an N-case regression of $\bar{X}^l_{21}$ on the K $\bar{X}^k_{1i}$ in group one and the J Z^j_{1i} in group three. The instruments for the M Z^m_2, the $\hat{Z}^m_2$, are the predicted values of the N-case regression of the Z^m_2 on the K $\bar{X}^k_{1i}$ and the J Z^j_1.

Consistent estimates of the coefficients can now be obtained by regressing the Y_{it} on the K X^k_{1it}, the L $\hat{X}^l_{2it}$, the J Z^i_1 and the M $\hat{Z}^m_2$.

If the number of variables in group one equals the number of variables in group four, then this is the best one can do. However, if there are more variables in group one than in group four, one can improve the efficiency of the estimates. Firstly, one has to calculate estimates of the variances of the error components. This is done by calculating error residuals, utilising the coefficient estimates above and the original data, and then making the calculations as in equation (17). One then transforms the dependent variables, the variables in groups one and three, and the instruments for the variables in groups two and four, in the same way as in the error components model. Finally, one performs a simple OLS regression on the resulting variables.

The Mundlak Mean Squared Error Estimator[18]

There is no easy transformation of the data which allows one to calculate the Mean Squared Error Estimator (MSEE) with a simple OLS regression. Instead, one must transform the data in two different ways, calculate the OLS regression on each, and then calculate a matrix weighted average of each.

Firstly, one calculates the OLSDV regressions. Secondly, one calculates what is called the 'between regression'. This can be done by regressing the $\bar{Y}_i$ on the $\bar{X}^k_i$, that is, an N-case regression using the within-unit means. Let us call the OLSDV results in matrix notation b^w, a $K + 1$-length column vector, and the results of the 'between' regression b^b.

To obtain the MSEE, one now needs to combine the two above. In matrix notation,

$$b^{\text{MS}} = Wb^b + (I - W)b^w,$$

with I in the $K + 1$ order-identifying matrix, and $W = V^w(M^b + V^w)^{-1}$. V^w is the variance of the within estimator, given by

$$V^w = \sigma_\mu^2 (X^{*'}X^*)^{-1},$$

with X^* defined as in equation (13). M^b is the mean squared error of the 'between' estimator, and is given by

$$M^b = pp' + V^b = pp' + (\sigma_\mu^2/T + \sigma_b^2)(\overline{X}'\overline{X})^{-1},$$

with V^b the variance of the between regression, $\overline{X}$ the $N \times (K + 1)$ matrix of within-unit means for the independent variables (used to calculate the 'between' regression), and p a $K + 1$-length column vector of the bias of the 'between' regression. Since σ_μ^2, σ_λ^2 and p are unknowns, they must be replaced by estimates. An estimate of σ_μ^2 can be derived from the formula given in equation (17), if one uses the b^w in calculating the residuals. An estimate of σ_b^2 can be obtained from the formula

$$\hat{\sigma}_b^2 = \frac{\sum\limits_{i=1}^{N} e_i^2}{N},$$

in which the e_i are the residuals from the regression calculating b^b. An estimate of p is calculated by

$$\hat{p} = b^b - b^w.$$

NOTES

1. See Kuh (1959) for an analysis and an example of this problem in which the data, both time-series and cross-section, have exactly the same source. Examples of this problem in fertility research can be found in Nerlove and T. P. Schultz (1970) and T. P. Schultz (1974a).

2. Aigner and Simon (1970) give a formal analysis of this point. The first example that follows differs on the surface from theirs, but not in essence, however, if one considers that educational levels are a function of lagged values of income. The second example more closely reflects their work.

3. The formula for the magnitude of the bias becomes more complicated if more variables are either included or omitted, but the same features are important. See Kmenta (1971, pp. 392–5) or Aigner and Simon (1970).

4. For an extensive discussion of this, see J. L. Simon (1977, 1974).

5. This example illustrates the cross-sectional case. A time-series example would exist if fertility were a function of an individual's relative income and also absolute income. If relative income stayed constant, then a secular shift in average income over time would allow one to identify the effect of absolute income.

6. See Chapter 8 by Boone Turchi for a more thorough discussion of specification.

7. A simple interaction term would be one way to accomplish this:

$$F = \beta_0 + \beta_1 \times I + \beta_1' \times PU \times I,$$

with PU being the per cent urban. The effect of a change in I would be $\beta_1 + \beta_1' \times PU$. One could then easily test to see if β_1' were significant.

8. See the first section of the appendix for the mathematical specification of the model and the error term which conforms to the above assumptions.

9. One can test for signficant differences across time-periods or units. See Maddala (1977, pp. 322–6) for this test within the time-series, cross-section framework, or consult most standard econometrics texts for the general type of test of the equality of coefficients. The types of differences emphasised here are differences in the slopes of the relationship, which usually also imply differences in the intercepts. Differences solely in the intercepts will be discussed in the error components approach. Another approach is to model the slopes as random variables about a common mean (see Swamy, 1971), but this will not be discussed here. The differences in slopes that concern us here are systematic ones.

10. See the second section of the appendix for the mathematical specification of the error term.

11. This topic is the main focus of Mundlak (1978).

12. The second section of the appendix contains a simplified method of computing the OLSDV estimates, which shows quite clearly that OLSDV utilises only the within-unit variation.

13. The third section of the appendix contains the details of computing the EC estimates.

14. Hausman (1978) specifies a large sample test to see if the unit and/or time effects are independent of the included variables.

15. Hausman and Taylor (1981) describe procedure which tests the assignment of variables into groups one and three. This test essentially

   compares the OLSDV coefficient to the coefficient produced by
   their method. If the two sets are significantly different, this is evidence
   of misspecification.
16. Only $N - 1$ $(T - 1)$ additional variables are specified in order to
   avoid perfect collinearity with the intercept term. The first unit
   (time-period) has been arbitrarily chosen as the unrepresented one.
17. See Nerlove (1971b) for the derivation of this result.
18. Only the model with unit-specific effects is considered here, although
   a model with only time-specific effects would be analogous. For the
   model with both, see Mundlak (1978).

7 Aggregate Data in Economic-Demographic Analysis

LEE E. EDLEFSEN and SAMUEL S. LIEBERMAN

This chapter treats issues which arise in the use of aggregate data in economic demography. The discussion focuses on fertility trends and patterns, though the analysis could be applied as well to migration and mortality. The chapter is divided into two sections. In the first section, an attempt is made to summarise current econometric and theoretical thinking on the use of aggregate data to estimate structural demand functions. The principal question addressed is the extent to which structural fertility relationships estimated with aggregate data are an accurate reflection of what is going on at the individual level. An important component of this question is whether or not such aggregate relationships can be used to test the implications of the micro-economic theory of fertility, which yields predictions about the nature of individual-level fertility 'demand' functions. The second section considers the estimation of aggregate reduced-form functions. Such functions are required when it is desired to estimate the total effects of variables (such as income) on fertility, rather than the partial effects which are given by structural relationships. Total effects can differ from partial effects when the fertility equation forms part of a general equilibrium system, in which case a change in income (for instance) may induce changes in prices and perhaps other variables which are held constant in structural functions. Discrepancies between total and partial effects can also arise when aggregate variables have direct, independent effects on individual fertility behaviour. There is almost no discussion in the literature of aggregation in these circumstances. Thus, in the second section, we simply attempt to sketch some of the issues involved, and to suggest what their implications might be. The most important implication deserves to be stated here: the problems introduced by aggregation depend crucially upon what types of questions the analyst is attempting to answer.

171

THE ESTIMATION AND INTERPRETATION OF STRUCTURAL DEMAND FUNCTIONS

Introduction

Micro-economic theory, as applied to fertility or other types of demographic behaviour, implies individual-level demand functions with the following general form:

$$Y_i = f(p, I_i, W_i), \tag{1}$$

where Y_i denotes, for instance, the fertility of the ith individual or couple, p denotes the vector of prices faced by the individual or couple, I_i denotes income, and W_i denotes a vector of other variables affecting Y_i. Let $\overline{Y}, \overline{I}$, and $\overline{W}$ denote group averages of the corresponding variables. The general question to be addressed in this section is: can a relationship among the aggregate variables be obtained which 'corresponds' to the individual-level relationship, and what is the nature of this correspondence in different circumstances? This question, as it is discussed in the literature, has two different though closely-related aspects. Firstly, what statistical problems are encountered in the use of aggregate data to estimate structural fertility (or other) relationships? Secondly, if utility-maximising behaviour is assumed, then what restrictions need be satisfied by individuals' preferences or by other aspects of the model to ensure that aggregate data perform as though generated by a single 'representative' individual? These issues are discussed separately.

Econometric Issues

Linear aggregation
Almost all of the literature on statistical aggregation is restricted to a consideration of linear equations. To be concrete, assume that the 'group' averages are formed by aggregating within time-periods. Thus, assume that at the individual-level there are N individuals, and that there are T time-periods. Let the individual-level equation for the ith individual in the tth time-period be

$$Y_{it} = \alpha_i + \beta_i p_t + \gamma_i I_{it} + \delta_i X_{it} + \epsilon_{it}, \tag{2}$$
$$i = 1, \ldots, N, \quad t = 1, \ldots, T,$$

where X_{it} represents the measurable variables affecting Y_{it}, and ϵ_{it} represents the error term. Thus, ϵ_{it} can be interpreted as representing the sum of those variables in W_{it} that cannot be measured. In what follows, the assumptions of the standard linear model will be maintained. Specifically, the measurable variables p_t, I_{it} and X_{it} will be assumed to be fixed (or uncorrelated with the error terms)[1] and the error terms ϵ_{it} will be assumed to have zero mean and a scalar variance–covariance matrix: $E(\epsilon_{it}) = 0$, $\text{Var}(\epsilon_{it}) = \sigma^2$, $\text{Cov}(\epsilon_{it}, \epsilon_{js}) = 0$, for all i, j, t, s. Note that in equation (2), individuals are allowed to have different behavioural coefficients (α_i, β_i, γ_i, δ_i), but these coefficients are assumed to not vary over time. Prices are assumed to be the same for all individuals, but the other independent variables are allowed to vary both over time and over individuals. Given this specification, group averages are defined by

$$\bar{Y}_t = \frac{1}{N} \sum_i Y_{it},$$

$$\bar{I}_t = \frac{1}{N} \sum_i I_{it},$$

$$\bar{X}_t = \frac{1}{N} \sum_i X_{it}.$$

Although groups here are defined explicitly in terms of time-periods, they could equally well be defined in terms of states, countries, cities, and so on.

A common procedure, when given aggregate data, is to estimate an equation of the form

$$\bar{Y}_t = a + bp_t + c\bar{I}_t + d\bar{X}_t + e_t. \tag{3}$$

The question which thus arises is: what is the relationship between the estimated coefficients of (3) and the 'true' coefficients, as given in equations (2). Obviously, there is no hope of recovering each individual's coefficients from aggregate data. However, under some circumstances, the estimated coefficients in (3) will be unbiased for the correct average of the individual-level coefficients. The most complete analysis of this issue has been given by Theil (1954; 1971, ch. 11).

Consider the summation over individuals of the equations in (2):

$$\frac{1}{N} \sum_i Y_{it} = \frac{1}{N} \sum_i \alpha_i + \frac{1}{N} \sum_i \beta_i p_t + \frac{1}{N} \sum_i \gamma_i I_{it} + \frac{1}{N} \sum_i \delta_i X_{it} + \frac{1}{N} \sum_i \epsilon_{it}. \tag{4}$$

This defines the true equation for the aggregate variables, $\bar{Y}_t$. Thus, at issue is the relationship between the 'true' aggregate equation, (4), and the estimates of the parameters of equation (3). Two separate questions are involved. Firstly, what can be said about the relationship between the coefficients in the aggregate equation (3) and the corresponding individual-level coefficients in (2). Secondly, what are the statistical properties of the estimators of the aggregate equation? Note that the first question does not, *per se*, involve any issues of statistical estimation. However, it must be answered before statistical questions can be addressed. Furthermore, when it is the case that aggregation is 'consistent', in the sense that (4) has the form of (3), then the statistical issues which arise are simply those which arise in the estimation of any linear equation. That is, in this case the second question does not, *per se*, involve any issues of aggregation.

To see the issues involved in answering the first question, consider in turn the terms on the right-hand side of (4). The first term is the average of all constant terms, and is just a constant term itself:

$$\frac{I}{N}\sum_i \alpha_i = \bar{\alpha} . \tag{5}$$

Thus, this corresponds directly to the parameter 'a' in (3). The second term is the average of the product of a parameter which varies over individuals and a variable which does not. Consequently, this sum equals the average of the parameter times the variable:

$$\frac{I}{N}\sum_i \beta_i p_t = \bar{\beta} p_t. \tag{6}$$

Thus, this corresponds directly to the term 'bp_t' in (3). The third and fourth terms in (4) are the ones which cause problems. Since both the parameters and the variables vary across individuals, these terms cannot, in general, be represented as the product of a constant parameter and the corresponding aggregate variable. What Theil shows, in effect, is that when there are any terms of this type in (4), then the OLS estimators of all the parameters will, in general, be biased as estimators of the average values of the individual-level parameters. Thus, even though there is no problem with the price term by itself, the expected value of the OLS estimator of b in (3) does not equal $\bar{\beta}$. It should be noted that Theil's analysis assumes that the regressors are fixed (or are uncorrelated with the error term) in the aggregate. Thus, there can be no problem of simultaneity bias (to be discussed below), and aggregation bias is the only issue.

The discussion above provides insight into circumstances in which there will be no aggregation bias (i.e. in which equation (4) has the form of equation (3)). Most obviously, if the individual-level parameters are the same for all individuals, then the aggregate equation is identical to every individual-level equation, and there is no problem of aggregation bias. Alternatively, if all of the independent variables are the same for all individuals in every time-period, then the aggregate equation has the form of equation (3), and the coefficients are the averages of individual-level coefficients. Again, there is no problem of aggregation.

The conditions noted above are unlikely ever to hold exactly in practice. However, these conditions can be relaxed substantially. Consider the term for income in (4). By the formula for a sample covariance this can be written as

$$\frac{1}{N}\sum_i \gamma_i I_{it} = \frac{1}{N}\sum_i (\gamma_i - \overline{\gamma})\,(I_{it} - \overline{I}_t) + \overline{\gamma}\,\overline{I}_t. \tag{7}$$

Consequently, if the sample covariance between the coefficients γ_i and the income variable I_{it} is zero in every time-period, then this term can be written in the desired form (i.e. $\overline{\gamma}\overline{I}_t$). This condition means that individuals' responses to income are not correlated with their level of income within the sample. If this condition holds for all variables, then there will be no aggregation bias.[2]

An alternative approach has been discussed by Lancaster (1966) and Chipman (1974). Each individual's share in total income is:

$$S_{it} \equiv \frac{I_{it}}{N\overline{I}_t}. \tag{8}$$

If this share does not vary over time ($S_{it} = S_i, t = 1, \ldots, T$), then

$$\frac{1}{N}\sum_i \gamma_i I_{it} = (\sum_i \gamma_i S_i)\overline{I}_t. \tag{9}$$

Since the share does not vary over time, the coefficient of $\overline{I}_t$ is a constant. It is the weighted average of the individual-level coefficients, where the weights are the shares. The mathematics is the same, though the intuition is somewhat different, for variables other than income (e.g. if educational levels are fixed for all individuals in the sample, then each individual's 'share' in 'total education' is fixed). If shares are constant for all variables, then the terms in (4) all reduce to share-weighted averages of coefficients times the aggregate variable. Thus, equation (4) will have the form of (3).

A difficulty with the above approach, of course, is that the share-weighted averages which are estimated are specific to the sample. Nevertheless, for some purposes this may not be a problem. For instance, the share-weighted average of income coefficients will be positive if all individual-level coefficients are. Thus, a test of the hypothesis that this coefficient is positive may be as appropriate as would a test of the hypothesis that the unweighted average is positive.

In any case, it seems plausible that as sample-size (N) grows, the weighted average coefficients should become more 'representative'. Theil (1971, ch. 11) has made this notion more precise by combining the two types of arguments made above. Once again, consider the income term for illustrative purposes. The following relationship is always true:

$$\frac{1}{N} \sum_{i=1}^{N} \gamma_i I_{it} = \sum_{i=1}^{N} \gamma_i S_{it} \bar{I}_t$$
$$= \bar{\gamma}\, \bar{I}_t + [\sum_{i=1}^{N} (S_{it} - \frac{1}{N})\ (\gamma_i - \bar{\gamma})]\ \bar{I}_t. \tag{10}$$

The term in brackets is N times the sample covariance between income shares and income coefficients.[3] Theil shows that if income shares and income coefficients are stochastically independent, then the coefficient of average income converges to $\bar{\gamma}$, the average of the individual parameters, as group-size (N) increases. Theil's result also holds if the level of income is stochastically independent of coefficients.[4]

For practical purposes, the important conclusions of the preceding analysis are as follows. (i) If there is no relationship between levels or shares of variables and the corresponding coefficients, then the coefficients of the aggregate relationship will be equal to (or will converge to, depending upon the exact assumptions) the group-averages of the individual-level coefficients. (ii) Even if there is such a relationship, if the shares are fixed then the aggregate coefficients will be equal to (or will converge to) the share-weighted average of the individual-level coefficients. In either case, OLS applied to the aggregate equation will provide unbiased (or consistent, depending upon the exact assumptions) estimators of the appropriate averages of the individual-level coefficients, as long as the independent variables are fixed or are uncorrelated with the error term.

Simultaneity bias

At the individual level, prices and perhaps income can plausibly be taken to be exogenous. Specifically, this means that the level of any individual's Y (e.g. fertility) will not have any effect on these variables. Thus, the assumptions of the standard linear model may be satisfied, and OLS will then provide unbiased estimators. The analysis of linear aggregation has proceeded so far on the assumption that the same thing is true at the aggregate level. This is far from an innocuous assumption. Indeed, for standard goods it is well known that prices are endogenous at the aggregate level, given that prices and aggregate quantities are determined by the equilibrium of market demand and supply. This leads to the well-known problem of simultaneity bias.

Nevertheless, the preceding analysis of aggregation bias still can be applied directly. Specifically, if the assumptions for consistent aggregation hold, then the coefficients of (3) will equal the appropriate average of the micro-level coefficients (at least in large samples). Given this, the issues of identification and estimation in the presence of simultaneity bias arise in the standard way and can be dealt with as usual.[5]

In any case, it is not obvious that simultaneity bias is always important in aggregate fertility equations. The important prices in such equations are wage rates and perhaps the prices of food, shelter, etc., and it could in some circumstances be argued that fertility in each period does not have causal effects on such prices, and also that it does not affect income. For instance, with respect to wage rates, it is likely that current fertility will affect the labour supply of some women. However, if this effect is small relative to total labour supply, then wages may not be affected. If this is the case, then wage rates can be treated as exogenous. Similar arguments might apply to income and other prices as well, in some situations.

Robinson's ecological fallacy argument

One of the most influential arguments concerning the use of aggregate data has been that of W. S. Robinson (1950). His article on the 'ecological fallacy' consisted primarily of a demonstration and a warning. He demonstrated that the simple correlation between two (specific) individual-level variables (denote this by $r_{\bar{x}\bar{y}}$) was smaller than the correlation between the corresponding aggregate ('ecological') variables $(r_{\bar{x}\bar{y}})$. He thus warned against the use of aggregate data to draw inferences about individual behaviour. Hanushek *et al.* (1972) state that: 'Robinson's article has been widely interpreted to demonstrate conclusively that: (i) aggregate (ecological) data are unsuitable for analyses of individual and household behaviour, and (ii) statistics estimated with individual or micro data are unambiguously better' (pp. 1, 2).

The issue raised by Robinson is, in fact, quite different than the issue of being able to obtain unbiased estimates of the parameters of an aggregate demand relationship such as (3). That is, he was concerned with the effect of aggregation on correlation coefficients rather than on regression coefficients. Correlation coefficients measure both the slope and the dispersion of a joint distribution, while regression coefficients measure only the slope. Thus, it is possible for correlation coefficients to vary dramatically over levels of aggregation, even though regression coefficients do not vary.[6]

For individual-level variables,

$$r_{yx} = b_{yx} \frac{S_x}{S_y},$$ (11)

where b_{yx} is the regression coefficient of y on x, r_{yx} is the correlation coefficient between y and x, and S_x and S_y are the sample standard deviations of x and y, respectively. The corresponding relationship for aggregate data is

$$r_{\bar{y}\bar{x}} = b_{\bar{y}\bar{x}} \frac{S_{\bar{x}}}{S_{\bar{y}}}.$$ (12)

The grouping of variables is often done in a way that maximises the between-group variance of the dependent variable y. If so, the standard deviation $S_{\bar{y}}$ may exceed S_y by more than $S_{\bar{x}}$ exceeds S_x. Thus, $r_{\bar{y}\bar{x}}$ will tend to exceed r_{yx} on these grounds alone, and this effect has no bearing on the relationship between the regression coefficients. Thus, Robinson's discussion really sheds no light on the issue of estimating an aggregate relationship such as (3).

Viewed in a slightly different way, the increase in the size of the correlation coefficient simply reflects the well-known fact that R^2s tend to increase when aggregate data are used (see Johnston, 1972, pp. 228-32). The R^2 is the square of the correlation coefficient between y and the estimated value of y, and in the case of just one independent variable, x, this is equivalent to the simple correlation between y and x.

Errors in variables

In the discussion of linear aggregation, it was assumed that all independent variables were measured without error. However, measurement problems are undoubtedly common when use is made of sample surveys. Consequently, it may be that estimators from such samples are seriously biased (see, for instance, Johnston, 1972), for a discussion of errors-in-variables bias). However, if it is the case that measurement errors are not systematically related to the groups used for aggregation, so that the errors 'average out' within groups, then aggregate regressions will be (asymptotically) free of such bias.[7] Thus, the existence of errors-in-variables bias at the individual level can constitute an argument in favour of using aggregate data. This point was made by Friedman (1957).

Omitted variables

Important variables are often unavailable in both aggregate data and in surveys of individuals, and it is difficult to say anything in general about the relative severity of this problem in these two situations. However, individual-level data do have one important advantage in this respect. Aggregation by reducing numerous pieces of information to a single sum may involve a drastic reduction in degrees of freedom. Thus, even if all the important aggregate variables are available, some may have to be dropped because of a lack of degrees of freedom for estimation of the parameters. In some situations, the bias induced by such omitted variables may be far more serious than aggregation bias *per se.*

Aggregation v. pooling

Given a true model such as (2), three estimation procedures can be distinguished: (i) estimation of a single aggregate relationship, as has been discussed, (ii) estimation of a single individual-level relationship, using pooled data for all individuals, and (iii) estimation of separate relationships for each individual. Implicit in some discussions in the literature is the assumption that the appropriate alternative to aggregate estimation is pooled, individual-level estimation. This is incorrect. Such a procedure will also yield biased estimators in general. This type of bias, and the circumstances in which it will not exist, are most commonly discussed in the literature in the context of models in which only the constant term varies over individuals (see especially Mundlak, 1979). In the context of model (3), it is always appropriate, of course, to estimate separate relationships for each individual (i.e. using the time-series of observations for each individual).[8]

Theoretical Issues

The focus of theoretical discussions of aggregation in the literature is somewhat different than is the focus of econometric discussions. Instead of investigating the circumstances in which aggregate coefficients will be an appropriate average of individual-level coefficients, the theoretical literature tends to focus on investigating the circumstances in which aggregate data will behave as though they were generated by a single, utility-maximising consumer. It is possible, as will be noted below, for aggregate data to have this property but for the aggregate relationship to bear no particular relationship to individual behaviour. However, there are assumptions, paralleling those made in linear statistical aggregation, which will ensure that aggregate relationships not only can be 'integrated' (i.e. generated by utility-maximisation), but also will appropriately reflect average individual behaviour.

Aggregate data act as though they are generated by maximisation of a utility function $U(\overline{Y}_1, \ldots, \overline{Y}_k)$ subject to the aggregate budget constraint ($\sum_i P_i \overline{Y}_i = \overline{I}$) if and only if: (i) aggregate demand is a function of prices and of aggregate income, $\overline{I}$; (ii) aggregate demand is homogeneous of degree zero in income and price; and (iii) the matrix of income-compensated price effects (i.e. the Hicks–Slutsky substitution matrix) is symmetric and negative semi-definite. Three different types of situations in which aggregate demand functions will satisfy these three conditions are discussed in the literature. These situations are discussed below in turn.

Identical individuals and identical constraints
In this situation, all individuals have identical demand functions and identical variables. Aggregate (per capita) demand is identical to every individual's demand, and there is no problem of aggregation. (Aggregate demand satisfies the three conditions since every individual's demand does.) This situation corresponds to the model with identical parameters and identical variables discussed in the context of linear statistical aggregation. However, linearity is not required here for consistent aggregation.

The required assumptions in this situation are highly restrictive. Nevertheless, Varian (1981) has argued that these assumptions might hold to a reasonable degree of approximation when aggregate behaviour is dominated by a large middle class with similar tastes and incomes.

Samuelson's condition
Samuelson (1956) showed that aggregate data will act as though they are generated by a single individual maximising a utility function subject to the aggregate budget constraint, if it is the case that there are lump-sum transfers made among individuals so as to maximise some concave objective function. For instance, the government may redistribute income in such a way as to maximise its social-welfare function. A variant of this argument has been used in the economic theory of fertility (see, for instance, Willis, 1973), to justify treating the family as a single maximising unit. Varian (1981) has extended Samuelson's argument to show that lumsum transfers are not required. Any set of instruments (taxes, subsidies, rationing, quotas, etc.) which can be used to affect individual behaviour, and thus allow some concave social-welfare function to be maximised, will work just as well.

It is important to note that under these conditions, aggregate demand will reflect the government's 'tastes', not individuals'. Aggregate demand will satisfy the three conditions noted above, but there need be no particular relationship between aggregate demand and individual demand. Indeed, it appears that it would be possible for aggregate demand to be 'rational' even though individual demand is not.

The Gorman–Lau conditions

The third set of conditions is more diverse than the other two. In general, this third set of conditions is derived from a consideration of the class of demand functions which can be both aggregated and integrated (i.e. generated by utility-maximisation).

The seminal work in this area is that by Gorman (1953). He investigated the class of demand functions which, when aggregated, yield a function of aggregate income. That is, he investigated the class of functions for which

$$\sum_i Y_i (P, I_i) = \overline{Y}_i (P, \overline{I}). \tag{13}$$

He showed that the only demand functions which satisfy this restriction (for all values of income) have the form

$$Y_i (P, I_i) = a(P)I_i + b_i(P), \tag{14}$$

where $a(P)$ is some function of P which does not vary among individuals, while $b_i(P)$ can vary. Note that the linear demand function (without 'X' variables, which will be discussed below) is of this type. More complicated functions are allowed as well. (For instance, $b_i(P)$ could be the sum of the logarithms of price, interactions of prices, etc.) The basic principle here is the same one encountered in the discussion of linear statistical aggregation. Since income can vary over individuals, it must have a coefficient which does not vary. Prices do not vary over individuals, and so the income coefficient is allowed to be a function of prices. There can also be a separate function of price which differs among individuals.

Gorman also showed that demand functions of the form of (14) can be generated by an indirect utility function of the form[9]

$$V_i(P, I_i) = A(P)I_i + B_i(P) \tag{15}$$

Thus, 'Gorman' functions are acceptable demand functions, satisfying the three required conditions. In addition, indirect utility functions of the

'Gorman' form can be aggregated to yield an aggregate utility function which is a function of aggregate income:

$$\sum_i V_i(P, I_i) = \overline{V}(P, \overline{I}) \tag{16}$$

(since the functional form of (15) satisfies the required aggregation conditions).

Finally, this aggregate indirect utility function will generate (by Roy's identity) the aggregate of the demand functions. Thus, the following result holds: demand functions can be aggregated consistently if they have the 'Gorman' form, and the resulting aggregate demand functions satisfy the three conditions for behaving as though they were generated by a single, utility-maximising individual. Furthermore, the aggregate (per capita) functions represent the appropriate average of the individual-level functions.

Variables other than price and income (i.e. the 'X' variables, which are often referred to in the theoretical aggregation literature as 'attribute' variables) can be introduced into the demand functions with no difficulty (see Lau, 1977a). The general form of the demand function is then

$$Y_i(P, I_i, X_i) = a(P)I_i + b_i(P) + C(P, X_i). \tag{17}$$

This function can be integrated and aggregated, and the aggregate can be integrated. The function $C(P, X_i)$ must be the same for all individuals, since the X_i are allowed to vary over individuals. There is no restriction that aggregate demand be a function of aggregate X_i, so it is not required that this function take the form of the sum of constant coefficients (across individuals) times the X variables (as is required in the case of income). However, aggregate demand must be a function of an additive index of individual attributes (i.e. $\sum_i C(P, X_i)$). Thus, aggregate demand in per capita terms can be a function of average education but not of median education. Alternatively, aggregate demand can be a function of the fraction of the population over age 65 (let $C(A_i) = 1$ if $A_i > 65$, 0 otherwise, where A_i denotes age), and separately of the fraction under age 15, but not of the ratio of those above 65 to those below 15 (see Lau, 1977b). (However, it can be a function of the proportion of the population above age 65 and below 15, since this can be generated by an additive function.)

The standard linear demand function thus satisfies the conditions for consistent statistical and theoretical aggregation, as long as the coefficients of income and of the attribute variables, X, are the same for all individuals.

The coefficients of price can vary. Note that there is thus no requirement, contrary to what is often asserted in the literature, that 'tastes' (i.e. utility functions) be the same for all individuals. Utility functions are allowed to differ to the extent that the coefficients of price (in both the indirect utility functions and the demand functions) can differ. It is true that this still implies strong restrictions on the way in which utility functions can differ among individuals. However, it is important to note that these restrictions apply *only to individuals with identical attributes*, since utility and demand are allowed to be functions of attributes. Clearly, this represents an enormous relaxation of the restriction that 'tastes' be identical among individuals.

It is sometimes asserted in the literature (see, for instance, Lau, 1977a; Shafer and Sonnenschein, 1981) that consistent theoretical aggregation required that individuals have identical, homothetic utility functions. This assertion arises when an additional restriction to those made above is placed upon demand functions. Specifically, if it is required that demand be zero when income is zero, then the terms $b_i(P)$ and $C(P, X_i)$ in (17) must be identically zero. Consequently, individual demand must have the form

$$Y_i(P, I_i, X_i) = a(P)I_i, \tag{18}$$

with a corresponding indirect utility function of the form

$$V_i(P, I_i, X_i) = A(P)I_i.$$

These utility functions are homothetic, and are identical across individuals. The 'zero' restriction is an implication of standard demand theory (since an individual's feasible set is the origin when income is zero). However, it seems to us that for practical purposes this is an unnecessarily strong restriction, if what we seek is a function which adequately represents demand over the range of typically observed incomes. As has been seen, when this restriction is relaxed, demand functions, and therefore utility, need no longer be either identical among individuals or homothetic.

The Gorman-Lau results just discussed seem to us to constitute the most important of the results in the literature on theoretical aggregation, at least from the point of view of applications to economic demography. However, these results can be extended in several ways, and it is worth noting them. Most importantly, at least some of the results of aggregation with coefficients and variables which are uncorrelated, or are distributed independently (as discussed in the context of statistical aggregation), carry over directly. We know of no discussions of this type in the literature, but the analysis is straightforward. Consider the linear model (2), with coefficients which vary over individuals. For every given individual (i.e. for any specific set of coefficients), this model is of the Gorman form and, thus, can be generated by utility-maximisation. If the coefficients are uncorrelated with (or are stochastically independent of) the levels or shares of the corresponding variables, then the aggregate equation will have the form of (or will converge to, depending upon the exact assumptions) equation (3). The coefficients of the aggregate equation will equal the averages of the individual-level coefficients. Most importantly, the aggregate equation also has the Gorman form, and thus can be generated by utility-maximisation. This constitutes an additional and substantial relaxation of the condition that individuals have identical tastes.

Chipman (1974) has analysed theoretical aggregation under the assumption that income shares are fixed for all individuals. This analysis, for the most part, parallels the discussion we have given for linear statistical aggregation with fixed shares and, thus, is not discussed here. Finally, Muellbaur (1975, 1976) and Lau (1977b) have analysed aggregation when the restriction is relaxed that aggregate demand be a function of aggregate income. Instead, they allow aggregate demand to be a function of more complicated indexes of income. Aggregate demand can no longer be generated by aggregate utility-maximisation, but they show that it can be generated by a function which is the sum of individuals' indirect utility functions, and which shares many of the properties of a true indirect utility function.

Summary

As a means of summarising the econometric and theoretical results on aggregation of structural demand functions, we shall review the conditions which are required for the consistent statistical and theoretical aggregation of the type of linear model (2) which is commonly formulated and estimated. The most comprehensive result seems to be: if individual-level coefficients are independent of the level or shares of the corresponding variables, then aggregate coefficients will be equal to (or will converge to as group-size increases, depending upon the exact assumptions) the average of individual-level coefficients. The aggregate relationship will satisfy all of the conditions imposed by utility-maximisation. It is not required that tastes (as represented by the coefficients) be identical across individuals, or that individuals have the same income and attributes, although it is required that the coefficients not be systematically related to the levels (or shares) of the variables. Even if coefficients are systematically related to the corresponding variables, if shares are fixed then the aggregate coefficients can still be interpreted as share-weighted averages of the individual-level coefficients. Under these conditions, the aggregate relationship will still have the Gorman form, and will still satisfy the conditions for utility-maximisation. In any case, as long as the true aggregate relationship has the form of (3) (fixed coefficients times the aggregate variables), then OLS will be an appropriate estimation procedure if the independent variables are uncorrelated with the error term. In the presence of simultaneity or other source of correlation of independent variables and the error term, then the standard results concerning identification and estimation apply.

Whether or not the above conditions should be considered to be highly restrictive depends to some extent on one's point of view. However, it seems to us that they are likely enough to be satisfied, or closely approximated, in typical situations, to justify the common practice of treating estimates of aggregate structural relationships as appropriate reflections of underlying individual-level behaviour.[10]

THE ESTIMATION AND INTERPRETATION OF REDUCED FORMS

Introduction

In the first section of this chapter, we discussed the general issue of estimating and interpreting structural demand (e.g. fertility) functions, given aggregate data. In this second section, we discuss the estimation and interpretation of other types of relationships. These other types of relationships can generically be thought of as 'reduced' forms, though we use this term somewhat loosely. These relationships contain quite different information than is contained in structural demand functions, and thus answer different questions. The theoretical and econometric issues involved correspondingly differ from those involved in the estimation of structural demand functions. Discussion of these issues in the literature (in the context of aggregation) is limited. Consequently, all we attempt to do in this section is to point out the general type of issue involved, to consider some circumstances in which it might arise, and to sketch some of the theoretical and econometric considerations which arise in the use of aggregate v. individual-level data in this context.

Structural demand functions, at both the individual and the aggregate level, describe behaviour as a function of prices, income and 'attributes'. The term 'attributes' here denotes individual-specific variables such as education, religion, family background, rural/urban residence, etc., as well as group- or society-specific variables such as government policy instruments (taxes, subsidies, rationing constraints, quotas, etc.) and perhaps others (as will be discussed below). Structural demand functions at the individual level, and sometimes at the aggregate level (as has been discussed) can be used to test the predictions of micro-economic theory. Regardless of the theoretical underpinnings, these functions yield the partial derivatives of the effects of the independent variables on the dependent variable holding constant the other independent variables. Thus, such relationships can be used to predict, for instance, the effect of income or of a government policy when prices and the remaining independent variables are fixed.

While such effects are of interest, we typically want to know more. That is, we typically want to predict the total effect of the income change or the policy, allowing all variables to adjust. These total effects are the sum of the partial direct effects given by the structural demand function and the indirect effects which arise when variables which are endogenous to the socio-economic system change. Depending upon the geographic and time-frame of the analysis, some or all prices may be endogenous, as may be some of the attributes such as individuals' levels of education, places of residence, and so on. These total effects[11] correspond to the partial derivatives of the appropriate reduced-form functions. When such total effects are desired, structural demand functions (and the corresponding micro theory) do not tell us what we want to know.

There appear to be two general types of circumstances in which total effects will differ from partial effects. The first arises when structural demand functions form part of a general equilibrium set of equations describing the behaviour of the entire socio-economic system. The second arises when aggregate variables enter directly into individual-level functions. These two circumstances are discussed below, in turn.

Reduced Forms of a General Equilibrium System

In standard general equilibrium analysis, the demand functions of individuals form one part of a system of equations in which prices and thus incomes are endogenous. It is possible to extend this type of model, at least in principle, to one in which some of the attributes of individuals (e.g. education, location) are endogenous (or alternatively their 'prices' could be treated as endogenous; the exact formulation of such a model is not important for our discussion). The reduced form(s) of such a model produces the total effects which we desire to estimate.

Such reduced forms are inherently aggregate. No issue of a correspondence between aggregate and individual-level reduced forms arises, because such individual-level relationships do not exist. It is true, of course, that some of the restrictions on individual-level and aggregate structural equations may carry over to aggregate reduced forms. The most important of these seem likely to be restrictions on functional form (specifically, if aggregate demand must be a function of all individuals' attributes, rather than of average attributes, then in general reduced forms must be also), though this issue does not appear to have been examined in any detail in the literature. There may also be some restrictions on aggregate reduced forms that must be satisfied if the underlying system is generated by utility- and profit-maximising households and firms, but, to the extent that anything is known about them, such restrictions appear to be weak.[12] The important point for our purposes is that aggregated data are essential for obtaining reduced forms. Even if we had individual-level data, and could estimate all of the individual-level structural equations of the general equilibrium system, it would still be necessary to aggregate those relationships to obtain the reduced forms. Given current knowledge, direct estimation of the reduced forms using aggregate data appears to be an appropriate procedure.

Reduced Forms when there are Individual-level Effects of Aggregate Variables

The hypothesis that aggregate variables may have direct effects on individual behaviour is common in sociology, where such phenomena are referred to as 'contextual' effects (see, for example, Hammond, 1973). This hypothesis is less common in economic analysis. However, labour economists sometimes include 'market variables' in individual-level equations in an attempt, for instance, to capture information about market constraints which is not completely transmitted by current, measured prices and incomes (see, for example, Nakamura *et al.*, 1979). In economic demography, Leibenstein's (1975a) theory of fertility might be interpreted as predicting that group income will have an effect on individual fertility over and above that of individual income. A similar effect seems implied by Duesenberry's (1949) relative income hypothesis. Regardless of their source, when such phenomena exist there will be a difference between partial and total effects even in the absence of general equilibrium considerations.

Imagine that average group income $(\overline{I})$ has a direct causal effect on individual fertility (Y), over and above the effect of individual income.

Then the true causal equation for the ith individual in year t is

$$Y_{it} = \alpha_1 I_{it} + \alpha_2 (\bar{I}_t) + X_{it}\beta + \epsilon_{it}, \tag{20}$$

where all variables are in mean deviations so that the constant is suppressed, $\bar{I}$ denotes average group income, and prices have been included among the X variables. The coefficients α_1, α_2 and β are assumed not to vary among individuals. Alternatively, they could be allowed to vary, but they could be assumed to be stochastically independent of the corresponding variables. This function can be generated by utility-maximisation, with an indirect utility function of the Gorman form discussed in the subsection on theoretical issues, and with $(\bar{I}_t)$ treated as an attribute variable. The coefficient α_1 gives the effect on Y of changing the income of a single individual, holding average income fixed, and corresponds to the conventional income effect of micro-economic theory. This parameter, plus the others, can be unbiasedly and consistently estimated by OLS at the individual level under the standard assumptions. When incomes of all individuals are changed by the same amount, the total effect of income (assuming no general equilibrium effect) is given by $\alpha_1 + \alpha_2$. Thus, both the partial and the total effects can be estimated from individual-level data in this model.

This model satisfies all of the conditions for consistent theoretical and statistical aggregation. However, in the aggregate it is no longer possible to distinguish between α_1, the effect of income acting through the budget constraint, and α_2, the effect of average income acting as an attribute. Specifically, the aggregate of (20) is

$$\bar{Y}_t = (\alpha_1 + \alpha_2) \bar{I}_t + \bar{X}_t\beta + \bar{\epsilon}_t. \tag{21}$$

This equation is, in effect, an aggregate reduced form. Assuming no simultaneity bias problems, or assuming that such problems can be dealt with by instrumental variable estimation, then the parameters can be estimated consistently. However, the coefficient of income cannot be interpreted as the simple effect of shifting the individual's budget constraint.[13]

An alternative model with some of the same characteristics is one in which the average value of fertility ($\bar{Y}$) has a direct causal effect on individual fertility. This situation might arise, for instance, if individual fertility were affected by group norms concerning fertility, and if group norms were a function of average group fertility. Then the individual-level equation for fertility would be

$$Y_{it} = \alpha I_{it} + \gamma(\bar{Y}_t) + X_{it}\beta + \epsilon_{it}, \tag{22}$$

where prices and attribute variables (including, perhaps, average income) are included among the X_{it}. Even though the error term, ϵ_{it}, must be correlated in small samples with average fertility ($\bar{Y}_t$), it can be shown that if the X_{it} are uncorrelated with all ϵ_{it} in large samples, and if the ϵ_{it} of different individuals are not correlated, then OLS will produce consistent estimators of the parameters of this equation. (The intuition is simple: in large samples an individual's error term will not be correlated with average fertility.)

This model can be generated by individual utility-maximisation, with (Y_t) treated as an attribute variable, and it can also be aggregated consistently, with the aggregate also generated by utility-maximisation. However, as in the previous model, the coefficient of aggregate income cannot be interpreted as measuring the partial (or micro) effect of income (and the same is true for the coefficients of prices and attributes as well). Specifically, when (22) is aggregated, the result is

$$\bar{Y} = \alpha \bar{I} + \gamma \bar{Y} + \bar{X}\beta + \bar{\epsilon},\tag{23}$$

which can be solved to yield the reduced form

$$\bar{Y} = \frac{\alpha}{1-\gamma}\,\bar{I} + \bar{X}\,(\beta\,\frac{1}{1-\gamma}) + \bar{\epsilon}.\tag{24}$$

Thus, it would be possible for the true macro effect of income $\left(\dfrac{\alpha}{1-\gamma}\right)$ to be negative even if the true micro effect (α) were positive.

A major implication of these two examples is that when aggregate variables enter individual-level equations, the desired total effects can be estimated using aggregate data, so long as the previously-discussed assumptions for consistent aggregation of structural demand functions are satisfied. At the same time, another implication is that the estimated effects in aggregate relationships can no longer be used to test the implications of micro-economic theory, even when the assumptions for consistent aggregation of structural demand functions are satisfied.

Summary

When the objective is to estimate total rather than partial effects, then the desired functions will be reduced form rather than structural equations. Two very different types of situations have been considered, in which a distinction between total and partial effects can arise.

In the first, structural functions form part of a general equilibrium set of equations describing the behaviour of the entire socio-economic system. Indirect effects then arise, which are added to the direct partial effects in order to obtain the desired total effects. Aggregation is necessary, since these effects can be derived only from aggregate reduced forms. No issue of a correspondence between aggregate and individual relationships arises. Furthermore, in standard economic models, there appear to be few restrictions imposed by underlying micro behaviour on aggregate reduced-form functions. Thus, for the most part, the issues of aggregation bias which arise in the context of structural equations do not arise here.

In the second of the situations considered, aggregate variables enter directly into individual-level structural equations. A distinction between total and partial effects then arises, even in the absence of general equilibrium effects. In the two examples considered, both partial and total effects can be estimated consistently from individual-level data, and the total effects can be estimated using aggregate data. When such effects exist, the coefficients of the aggregate relationship do not have the same interpretation as the corresponding individual-level relationship, even if the standard problems of aggregation bias do not arise.

CONCLUSION

It is important to distinguish between structural and reduced forms (i.e. between total and partial effects) in considering the problems which may arise in the use of aggregate data. Most of the literature concerning aggregation pertains only to the estimation of structural relationships. The general conclusion of our survey of this literature is that the problems encountered in using aggregate data for structural estimation are not as great as is commonly presumed. In any case, it is often the case that the questions posed by analysis require estimation of reduced forms rather than structural equations. If so, then the types of problems commonly discussed in the literature (in the context of structural estimation) may not arise at all. When reduced forms of general equilibrium systems are desired, then aggregation is required at some stage of the analysis, even if individual-level data are available. There appear to be no major problems with direct use of aggregate data to estimate the necessary reduced forms. When a difference between total and partial effects arises because aggregate variables enter individual-level structural equations, then both total and partial effects (in the examples we considered) can be estimated using individual-level data. However, total effects can be estimated directly by using aggregate data, and aggregate relationships cannot be used to test the implications of micro-economic theory.

It is not possible to give any blanket recommendations concerning the use of aggregate data. The problems encountered vary greatly with the circumstances and, most importantly, with the types of questions the analyst seeks to answer. However, our overall conclusion is that aggregate data are much more useful than they are often given credit for being.

NOTES

1. Fixed regressors along with $E(\epsilon_{it}) = 0$ will insure that OLS is unbiased. Alternatively, independence of regressors and error terms ensures unbiasedness. Lack of correlation between regressors and the contemporaneous error terms ensures consistency but not unbiasedness.
2. Strictly speaking, all that is required is that the sum over all variables of the covariance terms must be zero. Thus, there could be a non-zero covariance between income and its coefficient if this were offset by the covariances between other variables and their coefficients.
3. Comparison of equations (10) and (7) shows that this term is also equal to the sample covariance between level of income and the income coefficients.
4. Stochastic independence of levels and coefficients implies stochastic independence of shares and coefficients, but the converse is not true. Thus, independence of shares and coefficients is the weaker assumption, and Theil shows it is sufficient to give consistent aggregation in the sense already given.
5. However, it may be the case that there exist consistent estimators of the aggregate equation, in the presence of simultaneity bias, even if the assumptions for consistent aggregation do not hold. We know of no discussions of this in the literature, but consider a simple model in which income is the only independent variable. As noted, this aggregate equation can always be written as

$$\bar{Y}_t = \bar{\gamma}\,\bar{I}_t + [\sum_i (S_{it} - \frac{1}{N})\,(\gamma - \bar{\gamma})]\,\bar{I}_t + \bar{\epsilon}_t = \bar{\gamma}\,\bar{I}_t + \phi_t + \bar{\epsilon}_t,$$

where ϕ is as implicitly defined. Consistent estimation of $\bar{\gamma}$ will be possible if there exists an instrumental variable, Z_t, which is correlated with $\bar{I}_t$ but not with ϕ or ϵ_t. Such an instrument may exist even if the assumptions for consistent aggregation (e.g. plim $\phi_t = 0$) do not hold. This is true even though ϕ_t is the product of $\bar{I}_t$ and another variable.
6. This was pointed out by Goodman (1953, 1959).
7. Formally speaking, aggregation can be viewed as an instrumental variables procedure which will produce consistent estimators.

8. When repeated observations are not available for individuals, then this is, of course, not possible. This would be the case, for instance, when the individual-level data consist of a single cross-section, and aggregates are formed by grouping within states, cities, countries, etc.

9. An indirect utility function is derived by substituting demand functions into the direct utility function:

$$V_i(P, I_i) \equiv U_i \left[Y_{i1} (P, I_i), \ldots, Y_{ik} (P, I_i) \right].$$

Given an indirect utility function, demand functions can be derived by using Roy's identity:

$$Y_{ik} (P, I_i) = - \left[\frac{\partial V_i / \partial P_k}{\partial V_i / \partial I_i} \right] .$$

10. This conclusion has to be modified somewhat when aggregate variables enter individual-level demand functions, as is discussed in the second section.

11. This terminology obviously leaves something to be desired, since there are many possible 'total' effects, each corresponding to a different 'reduced' form, and thus to holding constant a different set of variables. Nevertheless, this terminology seems sufficiently informative for our purposes, and it seems preferable not to complicate the discussion too much.

12. The only studies of this issue that we are aware of are those by Hotelling (1932), Edlefsen (1981) and, indirectly, by Sonnenschein (1974).

13. This illustrates Leibenstein's (1975a) contention that the overall effect of income might be negative (i.e. if $\alpha_1 + \alpha_2 < 0$) even if the 'true' income effect is positive ($\alpha_1 > 0$). In Leibenstein's theory, the groups are not time-periods, as we have represented them here. However, that does not affect the basic argument.

8 Specification and Estimation of Models of Fertility

BOONE A. TURCHI

INTRODUCTION

In the past two decades, human fertility has become a subject of active concern to economic development planners and administrators throughout the Third World. It is widely agreed – although, some would argue, on the basis of relatively little evidence – that lower fertility rates would, in many cases, lead to a more rapid rate of economic and social development. This view has led to a growing emphasis on treating fertility-reduction policies as integral components of a nation's overall development strategy. Consequently, recent years have witnessed a new concern in the Third World and in donor nations with the introduction of programmes that will lead to lower aggregate fertility rates. Moreover, as the competition for scarce public development resources has intensified, more attention has been paid to the assessment of the productivity of these programmes relative to other socio-economic development projects.

The most common policy approach thus far applied has been *supply-oriented*. It has been assumed that the actual number of children born far exceeds the number that parents would have desired had they had available the means to control their fertility effectively. Under this assumption, the appropriate policy response has been viewed to be that policy which institutes programmes designed to supply the means of family limitation as cheaply, effectively and comprehensively as possible; hence the emphasis in the past decade on family-planning programmes, sterilisation clinics and abortion services.

In the face of the mixed success of these supply-side programmes, and because of the growing requirement that fertility policy be cost effective *vis-à-vis* other development programmes, the case can be made that a more comprehensive approach to fertility policy is desirable and necessary. This more comprehensive approach would include analysis of the determinants of the demand for children, and it might lead, in turn, to a more general interest in the manner in which socio-economic development policy now affects the demand for children, and the ways in which public programmes that are not specifically fertility-oriented might be altered to have a greater impact upon that demand. The kind of fertility research required by this new emphasis will be much more policy-oriented than previously, and the need for policy-relevance will have important consequences for that research.

This chapter assesses the implications for fertility research of a new emphasis on policy-relevance. It examines the problem of theory-development, model-specification and statistical-estimation in the context of policy-oriented research and attempts to offer guidance to those undertaking such research. In the remainder of this section, the importance of undertaking *causal* analyses of fertility is stressed, the problems introduced because of a necessary reliance upon non-experimental data are examined, and the essential role of theory in fertility research is emphasised. The second section sketches a theory of fertility that will serve as a basis for discussion in the following sections, and the third section treats the statistical problems inherent in analysing causal models with non-experimental data.

Causal Analysis and Fertility Research

At the outset, it is desirable to establish the connection between 'policy-relevant' fertility research and 'causal analysis'. Fertility research will be relevant to the policy process (i) if it assists in the precise identification of policy *targets*, and (ii) if it identifies policy *instruments* that make the most efficient use possible of scarce public resources. Ilchman (1975, p. 16) puts the requirements of policy-relevant fertility research quite well:

> To be useful to policymakers, the knowledge of the correlates of fertility should instruct those who must make choices, with or without such guidance, about their policy interventions: who might be the objects of intervention, what degree of change might be achieved by how much and what kind of resources, what methods of intervening make what difference to the outcome, how long the intervention should last until the behaviour is self-sustaining in enough people, what are the costs of intervention from the point of view of those who are the objects of intervention and the benefits to those who provide the means of intervening, whether enough resources are available publicly to achieve the purpose, and whether too many or not enough resources

are available to the objects of the intervention so that the desired behavior might not be forthcoming.

Clearly, the research described here as being policy-relevant is also causal research; it identifies those factors that, if altered, will directly lead to a change in the behaviour under study. Descriptive or correlational analyses of fertility are not sufficient to meet the needs of policy-relevant fertility research where explicit causal hypotheses must be formulated and tested.

This is not the place to attempt a precise definition of causation.[1] Instead, let us merely apply the functional notation

$$y = f(x, z)$$

to signify a causal relationship in which an effect variable (say a fertility indicator) is capable of being altered by cause variables x and z. Empirically, another variable, w, may be found to be historically associated with y without being a causal variable. For policy purposes, this association may, therefore, be irrelevant and/or misleading.

Causation in the natural sciences is often inferred as the outcome of carefully controlled experiments in which the effect of one variable on another can be isolated. In addition, the experiment that demonstrates a causal relationship between two variables is capable of repetition, a feature that allows confirmation of research findings by other scientists.

The controlled experiment 'is, in fact, nothing but a systematic way of collecting experience, and from a logical point of view the causal notions involved are of the same type as those which are all-pervading even in the earliest stages of prescientific experience, for example, "the water will boil if you put it over the fire" or "the crop will be larger if you manure the soil"' (Wold, 1954, p.166). However, the availability of controlled experiments is an advantage statistically, often allowing the application of simple techniques such as regression or analysis of variance.

In non-experimental situations such as fertility analysis, the researcher often has little or no control over how the data are collected, and the careful and often complex controls that can be applied in experimental situations are not available. Often, therefore, we find non-experimental data being analysed by statistical methods that are considerably more complex and difficult to apply than those commonly used in experimental research. Non-experimental data often are weak,[2] collinear and not precisely congruent with the underlying theory guiding the analysis. Consequently, social scientists often find themselves applying sophisticated statistical procedures to data of dubious quality and relevance.

The Role of Theory in the Modelling Process

Substantive theory plays a much more central role in non-experimental statistical research. In statistical inference proper, the model is given and not questioned. It is assumed that the variables included in the analysis, the functional forms applied, and the data-generation process are all proper and appropriate to the statistical procedure being employed. In non-experimental data analysis, these assumptions cannot be supported, and the primary issue is the specification of the causal hypothesis. This is fundamentally a problem of the substantive subject-matter theory, not of statistics. To avoid the misinterpretation and biases that arise in non-experimental statistical analysis, the subject-matter theory must be closely coordinated with that analysis. Thus, theory helps the non-experimental researcher to determine what variables need to be collected, how they ought to be grouped, which observations might not be generated by the process under study (i.e. identification of outliers), and what form the causal hypotheses might take. Finally, rigorous attempts to theorise are essential in non-experimental data analysis in order to establish criteria for choosing among competing theories. Because of the lack of controls and precise measurement in non-experimental data, careful theorising must be applied in order to allow the data to assist in the choice among competing theories.

SOME THEORETICAL CONSIDERATIONS

Because theory and estimation are so intimately related in non-experimental research, it is worthwhile devoting some effort to the development of a theoretical context that will serve as the basis for discussion in the following sections. Our theoretical approach will be that of the micro-economic theory of fertility, variants of which have been described and criticised in Chapters 3 and 4. Since our interest is in the estimation problems associated with empirical models of fertility behaviour, the choice of a prototype theory is not particularly critical, and the reader may wish to substitute his own theory in the following section.

The underlying axioms of behaviour that motivate the micro-economic model essentially state that individuals faced with limited resources, attempt to allocate those resources in a manner that will lead to a maximum in their perceived welfare. Children are argued to be contributors to their parents' perceived welfare by providing non-economic (or psychic) benefits and, possibly, economic benefits in the form of labour in family enterprises or wages from work outside the home. However, they are also costly in terms of time and monetary resources, and the parents must, therefore, weigh the benefits and costs of children in deciding on an optimal family-size. The implication of these assumptions about parental decision-making under resource constraint is that parents express a demand for children that is a function of their own relative preferences for children, the 'price' of a child, and economic resources available to the decision unit. This leads to the standard demand equation of consumer theory

$$D = f(NOC, PI, RP)$$

where D is the number of children demanded, NOC is the 'price' (or 'net opportunity cost') of a child, PI is a measure of resources, say permanent or potential income, and RP represents relative preferences for children.

Often in economic studies, preferences are assumed to be homogeneous, and the demand for a commodity is specified as being solely a function of differences in prices and incomes. Estimation of the demand function may then proceed in a straightforward way, with regression analysis or fairly simple modifications of it being the main analytical tool. However, in fertility studies, the issues are considerably more complex. Tastes for children may vary systematically over a population, and the opportunity cost of children is not a price determined in a market for traded goods. Moreover, even if relative preferences, opportunity cost (or price) of a child, and potential income are the direct determinants of the demand for children, fertility-reduction programmes may not be able to alter those variables directly, and the links between target variables and policy instruments must be identified. Policy considerations may therefore force the analyst to theorise about those factors that determine relative preferences, opportunity cost and potential income.

Suppose that, after reading the large sociological literature on fertility in Third World countries, the analyst proposes to add some new variables to his fertility model. The number of possibilities for modification is substantial. For example, a number of personal characteristics of individuals may affect their demand for children, either directly or through the preference, opportunity cost and income variables: education, place of origin, race, ethnic identity, size of family of orientation, religion, etc.

Social and economic conditions surrounding potential parents may affect the opportunity cost of a child: labour-market options for women, agricultural production practices in the region, or housing availability. Finally, elements of a couple's reproductive history might have influenced its current preferences regarding family-size: age of entry into sexual union, age of woman at first birth, or experience with infant- and child-mortality.

These background and contextual factors may systematically affect the demand for children, either directly or by affecting the proximate determinants of demand: preferences, opportunity cost and potential income. To include all of them, the analyst may build a causal model that indicates a specific hypothesis regarding how personal characteristics, contextual and environmental factors and reproductive history affect proximate variables and, ultimately, the demand for children. This model may then illustrate how public policy can affect the demand for children by, say, raising their opportunity cost, increasing women's labour-force opportunities, enforcing compulsory schooling, altering government housing projects to favour small families, and so on. Alternatively, public health policies designed to reduce infant- and child-mortality might reduce target fertility levels by raising probabilities of survival. The potential variety of programmes is quite large, and it is the task of the fertility analyst to estimate his model statistically in order to advise on the most fruitful policy options.

From a policy point of view, the model is now considerably richer than the unadorned economic model; a set of exogenous variables is hypothesised to act upon a set of endogenous variables, and the structural model developed by the analyst details specific hypotheses about these interrelationships. However, there is no longer a simple equation to be estimated statistically; in its place is a set of equations that form the structural model.[3] Unfortunately, simple statistical methods may not suffice if the estimated structural model is to give an unbiased view of the way in which exogenous variables affect fertility and other endogenous variables. In the following section, the statistical problems inherent in non-experimental statistical estimation of causal structural models are considered.

CAUSAL ESTIMATES FROM NON-EXPERIMENTAL DATA

Recursive Models and their Advantages

Because the analyst is often attempting to construct a causal chain linking policy-instruments to policy-targets via a set of intermediate variables, recursive simultaneous equations models have certain attractions.

A [deterministic] model is said to be 'recursive' if there exists an ordering of the endogenous variables and an ordering of the equations such that the ith equation can be considered to describe the determination of the value of the ith endogenous variable during period t as a function of the predetermined variables and of the endogeneous variables of index less than i. A model is said to be 'interdependent' if it is not recursive. (Malinvaud, 1966, p. 60.)

Suppose that the analyst, after an extended period of theorising, proposes a causal model of the demand for completed family-size as pictured in Figure 8.1. Suppose also that the analyst has been able to collect data that are very carefully matched to the theory so that theoretical variables are closely approximated with empirical analogues, the level of disaggregation is appropriate to the causal process under study, and the number of observations is ample for statistical analysis. It may then be possible to estimate a recursive model of the type shown in Figure 8.1.

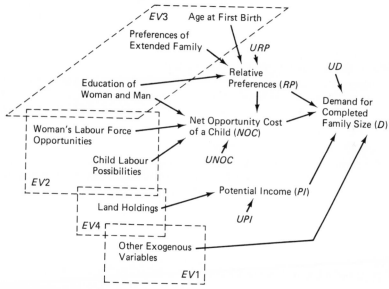

Structural Equations:
$D = f(RP, NOC, PI, EV1) + UD,$
$NOC = g(RP, EV2) + UNOC,$
$RP = h(EV3) + URP,$
$PI = j(EV4) + UPI.$

FIGURE 8.1 *Hypothetical causal model of the demand for children*

This model is an example of the class of micro-economic models described in the second section. The demand for a given completed family-size is determined by the proximate decision variables, Relative Preferences (*RP*), Net Opportunity Cost of a Child (*NOC*) and Potential Income (*PI*) of the family. There are, however, a number of exogenous variables identified that are thought to influence demand directly or indirectly through *RP*, *NOC* and *PI*. These values determine the behaviour of the individual fertility decision makers, but are not in turn determined by that behaviour. Four groups of exogenous variables are postulated; the groups are not mutually-exclusive – a variable may be a member of two or more groups – and the boxes representing the four groups *EV*1, *EV*2, *EV*3 and *EV*4 are shown intersecting, to represent the possibility of overlapping exogenous variable sets. The explicit exogenous variables shown in the boxes are included merely as examples of the sorts of exogenous variables that might be hypothesised to be significant determinants of the endogenous variables.

Figure 8.1 also lists the structural equations of the model. The demand for children is shown to depend upon all other endogenous variables (*RP*, *NOC*, *PI*), a set of exogenous variables (*EV*1) and a disturbance term (*UD*). The Net Opportunity Cost of a Child depends upon a set of exogenous variables (*EV*2) and upon parental relative preferences (*RP*), one of the endogenous variables in the system. Relative Preferences and Potential Income are both hypothesised to depend solely on exogenous variables and disturbances (*URP* and *UPI*).

Since causation is unidirectional, the model is recursive. Algerbraically, the recursiveness is manifested by the lower triangularity of the coefficient matrix of endogenous variables (Figure 8.2 Panel A). Moreover, if the errors in the four equations are independent of each other, the model is said to be 'fully-recursive'. Unidirectional causation and independence of error terms lead to a causal model with particularly appealing statistical properties. In particular, these assumptions imply that each equation in the system can be estimated independently with ordinary least squares (OLS). OLS will, at a minimum, provide consistent and asymptotically efficient estimates of the causal/structural parameters of the model, and, in some cases, the estimates will also be unbiased (Theil, 1971).

Thus, the availability of a complete and theoretiçally appropriate set of measures, an appropriately disaggregated data set, and an adequate sample-size, will lead to a statistical model that can be estimated simply and cheaply using computer programmes available in most places in the world. In this best of all possible non-experimental worlds, we are likely to obtain accurate measurement of structural coefficients of our causal

Panel A: Recursive Structural Model

$$\text{Let: } \mathbf{x}' = \{EV4, EV3, EV2, EV1\} \ (1 \times q),$$
$$\mathbf{y}' = \{PI, RP, NOC, D\} \quad (1 \times 4),$$
$$\boldsymbol{\epsilon}' = \{UPI, URP, UNOC, UD\} \ (1 \times 4).$$

Then the structural model may be written as

$\mathbf{By} = \mathbf{Tx} + \boldsymbol{\epsilon},$ where: $\mathbf{T}$ is a $(4 \times q)$ matrix of coefficients on the exogenous variables, and

$$\mathbf{B} = \begin{bmatrix} 1 & 0 & 0 & 0 \\ 0 & 1 & 0 & 0 \\ b_{31} & b_{32} & 1 & 0 \\ b_{41} & b_{42} & b_{43} & 1 \end{bmatrix} \quad \begin{array}{l} \text{(lower-triangular)} \\ (4 \times 4). \end{array}$$

Panel B: Interdependent Structural Model

$$\text{Let: } \mathbf{x}' = \{EV4, EV3, EV2, EV5, EV1\} \quad (1 \times (q + r)),$$
$$\mathbf{y}' = \{PI, RP, NOC, LFH, D\} \quad (1 \times 5),$$
$$\boldsymbol{\epsilon}' = \{UPI, URP, UNOC, ULFH, UD\} (1 \times 5).$$

The structural model is

$\boldsymbol{\beta} \mathbf{y} = \mathbf{Tx} + \boldsymbol{\epsilon},$ where: $\mathbf{T}$ is a $(5 \times (q + r))$ matrix of coefficients on the exogenous variables, and

$$\boldsymbol{\beta} = \begin{bmatrix} 1 & 0 & 0 & 0 & 0 \\ 0 & 1 & 0 & 0 & 0 \\ 0 & \beta_{32} & 1 & 0 & 0 \\ \beta_{41} & \beta_{42} & 0 & 1 & \beta_{45} \\ \beta_{51} & \beta_{52} & \beta_{53} & \beta_{54} & 1 \end{bmatrix} \quad (5 \times 5).$$

Panel C: Interdependent Latent Variable Model

Let $\boldsymbol{\eta}$ be a vector of latent variables representing $\{PI, RP, NOC, LFH, D\}$, the vector of endogenous variables.

The structural model is

$\boldsymbol{\beta}\boldsymbol{\eta} = \mathbf{Tx} + \boldsymbol{\epsilon},$ where $\boldsymbol{\beta}, \mathbf{T}, \mathbf{x}$ and $\boldsymbol{\epsilon}$ are defined as in Panel B.

The measurement model for the latent variables is:

$\mathbf{z} = \boldsymbol{\Lambda}\boldsymbol{\eta} + \boldsymbol{\mu},$ where $\mathbf{z}'$ represents the vector of indicator variables, $\{z_1, z_2, \ldots, z_m, LFH, D\} \ (1 \times (m + 2)),$ $\boldsymbol{\mu}'$ is a vector of residuals $(1 \times (m + 2))$, and

$$\boldsymbol{\Lambda} = \begin{bmatrix} \lambda_{11} & \lambda_{12} & \lambda_{13} & 0 & 0 \\ \lambda_{21} & \lambda_{22} & \lambda_{23} & 0 & 0 \\ \vdots & \vdots & \vdots & \vdots & \vdots \\ \lambda_{m1} & \lambda_{m2} & \lambda_{m3} & 0 & 0 \\ 0 & 0 & 0 & 1 & 0 \\ 0 & 0 & 0 & 0 & 1 \end{bmatrix} \quad ((m + 2) \times 5).$$

FIGURE 8.2 *Algebraic representation of three models*

model, so that we can provide accurate estimates of how changes in exogenous (policy) variables will ultimately affect the target variable, demand for children. This state of affairs comes about because we have (i) a comprehensive theory that has guided data collection, and (ii) a data set that faithfully represents the theory. That is, we have come as close to an experimental data set as is possible given the nature of our research. Because considerable effort has been expended on the theory and data-collection phases, the analysis phase is relatively straightforward and simple.

However, the world of non-experimental empirical research is hardly ever like the utopia just described. Even with enormous effort during the theory and data-collection stages, the non-experimental nature of the data makes it highly unlikely that controls will be sufficient to allow the application of simple estimation methods such as OLS. In particular, one almost always finds dependence between the errors of the structural equations (Theil, 1971, pp. 460–2). As a result, the covariance matrix of equation errors cannot be assumed to be diagonal, and OLS will, therefore, lead to biased and inconsistent structural coefficient estimates.

Consequently, even if the analyst is fortunate to possess a data set that fairly represents a recursive deterministic system, it is unlikely that the corresponding stochastic system of structural equations will support use of OLS. In order to achieve consistent estimates of the true structural parameters, the analyst will have to turn to more elaborate estimation techniques such as generalised least squares (GLS), or systems methods such as three-stage least squares (3SLS) or full-information maximum likelihood (FIML) (Lahiri and Schmidt, 1978).

Interdependent Simultaneous-equation Models

Unfortunately, the data available to a non-experimental researcher often will not allow him to construct even an empirical model that mirrors the hypothesised recursive structure of the theoretical model. The fertility model of Figure 8.1 was presented under the assumption that our theoretical hypotheses regarding the direction of causality could be adequately translated to the empirical data. Often, however, it is not possible to retain the recursive nature of theory in the empirical model because (i) causal precedence among empirical variables cannot be ascertained because of data measurement inadequacies, and/or (ii) the data are aggregated to the point that the aggregation obscures the causal chain inherent in the basic behavioural units, thus giving the appearance of interdependence.[4] Consequently, although the analyst may harbour theoretical views as to causal ordering, his empirical model must often incorporate mutual causation.[5]

Assume, for example, that in our previous model a woman must make an additional allocation decision, say regarding the number of labour-force hours to supply to the market each year. Theoretically, it may be the case that a woman first decides on a number of children demanded, and then decides on hours of labour force participation (or vice versa); however, data limitations may in fact rule out the distinction. Hence, the analyst may be forced to estimate a structural model that incorporates mutual causation among the endogenous variables. The result may be a model such as that pictured in Figure 8.3.

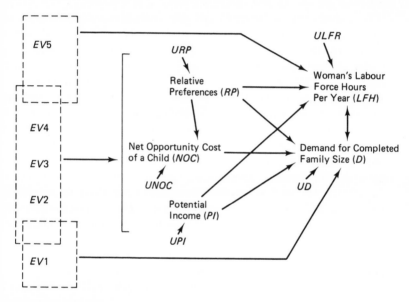

Structural Equations:
$D = f(LFH, RP, NOC, PI, EV1) + UD,$
$LFH = k(D, RP, PI, EV5) + ULFH,$
$NOC = g(RP, EV2) + UNOC,$
$RP = h(EV3) + URP,$
$PI = j(EV4) + UPI.$

FIGURE 8.3 *Model of fertility and labour-force participation*

The structural equation model is similar to the recursive model in Figure 8.1, except that a new equation explaining number of labour-force hours has been added. Labour-force hours (LFH) now determines and is determined by the demand for children (D), and the introduction of simultaneity into the system serves to disqualify OLS because error terms in the system are no longer independent of the explanatory variables of the model (Kmenta, 1971, pp. 531-4). The matrix representation of the model is presented in Panel B of Figure 8.2. The addition of an equation explaining labour-force hours increases the rank of the coefficient matrix of endogenous variables, and the interdependency of the system is indicated by the loss of triangularity in the coefficient matrix, β. Structural coefficients estimated by OLS are biased and inconsistent, and simultaneous-equations methods of estimation are therefore required (Theil, 1971, chs 9, 10; Kmenta, 1971, ch. 13; Schmidt, 1976, chs 4, 5).

The simultaneous estimation methods available range from single-equation methods such as two-stage least squares (2SLS) or limited-information maximum likelihood (LIML), to full systems methods that estimate the parameters of all equations in the model simultaneously – three-stage least squares (3SLS) and full-information maximum likelihood (FIML). All simultaneous methods yield biased coefficient estimates; however, if the model is correctly specified, they will yield consistent estimates. Thus, in the absence of specification error and harmful[6] multicollinearity, simultaneous methods are in general to be preferred to OLS.

However, the superiority of simultaneous estimation methods rests heavily upon the absence of specification error and serious multicollinearity. Summers (1965) found that multicollinearity sharply reduced the superiority of simultaneous estimation methods, and Quandt (1965) found in his Monte Carlo experiments that OLS might even be as satisfactory as 2SLS because the latter is seriously affected by multicollinearity. Misspecification due to missing variables or measurement error can also be expected to reduce or eliminate the superiority of simultaneous estimators. Because systems estimators such as 3SLS and FIML make use of all information in an equation system, the impact of misspecification in one equation is likely to be much more widely spread than in a single-equation method such as 2SLS. There are, unfortunately, no general demonstrations of the superiority of simultaneous-equation estimators in finite samples, particularly in the presence of multicollinearity and specification error. Since fertility data are often weak and collinear, the case for simultaneous methods is also not a strong one.

Moreover, simultaneous-equation estimation routines are rather more complex than simple regression routines. Often, full systems estimation packages such as 3SLS and FIML may not be available to analysts, and to the extent that the fertility data being analysed are weak and collinear, their unavailability may pose no great disadvantage.

Latent, Omitted and Badly-measured Variables

Until this point, we have assumed that our data set has contained all of the variables required by our theory of fertility. Moreover, we have also assumed that the required theoretical variables have been measured without error because the combination of measurement error and simultaneity has long been held to lead to intractable estimation problems (Kmenta, 1971, pp. 321-2, 596; Goldberger, 1964, pp. 387-8). Unfortunately, a major feature of non-experimental data sets, especially many of those dealing with fertility in Third World nations, is the absence of crucial theoretical variables and the presence of considerable measurement error in those variables that are available. Statistical tests of the micro-economic models of fertility are commonly hampered by the absence of variables such as potential income or the opportunity cost of children. Psychological variables, such as those measuring relative preferences for parenthood, versus other activities are also often omitted or poorly measured. These data-quality issues lead to serious problems of estimation and interpretation of statistical results.

For example, consider the impact that omission of a theoretically-relevant variable has on the interpretation of estimates from a simple structural model. Assume that the demand equation for children,

$$D = B1 \times P + B2 \times Y + U,$$

where D is the number of children demanded, P is the price (or opportunity cost) of a child, Y is potential income, and U is an unobserved and independently-distributed random disturbance, represents the true model of the demand for children. Assume also that the variables are scaled so that their expectations are zero. Then, the model specifies that price (P) and income (Y) combine to determine the demand for children, and the model generates a joint distribution of D and Y with

$$\sigma_{DY} = B2 \times \sigma_{YY} + B1 \times \sigma_{YP}$$

and

$$\sigma_{DD} = B2^2 \times \sigma_{YY} + B1^2 \times \sigma_{PP} + 2 \times B2 \times B1 \, \sigma_{YP} + \sigma_{UU}.$$

The linear regression of D on Y, with P omitted, is

$$E(D \mid Y) = (\sigma_{DY}/\sigma_{YY})Y = (B2 + gB1)Y,$$

where $g = (\sigma_{PY}/\sigma_{YY})$ is the slope of the regression of P on Y, and the sigmas represent the appropriate variances and covariances. The goal is to estimate structural parameter $B2$, but in the absence of the price variable, we estimate $B2 + g^*B1$, which clearly is not the same unless there is zero covariance between P and Y. Economists normally would anticipate that the income coefficient, $B2$, is greater than zero, the price coefficient, $B1$, is negative, and the covariance between price and income is positive. The net effect of the misspecification is, therefore, an estimated income coefficient that is biased toward zero.[7] In the total absence of a measure of P, it may not be possible to avoid biased estimates of the income parameter. However, a well-developed theory will at least alert the researcher to the problem of bias and allow an assessment of the probable direction of bias.

Often, the problem is not one of totally missing data, but of poorly-measured theoretical variables. Assume, for example, that although precise empirical analogues for Relative Preferences (RP), Net Opportunity Cost (NOC) and Potential Income (PI) are not available, a number of *indicators* of these variables are available in the data set. The theoretical variables of interest are now termed *latent* variables, because they do not exist in the data set, but the possibility exists that they can be measured by using linear combinations of the available indicators. The estimation problem has now become more complex. The researcher must find measures of the latent variables using the available indicators, and he must also estimate the structural system that explicitly includes the latent variables. The structural model of Figures 8.3 must be modified to account for the fact that some of the endogenous variables are now latent variables. Figure 8.4 is the result.

In this figure, all of the endogenous variables are defined to be latent variables (circled) while the exogenous variables (boxes) are assumed to be well-measured. The matrix version of the latent variable model is presented in Panel C of Figure 8.2. The structural model takes the same general form as the interdependent model of Figure 8.3, with the exception that the vector of endogenous variables is replaced by a vector of endogenous latent variables that must be represented by a set of indicator variables. The measurement model in Panel C represents the linear regression of the measured indicators on the set of hypothesised latent variables (factors).[8]

The model of Figure 8.4 is the latent variable model of Joreskog (1973, 1979), and it represents a major advance in the analysis of non-experimental data sets where measurement problems are present. The Joreskog model is, in fact, a combination of constrained factor analysis

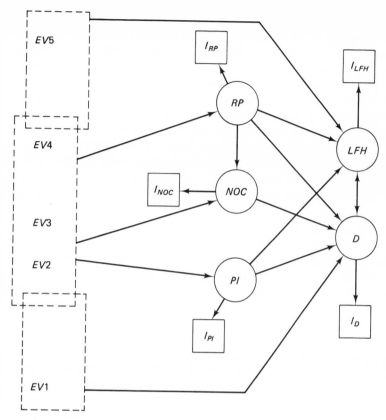

Latent variables: *RP, NOC, PI, LFH, D.*
Indicator variable sets: I_{RP}, I_{NOC}, I_{PI}, I_D, I_{LFH}.
Exogenous variable sets: *EV1, EV2, EV3, EV4, EV5.*

Error terms omitted for clarity; see Panel C of Figure 8.2.

FIGURE 8.4 *Latent-variable version of model in Figure 8.3*

(the measurement model) and structural equation estimation, and it represents a unification of two distinct branches of statistical estimation, psychometrics and econometrics. Moreover, it gives the non-experimental data analyst a powerful new tool to attack data sets that, for one reason or another, diverge considerably from well-controlled experimental data.

The price that is paid for this advance is a considerable increase in complexity of estimation. In most cases, resort must be made to a generalised form of full-information maximum likelihood estimation in order to achieve estimates of unknown coefficients. The problem of insuring identifiability is even more severe than in the standard interdependent structural equation case typified by the model of Figure 8.3, and the computer hardware and software requirements are such that many researchers in Third World settings may be unable to implement the methodology. Moreover, because estimation of latent-variable models requires a full-information method, it is subject to the same sorts of problems that affect other systems estimation methods. Nevertheless, latent-variable models offer the potential of significantly improved estimation of models using non-experimental data in the presence of measurement error and in the absence of precise measures of important theoretical variables.

Interpreting the Results

Fertility analysts and other users of non-experimental data ultimately must face the fact that specification of the model remains the most important and troublesome aspect of their research. The experimental scientist, through the design of his experiment, can produce a data set for analysis that is appropriate for only one theoretical specification. The non-experimental researcher, possibly having had no control over the generation of his data, has potentially a large number of models available that might fit the data more or less equally well.

Often, empirical research results on fertility are presented as if only one specification has been attempted, when in fact the published results are the outcome of an extensive process of data exploration. Because the weak, collinear nature of much fertility data leads to great instability in estimated coefficients as specification is altered, it is possible to search the data for the results that fit the analyst's preconceived ideas. If all researchers held the same set of preconceived ideas, reporting only one set of results from the specification search would not be such a questionable practice. Indeed, one would wonder why the empirical work is done at all if specification searches are carried out merely to satisfy preconceived ideas. However, prior opinions are generally not uniform, and the failure of an analyst to report the results of the entire search process is seriously misleading: someone with a different set of prior opinions might choose an entirely different set of results to report.

Consequently, an extremely important aspect of non-experimental data analysis is the interpretation and communication of results. Relatively little work has been done on this important topic; however, Leamer's (1978) contribution deserves special mention. Leamer attempts to provide a coherent and systematic methodology for the conduct of specification searches. He begins from a Bayesian framework; social scientists often bring prior opinions to their non-experimental data, and, because the sample results obtained from those data often conflict with those prior opinions, researchers are induced to test alternative specifications.

Leamer is not particularly upset by the prevalence of this 'data-mining' in social and economic research. Indeed, he sees it as a necessary outgrowth of the non-experimental context within which many social scientists work. Leamer is more concerned about the nature and strength of conclusions drawn from these specification searches, and his work is oriented toward elucidation of the way in which prior opinions should be combined with sample data and reported. He presents extensive theoretical results for the search process in the context of single-equation regression, and, although the theory has not been extended to simultaneous systems, Leamer's single-equation results are important guides for non-experimental data analysis.

SOME GENERAL CONCLUSIONS

From the preceding, it must be clear that the analyst of non-experimental data faces considerable difficulties in developing an accurate understanding of the causal processes underlying reproduction behaviour. Unlike the experimental scientist, who must spend considerable effort to design experiments that produce data allowing relatively simple statistical analysis, the social scientist, who deals with non-experimental data must expend considerable effort in the analysis-phase overcoming data problems. The statistical remedies applied rarely lead to the conclusive and replicable results that are common in the experimental sciences; nevertheless, social scientists have at their disposal an increasing array of statistical methods designed to overcome estimation problems inherent in non-experimental analysis.

Simultaneous-equation estimation techniques such as 2SLS, 3SLS and FIML offer the analyst the chance to model causal relations even when the data do not allow development of a causal hierarchy among endogenous variables. Generalisations of full-information maximum likelihood, such as Joreskog's LISREL, allow statistical estimation of structural models using data sets that do not contain precisely measured analogues to required theoretical variables. The price that must be paid for these new estimation techniques is increased computational complexity. Even in the best of circumstances, the estimation of structural models usually involves iterative maximisation routines that require computer resources that are often not yet available in the Third World.

Complicating the picture is the fact that systems methods of estimation do not yield unambiguously superior results if the data contain serious multicollinearity or if there is specification error in the statistical models. Systems methods, since they incorporate information from the entire set of equations, are much more prone to spread the effect of specification error and multicollinearity throughout the system. OLS, while it is biased and inconsistent in the structural-equations context, may in fact yield estimates of structural coefficients that are closer to the true values of those coefficients. The problem that the analyst faces, of course, is that there is no hard and fast rule available to guide him in choosing the proper estimation technique. The true coefficients are unknown, and the analyst is forced to assess the results of estimation with respect to his prior opinions regarding the sign and magnitude of the coefficients in question.

Unfortunately, this is not the same issue that Leamer addresses using Bayesian theory. His purpose is to demonstrate how prior opinions and sample results can be synthesised *given the proper choice of estimation method*. Statistical theory offers no firm guideline as to the choice of correct method, except in the case of well-specified and large data sets that are not beset by serious multicollinearity problems.

Because available non-experimental data usually will not allow the prior exclusion of alternative specifications, the use of subject-matter theory to choose the 'best' estimation method will continue to be extremely controversial. The analyst who chooses, say, the results of OLS over those of 2SLS, because the estimated signs and coefficient values reported by the former are more congruent with his prior theoretical expectations, is open to critiscism from other analysts whose prior opinions differ. There is, unfortunately, no unambiguous way to choose between prior opinions.

In spite of the difficulties just described, the situation is far from hopeless. Non-experimental social data have provided and will continue to provide considerable insight into the reproductive process, as the other chapters in this volume attest. The methods described in this chapter can be extremely useful if they are not misused. Misuse often occurs because, although estimations using many different specifications are attempted, only a few are reported. This practice leads to the often mistaken impression that the data support one theory strongly and alternative theories not at all. Ultimately, there is no single, easy answer to the question of appropriate analysis of non-experimental data. Instead, it must be reiterated that the quality of non-experimental data analysis is directly related to the rigour and completeness with which alternative theories are formulated, the care with which statistical estimation is performed, and, perhaps most importantly, the manner in which results are reported. Because of the difficulty in choosing among competing theories in social research, it is incumbent upon the analyst to report his statistical results in a way that allows others to test their sensitivity to alternative prior theories (Leamer, 1978).

In those situations where non-experimental data yield results that are insensitive to specification or to method of estimation, they provide information of immediate utility to the analyst or policy-maker. In those many cases where the results are not insensitive, non-experimental data may, at a minimum, allow the bounds of uncertainty to be narrowed while suggesting the shape of new procedures designed to collect more informative data.

If the demands of policy-makers and administrators for policy-relevant fertility research increase along the lines suggested in the first section of this chapter, new and difficult estimation problems will arise. At present, there is nothing routine or simple about the estimation of statistical models from non-experimental data. Nevertheless, the methods described here, applied with care and creativity, offer the possibility that demographic policy in the Third World can, in the next decade, be formulated on the basis of empirical findings of considerable strength regarding the underlying causal processes governing reproductive behaviour.

NOTES

1. See H. B. Simon (1968), Wold (1954) and Hicks (1979).
2. Non-experimental data will often be characterised as 'weak' in this chapter. By this term, we mean that the data often exhibit considerable measurement error, collinearity and low variance of explanatory variables. Moreover, sample-size is often insufficient for very precise estimation, and the data are often lacking precise empirical analogues for required theoretical variables.
3. Farooq's analysis of Nigerian household data (Chapter 12) in this volume could have been presented in terms of a set of structural equations. He chooses, however, to estimate a single-equation model, while recognising the statistical problems inherent in such a procedure.
4. Chapter 7, on aggregation, by Edlefsen and Lieberman in this volume discusses in some detail the conceptual and statistical issues associated with the use of aggregate data.
5. Chapter 17 by Winegarden in this volume makes use of a 'block recussive' structural system in which one of the behavioural equations may be estimated with OLS, while the remaining three interdependent equations must be estimated simultaneously. His analysis of cross-national data provides a good example of a situation in which use of aggregate data required simultaneous estimation methods. Farooq's

analysis of Nigerian household data also is a good example of the sorts of problems facing users of non-experimental data, even when the data are of relatively high quality.

6. The mere existence of collinearity in a data set is not necessarily harmful to statistical estimation. Theil (1971) shows that particular linear combinations of estimated regression coefficients may be well determined even if the individual coefficients are not. Moreover, individual coefficient estimates may not be severely degraded, depending upon the structure of the data matrix (Bauer, 1971).

7. This is likely to be a reason that numerous attempts by economists to measure the income elasticity of family-size have produced low or even negative income elasticities. See Turchi, 1975b, pp. 57–8.

8. Note that although the endogenous variables LFH and D are characterised as latent variables here, the measurement model constrains them to be equal to the measured variables I_{LFH} and I_O. The constraints are expressed in the last two rows and columns of the coefficient (or factor-loading) matrix.

9 Simulation Techniques in Fertility Analysis

GERRY B. RODGERS and RENÉ WÉRY

SIMULATION VERSUS ANALYTICAL SOLUTIONS

The use of simulation techniques in the social sciences is increasing, as larger and faster computers become more and more accessible. Simulation provides information about the characteristics and outcomes of a system by repeated numerical analysis. One proposed definition is given by Naylor: 'Simulation is a numerical technique for conducting experiments with certain types of mathematical models which describe the behaviour of a complex system on a digital computer over extended periods of time' (Naylor, 1971, p. 2). This gives a good idea of the practical consequences of a simulation approach, for the computer is an almost indispensible tool in this type of analysis. It is, however, debatable whether the use of a computer constitutes part of the basic definition of simulation – in principle, one can simulate on the back of an envelope. The fundamental aspect of simulation is rather the digital representation of a system, of which the behaviour is represented and analysed numerically.

Analytical techniques also provide information about the characteristics and behaviour of systems, but they do so through general solutions which transform a structural representation of a system into forms which can be readily utilised, or which provide general information about system behaviour. Thus an interacting set of relationships may be transformed into a reduced form which permits the impact of any exogenous change on all endogenous variables to be directly evaluated; or optima, or equilibrium paths which can only be inferred approximately from numerical techniques, may be determined exactly and in general.

Where analytical solutions are available, as in linear models, simulation techniques are wasteful, except in the obvious case where the quantitative values of a set of outputs corresponding to a particular set of inputs are required. On the other hand, analytical solutions of complex non-linear

213

systems may be extremely difficult if not impossible to find, and in any case intensive in the time of highly-skilled mathematicians. There is a large grey area, in which it is not clear which course is more efficient – to search for analytical solutions, or to grind out numerical outcomes. But it *is* clear that the cost of the latter approach is falling faster than the cost of the former, so that the economic case for simulation is becoming stronger. And models of social systems are becoming more complex, as researchers struggle to comprehend the broader interactions between their areas of interest. So it seems probable that the balance between analytical and simulation techniques is shifting in favour of the latter.

In the application of simulation to fertility analysis, a number of different issues arise. The value of simulation varies according to the questions posed and the form of the model. Broadly, we can separate models of the fertility of individuals from models of societal fertility levels. It is also useful to separate out the more direct, biological models of reproductive processes from models which relate fertility to broader social and economic change. Let us take first the traditional, direct model of biological components of fertility at the individual level, because this can illustrate some of our points fairly simply. In such models, fertility levels or changes are broken down into components corresponding to fecundability, exposure (sexual activity, contraception), spontaneous and induced abortion, etc. Exact accounting systems can be specified, for example

$$B_t = (1 - \beta_s - \beta_i)f_{(t-g)}p_{(t-g)}\sum_i(1 - \alpha_i)q_i.$$

The probability of a birth at time t (B_t) is equal to one minus the probabilities of spontaneous and induced abortions (β_s, β_i), times the frequency of sexual intercourse (f) lagged by the period of gestation (g) times the probability of conception without contraception (p), times one minus the efficiency of contraception of type i (α_i) times the probability of utilisation of that contraceptive (q_i) summed over all contraceptive methods. All of the variables on the right-hand side will also have their own sets of determinants, the variable p, for instance, depending on age, health, whether or not breastfeeding, timing in the menstrual cycle, fecundity of sexual partner, and so on. The process can be continued with a further set of determinants. How can simulation techniques help to understand these mechanisms?

There are several possibilities. If the model is simple, and the reduced form can be readily obtained, there is little that simulation can add. In a complex model, on the other hand, the partial relationship between fertility and a change somewhere in the system may be difficult to obtain

It is easy to visualise extension of the above model where this would be the case. For instance, the formulation above is exact only if the variables on the right hand side of the equation are independent. If this is not the case, the covariance of the independent variables needs to be introduced as a determinant of birth probability. Moreover, present fecundity and contraceptive use, among other variables, will vary with past fertility, while certain explanatory variables may be jointly determined. Thus a full understanding of the process of childbearing requires a mixed recursive-simultaneous stochastic model spanning several time-periods and with a fairly large number of endogenous variables.

The strategy to follow in this case has to be based on an appreciation of the uses to which the model is put, and the relative costs of different approaches. Some possible uses are: (i) estimation of the impact on fertility of an exogenous change (e.g. a policy change); (ii) analysis of the frequency distribution of the population according to their fertility; (iii) examination of the characteristics of the model with a view to identifying its implications and/or failings. For the first of these, simulation with the structural form provides essentially the same information as direct estimation from the reduced form, and the question is simply one of relative cost. For the second use, Monte Carlo techniques can be used to simulate frequency distributions, though this may be a long and rather expensive process. Analytical techniques are evidently superior in terms of information content; however, they rapidly become impractical with increasing model-size unless very simple distributions are assumed. The third case is perhaps the one for which analytical solutions are most desirable, since simulation is very much a second best compared with the full understanding of available solutions. Nevertheless, in complex systems, simulation may be the only option available. The alternative of simplifying the model to the point where an analytical solution can be found is sometimes available, but risks losing more through specification error than is gained from the analytical solution. In each case, then, there is a trade-off, and a decision needs to be made on a case-by-case basis.

A related issue concerns estimation techniques. In general, fully understood estimators with desirable properties are available only for highly restricted models. For complex models, the usual practice is to apply estimation techniques which are strictly valid only for relatively elementary situations. Analytical solutions and simulation techniques offer two quite different ways of approaching this problem. For instance, an analytical solution may provide a readily-estimated reduced form, the parameters of which may then be used to calculate the coefficients of the structural model – this principle underlying, for instance, the use of two-stage least squares for simultaneous models. A simulation approach, on the other hand, would involve an iterative procedure, in which a first round of coefficient estimates would be used to generate a set of model outcomes, which would in turn be compared with real-world observations. Various algorithms can be applied to modify coefficients so as to minimise the deviations of model outcomes from real data. These algorithms may involve not only coefficient changes, but also changes in model structure if numerical tests call the validity of the system into question.

Although the above discussion has been couched in terms of biological models of fertility, rather similar arguments can be extended to the behavioural micro models of household decision-making which have been much in evidence in the economic literature in recent years.[1] Here too, the fertility model is defined at the level of the individual, the models are potentially complex, and they may include several jointly-determined variables. The tendency in the formal literature has been to obtain analytical solutions for such models (which are in turn derived from standard economic assumptions about rational behaviour and utility maximisation). However, in principle, simulation techniques are available and can contribute.

At the macro level, some additional issues arise. Take first the type of model concerned with tracking the demographic characteristics of a population. The ideal way to do this is to incorporate in the model life-histories and demographic behaviour of all the individuals concerned. Since outcomes for each individual have stochastic components, and since the number of individuals is large (and they necessarily have widely varying demographic and personal characteristics), these models can be treated analytically only in special cases of mainly theoretical interest (notably stable populations). The normal approach is simulation, and a number of micro simulation models have been built (see Hammel *et al.*, 1976; Dyke and MacCluer, 1973; Menken, 1975; United Nations, 1979). This approach has several advantages. It permits not only the investigation of alternative age-structures and behaviour patterns, but also family formation and dissolution, migration, various other population disaggregations with interaction between them, and so on. The models themselves have the advantage of completeness, they permit a range of experiments, and clearly help understand both individual behaviour and – through aggregation across individuals – macro-demographic phenomena. But they also have one major disadvantage: to track a large population disaggregated in many dimensions requires enormous computer capacity and a considerable data-handling task. As a result, most micro simulation models to date have been fairly restricted in scope, though the potential for developing this class of model seems large.

The most common type of macro model is not based on micro simulation, but rather uses aggregate measures of fertility as both dependent and independent variables. The underlying model of fertility determination is usually based on micro-level theory, but the relationships are either estimated at or aggregated up to the macro level prior to insertion in the model. Where an aggregate model is specified in which fertility alone is a dependent varible, the arguments from simulation are fairly weak. Analytically tractable models are easier to specify at the macro level, since the theoretical constraints which restrict the specification of models of individual fertility behaviour are largely absent. But where fertility is treated as one element in a broader socio-economic model, the trade-off between model realism and model tractability once again emerges. Within a wider model of socio-economic change, fertility changes can have a variety of consequences, both direct (e.g. on female labour supply) and indirect (e.g. on government expenditure patterns). These consequences need to be brought into macro analyses even if the objective is only to explore the determinants of fertility or the response of fertility to policy interventions, because feedbacks to the determinants of fertility may well be important.

If, for instance, job opportunities for women are modified, a direct effect on fertility through conventional economic income and substitution effects can be foreseen. However, at the same time there may be, among other consequences, adverse side-effects on overall wage levels, which indirectly affect both fertility and mortality (and again affect fertility through the latter variable). In addition, the change in fertility in turn affects population-size and age-structure, with later consequences for schooling, labour-market entry, and the size of the fertile population. The fertility change may also have some long-term consequences for normative fertility behaviour, or may affect patterns of consumption and saving. A complete analysis of any given policy change on fertility levels requires the evaluation of these indirect effects.

In order to capture relationships such as these, complex models are required. It is true that much simpler models of economic-demographic interaction are often specified, in an attempt to investigate through analytical solutions the essentials of the problem. But the range of relevant relationships is wide, so that many endogenous variables are required, and non-linearities and simultaneities are frequent. Simple models may help understand particular phenomena. But if the linkages, both forward and backward, between fertility and other aspects of socio-economic change are to be understood, it is also necessary to build larger models, which can be analysed only through simulation techniques.

THE EFFECTS OF ECONOMIC POLICY ON FERTILITY:
ILLUSTRATIVE MACRO-SIMULATIONS

Introduction

In this section we present the results of some experiments with an economic-demographic model, which illustrate certain uses of simulation techniques in fertility analysis. The experiments themselves are designed to explore the impact of different types of policy measures on fertility. But in so doing, they also help to analyse the structure and validity of a number of different models of fertility.

The economic-demographic model which is used as the systems framework for the experiments is Bachue-Philippines. This model is described in greater or lesser detail elsewhere (Rodgers, Hopkins and Wéry, 1976, and 1978; Wéry, Rodgers and Hopkins, 1978). We shall give only a cursory outline here. Bachue-Philippines simulates the behaviour in the long run of both economic and demographic aspects of development, with particular concentration on employment and income distribution. It consists of three main subsystems. The first, economy, determines the level and pattern of demand and output by sector, using an input–output production system. It also determines the internal terms of trade and the distribution of value added among various population groups. The second subsystem, labour and income, determines employment, unemployment and wages in a number of socio-economic groups, and the household income distribution which they generate. Dualism and rural–urban differentiation characterise this subsystem. The third demographic subsystem tracks the population by age, sex, location and education. It incorporates endogenous marriage, fertility, mortality and migration. Each of the subsystems is quite disaggregated, and there are extensive interrelationships and feedbacks both within and between them.[2] The model has been estimated on the basis of Philippines cross-section and time-series data, supplemented for a small number of functions, notably the fertility function, by international data.

The 'reference run' or 'basic scenario' of Philippine development generated by the model is a development path on which modern, urban employment increases relatively rapidly up to the end of the twentieth century, with decreasing wage differentials, while constraints on food supply lead to rising relative food prices. Mainly as a result of these two factors, inequality slowly, but steadily declines. The Philippines enters the fertility phase of the 'demographic transition' but has not completed it by the year 2000. At the latter date, the country's GDP per capita is comparable with some of the more developed Latin American countries in the early 1970s, or with Spain, Greece or Japan in the early 1960s, though inequality is considerably greater. This reference run is intended not as a prediction, but as a standard of comparison against which can be compared the outcomes when variables in the model are modified to simulate policy changes; it is experiments of this type which we report later in this chapter. A selection of the quantitative outcomes of the reference run, for the years 1965, 1985 and 2000, is given in the first three columns of Table 9.2.

The Fertility Functions

Fertility is endogenous in Bachue-Philippines, and in the reference run a behavioural macro-function, estimated on the basis of international cross-section data, is included. However, for purposes of fertility analysis, it is desirable to explore variations in model response with respect to this relationship. One approach would be to treat the fertility function as stochastic, and undertake Monte Carlo tests. But this assumes the basic structure of the fertility function to be correct. We preferred to explore the consequences for model results of incorporating a variety of different fertility functions based on different theories, and using different independent variables, data sources and estimation methods. Six functions have been used for this chapter.[3] Although their content differs signficantly, they have in common that they are multivariate and that the explanatory variables can be generated endogenously in Bachue-Philippines. They all also incorporate an economic model of fertility – i.e. in each case economic factors are among those determining fertility, either through altering prices of time and the opportunity costs of child-care in a household decision model, or through modifying the benefits to parents of childbearing, or, implicitly, through changing social patterns and behaviour in such a way as to modify family and fertility norms.[4] The functions are summarised (in elasticity form) in Table 9.1; we discuss each in turn below.

TABLE 9.1 *Summary of the fertility functions – elasticities with respect to explanatory variables*

	RR^a		WB^b	$NS1^a$		$NS2^a$		WRL^b		WRH^b	
	Urban	Rural		Urban	Rural	Urban	Rural	Urban	Rural	Urban	Rural
1 % agriculture population	0.112	0.090									
2 Female LFPR	-0.104	-0.081		0.072	0.065	-0.338	-0.305	0.0	0.0	-0.3	-0.3
3 Life expectancy	-0.832	-0.749						0.0	0.0	0.1	0.1
4 % illiterate	0.243	0.089									
5 Income per capita			-0.20	-0.014	-0.005	0.039	0.014				
6 Newspaper circulation			-0.12								
7 Income of 40% poorest			-0.36								
8 Gini coefficient								0.3	0.3	0.9	0.9
9 Children school enrolement				-0.004	-0.002	-0.055	-0.023	-0.1	-0.1	-0.3	-0.3
10 Male wage											
11 Female wage								-0.1	-0.05	-0.3	-0.2
12 Child mortality								0.2	0.2	0.4	0.4
13 % married women				0.992	1.081	4.513	4.916				
14 Years of schooling				-0.181	-0.110	-0.447	-0.272				
15 Crude death rate lagged 3 years				0.062	0.094	0.040	0.059				
16 Crude death rate lagged 4 years				0.038	0.049	0.026	0.034				
17 % traditional employment								0.1	0.05	0.25	0.10

18 % unpaid family workers	−0.256	−0.366	−0.452	−0.645				
19 Household income					−0.2	−0.2	0.1	0.1
20 % women with less than primary education					0.15	0.10	0.4	0.3
21 % women with secondary school completed and more					−0.15	−0.10	−0.35	−0.30
22 Age at marriage					0.0	0.0	0.3	0.3
23 % secondary sector employment					−0.1	−0.1	−0.6	−0.4
24 % modern services consumption					−0.1	−0.1	−0.4	−0.3

[a]Elasticities computed using initial (1965) values in Bachue.
[b]Constant elasticities (bi-log formulation).
RR: Reference run Bachue function.
WB: World Bank function.
NS1: Nerlove and Schultz, Puerto Rico 1950–60, ordinary least squares.
NS2: Nerlove and Schultz, Puerto Rico 1950–60, instrumental variable estimates.
WRL: Wéry and Rodgers, low elasticities.
WRH: Wéry and Rodgers, high elasticities.

Reference run Bachue function (RR)
    Data base: international cross-section.
    Estimation method: multiple regression (ordinary least squares).
    Reference: Rodgers, Hopkins and Wéry (1976).

$$F = 4.67 - 0.0064 \ R + 0.016 \ I - 0.0446 \ e_0^0 + 0.0059 L_A,$$

where F is fertility (gross reproduction rate),
        R is labour-force participation rate for women aged 15–44,
        I is percentage of adult population which is illiterate,
        e_0^0 is life expectancy at birth (years),
        L_A is percentage of the labour-force in agriculture.

This function is based on data from 47 countries. It was used for the reference run of the model[5] because fertility functions based on Philippine cross-sectional data did not give results which seemed likely to persist over time.[6] The underlying model is a household decision one, but the selection of explanatory variables was severely constrained by the availability of comparable international data.

World Bank (WB)
    Data base: international cross-section.
    Estimation method: stepwise multiple regression (ordinary least squares).
    Reference: World Bank (1974, p. 147).

$$F = A Y^{-0.2} \ N^{-0.12} \ G^{-0.36},$$

where F is fertility (special index, approximation to the general fertility rate),
        A is a constant adjusted to give correct Philippine fertility at the origin,
        Y is income per capita,
        N is newspapers per 1000 population (mapped onto educational level in Bachue),
        G is distribution of income (share of bottom 40 per cent of households in total income).
    The function, based on data from 64 countries, was designed to demonstrate the impact of income distribution on fertility.

Nerlove and Schultz (1) (NS1)
    Data base: Puerto Rican municipio data for 11 years, 1950–60.

Estimation method: multiple regression (ordinary least squares).
Reference: Nerlove and Schultz (1970, p. 45).

$$F = 0.0647 \; L - 0.253 \; Y + 0.664 \; M_g + 0.751 \; M_c - 0.00358 \; E_c$$
$$- 0.79 \; E_a + 0.287 \; D_{t-3} + 0.173 \; D_{t-4} - 0.365 \; Z + C,$$

where F is the crude birth rate,
L is the female labour-force participation rate,
Y is income,
M_g, M_c are proportions married (legally, consensually),
E_c is adolescent education,
E_a is adult education,
D_{t-3}, D_{t-4} are crude death rates lagged three and four years,
Z is unpaid family workers,
C is a constant, adjusted to give initial Philippine values.

This fertility function is one component of a 25-equation model, also involving female labour supply, income, marriage and migration. The study combines a micro theory of fertility determination with an application to macro (municipality) data. Certain adjustments have been made to the independent variables of the function, in an attempt to allow for differences between Puerto Rican and Philippine conditions. This included the merging of M_g and M_c and their mapping onto age at marriage, and an indirect estimation of Z.

Nerlove and Schultz (2) (NS2)

Data base, estimation method and reference as above, except that a simultaneous equation estimation technique (instrumental variables) has been used, giving the following function:

$$F = C - 0.303 \; L + 0.714 \; Y + 3.02 \; M_g + 2.66 \; M_c - 0.05282 \; E_c$$
$$- 1.95 \; E_a + 0.182 \; D_{t-3} + 0.120 \; D_{t-4} - 0.644 \, Z.$$

The nature of the model is such that, on theoretical grounds, the simultaneous estimation technique is to be preferred.

(v) Wéry-Rodgers (1) - Low (WRL)

(vi) Wéry-Rodgers (2) - High (WRH)
Data base: none.
Estimation method: intuition and educated guesswork.

All the previous functions were empirically estimated. To round off the sequence of fertility functions, we have constructed two which are constrained by our imagination and experience and the availability of variables and policy instruments in Bachue-Philippines, rather than by data. These functions incorporate a wide range of variables which could be predicted as affecting fertility from standard models of fertility determination, with particular concentration on economic variables. Because the evidence is mixed, two very different estimates, 'low' and 'high', have been made. These, of course, are two from a large number of possibilities. The dependent variables are age-specific marital fertility rates, and the equations are log-linear (constant elasticity) in form. The independent variables include female labour-force participation, life expectancy, income inequality, child school enrolment, female wage, child mortality, extent of traditional sector employment, household income, female education, age at marriage, extent of secondary sector employment, consumption of modern services. Elasticities used are given in Table 9.1, last four columns; note that in some cases, rural and urban figures are different.

When each of the functions is built into Bachue-Philippines, the original reference run of the model is naturally modified. It is therefore instructive, as a first indication of the interaction between these fertility functions and the Bachue-Philippines system, to compare the different reference runs obtained by use of each fertility function.[7] The outcomes are summarised in Table 9.2. This gives, for the years 1965, 1985 and 2000, the absolute values of some 60 key variables in the original reference run of Bachue-Philippines (columns 2-4). Then, in columns 5-9, are given results using alternative fertility functions. Results are expressed as percentage differences from the original reference run in the year 2000. It can be seen that these differences are sometimes quite large. Fertility, as measured by the crude birth rate, declines relative to its initial value in all runs, but the extent of the decline varies quite considerably with the fertility function chosen. The standard reference run (RR) gives a decline over 1965-2000 in the crude birth rate of 27 per cent. Three of the other runs give declines greater than this, with the maximum reached by the Wéry-Rodgers high (WRH) function, which gives a fertility level in 2000 almost 40 per cent lower than the reference run RR, implying a 56 per cent decline in the crude birth rate over 1965-2000. The World Bank function (WB) gives fertility overall declining a little faster than in the

TABLE 9.2 *Reference runs with different fertility functions; basic reference RR in absolute figures for 1965, 1985, 2000; all other percentage comparison with RR in 2000*

	RR, 1965	RR, 1985	RR, 2000	WB	NS1	NS2	WRL	WRH
Demographic outcomes								
Urban population (thousands)	10549.000	24264.668	41042.625	-2.2	9.5	7.8	-5.9	-18.2
Rural population (thousands)	21608.000	34412.809	47097.609	-12.8	17.4	9.2	2.6	-16.7
Total population (thousands)	32157.000	58677.461	88139.688	-7.9	13.7	8.6	-1.4	-17.4
Crude birth rate	43.839	36.804	31.801	-8.0	22.8	18.6	-7.5	-39.4
Rural total fertility rate	7.301	5.730	4.860	-13.8	28.9	21.3	-10.4	-49.6
Urban total fertility rate	5.830	5.084	4.391	-2.6	28.1	25.8	-21.2	-52.6
Rural life expectancy	52.798	62.509	67.758	1.5	-1.0	0.1	-0.5	1.1
Urban life expectancy	59.494	63.943	68.160	0.2	-1.1	-1.1	0.5	1.6
% completed secondary educ., rural	8.523	19.058	25.143	-1.4	0.9	0.1	0.4	-0.7
% completed secondary educ., urban	37.818	46.529	52.461	-0.2	0.6	0.4	-0.0	-0.6
Net rural–urban migration (%)	0.661	0.720	0.718	-5.1	-4.7	-9.6	2.5	3.5
LFPR of rural females aged 15–44	46.047	46.147	46.800	2.3	-3.2	-2.8	0.2	5.5
LFPR of urban females aged 15–44	44.532	46.969	48.445	0.3	-2.6	-2.3	0.4	3.2
Economic structure (million pesos of 1965)								
Total value-added urban	12840.457	47289.207	137297.313	0.4	-1.4	-1.2	0.2	1.1
Total value-added rural	7400.059	21804.012	52258.113	-2.3	4.6	3.5	-0.0	-4.1
Investment as % of GDP	18.967	19.037	22.278	1.8	-3.4	-1.9	-0.1	2.9
Total government expenditure	2545.000	9905.055	30970.094	-5.1	7.8	4.6	-0.4	-10.6
Total government revenue	2234.635	9399.125	29365.676	-0.1	-0.7	-0.8	0.4	0.9
Total exports	4220.625	20791.070	63602.418	2.1	-3.6	-1.7	-0.1	2.9
Total imports	4869.207	18309.926	59252.914	0.4	0.0	-0.1	-0.3	0.7
Balance of payments	-503.495	2894.443	5464.348	20.1	-42.3	-19.4	2.0	26.8
Primary output % (sectors 1, 2, 3, 4)	27.719	23.848	20.239	-3.0	4.8	2.6	0.3	-3.9
Secondary output % (sectors 5, 6, 7, 8, 9)	21.159	24.341	27.032	0.9	-1.1	-0.4	-0.2	1.3

Tertiary output % (sectors 10, 11, 12, 13)	51.122	51.811	52.730	0.7	-1.3	-0.8	-0.0	0.8
Agriculture-industry terms of trade	1.000	1.425	1.556	11.0	4.4	16.7	-7.1	-4.1
Labour and employment (thousands)								
Primary sector employment (%)	56.274	53.389	48.018	-2.0	2.7	1.9	0.2	-1.6
Secondary sector employment (%)	14.079	14.306	15.952	1.1	-2.5	-2.5	0.3	2.3
Tertiary sector employment (%)	29.647	32.319	36.056	2.2	-2.5	-1.4	-0.4	1.1
Modern urban employment	1700.332	4370.888	8618.188	-0.7	0.1	-0.6	0.2	-0.3
Traditional urban employment	1174.426	2601.546	4521.313	-2.3	2.9	0.6	-0.2	-3.3
Mordern rural employment	1298.984	2357.057	3636.361	-1.3	-3.3	-3.9	1.4	4.9
Traditional rural employment	5640.996	9772.633	14201.848	-7.9	6.6	1.4	2.2	-5.1
Modern urban entrepreneurs/self-employment	239.891	603.912	1124.550	0.2	-0.4	-0.5	-0.0	0.5
Modern urban uneducated wage employment	560.952	1179.428	1982.817	-1.3	0.3	-0.0	-0.2	-1.1
Modern urban educated wage employment	899.490	2587.547	5510.813	-0.6	0.2	-0.8	0.5	-0.1
Modern rural wage employment	711.469	1359.852	2181.818	-1.2	-4.7	-5.5	1.6	6.6
Modern rural self-employment	587.514	997.205	1454.542	-1.4	-1.1	-1.6	1.0	2.5
Wages (in 1965 pesos)								
Modern-1 urban uneducated wage	1781.637	2538.444	4089.872	-1.3	-3.4	-6.0	2.3	3.6
Modern-1 urban educated wage	5648.156	7241.063	10461.188	-0.9	-4.7	-6.0	1.8	4.2
Modern-1 urban entrepreneurs income	16871.559	21291.398	29900.000	-3.0	-1.1	-3.8	2.0	0.2
Modern-2 urban educated wage	2475.541	2870.574	4179.563	-1.5	-3.3	-5.7	2.2	3.2
Modern-2 urban entrepreneurs income	7934.156	9887.094	15934.984	-2.5	-3.1	-6.1	2.5	2.7
Traditional urban mean earnings	1885.856	2554.561	4001.080	-1.4	-3.8	-6.2	2.3	4.1
Traditional urban educated earnings	4370.910	4562.832	6368.313	-1.0	-5.8	-7.2	2.3	6.2
Traditional rural earnings	872.401	1806.041	3170.527	10.9	2.6	12.2	-6.0	-3.6
Modern rural wage	1433.410	2738.742	4321.996	8.0	4.2	12.1	-5.1	-5.7
Modern rural self-employed earnings	1770.938	3789.672	6435.500	8.7	1.3	9.2	-4.9	-2.9

TABLE 9.2 (*continued*)

	RR, 1965	RR, 1985	RR, 2000	WB	NS1	NS2	WRL	WRH
Incomes (in 1965 pesos)								
Urban household income bottom decile	670.455	1004.762	1775.723	-0.5	-4.4	-6.4	1.8	3.9
Urban household income top decile	24518.141	33272.031	49230.000	-2.8	-1.1	-4.2	1.8	-0.1
Rural household income bottom decile	494.495	961.168	1621.268	5.8	3.3	9.4	-3.6	-3.3
Rural household income top decile	8487.492	17233.301	27886.680	3.8	3.0	7.7	-2.5	-2.3
Mean urban household income	6221.379	8631.313	13495.859	-2.1	-2.1	-4.9	1.8	1.1
Mean rural household income	2656.064	5288.938	8666.063	4.4	3.2	8.3	-2.8	-2.6
Mean urban income per adult equiv.	1241.704	1810.586	3014.186	0.0	-8.8	-10.0	5.8	16.2
Mean rural income per adult equiv.	619.174	1250.880	2236.763	12.9	-6.7	1.9	-4.1	9.2
Mean total income per adult equiv.	826.265	1482.796	2599.460	6.4	-8.2	-4.6	0.6	12.9
Urban Gini coefficient (after tax)	0.507	0.479	0.452	-0.6	1.0	0.8	-0.1	-1.2
Rural Gini coefficient (after tax)	0.423	0.428	0.419	-0.8	-0.2	-0.8	0.5	0.4
Total Gini coefficient (after tax)	0.499	0.471	0.459	-1.3	-0.2	-1.5	0.7	-0.1

reference run RR, especially in rural areas, largely because it includes a direct income effect; but results are quite close to RR. The Wéry–Rodgers low function (WRL) gives similar results in 2000 in terms of crude birth rate, but the time path is different – slower fertility change at first, but a more rapid decline over the 1990s, as evidenced by the larger changes in the total fertility rates. The two Nerlove–Schultz functions (NS1 and NS2), on the other hand, give fertility declines less than in the reference run; the decline over 1965–2000 is 14 per cent in NS2 and only 11 per cent in NS1. An idea of the reasons for these differences can be obtained by examining the elasticities in Table 9.1.

The large change in WRH can be traced to the large response to modernising economic structure, to female labour-force participation, to increased inequality and to increased education. In some cases, feedback loops are set up, so that the response of fertility to rising female labour-force participation in turn generates a further rise in the latter. The rather small responses of NS 1 and NS2 are partly due to the rather common pattern of small elasticities estimated in national cross-section. But there are also some effects of unexpected sign, notably the effects of unpaid family work, which, surprisingly, has a large negative impact. Increasing proletarianisation of the Philippine economy is then associated with higher fertility, which partly offsets the more conventional negative effects from declining mortality, rising age at marriage, and so on.

The effects on the rest of the economy of these changes are also quite diverse. It can be seen that in cases where fertility declines faster than in the reference run, there is a gain in income per adult equivalent overall by the year 2000, though only where the fertility decline is dramatic does the gain exceed 5 or 6 per cent. Nor are the gains evenly spread. In WB, they are entirely captured by rural areas, and urban household incomes fall (though the effects on the incomes of the urban poor are offset by improved urban income distribution). In WRL and WRH, the losers are the rural poor. In NS1, there are relative losses in income, which are particularly felt by the urban poor, although incomes per adult equivalent decline everywhere; while in NS2, rural incomes are up, especially among the poor, but all urban incomes are down. A number of different mechanisms contribute to these changes. Demographic change affects demand, particularly for food; thus falling birth rates reduce demand for agricultural output, agricultural prices and rural incomes. This is seen in, for instance, WRL where the fertility rate declines significantly faster than in the reference run only over 1985–2000. Here the terms of trade have declined as a result, and with them rural wages and incomes. In WRH and WB, the fertility decline is more rapid than in the reference run from the start. By the year

2000, the rural population and rural labour supply is lower – this can be seen in the primary sector employment figures – and this eventually reduces food output by more than the reduction in demand. When this occurs, the net effect is to raise the terms of trade, as can be seen in the case of WB, and with them rural incomes. In WRH, the supply effects do not dominate until after the year 2000, so the terms of trade are still somewhat down on the reference run in 2000. In NS1 and NS2, the demand effects still dominate, especially in NS2, where higher fertility has considerably raised the internal terms of trade. Feedbacks on migration, on labour supply, on government expenditure, on imports and exports, on output structure and on employment and wages can also be seen; we comment on some of these below in discussing policy experiments.

Policy Experiments

In this subsection we present two 'policy' experiments with Bachue-Philippines, each of which is implemented with each of the fertility functions described in the last subsection. Each experiment consists of one or more changes made exogenously to Bachue-Philippines, designed to reflect the direct or indirect effects of government policy instruments. The changes concern the following.

Education: the experiment consists of substantially increasing the rate of growth of enrolment and graduation in both secondary and primary school, especially in rural areas. The impact of the change is substantial; by the year 2000, in rural areas, 35 per cent of the population have completed secondary school,[8] as compared with 15 per cent in the reference run. The percentage of the population with less than primary education is 30 instead of 51. In urban areas, secondary completion is up from 43 per cent to 59 per cent, non-completion of primary down from 25 per cent to 14 per cent.

Egalitarian development: this experiment involves the application of a set of policies, representing a wide-ranging attempt to reduce income inequality and raise the incomes of the poorest 10 per cent. It includes progressive taxes, transfer payments to the poor, import substitution in food, higher exports, increased imports of some consumer goods, increased public investment, higher agricultural productivity growth, a public-works programme, increased migration, promotion of small-scale industry, some nationalisation of modern industry, high rates of education growth, increased labour absorption, and miscellaneous other policies bringing down wage variance. The programme is quite implausibly large, but is of interest if we wish to investigate the impact of a thoroughgoing attack on poverty.[9]

Results of the experiments are summarised in Tables 9.3 to 9.5. The results are presented policy by policy, and each table gives the effects of one policy change for each fertility function. Each policy is implemented in the year 1976 in the model, which is then run to the year 2000. The figures in the tables are percentages – they represent the percentage change in the variable concerned, in the year concerned, induced by the policy change. It is important to understand that the percentage figures in the tables refer to a static comparison, and not to changes over time. Comparisons are made for the years 1985 and 2000.

Education

The effects of the education change build up slowly, and are still rather small in 1985 for most functions. However, eventually they reach a respectable size in most cases, though still usually relatively small given the rather large education policy change assumed. The general effect, as expected, is for higher education to promote lower fertility. Table 9.3 summarises the effects on fertility in 1985 and 2000.

It can be seen that there is some diversity. In 1985, fertility in Nerlove-Schultz-2 (NS2) and Wéry–Rodgers high (WRH) is more responsive than in the others. These are functions which respond to child schooling rates rather than or as well as to adult education levels, and child schooling rates change with a much shorter lag. By the year 2000, however, adult education levels have changed sufficiently for some fertility response to be produced everywhere. The largest response in 2000 is in NS2, where the crude birth rate has been reduced by 20 per cent relative to the NS2 reference run. WRH, which showed the largest changes in 1985, seems relatively less responsive in 2000, but this is largely because it has reached replacement level fertility – a GRR of 1 – which is treated as a lower bound; this reduces the percentage change computed. Relatively large reductions in total population size are generated by NS 2, WRL and WRH, with the international cross-sections – RR and WB – and NS1 some way behind. The rural bias of the education policies is reflected in the relative changes in urban and rural fertility. This is seen in both 1985 and 2000 figures, with the rural change in fertility usually two to four times the urban change.

The diversity of the effects on fertility do not show up in equally diverse economic side-effects, because many of the effects of education on the economy are independent of the fertility change. However, there

TABLE 9.3 *Education experiment: effects on fertility in 1985 and 2000 (%)*

1985	RR	WB	NS1	NS2	WRL	WRH
Total population	0.0	−0.0	−0.0	−0.2	−0.3	−0.6
Crude birth rate	0.1	−0.6	−0.9	−4.0	−2.5	−6.2
Rural gross reproduction rate	0.0	−0.9	−1.0	−4.7	−3.5	−9.0
Urban gross reproduction rate	0.0	−0.1	−0.3	−2.0	−1.0	−2.4
Rural % completed secondary school	12.3	12.2	12.4	12.3	12.4	12.3
Urban % completed secondary school	1.5	1.5	1.5	1.5	1.5	1.5

2000						
Total population	−0.2	−0.7	−0.4	−2.9	−3.2	−4.9
Crude brith rate	−1.8	−2.3	−4.2	−19.9	−10.4	−5.8
Rural gross reproduction rate	−3.5	−5.4	−6.2	−27.9	−15.2	−15.8[a]
Urban gross reproduction rate	−1.0	−1.3	−2.3	−13.1	−8.2	−1.0[a]
Rural % completed secondary school	70.7	68.0	72.0	70.1	71.0	69.0
Urban % completed secondary school	13.0	12.7	13.1	12.8	12.9	12.7

[a] Percentage change affected by function hitting lower bound (gross reproduction rate = 1).

are certain interesting differences between fertility functions. A few key variables are reported in table 9.4. It can be seen that all functions agree that greater education leads to more equality, both within urban and rural areas and between them, but the extent varies. In Nerlove–Schultz-2 (NS2), and to a lesser extent in the Wéry–Rodgers functions WRL and WRH, the fertility decline is large enough to generate some limited gains in overall income per adult equivalent as well. As a result, the poor do reasonably well. Incomes in the lowest rural decile are up by 4–11 per cent. The rural rich usually also gain, but less, while the incomes of the urban poor are mostly little changed and the urban rich lose in all runs. Some of the variation can be attributed to the internal terms of trade, which eventually move in favour of agriculture when rural fertility declines, but this factor is fairly weak except in the very long term (after the year 2000). Rural–urban migration, which is promoted by higher education levels, also reduces the rural labour-force and therefore rural output. In NS2, where the fertility decline is largest in 2000, the shift in demand to urban areas is sufficiently large to promote modern urban employment and maintain urban relative to rural incomes; urban uneducated

TABLE 9.4 *Education experiment: effects on variables other than fertility (2000)*

2000	RR	WB	NS1	NS2	WRL	WRH
Net rural–urban migration	6.3	8.6	5.8	14.2	10.3	7.8
Agricultural-industry terms of trade	14.8	10.0	17.2	3.5	7.2	11.3
Modern urban employment	0.8	1.4	0.7	1.7	1.4	1.0
Traditional urban employment	−2.6	−2.1	−3.1	−2.6	−1.2	−1.2
Modern rural employment	−3.7	−2.9	−3.5	−0.6	−2.4	−2.4
Traditional rural employment	−4.2	−4.2	−4.8	−5.1	−4.1	−6.0
Modern urban uneducated wage	4.0	4.1	3.1	7.6	5.9	4.7
Modern urban educated wage	−10.5	−9.5	−10.8	−6.9	−8.5	−9.5
Urban traditional earnings	−3.0	−1.7	−3.9	0.6	−1.5	−1.7
Rural traditional earnings	12.9	9.5	14.2	4.3	7.2	11.4
Modern rural wage	11.1	7.6	12.0	2.4	5.8	7.9
Income of bottom urban decile	−0.9	0.1	−1.6	3.7	1.4	0.4
Income of top urban decile	−5.0	−3.9	−5.7	−1.6	−2.8	−4.4
Income of bottom rural decile	8.0	5.4	8.6	1.4	4.1	6.0
Income of top rural decile	4.4	2.8	5.0	−0.6	1.4	2.6
Mean urban income/adult equivalent	−3.9	−2.7	−4.2	2.3	−0.7	−1.4
Mean rural income/adult equivalent	6.0	4.7	8.0	7.7	5.7	8.9
Mean income/adult equivalent	0.7	0.8	1.7	5.2	2.5	3.5
Overall Gini coefficient	−2.2	−1.8	−2.5	−1.0	−1.4	−1.9

wages actually are increased more than rural wages and earnings. This leads to a continued high rate of migration.

Another experiment, not reported in detail here, but meriting a brief comment, involved an exogenous rise in female labour-force participation rates – this is commonly regarded as likely to influence fertility. Changes in birth rates were generally less than would be expected from the elasticities of female labour-force participation in the fertility functions, because indirect effects through wages, inequality, mortality, employment structure and other factors offset the direct effects. This illustrates the importance of examining the system of interrelationships as a whole rather than just the fertility function, when attempting policy assessments.

Egalitarian development strategy
In this experiment we look at the effects of a wide-ranging and implausibly

successful attack on poverty and inequality.[10] The effects on fertility vary from small to very large, but the conclusion is unanimous that fertility is reduced (see Table 9.5). Indeed, the birth-rate reduction ranges up to 30 per cent (WRH) in 1985. Rural fertility falls more than urban - this is hardly surprising since one of the main aims of the egalitarian strategy is to improve rural living conditions, in which it succeeds. Fertility decline in RR comes about largely through mortality change, although there are some secondary literacy and labour-force participation effects. Presumably, the inclusion of more independent variables in this function would have increased sensitivity. The WB function responds directly to income distribution, as well as to mean income per capita. Virtually all the independent variables in the WRL and WRH functions contribute to fertility decline; direct inequality effects, child mortality and employment structure are particularly important for WRH. The lack of impact on urban fertility in the WRL function can largely be traced to household income effects (with a negative elasticity in this function). It is interesting to note the mutual reinforcement between rural female labour-force participation increase and rural fertility decline in WRH. NS1 and NS2 respond much less than the others;[11] the main reason is that the egalitarian strategy promotes modern employment which, in the NS1 and NS2 functions, tends to increase fertility. Income effects also tend to raise fertility in NS2. However, the net change is still negative, because of the weight of mortality, marriage and education changes.

The differences between the various runs are sufficient to quite considerably affect certain outcomes by the year 2000; changes in the internal terms of trade, for instance, vary from 23 per cent (WB) to 46 per cent (WRH).[12] WRH hits the lower bound of the fertility function again; even so, it comes out well in terms of both income generation and poverty reduction, though it leaves more urban poverty than do either of the international cross-section runs. WRL, although it maintains the largest fertility reduction through to 2000, does not do particularly well in terms of either income or inequality. NS1 and NS2 do distinctly worse than the others in terms of both incomes and income distribution. Some of the income effects are due to the smaller fertility decline; however, they are also partly due to the additional imports, which are to some extent substituting for domestic production. Much of the difference in outcomes between the runs can be traced to terms of trade effects, since the terms of trade are fairly sensitive to fertility change. However, there are also dynamic interactions between fertility and the explanatory variables of the fertility functions which contribute significantly to the diverging outcomes.

TABLE 9.5 Egalitarian development: selected outcomes for 1985 and 2000 (%)

1985	RR	WB	NS1[a]	NS2[a]	WRL	WRH
Crude birth rate	-9.9	-12.9	-3.0	-1.6	-10.7	-29.4
Rural gross reproduction rate	-13.3	-15.9	-3.8	-1.9	-18.2	-42.3
Urban gross reproduction rate	-3.4	-7.5	0.8	1.4	-0.7	-16.1
Rural life expectancy	10.6	10.4	10.0	10.1	10.6	10.9
Urban life expectancy	2.9	3.4	2.5	2.5	2.6	3.5
% completed secondary school rural	2.4	2.4	2.5	2.5	2.5	2.4
% completed secondary school urban	-3.1	-3.3	-3.1	-3.1	-3.1	-3.2
Net rural–urban migration	56.8	59.1	57.2	54.7	54.7	59.6
Rural female labour-force participation	1.0	1.2	-1.0	-1.1	1.1	4.4
Urban female labour-force participation	-0.5	-0.4	-0.6	-0.7	-0.6	1.0
Primary sector output (%)	4.3	4.1	4.4	4.4	4.7	3.0
Agricultural-industry terms of trade	43.3	39.3	43.7	46.1	47.4	42.0
Modern urban employment	9.8	9.7	9.3	9.3	9.4	11.5
Modern rural employment	16.6	18.9	15.4	15.7	16.0	19.9
Modern urban uneducated wage	-18.9	-17.3	-19.0	-19.2	-19.7	-17.9
Modern urban entrepreneur income	-45.5	-44.5	-46.3	-46.4	-46.4	-44.9
Traditional urban earnings	-6.9	-5.1	-7.0	-7.4	-8.2	-4.8

Traditional rural earnings	43.5	39.7	42.6	45.0	45.2	41.2
Modern rural wage	15.8	15.5	13.7	16.3	16.4	16.1
Urban household income, bottom decile	17.6	19.7	17.2	16.4	15.9	19.8
Rural household income, bottom decile	82.8	81.3	81.0	84.0	84.2	81.0
Mean urban income/adult equivalent	−17.3	−15.4	−18.4	−18.8	−18.6	−15.4
Mean rural income/adult equivalent	40.2	41.1	35.2	36.6	40.1	43.1
Overall income/adult equivalent	10.6	11.0	8.7	8.4	10.2	12.0
Overall Gini coefficient	−25.5	−25.0	−25.9	−25.9	−25.8	−24.8
2000						
Crude birth rate	−11.6	−10.0	−1.2	−4.1	−17.6	−1.3
Agricultural-industry terms of trade	28.5	23.3	31.2	14.2	40.0	46.7
Modern rural employment	33.5	33.2	37.8	37.7	36.2	31.3
Urban household income, bottom decile	21.4	20.5	19.5	25.4	18.3	15.0
Rural household income, bottom decile	84.2	83.3	80.0	70.3	86.7	96.4
Urban income/adult equivalent	−22.6	−21.6	−26.2	−22.7	−24.7	−23.6
Rural income/adult equivalent	41.8	42.5	32.0	25.3	46.5	55.0
Overall income/adult equivalent	5.2	5.7	0.3	−0.4	5.7	9.0
Overall Gini coefficient	−31.5	−31.5	−31.2	−30.4	−31.5	−32.2

[a]Not strictly comparable with other runs – see note to text.

CONCLUSIONS

Although the results discussed above are experimental, they do indicate ways in which simulation techniques can be applied to draw conclusions with respect to (i) the choice of fertility function (and its estimation), and (ii) the effects of economic policy on fertility.

With respect to the choice of fertility function, there is a good deal of variation in the response of those used. On the whole, the functions based on international cross-section data (RR, WB) have a fairly smooth response to changes. Since fertility is explained by a small number of macro-variables, and these are highly aggregated, the scope for feedbacks is limited, and there is less tendency for the functions to respond abruptly to specific changes in the model – it is the aggregate consequences of particular policies which cause fertility to change. This is not true of the 'micro' functions, which have more diverse and less predictable responses. NS2 is more sensitive than NS1, and is also to be preferred to NS1 because it was estimated by simultaneous-equation techniques. However, its sensitivity is not uniform; the response of fertility in the education (and also labour-force participation) experiments was fairly large. But the more general changes in economic outcomes incorporated in the egalitarian development strategy generated rather small changes. One reason is the positive effect of income in this function, with a declining elasticity as income increases. More important is the inclusion of an employment structure variable for which the partial elasticity has the opposite sign to that predicted. Increasing the proportion of unpaid family workers reduces fertility in NS2 (and NS1), whereas the prediction of the Nerlove-Schultz theory is the reverse. A possible explanation is that unpaid family workers are acting as a proxy for an important variable omitted from the model.

The 'guestimate' WRL and WRH functions have responses which differ from the other micro functions, and from each other. The differences are most marked in the egalitarian strategy run, where many different changes cumulated to give large fertility responses, whereas in the NS functions some of the effects offset each other. The response of WRH to the egalitarian strategy is perhaps implausibly large, but the same is true of the strategy itself. An obvious next step would be to test model sensitivity to different parameters of WRL and WRH, so as to suggest the variables on which future research efforts should be concentrated. It would also be possible to refine parameter estimates by the iterative procedure noted in the first section, if there were an accurate time-series of birth rates and other important economic and demographic variables against which model results could be checked.

The differences in outcomes with the different versions of the model suggest some guidelines for the choice of fertility functions in models of this sort. The international cross-sections may be better at tracking long-term evolutions, but not at assessing shorter-term reactions to particular policy instruments, where direct effects will probably be lost. Micro functions have several advantages, and the experiments with WRL and WRH suggest that a satisfactory formulation can be found. However, they do run into estimation problems, partly because cross-sectional parameter estimates are not necessarily a good guide to changes over time, and partly because complex micro functions run into difficulties of specification, of data availability, and of multicollinearity. An example of the cross-sectional estimation problem is the positive income effect measured in NS2. This may well reflect relative, rather than absolute, income position, in which case increasing incomes of the population as a whole over time would not have the effects on fertility predicted by the cross-sectional coefficient of income. Other dynamic effects (expectations, changing norms) will also be omitted.

An illustration of the relative validity of different estimation techniques is the performance of the Bachue-Philippines reference run (using a fertility function based on international cross-section analysis), compared with observed changes in fertility in the Philippines.

World Fertility Survey data for 1977, together with earlier estimates, suggest that the total fertility rate in the Philippines has dropped sharply:

	1965	*1970*	*1977*
Survey estimates	6.3	5.9	5.0
Bachue-Philippines	6.8	6.6	5.9

The level of the Bachue estimates are consistently higher than the survey estimates, because of different data sources and internal corrections for consistency in the model. This apart, the pattern of fertility decline is reproduced in the model, with around two-thirds of the change suggested by the survey data. Behavioural fertility functions using cross-sectional Philippine national data, however, generate virtually no change in fertility levels over this period (see, for example, Kintanar *et al.*, 1974; also Rodgers, Hopkins and Wéry, 1978, ch. 6). In this case, then, the dynamics appear to be better represented by the internationally-based function, though improved, dynamically-specified national functions could certainly also be developed.

Another major issue is whether a fertility function should be estimated alone, or as part of a larger set of relationships. Theoretically, the case for the latter is strong if fertility and some other variable are simultaneously determined. Empirically, the simulations shed some light on this issue through the comparison of NS2 (estimated with simultaneous-equations techniques) with NS1 (estimated as a separate function).[13] Firstly, it can be observed that significantly different results are obtained with NS1 and NS2, with the demographic responses of NS2 larger on the education and labour-force participation experiments. But secondly, especially in the light of the comments made above, the results suggest that the static world of simultaneous household decision models is too restricted, and too sensitive to minor changes in model specification; only by looking at fertility within – and estimated as part of – a dynamic model which incorporates recursive relationships, structural changes and expectations can we hope to obtain adequate explanations of fertility – and fertility research is still far from this point.

In the meantime, what can we infer about the effects of economic policy on fertility in the case represented by the Philippine model? The evidence of the last section is unambiguous – there are such effects, and the impact on fertility is likely to be important in some cases. In particular, the egalitarian development path, which relies on employment generation and reduced income disparities, has by far the largest impact on fertility, enough to generate major modifications in the rate and nature of population growth with a majority of the fertility functions used.

A final comment is worth making on the importance of the fertility specification for model use. Our results suggest that the interactions between fertility and the rest of the socio-economic system generate development paths which diverge for different fertility functions (Table 9.2) and which generate significantly different appreciations of the impact of certain types of policies (Tables 9.3 to 9.5). There is therefore a strong case for careful endogenisation of fertility for large-scale simulation purposes.

NOTES

1. See, for instance, T. W. Schultz (1974) for a number of articles which are typical of the genre.
2. The model requires some 250 behavioural and accounting equations to describe it fully, and contains almost 2000 endogenous variables.
3. For a more detailed analysis using additional functions and making additional experiments, see Rodgers and Wéry (1977).
4. For more comprehensive surveys of fertility functions, see T. P. Schultz (1974b) and Research Triangle Institute (1971).

5. With minor corrections to give observed initial fertility.

6. We return to this point in the next section.

7. The use of these various functions in Bachue-Philippines should be treated as experimental. Imposing fertility functions estimated for Puerto Rico on a model estimated for the Philippines is not intended as a guide to policy-making in Puerto Rico, or for that matter in the Philippines. The objective is rather to explore the importance and implications of likely and plausible relationships between economic and demographic change.

8. With the original (RR) fertility function.

9. It is discussed in more detail in Hopkins, Rodgers and Wéry (1976).

10. Implausible not only because of the size of the changes made, but also because the country is running a massive balance of payments deficit and a large government deficit without doing anything about financing either. Since we are interested mainly in fertility, we have not made great efforts to solve this sort of problem.

11. Strictly, these are non-comparable with the rest, since the egalitarian strategy initially sent the model outside the bounds permited by its solution technique: additional food imports were required to get the model to run to 2000. This reduces the internal terms of trade, and thus reduces rural incomes relative to urban. The net effect is probably to slightly underestimate the fertility decline produced by egalitarian development.

12. The smaller change in NS2 is because the terms of trade are artificially modified as noted in the previous note.

13. Although the test is not entirely fair, since for a complete comparison the whole Nerlove–Schultz model should have been incorporated in NS2, rather than only the fertility function.

10 Some Aspects of Anthropological Contributions

CHRISTINE OPPONG

INTRODUCTION

This chapter is concerned with some of the advantages which might accrue to economic research and policy-making based upon it in the field of fertility behaviour, if more insights, both conceptual and methodological, were drawn from other disciplinary approaches. The particular approaches used here are those of social anthropology or comparative family sociology. These are especially appropriate since economists' interests in fertility behaviour extend beyond one culture or nation-state and thus require a thoroughly cross-cultural perspective.[1] At the same time, since data bases are admittedly inadequate and funds for collecting relevant new data limited, introduction to a range of flexible and relatively inexpensive techniques of data collection, which may be used to explore issues of special interest or policy-related concern, may help to extend the current range of questions examined by more conventional approaches pursued by economists.

Significantly, at the present time, it is frequently argued that there is a need for reconciliation among different disciplinary approaches (e.g. Burch, 1980). Associated activities which attest to the prevalence of such interests include the emphasis given to interdisciplinary debate[2] and attempts to develop conceptual models helping to explain differential fertility which incorporate social and cultural factors, as well as economic.[3] Economists often claim a high degree of cross-cultural applicability for their models, but a number of critics have argued that current economic models have not sufficiently taken into account the social, cultural and specifically familial contexts of fertility.[4]

Two major points have been made earlier in this volume about the sub-

240

ject matter and methods of economists' research on fertility. Firstly, economic research is concerned with the extent to which fertility behaviour is ultimately a rational or consistent response to perceived resource constraints and opportunity costs – attempting to provide insights into the extent to which fertility levels and changes are related to alterations in availability and allocation of scarce resources in money, material goods and time between potentially conflicting goals. Secondly, there is little tradition among economists of collecting and processing new field data for such research purposes. This gap restricts the number, range and type of variables considered for building models, and thus the array of policy options to which such models might be relevant.

Consequently, the goal of this chapter is to include in this series of mainly economic essays a discussion from a social-anthropological perspective, which calls attention to an alternative conceptual framework for examining potential connections between fertility-related expectations and behaviour and perceived resource scarcity at the micro level of the individual and domestic group. This is achieved through indicating how differences and changes in expectations (norms, values and perceptions) and behaviours associated with various roles (such as those of parent, spouse, child, kin, etc.) may be related to both resources on the one hand and fertility on the other, and form critical intervening links in chains of change, which more complex models are currently attempting to incorporate, relating changing phenomena both inside and outside the domestic domain (e.g. Bagozzi and Van Loo, 1978a, 1978b, 1980). At the same time, it briefly describes, for readers trained in other disciplines, some of the empirical techniques used by anthropologists in the field; noting their peculiar advantages for the study of norms, values and beliefs and activities associated with resources and procreation and its regulation. These include modes of data collection such as observation of natural life events and situations; purposeful selection of typical or deviant or contrasting cases or small analytical samples of events, people, domestic groups or communities for detailed study, the emphasis upon the value of qualitative as well as quantitative data and information about relationships or how things hang together in social systems. As Simmons has remarked, all of these research tools and modes of data collection can be important for the work of economists, just as the kinds of hypotheses derived from an anthropological or behavioural framework may be tested with the conventional tools of econometrics.

With these goals in view, we first look at some anthropological perspectives on fertility and then examine several conceptual problems currently confronted by economists and demographers, before going on to examine

the relevant concepts used by social-anthropologists and family sociologists. The variables and their definition, and the relationships that are of
primary concern to economic and demographic studies of fertility, include
such concepts as household, family, costs of parenting, sex roles and
marriage or conjugal-role relationships. Some indication is given of how
formulation of indices to facilitate measurement and comparison of aspects
of such phenomena is pertinent to examination of correlates of variations
and changes in fertility-related expectations and behaviour. These aspects
include such dimensions as the *openness* or *closure* of the conjugal family
unit, its functional boundedness in various areas of functioning, and the
jointness or *segregation* of the conjugal-role relationship (the extent to
which spouses flexibly share activities and responsibilities of various kinds).
Next we discuss briefly some of the empirical methods which are the
foundation of social-anthropological field-work. In the final section we
refer to some Ghanaian empirical studies, which illustrate the potential
value of these concepts and methods for economic-demographic work,
focusing on fertility and its regulation, and the research and policy implications of these.

Anthropological Approaches

Anthropologists feel that the main demographic patterns of any society
rest on a combination of social, cultural and psychological factors, and
that these can be uncovered only through the intensive methods of the
field anthropologist (e.g. MacFarlane, 1976). Numerous ethnographic
accounts have documented, albeit often in descriptive fashion, the sorts of
relationships observed between the resource system of a society, modes of
production, values and demographic processes, in particular procreation
within the context of marriage and domestic organisation. Recent sum-
maries of the trends observed in anthropological approaches to population
studies in general have indicated a wide range of interest, with two basic
themes permeating many of these studies; one being the way demographic
events influence social structure and ideology, and vice versa (see Reining,
1981). Such studies have been carried out using different levels of analysis
including individuals, domestic groups, communities, cultures, states and
globally.

A persistent theme of such studies is the existence of mechanisms
whereby a balance of some kind is maintained between available, finite
material resources, in land, food, etc., and population-size (at the domestic,
community or ethnic level) (e.g. Douglas, 1966). In contrast with scholars
of other disciplines, anthropologists have consistently supported the con-

tention that societies have 'always' controlled their own population growth, and some empirical work in this field shows the relevance of this hypothesis to the population dynamics of small groups (Reining, 1981, p. 40).

Discussions about factors constraining fertility include whether it is deliberate or incidental; whether it is the result of social or biological mechanisms, and the extent to which individuals or sets of people are making conscious decisions, rather than following the dictates of tradition or custom. The sorts of methods of fertility regulation which anthropologists have typically documented include pre-modern methods such as abortion, delayed marriage, enforced celibacy, residential separation of spouses, post-partum sexual taboos and breastfeeding. As Reining (1981, p. 89) has emphasised, anthropologists expect to find controls, both on the basis of previous empirical evidence and on the basis of their theoretical approach to the functioning of a society. The difficult task is to show how these controls work or how they change, in particular cultural contexts, or how they are related to the particular resource-base considered critical and to changes taking place in the latter.

It has been argued by anthropologists that a new 'cultural inventory' is a necessary pre-condition to modern contraceptive adoption (Epstein, 1977, pp. 226, 235). People need to have alternative choices and possibilities for calculation, as well as the opportunity and power to shape their own lives, and those of their children, and that only when their economic hopes and aspirations are raised in a context of scarce means do they start worrying about the potential future quality of life of their children (e.g. Das Gupta, 1977). Thus anthropologists are seen to share with economists an interest in relating resources of several kinds and expectations about them to differential and changing fertility. And in this endeavour power, control and the opportunity to choose are realised to be critical.

We shall turn next to some particular conceptual issues and methodological problems, currently the focus of scholarly concern and about which recent comparative anthropological work has something pertinent to contribute, in view of its cross-cultural perspective and multiple modes of data collection and analysis.

Conceptual Concerns: Family Phenomena

Certain concepts pertaining to role relationships and resources in the domestic domain recur frequently in the various writings of economists about fertility. They usually concentrate on couples who are married and include in their calculations the relative resources of each spouse in terms of occupation, income, age and education. Thus the marriage bond and conjugal resources are major foci. They view fertility as occurring in 'households' inhabited by 'families' and consider parenthood and parental inputs into childbearing and childrearing. Increasingly, the use of the resource time as well as money is calculated and considered.

For the most part, the implicit models of marriage, family and household organisation and parenthood utilised, consciously or unconsciously, are derived from western European and North American models. The latter assume a functionally individuated, nuclear family, of wife, husband and children, living in the same home with a segregated conjugal-role relationship, in which the husband is the major income-earner working outside the home, with little responsibility for tasks within the home, and the wife has major responsibility for domestic work. She may or may not generate income outside the home, depending upon a variety of preferences and constraints.

Assumptions built into this model and invalid in many cultural contexts include the ideas that conjugal solidarity in economic and other terms is stronger than sibling solidarity or that between any other combination of kin; that children are raised by their biological parents; that only mother's time is used for child-care; that the conjugal family is a functionally separate unit as regards maintenance, consumption, socialisation, and control over people and resources (e.g. Schultz, 1974). At the same time, there is the underlying assumption that the areas of productive work and income generation on the one hand, and home and procreation and socialisation on the other, are spatially and functionally separate and that one is mainly the preserve of men and the other largely the concern of women.

However, frustration in attempts to utilise such a model of the domestic domain in diverse studies, the barrage of criticism from scholars more accustomed to cross-cultural comparative data collection and analysis and exposure to the growing bodies of empirical evidence refuting such assumptions have led to a general mood of dissatisfaction regarding this model. Thus a growing sense of unease is apparent in the writings of economists and demographers as they write about 'household' behaviour and differential fertility in various cultures. Signs of such unease include worry about what should be the unit of analysis in empirical work, in view of the increasing dissatisfaction with the classical economic concept of the unitary, functionally-individuated, co-resident 'household'. Such concern is evident, for example in the qualms of Kuznets (1978) as he writes about the size and age-structure of family households, particularly with respect to the boundedness or 'closure' of domestic units. It is clear in the misgivings of Galbraith (1973, p. 36) as he discusses consumption and the concept of the household and the sexual division of tasks and resources. It is obvious in the writings of Leibenstein (1977), who remarks, regarding units of study, that in traditional economic theory pertaining to the household, the way in which individuals are related to economic decision-making units is not considered, with the consequence that traditional economic theory is unable to examine intra-household differences in preferences and values and how these may relate to economic decisions. However, as he argues, once the basic decision-making unit considered is the individual, then a much more realistic and detailed analysis is possible, because the behaviour and expectations of individuals can be considered, their roles and the ways they relate to others and to groups. Indeed, it is only when individuals are considered that an attempt can be made to study the functioning of highly complex domestic groups (or firms).

Similarly, there is an expressed realisation of the need to improve the sophistication of conceptual frameworks relating to family systems and kin ties so that their power for theory-building or data collection at the macro or micro level can be improved. Thus R. Freedman (1979, p. 65) notes the significance of the failure of classical demographic theory to deal empirically with changes in the family which might be among the links between macro-variables and fertility. Again, cultural variability in family systems is increasingly recognised, even though the extent of differences may not be fully perceived. Thus, Birdsall *et al.* (1979, p. 217) while recognising that '"families" are organised differently in different societies' still think that 'the nuclear family, with modest and variable extensions and adaptation, remains the predominant type'.

Related to these concerns is the growing recognition of the ambiguity and measurement difficulties encountered in attempts to index and compare central and critical concepts such as 'costs of parenthood', 'women's status', etc., increasingly used in economic-demographic analyses. These are problems which have been referred to in Part I of this volume and with which recent empirical analyses have been compelled to grapple (e.g. Maudlin, Berelson and Sykes, 1979), albeit unsuccessfully (Dixon, 1979). It is thus not surprising to find that numerous attempts have been made by economists and demographers, especially those involved in empirical work in diverse cultural contexts, to increase the complexity of the bounded, co-resident, conjugal family and household model in their studies. Such attempts have involved the dichotomisation of residence patterns, often contrasting 'nuclear' and 'extended'; a more careful examination of the directions of the flow of resources between kin and parents and children (e.g. Caldwell, 1982, 'wealth flows'); and realisation of the possibility of delegation of child-care to people other than the biological parents. Recently, Ben-Porath (1980) has begun to attempt a more sophisticated analysis of familial transactions.

All such attempts are steps towards making household models more flexible and more appropriate to diverse life situations, so that they might become more capable of dealing empirically and theoretically with very diverse domestic situations and relationships. And these are intimately involved in the complex processes of begetting, bearing and rearing children, the differential outcomes of which ultimately constitute diverse fertility levels and affect population growth.

We now turn to a set of variables and a conceptual framework which permit the required degrees of flexibility, complexity and detail needed for cross-cultural work.

ROLES, RELATIONSHIPS AND RESOURCES

Scholars from a variety of disciplines have, over the past few decades, proposed the relevance to fertility of a number of changing phenomena in the domestic domain pertaining to resource production, control, management, consumption and availability or perceptions about these, which, if they are to be adequately tested, require far more sophisticated models of roles, relationships and resources than those offered hitherto by economists. They include a range of propositions referring to role substitution, role activity delegation or sharing, changing status attached to roles (in terms of associated deference or prestige and control of resources and power over people), including increases in equality and changes in norms, values and perceptions about resources in time and money and how they should be spent – on whom and by whom. Before examining some of these hypotheses, a closer look at concepts relating to roles and statuses is required, since these and their associated attributes, including conflict, strain, stress, etc., form the potential building blocks and links in such new hypotheses.

Role theory offers a flexible and widely used set of concepts, which has been developed over several decades, providing a framework and a set of units for data collection and analysis by diverse methods of varying complexity and based on contrasting assumptions regarding the nature of social change (Biddle, 1979). The concepts allow the researcher to focus upon individuals, while at the same time placing them within their diverse economic, social and cultural contexts, including consideration of prescribed norms, tasts, preferences or values and perceptions and institutional frameworks of reciprocal rights and obligations and sets of relationships with significant others. Role theory also facilitates measurement and comparisons, of both behaviour and expectations including role strain (perceived inadequacy of resources), conflict and pressure towards change and innovation. Furthermore, role theory enables us to examine systematically issues of allocation of resources, choice, decision-making and power, essential to the documentation of dynamic systems.

Types of data which can be used with the framework include such a diverse array of materials as time budget series, interviews, observations, surveys, focused biographies, census materials, media and literature searches. Foci of study can include behaviours, resources and expectations. The concept of role focuses attention upon activities and expectations characteristic or observed among particular categories of people and relevant to certain contexts. Thus behavioural or expected roles can be studied. Role expectations include expressions of what ought to be (prescriptions), what is preferred (values), or what is seen to exist (perceptions). Conformity involves the idea of similarity and overlap between expectations and activities and the idea that the former moulds the latter. On the other hand, creativity, innovation or deviance are associated with changes in behaviour from customarily acceptable role models. Such is the case of innovators who decide to use modern contraceptive methods to control their fertility and cause it to be below traditionally-valued levels. It is recognised that in rapidly-changing, mobile and complex systems there are likely to be conflicting pressures upon individuals in terms of new role expectations, as well as changing opportunities or new resource constraints and areas of stress and strain, and in these phenomena are valuable pointers to possible directions of social change.

The framework is capable of providing needed links between observations at the micro and macro levels, between individuals, institutions and societal and cultural contexts.

Simple forms of role concepts are used in many studies, but they offer tremendous potential for increasingly complex and sophisticated analysis, as well as for subtle qualitative treatment (Nye, 1976). Recently a framework for comparative role analyses in relation to demographic change has been outlined, within the context of a global research programme on women's roles and demographic issues, which combines the above variables, providing a system of classification to facilitate such endeavours cross-culturally (Oppong, 1980). This framework includes consideration of the roles of parent, worker outside the home, worker inside the home, spouse, kin, community member and self-actualising individual. It combines several kinds of data, including information on resources, decision-making and control, as well as expectations indicating how multiple measures of sexual inequalities in the division of tasks and resources may be devised.

The cursory reference above to some current problems in the economic and demographic literature pertaining to the explanation of household behaviour in general and fertility in particular, indicates the potential range of utility of the role framework and its current relevance. It could be used to help solve several dilemmas.

(i) It can help to overcome the problem of the simultaneous examination of expectations, resources and behavioural phenomena.

(ii) It can facilitate a shift beyond the use of unitary co-residential household models towards a focus upon individuals as parents, spouses, workers outside the home, etc., but within their nexus of resources, relationships, etc., thus permitting a more complex conceptualisation of the domestic group (e.g. J. Goody, 1972).

(iii) It can make possible a more complex analysis of resource flows and transactions between individuals and within and between households, and the contracts which may exist between them, which are increasingly realised as critical by economists and demographers (e.g. Ben-Porath, 1980).

(iv) It could make feasible the kinds of studies of inertia and rational decision-making advocated in some quarters, especially through the mechanism of role strain (e.g. Leibenstein, 1980).

(v) It can provide meaningful measures of individuation or solidarity or individualism, called for by some hypotheses (e.g. MacFarlane, 1978a, 1978b).

(vi) It could make available a more realistic and systematic assessment of relative costs and opportunity costs of child-care, and who is providing the required resources in different cultural contexts (Oppong and Bleek, 1982; Oppong, 1983c).

(vii) It could incorporate the use of time-budget studies more meaningfully into appropriate socio-economic frameworks (e.g. Mueller, 1982).

(viii) Being culture-free, it could make possible the kind of detailed cross-cultural comparisons required to asses and contrast rates and directions of change and areas of difference in the relative status and power of the sexes (Oppong, 1983b).

With this sort of role framework in mind, we shall next turn to a brief consideration of several major hypotheses linking resources, parental roles and fertility. As we shall see, underlying each is the assumption that increasing costs, burdens, conflicts, stresses and strains associated with the maternal or paternal roles, either actual or perceived, lead to attempts to reduce these costs in one way or another, including lowering of fertility values and increased regulation of fertility, at least for those individuals who have the power, means and opportunities to do so.

Some Hypotheses Linking Parental Roles, Resources and Fertility

As we noted above, many economic models built to explain fertility have assumed that parents maintain and care for their own children and that the continuing flow of time and money inputs is from mothers and fathers to their offspring. Contrary empirical evidence from many contexts, however, has led to the widespread testing of a number of hypotheses, which envisage other types of transactions associated with parental roles. Some of these hypotheses are referred to here.

Parental status

A current theme attracting many researchers is that relating parental status, in terms of command over the labour and products of children, with high fertility values (e.g. Cain, 1977; Mueller, 1976; Turchi and Bryant, 1979). Time-use studies have underlined the importance of inputs of children's time to the farms and business enterprises of parents and kin, arguing that as this work becomes illegal or otherwise unavailable, as in contexts of universal primary education and wage employment for adults only, the economic value of children declines, the costs rise and fertility also declines (e.g. Bulatao, 1980). Thus, Caldwell's (1982) wealth flows argument has proposed that as children become the object of work and money costs, rather than producing resources for their parents' benefit, support for high fertility is likely to decline.

Furthermore, studies in some cultures focusing on the effects of education have indicated quantitative and qualitative differences in the content of parent-filial relationships with schooling; differences in time and knowledge devoted to the parental role and the quality of interactions, and the rising of parental aspirations for children's education, training and future occupations, which indicate a relative rise in the status of children *vis-à-vis* parents and point towards a growing emphasis on quality rather than quantity of children (e.g. Caldwell, 1979; Hill and Stafford, 1980; Levine, 1980).

Time-use studies, value of children psychological studies and observations of flows of wealth of different kinds and effects of education support the hypothesis regarding the dwindling of parental status *vis-à-vis* children (that is, increased equality) and fertility. There is, however, a lack of detailed studies illustrating the precise mechanisms whereby such changes occur at the level of activities and expectations, and identifying the individuals in selected populations who have already either suffered parental status loss or raised their aspirations for their children and adapted their behaviour accordingly.[5]

Individualism

A range of hypotheses are current which focus upon the effects of increasing individualism: the diminution of parental-role delegation of activities and responsibilities concerned with parenting, a pattern which has been widespread in many cultures (e.g. E. Goody, 1978). Such hypotheses link parents' increased personal responsibility with a rising perception of costs, whether in time or money, and a desire to limit fertility. Such personalisation of parental responsibilities, as Leibenstein has pointed out, is a critical policy-related phenomenon, since 'free riders' are less likely to care about restricting their procreative activities, than are those who are totally involved in assumption of related parental expenditures. Two main types of sharing and delegation have been identified and studied, the one involving the spouse and thus the conjugal division of labour and resources (aspects of what have been termed *jointness* and *segregation* of the conjugal-role relationship), and the second involving kin, servants, household members and others.[6] Diminished opportunities for delegation have been related to kin dispersal, schooling of children who are potential nurses, and changing norms about the propriety of such sharing or delegation. Historical evidence has been provided of the economic and affective changes over time associated with such a shift towards individualsim.[7]

Individualisation of parent–child ties is correlated with the dwindling strength of sibling group bonds. Causal mechanisms include social and spatial mobility of individuals and dispersal of kin, through education and individual opportunities for employment and income-generation. Thus, while the classical household model assumes individualism in terms of the parental role, historical and cross-cultural data show the diversity and complexity and importance of changes in this sphere, and the need for measurement and comparison. Again, more detailed studies of changing behaviour patterns and expectations in this regard are needed, which can be used to test the hypothesis of their association with differential fertility.

The sexual division of labour

Regarding parental inputs in time and money, the classical household model assumes the male is the main breadwinner, providing material resources to support offspring, and that the female is the nurturant mother and domestic worker, providing time. However, increasing bodies of data collected from around the world attest to the variety in the sexual and more specifically conjugal division of labour, both inside and outside the home, and the pervasiveness of change.

A subject which has been the focus of considerable research attention from economists and others has been the effects upon fertility-related behaviour and aspiration of women's paid work *outside the home*.[8] The underlying assumption here is one of role conflict; that the expectations and activities of the two roles are incompatible, that women cannot work outside the home and care for children and babies within it, and that the more women who work outside the home, the lower will be their fertility. However, realisation that many women of the world are engaged in production and income-generating activities, in contexts where these can be combined with child-care, has led to an increase in time-use studies and observation of activities to discover the extent of simultaneity of parental and occupational role activities.[9]

A subject which has been given less attention, especially in the developing world, is division of domestic labour between spouses, in particular time inputs into child-care. This is regrettable since several studies have shown that the more flexible and egalitarian the conjugal division of tasks, the lower are fertility expectations.[10] Significantly, such flexibility of allocation of role activities between spouses and the associated egalitarian decision-making processes have been linked to the similarity of resources in education and income. Such evidence provides important scope for the extension of research into sex roles and conjugal exchanges in relation to parental costs and fertility (e.g. Scanzoni, 1975, 1976a, 1976b and 1980; Bagozzi and Van Loo, 1980).

The individual self

Another theme in studies of industrial and post-industrial nations is the attempt to link the absolute decline in fertility aspirations with the individuals growing focus upon self. The latter involves the desire to spend as much time as possible upon leisure, rest and recreation or the desire to spend material resources upon personal status-enhancing attributes (expensive material goods) or costly-enjoyed activities, hence the lack of desire for offspring who would detract from available resources in money and time. Recent writers on this topic have noted that a profound cultural change has taken place in Europe associated with a marked demographic change – the decline in fertility. Responsible parenthood is no longer a universally valued goal, parental sacrifice is no longer a prescribed norm (Hawthorn, 1980; Ariès, 1981; Steiner, 1977).

In the developing world, one or two studies indicate a shift in norms, tastes and perceptions of a similar kind among deviant urban minorities. Individuals are depicted who reject local pro-natalist norms and values regarding marriage and parenthood and prefer to spend their time and money on individual material security, self-gratification and advancement (e.g. Dinan, 1983).

Such hypotheses linking changing roles and fertility cannot be tested using traditional economic household models and the stock lists of variables. They call for propositions regarding linkages between activities, expectations and resources (material and intangible, i.e. statuses) attached to roles, and differential and changing fertility aspirations and achievements, and for connecting changing parental-role activities and expectations with changes in other roles people play. To test such hypotheses, data are needed on time and money budgets, acquisition and control of resources, decision-making processes and changing norms, values and beliefs. Collection and analysis of such a battery of data is facilitated by adoption of the flexible set of concepts available from role theory and a battery of qualitative and quantitative research methods, already familiar to anthropological field-workers. It is to consideration of these methods that we shall now turn.

ANTHROPOLOGICAL METHODS AND RESEARCH DESIGN

Field-work

The importance of observing and documenting real-life situations, of seeing and describing behaviour as well as taking account of role expectations – norms, values and beliefs – are basic to the social anthropological approach. Thus a hallmark of anthropological field-studies is the necessity for a period of personal immersion in the real-life context of the people studied, with the idea that such face-to-face personal experience is vital for finding out what are really the fundamental questions, and consequently what are the variables and hypotheses which can be selected for more detailed and systematic study. This applies even though the field-worker may approach the field with a clear conceptual framework to assist in the collection and classification of information, or a theoretical model which already indicates the kinds of issues and connections selected for study.

Other characteristic features of anthropological field-work include its intensiveness and its smallness of scale, especially single-community studies entailing several months or years of residence, and the use of genealogical materials to provide an important framework for the collection of much behavioural data on patterns of production, ownership, inheritance, ritual behaviour, residence patterns, socialisation, etc.

In field-studies, it has been in the past common practice to take a holistic approach, that is, taking account of the total range of social and cultural phenomena which can be observed, rather than defining one narrowly-prescribed set of factors to be considered in isolation (which in the case of fertility has often been assumed to include parity on the one hand, and age, marital status, education, employment and income on the other). At the same time, the field-worker using an anthropological approach remains sensitive to the potential significance of unanticipated findings in the field, what have been called 'anomalous strategic data'.

Social events both large and small in scale provide important subjects for study, including birth, naming ceremonies, puberty rituals, weddings, funerals and court cases and disputes. A series of such selected events may themselves provide the major subject of study, as for instance, a set of legal cases, a series of funerals or puberty rituals. The study of important groups has been a central focus of concern, including domestic groups (households), descent groups (lineages and descending kindreds) and sibling groups; their formation, organisation and change over time.

Data Collection Techniques

Watching and listening are the basic field techniques, as is careful recording of all such observations. In the past, interviews with key informants have formed an important source of data. Ethnographers normally combine data from personal eye-witness observations with information gained from informants' descriptions. Life-history materials or focused biographies have also been an important type of field data. These are often useful for examining values and perceptions, as well as being accounts of past activities and events. They may, of course, focus on particular issues such as fertility (e.g. Reining *et al.*, 1977; Oppong and Abu, 1984). And, often, interview guides are used rather than questionnaires, encouraging people to talk on selected topics but leaving their responses free-flowing and open.

Surveys and censuses have been increasingly used as sources of information. There is, however, a pervasive feeling that reliance on one structured interview is likely to produce inadequate and distorted information.

Meanwhile, observation is limited to the range of the eyes and ears of the observer, who is thus constrained in the number of events and people that can be observed, hence the typical small size of the communities, neighbourhoods and sets of domestic groups or individuals studied by ethnographers.[11]

Data Analysis: Qualitative and Quantitative

Anthropologists, like other social scientists, use diverse methods in looking for meaningful patterns among the variables selected for study, including various kinds of quantitative analysis, such as tests of independence and measures of association and factor analysis, multiple regression, etc. What differentiates the anthropologist's approach from that of other social scientists using similar techniques, however, is that they generally also have plenty of contextual data as well, including descriptions of behaviour observed, language texts, focused interview materials, etc., which all may give support and weight to the statistical data. Thus, they avoid the problem of attaching too much meaning to the occurrence of chance, statistically-significant differences, which may easily occur in large samples of data.

The argument is not whether to use quantitative or qualitative data, but how most judiciously to mix and integrate them to develop useful and credible information. As Pelto and Pelto (1978) have noted, credibility of information about human behaviour can rest alone on neither 'purified numerical analysis' nor 'rich verbal description that ignores underlying questions of quantity and intensity'. The importance attached to numerical analysis and its sophistication in anthropological studies has varied in the past but is noted to be increasing. Interest in the study of change processes has no doubt led to an increased interest in quantification. In cases in which the universe studied is small, the total universe may be sampled. Sometimes a random representative or stratified sample is selected, or quota sample, when a goal is to study people who differ in some critical way such as age, social class, caste, etc. Another important kind of sample which may be used is the *analytical sample*, which is not necessarily randomly selected nor representative of any larger universe, but is chosen specifically for the exploration of selected variables and their potential linkages and correlations with other chosen factors.

Types of Research Design: Some Examples

Anthropologists use several sorts of research design when planning their studies. These include studies of single cases such as one individual, one family, household, kin group or village community, such as Bleek's (1975) study of a single West African lineage; comparisons and contrasts of several case-studies, as in a study of 12 married couples and their relationships and resources (Oppong, 1982); the cross-cultural (statistical) method, such as used in the study of patterns of post-partum abstinence in West Africa in Page and Lesthaege (1981), and the inter-regional comparison and intra-cultural analysis, such as the several cultures study of fertility in East Africa (Molnos, 1972).

ETHNOGRAPHIC EVIDENCE FROM GHANA

Now we turn to several sets of West African data which illustrate the potential usefulness of carrying out exploratory, small-scale research in depth, with analytical samples of purposively selected cases of several kinds; the aim being to increase understanding about systems of role relationships in the domestic domain, including resource acquisition, control and allocation, power and decision-making and reproduction. The context of these cases is Ghana, a country characterised by highly pro-natalist values in which observed completed marital fertility is estimated at 7.5 children per woman. There is, however, considerable contrast in fertility levels among different groups. The most marked difference is that between women in different kinds of employment. Female labour-force participation is quite high, with 64 per cent of women reported to be economically active. The majority of the women workers are engaged in agriculture (55 per cent), followed by sales (26 per cent) and production and related workers (15 per cent). Only a few women workers are classified as employees (salary/wage earners). Less than 3 per cent are in the professional, technical, administrative and clerical workers occupational category.

Female employees have a total fertility rate of 3.6. These are mainly women with some formal education who work as secretaries, receptionists, typists, clerks, nurses and teachers in government departments and private organisations. Self-employed women and family workers have the highest total fertility rate (6.4 and 6.6, respectively). These are mainly farmers and traders working with their children and kin, and several studies have shown how the latter rely on their own and fostered children to help them to run and develop their businesses and farms.

The cases which follow depict people from each of these two main contrasting employment and fertility regimes, farmers and employees. They document aspects of use of time, money and living space within the domestic domain; of the role activities and expectations of parents, spouses and offspring and kin, showing the contrasting relationships and exchanges occurring in different production contexts and how these appear to be related to changing attitudes and practices regarding parenthood and reproduction.

The first example focuses upon subsistence savannah farmers, among whom all members of the domestic group are mainly unpaid family workers subject to the authority of senior male kin. This material is relevant to arguments about intergenerational wealth flows and fertility; as an instance in which parents and kin perceive themselves and are observed to benefit from children's labour and thus maintain-high fertility values and reject the advent of schools which will change children's activities. The remaining examples are mainly of people for whom income-generation or procurement of a livelihood occur outside the domestic domain; people for whom 'work' and 'home' are separate, and whose own children do not assist them in productive and money-gaining activities, rather they go to school, have high achievement aspirations for educational qualifications and jobs, and cost their parents increasing amounts of time and money; depending, as we shall see, on the extent to which the mother or father uses her or his own resources and upon their rising aspirations in this regard. Thus, the second case is that of educated, urban migrants, among whom the men are employed as senior civil servants, earning relatively high government salaries and the women are in various occupations, with diverse claims to autonomy and economic independence. These data address issues concerning the conjugal division of labour and resources (*jointness*) and power and the functional individuation (*openness*) of the nuclear family. These sets of variables, as was noted above, have been found relevant to fertility and also to modes of production and migration. An unexpected outcome of this study was the salience of tension, conflict and change inadvertently observed, as decision-making processes unfolded during the period of intense observations. The third case is an analysis of changing normative prescriptions consequent upon successive generations of education regarding familial roles on the one hand, and family-size on the other. The data support the contention that changes in roles within the domestic domain are the intervening variables linking education, urbanisation, occupational change, etc., with fertility and family-size values. The fourth case is a study of government employees, nurses and clerks, living in the capital, Accra, who include both migrants and locals. Social and spatial mobility associated with changing interactions with kin and spouses are shown to be relevant to perceptions about availability of money and time, the costs of parenting and family-size values. The fifth and sixth cases are those of female and male teachers scattered in rural and urban areas around the country. Some are migrants; some are in their home towns. This study addresses issues of role strain, arising from the disintegration of traditional supports for high fertility and the perceived inadequacy of resources in money and time, and relates them to changing parental role behaviours and expectations, including family-size and fertility-regulation. The seventh case study is of particular methodological interest. It consists of focused biographies of educated Ghanaian women from two ethnic groups, the Ga and Dagomba, half of whom are living outside their home areas. It focuses upon fertility through in-depth examination of the maternal role and the changing values, prescriptions, perceptions and behaviours attached to it. The establishment of role profiles for each women is intended to demonstrate the extent to which the maternal role is salient and valued for these women, in contrast to their other six roles, and to examine how it is changing in contexts of social and spatial mobility.

As we shall note, a variety of methods of data collection were used in these several studies, including participant observation, focused interviewing, collection of genealogies, censuses of domestic groups, surveys, postal questionnaires, focused biographies and analysis of archival materials. The cases studied included individuals, couples, domestic groups, kin groups and communities. The cases were selected in various ways including purposively – with the help of local experts; randomly from known populations, and as total universes of given categories of subjects. Sample-sizes of people studied varied from a dozen to a thousand. All the cases were relatively small in scale, and in one way or another present evidence of the logic and processes involved in reproductive behaviour for the people concerned. They simultaneously seek to throw more light on the potential links between fertility and resources of several kinds, including the time available to parents from younger and older members of domestic groups and others; the money available to parents and the demands made upon it; and the changing tastes and values associated with education and mobility. Throughout, there is an assumption that female and male perspectives, values, resources and power in fertility-related decision-making need to be viewed dynamically in relation to each other, and, at the same time, that ethnic differences in behaviour and expectations need to be taken into account. The continuing focus is on the roles played by individuals in the domestic domain – their activities, norms, preferences and perceptions and status in terms of control of resources and power over people and social prestige – and how these change as altering modes of production and income-generating opportunities, education and migration have an impact.

Children: Allocation of Benefits

In the early 1960s, a small ethnographic study in the Muslimised traditional kingdom of the Dagomba in northern Ghana examined socialisation and education of children (Oppong, 1973). A variety of methods were used to collect the data for the study. These included participant observation, interviewing of key informants and others, collection of household censuses and genealogies, and several small select surveys of limited populations, including schoolchildren.

At the time of data collection, subsistence agriculture and animal husbandry and home-based crafts, such as leather-work, weaving, blacksmithing, butchering and barbering, were the main modes of gaining a livelihood. Schools were a new phenomenon and compulsion was required to recruit pupils. Adults complained that they needed the children's labour in the home and on the farm, where the young were observed to assist in carrying out the time-consuming tasks of water-carrying, fuel-collecting, food-processing, bird-scaring and poultry and animal husbandry, including cow-herding and caring for horses. So, few children, often only one or two from a sibling group, were allowed to go to school.

This is a culture in which numerous offspring are desired, barrenness is abhorred, and the only universal method of family-planning used is postpartum sexual abstinence.[12]

Wives return to stay with their parents and guardians after the birth of a child, especially that of the first or second. Ideally in a polygynous system, husbands do not suffer conjugal deprivation, and a mother returns to her husband when her child is walking and ready to be weaned. The way in which these practices provide an effective system of birth-spacing has recently been indicated (Gaisie, 1980). Kin and in-laws are nearby to see that these prescribed norms are adhered to.

The domestic group living in a mud-walled compound of varying size and complexity usually contains one or more conjugal families with monogamous or polygynous husbands. In some cases, adult brothers or father and sons live in the same household with their wives and all or some of their children. Women live with adult brothers or parents after childbirth, after divorce, widowhood or conjugal separation, and in this situation command a senior household position.

The important kin group for control over resources including professional skills and knowledge is the 'dang', the descending kindred composed of descendants of a common ancestor counted through male and female ties. Thus the children of brothers and sisters belong to a common 'dang'. Individuals belong to several such sets of kin. The strong bonds between brothers and sisters are strengthened even more in this sytem by fostering, the transfer of children, typically boys to mothers' brothers and girls to fathers' sisters, which occurs in a considerable minority of cases, up to one in four or more. Some children also stay with their grandparents. Such a pattern of fostering of children by non-parental kin has been documented among the neighbouring Gonja and in other West African communities, as well as in other parts of the world (Goody, 1978). Many reasons are given for the practice, including the advantages of training in crafts and specialist skills, such as divining, music and royal genealogies; of spreading resources through the kin group, of binding relatives more closely together in a system of considerable spatial mobility; and significantly of providing a critical source of child labour and assistance for people without young children in their homes to fetch and carry, etc. - help which, as we have noted, is crucial for the continuation of the traditional domestic and agricultural patterns of subsistence. Supporting this pattern of behaviour is the ideology that parents are not necessarily the best people to rear their own children. Ensuring its enforcement is the fact that parents do not have complete control of their children, who, like them, are subject to the overriding authority of elders of the kin group – their parents' senior siblings and their own parents and classificatory parents (i.e. uncles and aunts).

Thus the study described how, in such a system, children provide critical labour inputs to domestic groups and kin groups, the heads of which claim they cannot go to school or the survival of the group will be threatened. In this system, fertility is regulated only by customary spacing practices sanctioned by kin and community to benefit the health of mothers and babies, leading to prolonged birth-intervals. Meanwhile, the benefits accruing from children are spread among members of the kin group, in this case the descending kindred. Indeed, parents are sometimes virtually compelled, occasionally by supernatural sanctions, to send one or more children to a kinsman or woman. Thus parental and filial role substitution is of common occurrence.

These findings, like those of many other ethnographic descriptive studies of socialisation and the domestic domain in cultures of the developing world, demonstrated clearly both what important labour inputs children can provide in a subsistence economy and how erroneous are assumptions that parents always rear their own children or that conjugal families are residentially or functionally bounded groups.

This is a society in which the traditionally sanctioned norms for parental and conjugal roles prescribe that parents and children and husbands and wives should live separately with kin for specific periods of their lives, and that some children should spend most of their young lives with non-parental kin. These norms differ significantly in the several occupational and status groups within the society, according to the needs of particular professions and political posts, and thus call attention to the necessity of documenting carefully, in any particular cultural context, the amount of parental-role delegation or substitution present in different subgroups; the extent to which the 'costs' and 'benefits' of childrearing and child-labour are spread and to whom and in what circumstances.

Meanwhile, the traditional prescriptions and practices with regard to birth-spacing have apparently kept fertility levels lower than those of nearby ethnic groups, who do not have such norms and practices. A breakdown in these traditional practices may accordingly lead to higher fertility levels (Gaisie, 1980).

We turn next to samples of the socially and spatially mobile elements of the Ghanaian population, and see how configurations of roles and statuses are changing with consequent alterations in fertility-related expectations and activities.

Conjugal 'Jointness' and Nuclear Family 'Closure': Power Tension and Change

The next example dealing with urban conjugal-role relationships is relevant to our present concerns for several reasons (Oppong, 1982). Firstly, it is concerned with modes of documenting and measuring crucial variables, the relative flexibility of the conjugal division of labour termed *'jointness'* or *'segregation'*, and the boundedness of the conjugal family in terms of maintenance socialisation, etc., termed *'closure'* or *'openness'*. These have been related to family-size and fertility-regulation as we noted above (e.g. Liu, 1977). Thus it may serve to facilitate the study of differences and changes in important aspects of role relationships, including the kinds of role substitution or sharing of activities and resources between spouses and kin, which have been demonstrated correlates of differential fertility and which are in fact signs of the allocation of rewards and costs (e.g. Scanzoni and Szinovacz, 1980).

Secondly, since the study involved observation and open-ended repeated interviewing of wives and husbands in states of tension and conflict, it inevitably grew into a study of power and decision-making over time, thus demonstrating how the very dynamic change processes themselves might be documented; a topic which is currently of great interest to students of fertility (Hollerbach, 1980; Burch, 1980).

Thirdly, it involved an exchange perspective, which has been utilised in other studies attempting to relate types of conjugal-role relationships, both to the occupational structure, educational opportunites and kin networks and within the conjugal family, power relations, the division of labour and fertility (see Scanzoni, 1976a and 1976b; Bagozzi and van Loo, 1978a and 1978b).

How to measure differences and explain changes in conjugal family role and status systems has been a longstanding challenge to anthropologists, family sociologists and others, and is now beginning to be confronted by economists. These processes involve both the measurement of differences and changes within the domestic domain and the estimation of effects of externally-triggered factors, such as changes in modes of production involving individual resource control or autonomy, and changes in the relative status of one sex or the other or adults or children, through changes in chances for increasing skills, knowledge, wealth, prestige, etc., offered by education, employment or entrepreneurial opportunities. Much has been made of the potential relevance of such processes and changes to fertility, and these are obviously issues of critical interest to population scholars, including economists.

This problem of documentation and measurement of differences and changes was thus confronted in a field-study of family relationships in Accra carried out among suburban Akan migrants in the late 1960s (Oppong, 1982). The traditional patterns of domestic organisation and family relationships of one segment of the Akan had been studied and described over two decades earlier (Fortes, 1950, 1954). The Akan ethnic group is the most numerous in Ghana and constitutes over 40 per cent of the population. Traditionally, subsistence agriculturalists in the tropical rain forest and more recently engaged in cocoa cash-cropping, their system of kinship and marriage is characterised by matrilineages, corporate kin groups recruited through uterine ties, which own and manage substantial properties in land and housing and by polygyny. Inheritance is customarily matrilineal, property passing to siblings and children of female members of the sibling group. Traditionally, many marriages have been duolocal; that is, each spouse continues to co-reside with matri-kin, children staying partly with fathers and partly with matri-kin. The costs of their maintenance have been similarly spread. For purposes of sex, procreation, socialisation and maintenance of children, for production, management and ownership of resources, the conjugal family is not a *closed* or functionally bounded group. Wives and husbands cooperate in agriculture, but they own nothing together. Neither inherits the other's property, and they seldom traditionally live alone together. Conjugal role relationships may thus be characterised as *segregated* in each sphere, except for customary joint production of the wherewithal to maintain their common children. These traditional behaviour patterns and associated norms, values and perceptions persist to a considerable extent today.

The question asked in the study of Akan urban educated migrants was how the roles of parent, spouse, household member, kin, etc., are modified in a situation of migration and individual income-earning, when one or two or even three or more generations of education and social mobility have affected patterns of residence, modes of earning a livelihood, availability of resources, standards of living, opportunities for autonomy, aspirations and tastes. For education is correlated with individualism: with movement away from kin (Caldwell, 1969) and with individual employment and income-earning, rather than cooperation in enterprises with kin. And these factors have been hypothesised as being related to changing fertility levels as noted above.

Data to answer these questions were collected by several means, from migrant Akan men who were senior government employees living and working in Accra, and from their wives. Some information was collected through questionnaires, filled in largely by the respondents themselves. This mainly constituted reports of household behaviour and exchanges with kin, children, wives and others. In addition, a detailed panel of case-studies was collected over a 10-month period of repeated observations and focused interviewing in 20 households. Eventually, 12 of these couples and domestic groups were subjected to detailed analysis and comparison.

In order to form indices of the *jointness* of the conjugal-role relationship in several spheres, scores of financial provision, financial management and chore participation were derived. To measure the degree to which the conjugal family was financially a *closed* group, an index of financial *closure* was devised, which comprised information on education of children, remittances to kin and co-ownership of family property.

Analysis of the survey responses gave evidence of interesting correlations between generations of education and financial *closure* of the conjugal family. The latter in turn appeared to facilitate more syncratic decision-making by couples, which was also associated with more joint task performance (financial provision, management and chore performance, see Oppong, 1982, p. 143). Indeed, both case and survey data gave interesting indications of the dynamic and complex associations existing between relative *closure* and *jointness* of conjugal relationships in a number of areas, and also of marital power and decision-making and the apparent stability and harmony of husband–wife relationships.

Among the families surveyed, the use of child and adolescent labour from poorer homes was seen to prevent the time-strain pressures and opportunity costs which might have led to increased fertility regulation. Meanwhile, aspirations for high-status offspring in terms of education and level of maintenance meant that traditional high fertility ideals had already dropped towards an ideal family-size of four children because of financial constraints.

The modes of measurement and data collection and the over-all framework for analysis used in this study were subsequently found useful in other settings, in which they were related directly to questions regarding fertility.

Norms: The Chain of Change

The study of prescribed norms for familial roles has been a popular pastime in family sociology in North America. But much less has been done in this regard in other parts of the world. As we noted above, interest has been raised by several studies showing links between the patterns of such norms and fertility desires and ideals. In the study discussed here, a random sample of students at two universities provided the data and the issues of role delegation and substitutability and status were once more examined at the normative level, using a subset of nearly 400 single. childless young men (Oppong, 1975b). The hypothesis linking conjugal role *jointness* and smaller family-size values was examined. A score of *jointness* and *segregation* was seen to correlate with mean number of children advocated (Oppong, 1975a). Similarly, a correlation was found between approval of conjugal family *openness* ('extended family' norms) and large family-size values, and approval of *closure* (functionally-individuated nuclear family) and small family-size values (Oppong, 1974a). The *closure* scale indicated degrees of approval expressed regarding the playing of the conjugal and parental roles acrosss the boundaries of the nuclear family. The seven activity areas included childrearing, inheritance, decision-making, financial provision, sex and procreation, chore performance and co-residence.

At the same time, social and spatial mobility, as indexed by generations of education, were found to be associated with increasing approval of *jointness* and *closure* in terms of intergenerational transmission of property within the conjugal family and its residential separation from kin, as well as a more egalitarian relationship between spouses (Oppong, 1975b). Significantly, these norms were among those most closely associated with changing family-size desires. Since no direct correlation was found between generations of education and family-size values, further evidence was provided of the critical intervening nature of changing family norms, links in a chain of changing role expectations (Oppong, 1977a).

Mobility, Resource Scarcity and the Retreat from Parenthood

In many cultural contexts, the earliest signs of changes in attitudes and behaviour relating to fertility have been among the upper and middle classes, professionals, civil servants, clerks and teachers. Caldwell (1968b) demonstrated that such change was already taking place in Ghanaian towns in the 1960s. Large families were increasingly perceived as burdensome. It was thus decided to study a small sample of junior civil servants to explore changes, if any, occurring in their attitudes to fertility and its regulation. Two small independent samples of women and men were selected, specifically to explore variables correlated with differences in attitudes to family-size and -planning.

In this study, self-administered questionnaires were used, and these data were supplemented by focused interviewing. Several hypotheses were explored, and it was discovered that the most mobile sectors of the two populations in both social and spatial terms wanted fewer children than they thought ideal (Oppong, 1974b). The most mobile did not know more about contraception, nor was their greater readiness to seek promotion correlated with their smaller family-size desires. The critical link appeared to be economic constraints and insecurity. On the whole, migrants felt themselves to be in worse financial predicaments than the locals (cf. Caldwell, 1969). Significantly, those who were most mobile in both social and spatial terms were the ones shouldering the greatest burdens of help to kin. At the same time, they received the least financial help from kin. It was thus concluded that their feelings of economic insecurity and strain in relation to their kin responsibilities were a critical factor affecting their own parental-role expectations, and that a detailed analysis of flows of resources to and from kin should be studied further in relation to fertility desires and achievements.

Data from the married male subset of the sample also showed the relevance of exploring the effects of geographical and socio-economic mobility over two generations (Oppong, 1976). The two most mobile groups tended to be most ready to move elsewhere to improve their situation, and some of these had the biggest drain from kin on their resources. Simultaneous examination of mobility status and perceptions of financial status showed that locals with a good to fair assessment of their resources wanted the most children and in-migrants with illiterate parents and a poor perception of their financial status wanted the fewest

(3.9) (Oppong, 1976). This analysis again called attention to the need for more detailed studies of the availability of resources in money and time – the relative benevolence of the immediate environment – including data on the exchanges between kin and the availability of parental role substitutes – all of which are likely to affect resources and expectations for child-bearing and childrearing.

Women Teachers: The Crumbling of High-fertility Supports

The Ghanaian studies mentioned so far have clearly demonstrated the relevance of studying changes in role expectations and activities in relation to fertility. They have emphasised the critical importance of the type of employment and the availability and allocation of domestic resources, and the salience of role stress or perceptions of cost, as spurs to innovation and change. At the same time, the importance of the relative status of family members was emphasised, their control over resources, power over others and part played in decision-making. Spatial and social mobility entailed by schooling and the search for suitable employment were confirmed as important factors triggering off changes in resources and familial roles and relationships, which in turn affected family-size aspirations and achievements. It was therefore resolved to collect a systematic set of data focusing on these several issues, looking at a sample of women and men, rural and urban, migrant and non-migrant, and selected from among a group of potential innovators. Accordingly, a national sample of primary school teachers was chosen and data were collected through postal questionnaires and focused interviewing with a small subsample. We shall consider an analysis of role strain firstly among the women then among the men (Oppong, 1977b, 1983a and 1983b). The major factors precipitating change in this case again were education and employment as salary-earning government junior civil servants. Thus, many of the changes observed in domestic life were also responses to the pressures engendered by migration and the separation of work and home. For many were first generation employees coping with problems of job demands which their mothers and fathers before them had not faced, and at the same time enjoying positions of occupational prestige and individually-earned and disposable incomes, which although considered low were their own. Thus, the major questions the study set out to ask were how parental, conjugal and kin roles changed to adapt to new needs and aspirations. To what extent were traditional domestic and familial expectations and behaviour patterns fulfilled and followed; to what extent was there innovation and change? Both survey data and discursive interviewing provided overwhelming evidence of stress for women and men; both time-stress and money-stress. Individuals found themselves unable to fulfil all their customary obligations or to achieve their aspirations for themselves and their dependents. There was observed to be a considerable gap between norms and behaviour patterns reported and observed.

Thus among the women, mainly mothers as well as employees, inadequacy of time constituted a permanent stress factor, as they tried to cope with the conflicting demands of their roles as workers outside the home and as mothers. Expectations of customary forms of help from kin were not fulfilled, nor were new expectations regarding the joint role the spouse should play in child-care and domestic tasks. Similarly, in the financial sphere, gaps between norms and reality led to stress – demands of kin could not be fulfilled, husbands did not contribute enough; salaries were considered too low; so money issues were very salient and a substantial minority were in debt.

Such were their feelings of resource stress in a situation of continuing normative pressures for high fertility, that one in three admitted feeling they had too many children to care for. Sixteen per cent tried to solve their childrearing problems by sending one or more children to kin. Meanwhile, 68 per cent had children other than their own staying with them, many being responsible for their own sisters and sisters' children. At the same time, their aspirations for their own children's level of education was high and anxiety-provoking in a situation of economic strain. Thus it was not surprising that two out of five mentioned issues related to parenthood when asked to relate problems they had encountered. Texts recorded from teachers documented the extent of their problems and their strategies for coping. Many had neither adequate kin support nor assurance of dependability from their husbands, and they lived in a context lacking institutional supports, such as crèches and child allowances. And yet the ideal of the full-time income-earner and mother of at least four and preferably six children remained. However, as the composition of the domestic group and exchanges between kin altered, women were observed to find this ideal image increasingly hard to realise.

Significantly, it was the wives with lower than average fertility who were more likely to complain of resource constraints. At the same time they felt a greater sense of personal responsibility for household expenses and chores. They more often stated that husband and wife should share equally in the cost of raising children and less often than mothers with high fertility did they think that their husbands should help them with housework. Meanwhile more women with relatively high fertility had higher than average levels of legal and financial support and security in marriage. These findings were seen as being in line with other work linking indices of greater levels of personal responsibility (costs), with respect to domestic duties and tasks, and an increased demand for the individual's own resources and correspondingly less command over the resources of others, with smaller family-size ideals or lower fertility.

Male Teachers: Parental Costs and Fertility regulation

In the analysis of data from male teachers, supportive evidence was once more provided for hypotheses linking social and spatial mobility consequent upon generations of education and salaried employment with changes in familial roles and fertility, on the levels of both expectations and behaviour (Oppong, 1983b). And once more increasing costs of parenting and parental role strain figured prominently, as did the themes of conjugal familism, personal responsibility and sexual equality (see Figures 10.1 and 10.2). Thus, parental and grandparental education, which were themselves indices of social and spatial mobility in childhood, were associated at the level of norms and values, as well as behaviour with decreasing exchanges of time, goods, money, property and children between kin and the diminished sharing of responsibility for these by relatives. Meanwhile, conjugal sharing of domestic tasks increased with a greater blurring of the sexual division of labour in the home. On the behavioural level, fertility control was correlated with individualisation of the paternal role and acceptance of related responsibilities, a more flexible and active participation in domestic tasks and conjugal decision-making and the dwindling of wealth flows between kin. On the level of norms and values, approval of such increasing *closure* of the conjugal family and conjugal *jointness* and equality and individualised parental responsibility was associated with lower family-size preferences.

All these changes, of course, essentially involved greater time and material inputs associated with the paternal and conjugal roles, thus entailing relatively greater personal costs. At the same time, markedly higher aspirations for children's education, especially that of daughters, were associated with lower family-size preferences, and a high score on an index of child-care strain was correlated with fertility regulation.

Thus, once more hypotheses linking lower fertility desires and increased regulation with more individualism, growing equality of parents and children, wives and husbands and an increasingly flexible division of labour between spouses are supported. Significantly, men who participate more in domestic work, spending more time and effort on tasks in the home, are also among those with lower family-sizes, lower preferences and more

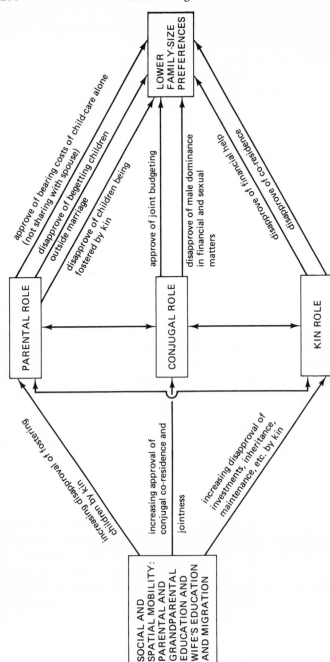

FIGURE 10.1 *Familial roles, changing norms and values, and lower family-size preferences*

SOURCE Oppong, 1983b.

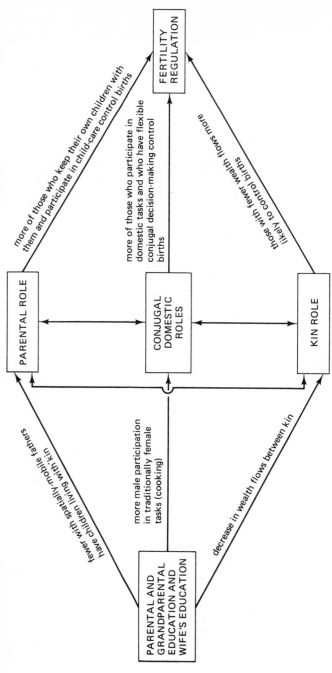

FIGURE 10.2 *Changing familial role behaviours and fertility regulation*

SOURCE Oppong, 1983b.

contraception. Again, in terms of sex-role norms, disapproval of male dominance in financial matters and sex is associated with lower family-size preferences, lower family-size and contraceptive usage. These data thus once more emphasise the relevance of studying the division of domestic and parental activities and power between women and men as well as that outside the home.

Maternal Values and Aspirations

The last data set mentioned is that of 60 focused biographies of Ghanaian educated women. In these, information on expectations and behaviour for seven roles was collected, focusing upon the maternal role and fertility. On the basis of these studies, both detailed and simplified modes of categorising data have been designed which facilitate quantification and comparison. The latter consists of role profiles which indicate levels of role rewards (status-economic and social), role strain and salience. A goal of this analysis is to uncover the causes and consequences of changing role priorities and values affecting motherhood, which may assist in the process of understanding differential and changing fertility, in particular the effects of perceived costs and opportunity costs. Once more, the sample comprises migrants and non-migrants, so that potential effects of mobility may be examined (Oppong and Abu, 1984).

These data provide connections between perceptions of time-strain, occupational/parental role conflict and smaller family-size desires. Thus, for instance, among Ga migrants in Tamale, those who report no feeling of time-strain desire 4.2 children; those who perceive a little time-strain want 4; those who perceive some want 3; and those who feel a lot of time-strain want 2. Again, some of the findings support the argument that declining family-size values are associated with changes in conjugal-role satisfactions and that high ranking of individual gratification in terms of personal leisure and pleasure are associated with voluntary termination of pregnancies which might interfere with the life-style (cf. Dinan, 1983).

CONCLUSION

It has been argued that current versions of economic demand theories of fertility still remain too heavily influenced by a Western world view, regarding among other things, family relations, thus hampering their capacity to contribute further to an understanding of the causes of high fertility in the developing world. It has thus been argued that fertility theories and models built to understand and measure factors influencing fertility must be developed initially with particular social and cultural and familial contexts in mind, but ultimately sufficiently complex and cross-culturally appropriate to deal with any situation.

Economic theories of fertility need to take account of an array of diverse cultural practices which may have profound effects upon the production, control and allocation of the scarce resources in money, material goods and time, with which the theories deal. These include the contrasting contents of marriage contracts – different in terms of the expected conjugal exchanges, the division of tasks, responsibilities, resources and power, the number and range of people affected and the set of people involved in the unions which may be monogamous, polygynous or polyandrous, and their length of duration. They include the degree of sibling solidarity expressed in joint production, management and intergenerational transmission of resources of various kinds, as well as shared responsibility for children. They include modes of reckoning descent and inheritance and the functioning of descent groups – including patrilineages, matrilineages, descending kindreds. They include the division of labour of different kinds between the sexes, age-groups, classes, castes. They include patterns of authority, sources of power over people, and control of resources and thus of dependence and autonomy. Such factors need to be taken into account if studies are to realistically index costs or prices of childbearing, or to document conjugal decision-making processes in contexts in which the roles of mothers-in-law or senior agnates and other senior kin are critical.

When researchers do not fully understand or are unaware of cultural and social phenomena in the context in which they are working, field-research focusing on individuals, the domestic groups, neighbourhoods and communities, which sifts through a wide range of information is required. Such a preliminary immersion in the range of potentially-relevant facts is needed before the right questions can be asked. Subsequently multi-method approaches are likely to lead to the richest and most meaningful data bases.

It has been argued that recent work which has seriously considered cultural differences has been productive of new understandings of fertility determinants, because it has taken into account the fact that many aspects of familial, sex and generational roles have very different expectations and associated activity patterns; different from the models used in much earlier work, such as the stereotypes of the division of labour and resources in the household used by classical new home-economists (G. Jones, 1977). Thus, it is once more argued that progress cannot be made in understanding differential and changing levels of fertility until more is known about flows and exchanges of resources within the domestic domain, between mates, parents and children, siblings and kin, and importantly until more is known about the way these exchanges themselves change and are affected by alterations in non-domestic spheres such as labour markets, migration patterns and education. Here is a fertile field for research, and we believe that it is one in which it will be beneficial for economists to join forces with anthropologists, psychologists, sociologists, demographers and others, if realistic and relevant research is to be conducted in diverse cultural settings which will be pertinent to policy requirements and welfare needs.

Thus the ultimate goal of this chapter has been to call attention, like G. Jones (1977, p. 38), to the necessity of understanding how economic factors in the domestic domain are important in determining fertility 'through the screen of culture and family structure'. It has been argued that for such understanding to be facilitated, new flexible models of role relationships and resources in the domestic domain need to be conceived, and that to test these models small sets of different types of empirical field data, both quantitative and qualitative, need to be collected. Illustrations of the form and content of such materials from one country, Ghana, have indicated their potential relevance. Ultimately, such studies should help to provide the kinds of materials required to shed more light on continuing and changing patterns of fertility behaviour, and expectations in contrasting subgroups and cultures (Miró and Potter, 1980a), and without such understanding, realistic and effective population policies will be difficult to devise or execute.

NOTES

1. Readers unfamiliar with the findings and methods of the discipline of anthropology may consult a recent research guide by Pelto and Pelto (1978).
2. See, for example, the array of papers from several disciplines presented at the IUSSP Seminar on Determinants of Fertility Trends: Major Theories and New Directions for Research, held in Bad Homburg, 14–17 April 1980, or the contributions to the workshop on the Anthropology of Human Fertility, held on 20–1 February 1981 at the National Academy of Sciences, Washington, DC.
3. See, for instance, Leibenstein (1975a, 1975b), Easterlin (1978), Bagozzi and Van Loo (1978a, 1978b), Bulatao (1981); and attempts

to include the effects of taste or preferences, social influence or reference groups and community-level variables.

4. See, for instance, G. Jones (1977), Bagozzi and van Loo (1978a, 1978b), Beaujot, Krotki and Krishnan (1978), Oppong (1983c).

5. Studies in this category would include those of Banks (1954) on Victorian England, and Caldwell (1968b) on Ghanaian suburban dwellers, among whom aspirations for an expensive quality of child-care and training is leading to lowering of fertility values from their traditionally high level.

6. Such diminution of parental-role delegation has been conceived in terms of 'conjugal familism' (e.g. Ryder, 1959; Petersen, 1961); lack of supportive kin and community assistance (Goldberg, 1960); the disintegration of lineage systems and the emergence of strong nuclear families (e.g. Fortes, 1954); increased 'closure' of the conjugal family (Oppong, 1982).

7. See MacFarlane (1978a, 1978b) on economic individualism and Stone (1977) on affective individualism. Both of these historical studies examine several centuries of evidence from English family life.

8. The literature on this subject is enormous; see Standing (1978), and Standing and Sheehan (1978).

9. For example, see DaVanzo and Lee (1978), Ho (1979).

10. See, for instance, studies by Scanzoni (1975, 1976a, 1976b), Tobin (1976), Rainwater (1965); see also Howell (1979).

11. Typical tools of research have been outlined in Chapters 5 and 6 of Pelto and Pelto (1978).

12. Note that here, as below, we use the 'anthropological present tense' even though a number of changes have occurred in the region in the intervening period consequent upon compulsory schooling, cash-cropping, large-scale farming; the introduction of new machinery and modes of production; and the growth of a class of landless labourers.

PART III:
EMPIRICAL EVIDENCE
FROM DEVELOPING
COUNTRIES

... every specific historic mode of production has its own special laws of population, historically valid within its limits alone. An abstract law of population exists for plants and animals only, and only insofar as man has not interfered with them.

> Karl Marx, *A Critique of Political Economy* (New York: The Modern Library, First Modern Library Edition, 1936) p. 693.

11 Problems of Interpretation and Specification in Analysing Fertility Differentials: Illustrated with Kenyan Survey Data

RICHARD ANKER

INTRODUCTION

High fertility rates and high population growth rates in the developing world have stimulated many studies of the factors determining fertility rates. Due to data limitations, much of the early multivariate research on fertility differentials was carried out at a fairly high level of aggregation and abstraction; in numerous regression analyses of fertility differentials, countries and regions of countries were used as the units of observation (see, for example, Adelman, 1963; Anker, 1978). Results from these analyses indicated that fertility rates tend to decline along with socio-economic development and accompanying changes in the economic costs and benefits associated with children, thus supporting, for example, the socio-economic theory of fertility and the demographic transition theory (Becker, 1960; Easterlin, 1975; Notestein, 1945).

Although regression results based on macro-level units of observation have been, in general, intuitively satisfying and consistent with theory, they leave much to be desired. Firstly, there is a problem of aggregation bias, because the unit of observation (e.g. country, state, district) is not the same as the unit upon which the theory is based (usually individual or household). (See Chapter 7 by Edelfsen and Lieberman, which discusses aggregation problems.) Secondly, macro-level analyses rarely take into consideration cultural and country-specific factors. Yet, relationships between socio-economic variables and fertility are known to vary from country to country and area to area, and historical experience has shown that there are many possible relationships between socio-economic development and fertility, including one path where socio-economic development causes fertility to rise (Nag, 1979). Thirdly, there are statistical problems associated with regression analysis of fertility differentials using macro-level data such as high levels of multicollinearity which make it difficult to separate out the independent effects of closely related variables; for example, because male and female education levels in societies are so closely related, it is sometimes impossible to attribute differences in fertility rates to one or the other of these education variables using macro-level data.

Micro household-level data, in contrast, are not subject to the above problems to the same extent as are macro-level data. Multicollinearity tends to be much lower in micro-level data, thereby increasing the analyst's ability to separate out the effect of one variable from that of another. Many more explanatory variables, including cultural and country-specific factors are available in micro data, thereby making it possible to investigate the extent to which the determinants of fertility are similar or different across major population subgroups. In addition, the theory and the data refer to the same micro-level of aggregation. For these and other reasons, much of the recent work on fertility differentials has been based on household micro-level data. The most ambitious endeavour of this type is, of course, the World Fertility Survey with household surveys in over 40 countries.

Unfortunately, in this rush toward the use of household survey data, insufficient attention has been given to problems associated with its use. Two of the more important problems in the use of household data for the regression analysis of fertility differentials are: (i) the importance of functional form and the use of non-linear relationships; and (ii) interpretation of observed relationships. This chapter, using ordinary least squares and data from a 1974 national household survey of Kenya, demonstrates how regression results are affected by the functional form used, how these analyses can be subjected to tests of robustness, and how these results can be interpreted for policy purposes.

The remainder of this chapter is structured as follows. In the next section, the data used are described, while in the third section, the theoretical model used in the regression analysis is described. The following section discusses questions related to the use of non-linear functional forms. The fifth section investigates questions related to the interpretation of results from multiple regressions analysis, and the next discusses the use of regression results for purposes of predicting likely future changes in fertility rates. Finally, a summary is presented and conclusions are drawn.

DATA

The data source of the empirical analysis in the fourth and fifth sections is the 1974 ILO/University of Nairobi Household Survey, which was a national representative sample of Kenya and was a joint effort of James C. Knowles, the author, and Professors S. Ominde and J. N. Muinde of the Department of Geography and Population Studies Centre of the University of Nairobi. Households in the survey were chosen using a stratified multi-stage sampling procedure. Firstly, two districts were randomly chosen from each of Kenya's eight provinces (except in Nairobi province which is co-terminous with Nairobi district). Then, within each sample district, sub-locations were classified into high, medium and low population density strata of approximately equal size, and one sub-location was randomly selected from each density strata. The sampled sub-locations included 36 rural and 9 urban sub-locations from all over Kenya. Lastly, within each sample sub-location, all households were enumerated and then selected. The total sample available for analysis consisted of 1170 households with at least one currently married woman of 15–49 years, and information on all of the variables used in the multivariate analysis. Nine hundred and ninety-eight households were drawn from rural areas, and 172 were from urban areas.[1,2]

Two questionnaires were administered to each sample household. Heads of household (usually, but not always, men) were asked questions regarding characteristics of the household and of the individuals belonging to it. Ever married women 15–49 years of age were asked questions about themselves and their children. Questionnaires were very wide-ranging in content, including economic, sociological, demographic and cultural questions. All of these factors, as will be shown below, were found to affect fertility rates in Kenya.

THEORETICAL MODEL

Since theoretical discussions and developments are presented elsewhere in this volume, the discussion here is brief. Parts of this short section draw on an earlier work (Anker and Knowles, 1982 and 1983), to which readers interested in further theoretical discussions of the variables used in the analysis, or for more detail of the analysis itself, should refer.

An eclectic approach is used in this chapter. The demand orientation of the economic theory of fertility, where households are seen as rational entities maximising their utility subject to various constraints, is extended in order to increase the theory's applicability to the situation in the developing world. Firstly, it is necessary to consider the important economic contributions children in developing countries make to their families. Indeed, the economic contribution of children to their parents is believed to be so important that it is frequently considered to be a major reason for high fertility rates in developing countries. In this study, we attempt to account for the economic contributions of children by including factors which should affect their economic output, such as the amount of land owned, the value of livestock owned, and the extent to which children are educated.

Secondly, factors affecting the supply of children must also be considered.[3] Some couples, as a result of poor health, high rates of infant mortality, and cultural constraints on fecundity and conception, have fewer children than they desire. The fertility and family-size of such couples is determined not by their desire for a certain number of children, as indicated in a model of utility-maximisation, but by involuntary restrictions on the supply of children.[4] In contrast, many couples have unwanted births. Factors related to fecundity and unwanted births (and thus to the supply of children) considered in the present study are: family-planning practices, wife's age, wife's health, polygamy and mortality.[5]

In the next two sections, fertility differentials are related to a number of micro-level explanatory variables (including several which are culture-specific) using ordinary least squares. Two explanatory variables which refer to the community or macro-level (average mortality rate in the sub-location of residence and average education level for children in the sub-location of residence) are also specified in the regression analyses, since macro-level factors are known to affect basic values and general economic conditions. The sample is restricted to African women, and separate analyses are carried out for various groups of women: all women (Table 11.1), rural and urban women as well as women from different tribes (Table 11.2). Names and definitions of variables used in the analysis are listed below.

CEB   total number of live births (the dependent variable)

AGE   age of woman in years

AGESQ   age of woman squared

EDW   number of standards of school completed by woman

EDWSQ   square of number of standards of school completed by woman

EDW1   binary variable indicating if woman has completed some school but is probably not functionally literate (1 if completed standards 1-4, 0 otherwise)

EDW2   binary variable indicating if woman is probably functionally literate but is not a primary school graduate (1 if completed standards 5 or 6, 0 otherwise)

EDW3   binary variable indicating if woman is a primary school graduate but has not completed 'O' levels in secondary school (1 if completed at least primary school but less than form IV, 0 otherwise)

EDW4   binary variable indicating if woman has completed 'O' levels in secondary school (1 if completed at least form IV, 0 otherwise)

EDH   number of standards of school completed by husband

EDHSQ   square of number of standards of school completed by husband

EDH1   binary variable indicating if husband has completed some school but is probably not functionally literate (1 if completed standards 1-4, 0 otherwise)

EDH2   binary variable indicating if husband is probably functionally literate but is not a primary school graduate (1 if completed standards 5 or 6, 0 otherwise)

EDH3   binary variable indicating if husband is a primary school graduate but has not completed 'O' levels (1 if completed at least primary school but less than form IV, 0 otherwise)

EDH4   binary variable indicating if husband has completed 'O' levels in secondary school (1 if completed at least form IV, 0 otherwise)

INCOME   household income per adult per annum, in hundreds of Kenyan shillings

LAND   number of acres of land owned by rural households, adjusted for climate potential of land (0 if urban)

URBAN   binary variable indicating urban residence of women (1 if urban, 0 otherwise)

MORT   inverse of child survival rate (i.e. total number of live births divided by total number of surviving children)

AVMORT03   average probability of a child dying before reaching three years of age in woman's sub-location of residence (macro variable)

LFAWAY   binary variable indicating if woman has worked away from home since being married (1 if worked away from home, 0 if not)

LFHOME   binary variable indicating if woman has worked since being married only at or near home (1 if worked only at or near home, 0 if not)

FPVISIT   binary variable indicating if woman reported visiting government family-planning clinic in two years before survey (1 if yes, 0 if no)

EDEXPECT   average number of years of schooling mother expects her children to complete

AVENROL   average enrolment rate for children 15–19 years of age in woman's sub-locations of residence (macro variable)

MIGRANT   binary variable indicating if woman is a migrant (1 if migrant, 0 if not)

FARMCPTL   value of livestock owned by rural households, in thousands of Kenyan shillings (0 if urban)

SIBLINGS   total number of living brothers and sisters of the husband and wife

POLYGMOS   binary variable indicating if woman's marriage is polygamous (1 if polygamous, 0 if monogamous)

HUSAWAY   binary variable indicating if husband is residing away from wife (1 if away, 0 if not)

GOODHLTH   binary variable indicating if woman characterised her health as 'good' or 'excellent' during previous 12 months (1 if yes, 0 if no)

POORHLTH   binary variable indicating if woman characterised her health as 'poor' or 'terrible' during previous 12 months (1 if yes, 0 if no)

LACTMO   number of months woman says that she normally breastfeeds her children

LACTMOSQ   square of number of months woman normally breastfeeds her children

LACTLOES   binary variable indicating if woman normally breastfeeds for less than six months (1 if yes, 0 otherwise)

LACTLO   binary variable indicating if woman normally breastfeeds for six to eleven months (1 if yes, 0 otherwise)

LACTHI   binary variable indicating if women normally breastfeeds for 13 to 18 months (1 if yes, 0 otherwise)

LACTHIES   binary variable indicating if woman normally breastfeeds for more than 18 months (1 if yes, 0 otherwise)

A priori expectations are that the following variables will be positively related to fertility: household income per adult (INCOME), husband's education (EDH), amount of land owned (LAND), value of livestock owned (FARMCPTL), wife's age (AGE), number of brothers and sisters of husband and wife (SIBLINGS), infant and child mortality (AVMORT03,

MORT) and good health of the wife (GOODHLTH). It is expected that the following variables will be negatively related to fertility: wife's education (EDW), urban residence (URBAN), wife's work especially if it is away from home (LFAWAY, LFHOME), high education expectations for the children (EDEXPECT, AVENROL), acceptance of modern family-planning methods (FPVISIT), migrant status (MIGRANT), polygamy (POLYGMOS), husband residing away (HUSAWAY), poor health of the wife (POORHLTH) and length of breastfeeding (LACTMO).

In the multivariate analysis which follows, ordinary least squares (OLS) is employed. There are several reasons for using this statistical model. Firstly, OLS is relatively easy and inexpensive to use, and statistical packages enabling its use are widely available. Secondly, virtually all analysts intending to do multivariate analysis are familiar with OLS - a point of no small importance, especially since we want to illustrate certain specifications and interpretation problems.

ESTIMATION OF NON-LINEAR RELATIONSHIPS

In social science research, for simplicity, behavioural relationships are often assumed to be linear. Thus, for example, one might consider the number of live births a woman has had (CEB) to be a linear function of her age (AGE), her education level (EDW), mortality experience among her children (MORT), the number of months she usually breastfeeds her children (LACTMO), the amount of land the family owns (LAND), and her husband's education (EDH). When we add to these basically interval variables several binary variables which take on the value 0 if the characteristic is not present and the value 1 if the characteristic is present - the woman's place of residence (URBAN), and whether the woman has worked near home (LFHOME) or away from home (LFAWAY) - we obtain a fairly comprehensive set of explanatory variables. Using the Kenyan survey data described in the second section, these variables are related to fertility using ordinary least squares, and these results are shown in equation (1) in Table 11.1. For the most part, results meet *a priori* expectations. Fertility is a positive and significant function of wife's age, husband's education, own mortality experience and amount of land owned; fertility is a negative and significant function of wife's education. Results are insignificant at the 0.10 level however for some explanatory variables: urban residence, length of breastfeeding and wife's work experience whether at home or away from home.

TABLE 11.1 *Alternative regressions on fertility (CEB) among married women in Kenya (t statistics in brackets)*

	Equation specification			
Independent variables	Linear specification of all variables (1)	Linear specification with age variable in quadratic form (2)	Quadratic specification of selected variables (3)	Binary specification of selected variables (4)
AGE	0.2093*** (28.25)	0.6859*** (13.17)	0.6843*** (13.18)	0.6797*** (13.00)
AGESQ	—	-0.0075*** (9.24)	-0.0075*** (9.24)	-0.0074*** (9.14)
EDW	-0.0592** (2.49)	-0.0538** (2.35)	0.0348 (0.71)	—
EDWSQ	—	—	-0.0117** (1.97)	—
EDW1	—	—	—	0.1085 (0.75)
EDW2	—	—	—	-0.1697 (1.00)
EDW3	—	—	—	-0.4341** (2.08)
EDW4	—	—	—	-1.0541** (2.40)

	(1)	(2)	(3)	(4)
EDH	0.0464** (2.25)	0.0384* (1.93)	0.0488 (1.13)	—
EDHSQ	—	—	−0.0013 (0.29)	—
EDH1	—	—	—	0.1286 (0.88)
EDH2	—	—	—	0.0753 (0.47)
EDH3	—	—	—	0.2502 (1.43)
EDH4	—	—	—	0.5226* (1.77)
MORT	0.5158*** (2.76)	0.4796*** (2.66)	0.4728*** (2.62)	0.5013*** (2.78)
LAND	0.0119*** (3.91)	0.0132*** (4.45)	0.0141*** (4.75)	0.0131*** (4.43)
URBAN	−0.2224 (1.25)	−0.2923* (1.70)	−0.2043 (1.18)	−0.2316 (1.33)
LFAWAY	−0.2111 (0.88)	−0.3446 (1.48)	−0.1408 (0.58)	−0.1848 (0.76)
LFHOME	0.1017 (0.77)	0.0375 (0.29)	0.0565 (0.44)	0.0615 (0.48)
LACTMO	0.0130 (1.51)	0.0070 (0.84)	0.0632*** (2.57)	—

TABLE 11.1 *(continued)*

Independent variables	Equation specification			
	Linear specification of all variables	Linear specification with age variable in quadratic form	Quadratic specification of selected variables	Binary specification of selected variables
	(1)	(2)	(3)	(4)
LACTMOSQ	—	—	−0.0018** (2.44)	—
LACTLOES	—	—	—	−0.7986*** (3.55)
LACTLO	—	—	—	−0.0459 (0.31)
LACTHI	—	—	—	−0.1705 (1.25)
LACTHIES	—	—	—	−0.2171 (1.44)
Constant	−2.6024	−9.5195	−9.9401	−9.2308
Joint F values (turning points)				
AGE, AGESQ	—	470.72*** (45.73)	469.01*** (45.62)	—
EDW, EDWSQ	—	—	4.31** (1.50)	—

EDH, EDHSQ	—	—	1.83 (19.02)	—
LACTMO, LACTMOSQ	—	—	3.32** (17.59)	—
EDW1 to EDW4	—	—	—	2.46**
EDW2 to EDW4	—	—	—	3.09**
EDW3, EDW4	—	—	—	3.71**
EDH1 to EDH4	—	—	—	1.02
EDH2 to EDH4	—	—	—	1.10
EDH3, EDH4	—	—	—	1.65
LACTLOES to LACTHIES	—	—	—	3.54***
LACTLOES, LACTHIES	—	—	—	6.29***
Summary statistics				
R^2	0.48	0.52	0.52	0.52
$\bar{R}^2$ (adjusted)	0.48	0.51	0.52	0.52
F	118.70***	123.14***	96.50***	66.50***
DF	1160	1159	1156	1150

— not specified
*** significant at the 0.01 level
** significant at the 0.05 level
* significant at the 0.10 level
SOURCE 1974 ILO/University of Nairobi Survey.

Since the real world is, of course, non-linear, we now proceed to specify in non-linear form four explanatory variables (wife's education, husband's education, wife's age and length of breastfeeding). The effects of wife's education and husband's education are likely to be non-linear, because any one-year increase in educational attainment has a different effect on a person's values and job-market prospects depending on the education level concerned; for example, completing two years of school rather than one year of school is usually much less important for an individual than completing seventh standard rather than sixth standard when the latter implies graduation from primary school. In addition, it usually takes several years of formal education for a person to become literate; as a result, completing one, two, three or even four standards of school may not have a lasting effect on an individual's ability to read or write. The relationship between wife's age and fertility should be non-linear because age-specific marital fertility rates are known to decline with age.[6] Finally, the length of time women normally breastfeed may be non-linearly related to fertility, partly because breastfeeding for a short period of time may not have much of an effect on the period of post-partum amenorrhoea, whereas the effect associated with breastfeeding for a very long period of time may be weakened because the frequency of suckling may become reduced.

Two commonly used non-linear functional forms are employed in Table 11.1 – a quadratic functional form and sets of binary variables. While other non-linear functional forms (such as log, inverse, jack-knife) could also have been specified, for simplicity attention is focused on quadratics and binaries, since they are the most commonly used in analyses of fertility differentials.

The quadratic form is the easier of the two to employ, and also requires the fewest degrees of freedom. For these reasons, it is frequently employed in the regression analyses of macro-level data where the degrees of freedom are normally fairly small. However, the quadratic form imposes a U-shaped or inverted U-shaped relationship on the data, a relationship which, as we shall see below, may be inappropriate.

Use of binary variables, on the other hand, is more flexible in that it does not impose a particular relationship on the data, but it is very demanding in terms of the sample-size required, and for this reason has come to be employed mainly in the regression analysis of survey data where samples are relatively large. Another disadvantage of binary variables is that information is, in a sense, 'thrown away', since no distinction is made among persons falling within binary categories. For example, in equation (4), Table 11.1, no distinction is made among women who have completed 1, 2, 3 or 4 school standards; all of these women are included in one binary variable (EDW1) and as a result it is not possible to observe differences in fertility among these women. For this reason, as will be shown below, when using binary variables, results can be affected by the manner in which variables are categorised.

Since the relationship between wife's age and total number of live births is obviously so strong, non-linear and non-behavioural in nature, the completely linear formulation of equation (1) in Table 11.1 is improved in equation (2) by including an AGESQ term. When this is done, the adjusted R^2 (i.e. the overall level of explanation attributable to all of the explanatory variables after adjusting for the degrees of freedom)[7] rises fairly sharply – from 0.475 in equation (1) to 0.511 in equation (2). Also as a result, the EDW and EDH coefficients become somewhat smaller, and the URBAN coefficient becomes significant at the 0.10 level in equation (2).[8]

When we add square terms (equation (3), Table 11.1) and sets of binary variables (equation (4), Table 11.1) for wife's education, husband's education and length of breastfeeding, there are several important changes in coefficients. For illustrative purposes, results from the non-linear formulations for wife's education, husband's education and breastfeeding from equations (3) and (4) are juxtaposed with results from their linear formulations (equation (2)) and are shown in Figures 11.1 to 11.3.

According to equation (2), husband's education is positively and significantly related to fertility. However, when a quadratic functional form is used as in equation (3), the relationship between husband's education and fertility is found to be insignificant. Specifying EDHSQ does not significantly improve the fit (t value 0.29), nor is the joint F value for both EDH and EDHSQ statistically significant at the 0.10 level (joint F value of 1.83).[9] Thus, as indicated in equations (2) and (3), husband's education and fertility are positively related but this relationship is not well represented by a quadratic form. In this regard, notice that the turning point (i.e. where the effect of husband's education changes direction from positive to negative) for the quadratic specification does not occur until EDH has a value of just over 19 – a value which is beyond its maximum value (university has value 14), again implying that the relationship between EDH and CEB is monotonic and positive in nature. Results for the binary formulation for husband's education are mixed; while joint F values for husband's education are insignificant at the 0.10 level, fertility is significantly higher when the husband is very well educated (EDH4), and there is a tendency for fertility to rise with increases in levels of husband's education.

For wife's education, all three formulations indicate that increases in

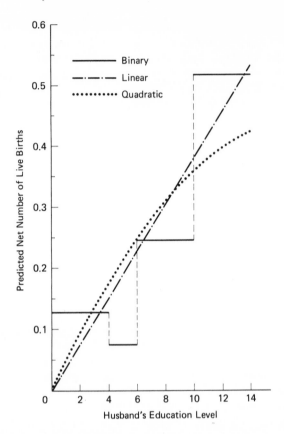

FIGURE 11.1 *Predicted net relationship between husband's education and total number of births, based on Table 11.1*

the wife's level of education have a significant negative effect on fertility. However, the two non-linear formulations indicate that this negative relationship does not begin until women have completed some education - approximately two standards according to the quadratic formulation, and approximately five standards according to the binary formulation. These relationships are shown graphically in Figure 11.2.

An interesting question is whether the binary formulation 'hides' important differences in the effect of wife's education *within* the category of women completing 1-4 standards so that, for example, a significant positive effect on fertility for standard 1 or 2 completed is counterbalanced by a negative (or null) effect for standard 3 or 4 completed. Such a pos-

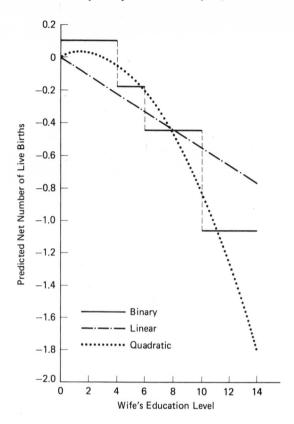

FIGURE 11.2 *Predicted net relationship between wife's education and total number of births, based on Table 11.1*

sibility is worth investigating because of findings from other studies in Africa where fertility is observed to be positively related to early increases in female education (for example, see the Nigerian study in this volume). To investigate this possibility, we re-estimated equation (4) after replacing EDW1 by two binary variables, one representing completion of standard 1 or 2 and the other representing completion of standard 3 or 4 (unreported regressions). The results indicate that fertility is significantly higher for women completing standard 1 or 2 (coefficient 0.4428, *t* value 1.86) compared to women who never attended school (i.e. excluded class), whereas for women completing standard 3 or 4, their fertility is virtually the same as for women who never attended school (coefficient 0.0369, *t* value 0.18).

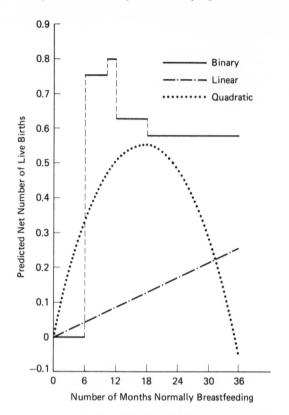

FIGURE 11.3 *Predicted net relationship between number of months breastfeeding and number of births, based on Table 11.1*

This is a good example of how the categorisation used in defining binary variables, for women who completed standards 1-4, as in equation (4), indicates that wife's education and fertility are negatively related after a threshold of about standard 7 is completed, and that there is no significant relationship between wife's education and fertility below this threshold. However, when the standard 1-4 category is subdivided (as discussed in the above paragraph), it appears that there is a small positive segment to the wife's education–fertility relationship.[10]

For breastfeeding, results differ so greatly between equations (2), (3) and (4), depending on the formulation used, that the analyst would draw completely different conclusions about the relationship between breastfeeding and fertility. Based on the linear formulation (equation (2)), one would conclude that there is no significant relationship between breast-feeding and fertility. Based on the quadratic formulation (equation (3)), one would conclude that increases in the period of time women normally breastfeed have the expected negative effect on fertility for periods beyond about 18 months, but that, for up to 18 months, length of breast-feeding and fertility are unexpectedly positively related. Lastly, based on the binary formulation (equation (4)), one would draw a third, and completely different conclusion – that the usual length of breastfeeding and fertility are not related except that women who usually breastfeed for less than six months have significantly lower fertility than other women. These results are shown graphically in Figure 11.3. Given that the positive segment of the breastfeeding–fertility relationship (as observed in equation (3)) results from low fertility among women who normally breastfeed for a short period of time (as observed for LACTLOES in equation (4)), a reasonable conclusion is that this positive relationship is not behavioural in nature; rather, knowing that a woman who normally breastfeeds for a short period of time helps identify relatively 'modern' women with relatively small family-size desires.

Since extended periods of breastfeeding are known to increase the post-partum amenorrhoea period, it is worth investigating whether the negative segment of the breastfeeding–fertility relationship (as observed in the quadratic formulation in equation (3)) is behavioural in nature, and thus, whether in the binary formulation LACTHIES 'hides' a strong negative effect on fertility of breastfeeding for periods longer than 18 months. For this reason, equation (4) was re-estimated after replacing LACTHIES by two binary variables, one representing women who normally breastfeed for 19-23 months and the other representing women who normally breastfeed for 24 or more months (unreported regressions). While the coefficient for normally breastfeeding 24 or more months was insignificant (coefficient 0.1186, t value 0.73), the coefficient for normally breastfeeding 19-23 months was significant at the 0.05 level (coefficient -0.6255, t value 2.22). Given that these results are internally inconsistent and that there are only 42 sample women who reported normally breastfeeding for 19-23 months, it seems that the negative segment of the lactation–fertility relationship (as observed in equation (3)) is probably a statistical artefact. In conclusion, the present analysis does not provide evidence that extended lactation significantly reduces fertility rates in Kenya – a conclusion which one would have drawn if the analysis were based on the linear (equation (2)) and binary (equation (4)) formulations but not if the analysis were based on the quadratic formulation (equation (3)).

What general lessons can be drawn from the above analysis? Is there a systematic way of establishing which functional form is the most appropriate?

First and foremost, there are theoretical considerations. If the analyst knows, or has strong reasons for believing, that an explanatory variable is related to fertility in a particular way, then a functional form which approximates this expected relationship should be specified. If, on the other hand, the analyst is uncertain as to the shape of the relationship – as is often the case in research on fertility differentials – it becomes more of an empirical question of which functional form best fits the data.

There are useful guidelines, however. One can inspect residuals (i.e. error terms in a regression) to ascertain how a particular explanatory variable is related to fertility. One can also use t values and F values in deciding which functional form best fits the data.[11]

For example, for the wife's education, all three formulations are significant at the 0.05 level, and as a result one cannot choose between them on this basis. On the other hand, the EDW–CEB relationship does appear to be non-linear based on the significance of the coefficient of EDWSQ in equation (3) and on the significance of the set of binaries in equation (4). However, significance levels are similar for these two non-linear formulations, and as a result do not provide a basis for choosing between them.

For husband's education, the quadratic formulation (equation (3)) does not provide a good fit – both the t value of the square term and the joint F value for the linear and square terms together are insignificant – indicating that the relationship between EDH and CEB is not quadratic. In the binary formulation, the joint F value is insignificant, but because one of the binary variables (EDH4) is significant, it is difficult to conclude that the linear form is superior to the binary form.

For breastfeeding, the linear formulation is insignificant and obviously inappropriate. On the other hand, both of the non-linear formulations, specified are significant. There is not, however, a very strong basis for choosing between the two non-linear formulations (based on significance tests), even though the binary formulation has a higher level of significance than has the quadratic formulation (0.01 compared to 0.05, respectively).

As shown above, use of statistics such as t values and F values can be helpful in establishing whether or not a relationship is linear or non-linear – although they are less helpful in establishing which non-linear function should be specified. Analysis of residuals (which we did not attempt) can also be useful in determining the type of curve which best fits the data. However, residuals, t values, joint F values, Durbin-Watson values and other statistics are not by themselves sufficient to determine which is the most appropriate functional form of regression analysis. Researchers must also take into consideration theoretical considerations, research objectives and the nature of the explanatory variables involved when making a decision about which functional form to use.

For large-scale household surveys and for explanatory variables which are basically interval in nature, it is not clear as to which functional form is best, although the author personally believes that binary variables are usually preferable. This is particularly true when one intends to re-estimate the relationship for various population subgroups[12] and also when the exact form of a relationship is not known and thresholds or other complicated types of relationships are suspected. On the other hand, when an explanatory variable is truly interval in nature (or if one is interested in elasticities), an analyst should seriously consider the use of a quadratic relationship (or other continuous functional forms, if necessary). For this reason, a quadratic formulation for wife's age was used in Table 11.1.

If an analyst uses sets of binary variables to represent explanatory variables, he or she should consider the following points.

(i) Interval and ordinal variables should be categorised using prior knowledge about where there are likely to be discontinuities in a variable's relationship to fertility. For example, for wife's and husband's education, one should take into consideration important levels in the school system (e.g. primary, secondary, tertiary, university) and whether or not respondents have completed them.

(ii) In categorising variables, one must remain cognisant of sample-size. Notice that for each of the binary variables specified in Tables 11.1 and 11.2, there are at least 10 respondents with this included characteristic and it is indicated if there are less than 30 respondents (a commonly used minimum). There are several reasons why it is necessary to pay attention to binary cell size. Firstly, results are more sensitive the smaller the cell size, implying that one must be cautious about drawing strong conclusions based on relatively few observations. Secondly, the analyst must realise that when analysing fertility differentials within population subgroups, sample-sizes decrease, and consequently certain binary variables will need to be deleted from these subgroup regressions due to a paucity of observations. The analyst then has the choice of either excluding respondents belonging to these deleted binary variable categories from the analysis altogether, or including them in an adjacent binary variable, as in Table 11.2.

(iii) The analyst should consider whether or not the categories employed conceal significant differences within each category. The possibility of

TABLE 11.2 Regressions on fertility (CEB) among married women in Kenya by residence and tribe (t statistics in brackets)

Independent variables	All women (1)	Urban women (2)	Rural women (3)	Tribe (rural only)			
				Kikuyu (4)	Luhya (5)	Luo (6)	Kamba (7)
AGE	0.669*** (12.83)	0.668*** (4.92)	0.639*** (11.33)	0.543*** (4.26)	0.530*** (4.29)	0.716*** (4.79)	0.435** (2.15)
AGESQ	−0.0072*** (8.99)	−0.0072*** (3.29)	−0.0069*** (7.88)	−0.0052*** (2.66)	−0.0044** (2.29)	−0.0083*** (3.52)	−0.0043 (1.39)
EDW1	0.002 (0.00)	0.451[a] (1.18)	−0.068 (0.44)	0.003 (0.00)	0.310[a] (0.87)	0.316 (0.75)	0.065[a] (0.13)
EDW2	−0.251 (1.49)	0.621 (1.55)	−0.381** (2.06)	−0.413 (1.19)	−0.296[a] (0.69)	−0.410 (0.89)	−0.624[a] (1.08)
EDW3	−0.486** (2.34)	−0.148 (0.35)	−0.547** (2.27)	−1.051**[a] (2.25)	−0.067[a] (0.15)	−0.588[a] (0.97)	−0.661[a] (0.93)
EDW4	−1.121***[a] (2.59)	−1.238*[a] (1.87)	−1.801***[a] (2.60)	−[b]	−[b]	−[b]	−[b]
EDH1	0.045 (0.22)	−0.479 (1.11)	0.126 (0.81)	0.088 (0.26)	0.240 (0.66)	0.591 (1.36)	−0.046 (0.10)
EDH2	−0.141 (0.87)	−0.607 (1.28)	−0.101 (0.59)	−0.385 (1.08)	0.041 (0.11)	1.349*** (2.68)	−0.355[a] (0.69)
EDH3	0.097 (0.55)	−0.031 (0.06)	0.099 (0.52)	0.101 (0.24)	−0.597 (1.33)	1.074** (2.31)	0.571[a] (0.97)
EDH4	0.280 (0.94)	0.335 (0.57)	0.091 (0.25)	1.027*[a] (1.77)	−[b]	−[b]	−[b]	−[b]

LAND	0.014*** (4.68)	—	0.014*** (4.46)	-0.009 (2.64)	0.005 (1.11)	0.030*** (2.64)	0.006 (0.72)
URBAN	-0.252 (1.28)	—	—	—	—	—	—
SIBLINGS	0.017 (1.56)	-0.004 (0.19)	0.020* (1.66)	0.048** (2.31)	-0.013 (0.47)	-0.044 (1.16)	-0.028 (0.58)
LFAWAY	-0.259 (1.06)	0.311 (0.82)	-0.684** (2.23)	-0.276[a] (0.61)	_[b]	_[b]	_[b]
LFHOME	0.155 (1.16)	0.504[a] (0.82)	0.027 (0.19)	0.262 (0.79)	-0.418 (1.15)	0.326 (0.79)	-0.744 (1.57)
AVENROL	0.015*** (4.04)	-0.010 (0.99)	0.018*** (4.65)	-0.063*** (3.90)	0.038*** (4.19)	0.036* (1.67)	0.154** (2.53)
EDEXPECT	0.092*** (3.32)	0.043 (0.54)	0.104*** (3.23)	0.091 (1.18)	0.123 (1.23)	0.015 (0.14)	0.161** (2.23)
FARMCPTL	-0.0001 (0.49)	—	-0.00001 (0.55)	0.00001 (0.84)	-0.00000 (0.08)	-0.00002 (0.81)	-0.00001 (0.33)
INCOME	-0.019 (0.94)	-0.061** (2.17)	0.002 (0.09)	0.001 (0.00)	0.157*** (2.66)	-0.062 (0.60)	-0.081 (1.23)
MIGRANT	0.057 (0.37)	0.822** (2.49)	-0.123 (0.69)	-0.558 (1.62)	0.164[a] (0.37)	0.096 (0.22)	_[b]
MORT	0.503*** (2.75)	3.143*** (3.39)	0.405** (2.14)	1.760** (2.26)	0.184 (0.51)	0.385 (1.11)	0.780 (0.82)
AVMORT03	0.506 (0.39)	-1.730 (0.29)	1.205 (0.89)	6.821* (1.71)	6.716 (1.51)	-3.123 (0.55)	90.666** (2.29)
FPVISIT	0.221 (1.36)	0.440[a] (1.24)	0.165 (0.91)	0.220 (0.79)	0.492 (1.02)	-0.465 (1.00)	0.287[a] (0.65)
POLYGMOS	-0.538*** (3.98)	-0.479[a] (1.34)	-0.559*** (3.71)	-0.374[a] (1.01)	-1.089****[a] (3.02)	-0.846** (2.21)	0.005[a] (0.00)

TABLE 11.2 (continued)

Independent variables	All women (1)	Urban women (2)	Rural women (3)	Tribe (rural only)			
				Kikuyu (4)	Luhya (5)	Luo (6)	Kamba (7)
HUSAWAY	-0.364* (1.82)	[b]	-0.342* (1.65)	-0.327 (1.11)	[b]	[b]	0.107[a] (0.26)
LACTLOES	-0.757*** (3.39)	0.051 (0.14)	-1.223*** (4.49)	[b]	[b]	-1.818***[a] (2.99)	[b]
LACTLO	-0.065 (0.44)	-0.256 (0.92)	-0.019 (0.11)	-0.272 (0.93)	0.031[a] (0.08)	0.194[a] (0.37)	-1.863***[a] (3.58)
LACTHI	-0.117 (0.87)	-0.056 (0.16)	-0.137 (0.94)	-0.261 (0.99)	-0.306 (0.91)	-0.212 (0.49)	-0.836[a] (1.62)
LACTHIES	-0.152 (1.02)	[b]	-0.141 (0.89)	[b]	-0.550 (1.36)	-0.177 (0.42)	0.104 (0.23)
GOODHLTH	0.091 (0.77)	0.021 (0.07)	0.063 (0.49)	0.352 (1.39)	0.223 (0.69)	-0.039 (0.97)	-0.342 (0.88)
POORHLTH	0.092 (0.66)	0.434[a] (0.93)	0.061 (0.38)	-0.149 (0.43)	0.596 (1.59)	0.065 (0.16)	-0.810* (1.86)
Constant	-11.385	-12.508	-11.050	-5.258	-11.571	-11.989	-20.764

Joint F statistics

EDW1 to EDW4	2.51**	2.45**	2.97**	2.00	0.56	0.77	0.75
EDW4, EDW3	3.73**	3.48**	3.76***	4.20**	0.02	0.65	0.47
EDH1 to EDH4	0.87	1.87	0.57	1.89	1.37	2.65*	0.91
EDH4, EDH3	1.04	1.39	0.25	2.79*	3.65*	0.76	2.23
LACTLOES to LACTHIES	3.00**	1.39	5.29**	0.67	0.24	2.70**	6.06***
GOODHLTH, POORHLTH	0.34	0.54	0.13	1.73	1.37	0.74	1.74

Summary statistics

R^2	0.55	0.65	0.54	0.63	0.73	0.60	0.56
$\bar{R}^2$ (adjusted)	0.53	0.58	0.53	0.57	0.68	0.52	0.45
F	44.38***	10.26***	38.35***	11.37***	13.95***	7.74***	5.09***
DF	1138	145	967	180	127	133	100

*** significant at the 0.01 level
** significant at the 0.05 level
* significant at the 0.10 level

− not specified
a less than 30 observations
b less than 10 observations
SOURCE 1974 ILO/University of Nairobi Survey.

this problem was investigated earlier in this section for breastfeeding and wife's education, and, indeed, it was found that within the first category of wife's education (completion of standards 1-4), completion of standard 1 or 2 had a much different effect on fertility than did completion of standard 3 or 4.

(iv) The analyst should also consider whether results for a set of binary variables are internally consistent. (This is automatically considered when estimating linear or quadratic functions.) It is not generally sufficient to find that the estimated coefficient for one binary category is statistically significant if this result cannot be rationalised with results for the other binary categories; the one significant result could be a statistical artefact. For example, results reported above for breastfeeding indicate that a small group of sample women who normally breastfeed for 19-23 months have significantly lower fertility than women who normally breastfeed for an average period of time (i.e. 12 months); on the other hand, the fertility of women who normally breastfeed 13-18 months or 24 or more months is not significantly different than for women who normally breastfeed for 12 months. Given the small sample-size involved (about 40 women report normally breastfeeding 19-23 months) and the inconsistency of these results with those for women who report normally breastfeeding for 13-18 months and for 24 or more months, it is not possible to conclude that there is a negative relationship between breastfeeding and fertility based on the significant result for this small group of women.

(v) Finally, when presenting results for binary variables (as well as quadratics), the analyst should include statistical measures of significance which refer to the *set* of variables (as well as for each variable separately). Again referring to results in Table 11.1, notice that at the bottom of Table 11.1, joint F values and turning points are presented.[13] The joint F values indicate whether or not *sets* of variables are statistically significant.[14] This information is important because it is possible for a set of variables to be significant even though each of the variables in the set is insignificant because of multicollinearity. It is also possible (although somewhat unusual) for a set of variables to be insignificant even though one or more variables in the set is significant (Kmenta, 1971).

PROBLEMS IN THE INTERPRETATION OF REGRESSION RESULTS

As shown in the previous section, interpretation of regression results depends on the functional form which is used. There are also other problems analysts must face in interpreting regression results. Some of these other problems are discussed below.

Firstly, observable variables in the social sciences are multidimensional in nature, the most important example in the fertility literature being wife's education. Education is said to change a woman's status and values away from a traditional life-style (which includes a large family-size) towards a life-style which includes higher status, a career and an increasing array of consumer goods. Education also increases a woman's income-earning potential and, as a result, the opportunity cost of withdrawing from the labour-force in order to care for children. Finally, education is said to increase a persons's willingness to accept (and to use efficiently) new products and procedures, including modern contraceptives. The interesting lesson for us here is that the observation of a relationship (e.g. between wife's education and fertility) does not indicate the reasons for this relationship.[15]

Secondly, even results which are statistically significant can be misleading. There may be specification errors whereby explanatory variables proxy for, and therefore, 'pick up' the effect of other theoretically important variables which are not specified due to a lack of data. For these reasons it is useful to test the robustness of regression results, especially for area and cohort life-cycle differences in behaviour. To illustrate this, we stratified sample households according to place of residence and tribal affiliation. Readers interested in life-cycle effects are referred to Anker and Knowles (1982), where separate analyses are performed for women in different age groups. We also expanded the list of explanatory variables to include additional theoretically important determinants of fertility. Variable definitions are provided in the third section, as are *a priori* expectations as to how these variables will be related to fertility. Regression results are shown in Table 11.2. For all sample women (equation (1), Table 11.2) notice that, except for husband's education (EDH1–EDH4), coefficients of variables which were previously reported in Table 11.1 are not greatly affected by specification in Table 11.2 of these additional explanatory variables, only those associated with children's education (AVENROL, EDEXPECT), polygamy (POLYGMOS) and separation of spouse (HUSAWAY) are statistically significant at the 0.10 level, and that, contrary to *a priori* expectations, AVENROL and EDEXPECT have positive (and significant) coefficients – indicating that higher educational expectations and educational attainment for children are associated with more - not less - fertility.

How much confidence can we place in the results shown in equation (1), Table 11.2? Is it possible to distinguish between several competing theories which could be used to explain the same observed relationships?

To help in answering these questions, we re-estimated equation (1) for rural and urban areas (equations (2) and (3), Table 11.2), and for each of the four largest tribes in Kenya (equations (4)-(7), Table 11.2). These results should increase our understanding of the underlying factors helping to determine fertility, since results for each of these population subgroups are expected to differ somewhat. For example, one would expect the relationship between wife's education (EDW1-EDW4) and fertility (CEB) to be stronger in urban than in rural areas, since education is a more important determinant of a person's income-earning capacity (and thus the opportunity cost of withdrawal from the labour-force) in urban areas where jobs requiring education are more readily available. For the same reason, the relationship between working away from home (LFAWAY) and CEB should be stronger in urban as compared to rural areas. In addition, work away from home would be more compatible with child-care in rural areas than in urban areas, since the extended family tends to be stronger and work tends to be closer to home in rural areas. Migrant status (MIGRANT) is expected to be positively related to fertility in urban areas, because migrants (mostly from rural areas) enter the urban area with a relatively traditional value system and a relatively large family-size, whereas in rural areas these factors are not as marked so that the disruption of family life and the achievement-orientation of migrants should cause a negative relationship in rural areas between migrant status and fertility. Lastly, the community level measures of mortality (AVMORT03) and school enrolment (AVENROL), which are measured at the sub-location level, should be less relevant (and thus weaker) for urban areas than for rural areas, since urban norms are probably established more on a city-wide basis than on a sub-location basis.

Also, except in the few instances where there may not be enough variation (or range) in the explanatory variable for a given tribe, one would expect the results to be similar in each of the tribes. The extent to which results are similar (or different) across the four tribes should increase (or decrease) our confidence in the earlier results for all rural women. In any case, it is important to consider tribal affiliation in Kenya, where there is such diversity among tribes in terms of culture, tradition, historical experience and physical environment. This is doubly important, because tribes in Kenya are concentrated in particular regions of the country, and it may be that micro variables which are highly related to area of residence (as well as macro variables which are, of course, region-specific) may have proxied for important unobserved regional factors which were not specified in the analysis of all rural women (equation (3), Table 11.2).

Results for all rural women (equation (3), Table 11.2) are very similar to those for all sample women, which is as expected, since rural women comprise 85 per cent of the total sample. Interestingly, however, LACTLOES, LFAWAY and wife's education (EDW2-EDW4) are much more strongly related to fertility in the rural sample than in the combined sample. These results indicate that fertility is significantly lower than average for a small, 'élite' group of rural women who are relatively well educated, who work away from home and who are untraditional in their breastfeeding practices.

For urban areas, results differ quite substantially from those for rural areas. Numerous explanatory variables are significant in one area and insignificant in the other. Although the small sample-size suggests that the urban results should be interpreted very cautiously, it does appear that the determinants of fertility are quite different in rural and urban areas of Kenya.

We hypothesised above that the negative relationship of wife's education to fertility would be stronger in urban areas than in rural areas. The fact that this is not the case (compare equations (2) and (3) in Table 11.2) implies that the economist's opportunity-cost explanation gains little support from these data. Furthermore, since family-planning acceptance rates are so low in Kenya, one is left with the likelihood that changes in status, tastes or values account for the observed negative relationship between wife's education and fertility among rural women.

Rural and urban results for LFAWAY and LACTLOES reinforce the impression that increases in education levels of rural women cause their desired family-size to change toward a smaller, although still quite large desired family-size. As hypothesised above, LFAWAY was expected to be more strongly related to fertility in urban areas than in rural areas, yet the opposite occurs. LFAWAY's estimated coefficient is negative (and significant at the 0.05 level) in rural areas and positive (although insignificant) in urban areas. Of course, work away from home and childcare may be compatible in both urban and rural areas of Kenya, where domestic servants are inexpensive, where older children often help take care of younger children, and where other adults in the extended family are frequently present.[16] Even so, why then is the relationship between LFAWAY and fertility negative and significant only in rural areas? One possible explanation is that rural Kenyan women who work away from home – agricultural work on one's own farm was generally considered as work near home – (only about 4 per cent of the rural sample, of whom one-third are school teachers) adopt a smaller family-size norm because their work affects their status, interests and values. Regardless of the reason for these results, it does appear that there exists a 'modernisation' lower fertility syndrome for a small but growing group of rural Kenyan women.

Three variables, namely EDEXPECT, AVENROL and LACTLOES, had unexpected (yet significant) signs in the analyses of all women and rural women (equations (1) and (3), Table 11.2). Also, SIBLINGS was significant at the 0.10 level in the analysis of rural women (equation (3), Table 11.2). In order to see how much confidence one can have in these results, we now look at regression results for the four largest tribes in Kenya (equations (4)–(7), Table 11.2). For SIBLINGS, the significant positive coefficient observed in the analysis for all rural women is seriously called into question since in three of the four tribes, SIBLINGS has an unexpected negative sign. For EDEXPECT, AVENROL and LACTLOES, however, the tribal analysis tends to confirm the existence of these unexpected relationships. EDEXPECT is positive in all four tribes; AVENROL is positive (and significant) in three of the four tribes; LACTLOES is negative and significant in the one tribe with a sufficient number of women in this category (i.e. at least ten women) and LACTLO is negative in two of the other three tribes. Given the consistency of these results and the small sample-sizes involved, it is unlikely that these results are statistical artefacts. Consequently, one must provide reasonable explanations for these results. As explained above, LACTLOES is probably indicative of atypical behaviour which is also accompanied by a lower family-size.

Results for EDEXPECT and AVENROL imply that at the time of the survey, parents viewed education for their children as a 'good investment'. This conclusion is consistent with the high rate of return to education previously found in Kenya (from 19.9 per cent for university to 55.1 per cent for 5–7 years of primary school, according to earlier studies; Carnoy and Thias, 1971, 1972), and the strong family ties in Kenya, where children are still expected to share part of their income with their parents. The rural and urban results are also consistent with this conclusion, since in rural areas (where EDEXPECT is significant), traditional values are strong and grown-up rural children are more likely to contribute part of their income to their parents than are urban children.[17]

PREDICTING FUTURE TRENDS IN FERTILITY RATES[18]

Most analysts discuss their regression results from the point of view of statistical significance, since they are interested in testing hypotheses – i.e. knowing the degree of confidence they can have that explanatory variable *x* is related to fertility in a particular direction. Some analysts go a step further, to report elasticities (the percentage change in fertility which is associated with a one per cent change in the explanatory variable). While both significance levels and elasticities are useful, neither is sufficient if one is to use regression results for understanding likely future changes in fertility.

Elasticities or coefficients tell only part of the story. The total effect of an explanatory variable is dependent on its coefficient (or elasticity) as well as how much the explanatory variable is likely to change. In addition, one must also consider the underlying reasons for an observed relationship, and should not blindly use them to 'predict' future changes in fertility. To illustrate this problem, consider the results in Tables 11.1 and 11.2 for the land ownership variable (LAND), a measure of wealth whose effect is believed to represent a positive income or wealth effect. Over time, along with population growth and a fixed stock of land, average farm-size is likely to decline, while average income levels are likely to rise due to capital investments and technological change. Thus, if the LAND coefficient represents a positive income effect, it should imply that fertility rates will rise in the future, along with economic development and increases in rural income – not that fertility rates will fall along with decreases in average farm-size. This is a good example of why one must think about the underlying reasons for the relationships which are observed, and why one should not blindly project out its likely effects.

Other examples of perverse 'predictions' – which would result if based on an uncritical use of estimated coefficients – involve FPVISIT, EDEXPECT and AVENROL. Increases in family-planning acceptance should help reduce fertility (or possibly have no independent effect), not increase fertility as would be 'predicted' based on results in Table 11.2. Rather, results for FPVISIT in Table 11.2 probably indicate that relatively fecund women with relatively high fertility are those most in need of family-planning. Also, future increases in school enrolment rates may help decrease (or at least not increase) fertility, as would be 'predicted' based on results in Table 11.2 (see note 17).

There are also other problems associated with estimating the likely effect on fertility of certain variables. For example, the predicted effect on fertility of husband's education based on its coefficient is likely to be overestimated, since husband's education is believed to represent a positive income effect, and, over time, male education levels in Kenya will increase much faster than will average income levels.

For wife's education, the likely effect on fertility of increases in female education will depend on what is the major reason for the observed negative relationship between wife's education and fertility. If this relationship is due to changing values or to changes in female status (as is argued in the previous section), then the effect of increases in wife's education based on the estimated coefficient should prove to be fairly reasonable. If, on the other hand, this relationship is due to the opportunity cost associated with the wife's possible withdrawal from the labour-force for child-care, then the estimated effect on fertility of wife's education is likely to be overestimated, since the relative level as well as the absolute level of education should be the main determinants of the opportunity-cost involved.

Finally of course, one must remain cautious in using, for purposes of prediction, estimated effects which are insignificant, since it is uncertain that these relationships even exist.

SUMMARY AND CONCLUSIONS

Increasingly, researchers have been turning to household survey data in order to test their hypotheses regarding the determinants of fertility. This interest in survey data has resulted partly from disenchantment with macro, aggregate-level data where multicollinearity problems are serious, where measurement error is an ever-present problem, and perhaps most importantly, where the theoretical models used to explain differentials in fertility rates are based on individual or household considerations (that is, at a different level of aggregation). This growing use of survey data is also related to such perceived advantages of survey data as its relatively low multicollinearity and thus the increased ability to separate out the effects of one explanatory variable from another; its richness, which allows researchers to investigate the importance of area- and culture-specific factors; its general provision of large sample-sizes, which allows researchers to investigate whether the determinants of fertility differ among major subgroups of the population; and finally, of course , its assurance that theory and data refer to the same level of aggregation.

Issues related to the estimation of non-linear relationships were taken up in the fourth section. Using the household survey data from Kenya described in the third section (which uses a broad eclectic approach, taking into consideration factors which are country- and culture-specific as well as factors related to the supply and demand for children), differentials in the number of live births sample women reported having were related to a number of demographic, social, economic and cultural explanatory variables using ordinary least squares. For three of these explanatory variables (wife's education, husband's education and length of time women normally breastfeed their children), three functional forms were used – linear, quadratic (i.e. U or inverted U-shape) and sets of binaries (i.e. no assumption on form of relationship). Interestingly, these regression results differed quite substantially. For husband's education, results from all three formulations indicated a positive relationship to fertility – although at first glance only the linear and binary formulations indicated that this relationship was statistically significant. For wife's education, results from all three formulations indicated a negative relationship to fertility – although the quadratic and binary formulations indicated that there was a threshold below which this relationship was non-negative. Indeed, on closer examination, it was shown that at first there was a significant positive relationship between wife's education and fertility. For breastfeeding, results for all three formulations differed. According to the linear formulations, there was no relationship; according to the quadratic formulation, the relationship was in the shape of an inverted U (i.e. positive then negative) with the turning point at about 18 months; according to the binary formulation, there was no relationship except that women who normally breastfeed for a very short period of time (i.e. less than 6 months) have significantly lower fertility.

The fourth section also contained a general discussion of the advantages and disadvantages of estimating non-linear relationships using sets of binaries or quadratics. It was noted that it is difficult to apply set rules in deciding which formulation is the most appropriate, although, for household survey data with large sample sizes, the flexibility of binary variables generally makes them the preferable form. It was also noted: that summary statistics such as joint F values and turning points should be calculated; that the categorisation of variables into sets of binary variables should be done so that they are meaningful; that consideration should be given to the possibility that binary variables conceal important fertility differences among women within each binary category; and that consideration should be given to whether or not results for binary categories within each set of binary variables are internally consistent.

In the fifth section, two frequently encountered additional difficulties in analyses of fertility differentials were discussed: (i) ascertaining the underlying reasons for observed relationships; and (ii) robustness and the degree of confidence one can place in regression results. Again, illustrations were provided using results from regression analyses of Kenyan data. Since there are *a priori* reasons for believing that results from rural and urban subsamples as well as for other population subgroups (such as by age, or by tribe) should differ from each other, the degree to which these expectations are confirmed or denied can be useful in helping researchers both to draw conclusions with regard to robustness of results and to choose between competing explanations. For these reasons, in that section similar regression equations were estimated for urban women, rural women and women in each of the four largest tribes in Kenya, and conclusions were drawn regarding the implication of these results.

Finally, the sixth section contained a discussion on the use of micro-level regression results for 'predicting' likely future changes in fertility. Results from Kenya (reported in the fifth section) were used to illustrate why analysts must know the underlying reasons for the observed relationships, as well as how rapidly the explanatory variables are likely to change in the future if they are to use their regression results for 'predicting' likely future trends in fertility.

In conclusion, the increasing use of houehold survey data to study fertility differentials should greatly improve our knowledge about fertility determinants, especially for specific countries. It is hoped that this chapter will be of use to researchers in overcoming some of the difficulties associated with regression analysis based on household survey data.

NOTES

1. Households in North-Eastern Province (which is inhabited mainly by nomadic people, and which comprises only about 2 per cent of Kenya's population according to the 1969 Population Census) are excluded from the analysis, because it is believed that the sample was non-randomly selected in this region.
2. Urban areas were purposely oversampled so that, rather than comprising approximately 10 per cent of the sample as in the 1969 Population Census, urban households comprise approximately 15 per cent of the households in the survey.
3. For a good discussion of how supply and demand factors can be incorporated into a uniform theoretical framework, see Easterlin (1975).
4. Analysing fertility differentials and *not* including variables which measure supply constraints creates a specification error, and coef-

ficients of the variables used in the analysis are biased if they are correlated with the unspecified supply factors. The size of this bias obviously is an empirical question, but there are *a priori* expectations. For example, since income should be positively correlated with measures of health and fecundity, not specifying supply factors should bias upward the estimated effect income has on fertility.

5. One important problem with the socio-economic theory of fertility not considered in this chapter is the assumption that the household is a homogeneous unit. Thus, differences in family-size desires of various household members, especially husband and wife (except in so far as this is captured by differences in their education), are implicitly assumed to be non-existent. For a discussion of this point see Birdsall (1976), Anker (1982) and Oppong (1978).

6. The estimated coefficient for wife's age in Tables 11.1 and 11.2 is an estimate of the age-specific marital fertility rate. This can be demonstrated by taking the first derivative of wife's age with respect to number of live births she has had.

7. Results are virtually the same when a set of binary variables is used to represent wife's age (unreported regressions), rather than AGE and AGESQ as in equations (2)–(4) in Table 11.1. In the remainder of the chapter, the quadratic form rather than the binary form is used for wife's age, for three reasons. Firstly, results for the quadratic form are easier to present. Secondly, the adjusted R^2 is slightly higher for the quadratic form as compared to the binary form (0.511 compared to 0.508 based on equation (2)). Thirdly, for an interval variable such as wife's age, where each value (i.e. year) has a definite meaning, use of a binary form would be inappropriate and equivalent to throwing away information, since each year of age implies more births on average, whereas binary variables implicitly assume that the number of births is the same for all women, regardless of age, within each binary category.

8. As estimated in Table 11.1 for wife's age, the linear formulation underestimates fertility at the younger ages (below about 32 years) and overestimates fertility at the older ages (above about 32 years), as compared to the quadratic formulation. For this reason, when the quadratic formulation for wife's age is used in equation (2), changes in coefficients are largest for variables which are the most highly related to age (e.g. wife's education, husband's education, wife's labour-force participation).

9. For any one variable, the student t values as shown in brackets in Table 11.1 is equal to the square root of the F value. This relationship between t values and F values does not hold for sets of variables, as shown at the bottom of Tables 11.1 and 11.2.

10. Because the number of women in the sample who completed standard 1 or 2 is small (only 44 women for the total sample), analysis in the fifth section (where fertility differentials within population subgroups are analysed) continues to use the EDW1 binary variable. As an indication, note that for rural women, when the formulation in equation (3) in Table 11.2 (unreported regression) is used with binary variables

representing women who completed standard 1 or 2 and women who completed standard 3 or 4 replacing EDW1, neither coefficient is significant at the 0.10 level (*t* values 0.88 and 1.11, respectively), although their estimated signs do indicate a non-monotonic relationship (0.2199 and −0.1959, respectively). For the urban sample, as there are less than 10 women who have completed standard 1 or 2, this issue was not investigated.

11. The Durbin–Watson statistic (which is frequently used in analysing time-series data) has been recommended as a useful tool to test for non-linearity (Kmenta, 1971; Lansing and Morgan, 1973; Prais and Houthakker, 1955). The Durbin–Watson statistic indicates if there is serial correlation between residuals when the residuals are arranged according to the size of the explanatory variable – which would, of course, be the situation for non-linear relationships. However, our experience with the usefulness of this statistic is not very satisfactory. Based on equation (2), Table 11.1, the Durbin–Watson statistic is 1.84, 1.85 and 1.91 for EDW, EDH and LACTMO respectively – rejecting in each instance the likelihood of non-linearity. Yet, according to equations (3) and (4), at least EDW and LACTMO are non-linearly related to fertility. Similarly, the Durbin–Watson statistic (1.78) for AGE in equation (1) does not indicate non-linearity. It seems that for micro data with large sample-sizes (especially when these data are clustered around particular values or in a fairly small range), the Durbin–Watson statistic is not sufficiently sensitive to be a useful test for non-linearity.

12. Since some relationships will differ across population subgroups, it is often inappropriate to impose on the data one specific functional form based on a detailed analysis of all sample women. In this situation, the flexibility of binaries can be very useful, since the shape of the functional relationship is allowed to differ across the various population subgroups.

13. It is useful to calculate turning points for quadratic formulations, since it is common for a turning point to occur at a value which is not found in the real world – thereby indicating that, in fact, the relationship is monotonic. An example of this is provided in equation (3), Table 11.1, where the turning point for husband's education is about 19 whereas the maximum possible value of husband's education is only 14.

14. It is also useful to calculate joint *F* values for subsets of binary variables, because inclusion of an insignificant binary variable in the set 'unfairly' reduces the significance of the set as a whole (see the end of Table 11.1). While it is possible to drop insignificant categories (thereby often causing them to become part of the excluded class), this procedure would not be justified when one is interested in observing thresholds and non-linearities.

15. Thus, for examples, economists, sociologists and demographers tend to interpret the same observed negative relationship between fertility and wife's education as confirmation of *their* hypotheses on opportunity costs, tastes and family-planning, respectively.

16. In a separate analysis of the determinants of female labour-force participation in Kenya (Anker and Knowles, 1978), neither family-size nor the presence of young children in the household was found to have a significant effect on whether or not Kenyan women were in labour-force.

17. With time, as the job-market for educated Kenyans deteriorates, the relationship between children's education and fertility should become negative. If so, educating children should become a major economic burden on parents, which in turn should help to reduce fertility rates.

18. The discussion in the sixth section ignores the serious problems associated with the use of point-in-time cross-section results for purposes of predicting changes over time. This problem is discussed in Chapter 6 in this volume.

12 Household Fertility Decision-making in Nigeria

GHAZI M. FAROOQ

INTRODUCTION

This chapter, based on a national household fertility, family and family-planning (FFFP) survey, 1971–5, is an attempt to provide an understanding of household reproductive behaviour in a traditional African society that is currently undergoing rapid social and economic transformation. Nigeria, like most of sub-Saharan Africa (Adegbola, 1977), has high levels of both fertility and mortality. The crude birth rate, one of the highest national fertility rates in the world (Ekanem and Farooq, 1977), is estimated to be slightly in excess of 50 per thousand population. However, a preliminary bivariate analysis of the present data in an earlier paper showed that south-western Nigerian households are *not* engaged in uncontrolled reproductive behaviour. Parents do have a conception of desired family-size, and do desire and practise fertility limitation (Farooq, Ekanem and Ojelade, 1977). This chapter goes an important step further in that, through an extensive use of multivariate regression analysis, it estimates a model of the socio-economic and cultural determinants of fertility, and attempts to delineate the different fertility concepts relevant to a traditional African society.

The postulated relationships as well as the analytical framework used in this chapter differ in some respect from a pure utility-maximisation approach. A model of African fertility behaviour must be differentiated from a conventional Western model by its treatment of the important socio-cultural and biological variables which are more important in Africa than in the industrialised countries. In fact, the reproductive experience of many households may be a function more of supply factors than of demand ones. The changes associated with the social and economic development process may also produce different fertility behaviour from that conventionally expected in the light of experience elsewhere.

The rest of the chapter is organised as follows: the next section briefly describes the survey and types of information collected. Different fertility indices are discussed, especially as they relate to demand and supply aspects of fertility in the context of Nigeria. The third section outlines the important theoretical elements and the postulated relationships between fertility and various exogenous variables. The fourth section deals with the empirics of the relationships outlined in the section preceding it. The final section presents the major findings of the study, their policy implications, and the likely future trend of fertility.

DATA AND FERTILITY CONCEPTS

The Survey

The national FFFP Survey was carried out during 1971–5 by the Institute of Population and Manpower Studies at the University of Ife, with the aid of a grant from the Population Council. Data used in this chapter are drawn from the survey conducted during July and August 1971 for 3013 sample households under the Western Phase, which covered the four states of south-western Nigeria.[1,2] The estimated fertility behaviour equations for eastern Nigeria based on the data collected under the Eastern Phase, 1972–3, for 1725 sample households in the three eastern states are reported elsewhere (Farooq, 1980).

The purpose of the FFFP Survey was 'to obtain reliable information on demographic, social and economic traits of Nigeria's people, and, most especially, upon their fertility behaviour and prospects for its change' (Acsadi *et al.*, 1972, p. 156). This was the first comprehensive demographic survey for the country.[3] Essentially a fertility survey, it concentrated on *household* fertility behaviour and attitudes. Thus, there had to be at least one *eligible woman*, defined as currently married and below age 50, and one *eligible man*, defined as husband of the eligible woman (or women), in a household for it to be included in the enumeration.

Three separate types of schedule were administered for each sample household: one household questionnaire, a male questionnaire for every eligible male respondent, and a female questionnaire for every eligible female respondent. The household and female questionnaires were the major sources of data for this chapter. The female questionnaire provided the main source of information for this analysis since, besides the fertility and pregnancy history of women, it contained the crucial questions on desired family-size, ideal family-size and family-planning. It also provided more details on social and economic variables than did the household or male questionnaires. Unfortunately, the female questionnaire was not completed for about one-quarter of the eligible women. Quite frequently in polygynous households, only one or at most two women provided information. Hence, the detailed analyses of realised fertility, i.e. number of live births or children ever born alive per eligible women (CEB), and family-size preferences are limited to the sample of 3400 wives from 3013 sample households who completed the female questionnaire. The number of actual observations for statistical analysis is about 3000 after exclusion of cases with missing or erroneous data.

From the household questionnaire it was possible to obtain for each of the eligible women information on CEB, the number of deceased children, sex of children and a variety of socio-economic variables (the array of exogenous variables being considerably shorter than that from the female questionnaire). Hence, an analysis of CEB was also carried out for the complete sample of about 4400 wives, including many of the polygamously married women who did not complete the female questionnaire but for whom fertility information was available from the household questionnaire.

Besides the above limitations, some important variables, as pointed out in the next section, were also excluded from the inquiry. The pregnancy history was found to be incomplete for many women, and, therefore, was not usable. Despite the extra care taken, there appears to have been some under-reporting of deceased children and hence CEB, particularly among older, illiterate women.[4] Specific data limitations and errors as they affect this chapter's framework or results are pointed out where appropriate in the next two sections. However, it should be mentioned that, by and large, the quality of data was found to be quite reasonable, and that the survey *does* afford information for a fairly comprehensive analysis of the more important socio-cultural and economic determinants of household decision-making regarding fertility.

Measurement of Fertility as the Dependent Variable

In measuring fertility as the dependent variable, the Nigerian survey allows the use of two concepts, the first relating to actual or realised fertility behaviour, and the second to family-size preferences. Indices of actual fertility behaviour are computed from the reproductive histories of wives – the measure used here is the number of live births or CEB. One possible measure of family-size preferences is derived from the woman's or couple's response concerning ideal family-size. However, eligible women were also asked a question on 'additional children wanted'. This then provides an alternate measure of family-size preference – adding the number of additional children wanted to the number of existing children (i.e. surviving births) gives an index of 'desired family-size'. The advantages and disadvantages of CEB, ideal family-size or desired family-size as the dependent variable for this analysis are discussed below.

It can be easily visualised that although a couple at any given time may have some idea of the number of children it would like to have, this number itself can change with the actual fertility experience, i.e. the number of pregnancies, birth parity order, relationships of parents with existing siblings, and so on. In this sense, as also argued by Namboodiri (1972, pp. 194–9), the concept of ideal family-size used in many household fertility surveys may not provide an accurate measure of the number of children a couple wishes (see also Laing, 1970; Hauser, 1973; G. B. Simmons *et al.*, 1978, pp. 141–53). This applies equally to the present study. In the Nigerian survey, the question on ideal family-size was put to eligible women as follows: 'I would like to ask more generally, what do you think is the ideal (generally desirable) number of children for a woman in this area to have?' The response to such a question could very well apply to some hypothetical ideal family, which may not necessarily share the respondent family's social, economic, cultural and demographic milieu.

Most economic analyses of fertility behaviour take an index of actual fertility behaviour such as the number of live births as the dependent variable (for references, see T. P. Schultz, 1974a). In the case of Nigeria, it may be argued that the number of live births may be more a measure of supply than demand for children. Given that medical, health and other such social amenities are relatively scarce, the incidence of sterility, subfecundity and pregnancy wastages are claimed to be quite high; also, the infant and child mortality level is high (Ekanem and Farooq, 1977). Customs such as post-natal sexual abstinence, which may last over long periods of breastfeeding (an average of two to three years in the Yoruba society), are said still to persist. Hence, if the high-fertility attitude of the society persists, many couples would strive to produce as many children as possible. If true, an appropriate measure of family-size preference may better approximate the demand for children and, therefore, may have more meaningful implications for policy consideration.

In any case, preferences concerning family-size could be conceived as influencing actual fertility experience, and vice versa. Namboodiri, among others, makes a strong case that the determinants of family-size preferences are interrelated with those of actual fertility behaviour, and that 'a study of one, therefore, cannot be completely divorced from that of the other' (Namboodiri, 1972, pp. 195–6).[5] Actual household fertility experience in Nigeria was observed to be consistent with family-size preferences (Farooq, Ekanem and Ojelade, 1977). In this chapter, fertility behavioural equations are estimated using two measures, namely CEB and desired family-size. The latter, as defined above, appears to be, *a priori*, a more appropriate family-size preference variable than does ideal family size.[6] It takes into account the actual fertility experience that could safely be assumed to influence the household's preferences regarding additional children. Above all, this measure reflects the respondent family's social and economic characteristics.

It is important to point out that typically in an African survey, questions on preferences of family-size elicit a large non-numerical response, almost entirely couched as 'up to God'.[7] This survey fared comparatively better, in that about three-fifths of the eligible women gave quantitative answers to the question on number of additional children wanted. Desired family-size equations are estimated in two different ways: (i) excluding eligible women whose response was 'up to God', and (ii) including these women by assigning to additional children wanted a fixed numerical value equal to the average top 10 per cent figure obtained from those with numerical responses in urban and rural areas, separately. The second measure in essence assumes that most of these women prefer large families (that is, as many children as God will provide).

THEORETICAL CONSIDERATIONS FOR THE EXPLANATORY VARIABLES AND THEIR SPECIFICATION

As pointed out in the introductory section, Nigerian society differs sufficiently in various aspects from a typical Western one that an application of the usual economic model of fertility to Nigeria might very well be misleading. This does not mean that economic factors are not important, or that the use of theoretical economic constructs is to be completely ruled out. What seems to be needed is a more integrated economic-sociological framework that would allow for consideration of all relevant factors, be they economic, cultural, psychological or biological. This section outlines a model of fertility determination in terms of the exogenous factors expected to be important, their measurement and expected relationships with fertility behaviour and among themselves. These are grouped as socio-economic, cultural, mortality, biological, life-cycle and family-planning factors. Variables relevant to only actual fertility behaviour (or family-size preference) are so identified. Under appropriate headings, there are also discussions of the important missing variables.

Socio-economic Factors

The choice of variables here largely emanates from the economic theory of fertility decision-making that associates reproductive behaviour with the parents' socio-economic characteristics. This theory is well expounded in the literature (see Chapter 2). Below, is a discussion of socio-economic factors that are considered to be relevant in the context of the Nigerian society.

Income and relative economic status
Holding tastes and all other factors constant, high income households are expected to have a larger demand for children than have low-income households (J. L. Simon, 1974). On the supply side also, *ceteris paribus*, relatively higher income levels could be expected to contribute positively to the natural fertility level. In the survey, information on current annual income was collected for both husband and wife (but not for other members of the household). The wife's income was, however, found to be highly correlated with her education attainment level and her economic activity status, but was less accurately reported.[8] Therefore, regression equations containing an income of wife variable are not reported. As discussed below, wife's education level may be a good proxy for wife's income and 'permanent' income. Husband's current income is sometimes assumed to be a proxy for 'permanent income', which is theoretically a more correct variable (children involve relatively long-term expenditure commitments, which then should be related to long-term income prospects). As a more appropriate measure of permanent income, 'quality' of husband's labour activity is also used (that is, whether he was reported to be engaged in a formal economic activity or in an informal economic activity). It can be readily seen that long-term income potential of a man employed in the formal economic sector could be expected to be larger than if he were employed in the informal economic sector. Husband's education status is also sometimes used as a measure of permanent income. Unfortunately, the coding and data files' construction was such that the survey information on this variable could not be exploited. Hence, relevant income variables used in this study are husband's current income and type of his

economic activity. Two different questions were asked in the survey on the wife's perception of her household's standard of living. The questions were as follows. 'Would you say that your present level of living is adequate for the things an average family needs, or worse than that?' (This provides a measure of 'peer comparative economic status'.) 'Do you think your present standard of living is better or worse than it was in the past or just the same?' (This provides a measure of 'time comparative economic status'.)

These subjective measures of the household's relative economic status, like the income variable, are expected to be positively related with fertility behaviour (D. Freedman, 1964). This is true, of course, if the larger resources' 'quality' effect on children (i.e. resources spent on improving the quality of children) does not dominate the 'quantity' effect (i.e. resources spent on having additional children).

Education

In a developing society like Nigeria, education of the wife could be expected to be one of the most important environmental factors shaping the household fertility decision-making and behaviour. Operating as a composite variable,[9] education has negative as well as positive effects on the fertility level and family-size preferences. On balance, the negative effects may be stronger than the positive effects.

Negative effects of education on fertility work largely through the influence of education on tastes and aspirations for material well-being,[10] and on the opportunity-cost of children. Increasing education could be expected to improve not only the employability of the wife by opening up various alternate avenues of employment, but also her income level in her sector of employment. Wife's education also may serve as a proxy for the parents' expectations concerning their children's education (women with higher education likely desire higher education for their children). If this is true, more education for children means a larger price effect and a lower income utility, since their entry into the labour market is inadvertantly delayed. In the case of actual fertility experience, the negative effect of women's education is also likely to be accentuated by the positive correlation between education level and approval of family limitation, knowledge and effective practice of contraception.

Positive effects of education on fertility work through an income effect and, in the case of Nigeria, also through the influence that education has in weakening the otherwise widely-held practice of lactation taboos, any relaxation of which will help shorten the post-partum sexual-abstinence period. Education, as in the case of the income variable, also contributes to raising the natural fertility level, through its influence on nutrition, personal hygiene and health, which may help reduce incidences of sterility and pregnancy wastages.

In situations where desired family-size exceeds the actual number of children the couples can produce, any increase in natural fertility will result in increasing the actual fertility level. The hypothesis advanced here is that up to a certain level, x, increases in the education attainment level would be related to an increase in fertility, but after that level, the negative effects of education begin to overcompensate for the positive ones. This hypothesis, which is referred to as a 'threshold hypothesis' for the purpose of this chapter, is tested by using four binary education variables (see Table 12.1 – variable dictionary).

Women's work participation

Wife's labour-force activity is a more direct measure of opportunity cost of children than is education *per se*.[11] However, in a society like Nigeria, such an opportunity cost of children may largely be compromised on two accounts. Firstly, given the strong familial ties and importance of tribal links, the joint or extended family system is a very common feature of the Nigerian society. (According to Caldwell, 1977a, the concept of 'nuclear' family may be more or less irrelevant.) Under the extended-family system, there is available a ready and relatively cheap provision of baby- and child-care, which allows for an easy substitution of the woman's role in home and market economic activity. Secondly, if a woman is engaged in farming or retail trading activity (as is the case for the majority of working wives, 55 per cent in urban areas and 77 per cent in rural), these activities are observed to be not very incompatible with her reproductive (and home) activity. On balance, such labour activity, by contributing to the family's financial resources, may also have a positive effect on fertility, which may overcompensate for the substitution effect of work participation.

Such might not be the case if a woman is engaged in a formal economic activity and is reported to be in occupational categories such as 'professional, administrative and clerical workers', 'other sales workers' and 'craftsmen, production process, transport and service workers'. However, there may be a high correlation between education level and reported occupation. As mentioned before, education may serve as a proxy for labour quality and, especially in the urban setting, higher education means more of the labour-market being accessible to a woman, particularly job opportunities in the formal sector. As an alternative to the five occupational groupings available, the following binary variables are used to measure the wife's work-participation effect: (i) not in labour-force, (ii) labour-force participation in formal sector, and (iii) labour-force participation in informal sector. (One of the three categories is treated as excluded, depending on the stipulated relationships in a given equation.) The relationship of the first and third variables with fertility behaviour is *a priori* indeterminate, but in case of the second, it is expected to be negative.

Important variables not available for analysis
Two important micro variables not accounted for in this analysis are children's education and the household's migration status. Children's schooling is a measure of child quality, in the sense that a trade-off 'à la Becker' exists between quantity and quality of child services produced. Child education level may also be a rough measure of school expenses and hence child-cost. However, such effects may be picked up by the woman's educational level.

Among the various kinds of migration, the rural–urban migration phenomenon may be most important for influencing the fertility behaviour of the migrant households through structural and attitudinal changes, changes in income, opportunity-cost of children and the like. Overall net effects of migration-related factors on fertility behaviour are probably negative in the long run, but over the short and medium terms, the direction of relationship is not clear (Stark, 1978).

Additionally, the importance of children's wages and employment factors as they influence the household fertility decision in developing countries cannot be underestimated. Unfortunately, most surveys like this one do not collect much usable information on these parameters.

Given the lack of secondary data, no information was available on *community-level* variables such as mortality, school enrolment rates, land availability, agricultural productivity, income distribution, and the like. Such variables, approximating the community environment for the household, have obvious implications for any demographic decision-making problem of the household. Non-inclusion of the relevant macro variables should, therefore, be taken as a major limitation of the present study.

Cultural Factors

Practice of polygyny
Polygyny is very widely practised in the Nigerian society.[12] The survey reported that about two-fifths of eligible women in urban areas and three-fifths in rural areas were in polygynous marriages (see Table 12.1). Based on the results of the earlier study (Farooq, Ekanem and Ojelade, 1977), the relationship between polygyny and realised fertility (CEB) is expected

to be negative, partly due to polygynous wives being comparatively more subjected to coitus and thus fertility-restricting customs and practices than monogamous wives, and partly because they also tend to have a larger incidence of sub-fecundity (see also Olusanya, 1971a). The relationship between polygyny and family-size preference is, however, expected to be positive, as more children may be seen by polygynous wives as emotional and status security safeguards.

It is pertinent to point out that a typical polygynous household set-up is such that the fertility decision-making may be more a wife-specific phenomenon than a joint husband–wife one. In many instances, it is primarily the wife who bears the brunt of the child-cost – this factor is perhaps partly responsible for the high female labour-force participation observed for this society. However, husbands placed in the upper socio-economic echelons, having either single or multiple wives, are likely to be contributing to the household budget for childbearing and childrearing.

Religion

South-western Nigeria is a multiple-religion society, with 32 per cent of respondents being Muslim, 55 per cent Christian, and the rest pagan. Caldwell (1968a, p. 618) has observed that Muslims in tropical Africa tend to both desire and attain larger numbers of children than do the other religious groups. This hypothesis is tested in the present study.

Sex preferences

Among more traditional societies, a preference for boys over girls is usually observed. The Nigerian survey provides information on the sex distribution of CEB. In order to test the significance of sex-preference on fertility behaviour, three binary variables were used: (i) excess of male CEB or female CEB, i.e. excess of either sex, (ii) excess of male CEB, and (iii) excess of female CEB. Only the third variable was found to be significant, implying that when a couple had more female children than male, it attempted to produce more births to have male offspring. (This does not imply, however, that the couple will try to balance the number of sons and daughters.) It should be mentioned that, theoretically, it is the sex distribution of surviving children and *not* of children ever born that is the more appropriate variable. Unfortunately, information on sex of deceased children was not available.

Besides the above factors, there are also coitus-related customs, which will be discussed under the biological factors.

Mortality Factors

In both demographic and economic studies, a positive relationship between infant-child mortality and fertility is emphasised. This is based essentially on the premise that the higher the infant and child mortality, the larger will be the number of live births necessary for obtaining the desired number of surviving children. Hence, from the survey data, if the child survival rate is estimated as 1 minus (deceased children/CEB), the number of live births needed to produce x surviving children equals x times the reciprocal of the child survival rate. The reciprocal of the child survival rate is, therefore, included in the CEB function. This is a rough measure of 'safety factor' or 'replacement factor' (Harman, 1970; Snyder, 1974).[13]

Biological and Life-cycle Factors

It is important to account for biological factors in fertility analyses, as they regulate the human reproduction process and determine fecundity, and hence the potential supply of births or the natural fertility level. The factors discussed above are largely behavioural, and modify the extent to which natural fertility is realised.[14] Biological factors which are potentially important determinants of Nigerian fertility include temporary sterility associated with breastfeeding and permanent or secondary sterility associated with aging.

In Nigeria, social customs regarding breastfeeding and marital sexual abstinence are significant determinants of fertility. Traditionally, the duration of breastfeeding is about 30 months. During this period, sexual relations are considered to be harmful to the health of the child (Olusanya, 1971b). The traditional period of abstinence is up to 3 years, and exceeds that of amenorrhoea and lactation (Orubuloye, 1979). Even if the coitus-controlling tradition were not strictly adhered to, breastfeeding, by reducing female fecundity, influences child-spacing, and most probably the total number of live births as well.[15] The breastfeeding effect has two components: the first relating to its effect on amenorrhoea (usually referred to as lactation anemorrhoea), and the second relating to a continuation of the lactation taboo after menstruation starts. Since a question on the duration of amenorrhoea pertaining to the last birth was included in the survey, it is possible to test for the relevance of the two effects by using (i) duration of amenorrhoea, and (ii) duration of breastfeeding minus duration of amenorrhoea variables. Among the Yoruba wives, there is also said to be a high frequency of terminal sexual abstinence, in many cases before the onset of menopause, because 'the family system could not stand the stress of her having parallel maternal and grandmaternal responsibilities and obligations' and 'for personal reasons such as being too old now for the worry of raising more children' (Caldwell, 1977a, pp. 9, 14; see also Caldwell and Caldwell, 1977).

A quadratic age variable is introduced to measure the terminal sexual-abstinence effect as well as that portion of sterility and subfecundity that may result from increasing age. (A direct question was asked concerning sterility, but the quality of response was found to be unsatisfactory.) It could readily be visualised that actual fertility experience is a convex-increasing function of age – CEB increasing with age but the *change* in the slope of the age coefficient being negative. Both age and age squared are, therefore, included in CEB equations.[16]

For the functional specification of CEB, it may be important to account for the household's stage in the life-cycle. So, besides the wife's age, her age at first marriage is included as a relevant life-cycle variable, though it should be noted that age at marriage, to some extent at least, is a decision variable itself, as it might be influenced by such factors as female education and labour-force participation. The wife's age minus her age at marriage gives the duration of marriage (in the present case, within the fecund age limit) and if some estimate of average birth interval were to be available, other factors being constant, the approximate number of births could be obtained (i.e. dividing duration of marriage in years by average birth interval). Hence, whereas age of wife is expected to have a positive effect on CEB, age at marriage should have a negative effect. Age at marriage also may serve as the relevant proxy for the woman's age at first birth.

Age factors are included in the desired family-size equations also, as age of wife may have an important bearing upon the number of additional children wanted. The number of living children in the index of desired family-size would, of course, be partly dependent upon the age factor. Also, with increasing age, the tendency to rationalise existing number of children as the desired number usually becomes marked.

Family-planning Factors

From the theoretical point of view, if, for a given couple, the biological reproduction maximum is greater than the number of children it wants based on socio-economic environmental factors, then some contraceptive practice has to be adopted by the couple in order to control the supply of children. In the Nigerian survey, more than one-half of the urban eligible women and more than one-third of the rural ones approved of family limitation practices to 'have just the number of children that they want, and have them when they want them'. Most respondents had a knowledge of traditional methods such as abstinence, breastfeeding and rhythm, but only slightly more than one-tenth were aware of modern methods. More than one-half of the respondents had actually practised fertility control, mainly abstinence – less than 5 per cent had ever used a modern method (Adeokun and Ilori, 1976).

Three separate family-planning variables will be used in this analysis: attitude towards, knowledge of, and practice of family-planning. The attitude variable is a proxy for the demand for family-planning, with knowledge and practice measuring the extent to which conscious family limitation is known and practised. It is obvious that the three variables are intercorrelated, and hence the estimated parameters need to be interpreted with caution. All three variables usually are expected to be negatively related to current fertility behaviour. But in situations such as the present one, where the dependent variable is CEB and where the question of fertility limitation may arise only when a sufficient number of live births have been obtained (i.e. family-planning is not used for spacing), the family-planning variables may very well be positively related to CEB. Therefore, *a priori*, the causality is indeterminate.

EMPIRICAL RESULTS

Table 12.1 provides the dictionary of variables for which information was available from the household questionnaire. Although fewer exogenous variables are covered for the household questionnaire than for the female questionnaire, the number of eligible women in the sample is much larger. In the estimation of actual fertility behavioural equations (Tables 12.2 and 12.4), this larger sample is probably more truly representative of the population, in the sense that the coverage of wives in polygamous marriages is more complete. Note that in the complete sample, 40 per cent of wives in urban and 58 per cent in rural areas are reported to be polygamously married compared with the corresponding figures of 29 and 51 per cent in the partial sample. Table 12.1 also presents a description of the variables collected in the female questionnaire. This data set provides the empirical base for estimation of the fully-specified CEB equations (Tables 12.3 and 12.5) and desired family-size equations (Tables 12.6 and 12.7). The means and standard deviations of each variable used in the urban and rural equations are also shown in Table 12.1.

TABLE 12.1 *Definitions, means and standard deviations of the variables used in estimation of fertility equations for south-western Nigeria: complete sample (based on household questionnaire) and partial sample (eligible women[a] who completed female questionnaire)*

Variable symbol (1)	Definition (2)	Mean/(standard deviation)			
		Complete sample		Partial sample	
		Urban (3)	Rural (4)	Urban (5)	Rural (6)
Endogenous dependent					
CEB	Number of children born alive	3.03 (2.23)	3.45 (2.66)	3.21 (2.21)	4.23 (2.45)
DFS1[b] DFS2[c]	Surviving children + additional children wanted	–	–	7.62 (2.70)	8.99 (3.11)
DFS2[c]	Same as above	–	–	6.59 (2.66)	7.52 (3.26)
Exogenous independent					
EDW1	1 if wife has some formal education (1–5 standards), 0 otherwise	0.13 (0.34)	0.07 (0.25)	0.14 (0.35)	0.06 (0.24)
EDW2	1 if wife has completed primary schooling (6–9 standards), 0 otherwise	0.18 (0.38)	0.10 (0.30)	0.20 (0.40)	0.11 (0.31)
EDW3	1 if wife has completed secondary schooling (10–12 standards), 0 otherwise	0.09 (0.29)	0.02 (0.15)	0.10 (0.30)	0.03 (0.17)
EDW4	1 if wife has higher education (13+ standard), 0 otherwise	0.03 (0.18)	0.02 (0.13)	0.04 (0.20)	0.02 (0.14)

TABLE 12.1 (*contd.*)

Variable symbol (1)	Definition (2)	Mean/(standard deviation)			
		Complete sample		Partial sample	
		Urban (3)	Rural (4)	Urban (5)	Rural (6)
LFNOTACT	1 if wife is not in labour-force, 0 if in labour force	0.23 (0.42)	0.20 (0.40)	0.22 (0.41)	0.19 (0.39)
LF. INFORMAL	1 if wife is engaged in an informal labour activity, 0 otherwise	..	–	0.49 (0.50)	0.68 (0.47)
LF. FORMAL	1 if wife is engaged in a formal activity, 0 otherwise	0.26 (0.44)	0.12 (0.32)	0.28 (0.45)	0.13 (0.33)
HLF. FORMAL	1 if husband is engaged in a formal economic activity, 0 otherwise	–	–	0.59 (0.49)	0.30 (0.46)
H. INCOME	Total income of husband during the 12-month period preceding survey (in 1000£; 1£=2 Naira)	3.04 (2.37)	–	3.20 (2.46)	–
POLYGMOS	1 if wife reported to be in polygamous marriage, 0 otherwise	0.40 (0.50)	0.58 (0.49)	0.29 (0.45)	0.51 (0.50)
MOREGIRLS	1 if female CEB greater than male CEB, 0 otherwise	0.31 (0.46)	0.30 (0.46)	0.32 (0.47)	0.34 (0.47)
MORT	Inverse of child survival rate	1.14 (0.68)	1.20 (0.89)	1.26 (0.61)	1.42 (0.88)

AGE	Age of wife in years	28.47 (6.92)	29.84 (7.83)	29.15 (6.64)	31.08 (7.72)
AGESQ	Age squared	858.25 (431.17)	951.42 (498.65)	893.58 (424.09)	1025.44 (508.74)
AGEMAR	Wife's age at first marriage	–	–	18.86 (3.70)	17.62 (3.92)
PEERSTD	1 if level of living better from that of an average family, 0 otherwise	–	–	0.18 (0.38)	0.22 (0.42)
MUSLIM	1 if wife Muslim, 0 otherwise	–	–	0.37 (0.48)	0.29 (0.47)
LACTHI	1 if breastfed last child 2 years or more, 0 if less than 2 years	–	–	0.23 (0.42)	0.36 (0.48)
FPAPROVE	1 if wife approves family limitation, 0 otherwise	–	–	0.46 (0.50)	0.34 (0.47)
FPKNOWMD	1 if wife knows one or more modern methods of contraception, 0 otherwise	–	–	0.25 (0.43)	0.11 (0.31)
EVERUSE	1 if wife ever practised contraception including abstinence, 0 otherwise	–	–	0.80 (0.40)	0.71 (0.45)

[a] Currently married women aged 15 to 49 years
[b] Including women with response 'Up to God' (see the subsection entitled 'Measurement of fertility as the dependent variable')
[c] Excluding women with response 'Up to God'
– Not available

Fertility equations are calculated separately for urban and rural areas. As shown in Table 12.1, the mean and standard deviation values for various variables are quite different between urban and rural samples. This is especially true for education, wives' and husbands' engagement in formal economic activity, incidence of polygyny, proportion Muslim, breast-feeding, approval of family limitation and knowledge of modern contra-ceptive methods.

Before we turn to the discussion of empirical results, it needs to be pointed out that the regressions in Tables 12.2 and 12.7 are estimated by the method of ordinary least squares. Since some of the variables that are treated as exogenous in these equations (e.g. female work-participation, age at marriage and family-planning) might themselves be affected by some of the included independent and/or dependent variables, i.e. since they are endogenous variables in the real sense, interpretation of the results requires a cautionary note as estimates of the parameters may have a 'simultaneity bias'. (For a discussion of alternative approaches to specifying fertility models, see Chapter 8 by Turchi.) However, in dealing with societies such as Nigeria, where complex cultural patterns and traditional values may still prevail and for which not much empirical quantitative evidence is available on how fertility and various other decisions are made by a typical house-hold and how these decisions interact with each other, it may be reason-able to identify determinants of fertility in a single-equation model rather than study fertility as part of an incorrectly specified simultaneous-equation framework. Also, the data limitations of the present survey do not permit empirical specification of a full model. As may be clear from the discussion in the previous section, a conscious effort is, however, made to at least minimise the multicollinearity problem.

The Determinants of Cumulative Fertility: Urban Results

Results from the regression of CEB on different sets of exogenous variables are given in Table 12.2. Equation (1) refers to the total sample of eligible women (for whom the household questionnaire was completed), and equations (2)–(4) pertain to three age cohorts of women. One main pur-pose of the age-specific equations is to pick up the interaction effects related to the wife's stage in the life-cycle. By and large, the validity of the theoretical framework outlined in the previous section appears to be well borne out by the estimated regression coefficients.

Socio-economic factors are quite relevant, particularly husband's income and wife's education level. The coefficient of 0.058 for H. INCOME signifies that, *ceteris paribus*, if the husband's income is higher by £1700, it has the equivalent effect of adding one extra live birth. Education binary variables appear to support the threshold hypothesis – fertility increases initially with education (although parameter estimates are not statistically significant for EDW1 and EDW2, particularly for EDW2) until the threshold level is obtained with completed primary education, and then starts decreasing.[17] The range of education effect is wide indeed compared with the excluded group of uneducated women – the regression coefficients decline in a systematic manner from 0.19 for EDW1 to −0.65 for EDW4. So women with higher education will have, on the average, two-thirds of a live birth less than uneducated women, and almost one less than women with little education.

Overall, female work-participation does not appear to have much of an effect on CEB except when the wife is engaged in the formal sector (LF.FORMAL is significant only at the 10 per cent level). Although LF. FORMAL is positively correlated with education, the multicollinearity problem is not very serious (the first-order correlation coefficient between LF.FORMAL and EDW4 is 0.19).[18] The trade-off between participation in formal economic activity and childbearing/rearing is clearly revealed only in the youngest age group (equation (2)). Another important observation is that whereas the impact of non-work participation on CEB is, as expected, positive in the 25–34 age-sample (equation (3)), it is negative and significant in the case of the 15–24 sample. An explanation is not difficult to find. Since the LFNOTACT coefficient can alternatively be interpreted as largely measuring the influence of wife's labour engagement in traditional activities (the excluded category), the hypotheses advanced in the previous section of a positive fertility effect of wife's labour engagement operating through an improvement of the household budget constraint, and of traditional economic activities not being overtly incompatible with childrearing, appear to be relevant for the young-wife households. It is pertinent to note that the joint F statistics for LFNOTACT and LF.FORMAL show that these labour-force participation variables taken together are significant at the 5 per cent level for the total sample and at the 1 per cent level for age-groups 15–24 and 25–34.

Regressions not shown here suggest that fertility is related to women's occupations. Women who work in farming or agriculture have relatively high fertility in both urban and rural areas. The regression coefficient for 'petty traders' occupation was negative in both urban and rural samples, but the coefficients were small and not significant. Women working in the 'professional, administrative and clerical workers', 'other sales workers' or 'craftsmen, production process, transport and service workers' occupations had relatively low fertility. These results are consistent with the positive association between education level and fertility, as mentioned before.

TABLE 12.2 *Regressions on fertility (CEB) among urban women in south-western Nigeria by age: complete sample of eligible women*[a] *(standard errors in brackets)*

Explanatory variable	Total (1)	Age groups 15–24 (2)	25–34 (3)	35–49 (4)
Constant	−4.917	−1.288	−3.527	−0.852
EDW1	0.195 (0.137)	0.028 (0.117)	0.029 (0.200)	0.959* (0.436)
EDW2	0.034 (0.127)	0.049 (0.103)	−0.083 (0.183)	0.513 (0.463)
EDW3	−0.234 (0.169)	0.048 (0.135)	−0.346 (0.228)	x
EDW4	−0.654* (0.265)	−0.409[b] (0.274)	−0.925**[b] (0.329)	x
LFNOTACT[1]	0.109 (0.116)	−0.191* (0.098)	0.272+ (0.165)	0.126 (0.412)
LF.FORMAL[1]	−0.170+ (0.105)	−0.198* (0.101)	−0.183 (0.143)	−0.041 (0.326)
H.INCOME	0.058** (0.019)	0.027 (0.019)	0.073* (0.027)	0.088+ (0.056)
POLYGMOS	−0.417** (0.095)	−0.063 (0.088)	−0.400** (0.134)	−0.918** (0.285)
MOREGIRLS	0.371** (0.095)	−0.014 (0.090)	0.366** (0.132)	0.714* (0.292)
MORT	1.117** (0.067)	1.333** (0.075)	1.387** (0.109)	0.842** (0.147)
AGE	0.303** (0.046)	0.076** (0.019)	0.177** (0.023)	0.112** (0.034)
AGESQ	−0.002** (0.001)	–	–	–
$\bar{R}^2$	0.47	0.51	0.29	0.17
F	105.08	40.41	26.17	6.82
Average CEB	3.03	1.47	3.14	4.93
No. of observations	1399	420	676	303

Notes to Table 12.2 are on p. 331.

Turning to cultural variables, both POLYGMOS and MOREGIRLS come out with expected signs and are significant at the 1 per cent level. This shows the relevance of cultural factors in a traditional society, and suggests the problems of applying the pure home-economics models to developing countries. On the average, a wife in the polygnous union will have more than two-fifths of a live birth less than a monogamous wife. Male sex preference is strong with more than one-third of a live birth extra produced in cases where female children are more numerous than male. Since this variable is a life-cycle variable, one would expect that the sex imbalance among children produced would display a markedly increasing influence on births with the age of woman. Hence, whereas for wives in the 15-24 age-group no relationship is observed, the parameter estimate of MOREGIRLS is 0.37 for the 25-34 age-group and almost doubles to 0.71 for the 35-49 group. This last age-group signifies the final reproductive stage in a household's life-cycle.

After AGE, MORT adds the most to the overall explanatory power of the equation (in terms of R^2) accounting for about 11 per cent of the total variance in CEB. Caution is advised in the interpretation of the MORT variable. Since MORT is constructed using CEB, and is thus correlated with the error term, the coefficient estimate is biased (see also Williams, 1977). There appears to be a tendency among couples to replace deceased children with additional births. The replacement effect seems strongest for the first two age-groups – lower MORT value for the 35-49 sample (about 40 per cent lower than that for the 25-34 age-group), which implies that these women are less able to achieve replacement. Elasticity of CEB with respect to MORT calculated at the sample mean for the 15-24, 25-34 and 35-49 age-groups is 0.83, 0.65 and 0.25, respectively. These elasticity values may underestimate replacement since the process is incomplete at the date of interview and, more importantly, MORT includes both infant and child deaths at later ages. The elasticity would be much larger if only infant mortality were considered, as it is relatively easier to replace infant

---

[1]   The joint F statistics calculated for LFNOTACT and LF. FORMAL show them to be significant at the 5 per cent level in equation (1) and at the 1 per cent level in equations (2) and (4).

The following notes also apply to Tables 12.3 to 12.7

For explanation of the notations used, see Table 12.1.

** Significant at the 1 per cent level; * at the 5 per cent level; [+] at the 10 per cent level (two-tail test).

$\bar{R}^2$ is R^2 adjusted for degrees of freedom

[a] Currently married women aged 15–49 years

[b] Less than 30 cases

[x] Not reported, as less than 12 cases

deaths, and there may also be a greater motivation for doing so.[19] The replacement effect of infant mortality would be particularly strong in the Nigerian cultural situation as sexual relations normally resume immediately if an infant dies.

The coefficient estimates for AGE and AGESQ are consistent with the *a priori* expectations. It may be interesting to mention that for a micro data set, R^2 of 0.47 for equation (1) in Table 12.2 is relatively high and suggests that the equation is statistically a good fit. However, this is partly due to the inclusion of the non-behavioural variable age, which largely measures the physiological and the terminal sexual-abstinence effects. In this equation, when re-estimated excluding the two age variables, the variance explained by socio-economic factors is increased to 4.5 per cent from 1 per cent, and that explained by cultural factors to 2.3 per cent from 1.1, while the value of the R^2 is reduced to 0.28.

A comparison among the three age equations reveals some important variations. Whereas the set of socio-economic variables emerges as quite significant for the younger age-cohorts of 15–24 and 25–34 years, such is not the case for the older cohort, 35–49, for whom only EDW1 and H. INCOME appear to be somewhat relevant. This result seems to be consistent with the relatively recent onset of the socio-economic transition phenomenon in the society. Note also the dominating effect of cultural factors on the CEB of the 35–49 age-group, an influence absent in the case of the 15–24 cohort. As far as the coefficients of cultural factors are concerned, there is a distinct and clear-cut upward trend with age. All in all, the fertility decision model appears to apply best in the middle age-group. This should not be surprising, since, at the early ages, reproductive experience may depend, to some extent at least, upon factors such as age at marriage and biological maxima, and the factors that influence child-spacing. The fertility equation for older ages, on the other hand, includes certain explanatory variables that may or may not have the same values as those held during the actual reproductive experience; also, the recall error is likely to be more serious than among younger ages. (This may be partly responsible for the large estimated coefficient for EDW1, positive and significant, as the reporting of retrospective fertility by educated women might have been more complete than by uneducated women.)[20] Hence, from both sides, 25–34 age-cohort equations represent a better approximation of the fertility behaviour model except that fertility is incomplete for this age-group.

Table 12.3 presents CEB equations estimated with the smaller samples of women for whom the female questionnaire was completed. If, along with the decrease in sample-size (from 1399 to 773 wives), there were also significant sample variations, parameter estimates would be different. Equation (1), including exactly the same variables as equation (1) in Table 12.2, is designed to test this possibility. Socio-economic variables behave more or less in the same way, except that the regression coefficient for LFNOTACT becomes more substantial (though being significant only at the 10 per cent level). But there are substantial declines in the POLYGMOS, MOREGIRLS and MORT coefficients. The POLYGMOS parameter decreases in absolute size to one-third (from -0.42 to -0.14), which may be a direct result of exclusion of a large number of polygamously married women from the sample. It remains altogether insignificant when other variables are added to equation (1) - see equation (2). This variable, however, remains important for the older age-group, 35-49 (equation (5)). MOREGIRLS becomes insignificant for the total sample as well for all age-groups.

Equation (2) gives the results for a more fully-specified model along the lines of the theoretical framework developed in the previous section. A comparison of equation (2) with equation (1) shows that parameters are altered to a varying extent when additional variables are included. This is also true for rural equations (Tables 12.4 and 12.5). The addition of relevant variables like age at marriage, comparative economic status and the duration of breastfeeding affects both the size of the coefficients and the significance levels of high education, female work-status, MOREGIRLS and MORT. AGEMAR, as expected, displays a negative and significant impact on CEB for all age-groups. Since AGEMAR may be approximating the wife's age at first birth, its computed effect emerges as more substantial for the younger age-groups than for the 35-49 group. The estimated coefficient of -0.184 means that, *ceteris paribus*, a delay in marriage of five to six years has the equivalent effect of one less live birth in the 25-34 sample. This effect (especially in the case of the 15-24 age-group) is less than one might have expected, and could partly be due to underestimation of the age at marriage and adolescent sterility. It is important to mention that including the age-at-marriage variable does not seem to cause serious simultaneity bias referred to earlier. If anything, its exclusion from the regression equations may bias the estimators due to the statistical problem of omitted variables.[21]

The subjective variable 'peer comparative economic status' emerges significant for the total sample, adding further to the relevance of socio-economic factors in the fertility decision problem.[22] Although positive in all three age-groups, PEERSTD is significant only for the 35-49 age-group, where, *ceteris paribus*, a respondent who considers her family's level of living better than the average level has produced slightly more than one

TABLE 12.3 *Regressions on fertility (*CEB*) among urban women in south-western Nigeria by age: partial sample consisting of the eligible women[a] who completed the female questionnaire (standard errors in brackets)*

Explanatory variable	Total		Age groups		
	(1)[1]	(2)	15-24 (3)	25-34 (4)	35-49 (5)
Constant	−6.568	−5.739	−1.505	−1.279	2.779
EDW1	0.186 (0.153)	0.202 (0.173)	0.257 (0.183)	0.116 (0.230)	0.297[b] (0.512)
EDW2	0.058 (0.139)	0.073 (0.160)	0.192 (0.156)	0.056 (0.212)	−0.196[b] (0.531)
EDW3	−0.247 (0.189)	−0.292 (0.215)	−0.105 (0.211)	−0.299 (0.246)	x
EDW4	−0.644* (0.287)	−0.432+ (0.310)			
LFNOTACT[2]	0.206+ (0.128)	0.300* (0.142)	0.116 (0.142)	0.264 (0.182)	0.782 (0.512)
LF. FORMAL[2]	−0.155 (0.126)	0.011 (0.134)	−0.026 (0.160)	−0.009 (0.167)	0.185 (0.395)
H. INCOME	0.072** (0.023)	0.043+ (0.025)	0.045 (0.032)	0.037 (0.030)	0.073 (0.076)
POLYGMOS	−0.138 (0.115)	−0.151 (0.124)	0.019 (0.151)	0.053 (0.159)	−0.601+ (0.344)
MOREGIRLS	0.243* (0.109)	0.168 (0.114)	−0.099 (0.126)	0.200 (0.145)	0.411 (0.352)
MORT	0.892** (0.081)	0.523** (0.092)	0.832** (0.156)	0.589** (0.139)	0.495** (0.187)
AGE	0.410** (0.054)	0.557** (0.062)	0.201** (0.034)	0.265** (0.027)	0.082* (0.040)
AGESQ	−0.004** (0.001)	−0.006** (0.001)	−	−	−
AGEMAR	−	−0.150** (0.015)	−0.139** (0.025)	−0.184** (0.020)	−0.078* (0.037)
PEERSTD	−	0.259+ (0.140)	0.080 (0.153)	0.091 (0.173)	1.029+ (0.533)
MUSLIM	−	−0.160 (0.125)	−0.027 (0.141)	−0.170 (0.161)	−0.210 (0.363)

LACTHI	–	-0.237^{+}	0.216	-0.547^{**}	-0.178
		(0.140)	(0.184)	(0.182)	(0.366)
FPAPROVE	–	0.235^{*}	0.084	0.093	0.669^{*}
		(0.111)	(0.123)	(0.141)	(0.344)
FPKNOWMD	–	-0.011	0.098	0.022	-0.201
		(0.130)	(0.133)	(0.165)	(0.442)
EVERUSE	–	-0.060	0.248	-0.044	-0.344
		(0.149)	(0.160)	(0.196)	(0.449)
$\bar{R}^2$	0.49	0.51	0.37	0.36	0.11
F	82.91	43.57	7.27	14.57	2.22
Average CEB	3.21	3.53	1.84	3.45	5.46
No. of observations	1021	773	183	414	176

[1] Same specification as equation (1) in Table 12.2.
[2] The joint F statistics calculated for LFNOTACT and LF. FORMAL show them to be significant only in equations (1) and (2) at the 10 per cent level.
For other notes, see Table 12.2.

extra live birth.[23] Causality in the case of this age-group could also be reversed, i.e. the wife feels she is better off because she has more children.

An unexpected relationship is observed between the practice of Islam and fertility – the impact of being Muslim is negative, though not significant. More discussion of this variable follows in the subsequent sub-section.

The hypothesis about breastfeeding is supported. This variable appears to be pertinent to the most fecund age-group of 25–34 years. A wife breastfeeding the last child for two years or more[24] would have, on average, above one-half live birth less than the women not adhering to the social custom of prolonged breastfeeding. Splitting of the breastfeeding effect into amenorrhoea and lactation taboo yielded correct signs for the two coefficients, but did not improve the equation specification. This might be due to data problems, as many women either did not respond to the question on amenorrhoea, or gave erroneous information in that the duration of amenorrhoea reported was too long (or too short) to be biologically possible.

Finally, as regards the family-planning variables, only the attitudinal variable is significant. FPAPROVE displays a positive influence, and its impact is substantial (significance level close to 5 per cent) in the older age-group. This result is not surprising, as in a society characterised by high-fertility norms, consideration of family-limitation would arise only when the couple had achieved a sufficient number of children.[25]

As a very brief summary of the above results, it can be stated that the urban reproduction experience is not completely determined by biological and cultural factors. It is also systematically related to demand-specific socio-economic environmental factors. So, whereas the practice of polygyny, excess of female over male children, age, age at marriage and prolonged breastfeeding customs are important factors influencing CEB, the wife's education attainment level and her work status, husband's income and to some extent peer comparative economic status also exert significant effects. The infant-child mortality variable, which measures the biological and behavioural components of replacement, also comes out as important, though the replacement of children who die is far from complete. Basically similar results were obtained for eastern Nigeria (see Farooq, 1980).

The Determinants of Cumulative Fertility: Rural Results

Table 12.4 gives regression equations for the complete rural sample corresponding to the ones for urban in Table 12.2. As in the urban cases, parameter estimates for education binaries show the non-linear effects of education attainment. In fact, the positive impact of some formal education versus none, as measured by EDW1, is much more substantial and significant than was observed for urban wives. The effect of EDW1 on the reproductive performance of wives in both the 25–34 and 35–49 cohorts is considerable and significant, which was not the case for the urban 25–34 age-group. Though perhaps influenced by a comparatively better reporting of CEB by educated women than by the uneducated ones, the significance of the EDW1 parameter may be at least to some extent real. If true, this education effect probably works largely through its contributing to an improved fecundity level and perhaps also its capturing the land-holding effect. Non-statistical significance of high education effect probably works largely through its contributing to an improved fecundity level and perhaps also its capturing the land-holding effect. Non-statistical significance of high education (as well as LF.FORMAL) in the age-specific equations could be due partly to fewer observations on these variables – coefficient signs are negative as expected, and coefficient sizes are large. The labour-activity variable LFNOTACT, as in the urban case, is relevant for young wives – their work participation (mostly farming) adds sufficiently to the household's

TABLE 12.4 *Regressions on fertility (*CEB*) among rural women in south-western Nigeria by age: complete sample of eligible women*[a]
(standard error in brackets)

Explanatory variable	Total (1)	Age groups		
		15-24 (2)	25-34 (3)	35-49 (4)
Constant	-4.085	-1.125	-4.052	-0.775
EDW1	0.299[+] (0.165)	-0.108 (0.158)	0.516* (0.246)	0.894[+] (0.480)
EDW2	0.067 (0.141)	0.075 (0.125)	0.210 (0.207)	0.128 (0.550)
EDW3	-0.588* (0.270)	-0.280[b] (0.209)	-0.407 (0.270)	-0.686[b] (1.304)
EDW4	-0.527[+] (0.316)			
LFNOTACT[1]	-0.108 (0.107)	-0.184[+] (0.110)	0.001 (0.153)	-0.171 (0.294)
LF. FORMAL[1]	-0.010 (0.116)	0.088 (0.126)	-0.209 (0.166)	-0.189 (0.333)
POLYGMOS	-0.226** (0.084)	0.130 (0.098)	-0.192[+] (0.118)	-0.619** (0.210)
MOREGIRLS	0.404** (0.089)	-0.014 (0.112)	0.307* (0.122)	0.753** (0.217)
MORT	1.151** (0.049)	1.401** (0.079)	1.130** (0.071)	1.042** (0.097)
AGE	0.262** (0.039)	0.067** (0.021)	0.215** (0.022)	0.118** (0.025)
AGESQ	-0.002** (0.001)	-	-	-
$\bar{R}^2$	0.47	0.43	0.30	0.22
F	185.20	50.03	49.11	21.87
Average CEB	3.45	1.48	3.43	5.25
No. of observations	2270	586	1027	657

[1] The joint *F* statistics calculated for LFNOTACT and LF. FORMAL show them to be significant only in equation (2) at the 10 per cent level.
For other notes, see Table 12.2.

resource base, to produce, on average, an additional two-fifths of a live birth, other factors being constant. Perhaps women with children are even expected to work. The joint F test on LFNOTACT and LF.FORMAL shows these labour activity variables to be significant only for the 15-24 age-group.

Cultural factors, particularly MOREGIRLS, show strong influences on reproduction – the impact becoming more pronounced and significant with age, as expected. MORT coefficients for the total sample and age-groups 15-24 and 35-49 are larger than the urban ones, reflecting the comparatively higher level of infant-child mortality in rural areas. However, the elasticities of CEB with respect to MORT are not very different from the urban ones. Elasticity values are 0.82, 0.41 and 0.29 for age-groups 15-24, 25-34 and 35-49, respectively.

A comparison of equation (1) in Table 12.5, which provides the estimated equations based on rural wives who completed female questionnaires, with the corresponding equation in Table 12.4 reveals an interesting result. The impact of education variables is more pronounced, especially EDW1 and EDW3. Otherwise, results are similar to the urban ones, in that coefficient estimates for POLYGMOS, MOREGIRLS and MORT decrease in magnitude, and POLYGMOS becomes significant. However, in the fully specified CEB function (equation (2)), POLYGMOS registers as a significant factor at the 10 per cent level. In the age-specific equations, it is not significant, not even for the older age-group, which is contrary to the case in urban equation (5) (Table 12.3). On the other hand, male preference attitude remains as a significant factor for the 35-49 age-group, which was not the case for urban wives.

AGEMAR is significantly and negatively associated with CEB, although the effect, unlike the urban case, is more substantial for the youngest age-group than for the 25-34 age-group. This may be partly because of a comparatively younger average age at marriage in rural areas (17.6 years versus 18.9 – see Table 12.2). PEERSTD, relevant to only the 35-49 age-group, enters with an unexpected negative sign, but is significant only at the 10 per cent level. Overall, the demand-specific socio-economic variables appear to be not as important as in the case of the urban sample.

An important result is the unexpected negative impact of MUSLIM on CEB. It is highly significant for the total sample and, unlike in the urban case, is important for the 25-34 and 35-49 age-groups. Hence, in the context of Nigerian society, one can seriously question the otherwise widely-held contention that the Muslim traditions are more associated with high fertility than are those of other religious groups. Also, there is no evidence

TABLE 12.5 *Regressions on fertility (*CEB*) among rural women in south-western Nigeria by age: partial sample consisting of the eligible women[a] who completed the female questionnaire (standard errors in brackets)*

Explanatory variable	Total		Age groups		
	$(1)^1$	(2)	15-24 (3)	25-34 (4)	35-49 (5)
Constant	−5.448	−3.950	−0.741	−1.801	1.604
EDW1	0.316⁺ (0.186)	0.154 (0.228)	−0.087[b] (0.239)	0.274[b] (0.316)	0.051[b] (0.575)
EDW2	−0.002 (0.060)	0.003 (0.020)	0.027 (0.185)	0.088 (0.247)	x
EDW3	−0.766** (0.288)	−0.326 (0.365)	x	−0.248 (0.323)	x
EDW4	−0.627⁺ (0.349)	−0.579[b] (0.393)			
LFNOTACT[2]	−0.021 (0.128)	0.117 (0.149)	−0.159 (0.169)	0.315⁺ (0.193)	0.088 (0.355)
LF.FORMAL[2]	−0.103 (0.160)	0.031 (0.185)	0.086[b] (0.211)	−0.215 (0.236)	0.227[b] (0.435)
POLYGMOS	−0.134 (0.097)	−0.192⁺ (0.112)	0.190 (0.141)	−0.184 (0.142)	−0.429 (0.255)
MOREGIRLS	0.262* (0.103)	0.132 (0.116)	0.079 (0.145)	−0.107 (0.149)	0.478⁺ (0.262)
MORT	0.823** (0.057)	0.617** (0.065)	0.996** (0.116)	0.764** (0.088)	0.419** (0.121)
AGE	0.365** (0.047)	0.420** (0.059)	0.201** (0.038)	0.260** (0.026)	0.125** (0.031)
AGESQ	−0.003** (0.001)	−0.003** (0.001)	–	–	–
AGEMAR	–	−0.124** (0.015)	−0.164** (0.025)	−0.149** (0.019)	−0.078** (0.030)
PEERSTD	–	−0.192 (0.136)	0.010 (0.174)	0.053 (0.169)	−0.604⁺ (0.323)
MUSLIM	–	−0.374** (0.127)	−0.353* (0.174)	−0.451** (0.165)	−0.399 (0.278)
LACTHI	–	0.092 (0.122)	0.061 (0.169)	−0.128 (0.161)	0.358 (0.266)

TABLE 12.5 (*contd.*)

Explanatory variable	Total		Age groups		
	$(1)^1$	(2)	15-24 (3)	25-34 (4)	35-49 (5)
FPAPROVE	–	0.232* (0.118)	−0.050 (0.150)	0.078 (0.154)	0.618* (0.267)
FPKNOWMD	–	−0.124 (0.177)	0.001^b (0.215)	−0.206 (0.222)	−0.070 (0.432)
EVERUSE	–	0.131 (0.128)	0.219 (0.162)	0.065 (0.165)	0.086 (0.283)
$\bar{R}^2$	0.48	0.48	0.43	0.35	0.13
F	146.59	58.59	10.49	17.70	4.27
Average CEB	3.91	4.25	2.10	3.85	6.01
No. of observations	1603	1067	204	501	362

[1] Same specification as equation (1) in Table 12.4.
[2] The joint F statistics calculated for LFNOTACT and LF.FORMAL show them to be significant only in equations (3) and (4) at the 10 per cent level.
For other notes, see Table 12.2.

of a conclusive negative *or* positive relationship between MUSLIM and desired family-size (Table 12.7).[26]

The family-planning variables behave more or less in the same manner as in the case of urban wives – FPAPROVE is the only significant variable, and is positively associated with the fertility level.

LACTHI displays a substantial *but* positive and significant impact on reproductive experience of the 35–49 age-cohort. Given the history of comparatively backward (relative to the present situation) medical, health and social conditions, women in this cohort have probably had a high incidence of sterility, pregnancy wastage and sub-fecundity.[27] Thus, LACTHI may be measuring the fecundity effect. Such results provide an element of justification for the proposition that actual fertility levels for some segments of the rural population may be determined more by biological than by choice variables. Also note that in terms of both R^2 and F, the equation for the 35–49 age-group is weak as compared with the corresponding urban equation.

Family-size Preferences

As discussed in the second section, desired family-size (DFS) is used as the relevant measure of family-size preferences. Table 12.6 shows the estimated DFS equations for the urban sample, and Table 12.7 for the rural sample. Equations (1) in the two tables pertain only to the sample of women who gave quantitative answers to the question on additional children wanted, whereas in the estimation of equations (2) to (5), women who gave the non-numerical response of 'up to God' are included (by assigning to additional children wanted by them a numerical value equal to the average top 10 per cent figure obtained from the women who gave numerical responses – see the second subsection of the second section). Comparisons of equation (1) with equation (2) in both Table 12.6 and Table 12.7 do not reveal substantial differences between the two samples, and, if anything, the explanatory powers of equations (2) are slightly better than those of equations (1) (note the R^2 and F values). The discussion of results below, therefore, pertains to the sample including women with the response 'up to God'.

For both urban and rural samples, female education level emerges among the more pervasive influences on DFS. All the education variables are significantly and negatively associated with DFS in all ages. (The only exceptions are the rural 25–34 and 35–49 age-equations, where EDW1 is found to be insignificant: in the case of the 35–49 age-equation, however, this may be due to the limited number of observations.) In the urban sample, compared to women with no education, women with some formal education prefer, on the average, one less child, and women with higher education almost two fewer children – increasing education level has a consistently increasing negative impact on family-size preference. The increasing trend is slightly more marked for rural wives with absolute size of coefficients increasing from −0.67 for EDW1 to a remarkable level of −2.75 for EDW3 and −2.28 for EDW4. It is pertinent to point out that evidence of the substantial negative effect of EDW1 (and EDW2) on DFS (in both rural and urban samples), when compared with the evidence of positive association of this variable with actual reproductive experience, seems to confirm the contention that some formal education may contribute to, *inter alia*, an improvement in the natural fertility level.

The joint F statistics for the set of education binary variables in Tables 12.6 and 12.7 show that education attainment is highly significant in influencing the attitudes of both urban and rural wives towards the desired number of children. Conceptually, the joint F test on education variables

TABLE 12.6 *Regressions on desired family-size (DFS) among urban women in south-western Nigeria by age: partial sample consisting of the eligible women[a] who completed the female questionnaire (standard errors in brackets)*

Explanatory variable	Total		Age groups (including 'up to God')		
	Excluding 'up to God' (1)	*Including 'up to God'* (2)	*15-24* (3)	*25-34* (4)	*35-49* (5)
Constant	4.404	1.253	6.278	7.728	16.834
EDW1	−1.027** (0.329)	−1.050** (0.264)	−0.669[+] (0.397)	−1.388** (0.394)	−0.720[b] (0.674)
EDW2	−1.208** (0.307)	−1.034** (0.244)	−0.855* (0.338)	−0.841* (0.372)	−1.862[b]** (0.707)
EDW3	−1.318** (0.371)	−1.746** (0.320)	−1.265** (0.433)	−1.894** (0.405)	x
EDW4	−1.674** (0.546)	−1.939** (0.483)			
LF.INFORMAL	0.229 (0.220)	0.436* (0.174)	0.171 (0.266)	0.688** (0.253)	0.044 (0.461)
H.INCOME	−0.119* (0.047)	−0.092* (0.038)	−0.146* (0.064)	−0.061 (0.053)	−0.040 (0.098)
HLF.FORMAL	0.160 (0.241)	0.135 (0.189)	0.040 (0.286)	−0.066 (0.281)	0.360 (0.470)
PEERSTD	−0.013 (0.265)	−0.053 (0.219)	−0.027 (0.331)	−0.001 (0.304)	−0.396[b] (0.693)
POLYGMOS	0.026 (0.250)	−0.051 (0.194)	0.355 (0.319)	−0.029 (0.282)	−0.712 (0.467)
MUSLIM	0.704** (0.248)	0.411* (0.190)	0.332 (0.290)	0.591* (0.280)	0.201 (0.482)
AGE	0.206[+] (0.106)	0.447** (0.090)	0.065 (0.061)	0.012 (0.045)	−0.207** (0.054)
AGESQ	−0.003[+] (0.002)	−0.007** (0.001)	–	–	–
Joint F statistics					
EDW1 to EDW4	10.59[c]	5.61[c]	–	–	–
EDW1 to EDW3+4[d]	–	–	6.85[c]	12.66[c]	4.99[c]
$\bar{R}^2$	0.12	0.14	0.09	0.14	0.09
F	7.54	13.33	3.68	8.43	2.88
Average DFS	6.59	7.62	6.89	7.80	8.28
No. of observations	597	932	286	462	183

[c] Significant at the 1 per cent level. [d] EDW3 + 4 = EDW3 + EDW4.
For other notes, see Table 12.2.

is relevant here because the influence of education on DFS is associated largely with the changes in relative tastes and preferences that education may generate. Unlike the case of CEB, the normal substitution effects of education on the number of children wanted are less likely to be impaired by the indirect positive effects of education operating through its influence on some intervening variables.[28]

Wives' work participation in the informal sector, LF. INFORMAL, has a significant and positive impact on DFS of urban wives and is relevant to the 25-34 age-group.[29] This may be due to two factors: (i) childrearing activity does not hamper female work participation and, perhaps more importantly, (ii) the children help their mothers in the family retail or petty-trading concerns.

In the case of the rural sample, the impact of a husband being engaged in formal labour activity on DFS is negative and significant particularly in the 25-34 age-group. It is interesting to observe also that rural wives belonging to this age-cohort who consider their standard of living to be better than average prefer a larger family, other factors being constant. HLF. FORMAL and PEERSTD do not appear to be important in the urban behaviour.

There is no statistically significant negative *or* positive relationship between the wife being Muslim and DFS in the rural sample (Table 12.7). However, in the case of the urban sample, the MUSLIM variable has a negative (though not significant) impact on CEB but a positive association with DFS (Table 12.6). Note that the relationship between MUSLIM and such factors as female education level, husband's income and female engagement in the formal labour activity is negative.[30] Hence, it can be argued that the positive relationship observed between MUSLIM and DFS is probably due more to the comparatively low socio-economic status of Muslim households than to the religion *per se*.

Contrary to *a priori* expectations, POLYGMOS factor does not exert much influence upon family-size preferences. It is interesting to note, though, that for the 35-49 age-group, the relationship is negative for both urban and rural samples (significant only in the latter case). These women may be rationalising their smaller number of children. This rationalisation hypothesis advanced in the previous section appears to be verified by the AGE variable - AGE coefficients for the 35-49 age-group are negative and significant (see equation (5) in Tables 12.6 and 12.7). For the sample as a whole, DFS increases with age, but solving for AGE and AGESQ gives the inflection point (that is, where the change in the slope of the age function becomes negative) at age 32 for urban and 32.7 for rural wives.

TABLE 12.7 *Regressions on desired family-size (*DFS*) among rural women in south-western Nigeria by age: partial sample consisting of the eligible women[a] who completed the female questionnaire (standard errors in brackets)*

Explanatory variable	Total		Age groups (including 'up to God')		
	Excluding 'up to God' (1)	Including 'up to God' (2)	15–24 (3)	25–34 (4)	35–49 (5)
Constant	4.834	3.185	7.708	6.007	13.762
EDW1	−0.768[+] (0.475)	−0.669* (0.332)	−1.101* (0.450)	−0.248 (0.507)	−0.864[b] (0.835)
EDW2	−0.756[+] (0.391)	−1.030** (0.285)	−1.234** (0.363)	−0.834* (0.418)	x
EDW3	−2.215** (0.623)	−2.751** (0.502)	−1.739**[b] (0.563)	−2.835** (0.529)	x
EDW4	−2.108**[b] (0.737)	−2.280** (0.566)			
LF.INFORMAL	−0.424 (0.276)	−0.113 (0.187)	0.397 (0.280)	−0.127 (0.280)	−0.762[+] (0.413)
HLF.FORMAL	−0.684* (0.291)	−0.450* (0.201)	−0.271 (0.306)	−0.628* (0.297)	−0.302 (0.454)
PEERSTD	0.615* (0.307)	0.573* (0.206)	0.418 (0.339)	0.642* (0.296)	0.527 (0.458)
POLYGMOS	−0.008 (0.253)	−0.201 (0.168)	0.286 (0.274)	−0.157 (0.247)	−0.611[+] (0.356)
MUSLIM	0.339 (0.283)	0.001 (0.185)	−0.246 (0.312)	0.044 (0.273)	0.021 (0.380)
AGE	0.256* (0.125)	0.392** (0.081)	0.032 (0.059)	0.132** (0.045)	−0.087* (0.043)
AGESQ	−0.005** (0.002)	−0.006** (0.001)	–	–	–
Joint F statistics					
EDW1 to EDW4	10.21[c]	3.25[d]	–	–	–
EDW1 to EDW3+4[e]	–	–	5.75[c]	9.76[c]	0.58
$\bar{R}^2$	0.06	0.08	0.07	0.09	0.03
F	4.82	11.32	3.89	7.67	1.34
Average DFS	7.50	8.98	8.07	9.24	9.34
No. of observations	711	1353	337	619	397

[c] Significant at the 1 per cent level.
[d] Significant at the 5 per cent level.
[e] EDW3 + 4 = EDW3 + EDW4
For other notes, see Table 12.2

CONCLUSION AND POLICY IMPLICATIONS

Based on the Western Phase data from the national household fertility, family and family-planning survey, 1971, urban and rural actual fertility (CEB) and family-size preference behavioural equations have been estimated for south-western Nigeria. The theoretical framework of socio-economic and cultural determinants of reproductive behaviour outlined in the third section appears to have reasonable empirical validity as discussed in the previous section. Also, the CEB regression results obtained for eastern Nigeria (Farooq, 1980), based on the Eastern Phase data, 1972-3, are found to be largely consistent with those for the south-western region. Socio-economic factors are, by and large, relevant to household fertility decision-making in Nigeria. Below, an attempt is made to bring out the relevance of different policy options to reproductive behaviour in the light of empirical results obtained by the present study.

Among the socio-economic factors, female educational attainment exerts the most pervasive influence on both CEB and desired family-size (DFS). Whereas the effect on DFS is conclusively negative for all the different levels of education attainment, the effect on CEB of some formal schooling (versus no education) is positive and particularly so among the rural women. This means that even a little education helps to reduce the otherwise large incidence of sterility, sub-fecundity and social practice of marital sexual abstinence; and improves permanent income, health, personal hygiene, nutrition and the like – all of which result in increasing the natural fertility level. Hence, in the case of households with DFS greater than living children, an increase in natural fertility would be translated into a larger number of live births.

As to the likely future trend in fertility, it may be noted that an earlier study (Farooq, Ekanem and Ojelade, 1977) showed that whereas most urban couples seem to be able to achieve the desired number of children, such was not the case for many rural couples. If true, with increasing socio-economic advancement the urban fertility may decline, since DFS would be reduced. Conversely, in the short run at least, there is the possibility of rural fertility rising as the combined result of increasing education opportunities for women, and concomitant effects on female fecundity, curtailment in the practice of polygyny (which was noted to be negatively associated with CEB) and continuation of male sex-preference (which has positive influence upon CEB). It is pertinent to add here that with the adoption of the free 'Universal Primary Education' scheme, at least the lower education level will increase among the female population. However, given the strong negative impact of primary and lower educational attainment on family-size preferences, it is quite conceivable that a decrease in DFS may occur along with the increase in natural fertility. Hence, on balance, there might be only a slight or no increase in rural fertility. In the medium and long runs, the rural fertility can be expected to follow the downward urban fertility trend.

Female secondary or higher education attainment level not only has a direct impact on fertility, in that it displays a very large negative impact on DFS, but it also may exert important influences on the quality of female work participation (in terms of increasing female engagement in the formal labour-market) and age at marriage (i.e. delaying marriage), which in turn have been observed to influence actual fertility behaviour. Hence, by all indications, it seems that a wider role for female education (formal schooling as well as adult education programmes) has to be included in the complex of 'comprehensive population policies' of interest to the policy-makers.

Female labour involvement in the traditional economic activities of farming and retail/petty-trading exerts, if any, a positive influence on family-size preferences and actual fertility. Particularly during the 1970s, there was an increasing emphasis upon rapid industrial development (so much so that there is a general criticism that the agricultural sector is being ignored). If the national industrialisation and labour policies are designed to include a well-defined objective of improving the role of women in terms of better job-opportunities in the formal labour-market, future fertility behaviour is likely to be subjected to some important structural changes.

In recent years, there have been increasing federal budget allocations for expanding basic social welfare services in order to improve the national health standards. In both urban and rural areas, the emphasis is on providing safe drinking water, and medical and health services. The needs for maternal and child health-care seem to be receiving their due recognition. These efforts are likely to improve female fecundity and reduce pregnancy wastages on the one hand, and reduce the present high infant-child mortality on the other. In fact, the survey found that three-quarters of the rural and four-fifths of the urban respondents already felt that children had better chances of surviving to adulthood 'than when they were children'. A decline in infant-child mortality is likely to reduce the perceived extent of excess fertility required to ensure the desired number of children. Hence, along with female education and work status, medical and health services should also be included among the 'comprehensive' population policy variables.

Finally, it was observed that the attitude towards family-limitation was positive when the couples were able to beget a sufficient number of live births. Hence, as a corollary to improved natural fertility, there would be an expanding scope for an active family-planning/welfare policy aimed at improving information/knowledge of modern contraceptive methods, and ready access to modern contraception and the necessary follow-up clinical services. Such services will be needed to offset the increase in fertility which may occur when the present fertility-reducing effects of customs such as prolonged breastfeeding and post-partum sexual abstinence are reduced as a by-product of the national social and economic development process.

NOTES

1. For details of this survey, including the questionnaire, sampling design, errors and biases, see Acsadi *et al.* (1972, chs 5–9). Among the three survey phases covering respectively the south-western, eastern and northern regions (field-work was carried out in this order), the one for south-western Nigeria generated by far the most reliable information. This was largely due to the geographical proximity of the survey project headquarters (the University of Ife) to the survey area and to the absence of language or ethnic barriers. Control over the field-work was also comparatively better. Only south-western Nigeria was, therefore, selected for detailed study. Also, among the three regions, the south-west is the most homogeneous with respect to ethnic affiliation (Ekanem, 1972, ch. 4).
2. Covering the area south-west of the river Niger, south-western Nigeria includes the four former states of Lagos, Western (further subdivided in April 1976 into Ogun, Ondo and Oyo states), Kwara and Mid-west. It contains approximately 30 per cent of the country's population and is the land of the Yorubas – one of the three major tribes. In fact, the Yoruba tribe is among the largest tribes in Africa south of the Sahara.
3. For limitations of the national censuses and of earlier demographic surveys, see Ekanem and Farooq (1977), and references therein.
4. The details of errors and biases in the survey data are contained in earlier publications (Acsadi *et al.*, 1972; Ekanem and Farooq, 1977).

5. He reasons that the use of family-size preference as a dependent variable in the economic analysis of fertility is consistent with the view that a knowledge of the determinants of individual preference systems is necessary in order to understand consumer behaviour.

6. Rodgers (1976), in a study of Thailand, also found that 'desired additional children' was measured more accurately than ideal family-size.

7. In an earlier study, it was suggested that such a response is not necessarily due to the lack of understanding. 'A large proportion of non-numerical response is a way of avoiding direct confrontation with an issue that is believed to be beyond the respondent's control. Expressing opinions about the future in terms of number of additional children desired may also be considered premature, especially given the high incidence of miscarriage and infant mortality' (Farooq and Adeokun, 1976).

8. Income was among the least accurately reported variables in the survey (Acsadi *et al.*, 1972, p. 200). Only in the case of urban husbands was income measurement found to be sufficiently reasonable for it to be included in the present analysis.

9. Education usually emerges as a strong index of socio-economic status, modernisation and development level, and attitudinal changes in fertility and differential studies (Farooq and Tuncer, 1974; Holsinger and Kasarda, 1976; Graff, 1979, and references therein).

10. Traditional cultural values and norms are also likely to change with increasing education. Caldwell (1977a, p. 9) associates extent of imported 'Westernisation' and imported values with education.

11. Opportunity-value of a person's time expended in non-market activities is equal to the market wage that he would earn from his labour-market activities (Becker, 1965).

12. For marriage practices in Nigeria, see Morgan (1975, pp. 199–206). It is interesting to mention that polygyny is prevalent among all religious groups.

13. Apparently, in both the Harman (1970) and Snyder (1974) studies, replacement factor was not defined for cases where no live birth survived. Exclusion of these cases (if true) from the sample introduced, according to Williams (1977), a serious bias in the estimated coefficient. In the present study, for 100 per cent child mortality cases the value of the observation is taken as equivalent to CEB (or deceased children). However, there were very few such cases in the sample.

14. For a full exposition of biological factors and their importance, see the paradigm-setting studies of Easterlin (1978) and Davis and Blake (1956).

15. For a review article on the fertility-reducing effect of prolonged breastfeeding, see Van Ginneken (1974).

16. Age being associated with birth-cohort effects also 'may capture time variant determinants of fertility' (T. P. Schultz, 1974b, p. 7).

17. A joint F test for the set of four education binary variables shows it to be not significant at the 5 per cent level, but the subset EDW3 and EDW4 is found significant at the 5 per cent level. The corresponding joint F statistics for education variables in the rural equations (Table

12.5) found them to be not very significant. These results, however, are not to be interpreted to mean that education is of a limited relevance to fertility behaviour. The sign/size of individual education parameters are quite consistent across age-groups and rural/urban samples. The results obtained (Tables 12.2 to 12.5) clearly confirm the non-linearity in the relationship between education and fertility. Statistically, t statistics are more relevant than the joint F statistics.

18. Female education may be collinear to a limited extent with H.INCOME (first-order correlation coefficients between H.INCOME and EDW3 and EDW4 are 0.17 and 0.19, respectively). It is interesting to report that regression parameters for EDW3 and EDW4, in absolute size, decrease when LF.FORMAL and LFNOTACT are introduced to the equation, but they increase again closer to their previous levels when H.INCOME variable is added. EDW1 and EDW2 remain more or less stable.

19. See also Harman (1970, pp. 33–7).

20. The $\bar{R}^2$ and F values obtained are also comparatively very low, signifying that the equation is rather weak.

21. This was tested by re-estimating equation (2) in Tables 12.3 and 12.5 with AGEMAR omitted. Comparison of the urban equation with the original one in Table 12.3 shows it to be statistically much weaker with lower R^2 (0.45 versus 0.51) and F values (36.2 versus 43.6), and, perhaps more seriously, it generated larger standard error for every regression parameter. Most coefficients remained stable in size. The only coefficients affected substantially by the exclusion of AGEMAR were those of EDW3 and EDW4 (coefficients increasing in absolute size to -0.63 and -0.83 from -0.29 and -0.43, respectively), and age variables (AGE and AGESQ coefficients decreased in absolute size to 0.46 and -0.004 from 0.56 and -0.006, respectively); the intercept value is altered to -6.98 from -5.74. Note also that first-order correlation coefficients between AGEMAR and EDW3, EDW4, AGE and AGESQ (0.15, 0.16, 0.12 and 0.13, respectively) are not very high. The estimated parameters in rural CEB equation (2), Table 12.5, are affected even less than in the urban case when AGEMAR is excluded from the regression calculations. Only EDW2, EDW3 and EDW4 coefficients and intercept value changed, with all increasing in absolute size. As in the urban case, standard errors for all parameters increased, and $\bar{R}^2$ and F values decreased substantially, signifying a weaker statistical equation than the original one including the age-at-marriage variable.

22. Among other economic status variables, 'time-comparative economic status' could not be used, as almost all the respondents claimed that their present level of living was better than it was in the past, and HLF.FORMAL was observed to be not important (regression results not included here).

23. Along with PEERSTD, another comparative economic status binary was used to measure the effect of the respondent considering the family level of living being the *same* as that of an average family. This variable proved to be redundant, as the estimated coefficient size was

very small (0.045) and the standard error value too high (0.121). This was also the case in the rural sample.

24. It is probably safe to assume that if a woman with a multiple number of children breastfed her *last* child for a relatively long period, she would have done so for her preceding children as well. Hence, the variable used here may be a good proxy for the lifetime practice of prolonged breastfeeding.

25. Family-planning variables do not add much to the fertility explanation, but *do* improve fertility functional specification. Equation (2) in Table 12.3 (and in Table 12.5), re-estimated excluding the family-planning variables, depicts slight decreases in the intercept value and coefficient sizes for EDW3, MOREGIRLS and POLYGMOS and slight increases in absolute sizes of coefficients for EDW4, LACTHI and PEERSTD. On balance, standard errors become worse and $\bar{R}^2$ decreases slightly. More or less the same pattern was observed for the rural sample.

26. The possibility that this result is due to a high incidence of sub-fecundity (including sterility) among Muslim women was considered. The rural sample was partitioned into fecund and sub-fecund sub-samples. The sub-fecund sample was defined as consisting of those women whose desired family-size (DFS) was greater than two, but had not achieved a CEB of at least two by age 30. This was repeated for ages 25 and 35. An F test was utilised to test the hypothesis that the coefficient of the variable MUSLIM was different for the two groups using the total sample specification (2). In all cases, this hypothesis was rejected. As might be expected, the overall relationship is significantly different for these 'high' and 'low' fertility groups, as verified by an additional F test. The estimated coefficient on MUSLIM, however, changes very little in magnitude or in significance. The incidence of sub-fecundity, as defined above, was low, 7 per cent among women aged 30 or more, and less than 20 per cent among women aged 35 or more.

27. In an earlier paper (Ekanem and Farooq, 1977), it was observed that mortality level was higher in rural areas, and pregnancy wastage quite high.

28. Education variables in the case of CEB equations were capturing, also to a varying degree, the associated changes in permanent income, female fecundity, observance of traditional sexual-abstinence practices, and the like.

29. LF. FORMAL is not included in the equations as it is collinear with education attainment level, and in the way it is constructed as a binary variable, it is highly collinear with LF. INFORMAL.

30. For the urban sample, first-order correlation coefficients between MUSLIM and EDW1, EDW2, EDW3, EDW4, H. INCOME and LF. FORMAL are -0.18, -0.20, -0.14, -0.13, -0.29 and 0.7, respectively.

13 Demand for Children in Rural India*

M. T. R. SARMA

INTRODUCTION

The situation in India illustrates the difficulty faced by political leaders and administrators in many developing countries in choosing a strategy for dealing with population growth. At the 1974 United Nations World Population Conference in Bucharest, a member of the Indian delegation stated, 'Population policy . . . cannot be effective unless certain concomitant economic policies and social programmes succeed in changing the basic determinants of high fertility. It has truly been said that the best contraceptive is development.' However, in 1976, during the period of emergency rule in India, a vigorous programme of compulsory sterilisation was officially advocated in some States.[1] An official statement on national population policy was made, to the effect that '[t]o wait for education and economic development to bring about a drop in fertility is not a practical solution'.

The adoption of policy options such as compulsory sterilisations during the period of emergency in 1976 in India and the emphasis on the *supply* of birth-control services in the past perhaps reflects a natural but nonetheless one-sided technocratic view of what is essentially a social problem. This approach is perhaps understandable, because, as T. P. Schultz (1974b) put it:

*This case-study is based on the author's earlier work as a Research Associate at the Economic Growth Center, Yale University, New Haven, Connecticut, USA, for which partial support was received from the USAID and the Rockefeller Foundation Grant No. 70051. The author is grateful to Richard Beach and Ruth Daniel for the able research assistance, and to T. Paul Schultz, Mark Rosenzweig, T. W. Schultz, Finis Welch, William P. Butz, Yoram Ben-Porath, and Robert Willis for the comments and suggestions on an earlier draft of this chapter which was presented at the Labour and Population Workshop at Yale and the Agricultural Economics Workshop at the University of California, Los Angeles.

351

it seems far simpler to promote a better birth control technology than to learn why parents want the number of children they do and be prepared to promote the desirable social and economic changes that will modify those reproductive goals. For example, expenditures on family planning that seek to lower the *supply* price of modern birth control technology, reducing the cost (pecuniary and subjective) of restricting fertility, is a widely approved policy response. Alternatively, expenditures on, say, public health and nutrition programs that seek to reduce child death rates, contributing to a downward shift in parent *demand* for numbers of births, is thought to be counter-productive or at best a controversial policy strategy. [However,] *both sets of policy options – the 'supply' and 'demand' sides – need further elaboration and quantitative study to enable decision-makers to select an equitable and efficient mix of family planning and development policies for each social setting.* (Emphasis added.)

Even though some people may believe that the crux of the population problem in low-income countries like India lies in the field of politics rather than in the field of economics,[2] an attempt is made in this case-study to examine some economic determinants of fertility in rural India, in the belief that knowledge of factors that influence the decisions of parents with regard to fertility is important for appropriate population policy.

The data analysed in this chapter are obtained from an All-India sample survey of rural households for 1970–1, known as Additional Rural Incomes Survey (ARIS), conducted by the National Council of Applied Economic Research (NCAER) with financial support of the USAID (Contract No. AID-386-1620).[3]

An attempt is made in this case-study to explain the demand for children by parents in rural households in India, utilising the economic framework of household choice in a resource-constrained environment. This economic framework follows the seminal work of Becker (1960, 1965) and is typically stated in terms of a utility function maximised subject to a full-income budget constraint expressed in terms of the value of income produced by non-labour assets plus the value of the time of family members utilised in the production of home-produced goods and the production of market goods. In this framework of analysis, theoretically the number of children a couple (or household) produces in its lifetime is a home-produced good from which the couple derive utility, and that choice is subject to usual cost–benefit considerations. The analytical basis for this case study, as T. W. Schultz (1974) put it, rests on the economic postulate that the reproductive behaviour of parents is in large part a response to the underlying preferences of parents for children . . . . Thus, in thinking about the economics of fertility, social cost and benefits aside, the analytical key in determining the value of children to their parents is in the interactions between the supply and demand factors that influence these family decisions.

Although the relevance or appropriateness of the economic models of fertility formulated on the basis of the theory of allocation of time is still debatable, an attempt is made in this study to apply this framework to the analysis of fertility behaviour in rural India. (A more detailed discussion of the new home-economics family of models is contained in Chapter 2 and the appendix to that chapter.)

In this first attempt at analysis of the new set of micro data, it seems reasonable to estimate the coefficients of a multiple regression equation by the ordinary least squares (OLS) method, in which the number of children demanded by parents is regressed on all exogenous variables for which data are available in the ARIS, and which are thought to affect reproduction, directly or indirectly.

The variables that enter the regression analysis of determinants of the number of children ever born to eligible women (i.e. in the age-group 35–49 years and currently married) in rural households in India and the empirical results obtained are discussed in the next section.

EMPIRICAL RESULTS

The variables used in the regression analysis of the demand for children (the number of children ever born per woman) in the landed and landless households of rural India are defined and their sample means and standard deviations listed in Table 13.1.

It is relevant to note that the analysis is restricted to the women in the age-group 35–49 years mainly because for this age-group we can reasonably assume that women are close to their completed fertility. Unfortunately, lack of reliable data in the sample survey on the family-size preferred or 'additional children desired' has forced us to consider only 'children ever born' as the dependent variable.

The empirical results of the analysis of the data on the fertility behaviour of rural households in India are presented separately for landed and landless households. In an agrarian society like India, land undoubtedly

TABLE 13.1 *Means and standard deviations of variables used in regressions for different age-cohorts of women in landed and landless households in rural India*

Variable	Definition	Women in landed households				Women in landless households			
		35–9	40–4	45–9	35–49	35–9	40–4	45–9	35–49
CEB	Children ever born in 1971 (i.e. as on 30 June 1971)	4.42 (1.94)	4.79 (2.16)	4.92 (2.40)	4.69 (2.16)	4.27 (2.18)	4.46 (2.31)	4.92 (2.53)	4.50 (2.34)
EDW1	Education level of women – 1 if primary or below – 0 otherwise	0.08 (0.27)	0.04 (0.19)	0.04 (0.20)	0.05 (0.23)	0.13 (0.34)	0.07 (0.25)	0.11 (0.32)	0.11 (0.31)
EDW2	Education level of women – 1 if above primary but below matric. – 0 otherwise	0.04 (0.20)	0.03 (0.16)	0.02 (0.15)	0.03 (0.17)	0.04 (0.18)	0.04 (0.19)	0.04 (0.19)	0.04 (0.19)
EDW3	Education level of women – 1 if matric. and above – 0 otherwise	0.01 (0.11)	0.01 (0.12)	0.01 (0.96)	0.01 (0.11)	0.04 (0.20)	0.01 (0.11)	0.02 (0.15)	0.03 (0.16)
EDH	Education level of husband – 1 if primary or above – 0 otherwise	0.64 (0.48)	0.68 (0.47)	0.77 (0.42)	0.69 (0.46)	0.63 (0.48)	0.63 (0.48)	0.71 (0.45)	0.65 (0.48)
IADP	If parents live in the intensive agricultural development programme district – 1; otherwise –0	0.19 (0.39)	0.24 (0.43)	0.24 (0.43)	0.22 (0.41)	0.27 (0.44)	0.23 (0.42)	0.26 (0.44)	0.25 (0.44)
AGE	Age of the woman in completed years as on 30 June 1971	36.35 (1.40)	40.87 (1.29)	46.29 (1.41)	40.67 (4.28)	36.06 (1.35)	40.91 (1.32)	46.29 (1.48)	40.41 (4.29)
LAND	Gross area cultivated by the household, in hectares	5.28 (4.99)	4.77 (4.54)	4.73 (4.83)	4.96 (4.81)	0	0	0	0
FARMCAPTL	Value of farm implements, including tractor owned by the household, in thousand rupees	1.89 (3.45)	1.42 (2.53)	2.31 (4.32)	1.86 (3.50)	0	0	0	0
DISTANCE	Distance of the village in which parents live to the nearest town, in kilometres	28.46 (107.00)	21.42 (54.79)	25.61 (78.77)	25.37 (85.00)	27.76 (100.81)	28.72 (105.67)	33.92 (122.88)	29.69 (108.62)

SCHOOL	If there is an educational institution in the village where the parents live – 1; otherwise – 0	0.90 (0.31)	0.90 (0.30)	0.95 (0.21)	0.91 (0.28)	0.95 (0.22)	0.94 (0.24)	0.96 (0.19)	0.95 (0.22)
FACTORY	If there is a registered factory in the village or neighbouring village – 1; otherwise – 0	0.06 (0.22)	0.05 (0.22)	0.04 (0.19)	0.05 (0.21)	0.15 (0.36)	0.10 (0.30)	0.11 (0.32)	0.12 (0.33)
LIVESTOCK	Value of livestock owned by the household, in thousand rupees	0.90 (1.41)	0.88 (1.45)	1.04 (1.55)	0.93 (1.47)	0.13 (0.52)	0.17 (0.76)	0.11 (0.42)	0.14 (0.59)
HOSPITAL	If a health centre exists in the village where the parents live – 1; otherwise – 0	0.23 (0.42)	0.16 (0.36)	0.26 (0.44)	0.22 (0.41)	0.45 (0.50)	0.39 (0.49)	0.44 (0.50)	0.43 (0.49)
ELECTRIC	If the household used electricity – 1; otherwise – 0	0.30 (0.46)	0.24 (0.43)	0.28 (0.45)	0.28 (0.45)	0.52 (0.50)	0.45 (0.50)	0.50 (0.50)	0.49 (0.50)
DEATHRATE	Child death rate = no. of children dead / no. of children ever born	0.08 (0.16)	0.09 (0.16)	0.09 (0.15)	0.08 (0.16)	0.07 (0.16)	0.10 (0.20)	0.13 (0.19)	0.09 (0.18)
NORTH	If the parents live in the northern region[a] – 1, otherwise – 0	0.36 (0.48)	0.34 (0.47)	0.32 (0.47)	0.34 (0.47)	0.24 (0.43)	0.31 (0.46)	0.31 (0.46)	0.28 (0.45)
SOUTH	If the parents live in the southern region[b] – 1; otherwise – 0	0.22 (0.42)	0.27 (0.44)	0.21 (0.41)	0.23 (0.42)	0.40 (0.49)	0.30 (0.46)	0.34 (0.47)	0.35 (0.48)
EAST	If the parents live in the eastern region[c] – 1; otherwise – 0	0.17 (0.38)	0.15 (0.36)	0.17 (0.38)	0.17 (0.37)	0.19 (0.35)	0.18 (0.39)	0.16 (0.37)	0.16 (0.37)
Number of observations		433	357	321	1111	198	176	131	505

[a] Haryana, Himachal Pradesh, Jammu and Kashmir, Madhya Pradesh, Punjab, Uttar Pradesh.
[b] Andhra Pradesh, Kerala, Mysore (Karnataka), Tamil Nadu.
[c] Assam, Bihar, Orissa, West Bengal.

The western region, consisting of Gujarat, Maharashtra, and Rajasthan states, is omitted from the regression equations. The standard deviations of the variables are reported in Parentheses beneath the means. The values are unweighted.
SOURCE Additional Rural Incomes Survey, Third Round, 1970–1, National Council of Applied Economic Research, New Delhi.

provides an important basis for social cleavages. It is also felt that partitioning of all rural households into those who are cultivators (landed households) and those who are not (landless households) will allow the measurement of the impact of agricultural development programmes, e.g. of the so-called 'green revolution', on fertility. Theoretically, one could hypothesise that by differentiating the rural households by land-holding status, it will be possible to test whether land and children are complementary factors of production in agriculture, so that increases in land generate a derived increase in demand for children (see Rosenzweig and Evenson, 1977). *A priori*, one could hypothesise that agricultural development would increase the marginal productivity of labour, including that of children employed in agriculture. Thus, the economic value of children would increase, imparting a positive effect, other things remaining the same, on the demand for children among parents who are cultivators. Therefore, landed households (parents) in the present analysis are defined by the characteristic that they have at least one household member who combines part of his/her time with the land cultivated by the household (LAND) along with other farm assets used in production (FARMCAPTL) for purposes of generating farm income. Hence, for the landed households, the effects of the size of the cultivated area (LAND) and the amount of farm assets (FARMCAPTL) on the demand for children are estimated. These exogenous variables are expected to show positive (wealth) effects on fertility.

Four levels of schooling variables for women's education are used as exogenous variables in the regression equations: (i) illiterate or literate with no formal schooling; (ii) some but no more than primary schooling (EDW1); (iii) schooling above primary but below matric. (EDW2); and (iv) matriculation and above (EDW3) to capture potential non-linear schooling effects, as found by Ben-Porath (1975) for Israel. (See also Chapters 11 and 12.) However, for men's educational level, only a single dummy variable for all educational categories above illiteracy was used in the regression analysis, because it was found that alternative measures similar to women's education did not produce any significant difference in the variance explained by the regression equation. Theoretically, the negative effects on fertility level and family-size preferences of women's education variables are expected, on balance, to be stronger than the positive effects. However, the men's education (representing the income effect) is expected to be positively associated with the number of children ever born per woman. In the ARIS, information on current annual income of the household was collected, and it was found to be positively correlated with the education level of the husband. Husband's education level is assumed to be a proxy for permanent income of a couple. Holding tastes and all other factors constant, higher-income households are expected to have a larger demand for children than have the low-income households. Classification of households by caste or religion, potentially important for the study, was not possible due to lack of relevant data in the ARIS data files.

In addition to the empirical testing of the hypothesis relating to the effects of the education of women and men on their fertility (the number of children ever born per woman), the ARIS data enable us to establish the relationship between fertility and child-mortality. Although the economic theory of household choice does not indicate the nature of the relationship between fertility and child-mortality, one could expect, *a priori*, that the relationship would be positive (see T. P. Schultz, 1974b; Ben-Porath and Welsh, 1972; and Chapter 3 and case-studies in this volume). In the present analysis of ARIS data, the child-mortality variable is defined as the ratio of the number of children dead to the number of children ever born per woman (DEATHRATE). There are usually problems in interpretation of the statistical results when the child-mortality variable is measured in this way. However, it is important to assess the impact of this variable on the fertility of rural households in India.

In order to measure the effect of the new agricultural development programmes on fertility of women in rural India, the IADP (Intensive Agricultural Development Programme) variable is included in the regression equations. However, the IADP was introduced in India only at the beginning of the 1960s, generally in one district in each of the 16 major states in India. Therefore, although one could expect a positive association between IADP, which is expected to increase the incomes of rural households, and the demand for children in rural households, the completed fertility of women in the age-group 35–49 years may not provide a good basis for testing this hypothesis.

The value of livestock of the household (LIVESTOCK) is expected to reflect the influence of the economic contribution of children because herding of cattle is one of the important tasks performed by children in rural India. Therefore, the hypothesis that LIVESTOCK is positively associated with fertility is tested in the present analysis.

The analysis also makes use of variables representing the community characteristics for which sample survey data are available and which may influence the fertility decisions of the household, such as the existence of a factory in the village where the couple lives (FACTORY), the existence of a health centre in the village (HOSPITAL), the presence of an educational institution in the village (SCHOOL), the use of electricity

(ELECTRIC), and the distance of the village in which parents live to the nearest urban centre (DISTANCE).

The FACTORY variable is expected to measure the effect of the availability of non-agricultural job opportunities for children and, therefore, *a priori*, expected to have a positive influence on the demand for children.

The effect of HOSPITAL on fertility is difficult to predict when we are controlling for the effect of child-mortality along with other factors. If the parents take advantage of this institutional facility to acquire knowledge and use of contraceptive methods to limit family-size, this may have a negative effect, whereas if it improves the health of children by reducing the sickness and loss of work, it may improve the productivity of children in rural areas and thus have a positive effect on the demand for children.

The existence of an educational institution in the village (SCHOOL), while it does not reflect the quality of schooling available to children, does reflect the opportunities for improving the productivity of children and thus increasing their economic value in the long run. The impact of education on the demand for children in rural India clearly has policy implications.

The effect of the use of electricity (ELECTRIC) in rural areas on the demand for children is also difficult to predict. This variable could be positively associated with fertility if the use of electricity is for irrigation which increases the productivity of labour, including that of children employed on the farm.

The DISTANCE variable is used here as a proxy for the cost of migration and better employment opportunities in urban areas. One could, therefore, expect that if the distance between the place of residence and the nearest urban centre increases, then it will have a negative impact on the demand for children, other things remaining the same.

AGE (age of the woman in completed years), is used in the regression equations to control the effect of biological factors, since the women in the sample are in the childbearing period.

Table 13.2 shows the OLS estimates of the regressions on children ever born per woman in the cultivator households and non-cultivator households separately for women in the age-groups 35–9 years, 40–4 years, 45–9 years, and for the pooled sample aged 35–49.

The women's education variables are generally negatively associated with fertility, controlling for the effect of other variables, although the coefficient is not statistically significant in some cases. For the women in landed households in the age-group 35–9, higher level of schooling (EDW3) turned out to be statistically significant and negative. The regression

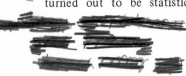

analysis for the pooled sample of women in landed households in the 35-49 age-group shows that the negative effect of women's educational level on fertility increases with the level of education. In other words, if women in the landed households are educated beyond primary level, there will be a statistically significant negative effect on their fertility, other things remaining the same.

For the women in landless households, the influence of women's education variables on their fertility turns out to be statistically insignificant, although they generally have negative signs. The coefficients in Table 13.2 for the pooled sample of the 35-49 age-group, in particular, exhibited an increasing tendency as the level of education increased. These results could perhaps be interpreted to show that the opportunity cost of the mother's time in bearing and rearing children in landed households is relatively more important than in landless households. This finding suggests that, *ceteris paribus*, increasing women's education would reduce the fertility for landed households.

The men's education variable turned out to be statistically significant and positive in both landed and landless households, for all age-cohorts. Thus, the hypothesis that the growth in men's education, which may be considered as a proxy for income, is associated with increased demand for children, other things remaining the same, cannot be rejected.

Child-mortality (DEATHRATE) is found to be positively associated with cohort-fertility in both landed and landless households. It may be of some interest to note that in Table 13.2, the size of the coefficient of DEATHRATE increases as the cohort ages in the landed households, whereas there is no such tendency to be observed for women in the landless households. The coefficients for women in the landless households in the age-groups 35-9 and 40-4 years appear to be relatively large, indicating perhaps a relatively quicker response to the incidence of child-mortality in landless households compared to landed households. The elasticity coefficients of fertility with respect to DEATHRATE calculated at their mean values are 0.073, 0.088 and 0.113 for the women in age-groups 35-9, 40-4 and 45-9 years, respectively, in the landed households, whereas the corresponding elasticity coefficients are 0.087, 0.136 and 0.167 for women in landless households.

As one might expect, AGE turned out to be significantly positive for women in the age-group 35-9 years in both landed and landless households. However, for women in older age-groups, this variable turned out to be either negative or not statistically different from zero.

The LIVESTOCK variable is an important factor affecting the demand for children only in the case of women in the age-group 45-9 years in landless households.

TABLE 13.2 *Regressions on children ever born among currently-married women in landed and landless households in rural India by age*

Explanatory variable	Landed households				Landless households			
	Age group			Pooled 35–49	Age group			Pooled 35–49
	35–9	40–4	45–9		35–9	40–4	45–9	
EDW1	0.52 (1.51)	−0.46 (−0.79)	−0.92 (−1.50)	−0.16 (−0.59)	−0.39 (−0.80)	0.93 (1.26)	−0.58 (−0.74)	0.12 (0.33)
EDW2	0.12 (0.27)	−0.60 (−0.81)	−1.47 (−1.72)	0.39 (−1.10)	1.07 (−1.32)	0.09 (0.10)	−0.98 (−0.82)	−0.19 (0.36)
EDW3	−2.10 (−2.67)	−0.89 (−0.94)	−0.34 (−0.27)	−1.17 (−2.10)	−0.43 (−0.53)	0.30 (−0.17)	−2.09 (−1.40)	−0.24 (−0.37)
(a)	3.4	0.62	1.61	1.82	0.68	0.54	0.85	0.15
EDH	0.66 (3.40)	1.01 (4.16)	1.32 (4.44)	0.93 (6.87)	1.38 (4.12)	0.95 (2.61)	1.10 (2.04)	1.10 (4.94)
IADP	0.28 (1.16)	0.32 (1.18)	0.10 (0.33)	0.15 (1.00)	−0.34 (−0.98)	−0.12 (−0.30)	−0.03 (−0.05)	−0.12 (−0.52)
AGE	0.15 (2.39)	0.12 (1.37)	−0.10 (−1.09)	0.03 (2.32)	0.26 (2.45)	−0.09 (−0.68)	−0.25 (−1.59)	0.03 (1.45)
LAND	0.04 (2.36)	0.04 (1.47)	0.01 (0.44)	0.04 (2.95)	—	—	—	—
FARMCAPTL	0.08 (1.90)	−0.20 (−2.15)	0.02 (0.54)	0.03 (0.94)	—	—	—	—
DISTANCE (c)	−0.01 (−0.16)	0.08 (0.41)	−0.08 (−0.53)	−0.05 (−0.66)	−0.28 (−2.03)	−0.17 (−0.94)	−0.09 (−0.48)	−0.21 (−2.33)
SCHOOL	−0.26 (−0.82)	−0.06 (−0.17)	0.06 (0.09)	−0.02 (−0.76)	−0.78 (−1.15)	0.51 (0.73)	−1.56 (−1.35)	−0.36 (−0.80)

FACTORY	0.85 (2.04)	1.15 (2.22)	-0.84 (-1.25)	0.63 (2.12)	-0.06 (-0.12)	-0.10 (-0.17)	-0.39 (-1.25)
LIVESTOCK	-0.10 (-0.97)	0.30 (1.82)	0.16 (1.29)	0.01 (0.17)	-0.16 (-0.59)	0.06 (0.21)	0.17 (1.04)
HOSPITAL	0.48 (2.09)	0.72 (2.22)	-0.10 (-0.34)	0.36 (2.29)	0.10 (0.30)	0.25 (0.63)	0.40 (1.77)
ELECTRIC	-0.34 (-1.55)	-0.44 (-1.59)	-0.23 (-0.75)	-0.33 (-2.20)	0.63 (1.71)	-0.10 (-0.25)	0.45 (1.89)
DEATHRATE	0.61 (1.06)	2.10 (3.14)	3.84 (4.63)	2.07 (5.32)	3.97 (4.26)	3.78 (4.26)	3.28 (5.95)
NORTH	-0.16 (-0.64)	-0.79 (-2.53)	-1.19 (-3.42)	-0.62 (-3.62)	-0.75 (-1.69)	-0.49 (-0.98)	-0.73 (-2.50)
SOUTH	-0.77 (-2.67)	-0.77 (-2.37)	-1.28 (-3.40)	-0.94 (-5.03)	-0.99 (-2.21)	-1.43 (-2.69)	-1.39 (-4.61)
EAST	-0.26 (-0.92)	-1.16 (-3.10)	-1.38 (-3.59)	-0.89 (-4.55)	-0.52 (-1.06)	0.65 (-1.18)	-0.73 (-2.23)
(b)	*2.59*	*3.94*	*6.61*	*10.93*	*1.75*	*2.61*	*7.10*
Intercept	-1.55 (-0.64)	-0.50 (-0.14)	8.88 (2.12)	2.86 (4.54)	-5.03 (-1.28)	7.22 (1.35)	3.03 (3.02)
R^2	0.14	0.18	0.24	0.14	0.26	0.24	0.20
F statistic	3.82	4.02	5.44	10.21	3.98	3.14	7.55
DF(n_1, n_2)	(19,414)	(19,388)	(19,302)	(19,109)	(17,181)	(17,159)	(17,468)
SEE	1.84	2.01	2.15	2.02	1.96	2.12	2.13
$\bar{R}^2$	0.11	0.12	0.20	0.13	0.20	0.16	0.17

t statistics are reported in parentheses beneath regression coefficients.
R^2 is R^2 adjusted for degrees of freedom.
(a) *F* statistic for the set of coefficients of women's education with (3, n_2) degrees of freedom.
(b) *F* statistic for the set of coefficients of regions north, south, east with (3, n_2) degrees of freedom.
(c) The coefficient of DISTANCE is to be multiplied by 10^{-2}.

IADP turned out to be positively associated with fertility of women in landed households, and has a negative sign for its coefficient in the case of women in landless households. However, the regression coefficients are not significant. Hence, this factor is not yet very important in influencing the fertility decisions of the parents.

The presence of a health centre in the village (HOSPITAL) has a positive influence on the demand for children, whereas the existence of an educational institution (SCHOOL) has no influence, with its coefficient being insignificant.

Contrary to our hypothesis, the electricity variable (ELECTRIC) has a significant negative impact on demand for children for landed households in rural India, whereas it has no statistically significant effect for landless households. It seems that any income effect on demand for children is smaller than the negative modernisation effect of electrification. The existence of electricity releases children from work to study longer, which increases the costs of rearing children.

The distance variable (DISTANCE) turned out to be negatively associated, as expected, with the demand for children; however, it is significant only for landless households. The migration factor or value of employment opportunities for children in urban areas may be relatively more important for landless parents than for those who have landed interests in the village.

The farm assets (FARMCAPTL) variable turned out to be statistically significant and positive for women in the younger age-cohort (35-9), but negative in the case of women in the 40-4 age-group and not significant for women in the 45-9 age-group. These results are difficult to interpret. One could speculate that the investment in farm assets is a complementary good which increases the productivity of children on the farm only when the parents are relatively young, whereas it becomes a substitute for children by the time parents become older.

An attempt is made to include in the regression equations presented in Table 13.2 dummy variables for the regions (north, south, east, west) in which the parents live in order to test whether there are any significant regional differences associated with the socio-cultural factors that affect the demand for children in rural India. The regression coefficients for the regions relative to the western region, which was omitted, turned out to be statistically significant and negative. The western region, which includes Rajasthan, has relatively higher fertility than other regions. In the case of landless households particularly, the negative coefficient for the southern region turned out to be relatively larger, indicating that fertility is relatively lower in south India than in other regions, if all other things remain the same. This finding is consistent with the fact that in Kerala state in the south, the birth rate started to decline relatively earlier than in other states in India (United Nations, 1975).

SUMMING UP

The main objective of this case-study is to estimate the nature of the influence of certain exogenous factors that affect the demand for children such as parental educational level, land-holdings, child-mortality and community-level indicators of socio-economic development in rural India.

The underlying hypothesis for this analysis is that childbearing and childrearing absorb a substantial fraction of the family's available time and income, and the reproductive behaviour (number of live births demanded by parents) significantly affects the welfare of parents. Hence, one can regard reproductive behaviour as a response to the relative scarcity of resources available to the household, and the associated costs of children. This approach perhaps may still be considered as incomplete because it ignores the biological features of the reproductive process that determine the supply of births.

The results of the analysis presented in this study reveal that, controlling for the effect of other variables:

(i)   an increase in husband's education, which may be considered as a proxy for income, increases the demand for children (as measured by the children ever born to his wife);

(ii) an increase in the education of the women reduces fertility (i.e. children ever born), particularly in landed households;

(iii) an increase in the amount of land cultivated by the household increases the demand for children (i.e. fertility);

(iv) fertility is generally higher in those rural households, whether they are cultivators or non-cultivators, that experience higher child-mortality rates, indicating that a reduction in child-mortality levels may reduce the fertility of women in rural India; and

(v)   the distance from the village where the couple lives to the nearest urban centre, representing the cost of migration or obtaining employment opportunities in urban areas, has the anticipated negative association with fertility.

In conclusion, this case-study suggests that parents in rural India, in deciding the number of children they will have, respond to the advantages and disadvantages of having children. Therefore, one can hope that further testing of the findings reported here and the related issues in the economic framework of household behaviour will provide useful.insights for formulating appropriate policies in India.

NOTES

1. Implementation of the family-planning programme under the Indian constitution, is largely the responsibility of the state governments. The tardy progress made in this field is partly because public approval and acceptance of this are largely missing, while the policies and programmes are prepared from the top by the central government. See, for an elaboration of this, Jagannadham (1973).
2. See, for example, Demeny (1976), who stated that '[t]he economic theory of fertility presented by Schultz had a potentially important role to play in clarifying the central issues of population policy, *even though the crux of the problem lay in the field of politics rather than in the field of pure theory of econometrics'*. (Emphasis added.)
3. See Sarma *et al.* (1975) for the sampling design, concepts and definitions used in the ARIS, and Sarma (1976) for an analysis of the effects of children on selected items of consumption expenditure based on the ARIS data. Funds for additional coding of the data were provided by Resources for the Future, Inc.

14 Differential Fertility in Rural Turkey

SAMUEL S. LIEBERMAN and
RICHARD T. MONTEVERDE

Turkish census and survey data reveal extensive variation in fertility at both the household and the community level. This chapter attempts both a theoretical and empirical accounting for these variations. Reconciling household- and community-level variation in fertility is one of the important unfinished tasks for social scientists and demographers, and the situation in Turkey represents an ideal setting for a preliminary examination of some of the major issues involved in this research agenda. The theoretical framework used in the chapter is eclectic.

Our point of departure for the discussion is the work done during the past 10 years reassessing the use of aggregate data in fertility analysis. For example, Hermalin (1975) upholds the use of aggregate data in macro-level analyses in the tradition of the demographic transition theory. He concludes that for a number of fertility-related research issues, aggregate-level analysis may be the preferable mode of inquiry. Ronald Freedman (1974) recommends that survey data on the attributes of individuals and households be supplemented with information on the characteristics of population aggregates taken from census reports or collected through community modules attached to household surveys. He suggests that aggregate-level variables may serve as indicators of norms and shared attitudes bearing on individual fertility in particular social settings. Turkish census and survey data provide an opportunity to explore many of the points raised by Freedman and Hermalin in regard to the use of aggregate- and household-level data.

THE SETTING: DEMOGRAPHIC AND SOCIO-ECONOMIC PATTERNS

Population phenomena in Turkey have been analysed extensively at the national level. High growth rates, declining mortality and fertility rates, and ongoing urbanisation figure prominently in the recent demographic experience of the country. Population growth has been rapid, averaging approximately 2.5 per cent per year over the last 50 years.[1] This sustained growth rate can be attributed to improvements in life-expectancy following the proclamation of the Republic in 1923, and the re-establishment of civil order. The régime of Kemal Ataturk (1923–38) initiated public health and village uplift measures, as well as land reclamation schemes. In the 1950s, mortality fell rapidly with the extension of disease eradication programmes, investments in medical facilities, and gains in education and levels of living. Mortality declined more gradually in the 1960s and early 1970s (Shorter, 1969; Macura, 1974). Similarly, fertility has fallen steadily since the late 1940s (Shorter, 1969; Farooq and Tuncer, 1974). Although opinions differ on the current level of fertility in Turkey, most estimates place the crude birth rate at between 33 and 36 per thousand (Ozbay, Shorter, and Yener, 1977; Hacettepe Institute of Population Studies, 1980).

Population growth has been unevenly distributed. The urban population, which remained roughly 18 per cent of the population during the first 25 years of the Republic, began to increase rapidly in the 1950s (Shorter and Tekce, 1974). Fed by migration from rural areas, the urban population reached 38 per cent in 1970, 42 per cent in 1975 and close to 50 per cent in 1980 (United States Bureau of the Census, 1980). Within rural areas, increase in numbers has resulted in both the expansion of existing settlements and the creation of new ones. Throughout the 1940s and even the 1950s, the sedentarisation of nomads, the resettlement of former Greek and Armenian villages, and the opening up of an Anatolian inner frontier by migrants from within Turkey as well as by immigrants from the USSR and Eastern Europe, all contributed to variation in rural population growth.[2]

Differential rates of migration from and within rural areas are not the only source of variation in rural growth rates. Longstanding geographical differences persist in mortality rates, linked to differences in public health improvements, ecological conditions, and socio-cultural patterns in a heterogeneous population (Macura, 1974, 1975). Regarding fertility patterns, recent findings suggest the maintenance of regional and provincial differences that can be traced back to the 1935–45 period. Fertility differences at subnational levels – units of analysis include regions, provinces, villages, and households – have been attributed to the growth of industrial and urban centres and the expansion of educational facilities in different sections of the country (Farooq and Tuncer, 1974; Tuncer, 1977). Yet, among areas demarcated according to patterns of agricultural production and social organisation, little is known about variation in fertility or about differences in mortality and migration.

Fortunately, the 1970 census provides data on rural counties that allow demographic rates to be related to various economic and social factors, including previously neglected indicators of agricultural production and social organisation.[3] However, before proceeding with an econometric analysis, it is useful to look at regional differences revealed by the county-level data.

Regional values for a number of agricultural and non-agricultural indicators appear in Table 14.1. Significant variation occurs in the level of social development as measured by literacy rates for different age-groups. Literacy rates for older women (LIT 45-9) are low throughout the sample counties. For the younger cohort (LIT 15-19), relatively high rates are recorded in the Aegean and the West-central agricultural regions, and extremely low rates are found in the South-east. The extent of a region's orientation to agriculture is measured by the proportion of the male labour force in non-agricultural employment (NON-AG-EMP). All regions are predominantly agricultural, since the sample consists of rural counties. Information is provided on regional agricultural resource potential, technology and social organisation, through indicators of resources (AV. LAND), rainfall (RAIN), land fragmentation (FRAGMENT), the distribution of land-ownership (GINI), and agricultural wage labour (AG-WAGE-EMP). (Precise definitions of indicators are given in Table 14.3.)

These indicators represent the diversified agricultural and social structure of the country. Contrasts can be drawn between the interior areas – the South-east, East-central, North-east, and West-central regions – and the coastal zones – Aegean and Black Sea regions. In interior areas, animal husbandry and extensive cultivation of cereals dominate. Most families own some land, and *ad hoc* rental and sharecropping arrangements roughly equal the size of operational holdings. Family members provide labour, occasionally supplemented by arrangements with other residents of small nucleated village settlements. Villages are close-knit social groups; village organisation and social processes – including forms of consultation and shared decision-making, institutionalised security guarantees and sanctions applied by the community – have a significant influence on production decisions and on household social and demographic behaviour.[4]

Within the interior, important differences exist in the history of settlement and the present availability of agricultural resources. In a number of areas, land was freely available until recently (Stirling, 1965), while elsewhere opportunities to extend cultivation were exhausted two or three generations ago. Tenurial practices and the distribution of wealth and

TABLE 14.1 *Means and standard deviations of social, economic and agricultural indicators by region, 1970*

Regions**	Number of rural counties	Social, economic and agricultural indicators*						Percent literate women ages	
		% Male labour-force outside agriculture	Crop-land per farm family (hectares)	rainfall (millimetres)	Land fragments per land-owning family	% Male agricultural waged labour	Inequality of land-ownership	15–19	45–9
		NON-AG-EMP	AV. LAND	RAIN	FRAGMENT	AG-WAGE-EMP	GINI	LIT 15-19	LIT 45-9
Coastal zones									
Aegean	49	0.35 (0.10)	20.7 (6.6)	715 (184)	3.5 (0.5)	0.17 (0.10)	0.51 (0.04)	0.63 (0.12)	0.24 (0.10)
Black Sea	37	0.25 (0.11)	11.3 (7.1)	1079 (528)	3.6 (1.2)	0.04 (0.02)	0.36 (0.08)	0.28 (0.12)	0.09 (0.04)
Interior areas									
South-east	25	0.25 (0.14)	60.6 (32.0)	578 (213)	4.6 (1.2)	0.08 (0.04)	0.57 (0.11)	0.12 (0.05)	0.04 (0.02)
East-central	33	0.23 (0.10)	30.2 (16.9)	452 (120)	6.1 (1.0)	0.04 (0.03)	0.44 (0.06)	0.32 (0.09)	0.09 (0.04)
North-east	41	0.25 (0.14)	45.4 (24.3)	409 (125)	5.7 (1.1)	0.03 (0.03)	0.46 (0.06)	0.29 (0.12)	0.08 (0.04)
West-central	44	0.29 (0.10)	46.0 (33.4)	409 (108)	5.7 (1.3)	0.07 (0.03)	0.46 (0.06)	0.48 (0.12)	0.14 (0.05)
Total sample	229	0.28 (0.12)	32.6 (26.7)	628 (366)	4.8 (1.5)	0.08 (0.08)	0.46 (0.09)	0.39 (0.19)	0.12 (0.09)

* Definitions and derivations of variables are taken up in Table 14.3.
** By region, the provinces included in the sample are: Aegean – Aydin, Izmir, Manisa, Mugla; Black Sea – Ordu, Rize, Samsun, Trabzon; South-east – Diyarbakir, Siirt, Urfa; East-central – Elazig, Sivas, Tokat, Yozgat; North-east – Agri, Erzincan, Erzurum, Kars; West-central – Afyon, Kayseri, Konya, Nevsehir.

SOURCE   Data are from the 1970 National Census of Turkey, and from Village Inventory Studies carried out in the late 1960s.

power within villages also differ between interior zones. For example, absentee landlords who hold sway over an entire village are present only in the South-east; in the East- and West-central regions, land and status are shared more equally.

In contrast, in coastal areas, climate, soil and location have contributed to a productive, specialised, and market-oriented agriculture. The most prosperous areas border on the Mediterranean and the Aegean, where the climate is suitable for cereals, tobacco (TOBACCO), cotton (COTTON), figs and citrus fruits (CITRUS). Farms tend to be relatively large in size, and farmers rely on mechanical aids and modern inputs. The village form of settlement predominates, but the organisation of agriculture depends on market processes and farm-enterprise decisions.[5] Wage labour is extensively used, supplied both by local residents and by migrants who are hired at seasonal intervals. In the other coastal region, the humid areas along the Black Sea, hazelnuts (HAZELNUT), tea (TEA), tobacco (TOBACCO), and citrus crops (CITRUS) are grown. Here, the terrain is hilly, and people are settled in small, dispersed hamlets. Holdings are small and fragmented, and productivity is low. The organisation of agriculture revolves less around a village community than around the deployment of family labour to produce, harvest and market crops through specialised government agencies.

Table 14.2 summarises regional differences in overall growth rates and in migration, mortality and fertility rates. Population growth (PG) in the sample of rural counties was generally rapid in the 1960–75 period. The South-east, where investments in irrigation made new lands available in the 1960s and 1970s, emerged as an area of above-average growth. Net outmigration (OM) was heaviest from countries of the East-central, West-central and Black Sea regions. The mortality index Q2, the probability of dying before age 2, divides the counties into groups of lower risk – those in the South-east, Aegean and Black Sea regions – and higher risk – those in the East- and West-central and North-east regions.

Fertility rates, which have long been recognised as differing between urban and rural areas in Turkey, vary extensively between rural counties in the sample. Furthermore, the rates conform to a pattern of regional variation discovered in early censuses and recent surveys (Shorter, 1971; Farooq and Tuncer, 1974; Toros, 1978; Hacettepe Institute of Population Studies, 1980). The measures of overall fertility adopted in Table 14.2 include CF, completed fertility (the average number of children ever born to women aged 45–9), and I_f, a standardised index of current fertility (defined in Table 14.3). Low and moderate levels of completed fertility, CF, are recorded for the Aegean and Black Sea regions, respectively; relatively high levels are found elsewhere. Current fertility, I_f, generally con-

TABLE 14.2 Demographic rates in Turkey's rural sector: means and standard deviations by region

Region**	Demographic indicators*						
	Population growth 1960–75 PG	Index of outmigration OM	Infant mortality to age 2 Q2	Completed fertility CF	Index of current fertility I_f	Index of marital fertility I_g	Index of proportion married I_m
Coastal zones							
Aegean	1.30 (0.12)	1.01 (0.10)	0.15 (0.02)	4.47 (0.72)	0.38 (0.30)	0.47 (0.07)	0.81 (0.02)
Black Sea	1.34 (0.16)	1.33 (0.25)	0.15 (0.05)	5.55 (0.60)	0.51 (0.05)	0.62 (0.05)	0.82 (0.03)
Interior areas							
South-east	1.52 (0.29)	1.22 (0.12)	0.15 (0.03)	6.21 (0.51)	0.60 (0.06)	0.71 (0.07)	0.86 (0.01)
East-central	1.22 (0.19)	1.41 (0.21)	0.22 (0.03)	6.26 (0.48)	0.56 (0.06)	0.66 (0.07)	0.85 (0.01)
North-east	1.31 (0.23)	1.30 (0.19)	0.23 (0.05)	7.01 (0.71)	0.65 (0.10)	0.77 (0.11)	0.84 (0.02)
West-central	1.34 (0.17)	1.36 (0.23)	0.20 (0.03)	6.14 (0.70)	0.51 (0.07)	0.60 (0.09)	0.85 (0.02)
Total sample	1.32 (0.20)	1.26 (0.24)	0.18 (0.05)	5.87 (1.06)	0.52 (0.11)	0.62 (0.12)	0.83 (0.03)

* Definitions and derivations of variables are taken up in Table 14.3 and the Appendix. Data are from the 1960, 1970 and 1975 National Censuses of Turkey.

** For provinces included in each region, see note to Table 14.1.

forms to the same pattern, except that the west-central region emerges as an area of moderate fertility.

Looking closer, the index of current fertility, I_f, can be decomposed into indices of marital fertility, I_g, and proportions married, I_m. Chapter 5 contains a detailed discussion of these indices. The marriage index is generally high, and varies only slightly by region.[6] By contrast, the index of marital fertility, I_g, varies substantially across rural regions, following a pattern similar to the indices of overall fertility, CF and I_f. Marital fertility is especially low in the Aegean region, intermediate in provinces of the West-central region and in counties scattered throughout the Black Sea region, and substantially higher in the counties of the South-east and North-east regions.[7] Of course, fertility rates also vary within counties. Both small-scale studies and national demographic surveys have documented significant differences between communities and within communities at the household level.[8]

In the sections that follow, different models and levels of analysis are used to account for cross-sectional patterns in county-level fertility rates. and for differences in household-level fertility which underlie the aggregate patterns. The approach involves first the specification of a community model of aggregate, demographic flows. This macro-level framework is compared briefly with other approaches to aggregate data, and then applied to data for the sample of counties. In a subsequent section, factors influencing fertility behaviour at the micro level are distinguished. Survey data for a sample of households are explored. To strengthen the micro-level analysis, the survey data are augmented through the inclusion of a number of community-level (aggregate) indicators. In the concluding section, results are reviewed, and the implications of the research strategy adopted are considered.

THE COMMUNITY MODEL: AGGREGATE-LEVEL ANALYSIS

The community framework, which we use to interpret aggregate patterns, is more akin to traditional demographic transition theory models than to the micro-analytic approach to aggregate data developed by T. P. Schultz (1969a, 1972).[9] In papers by Schultz and others of the new household-economics school of fertility analysis, aggregate indicators are used to test predictions – such as the suggested association between female educational attainment, opportunity-costs, and reproductive behaviour – derived from the micro-economic theory of fertility.[10] Having been evaluated through

TABLE 14.3 *Names and definitions of variables: county data set*

Social, economic, and agricultural indicators

LIT 15–19	Literacy rate of women aged 15–19
LIT 45–9	Literacy rate of women aged 45–9
NON-AG-EMP	Proportion of male labour-force employed outside agriculture
AV.LAND	Average number of hectares of crop-land per farm family
RAIN	Average number of millimetres of rainfall per year
FRAGMENT	Average number of land fragments per land-owning family
AG-WAGE-EMP	Proportion of male labour force in agriculture working for wages
GINI	An index of the degree of inequality in the ownership of land, in terms of a gini coefficient

Dummy variables representing regions and localities

S-EAST	County located in South-east region
E-CENTRAL	County located in East-central region
N-EAST	County located in North-east region
COTTON	Cotton grown in county
CITRUS	Citrus fruits grown in county
TOBACCO	Tobacco grown in county
HAZELNUT	Hazelnuts grown in county
TEA	Tea grown in county

Demographic indicators

PG	Population growth from 1960 to 1975 (in per cent)
OM	An index of net outmigration, the ratio of the number of women aged 25–34 to men of the same ages*
Q2	An index of mortality conditions, the probability of dying before reaching age 2*
CF	Completed fertility, the average number of children ever born to women aged 45–9
I_f	A standardised index of current overall fertility.* $I_f = \Sigma B_i / \Sigma W_i F_i$, where B_i is the number of legitimate births in each 5-year age-interval between ages 15 and 49, W_i is the number of women in each age interval, and F_i is the marital fertility rate of Hutterite women in each age interval. Also, $I_f = I_g \times I_m$.

I_g A standardised index of current marital fertility.* $I_g = \Sigma B_i /$ $\Sigma m_i F_i$, where m_i is the number of married women in each age-interval. B_i and F_i are defined above under the definition of I_f.

I_m An index among women in childbearing ages of the proportion married and average age of marriage. $I_m = \Sigma m_i F_i /$ $\Sigma W_i F_i$. m_i, F_i and W_i are defined above under the definitions of I_f and I_g.

---

*See the Appendix for assumptions involved in the derivation and use of these variables.

such empirical exercises, micro hypotheses are then linked to broad, often implicit, assumptions about trends in economic growth, market and institutional responses to population growth, and structural changes, to provide a basis for predictions about aggregate fertility trends. For example, Schultz's conclusions and policy recommendations in regard to Egyptian fertility depend on a continuing pattern of 'development and industrilization' (T. P. Schultz, 1972, p. 440).

Our rejection of this sort of micro-based interpretation of aggregate phenomena derives from the *ad hoc* treatment of the social adjustments and economic-demographic linkages – encompassing what economists conventionally refer to as aggregation mechanisms – assumed to be at work in the background. Rather than introduce information on economic pressures, structural conditions, and market and institutionally mediated 'adding up' processes in a selective and unsystematic fashion, community indicators are used to identify and explore the aggregate-level economic-demographic system.[11]

As in demographic transition theory, the community approach focuses on aggregate-level associations between demographic flows and structural features and processes in societies. The transition theory posits a connection between trends in fertility and mortality and societal processes of industrialisation, urbanisation, education, and modernisation of ideas and beliefs. Accordingly, a significant association at the provincial level in Turkey has been found between fertility and the literacy rate.[12] The 'modernisation' process which contributes to fertility differentiation in Turkey appears, however, to diverge from that which is depicted in transition theory, in as much as applications to Turkish demographic and development patterns have failed to demonstrate significant cross-sectional linkages between fertility rates and levels of industrialisation and urbanisation (Farooq and Tuncer, 1974).

The community model, while incorporating transition theory factors – levels of mortality, literacy and non-agricultural employment – introduces social processes and structural features characteristic of agricultural areas. As in transition theory, there is an assumption of rational decision-making in behaviour.[13] Also drawn from transition theory is an assumption of equilibrating responses and accommodating adjustments at the community level to pressures and repercussions stemming from population growth and other structural changes.[14]

In the model, the processes determining community population-size respond to the average standard of living in different localities. Community demographic control mechanisms are activated when the standard of living is threatened by population growth or other changes. Limits on growth are set by constraints on a locality's output defined by natural conditions, availability of land and other resources, level of technology, and institutions that organise economic life. Demographic control mechanisms – migration, marital fertility and timing of marriage – are set in motion in a variety of ways. For example, individual-level marriage and migration behaviour respond to changes in the terms and arrangements governing land-use, while fertility may adjust to changes in labour-supply and -demand. Community demographic rates result from an adding-up of individual-level decisions and outcomes. But, in what is a crucial characteristic of the community model, the aggregation process is recognised explicitly as being complex and interactive, involving numerous offsetting and compounding micro decisions and adjustments.

Specifications of the community model must take into account processes and interactions characteristic of the experience of individual countries. In the Turkish case, as noted above, the phenomena of interest include secular declines in aggregate mortality and fertility, rural-urban migration on a large scale, and intrarural differences in fertility and other demographic rates. Also recall that differing rates of population growth within the rural sector have been accompanied by variation in the extension of cultivation and the intensification of production. In terms of the community framework, we have clues as to why rural areas in Turkey turn to demographic control mechanisms to differing degrees.

In general, the community model would be composed of equations for net outmigration, fertility and other demographic rates, with each rate representing a flow that responds to specific community characteristics and the level of application of alternative demographic controls. In the initial model presented below, fertility and net outmigration flows control community growth, with fertility playing a passive role in the system.[15] The net outmigration (OM) flow is the outcome of agricultural and non-agricultural conditions reflecting community capacity to support a larger population. The fertility (CF) flow responds to predetermined mortality conditions and educational levels, both transition theory factors, and to the net outmigration flow, but only indirectly through net outmigration to community agricultural and non-agricultural characteristics.

The basic model is stated formally as follows:

$$OM = f(\text{NON-AG-EMP, AV. LAND, RAIN, FRAGMENT, AG-WAGE-EMP,} \quad (1)$$
$$\text{GINI, S-EAST, E-CENTRAL, N-EAST, COTTON, CITRUS,}$$
$$\text{TOBACCO, HAZELNUT, TEA}),$$

$$CF = f(\text{LIT 45-9, Q2, OM}). \quad (2)$$

The variables are reintroduced in the text below; more precise definitions are left to Table 14.3. Variable means and standard deviations appear in Tables 14.1 and 14.2.[16] Data are observations for counties tabulated in the 1970 census.[17] Counties are administrative and political units; each is relatively uniform in economic and cultural characteristics. Counties are treated as communities, although they themselves are aggregates of smaller administrative units.

Regression findings for equation (1) are presented in Table 14.4 (column 1). Results show that outmigration (OM) is more substantial where there are less non-agricultural employment (NON-AG-EMP), fewer resources – less land – on average per farm family (AV. LAND), less rainfall (RAIN), and widespread fragmentation in landholdings (FRAGMENT), an indicator of the intensity of cultivation. Migration flows are related inversely also to indices of the qualitative differences in social organisation in agriculture – the proportion of the agricultural labour-force that works for wages (AG-WAGE-EMP) and the Gini coefficient of inequality in land-ownership (GINI).

Moreover, after the above agricultural and non-agricultural conditions are taken into account, migration flows are found to be influenced by cropping patterns and by other unspecified conditions in different regions. Cropping patterns and other conditions are represented by dummy variables which indicate the cotton (COTTON), citrus (CITRUS), tobacco (TOBACCO), hazelnut (HAZELNUT) and tea (TEA) producing areas of the Aegean and Black Sea regions, and three of the four interior regions the South-east (S-EAST), East-central (E-CENTRAL) and North-east (N-EAST).[18] The extent of migration is relative to the omitted wheat-growing West-central region. Compared to the migration from this region, there is a large net outflow from tea-growing areas along the Black Sea, whereas

TABLE 14.4 *Regression results, community model: dependent variable, OM (t statistics in parentheses)*

Explanatory variables	(1)	(2)	(3)	(4)	(5)
NON-AG-EMP	−0.05 (−2.03)**	−0.05 (−1.77)*	−0.05 (−1.78)*	−0.04 (−1.43)	−0.03 (−1.03)
AV.LAND	−0.02 (−0.94)	−0.04 (−1.92)*	−0.05 (−2.45)**	−0.02 (−1.27)	−0.03 (−1.47)
RAIN	−0.05 (−1.27)	−0.03 (−0.84)	−0.02 (−0.42)	−0.04 (−1.07)	−0.03 (−0.92)
FRAGMENT	0.10 (2.22)**	0.12 (2.73)**	0.15 (3.17)**	0.11 (2.42)**	0.11 (2.51)**
AG-WAGE-EMP	−0.03 (−2.21)**	−0.02 (−1.37)	−0.01 (−0.49)	−0.03 (−2.01)**	−0.03 (−1.81)*
GINI	−0.12 (−1.85)*	−0.11 (−1.80)*	−0.11 (−1.71)*	−0.12 (−1.86)*	−0.12 (−1.83)*
S-EAST	−0.04 (−0.96)	−0.05 (−1.27)	−0.06 (−1.45)	−0.07 (−1.73)*	−1.10 (−2.09)**
E-CENTRAL	0.03 (0.85)	0.01 (0.28)	0.003 (0.08)	0.01 (0.18)	−0.01 (−2.32)**
N-EAST	−0.06 (−1.71)*	−0.09 (−2.51)**	−0.11 (−2.97)**	−0.10 (−2.61)**	−0.12 (−2.95)**
COTTON	−0.04 (−0.86)	−0.02 (−0.41)	−0.01 (−0.20)	−0.01 (−0.25)	0.01 (0.12)
CITRUS	−0.18 (−3.22)**	−0.14 (−2.54)**	−0.12 (−2.09)**	−0.18 (−3.24)**	−0.18 (−3.20)**
TOBACCO	−0.18 (−4.42)**	−0.11 (−2.49)*	−0.07 (−1.31)	−0.12 (−2.85)**	−0.09 (−1.81)*
HAZELNUT	−0.02 (0.39)	−0.02 (−0.36)	−0.02 (−0.44)	−0.03 (−0.48)	−0.03 (0.54)

	(1)	(2)	(3)	(4)	(5)
TEA	0.15 (1.96)**	0.14 (1.84)*	0.12 (1.54)	0.14 (1.87)*	0.14 (1.80)*
CF	–	0.27 (2.88)**	–	–	–
$\hat{C}F$	–	–	0.49 (3.28)**	–	–
I_f	–	–	–	0.19 (2.87)**	–
$\hat{I}_f$	–	–	–	–	0.31 (2.79)**
Intercept	0.20	−0.30	−0.68	0.32	0.40
R^2	0.408	0.431	0.437***	0.430	0.429***

* Coefficient is significant at the 0.10 level of confidence.
** Coefficient is significant at the 0.05 level of confidence.
*** R^2 based on instruments.

movement from citrus- and tobacco-growing areas, which attract some migrants, is much lower. On the plateau, migratory movements are less important in the remote North-eastern and South-eastern provinces.

A second factor in community population growth, represented by equation (2), is fertility. As seen in Table 14.5 (column 1), fertility flows (CF) are restricted where literacy (LIT 44-9) is more extensive and where mortality (Q2) is lower. Fertility responds directly to the index of long-term, net outmigration (OM). Irrespective of literacy and mortality levels, areas of higher net outmigration replace population loss through higher fertility. Interpretations follow of the causal relationship between fertility and the literacy, mortality and outmigration variables.

The influence of the literacy variable in the fertility equation is close to that discovered in studies of Turkish data using observations for samples of both urban and rural localities (Farooq and Tuncer, 1974; Tuncer, 1977). In the present study, literacy emerges as a factor that discourages fertility and population growth *within* a sample of rural communities. Similar to its role in transition theory, literacy is regarded as a powerful mechanism and composite indicator of changes in consumption standards, patterns of work and family organisation, and general acceptance within communities of contraception.

The finding of a positive relation between fertility and child-mortality reflects individual-level responses or community-level adjustments, or both. For example, the cessation of lactation following an infant death leads to hormonal changes that induce early resumption of ovulation. In the absence of fertility control, this individual-level mechanism results in a shortening of intervals between births (Adlakha, 1973). Community-level effects may operate through the influence of average mortality experience on expectations in regard to the death of children, and on fertility norms and attitudes towards contraception.

Finally, the results show that a significantly pro-natal factor in agricultural communities is the level of net outmigration. In the basic model, outmigration is the principal link between local agricultural conditions and fertility. A number of mechanisms in the agricultural economy contribute to the aggregate-level fertility response. A flow of remittances from migrants may influence fertility through a wealth effect and by demonstrating the value of children as long-term security assets and insurance investments. Labour scarcities in areas of heavy net outmigration may increase the value of child and other family labour, and make it easier to establish grown children in occupations or on land-holdings of their own. A premium placed on family labour may also be a reflection of the dissolution of ties of mutual aid in chronic outmigration areas.

In the basic model, the rural demographic system is activated by migration flows of varying magnitude. This formulation fits roughly the pattern of rural growth and fertility differentiation in the recent years of extensive rural–urban and international migration flows. But the picture presented of fertility responding to education, mortality conditions and net out-migration is too simplistic. Fertility differentials existed in Turkey prior to the upswing in rural–urban migration in the 1950s. This suggests closer examination of the determinants of differential fertility. Also, the possibility that migration flows themselves respond to differences in fertility and growth must be considered. Such differences are captured, to a degree, through variables that are included in both the migration and fertility equations, but important additional influences are lost unless the fertility variable is included in the migration equation.

In equations (3) and (4), fertility indices, CF (completed fertility) and I_f (current fertility) are introduced into the estimated relation for the out-migration flow (formerly equation (1)).

$$\text{OM} = f(\text{NON-AG-EMP, AV.LAND, RAIN, FRAGMENT, AG-WAGE-EMP,} \quad (3)$$
$$\text{GINI, S-EAST, E-CENTRAL, N-EAST, COTTON, CITRUS,}$$
$$\text{TOBACCO, HAZELNUT, TEA, CF}),$$

$$\text{OM} = f(\text{NON-AG-EMP, AV.LAND, RAIN, FRAGMENT, AG-WAGE-EMP,} \quad (4)$$
$$\text{GINI, S-EAST, E-CENTRAL, N-EAST, COTTON, CITRUS,}$$
$$\text{TOBACCO, HAZELNUT, TEA, } I_f).$$

As seen in Table 14.4 (columns 2 and 4) both fertility indices are statistically and quantitatively significant in the outmigration equation. The other explanatory variables are roughly similar in quantitative and statistical significance, with few exceptions. AG-WAGE-EMP loses significance in the equation containing CF (compare columns 1 and 2), and NON-AG-EMP loses significance when I_f is included (compare columns 1 and 4). The coefficients (and significance) of regional and crop dummies change as well. By adding fertility variables, the effects of differences in the long-term growth of the community labour-force on migration flows are considered. Migration decisions are seen as responding to poor returns in labour-markets or sharecropping, and to difficulties in acquiring land.

The inclusion of fertility variables in the OM equation complicates the model in several respects. Firstly, the revised model depicts a system in which the pattern of causation between migration and fertility is no longer recursive but mutually determined. Since ordinary least squares is now inappropriate as a statistical method of estimation,[19] two-stage least

TABLE 14.5 *Regression results, community model: dependent variables,* CEB, I_f *(t statistics in parentheses)*

Explanatory variables	CF (1)	CF (2)	I_f (3)	I_f (4)
LIT 45-9	-0.12 (-11.94)**	-0.05 (-3.75)**	-	-
LIT 15-19	-	-	-0.07 (-2.68)**	-0.10 (-3.39)**
Q2	0.33 (11.28)**	0.23 (7.55)**	0.30 (6.14)**	-
AV.LAND	-	0.10 (10.57)**	0.06 (3.76)**	0.04 (2.51)**
RAIN	-	-0.01 (-0.43)	0.02 (0.74)	-0.01 (0.33)
FRAGMENT	-	-0.16 (-5.44)**	-0.15 (-3.15)**	-0.06 (-1.27)
S-EAST	-	0.04 (1.21)	0.21 (3.89)**	0.11 (2.07)**
E-CENTRAL	-	-0.002 (-0.10)	0.04 (1.31)	0.08 (2.21)**
N-EAST	-	0.11 (4.91)**	0.17 (5.34)**	0.20 (5.69)**
COTTON	-	-0.03 (-1.04)	-0.05 (-1.31)	-0.08 (-1.87)*
CITRUS	-	0.07 (1.87)*	0.25 (4.28)**	0.16 (2.58)**
TOBACCO	-	-0.02 (0.86)	-0.03 (-0.76)	-0.11 (-2.34)**

HAZELNUT	–	0.07 (2.29)**	0.11 (2.29)**	–0.01 (0.33)
TEA	–	–0.03 (0.79)	–0.04 (0.63)	–0.12 (–1.63)*
OM	0.17 (3.89)**	–	–	–
ÔM	–	0.72 (6.59)**	0.93 (5.68)**	0.70 (4.01)**
Intercept	2.01	1.77	–0.65	–0.96
R^2	0.612	0.803***	0.715***	0.663***

* Coefficient is significant at the 0.10 level of confidence.
** Coefficient is significant at the 0.05 level of confidence.
*** R^2 based on instruments.

squares is used.[20] In Table 14.4 (columns 3 and 5), CF and I_f have been replaced by estimated values, $\hat{C}F$ and $\hat{I}_f$. Note, firstly, that the overall statistical and quantitative significance of the explanatory variables is maintained in the new relationships. Secondly, the enhanced role accorded to fertility in the revised formulations suggests a review of the original specification of the fertility equation. In equations (5) and (6), new fertility equations are specified to accompany equations (3) and (4) in the revised model.

$$CF = f(\text{LIT 45-9, Q2, AV.LAND, RAIN, FRAGMENT, S-EAST,} \tag{5}$$
$$\text{E-CENTRAL, N-EAST, COTTON, CITRUS, TOBACCO,}$$
$$\text{HAZELNUT, TEA, } \hat{O}M),$$

$$I_f = f(\text{LIT 15-19, Q2, AV.LAND, RAIN, FRAGMENT, S-EAST,} \tag{6}$$
$$\text{E-CENTRAL, N-EAST, COTTON, CITRUS, TOBACCO,}$$
$$\text{HAZELNUT, TEA, } \hat{O}M).$$

The literacy, mortality and (now estimated) migration variables of the original CF specification are retained. A set of agricultural variables has been added. In the equation for current fertility, I_f, variable LIT 15-19, literacy of women aged 15-19, replaces variable LIT 45-9; otherwise the specifications are identical.

Results for equations (5) and (6) appear in Table 14.5 (columns 2 through 4). In the estimated CF relationship, the sign and significance of the literacy variable is as it is in the initial specification, although the size of the coefficient has declined. The positive impact of child-mortality on fertility is maintained in the new specification. The significance and strength of the mortality variable in the I_f equation is to some extent an artefact of the use of Q2 in estimating current fertility (see the Appendix); accordingly, we present results for I_f with and without the Q2 variable (in columns 3 and 4, respectively).

An interesting finding is that two of the variables that measure the capacity of community agriculture to support a larger population, AV. LAND and FRAGMENT, are significantly related to both fertility indices. (RAIN, the third resource intensity variable, is included as a control variable.) These results are broadly comparable with a body of findings linking rural fertility differences in a number of countries to the relative availability of land between frontier and settled agricultural areas (Easterlin, 1971, 1976; Merrick, 1978). The mechanisms invoked in such studies – scarcity of land influences ages of marriage and marital fertility by reducing child-labour contributions and possibilities of establishing offspring on farms of their own – may be salient in view of the Turkish experience of settling various, sometimes highly localised, internal frontiers.

Reviewing the influence of agricultural variables differentiated on a regional basis, fertility is higher in the wheat-growing regions of the South-east and North-east, and in the areas where citrus fruits and hazelnuts are important crops.[21] Finally, the regression results show that the OM variable is still highly significant and makes an important contribution to the explanatory power of the fertility equation. Migration has a strong impact even after literacy, mortality and direct fertility–agriculture linkages have been taken into account.

The community models discussed above rest on a feedback mechanism which balances aggregate fertility and migration flows so as to stabilise population growth. But the overall fertility flow is itself a complex demographic variable dependent on the age-specific rates of both marital fertility and marriage. Specifically, the index of current fertility, I_f, is defined as the product of indices of marital fertility, I_g, and proportions married, I_m. The component rates are subject to separate influences; each can be treated as representing a specific form of community population control.

In equation (7), a relationship for marital fertility, I_g, is specified, whose independent variables are identical to those for I_f in equation (6).[22]

$$I_g = f(\text{LIT 15-19, Q2, AV. LAND, RAIN, FRAGMENT, S-EAST,} \qquad (7)$$
$$\text{E-CENTRAL, N-EAST, COTTON, CITRUS, TOBACCO,}$$
$$\text{HAZELNUT, TEA, ÔM).}$$

Results which are displayed in Table 14.6 (column 1 (without Q2), column 2 (with Q2)) are generally similar in sign and significance of coefficients and in overall strength of relationship with the above findings for the I_f equation (Tables 14.5, columns 3 and 4). Evidently, the feedback mechanisms linking overall fertility and migration flows work, at least in part, through the marital fertility component.

As regards the proportions married, I_m, findings for a specification along the lines of the I_f and I_g equations appear in Table 14.6, column 3. An alternative specification replaces variables AV. LAND, RAIN and FRAGMENT with variables NON-AG-EMP, AG-WAGE-EMP and GINI, and the estimated values for net outmigration (ÔM) and fertility (ĈF):

$$I_m = f(\text{LIT 15-19, Q2, NON-AG-EMP, AG-WAGE-EMP, GINI, S-EAST,} \qquad (8)$$
$$\text{E-CENTRAL, N-EAST, COTTON, CITRUS, TOBACCO,}$$
$$\text{HAZELNUT, TEA, ĈF, ÔM).}$$

TABLE 14.6   *Regression results, community model: dependent variables, I_g, I_m (t statistics in parentheses)*

Explanatory variables	I_g (1)	I_g (2)	I_m (3)	I_m (4)	I_m (5)
LIT 15-19	−0.07 (−2.70)**	−0.05 (−2.08)**	−0.03 (−6.25)**	−0.02 (−3.22)**	−0.01 (−2.13)**
Q2	—	0.22 (4.65)**	0.06 (4.13)**	0.06 (7.26)**	0.06 (6.13)**
AV.LAND	0.05 (2.61)**	0.06 (3.65)**	−0.002 (−0.67)	—	—
RAIN	0.001 (0.03)	0.03 (0.85)	−0.01 (−2.17)**	—	—
FRAGMENT	−0.07 (−1.50)	−0.14 (−2.92)**	0.004 (0.50)	—	—
NON-AG-EMP	—	—	—	−0.01 (−2.81)**	−0.01 (−2.36)**
AG-WAGE-EMP	—	—	—	−0.01 (−2.67)**	−0.003 (−1.12)
GINI	—	—	—	0.02 (1.91)*	0.03 (2.30)**
S-EAST	0.10 (1.79)*	0.17 (3.17)**	0.02 (2.21)**	0.02 (2.13)**	0.03 (2.86)**
E-CENTRAL	0.07 (2.24)**	0.05 (1.51)	−0.003 (−0.50)	−0.001 (−0.83)	−0.01 (−1.48)
N-EAST	0.21 (6.09)**	0.18 (5.61)**	−0.02 (−3.51)**	−0.02 (−3.97)**	−0.02 (−3.71)**
COTTON	−0.06 (−1.42)	−0.04 (−9.25)**	−0.02 (−2.88)**	−0.02 (−2.25)**	−0.01 (−1.63)
CITRUS	0.14 (2.34)**	0.21 (3.62)**	0.02 (1.82)*	0.01 (1.34)	0.03 (2.60)**

TOBACCO	-0.12 (-2.54)**	-0.06 (-1.31)	0.01 (0.7)	-0.0002 (-0.04)	0.02 (2.18)**
HAZELNUT	0.06 (1.18)	0.13 (2.56)*	-0.02 (-1.78)*	-0.02 (-2.78)**	-0.02 (-1.94)**
TEA	-0.11 (1.71)*	-0.05 (0.75)	0.03 (2.08)**	0.03 (2.52)**	0.02 (1.90)*
$\hat{C}_O$	0.64 (3.78)**	0.82 (4.93)**	–	–	0.06 (1.78)*
$\hat{C}_F$	–	–	–	–	0.04 (1.39)
Intercept	-0.81	-0.58	-0.02	-0.11	-0.18
R^2	0.627***	0.663***	0.515	0.548	0.569***

* Coefficient is significant at the 0.10 level of confidence.
** Coefficient is significant at the 0.05 level of confidence.
*** R^2 based on instruments.

Results suggest that higher literacy and lower mortality affect fertility through marriage (Table 14.6, columns 4 and 5).[23] The association between education and delay of marriage has been found in other studies of Turkish data (Ozbay, 1979). The marriage–mortality linkage may reflect social and economic obstacles to marriage encountered in areas where parents have greater chances of surviving to old-age.

Also noteworthy is the general significance of NON-AG-EMP, AG-WAGE-EMP and GINI, variables which are important in the OM equation but which are not related in a significant fashion to the marital fertility variable (not shown in Table 14.6). These results indicate that delay of marriage is more the norm in areas of more extensive non-agricultural employment and agricultural wage-work and greater equality in land-ownership. Wage-work in agricultural and non-agricultural activities provides short-run alternatives to marriage. Postponement of marriage in areas of more equal distribution may be in response to the expectation that a standard portion of land will be assigned to or purchased for prospective couples. Alternatively, delay of marriage may follow from the greater incidence of social modernisation effects associated with literacy in communities of relatively equal social structure. Marriage rates are also likely to be affected by the particular requirements of community agriculture; these considerations may explain the significant differences in I_m by cropping region. Other things being equal, marriage is earlier and more extensive in the South-eastern region and in the citrus- and tea-growing areas of the Black Sea coast.

We have also evaluated the proposition that I_m adjusts to levels of migration and fertility. As seen in Table 14.6 (column 5), I_m is significantly and directly related to $\hat{O}M$, but not significantly related to the measure of fertility, $\hat{C}F$. The I_m-OM relationship suggests that age and extent of marriage respond in an equilibrating fashion in areas of population loss due to net outmigration.

Thus far, attention has centred on interpretations of aggregate demographic flows. In the remainder of the chapter, data bearing on another set of issues related to the community model are explored. The focus is on decisions and demographic responses at the micro level that produce aggregate patterns.

THE MICRO MODEL

The community approach to aggregate demographic patterns rests on an assumption of rational micro-demographic responses to changing structural conditions. Although some possible patterns of adjustment in marriage, fertility and migration behaviour were described in the preceding discussion, no systematic attempt was made to distinguish among the factors affecting individual-level demographic choices and responses. Indeed, the multiplicity of processes and adjustments reflected in aggregate patterns is an argument against the specification of micro-level relationships on aggregate data. In this section, individual- and aggregate-level data are used to examine processes and influences bearing on fertility within households. Of interest are the micro-level mechanisms and statuses that underlie the persistent aggregate-level associations between fertility and measures of literacy, mortality and agricultural production capacity.

The theoretical underpinning of this section is provided by a micro-economic model of fertility behaviour similar to that of the new household-economics approach. In the micro framework, investments in children are governed by the availability of resources, household access to information, and the costs and utilities derived from children relative to other sources of satisfaction. The economic model posits associations between fertility and variables such as expected lifetime family income and the prices of inputs used in the childbearing and childrearing process – including the amount and quality of time contributed by parents.

Such elements in the decision-making model as prices, incomes, tastes and information are measured through household survey data or, as in the above-mentioned works of Schultz and others, through indicators of average conditions found in aggregate data sources. Population economists generally stress the superiority of survey-based measures of variables over aggregate-level indicators. Survey data are preferred because they permit, at least potentially, a closer representation of household conditions and because household-level inquiries typically provide a larger number of observations. But even where household-level data are available, aggregate rates can provide valuable supplementary information on the variables in the household decision-making model. Thus, aggregate rates can serve as indicators of long-term income-earning opportunities, price movements, and so forth. In addition, aggregate data can provide information normally unavailable through survey instruments. In this regard, aggregate data describe structural features of markets and local institutions that affect prices and incomes of micro-units. Furthermore, this level of data represents group characteristics and shared views and values that shape individual perceptions and tastes. Applications of new household-economics to aggregate phenomena typically fail to differentiate among diverse household characteristics (such as opportunity-costs) and broader features of local economic and social settings – all reducible ultimately to individual price, income, taste and information effects – that are captured in aggregate data. (This point is discussed further in Chapter 7.)

In short, aggregate-level data, which are introduced below along with survey responses in a micro-level relationship, can serve as a useful source of information on various price, income and taste influences on fertility choices. As just noted, our interpretation of the impact of aggregate rates in a micro specification diverges from the new household-economics view of community indicators as direct proxies for incomes, opportunity-costs and other price factors in a partial equilibrium framework. On the other hand, the approach to community-level indicators also differs from that of sociologists such as Freedman, who favour inclusion of aggregate data in micro-level analysis to capture 'neighbourhood' effects. Such 'contextual' factors supposedly represent influences and processes exogenous and supplementary to the personal attributes and orientations thought to be reflected in household surveys alone.[24] While accepting that aggregate variables capture important structural and social interaction features of local settings, it is unhelpful to distinguish between internally- and externally-determined factors (as compared with price, income and taste factors), and unrealistic to expect personal attributes and socially-transmitted characteristics and capacities to be accurately measured and differentiated through survey and aggregate-level data.

The following analysis draws on the responses of 1782 currently-married women who were interviewed in the 1973 Hacettepe survey.[25] The women were all between the ages of 25 and 49, and each had had at least one live birth. The discussion focuses on the determinants of differences in the number of children ever born or, equivalently, the number of live births, NOLVBR, for the subsample of 617 women who were living in localities for which there are county-level data.

The model to be estimated is as follows:

$$\text{NOLVBR} = f(\text{AGE, AGESQ, EDW1, EDW2, EDW3, EDH1, EDH2, EDH3,} \quad (9)$$
$$\text{EDH4, WKOWNLAND, HHSS, FATHLIT, DS-ED-GIRL,}$$
$$\text{LFP-PAID, AV. LAND, OM, LIT 45-9, Q2}).$$

Variables consist of indicators drawn from the household survey plus four previously-used county-level indicators – AV. LAND, OM, LIT 45-9 and Q2. Variables are defined in the text below and more precisely in Table 14.7. Variable means and standard deviations are also shown in Table 14.7, and the variables' correlations appear in the Appendix table.

Variables age (AGE) and age-squared (AGESQ) are introduced to control for age differences as well as life-cycle and cohort effects.[26] In a specification that omits separate terms for duration of marriage or labour-force experience, AGE and AGESQ also reflect differences in the period of exposure to the risk of pregnancy, the likelihood (which declines non-linearly with age) that women will bear additional children, age-related differences in incomes, and other time-dependent effects.[27]

The Hacettepe survey provides neither reliable income estimates nor detailed accounting of income sources. Nevertheless, dummy variables EDH1 to EDH4, corresponding to levels of husband's education, variables WKOWNLAND (work own land) and HHSS (household social security), and county-level variables AV.LAND and OM, are available as indicators of present and expected income, occupation, sector of employment and the role played by children in household economic activities. The relationships between each of these variables and fertility are shown in Table 14.8. In both the full sample of households (column 1) and the subsample for which there is also county-level data (column 2), fertility is increasingly inversely related to higher levels of husband's education, but varies directly with WKOWNLAND, HHSS, AV.LAND and OM.

Variable WKOWNLAND, by identifying families owning some or all of the land they cultivate, also indicates households whose fertility intentions are shaped by their reliance on family members for labour and by opportunities for children to make an economic contribution to the family. HHSS, the social security variable, takes account of the need and intention to rely on family members for support in old-age rather than on savings, rental income or a pension. Variables WKOWNLAND and HHSS maintain statistical and quantitative significance after AV.LAND and OM are introduced (compare columns 2 and 3).

Variables AV.LAND and OM provide additional information on the economic position and options of households within the respondent's locality. AV.LAND serves as an indicator of land availability and agricultural opportunities. Also, a wealth effect is likely to be captured in the coefficient for AV.LAND which serves as an indicator of both size of holding and level of income in farming households. As a measure of land availability and the relative ease of establishing children on their own holdings, AV.LAND captures the bequest effect discussed by Easterlin (1971, 1976) and Merrick (1978). Analogous to AV.LAND, variable OM, a measure of the extent of net outmigration in communities, serves as an indicator of 'settlement' possibilities and employment opportunities (labour-market tightness) for family members within their local communities, and of levels of income from non-local employment and the resultant remittances to individual households.

Variables EDW1, EDW2 and EDW3 (education of wife, levels 1 to 3)

TABLE 14.7 *Variable definitions, means and standard deviations: the micro model*

Variable names	Definitions	Means (standard deviations in parentheses)	
		Total sample	County subsample
Demographic variables			
NOLVBR	Number of live births	4.68 (2.53)	5.15 (2.63)
AGE	Age of woman	35.3 (6.50)	35.50 (6.50)
AGESQ	Age of woman squared	1291.6 (467.90)	1300.40 (469.20)
SURRATE	The ratio of the number of surviving children to the number of household births	0.83 (0.20)	0.82 (0.20)
Socio-economic dummy variables			
EDH1	Husband attended only some primary school	0.12 (0.32)	0.13 (0.33)
EDH2	Husband completed primary school	0.44 (0.50)	0.39 (0.49)
EDH3	Husband completed junior high school	0.06 (0.24)	0.07 (0.25)
EDH4	Husband completed at least high school	0.10 (0.29)	0.08 (0.27)
WKOWNLAND	Respondant's household cultivates agricultural land of which some or all is household-owned	0.27 (0.45)	0.37 (0.48)
HHSS	Respondant aspects to rely primarily on children in old age	0.75 (0.43)	0.74 (0.44)
EDW1	Woman attended only some primary school	0.11 (0.32)	0.09 (0.29)
EDW2	Woman completed primary school	0.24 (0.43)	0.19 (0.39)
EDW3	Woman completed at least junior high school	0.05 (0.23)	0.04 (0.21)
FATHLIT	Woman's father was literate	0.49 (0.50)	0.45 (0.50)

DS-ED-GIRL	Desire for daughter to attain at·least a junior high school education	0.39 (0.49)	0.37 (0.48)
LFP-PAID	Woman's participation in labour-force as paid worker	0.10 (0.30)	0.12 (0.32)

Variables indicating conditions in the woman's county of residence

AV.LAND	Average amount of crop-land per farm family (hectares)	—	32.9 (26.5)
OM	Index of net outmigration	—	1.32 (0.31)
LIT 45–9	Literacy rate of women aged 45–9 (in per cent)	—	17.8 (18.7)
Q2	The probability of dying before reaching age 2	—	0.19 (0.04)

Number of respondants	1782	617

TABLE 14.8   Regression results, micro model: dependent variable, number of live births (NOLVBR) (t statistics in parentheses)

Explanatory variables	(1) Full sample	(2) Subsample	(3) Subsample with community variables	(4) Full sample	(5) Subsample	(6) Subsample with community variables
	without household mortality variable (SURRATE)			with household mortality variable (SURRATE)		
AGE	0.70 (8.50)**	0.78 (5.23)**	0.79 (5.52)**	0.71 (9.17)**	0.80 (5.84)**	0.80 (5.99)**
AGESQ	-0.01 (-6.92)**	-0.01 (-4.31)**	-0.01 (-4.49)**	-0.01 (-7.65)**	-0.01 (-4.93)**	-0.01 (-4.98)**
SURRATE	-	-	-	-3.83 (-16.36)**	-4.44 (-10.66)**	-4.09 (-9.98)**
EDH1	-0.48 (-2.86)**	-0.58 (-2.03)**	-0.48 (-1.73)*	-0.42 (-2.65)**	-0.47 (-1.80)*	-0.44 (-1.71)*
EDH2	-0.68 (-5.42)**	-0.79 (-3.58)**	-0.66 (-3.07)**	-0.57 (-4.84)**	-0.61 (-2.98)**	-0.53 (-2.66)**
EDH3	-0.81 (-3.51)**	-0.71 (-1.78)*	-0.65 (-1.68)*	-0.77 (-3.58)**	-0.65 (-1.78)*	-0.63 (-1.77)*
EDH4	-0.75 (-3.30)**	-1.19 (-2.72)**	-1.29 (-3.06)**	-0.65 (-3.07)**	-0.75 (-1.86)*	-0.90 (-2.30)**
WKOWNLAND	0.57 (5.08)**	0.68 (3.53)**	0.55 (2.90)**	0.45 (4.25)**	0.56 (3.20)**	0.48 (2.73)**
HHSS	0.84 (6.55)**	0.83 (3.62)**	0.76 (3.46)**	0.83 (6.94)**	0.81 (3.82)**	0.75 (3.69)**
EDW1	-1.00 (-6.27)**	-1.10 (-3.60)**	-1.00 (-3.40)**	-0.74 (-4.94)**	-0.74 (-2.63)**	-0.67 (-2.46)**
EDW2	-1.54 (-11.63)**	-1.60 (-6.17)**	-1.26 (-5.02)**	-1.31 (-10.56)**	-1.33 (-5.58)**	-1.07 (-4.58)**
EDW3	-2.25 (-8.35)**	-2.14 (-4.12)**	-1.74 (-3.50)**	-1.92 (-7.61)**	-1.70 (-3.55)**	-1.39 (-3.01)**
FATHLIT	-0.27 (-2.60)**	-0.06 (-0.31)	-0.09 (-0.51)	-0.15 (-1.51)*	0.13 (0.75)	0.09 (0.53)
OS-ED-GIRL	-0.54 (-4.90)**	-0.52 (-2.61)**	-0.41 (-2.15)**	-0.50 (-4.87)**	-0.59 (-3.21)**	-0.49 (-2.74)**
LFP-PAID	-0.38 (-2.30)**	-0.43 (-1.57)	-0.16 (-0.62)	-0.31 (-2.05)**	-0.35 (-1.41)	-0.18 (-0.73)
AV.LAND	-	-	0.01 (3.50)**	-	-	0.01 (2.96)**
OM	-	-	0.74 (2.49)**	-	-	0.88 (3.20)**
LIT 45-9	-	-	-2.25 (-4.20)**	-	-	-1.68 (-3.37)**
Q2	-	-	2.80 (1.37)	-	-	0.44 (0.23)
Intercept	-9.11	-10.48	-14.65	-5.93	-7.17	-10.52
R^2	0.365	0.357	0.419	0.449	0.459	0.502
N	1782	617	617	1782	617	617

* Coefficient is significant at the 0.10 level of confidence.
** Coefficient is significant at the 0.05 level of confidence.

represent increasing levels of female educational achievement. The coefficients of variables EDW1 to EDW3 measure the fertility effects of different educational levels in comparison to women without any schooling. Even a limited encounter with formal education has a substantial negative effect on fertility; the impact on fertility grows for women educated to at least the third level (EDW3, completion of junior high school). The indicators of female educational attainment – representing tastes for consumption and leisure alternatives to childrearing, opportunity-costs, and effective knowledge of modern contraceptive methods – have the largest fertility impact in a regression that includes other indicators of both educational background and aspirations, and female employment experience.

Fertility and the educationally-related family background variables, FATHLIT (father literate) and EDH1 to EDH4 (education of husband, levels 1 to 4), are inversely related. These variables are moderately correlated with variables EDW1 to EDW3. Thus, they may influence fertility indirectly through the level of female educational attainment. The direct influence of these variables very likely reflects a mixture of status (tastes) and income effects on fertility. The variable FATHLIT, which is statistically significant only in the regression for the total sample, represents the higher consumption standards and the distinctive pattern of family life and child-rearing that women raised in literate households have encountered in their youth (and later in life). The indicators for the educational achievement levels of husbands (EDH1 to EDH4), as mentioned above, serve as proxies for levels of occupational and status attainment and permanent income associated with economic endeavours in the secondary and tertiary sectors.

The DS-ED-GIRL (desired education for girls) variable characterises respondents according to the aspirations expressed for the education of daughters. Although the variable reflects to some degree the educational levels of female respondents, their fathers and husbands, and to a lesser extent the level of literacy in the surrounding community,[28] the negative sign of the coefficient of DS-ED-GIRL is attributable to the perceived costs of investing in the education of children, and reflects a diminished economic role in households for daughters, as well as concomitant changes in their social status.

Only a small proportion of women reported labour-force activities; labour-force status is indicated in the survey by the LFP-PAID (labour-force participation paid) variable. Such labour-force participation is not closely associated with intermediate or higher levels of educational attainment. The negative association between employment and fertility has been linked in the general literature to opportunity-costs and to the incompatibility of labour-force participation and childrearing (Chaudhury, 1979). However, the decline in the statistical and quantitative significance of LFP-PAID when LIT (literacy) is added to the regression leads to the hypothesis that in Turkey, LFP-PAID represents primarily tastes and information effects; employment constitutes a mechanism analogous to schooling, through which women encounter new attitudes, alternative consumption possibilities, and information on more effective means of controlling fertility. Furthermore, the dominance of LIT over LFP-PAID suggests employment is only one among many mechanisms or channels through which new knowledge and attitudes are absorbed.

Alternatively, LIT may be a proxy for work opportunities for women who are not presently active in the labour-force, but who are limiting fertility in expectation of future labour-force involvement. Therefore, LIT may be a superior indicator of a woman's opportunity costs than LFP-PAID, which measures only opportunity-costs for current income-earners. If this hypothesis is correct, opportunity-costs are important, and are best indicated by LIT, and tastes and information effects on fertility are best captured in the education of wife variables EDW1 to EDW3. (The results for variable LIT confirm and extend the finding of other studies of Turkish data in regard to the impact of average educational levels on individual fertility.)[29]

Variable Q2, an index of the average level of mortality in localities, represents differences in household experiences and expectations of child-mortality. The sign of variable Q2 in Table 14.8, column 3, suggests that individual fertility tends to be higher in communities with relatively low survival rates for children. This finding may be the result of higher target levels of fertility in households that anticipate a certain number of infant and child deaths on the basis of perceptions of community mortality levels. Alternatively, the household's own mortality experience could lead to efforts to replace some or all of these who did not survive.

The introduction into equation (9) of the variable SURRATE, the child-survival rate within individual households, offers a means of distinguishing between individual- and community-level adjustments. The use of SURRATE, however, is fraught with statistical problems, notably the likely correlation between the variable and the disturbance term of the regression from the under-reporting of the number of deaths being reflected in errors in measuring the dependent variable NOLVBR, the number of live births.[30] The results shown in Table 14.8 lend support to the replacement hypothesis; variable SURRATE, the child-survival rate within households, is statistically and quantitatively significant in columns 4 to 6 of Table 14.8. Moreover, Q2 loses statistical significance and quantitative impact in the presence of SURRATE (compare columns 3 and 6).

Finally, the introduction of aggregate indicators into the micro specification results in a significant increase in the explained variance of fertility. In summary, the inclusion of community-level variables within a micro framework yields a richer understanding of fertility determinants than is possible within a standard micro interpretation or by adhering strictly to a correspondence of household-level data to internal influences and aggregate-level data to external influences.

CONCLUSION

This study calls attention to aggregate- and micro-level variations in fertility in Turkey, and pursues a two-stage approach to explain the findings. Firstly, a community-level framework – a macro-level approach with affinities to demographic transition theory – is adopted to account for cross-sectional variations in fertility rates at the county level. The community model represents a form of aggregate analysis that has been displaced in recent years by the questionable practice of testing micro hypotheses on aggregate data and then adducing micro interpretations of aggregate patterns. Apart from the methodological problems inherent in specifying and verifying micro theory on aggregate data, the subsequent application of micro reasoning to aggregate phenomena involves numerous implicit and, thus, unexamined and potentially misleading assumptions about structural features and economic-demographic interactions in societies. In a community model, on the other hand, societal characteristics, aggregation procedures and aggregate-level economic-demographic mechanisms are taken into account explicity, and indeed become the object of study. Aggregate fertility and migration flows are treated as variables in themselves, not as proxies for micro-level choices, and are seen as resulting from or being conditioned by aggregate pressures and structural adjustments.

All in all, rural fertility in Turkey seems to have responded to a variety of opportunities and stimuli at the community level. Fertility has been influenced by developments such as the emergence of a strong central government that raised educational levels and mobilised the rural population, and by the growth of job opportunities for rural migrants in the urban sector. These national development processes have interacted with local conditions and processes, and have thus had a differential impact on fertility. Fertility levels have also adjusted to opportunities for agricultural expansion, which vary according to the availability of land, ecological conditions, and technological and market developments.

The community model lends itself to further elaboration, according to the scope and quality of the data sources. For example, with agricultural census data, it would be possible to capture with greater precision the diverse ecological, resource and organisational conditions of rural Turkey; an effort could be made to examine production and organisational adjustments and accommodations within communities to differential patterns of demographic change.[31] Likewise, an attempt could be made to investigate the factors, now assumed to be determined outside the model, that account for differences in county mortality levels. Information on the level and timing of investments in public health and medical facilities, ecological differences and differences in nutritional levels and in patterns of child-care would be essential in such an exercise.

The community responses featured in the first phase of empirical work derive from a host of individual-level decisions and adjustments. In the second phase of data analysis, both household survey information and county-level indicators are used to represent factors bearing on household fertility behaviour. The micro-economic theory of fertility provides the framework for discussion in this part of the study. Aggregate variables serve to supplement indicators drawn from a 1973 demographic survey of households. The use of household- and county-level data in such a fashion corresponds to recent efforts to capture so-called contextual effects on fertility behaviour while controlling for the innate orientations and characteristics of individuals. However, aggregate indicators are not assigned the exclusive task of representing influences – information flows, norms and attitudes, and opportunities – emanating from the local community and social milieu, which are captured to some extent through indicators drawn from the household survey. Rather, community-level variables are also seen as providing crude estimates of individual income levels and other attributes, and as serving as indicators of channels and patterns of influence and opportunity not fully reflected in survey data.

Micro results show the expected relationships between fertility and such conventional micro-level variables as wife's and husband's educational attainment and wife's labour-force status. Besides introducing age and mortality variables to control for demographic processes, other variables outside the standard micro-economic specification were included – WKOWNLAND, HHSS, FATHLIT, DS-ED-GIRL. These variables, along with a set of aggregate indicators, offered opportunities to distinguish between multiple interpretations of single variables, and to explore new hypotheses. The micro variables WKOWNLAND and HHSS, and the aggregate variables

AV.LAND and OM, provided a chance to understand household decision-making as it proceeds in a setting of less than perfect information and access to markets. The introduction of an aggregate literacy variable enabled us to formulate hypotheses on the tastes and opportunity-cost effects of female education and labour-force participation. The inclusion of both individual- and community-level mortality variables allowed us to test between alternative mechanisms of mortality–fertility response.

The interpretation of variables in a mixed micro–aggregate model needs to proceed with extreme care. While aggregate indicators may be usefully retained in household-level analysis, a further benefit of the approach is to suggest questions to be pursued and probed in depth in micro-level studies.

APPENDIX: CONSTRUCTION OF MORTALITY, MARITAL FERTILITY AND NET OUTMIGRATION INDICES

Mortality

The value of $q(2)$ (our variable Q2) is estimated for each county from the proportions of children who died for women in different age-groups. Multiplying factors used in the calculation were derived by Trussell, using linear regression techniques on a set of model fertility schedules (Trussell, 1975). In our study, the factor K2 for each county is estimated from the formula

$$K2 = -0.2343(P1/P2) - 0.0601(P2/P3) - 0.0234 \log_e(P1/P2) - 0.0384 \log_e (P2/P3) + 1.0429,$$

where P1, P2, P3 are average parities in the age intervals 15-19, 20-4, 25-9, and the coefficients are those estimated by Trussell for the East mortality pattern. The estimate of $q(2)$ is derived as follows: Q2 = K2 × D2, where D2 is the proportion of children born alive who died, for women aged 20-4.

Marital Fertility

We have used the age distribution of women in each county, Hutterite age-specific fertility rates, and an estimate of the number of babies born per

APPENDIX TABLE Correlation matrix for variables in micro analysis, community subsample

	(1)	(2)	(3)	(4)	(5)	(6)	(7)	(8)	(9)	(10)	(11)	(12)	(13)	(14)	(15)	(16)	(17)	(18)	(19)
(1) NOLVBR	1.00																		
(2) AGE	0.31	1.00																	
(3) SURRATE	-0.47	-0.12	1.00																
(4) EDH1	0.05	0.06	-0.04	1.00															
(5) EDH2	-0.16	-0.10	0.10	-0.30	1.00														
(6) EDH3	-0.08	-0.01	0.02	-0.10	-0.21	1.00													
(7) EDH4	-0.24	-0.06	0.20	-0.11	-0.24	-0.08	1.00												
(8) WKOWNLAND	0.28	0.10	-0.15	0.12	-0.06	-0.16	-0.21	1.00											
(9) HHSS	-0.07	-0.45	0.09	-0.05	0.02	0.06	-0.15	-0.05	1.00										
(10) EDW1	-0.10	0.01	0.10	0.05	0.08	0.05	-0.07	-0.08	-0.03	1.00									
(11) EDW2	-0.29	-0.07	0.16	-0.09	0.18	0.11	0.18	-0.16	0.16	-0.15	1.00								
(12) EDW3	-0.21	0.02	0.15	-0.06	-0.12	0.04	0.49	-0.15	0.07	-0.07	-0.10	1.00							
(13) FATHLIT	-0.18	0.00	0.19	-0.14	0.14	0.13	0.25	-0.10	0.12	0.01	0.25	0.16	1.00						
(14) DS-ED-GIRL	-0.24	0.04	0.09	-0.03	-0.00	0.16	0.29	-0.18	0.10	-0.01	0.24	0.27	0.22	1.00					
(15) LFP-PAID	-0.06	0.03	0.02	0.03	-0.00	-0.06	0.01	0.05	-0.02	0.00	-0.10	0.14	-0.03	0.07	1.00				
(16) AV. LAND	0.16	-0.10	-0.10	-0.02	-0.10	-0.02	-0.06	-0.13	0.03	0.02	-0.08	-0.07	-0.10	-0.12	-0.11	1.00			
(17) OM	0.18	-0.04	-0.01	0.04	-0.01	0.03	0.03	0.10	0.03	-0.03	-0.10	-0.03	0.03	-0.05	-0.02	-0.04	1.00		
(18) LIT 45-9	-0.32	0.08	0.20	-0.01	0.09	0.08	0.05	-0.23	-0.04	0.05	0.18	0.11	0.06	0.16	0.09	-0.23	0.10	1.00	
(19) Q2	0.07	0.02	-0.12	-0.07	0.06	0.03	0.01	0.10	0.01	0.01	-0.01	-0.00	0.08	0.04	-0.11	-0.26	0.10	0.20	1.00

year, in order to calculate I_g. The annual number of births is estimated by 'surviving' forward the number of males aged 0-9. The number of male births, B_m, is derived from $B_m = \dfrac{B_s}{P_0}$; B_s is the number of living males aged 0-9, and P_0 expresses survival possibilities from birth to each age 0-9 in varying mortality regimes in areas where the rate of population growth is assumed to be 2.5 per cent. To derive P_0, we rely on the equation

$$P_0 = 0.9986 - 0.8874\,Q_2,$$

where the constants are taken from a linear regression of P_0 on $q(2)$ values for different mortality levels in the 'East' model life tables. We multiply B_m times a factor of 2.05 to obtain total births.

Net Outmigration

In the absence of estimates of intercensal or lifetime migration rates by county, the sex ratio for the ages 25-34 is adopted as a proxy. An underlying assumption is that migration is initiated by male household members, to be followed at a later date by women and children. Less significant assumptions are that across the sample, sex ratios at birth and the survival chances to age 35 of women to men are identical. At the provincial level OM, the proxy, is highly correlated ($r = 0.65$) with estimates of the intercensal (1960-5) outmigration rate.

NOTES

1. Growth in numbers in the newly-independent Turkish state followed a population decline in Asia Minor during the latter years of the Ottoman empire. Population is estimated to have fallen from 15.7 million in 1914 to 13.6 million in 1927 (Dewdney, 1972) as a consequence of continuous warfare and internal strife in the 1911-25 period and the mass migration of members of minority groups. The Armenian population alone was reduced from an estimated 1.5 million at the beginning of the First World War to a small handful by 1923 (Fry, 1929).
2. The anthropological literature documents extensions of the margin of cultivation in indigenous communities (Stirling, 1965), the founding of offshoot villages (Hutteroth, 1974), the settlement of nomadic and semi-nomadic tribes (Kolars, 1974), and the acquisition of occupation and cultivation rights by refugee groups (Magnarella, 1979).
3. A rural county is defined to be one in which at least 40 per cent of the male labour-force works in agriculture. Our 229 counties represent

six regions in a widely applied nine-region scheme based on ecological and agricultural factors.

4. Kolars provides an interesting account of the gatherings and interactions which produce a village consensus on particular modes of action. The processes through which individual villagers receive the sanction of important kinsmen and community leaders and offers of assistance in particular initiatives from other community members are also described (Kolars, 1974). Stirling's village study deals with the functional and effective links which bind villagers together, and with the extent to which individual behaviour is constrained by such ties. Stirling reports that 'any signs of unusual conduct will immediately lead to detailed and widespread discussion. If people take, as they are almost certain to do, the view that the innovation is malicious, pretentious, dangerous, impious or absurd, the innovator . . . has to face criticism, ridicule, or even ostracism' (Stirling, 1965, pp. 290–1).

5. Kolars describes the transition to a specialised, market-oriented agriculture in a community in the Mediterranean province of Antalya (Kolars, 1974).

6. Considerably more variation exists in the marriage index at the county level. Values of I_m approach 0.9 in the South-east and North-east regions, whereas values in the 0.74 to 0.80 range are not uncommon in the Black Sea and Aegean regions.

7. In the Aegean region, 32 of 49 counties have I_g values below 0.5, and 11 counties scored below 0.4. In counties in the West-central and Black Sea regions, I_g values are frequently in the 0.45 to 0.60 range. (Values of I_g below 0.6 are indicative of conscious fertility limitation.)

8. For example, Ozbay (1979) reports on fertility differences found in a 1976 survey in 30 communities chosen according to the average level of education of village residents.

9. A preliminary statement and application of the community framework appears in Lieberman (1980).

10. Other early examples of micro interpretations of aggregate patterns include DaVanzo (1972) and Wilkinson (1973).

11. One alternative to the paradigm of ongoing industrialisation and urbanisation is the pattern of rural structural change which is featured in the recent literature on American fertility decline (Easterlin, 1971, 1976). We refer to the process of opening up and settlement of frontier areas and the subsequent increase in population density and land values (see Merrick, 1978, for an application to Brazil). As a structural mechanism leading to fertility decline, the opening-up/settlement process may be relevant in the Turkish case, but only when the various forms of settlement – extension of cultivation in existing communities, founding of offshoot villages, establishment of refugee colonies, and so forth – and abandonment of land (through outmigration) are kept in mind, and considered in conjunction with developments such as intensification of agricultural production in various areas and the spread of educational institutions. Hutteroth (1974) discusses the different groups and mechanisms involved in settling Anatolia.

12. The literacy rate is treated by transition theorists as a prime socialising factor and a multidimensional indicator of breakdown in the extended

family system, widespread access to new technologies and goods, rising consumption standards, and other modernising adjustments in norms and social codes bearing on fertility (see Graff, 1979).

13. Davis, for example, emphasises the element of individual calculation in demographic behaviour in his discussion of transition theory (Davis, 1963).

14. The notion of demographic transition as an equilibrating societal response is introduced in Davis (1949).

15. The model has a 'recursive' formulation, in that causation runs from the exogenous explanatory variables to the first dependent variable, OM (outmigration), and then from a combination of exogenous variables and the first dependent variable, OM, to the second dependent variable, CF (completed fertility).

16. We have opted for a double-log specification in which the marginal impact of each variable changes according to the levels of the other variables in the model; since the model is recursive in form and with error terms assumed to be uncorrelated, ordinary least squares may be applied to estimate each equation. A discussion of the construction of fertility, migration and mortality indices appears in the Appendix.

17. Supplementary information on land-ownership is from Village Inventory studies carried out in the late 1960s by the Ministry of Village Affairs. The quality of Inventory data has been assessed and found acceptable in studies by Boratov (1972) and Miller and Cetin (1974).

18. Apart from differences in cropping patterns and techniques, regional dummies may reflect ethno-linguistic differences and differences in location with respect to major urban centres.

19. With the model no longer considered to be recursive in form, there is a likelihood that the error terms may be correlated with the 'independent' variables in each of the estimated equations; in this situation, ordinary least squares leads to estimates which are biased and inconsistent even for large samples.

20. Two-stage least squares is a technique designed to estimate a model in which the dependent variables are jointly determined. In the first stage, the dependent variables which appear as explanatory variables in equations of the model are regressed on the full set of exogenous variables. The resulting estimated values of the dependent variables, now uncorrelated with error terms, are introduced in the second stage in the original equations of the model, wherever they appear as explanatory variables. Each equation is then estimated by ordinary least squares. To ensure that the equations can be 'identified', i.e. distinquished from one another, certain variables are excluded from each relation. Excluded from the fertility equation are AG-WAGE-EMP, GINI and NON-AG-EMP, which represent conditions of primary impact on migration flows; excluded from the migration equation are Q2 and LIT 45-9, indices of mortality and educational levels which have special significance for fertility flows.

21. The regional dummy variables may reflect differences in resources in communities, and, as mentioned above, effects due to differences in labour requirements according to cropping patterns and cultural-linguistic differences.

22. The method of estimation is two-stage least squares.
23. The method of estimation is two-stage least squares.
24. See, for example, R. Freedman (1974), S. B. Lee (1977) and Nizamuddin (1979).
25. The 1973 survey was the third national survey of Turkey's population. We have used the responses to the male and female questionnaires from among the 6500 households selected in a multi-stage, stratified, random-sampling procedure. For details of sample design, questionnaire content and so forth, see Uner (1978). Women of ages less than 25 have been excluded from the sample in the present study because their cumulative fertility is more a reflection of timing and spacing considerations than of targets for completed family size (see Edlefsen, 1981).
26. Edlefsen (1981) argues that inclusion of age terms reduces the effect and biases the coefficients of other independent variables which change systematically with time. On balance, we feel that the biases introduced by excluding age variables, including the attribution of various life-cycle and cohort-specific effects to individual variables such as educational attainment, are likely to be more severe.
27. Age of marriage, a proximate determinant of fertility, is viewed in the micro-level analysis as endogenous to the fertility decision. In other words, age of marriage is seen as dependent on family-size targets arrived at by individuals who face differing constraints and opportunities (see DeTray, 1977). With the exclusion of an age/duration of marriage term (to avoid bias arising out of the simultaneous relationship with fertility), the dependent variable NOLVBR is understood to reflect controls on fertility within marriage as well as restraints associated with the timing of marriage.
28. Correlation coefficients between DS-ED-GIRL and EDW1 to EDW3, FATHLIT, EDH1 to EDH4 and LIT 45-9 are of the order of 0.2 or less.
29. See Ozbay (1979).
30. The interconnected difficulties of measuring individual fertility and mortality levels represent a classic errors-in-variables problem. Another estimation problem involves the non-behavioural relationship between fertility and child-mortality that arises from the differing relative probabilities of large and small families being observed at limiting values of the mortality variable (DeTray and Khan, 1977; Williams, 1977). In addition, a simultaneity bias may be present, in that SURRATE may depend on NOLVBR – both shorter birth intervals and higher birth orders result in higher infant-mortality. In the face of these difficulties, DeTray and Khan (1977, p. 323) suggest that direct evaluation of relationship between completed fertility and mortality is an 'impossible task'. We have elected to present results with and without SURRATE, and to observe the response of other exogenous variables to inclusion of the mortality indicator.
31. In a long-term perspective, variables such as AV. LAND, FRAGMENT and GINI, which are treated as exogenous in this chapter, may be seen as endogenous to the economic-demographic system.

15 Marital Fertility and Employment in Non-agricultural Sectors in Yugoslavia

MIROSLAV MACURA

This chapter deals with the determinants of marital fertility and employment of married women in non-agricultural sectors in Yugoslavia.[1] It attempts to account for intercommunity variations in the period measures of marital fertility and employment of married women at the beginning of the 1970s. The chapter focuses on the early (20-4) and intermediate (25-34) childbearing years – the years to which most of the legitimate childbearing in non-agricultural sectors is confined. It is primarily concerned with marital fertility, and analyses it jointly with female employment because *a priori* reasoning and empirical evidence suggest that they are closely interrelated. The two variables are treated as being simultaneously determined under influence of economic, social, psychological and cultural factors. The theoretical framework underlying the analysis borrows from the 'new home-economics' and elaborates on several determinants which do not belong to the theory.[2] Hypotheses derived from the theoretical considerations are tested against a cross-section of community-level data obtained by aggregating individual census and vital statistics returns and secondary information on social and economic indicators.

The analysis is restricted to non-agricultural sectors because, as argued below, variations in non-agricultural marital fertility contribute to variations in overall fertility in Yugoslavia far more than do variations in agricultural marital fertility or nuptiality. The importance of non-agricultural marital fertility derives to a large measure from the high proportion of population of childbearing years which belongs to non-agricultural sectors.

The proportion at the national level was around 0.69 in 1971. At the regional level (regions are defined below), it ranged between 0.55 and 0.86.

Yugoslavia differs in several respects from developing countries on which the present volume focuses. The level of socio-economic development attained is typical of a semi-industrialised, medium-income country. The secular fertility decline has seemingly approached its end, while mortality is almost universally low.

The chapter is structured as follows: the section below describes the marital fertility measures used, data sources and variations in overall and marital fertility. The second section elaborates on the theoretical determinants of marital fertility and employment of married women. Regression results are discussed in the third section, and the final section summarises the findings.

MARITAL FERTILITY MEASURES, FERTILITY VARIATIONS AND DATA SOURCES

Marital Fertility Measures

The present analysis draws on Coale's discovery of an approximate relationship existing between any age schedule of marital fertility and the corresponding age schedule of natural fertility (Coale, 1971). The relationship, called the Coale marital fertility model, is not widely known and will, therefore, be described in some detail. The relationship is as follows:

$$r_i = Mn_i e^{mv_i}, \quad i = 1, 2, \ldots, 7,$$

where $i = 1, 2, \ldots, 7$ are age-groups 15-19, 20-4, ..., 45-9, r_i is marital fertility rate of age-group i, n_i is natural fertility rate of age-group i, v_i is average exponential deviation between marital fertility rate of age-group i (which belong to 43 schedules used by Coale) and natural fertility rate of the same age-group, M is a parameter representing ratio of marital to natural fertility rate at age-group 20-4, and m is a parameter representing exponential deviation between marital and natural fertility rates at age-groups 25 and over.[3]

M and m are measures of the level of marital fertility schedule and the degree of fertility control within marriage over the age-range 25+.

Corresponding to any given age schedule of marital fertility are unique M and m. And, conversely, any given M and m imply a unique schedule. Thus, the two parameters are capable of fully describing the age schedule of marital fertility. The higher the level of the schedule, the greater the M; the larger the degree of fertility control within marriage, the greater the m. When $M = 1$, the level of the marital fertility schedule equals that of the natural fertility schedule, and when $m = 0$, the degree of fertility control equals that under natural fertility (that is, the control is absent). Figure 15.1 illustrates how the levels and degrees of control of marital fertility, the latter being reflected by the shapes of the schedules, are related to M and m.

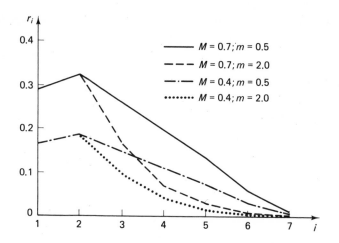

FIGURE 15.1 *Age schedules of marital fertility underlied by different combinations of M and m*

In the present analysis, M and m are used as dependent fertility variables for the early (20-4) and intermediate (25-34) childbearing years, respectively. The analysis is based on the premise that the relationship between overall marital fertility, measured, say, by total marital fertility rate, and factors affecting it is linear. The implication of the premise is that the relationships between M and m, on the one hand, and factors affecting them, on the other, are respectively linear and non-linear. (This is the consequence of the linear and non-linear relationship existing between total marital fertility rate on the one hand, and M and m on the other.) The use of the premise as the basis of the analysis requires a transformation of m. Figure 15.2 illustrates that the logarithmic transformation is an appropriate one. It shows that, if the total marital fertility rate, $TMFR$, is assumed to be a linear function of an independent variable, X, then the relationship between ln m and X is approximately linear. This approximate linearity between ln m and X holds irrespective of values of M or parameters in the linear equation relating *TMFR* and X.

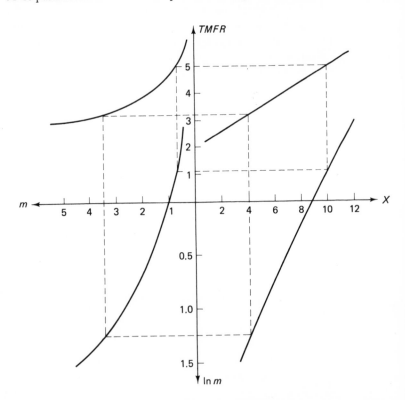

FIGURE 15.2 *Illustration of approximately linear relation between ln m and X when relation between TMFR and X is linear; TMFR = 2.0 + 0.3X and M = 0.6*

Recent Temporal and Regional Fertility Variations

The intermediate to low fertility that prevails in present-day Yugoslavia is a consequence of a secular fertility decline shared by all regions.[4] In the more developed regions, the fertility decline probably started around the turn of the century and gradually brought fertility down to low levels by the mid-1950s.[5,6] In all the more developed regions, except Slovenia, further decline brought fertility below replacement level by 1970 (see Table 15.1). In the less developed regions, the decline began much later, probably around or just after the Second World War. The date of onset varied

TABLE 15.1 Total fertility rates, 1950–75, and marital fertility indices for non-agricultural sectors, 1971: Yugoslavia and regions

Year/ fertility index	Yugoslavia	More developed regions				Bosnia-Herzegovina	Less developed regions		
		Croatia	Inner Serbia	Slovenia	Voivodina		Kosovo	Macedonia	Montenegro
Total fertility rates, 1950–75									
1950	4.30	3.24	3.72	3.15	3.43	5.89	9.74	6.64	5.52
1955	3.37	2.63	2.50	2.59	2.50	4.82	7.91	5.54	4.76
1960	2.88	2.19	2.12	2.19	2.19	4.06	7.35	4.38	3.77
1965	2.71	2.21	2.05	2.45	2.13	3.51	6.11	3.79	3.13
1970	2.29	1.81	1.87	2.11	1.70	2.67	5.51	2.98	2.63
1975	2.28	1.92	1.90	2.17	1.82	2.37	5.28	2.71	2.35
Marital fertility indices for non-agricultural sectors, 1971									
TMFRt	2.74	2.12	1.81	2.87	1.83	2.90	3.90	3.27	3.45
M	0.56	0.53	0.46	0.64	0.47	0.65	0.72	0.71	0.72
m	1.51	2.36	2.48	1.79	2.52	1.85	1.17	1.67	1.57

from one region to another, but once under way, the decline was rapid. As a result, in all less developed regions, except Kosovo, fertility was at or approaching a low level by 1975.

During the 1950s and 1960s, in all regions, the fertility decline was caused almost entirely by a reduction in marital fertility. Changes in nuptiality, confined mainly to the more developed regions, tended to temper the impact of marital fertility reduction on the overall fertility decline (Macura, 1980, 1982). Gradually, they brought about a convergence of the proportions of women married in the different regions. Simultaneously, the proportion of population in non-agricultural sectors increased sharply. As a result, variations in non-agricultural marital fertility emerged as a principal determinant of overall fertility variations. It is for this reason that the present analysis focuses on non-agricultural marital fertility and its determinants.

Marital fertility in non-agricultural sectors, represented by a truncated total marital fertility rate, *TMFRt*, was relatively low in 1971.[7] In the country as a whole, it varied considerably across the regions, being consistently lower in the more developed ones (Table 15.1). In Croatia, Inner Serbia and Vojvodina, it was very low even by contemporary European standards.[8] Behind these variations in marital fertility were equally pronounced variations in levels and age patterns of marital fertility schedules, represented by M and m (Table 15.1). M varied within a broad range, from 0.46 in Inner Serbia to 0.72 in Kosovo and Montenegro; m ranged between 1.17 in Kosovo and 2.52 in Vojvodina.

Data Sources

Information used in the present study comes from a data base developed for the construction of the demographic-economic simulation model Bachue-Yugoslavia (Macura *et al.*, 1977). The data base draws on three statistical sources: the 1971 Census of Population and Housing, the 1970–2 Vital Statistics and 1968–71 secondary socio-economic data. It was developed on the premise that, whenever feasible, various statistics should be specially processed to remove major limitations in official tabulations.

The data refer to 79 demographic regions of Yugoslavia, defined as geographical units consisting of contiguous communes which share similar socio-economic and demographic characteristics (Centar za demografska istrazivanja, 1963).[9] They come mostly from the 1971 census, by far the richest of the three sources. Census-based data were generated by utilising information on various personal characteristics – age, sex, marital status, residence, economic sector, employment, unemployment, educational attainment, school attendance and ethnicity – and those on ever-born and living children, as well as housing. Data obtained from the vital statistics are those on legitimate births. Information drawn from published socio-economic statistics deals with employment change, children in day-care centres and indicators of the availability of medical services pertaining to childbearing.

Births and infant-deaths in the 1970–2 vital statistics were erroneously distributed between the non-agricultural and agricultural sectors. This made it impossible to obtain marital fertility and infant mortality measures directly from tabulations based on individual vital statistics returns. They were therefore reached by indirect estimation. M and m were derived by a technique expressly developed for this purpose (Macura, 1979) using the census and vital statistics. Infant mortality rates were obtained by applying the Sullivan age model (Sullivan, 1972) to the census data.

The data used in the analysis refer, as a rule, to the non-agricultural sectors. Where necessary, they reflect characteristics of married couples in their early and intermediate childbearing years. Though prepared with caution, the data suffer from some limitations. They provide only proxies and not direct measures of certain key theoretical concepts. In some instances, it is necessary to make use of variables which proxy for two or more concepts, and, conversely, some concepts are approximated by more than one variable. Separate estimation of micro and macro effects is precluded. Last, but not least, collinearity among certain variables tends to be strong.

THEORETICAL FRAMEWORK

In view of the growing evidence which suggests that reproduction and other outcomes of household behaviour are interdependent, marital fertility and employment of married women are treated as jointly determined. The underlying theoretical premise is that forces shaping marital reproduction and married women's employment at the community level are broadly those operating at the household level. The theoretical framework advanced here draws on the 'new home-economics' but elaborates on determinants which are not part of this approach. Thus, it postulates that both childbearing and female employment are affected by incomes, costs and preferences, and by social, cultural and psychological factors. The framework sees children as 'normal goods', but considers the assumption of invariability of preferences among the couples overly restrictive. In the spirit of the 'social determinants school of thought', this framework recognises that preferences may well vary across communities, for social and cultural reasons. It further recognises that responses of couples to various factors concerning reproduction and female employment may also differ across the communities, for the same reasons. Variables considered important in influencing marital fertility and employment of married women in the Yugoslav setting are defined in Table 15.2 and discussed below. Also shown in the table are means and standard deviations of the variables.

Hypotheses derived from the theoretical considerations are tested separately for the early (20-4) and intermediate (25-34) childbearing years by estimating simultaneous-equation models of marital fertility and married women's employment for the two age-groups. The endogenous fertility variables of the two models are M and m, respectively. The estimation of the separate models for the two age-groups is expected to reveal that factors affecting fertility and female employment differ according to the stage in the life-cycle under consideration. For example, one may plausibly expect that decisions concerning first- and possibly second-order births, most of which occur during the early childbearing years, are shaped by forces that differ, at least partially, from those influencing decisions regarding higher-order births.

Theoretical Determinants of Marital Fertility

The income that married couples in their early and intermediate child-bearing years command in a community consists largely of earnings accruing to husbands and working wives. In the absence of a direct measure, the income of married men is proxied by their educational attainment expressed in terms of the average number of grades completed (denoted by EDM 20-4 and EDM 25-34, for the early and intermediate childbearing years, respectively). The net effect of the husband's education variable is unclear. On the assumption that children are 'normal goods', the effect of male education on marital fertility is expected to be positive.[10] However, male education may also proxy for other factors, such as preferences for fewer and better-educated children, and, hence, a negative effect of the variable should not be ruled out. The income accruing to wives, and the pecuniary and psychic costs which couples sustain as a result of wives' employment, depend largely on the extent to which wives work. Hence, their net income is proxied by the proportion of married women who are gainfully employed (denoted by EMW 20-4 and EMW 25-34 for the early and intermediate childbearing years, respectively). The effect of female employment on marital fertility could be positive or negative, depending on comparative strengths of income and cost effects.

Direct child-costs born by parents consist largely of educational- and nurture-costs. The former are comparatively small in Yugoslavia, as education is public and largely free. Nevertheless, the direct costs do depend directly on the extent of schooling – longer schooling implies a longer period during which both nurture- and educational-costs are incurred. The changes in these costs are proxied here by a variable measuring the changes in the extent of secondary and tertiary schooling across younger adult cohorts. The variable, denoted by SCHOOLING, is the ratio of the proportion of secondary and tertiary school graduates among persons aged 20-4 to the proportion among persons aged 30-4. Since parents are likely to desire fewer children when they anticipate future increases in direct child-costs resulting from the expansion of child-education, SCHOOLING is predicted to have a negative effect on marital fertility.[11]

Opportunity-costs of children largely equal net income (income less employment-related costs) foregone on the part of women not working because of children. Average education of married women (EDW 20-5 and EDW 25-34) is taken to proxy for the opportunity-costs of children, and is expected to have a depressing effect on marital fertility. This effect is also expected because married women with more education probably know more about modern contraceptives, use more efficient methods, and are likely to follow higher standards of childbearing, entailing greater child-costs.

Available evidence (D. Freedman, 1975) suggest that consumption levels and aspirations have a negative effect on fertility. The effect presumably arises and becomes diffused as production and marketing of modern consumer-goods, primarily durable, spread. This process was well under way in Yugoslavia during the 1960s, when the pattern of industrial production was shifting towards consumer-good and away from producer-good industries. The variable defined as dwellings in square metres per capita in urban areas (DWELLING) proxies both for consumption of one of the major durables – housing – and for consumption of related products – furniture, household appliances and the like. The variable is expected to be negatively related to marital fertility.[12]

To reduce incompatibility between women's work away from home and childbearing, parents in non-agricultural sectors in Yugoslavia rely mainly on day-care centres. When the day-care services are readily available (and inexpensive), they make childbearing easier and presumably encour-

TABLE 15.2 *Definitions, means and standard deviations of variables*

Symbol	Definition	Mean	Standard deviation
M1	Coale's M	0.5870	0.1183
M2	Coale's m	2.6825	1.5565
EMW 20–4	Proportion employed among married women aged 20–4	0.3825	0.1656
EMW 25–34	Proportion employed among married women aged 25–34	0.3788	0.1660
EDM 20–4	Average education[a] of married men aged 20–4	8.5075	0.6768
EDM 25–34	Average education of married men aged 25–34	8.2801	0.7385
EDW 20–4	Average education of married women aged 20–4	7.8207	1.1911
EDW 25–34	Average education of married women aged 25–34	6.2772	1.4241
UNEMPW 20–4	Unemployment rate among married women aged 20–4	0.0620	0.0461
UNEMPW 25–34	Unemployment rate among married women aged 25–34	0.0124	0.0093
SCHOOLING	Ratio of proportion of secondary and tertiary school graduates among persons aged 20–4 to the proportion among persons aged 30–4	1.6922	0.2618
DWELLING	Dwellings in square metres per capita in urban areas	13.2397	2.2543
DAYCARE	Proportion of children aged 0–4 in day-care centres	0.1241	0.1073
DIVORCE	Ratio of currently divorced to ever-married women aged 25–44	0.0350	0.0159
INFMORT	Infant mortality rate	0.0445	0.0249

Variable			
GYNAE	Gynaecologists and obstetricians per thousand married women aged 20–44	0.5428	0.2400
EMGROWTH	Employment growth rate	0.0403	0.0229
SHARE	Share of employment in industries and services having 40 per cent or more women workers	0.4149	0.0767
CROAT	Dummy variable indicating if demographic region belongs to regions predominantly inhabited by Croats (1 if yes; 0 if no)[b]		
MUSLIM	Dummy variable indicating if demographic region belongs to regions predominantly inhabited by Muslims (1 if yes; 0 if no)		
SLOVEN	Dummy variable indicating if demographic region belongs to regions predominantly inhabited by Slovenians (1 if yes; 0 if no)		
ALBTURK	Dummy variable indicating if demographic region belongs to regions predominantly inhabited by Albanians and Turks (1 if yes; 0 if no)		
MACEDON	Dummy variable indicating if demographic region belongs to regions predominantly inhabited by Macedonians (1 if yes; 0 if no)		
HUNGAR	Dummy variable indicating if demographic region belongs to regions predominantly inhabited by Hungarians (1 if yes; 0 if no)		
MONTENEG	Dummy variable indicating if demographic region belongs to regions predominantly inhabited by Montenegrins (1 if yes; 0 if no)		
TRAD	Dummy variable indicating if demographic region belongs to regions predominantly inhabited by 'traditional' ethnic groups (1 if yes; 0 if no)[c]		

[a] Average education is expressed in terms of the number of grades completed.
[b] Excluded group of demographic regions consists of regions predominantly inhabited by Serbs.
[c] Excluded class of demographic regions consists of regions predominantly inhabited by 'modern' ethnic groups.

age fertility. To examine whether this is indeed so, a variable measuring proportion of children in day-care centres (DAYCARE) is used.

Marriage instability can be expected to exert a negative effect on marital fertility. Couples living in unstable unions may be cautious about childbearing, for a variety of psychological reasons. Besides, the women may exercise caution since it is usually they who, after divorce, assume most of childrearing obligations and a disproportionate share of child-rearing costs. On the other hand, if remarriages are relatively frequent no matter whether divorcees have children or not, the constraints on childbearing in unstable unions are likely to be less severe. Therefore, *ceteris paribus*, one would expect marital fertility to be lower in communities where unions are comparatively unstable and/or remarriages among divorcees rare. This hypothesis is tested by employing the variable defined as the proportion of currently-divorced among ever-married women aged 25–44 (DIVORCED).

Among the three positive effects (physiological, insurance and replacement) that infant and early-childhood mortality may exert on fertility (Friedlander, 1977), only the replacement effect is likely to operate in non-agricultural sectors in Yugoslavia. This is so both because uncontrolled fertility and lengthy lactation are virtually non-existent, and because of the provision of universal old-age security. The variable INFMORT is used to test for the existence of this effect. Derived from census data on ever-born and living children of women aged 20–4, it represents infant and early-childhood mortality, lagged a few years.

Ethnic, linguistic and religious diversity is rather large in Yugoslavia. Social norms, values and mores are known to differ at least among certain socially and culturally distinct population groups. This socio-cultural diversity is probably associated with genuine differences in preferences among the groups. In order to test for these differences, demographic regions are classified into eight groups, namely those predominantly inhabited by Serbs, Croats, Muslims, Slovenians, Albanians and Turks, Macedonians, Hungarians, and Montenegrins, and seven dummy variables on the intercept – CROAT, MUSLIM, SLOVEN, ALBTURK, MACEDON, HUNGAR, MONTENEG – are defined and used; the excluded group of demographic regions consists of regions predominantly inhabited by Serbs.[13] The socio-cultural diversity is probably also associated with the differences in fertility responses on the part of the couples. To test for these differences, the eight groups are collapsed into two broader classes of regions, those predominantly inhabited by 'modern' and those inhabited by 'traditional' ethnic groups, and a single dummy variable on the slope, denoted by TRAD, is defined and used. Serbian, Croatian, Slovenian and

Hungarian groups are regarded as 'modern', Muslim, Albanian-Turkish, Macedonian and Montenegrin as 'traditional'. The dummy variable uses the 'modern' class as the excluded class.

Fertility determinants discussed so far are those considered to influence desired fertility. A partial exception is education of married women which, as stated earlier, probably proxies for knowledge, extent of use, and the use-effectiveness of modern contraceptives, among other things. Another variable which proxies for the use of modern contraception is the variable defined as the ratio of the number of gynaecologists and obstetricians to married women in their reproductive years (GYNAE). The variable also proxies for access to treatment for infertility and induced abortion. The mix of these services is likely to raise fertility among some couples and reduce it among others. As a result, the net effect of the variable on marital fertility is not predictable.

Theoretical Determinants of Employment Participation of Married Women

One of the likely determinants of employment of married women is the income of married couples other than that earned by the women themselves. This income is approximated here by average education of married men (EDM 20-4 and EDM 25-34), both because the predominant type of family in non-agricultural sectors is the nuclear family, in which, as a rule, only adults work, and because the incomes of husbands are well approximated by their education. In communities where the average education level of married men is comparatively high, the women are probably less motivated to work in order to augment family resources.

Work at home on the part of women entails indirect costs, which are approximated by married women's average educational attainment (EDW 20-4 and EDW 25-34). The greater the costs, the stronger are incentives for women to work. It is therefore expected that education of married women has a positive effect on their employment. The same effect is also expected because education, in addition to developing skills, enhances preferences for career work and possibly taste for women's economic independence *vis-à-vis* men. In addition, higher educational attainment, as a rule, promises more gratifying jobs and thus, probably, further contributes to higher employment.

The extent to which women in a community are employed is to a large measure influenced by conditions prevailing in the local labour-market. If jobs are relatively scarce, then the proportion of employed women is likely to be low. This is mainly the consequence of women's status as secondary workers. The relative scarcity of jobs is measured by the unemployment rate of married women (UNEMPW 20-4 and UNEMPW 25-34). On the other hand, if employment opportunities expand rapidly, women are likely to benefit. The expansion of employment opportunities in the labour-market is proxied by the employment growth rate (EMGROWTH). In addition, if the industry mix in the community favours women, then the proportion of employed women should be relatively high. The variable defined as the share of employment in industries and services that predominantly hire female labour (SHARE) represents the industry mix. Our expectation is that the unemployment rate is negatively related, and that the employment growth rate and the industry mix variable are positively related to married women's employment.

In most circumstances, childbearing and childrearing are incompatible with women's work away from home. At the same time, they entail costs and consequently motivate women to work and help meet the costs. The strengths of these two opposite effects depend on the circumstances under which couples live and work, and the net effect of reproduction on married women's employment can not be predicted *a priori*. To assess the effect, M1 and M2 are used as variables explaining variations in employment of married women in their early and intermediate childbearing years.

Expanding production and marketing of modern consumer-goods in the 1960s might have affected not only reproduction but also female employment. Adoption of new consumption norms and rising consumption aspirations could have strengthened preferences for market-work among the married women, since it was only through higher incomes that the new norms could be followed and aspirations fulfilled. Therefore, variations in married women's employment in the early 1970s may be partly explained by the differences in consumption levels, proxied by dwellings per captia (DWELLING).

Provision of child-care services in a community, as hypothesised earlier, reduces incompatibility between market-work of mothers and childrearing. Hence, when child-care services (DAYCARE) are more readily available in a community, proportions working among married women can be expected to be higher.

The marital instability and the likelihood of remarriage may influence female employment as well as fertility. As alimony payments are typically scanty in Yugoslavia, women living in unstable unions may be obliged to work to assume a steady income. Therefore, it is possible that the proportion of currently-divorced among ever-married women (DIVORCE) is positively related to married women's employment.

Social and cultural diversity in Yugoslavia probably influences employment of married women for the same reason that it affects marital fertility. Therefore, the same dummies used in the fertility equations are used to capture effects of this diversity on married women's employment. In particular, the dummies on the intercept are used to capture probable differences in preferences for market-work, and the dummy on the slope to test for differential female-employment responses.

MODEL SPECIFICATIONS AND EMPIRICAL RESULTS

Model Specifications

Based on theoretical considerations presented in the previous section, two models of simultaneous determination of marital fertility and employment of married women are postulated for early and for intermediate childbearing years. Results presented below are obtained by estimating the two models, referred to as specifications A and B. Specification A, which includes all relevant variables, is as follows.

(i) For the early childbearing years (20-4):

M1 $= f$ (EMW 20-4,   EDM 20-4,   TRAD. EDM 20-4,   EDW 20-4, TRAD. EDW 20-4,   SCHOOLING,   TRAD. SCHOOLING, DWELLING,   TRAD. DWELLING,   DAYCARE,   TRAD. DAYCARE,   DIVORCE,   TRAD. DIVORCE,   INFMORT, TRAD. INFMORT,   GYNAE,   TRAD. GYNAE,   CROAT, MUSLIM,   SLOVEN,   ALBTURK,   MACEDON,   HUNGAR, MONTENEG),

EMW 20-4 $= f$ (M1,   EDM 20-4,   TRAD. EDM 20-4,   EDW 20-4,   TRAD. EDW   20-4,   UNEMPW   20-4,   TRAD.   UNEMPW   20-4, DWELLING,   TRAD. DWELLING,   DAYCARE,   TRAD. DAYCARE,   DIVORCE,   TRAD. DIVORCE,   EMGROWTH, TRAD. EMGROWTH,   SHARE,   TRAD. SHARE,   CROAT, MUSLIM,   SLOVEN,   ALBTURK,   MACEDON,   HUNGAR, MONTENEG).

(ii) For the intermediate childbearing years (25-34):

$$\ln M2 = f(\text{EMW 25-34, EDM 25-34, TRAD. EDM 25-34, EDW 25-34,}$$
TRAD. EDW 25-34,   SCHOOLING,   TRAD. SCHOOLING,
DWELLING,   TRAD. DWELLING,   DAYCARE,   TRAD.
DAYCARE,   DIVORCE,   TRAD. DIVORCE,   INFMORT,
TRAD. INFMORT,   GYNAE,   TRAD. GYNAE,   CROAT,
MUSLIM,   SLOVEN,   ALBTURK,   MACEDON,   HUNGAR,
MONTENEG),

$$\text{EMW 25-34} = f(\ln M2,   \text{EDM 25-34,   TRAD. EDM 25-34,   EDW 25-34,}$$
TRAD. EDW 25-34, UNEMPW 25-34, TRAD. UNEMPW 25-34,
DWELLING,   TRAD. DWELLING,   DAYCARE,   TRAD.
DAYCARE,   DIVORCE,   TRAD. DIVORCE,   EMGROWTH,
TRAD. EMGROWTH,   SHARE,   TRAD. SHARE,   CROAT,
MUSLIM,   SLOVEN,   ALBTURK,   MACEDON,   HUNGAR,
MONTENEG).[14]

Specification B differs from specification A in so far as it excludes some variables included in A. Excluded variables are those which, upon inspection of coefficients of specification A, appeared as unlikely determinants of marital fertility and/or employment of married women.

The models were estimated by two-stage least squares. Results for marital fertility and female employment are discussed separately.

Marital Fertility Results

The results (Tables 15.3 and 15.4) largely confirm the hypotheses advanced in the above section concerning the effect of various factors on fertility behaviour within marriage.[15,16] Thus, they provide fairly strong support for the hypothesis on the positive income effect. With one notable exception, educational attainment of married men is positively related to marital fertility. For the intermediate childbearing years, the results clearly reveal the positive effect and suggest that the effect probably differs between the 'modern' and 'traditional' ethnic groups. This is implied by the negative and highly significant coefficient of EDM 25-34 in both specifications; the coefficient suggests the positive effect of male education on marital fertility (negative effect on *m*) in 'modern' ethnic groups. It is further implied by the coefficient of TRAD. EDM 25-34, which is positive and smaller in absolute size than the respective coefficient

TABLE 15.3 *Regressions on marital fertility during early childbearing years: dependent variable, M1 (t values in brackets)*

Explanatory variables	Specification	
	A	B
EMW 20-4	0.477***	0.455***
	(3.14)	(3.03)
EDM 20-4	0.058	0.058*
	(1.42)	(1.69)
TRAD. EDM 20-4	−0.129**	−0.100**
	(2.15)	(2.20)
EDW 20-4	−0.100**	−0.084**
	(2.51)	(3.03)
TRAD. EDW 20-4	0.013	—
	(0.23)	
SCHOOLING	0.029	—
	(0.44)	
TRAD. SCHOOLING	0.069	—
	(0.68)	
DWELLING	−0.034***	−0.034***
	(2.68)	(2.98)
TRAD. DWELLING	0.039**	0.028
	(1.80)	(1.49)
DAYCARE	0.368**	0.324**
	(2.30)	(2.34)
TRAD. DAYCARE	−0.729	—
	(1.26)	
DIVORCE	−5.044***	−4.813***
	(4.24)	(6.07)
TRAD. DIVORCE	11.187**	6.134**
	(2.36)	(2.46)
INFMORT	−0.446	—
	(0.29)	
TRAD. INFMORT	0.261	—
	(0.13)	
GYNAE	0.059	—
	(1.14)	

TABLE 15.3 (*continued*)

Explanatory variables	Specification	
	A	B
TRAD. GYNAE	−0.024 (0.17)	—
CROAT	0.027 (0.71)	0.023 (0.68)
MUSLIM	−0.014 (0.03)	0.225 (0.64)
SLOVEN	0.002 (0.03)	0.006 (0.10)
ALBTURK	0.267 (0.52)	0.384 (1.01)
MACEDON	0.278 (0.55)	0.411 (1.04)
HUNGAR	0.285 (0.57)	0.473 (1.25)
MONTENEG	−0.005 (0.07)	−0.001 (0.02)
CONSTANT	1.214*** (3.49)	1.165*** (4.97)
R^2 based on instruments	0.84	0.82
F	11.41***	18.11***
DF	54	62

*** Significant at the 0.01 level
** Significant at the 0.05 level
* Significant at the 0.10 level

of EDM 25–34 in either specification, but significant only in specification B. This indicates that it is fairly likely that the effect of male education in the 'traditional' groups is positive but weaker than that in the 'modern' groups; the size of the coefficient pertaining to married men's education in 'traditional' groups is the sum of the coefficients of EDM 25–34 and TRAD. EDM 25–34.

TABLE 15.4 *Regressions on marital fertility during intermediate childbearing years: dependent variable, M2 (t values in brackets)*

Explanatory variables	Specification	
	A	B
EMW 25–34	−1.605*** (2.45)	−1.695** (2.63)
EDM 25–34	−0.756*** (6.44)	−0.674*** (7.66)
TRAD. EDM 25–34	0.417 (1.52)	0.204* (1.81)
EDW 25–34	0.486*** (3.62)	0.503*** (5.13)
TRAD. EDW 25–34	−0.015 (0.06)	—
SCHOOLING	−0.239 (0.86)	—
TRAD. SCHOOLING	0.722* (1.96)	0.538** (2.53)
DWELLING	0.099** (2.11)	0.088** (2.56)
TRAD. DWELLING	−0.054 (0.59)	—
DAYCARE	−1.116* (1.87)	−1.173** (2.38)
TRAD. DAYCARE	−0.126 (0.05)	—
DIVORCE	10.967** (2.26)	12.031*** (3.57)
TRAD. DIVORCE	−12.925 (0.71)	—
INFMORT	−0.998 (0.18)	—
TRAD. INFMORT	−10.203 (1.47)	−10.161*** (2.71)
GYNAE	0.079 (0.41)	—

TABLE 15.4 (*continued*)

Explanatory variables	Specification	
	A	B
TRAD. GYNAE	0.138 (0.26)	—
CROAT	−0.268* (1.89)	−0.261** (2.18)
MUSLIM	−2.975 (1.57)	−2.028* (1.78)
SLOVEN	−0.427* (1.74)	−0.328 (1.59)
ALBTURK	−2.550 (1.27)	−1.310 (1.03)
MACEDON	−3.385* (1.74)	−2.184* (1.78)
HUNGAR	−3.450* (1.81)	−2.421** (2.04)
MONTENEG	−0.687** (2.65)	−0.589** (2.52)
CONSTANT	3.675** (2.66)	2.631*** (3.60)
R^2 based on instruments	0.85	0.84
F	12.33***	19.88***
DF	54	62

*** Significant at the 0.01 level
** Significant at the 0.05 level
* Significant at the 0.10 level

During the early childbearing years, the support for the hypothesis is weaker. The positive effect of married men's education is revealed only among the 'modern' ethnic groups. Among the 'traditional' groups, the variable exerts a negative effect. It could be that the education of married men in the 'traditional' groups represents a preference for fewer children, at least in the early years of childbearing, in addition to their income, and that the negative influence of the former factor is stronger than the positive effect of the latter.

Additional support for the positive income effect is provided by the results pertaining to employment of married women. These suggest that the income of married women, represented by the proportion employed among the women, has a positive effect on marital fertility. In other words, the positive effect of income accruing to married women appears to outweigh the negative effect of pecuniary and pyschic costs associated with their employment. This applies both to the early and the intermediate childbearing years. However, the results do not permit the establishment of whether the positive net effect exists in both the 'modern' and 'traditional' ethnic groups.

Changes in direct child-costs apparently do not affect fertility decisions within marriage in the early childbearing years. This is suggested by results of specification A regarding the SCHOOLING variable. These changes do not affect fertility decisions during the intermediate years among the 'modern' ethnic groups either. Only among the 'traditional' groups do changes in direct child-costs appear to exert expected negative effects on marital fertility in the intermediate years. The absence of the effect in the early childbearing years is perhaps not surprising, since it is plausible that at the early stage of the family-building cycle (when mostly first-order children are born), couples are not concerned with the long-term cost implications of their fertility decisions. It is, however, surprising that the effect is non-existent at the intermediate childbearing years among the 'modern' ethnic groups.

Average educational level of married women, as expected, is negatively related to marital fertility, at the early as well as intermediate childbearing years, and for the 'modern' as well as 'traditional' ethnic groups.

The results provide ample confirmation of the hypotheses concerning the influence on marital fertility of consumption levels (DWELLING) and availability of child day-care services (DAYCARE). The former tends to discourage, and the latter to encourage, childbearing during both the early and intermediate years among the 'modern' as well as 'traditional' groups. Similarly, marriage instability (DIVORCE) usually influences marital fertility negatively. The exception is the positive effect of DIVORCE in the early childbearing years among the 'traditional' ethnic groups.

Infant-mortality (INFMORT) does not seem to influence fertility decisions during the early childbearing years, or during the intermediate years in the 'modern' groups. It is only during the intermediate years among the 'traditional' groups that infant-mortality has the predicted positive effect. This result of specification B was achieved, however, only after INFMORT, which happens to be highly collinear with TRAD. INFMORT, was excluded (first-order correlation coefficient between the two is 0.92). These results suggest that the replacement effect is absent at the very beginning of the reproductive period, and that it exists in the intermediate years only among 'traditional' groups, where infant-mortality is still relatively high.

It was argued above that dummies on the intercept are likely to capture effects of socially- and culturally-related differences in preferences. The results indicate that they do so, and also that the effects are not all that widespread. In the early childbearing years, the effects appear to be absent. This is probably not surprising, since socially- and culturally-related preferences are much more likely to operate beyond the early years. In the intermediate years, it seems that couples in several ethnic groups favour higher marital fertility (less control) than those in the reference group, Serbs. This is clearly true of couples belonging to Croatian, Macedonian, Hungarian and Montenegrin groups.

Lastly, access to various medical services pertaining to reproduction, proxied by the number of gynaecologists and obstetricians per thousand married women (GYNAE), appears to have no bearing on marital fertility. If these services do influence reproduction, their positive and negative effects seem to be cancelling out.

Employment Participation Results

The results (Tables 15.5 and 15.6) are consistent with some of the hypotheses advanced. As hypothesised, income other than that accruing to married women, proxied by the educational attainment of married men, has a negative effect on employment of married women. This is true in both the early and intermediate childbearing years. In addition, the effect differs markedly between the 'modern' and 'traditional' ethnic groups.

The average educational attainment of married women is positively related to their employment during both the early and intermediate childbearing years, and its effect differs between the 'modern' and 'traditional' groups.

Labour-market conditions are also found to have a significant bearing on employment of married women. Scarcity of jobs, proxied by unemployment rates, has a predicted negative effect on female employment. In the early childbearing years, this is true among the 'modern' ethnic groups, but seemingly not among the 'traditional' ones. In the intermediate childbearing years, the negative effect is found for both types of groups. Employment expansion, proxied by employment growth rate, has a predicted positive effect, but only during the early childbearing years among the 'traditional' groups. Presence of industries and services favouring female labour also has the expected positive effect during both the early

TABLE 15.5 *Regressions on employment of married women during early childbearing years: dependent variable, EMW 20-4 (t values in brackets)*

Explanatory variables	Specification	
	A	B
M1	0.695 (1.26)	0.060 (0.45)
EDM 20-4	−0.094** (2.29)	−0.102*** (4.25)
TRAD. EDM 20-4	0.129* (1.80)	0.084** (2.09)
EDW 20-4	0.169*** (4.88)	0.152*** (6.40)
TRAD. EDW 20-4	−0.082 (1.17)	−0.119*** (3.58)
UNEMPW 20-4	−0.882** (2.97)	−0.894*** (4.54)
TRAD. UNEMPW 20-4	0.785 (0.94)	1.039* (1.82)
DWELLING	0.028 (1.21)	—
TRAD. DWELLING	−0.038 (1.51)	—
DAYCARE	−0.339 (1.23)	—
TRAD. DAYCARE	0.408 (0.63)	—
DIVORCE	3.084 (1.17)	—
TRAD. DIVORCE	−5.454 (1.10)	—
EMGROWTH	0.055 (0.13)	—
TRAD. EMGROWTH	1.478 (1.43)	1.425** (2.42)
SHARE	0.190 (0.70)	0.460*** (4.28)

TABLE 15.5 (*continued*)

Explanatory variables	Specification	
	A	B
TRAD. SHARE	−0.072 (0.20)	—
CROAT	−0.030 (0.52)	0.026 (1.20)
MUSLIM	0.097 (0.21)	0.034 (0.18)
SLOVEN	0.122 (1.33)	0.219*** (6.33)
ALBTURK	−0.143 (0.29)	−0.101 (0.49)
MACEDON	−0.100 (0.19)	−0.017 (0.08)
HUNGAR	−0.164 (0.31)	−0.633 (0.30)
MONTENEG	0.010 (0.13)	0.026 (0.53)
CONSTANT	−1.023 (1.39)	−0.134 (0.70)
R^2 based on instruments	0.91	0.94
F	22.51***	64.49***
DF	54	62

***Significant at the 0.01 level
** Significant at the 0.05 level
* Significant at the 0.10 level

and intermediate years. The effect seems to vary between the 'modern' and 'traditional' groups in the intermediate years.

However, childbearing and childrearing appear to be unrelated to employment of married women. Similarly, consumption levels, availability of day-care services and marital instability are consistently insignificant in estimated equations. It is likely that all this is the consequence of the use of aggregate data, which makes it impossible to capture effects of the variables which may be influential at the micro level.

TABLE 15.6 *Regressions on employment of married women during intermediate childbearing years: dependent variable, EMW 25-34 (t values in brackets)*

Explanatory variables	Specification	
	A	B
ln M2	0.003 (0.04)	−0.012 (0.29)
EDM 25-34	−0.089** (2.46)	−0.085*** (2.73)
TRAD. EDM 25-34	0.112** (2.11)	0.060 (1.56)
EDW 25-34	0.122*** (5.28)	0.135*** (6.10)
TRAD. EDW 25-34	−0.103* (1.78)	−0.048 (1.52)
UNEMPW 25-34	−1.888* (1.89)	−2.243*** (2.95)
TRAD. UNEMPW 25-34	0.816 (0.40)	—
DWELLING	−0.007 (0.68)	—
TRAD. DWELLING	−0.007 (0.41)	—
DAYCARE	0.115 (0.84)	—
TRAD. DAYCARE	0.565 (1.00)	—
DIVORCE	0.589 (0.60)	—
TRAD. DIVORCE	−0.321 (0.10)	—
EMGROWTH	0.244 (0.92)	—
TRAD. EMGROWTH	0.588 (0.93)	—
SHARE	0.623*** (5.52)	0.560*** (5.74)

TABLE 15.6 (*continued*)

Explanatory variables	Specification	
	A	B
TRAD. SHARE	−0.383	−0.320*
	(1.63)	(1.81)
CROAT	0.056	0.013
	(1.63)	(0.65)
MUSLIM	−0.173	−0.081
	(0.62)	(0.39)
SLOVEN	0.142***	0.086**
	(2.67)	(2.06)
ALBTURK	−0.302	−0.161
	(1.03)	(0.74)
MACEDON	−0.204	−0.100
	(0.67)	(0.49)
HUNGAR	−0.239	−0.148
	(0.83)	(0.69)
MONTENEG	0.013	−0.008
	(0.22)	(0.17)
CONSTANT	0.150	0.036
	(0.67)	(0.19)
R^2 based on instruments	0.96	0.95
F	52.89***	88.96***
DF	54	63

***Significant at the 0.01 level
** Significant at the 0.05 level
* Significant at the 0.10 level

Finally, concerning the influence of socially- and culturally-related preferences for market-work among married women, one specific finding stands out clearly. Employment among Slovenian women tends to be higher than for other groups, for reasons which are apparently social and cultural in nature. This is evident during the early as well as intermediate childbearing years.

SUMMARY

The purpose of this analysis was to account for intercommunity variations in period measures of marital fertility and employment of married women during the early (20-4) and intermediate (25-34) childbearing years in non-agricultural sectors in Yugoslavia in the early 1970s.

Results pertaining to marital fertility indicate that a number of factors ranging from economic to cultural, account for variations in the level as well as degree of control of marital fertility. They suggest that income of married men, proxied by their educational attainment, encourages reproduction during the intermediate childbearing years. The results are less conclusive for the early childbearing years, largely because of the negative effect of married men's education among the 'traditional' ethnic groups.

Contrary to numerous empirical findings, work away from home among married women appears to be positively associated with childbearing. The positive effect of income earned by working wives in the non-agricultural sectors in Yugoslavia is obviously stronger than the negative effect deriving from employment-related pecuniary and psychic costs. This may well be the consequence of an almost universal job-security as well as prolonged paid maternity leave enjoyed by working women in the non-agricultural sectors.

Changes in direct child-costs are found to have the predicted impact on fertility decisions during the intermediate childbearing years, though only among the 'traditional' ethnic groups. Opportunity-costs of children, as measured by the inadequate education proxy, also appear to exert a negative effect on childbearing during the early and intermediate years, in both 'modern' and 'traditional' groups.

Further, it seems fairly certain that consumption of modern consumer-goods does lead to lower fertility, by altering preferences for children versus goods, and that availability of day-care services encourages reproduction. This applies to both segments of the childbearing span and to both types of ethnic group. Furthermore, marriage instability and likelihood of remarriage appear to exert expected negative and positive effects on childbearing, respectively, with the exception of the 'traditional' ethnic groups for the early childbearing years.

Infant mortality affects marital fertility in the predicted fashion, but only during the intermediate childbearing years among the 'traditional' groups. Availability of medical services pertaining to reproduction apparently does not influence childbearing, which is somewhat surprising in view of the rather widespread resort to induced abortion in Yugoslavia.

Preferences related to social and cultural traits have a bearing on child-bearing, though only during the intermediate childbearing years.

Results referring to employment of married women indicate that the extent to which women work largely depends on incomes, costs and labour-market conditions. Income other than that earned by the women themselves is inversely related to their employment. Costs of economic inactivity on their part tend to encourage their employment; this is suggested by the positive effect of married women's education on their employment. The same result seems to indicate that taste for career-work and education-related attractions of market-work are stronger among better-educated women.

Lack of employment opportunities tends to discourage married women's employment, except among women during the early childbearing years in the 'traditional' ethnic groups. Contrary to this, employment expansion tends to encourage it, but only among the women just referred to. The presence of industries and services which largely rely on female labour is beneficial to employment among all groups of women. However, other factors considered as likely determinants of married women's employment are found to have no bearing on it. The exceptions are socially- and culturally-related preferences for market-work.

In conclusion, minor exceptions aside, the analysis shows that incomes and costs influence marital fertility and married women's employment in non-agricultural sectors of Yugoslavia in the way predicted by the 'new home-economics'. However, it also indicates that fertility behaviour is affected by a number of other factors – psychological, social and cultural – some of which seem to operate through preferences. Thus, variables which do not typically appear in empirical studies of fertility behaviour – those representing consumption levels, day-care services, psychological and economic motives against childbearing resulting from marriage instability and likelihood of remarriage – all appear to be important fertility determinants. The analysis further shows that labour-market conditions have a rather substantial impact on married women's employment behaviour, together with a limited influence of social and cultural factors. It also suggests that some of the factors, including childbearing and childrearing, do not affect this behaviour. It is possible, however, that the use of the community data made it impossible to uncover some of the effects that probably do exist at the individual level. In addition, specifications of the models that allow for estimation of separate effects for 'modern' and 'traditional' ethnic groups proved useful. The results do reveal that responses to the same factors differ to some extent among the two broad classes of ethnic groups. Furthermore, estimation of marital fertility and female employment models for the early and intermediate years separately revealed that some factors, notably changes in direct child-costs, infant-mortality and socially- and culturally-related preferences, affect reproduction only over one part of the childbearing age-span.

NOTES

1. Non-agricultural sectors are defined as all sectors except traditional, peasant agriculture. They include modern, socialised agriculture, which is a comparatively small sector.
2. For the discussion of the 'new home-economics' and alternative theoretical approaches to fertility determinants, see Chapter 2.
3. Originally, Coale proposed that estimates of the parameters, $\hat{M}$ and $\hat{m}$, of a given marital fertility schedule, r_i, $i = 1, 2, \ldots, 7$, be obtained in a stepwise fashion as follows:

$$\hat{M} = r_2/n_2$$

and

$$\hat{m} = (m_4 + m_5)/2,$$

where

$$m_i = (\ln(r_i/(Mn_i)))/v_i, \quad i = 4, 5$$

(see Coale, 1971). More recently, Coale and Trussell (1978) have proposed an alternative procedure which yields $\hat{M}$ and $\hat{m}$ simultaneously.
4. Yugoslavia consists of six federal republics: Bosnia-Herzegovina, Croatia, Macedonia, Montenegro, Serbia and Slovenia. Serbia consists of autonomous provinces Kosovo and Vojvodina and the rest of the republic, Inner Serbia. Regions referred to above are republics other than Serbia and the three divisions of Serbia. Croatia, Inner Serbia, Slovenia and Voivodina are regarded as the more developed regions, Bosnia-Herzegovina, Kosovo, Macedonia and Montenegro as the less developed ones.
5. For simplicity of exposition, the following, somewhat arbitrary, definitions of fertility levels are used: low fertility is defined as that associated with total fertility rate $(TFR) \leqslant 2.5$, intermediate with $2.5 < TFR \leqslant 5.0$ and high with $TFR > 5.0$.
6. Reliable fertility data prior to 1950 are unavailable. Therefore, much of the writing on fertility-change before this year is based on educated guesses rather than facts.
7. $TMFRt$ is computed as the sum of five-year age-specific marital fertility rates from age 20 onwards, multiplied by 5. It does not reflect

fertility below 20, which pertains to a small number of women and can take on a wide range of values, depending on the frequency of premarital conceptions leading to marriage. Thus, *TMFRt* represents true marital fertility variations in a better way than the standard measure – total marital fertility rate.

8. Among 15 selected low-fertility national populations of Europe, only the German Democratic Republic had marital fertility (1974) below that of Croatia, Inner Serbia and Vojvodina (1971).

9. The commune is the smallest administrative unit in Yugoslavia.

10. Specifically, EDM 20-4 and EDM 25-34 are expected to have respectively positive and negative effects on M1 and M2, defined as Coale's *M* and *m* in Table 15.2.

11. Returns to education in Yugoslavia accrue as a rule to children and not parents since the children leave parental households once they complete their education and then enter the labour-force and marry. Therefore, outlays on rearing and educating children are typically viewed by parents as costs and not as investment.

12. For several reasons, however, the variable is an imperfect proxy. Firstly, due to data limitations, it refers to only the urban areas. Secondly, a part of housing construction in non-agricultural sectors is financed from public and not household sources. And thirdly, to some extent, the variable also represents physical dwelling space, which may be positively related to fertility.

13. Muslims, who are mainly of Serbian and Croatian origin, are defined as an ethnic group by the 1971 Census of Population and Housing.

14. To clarify how each of the two models is specific, let us consider a simple simultaneous-equation model with two endogenous variables, Y_1 and Y_2, four exogenous variables, X_1, X_2, X_3 and X_4, plus a dummy on the intercept, I and a dummy on the slope, S:

$$Y_1 = a_1 + b_1 Y_2 + (c_1 + d_1 S)X_1 + (e_1 + f_1 S)X_2 + g_1 I,$$
$$Y_2 = a_2 + b_2 Y_1 + (c_2 + d_2 S)X_3 + (e_2 + f_2 S)X_4 + g_2 I.$$

The model can be rewritten as follows:

$$Y_1 = a_1 + b_1 Y_2 + c_1 X_1 + d_1 SX_1 + e_1 X_2 + f_1 SX_2 + g_1 I,$$
$$Y_2 = a_2 + b_2 Y_1 + c_2 X_3 + d_2 SX_3 + e_2 X_4 + f_2 SX_4 + g_2 I;$$

or expressed in a more general form:

$$Y_1 = f(Y_2, X_1, SX_1, X_2, SX_2, I)$$
$$Y_2 = f(Y_1, X_3, SX_3, X_4, SX_4, I).$$

It was this general form that was used above to define the models pertaining to the early and intermediate childbearing years.

15. The discussion of the results draws more heavily on estimates of specification B than those of specification A, since the former are gener-

ally superior to the latter. It may be noted at this point that the specification A estimate of the marital fertility equation for the early childbearing years pertaining to the 'traditional' ethnic groups suggests that the equation is not overidentified and that the results are not valid in this particular instance.

16. t and F tests as well as R^2 are not strictly valid when using two-stage least squares. Keeping this in mind, they are nevertheless employed here in order to make the interpretation of the results possible.

16 A Comparative Study of Costa Rica and Mexico*

ANDRAS UTHOFF and GERARDO GONZÁLEZ

INTRODUCTION

Why, when and how fertility rates will begin to decline in the Third World countries, and how quickly this final stage of demographic transition will come about, are unknown quantities of outstanding worldwide significance, from both the scientific and political points of view. Hence, in-depth studies of the countries which in recent years have shown a marked reduction in their rates of population growth will be useful for attaining a global understanding of these complex processes and acquiring knowledge for formulation of more efficacious population policies, designed to induce and regulate demographic transition.

Within Latin America, Costa Rica offers the most obvious example of a spectacular fall in the population growth rates. As can be seen in Figure 16.1, towards the end of the 1950s crude death rates had already dropped to decidedly low levels (10 per thousand per annum), generating an exceptionally rapid population growth (about 3.8 per cent per annum). At this point, a swift and steady decline in the birth rate began which, in the short space of a decade, brought about a change that in the developed countries had taken half a century.

Mexico is one of the countries of the region which contrasts most sharply with Costa Rica. While the course followed by the crude death rate was parallel and close to the corresponding trend in Costa Rica (the vital statistics published also show a marked reduction of infant mortality in 1970-3), the crude birth rate remained at more than 42 per thousand.

* This paper is based on the results of an earlier joint paper prepared by the authors for the ILO while working in CELADE; see Uthoff and González (1976).

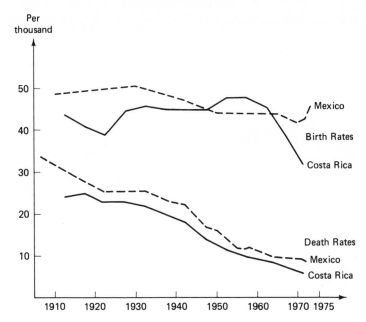

FIGURE 16.1   *Crude birth and death rates in Costa Rica and Mexico,*
1910-73

SOURCES   Costa Rica: Direccion General de Estadística y Censos,*Informes
estadísticos y anuarios estadiscicos*, taken from Paulo Campanario, 'Caracterización demográfica de Costa Rica, proyecto, Estrategias de Desarrollo
y Políticas de Población, CELADE (unpublished).

Mexico: Death Rates before 1950, Anuarios estadísticos de los Estados
Unidos Mexicanos', taken from El Colegio de México, *Dinámica de la
población de México*, 1970, cuadro II-1. Birth Rates before 1950, El
Colegio de Mexico, *op. cit.*, cuadro III-2. 1950-73, Dirección General de
Estadísticas, *Estadísticas Vitales*, serie I, 1, 1975, cuadro 1.

In fact, it registered an increase over the period 1970-3 reaching 45.8
per thousand population in 1973. This phenomenon is observable even in
the Federal District, in which, in view of its metropolitan character, a
decrease might have been expected otherwise. Here, too, the birth rate
climbed from 41.3 in 1970 to 43.8 per thousand in 1973.[1]

This is not the place for a detailed discussion of whether this increase
in the birth rate is real or merely a statistical artefact in terms of how far it
reflects a change in the age structure of the female population of childbearing age or is a result of an improvement in the recording of vital
statistics, etc. What can be maintained, for the moment, is that whereas in

Costa Rica the birth rate has been declining significantly since the 1960s, in Mexico there has been no significant change up until 1973.[2] This fact emerges even more clearly from a comparison of age-specific fertility rates in the two countries for the years 1960 and 1970(71)– see Figure 16.2.

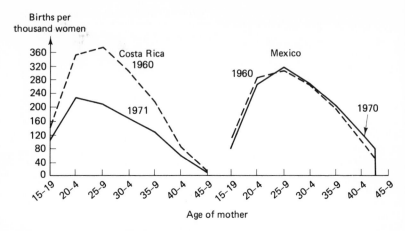

FIGURE 16.2 *Age-specific fertility rates*

SOURCE United States Bureau of the Census, *World Fertility Patterns,* 1974.

The problem to be dealt with in this chapter can be summed up in the following question: Why is it that the fertility level has declined in Costa Rica and not in Mexico? Only the intercensal period will be considered, and the approach will be four-fold: to describe the measurements of fertility that will be used; to discuss the profile of fertility in both countries; to indicate the factors operating to produce skewness in the distribution of women by the number of children ever born in both countries; and to assess, in light of the above, the importance of these factors to the changes in fertility during the intercensal period.

The chapter is centred on the interaction between women's *contemporaneous* participation in economic activity and two other variables related to fertility, namely marital status and education. The first is an intermediate variable, which facilitates continuous exposure to stable sexual unions (of particular importance in traditional societies like those of Latin America); the second is a determinant variable, which is observed as having a negative correlation with fertility, and has been associated with hypotheses relating to the value of the mother's time (opportunity-costs) or to social status.

The main changes which have happened during the intercensal decade are summarised in Tables 16.1 and 16.2. The most important changes which also show to be statistically significant are those by marital status, education and age. Changes in labour-force participation rates for women

TABLE 16.1   *Changes in female population composition: Mexico City, 1960–70*

	Women aged 15–49			Standard deviation	t statistic
	1960	1970	Difference		
Labour-force participation					
Economically active	0.333	0.338	+0.005	0.005	+ 1.00
Non-economically active	0.667	0.662	−0.005	0.005	− 1.00
Marital status					
Single	0.390	0.387	−0.003	0.005	− 0.60
Married or in stable union	0.556	0.539	−0.017	0.006	− 2.83
Widowed, separated or divorced	0.054	0.074	+0.020	0.003	+ 6.67
Education					
None (00)	0.169	0.136	−0.033	0.004	− 8.25
Lower primary (01–03)	0.228	0.191	−0.037	0.005	− 7.40
Higher primary (04–06)	0.371	0.451	+0.080	0.005	+16.00
Lower secondary (07–09)	0.073	0.046	−0.027	0.003	− 9.00
Higher secondary (10–12)	0.111	0.093	−0.018	0.003	− 6.00
University (13 and over)	0.048	0.083	+0.035	0.003	+11.67
Age					
15–19	0.214	0.241	+0.027	0.005	+ 5.40
20–24	0.195	0.203	+0.008	0.004	+ 2.00
25–29	0.167	0.156	−0.011	0.004	− 2.75
30–34	0.140	0.117	−0.023	0.004	− 5.75
35–39	0.122	0.113	−0.009	0.004	+ 2.25
40–44	0.085	0.094	+0.009	0.003	+ 3.00
45–49	0.077	0.075	−0.002	0.003	− 0.67

SOURCE: OMUECE, Mexico, Capital 1960–70; CELADE, Banco de Datos.

aged 15–49 do not show to be statistically significant. The extent to which these changes are related to the observed trend in fertility during the intercensal period will be examined below.

THE MEASUREMENT OF FERTILITY AND ITS DECOMPOSITION

The study is based on samples drawn from the censuses of 1960 and 1970 in Mexico and of 1963 and 1973 in Costa Rica.[3]

The fertility measure used is that of number of live births or children

TABLE 16.2 *Changes in female population composition: San Jose de Costa Rica, 1963-73*

	Women aged 15-49				
	1963	1973	Difference	Standard deviation	t statistic
Labour-force participation					
Economically active	0.368	0.378	+0.010	0.009	+ 1.11
Non-economically active	0.632	0.622	−0.010	0.009	− 1.11
Marital status					
Single	0.444	0.487	+0.043	0.009	+ 4.78
Married or in stable union	0.482	0.464	−0.018	0.009	− 2.00
Widowed, separated or divorced	0.074	0.049	−0.025	0.004	− 6.25
Education					
None (00)	0.048	0.032	−0.016	0.003	− 5.33
Lower primary (01–03)	0.193	0.125	−0.068	0.006	−11.33
Higher primary (04–06)	0.440	0.399	−0.041	0.009	− 4.55
Lower secondary (07–09)	0.110	0.115	+0.005	0.006	+ 0.83
Higher secondary (10–12)	0.149	0.228	+0.079	0.007	+11.29
University (13 and over)	0.059	0.101	+0.042	0.005	+ 8.40
Age					
15–19	0.223	0.256	+0.033	0.008	+ 4.1
20–24	0.187	0.208	+0.021	0.007	+ 3.0
25–29	0.147	0.146	−0.001	0.006	− 0.2
30–34	0.139	0.113	−0.026	0.006	− 4.5
35–39	0.116	0.109	−0.007	0.006	− 1.2
40–44	0.102	0.093	−0.009	0.005	− 1.8
45–49	0.087	0.075	−0.012	0.005	− 2.4

SOURCE   OMUECE, Costa Rica, Capital, 1963–73; CELADE, Banco de Datos.

ever born per woman, grouped in quinquennial age-groups and by a breakdown according to contemporaneous labour-force participation, marital status and education. In contrast to other types of fertility data from censuses, the number of children ever born represents *cumulative* fertility. The number of children ever born per 1000 women 50 or more years old is also the *completed* fertility rate, and, when only female children ever born are counted, is also equivalent to the *gross reproduction rate.* The most important use of these data is that they provide information on the extent of childlessness in a population as well as on the distribution of mothers by number of children. This last property is what primarily justifies its use in this study, because the chapter will be centred on the assessment of the importance of contemporaneous labour-force participation, education and marital status in the production of skewness in the distribution of mothers by number of children.

In both countries, the questions on children ever born were asked of those women who at the moment of the census were or had been married, were consensually married or were single, with a very low non-response rate. Intertemporal comparisons in each country on the reported children ever born are not considered, because the information on the number of children ever born was affected by differences in definitions and scope; the most important was the inclusion of stillbirths in the 1960s censuses. This study analyses only the information on the number of children ever born *alive*, reported in the 1970 census in Mexico and in the 1973 census in Costa Rica.

Based on the distribution of women by their number of children ever born, the assessment of factors producing skewness on such a distribution is performed. A useful inequality index for this purpose is that developed from information theory, elaborated by Theil (1967, ch. 4). It may be written as

$$T = \sum_{i=1}^{W} Y_i \log \frac{Y_i}{X_i},\tag{1}$$

where Y_i is the fertility share and X_i the population share of individual woman i, and W is the total number of women of childbearing ages. This index will be used in the analysis of the distribution of women by the number of children ever born. Hence, Y_i should be interpreted as the share of children ever born attributable to woman i. The population share of woman i is obviously $1/W$. T reaches a minimum value of zero when $Y_i = X_i$ for all i (i.e. when fertility shares are equal to $1/W$ for each woman in the population). This is equivalent to a situation in which all women are of the same class of fertility. A maximum value of $\log W$ is attained when all children ever born are attributable to one woman.

Like the Gini coefficient, this inequality measure is distribution-free. Its principal attractions are its convenient aggregation properties (see Theil, 1967, p. 106).

With the identification of appropriate fertility classes, T may be written as

$$T = \sum_{j=1}^{N} Y_j \log \frac{Y_j}{X_j} + \sum_{j=1}^{N} Y_j T_j,\tag{2}$$

where Y_j and X_j are the fertility and population shares of class j, respectively, and T_j is the inequality of fertility within class j. In this analysis, the classes are 0, 1, 2, . . . , 9 or more children ever born. All individuals are located on their respective class means, which means that there is zero within-fertility-class variation.[4] This implies that equation (2) may be reduced in this case to

$$T = \sum_{j=1}^{N} Y_j \log \frac{Y_j}{X_j} . \tag{2'}$$

Thus, equation (2') permits determination of total inequality in the distribution of women by children ever born considering variation between fertility classes alone. The index is to be applied to the distribution of women by their number of children born within each quinquennial age-group.

Following Fishlow (1972), equation (3) enables us to determine how much of the total inequality T, as given in (2'), is due to fertility variations among different labour-force status means and education-class means:

$$T_{km} = \sum_{k=1}^{K} Y_{k.} \log \frac{Y_{k.}}{X_{k.}} + \sum_{m=1}^{M} Y_{.m} \log \frac{Y_{.m}}{X_{.m}} + \left[\sum_{k=1}^{K} \sum_{m=1}^{M} Y_{km} \log \frac{Y_{km}}{X_{km}} - \sum_{k=1}^{K} Y_{k.} \log \frac{Y_{k.}}{X_{k.}} - \sum_{m=1}^{M} Y_{.m} \log \frac{Y_{.m}}{X_{.m}} \right], \tag{3}$$

where Y_{km} and X_{km} are the fertility share and population share, respectively, of labour-force status class k and education class m. We also have

$$Y_{k.} = \sum_{m=1}^{M} Y_{km} \quad \text{and} \quad X_{k.} = \sum_{m=1}^{M} X_{km}$$

as the fertility and population shares of labour-force status class k, irrespective of education, and

$$Y_{.m} = \sum_{k=1}^{K} Y_{km} \quad \text{and} \quad X_{.m} = \sum_{k=1}^{K} X_{km}$$

as the fertility and population shares of education class m, independent of labour-force status.

The difference between (2') and (3) is due to the variation in fertility classes within the K-times-M labour-force status–education cells, and is due to omitted characteristics, operating to produce variation in fertility within such cells. This is the 'within' component. The terms in equation (3) further partition the total explained inequality into three components. The first term is the weighted difference in the average number of live births between the different labour-force status groups relative to the total average; the second is a similar variation in the average number of live births between the different educational classes around the total average; and the third is the interaction between these two variables in the determination of fertility differentials.

This method was applied to women aged 15–49, grouped by quinquennial age-groups, in the two capital cities: San Jose in Costa Rica and Mexico City in Mexico. The variables considered for the decomposition exercise were those of contemporaneous labour-force participation (in labour-force and not in labour-force), educational levels (0–3, 4–6 and 7 or more years of instruction) and marital status ('single', 'legally married or in consensual union' and 'separated, widowed or divorced'). The method is applied for two variables each time. That is, triple interactions were not studied.[5]

The Theil decomposition method measures the level of association between the fertility inequality (differentials) and the dispersion registered by the other related variables. For its application, there is no need to specify a formal model relating fertility to the explanatory variables. In this sense, this method is different from regression analysis. It detects only the existence and magnitude of the associations between each variable and the fertility inequality, not the direction of such associations, which can be inferred by looking at fertility levels among subgroups. This constitutes a limitation for the analysis of scaled variables (such as education), but facilitates the joint analysis of scaled and non-scaled variables (marital status and labour-force participation), particularly when there is room for natural discrete partitions.

This method is applied in the belief that we are not able, at this moment, to translate our hypotheses in terms of parameters to be estimated in a formal model. On the contrary, we are at the stage of examining, with some preconceived ideas, the nature of the dependencies or associations which actually exist.

By construction from $(2')$ and (3):

$$0 \leqslant T_{km} \leqslant T. \tag{4}$$

The nearer T_{km} gets to T, the larger the explanatory power of the factors producing the observed inequality. Given that T-maximum depends on the number of cases (recall that T-maximum is equal to log W) for intercountry and intertemporal comparisons, the relative importance of each component is reported by simply dividing T_{km} by T in all years and in each country.

EDUCATION, MARITAL STATUS AND LABOUR-FORCE PARTICIPATION AS DETERMINANTS OF DIFFERENTIAL FERTILITY

Tables 16.3 to 16.5 provide evidence of significant fertility differentials among women grouped by education-attainment levels, marital status and contemporaneous participation in economic activity. Only double- cross-tabulations were obtained for each quinquennial age-group, crossing contemporaneous labour-force participation status with education (Table 16.4) and with marital status (Table 16.5).

As shown in Tables 16.3 and 16.4, fertility appears above average among non-economically active women in all the age-groups. Nevertheless, when women are categorised by educational level, then among the non-economically active, those with high levels of education exhibit below-average fertility rates. Education not only shows a negative correlation with fertility in all age-groups, but also influences fertility with the same pattern within the two labour-force status groups. High fertility rates appear to be characterised by low levels of education attainment and relatively smaller opportunities for work. Thus, the problem of fertility in both countries may be associated with low opportunity costs of time due to the lack of jobs available for the mainstream of the less-educated women.

When the relation between fertility and labour-force participation is analysed by marital status, fertility rates systematically appear to be below average for those women who are economically active, with some minor exceptions. However, the fertility rates differ not only by labour-force

TABLE 16.3   *Average number of live births per 100 women by age,
labour-force participation and occupation*

Age	Active					Non-active	Total
	M	C	A	O	Total		
San Jose (1973)							
15–19	10.0	6.4	6.7	7.0	6.9	10.0	9.1
20–24	23.1	24.7	41.7	50.4	35.7	92.6	66.4
25–29	90.4	104.3	117.9	133.6	110.6	229.8	175.0
30–34	161.7	181.7	315.1	238.8	210.8	373.1	305.3
35–39	257.3	235.9	293.5	321.7	280.4	454.9	392.0
40–44	268.1	317.9	315.4	334.4	310.6	544.0	468.1
45–49	248.3	242.6	262.8	397.7	305.5	520.0	460.5
Mexico City (1970)							
15–19	10.8	3.4	5.6	7.7	6.5	21.3	16.2
20–24	18.2	20.8	30.3	55.9	34.3	159.2	107.7
25–29	62.4	97.4	115.5	146.0	107.9	296.2	234.1
30–34	155.7	217.2	270.7	264.4	229.2	450.0	382.9
35–39	383.4	343.6	346.8	419.7	365.1	535.4	484.8
40–44	283.0	399.3	391.5	442.2	376.3	583.1	522.5
45–49	287.1	389.4	381.1	415.3	382.0	563.4	507.2

M = Managers or professionals
C = Office clerks, saleswomen, drivers
A = Craftworkers, operators
O = Others

SOURCE   OMUECE, CELADE; San Jose, Costa Rica, 1973; Mexico 1970.

participation status. Within both economically- and non-economically-active women, much more important appear to be the fertility differentials between the single women and the rest, especially in Mexico City. Hence, much of the observed differentials which are attributed to labour-force participation in the aggregate can also be ascribed to marital status. The composition of labour-force participation by marital status may be an important factor explaining fertility differentials.

In order to assess the importance of these factors[6] in the determination of fertility differentials, the Theil fertility inequality index decomposition was applied within each quinquennial age group. Table 16.6 reports on the *between* labour-force participation status inequality component as a percentage of total inequality (column 1), and also on the *between* 2-times-6 labour-force status–education fertility rates differences with respect to the

TABLE 16.4 *Average number of live births per 100 women by age, education and labour-force participation*

Age/ Education	San Jose			Mexico City		
	Active	Non-active	Total	Active	Non-active	Total
15–19 years						
0–3	9.6	20.8	14.9	10.5	50.0	30.7
4–6	6.7	24.7	15.4	5.1	22.3	15.9
7 and over	6.1	3.9	4.2	3.6	7.0	6.4
20–24 years						
0–3	51.9	132.4	97.1	75.6	208.3	164.6
4–6	52.9	122.8	92.9	28.7	154.9	103.6
7 and over	22.3	60.5	41.9	14.9	97.8	55.4
25–29 years						
0–3	185.5	245.0	223.9	175.9	347.8	300.7
4–6	113.0	257.1	200.5	102.2	283.8	227.5
7 and over	95.0	195.4	141.0	55.4	227.1	149.3
30–34 years						
0–3	269.6	479.9	414.2	299.0	515.8	458.5
4–6	255.9	368.2	328.7	232.6	429.3	375.3
7 and over	162.5	300.0	225.6	138.3	325.0	239.5
35–39 years						
0–3	364.7	550.4	500.3	467.0·	620.8	581.0
4–6	283.2	455.3	400.0	331.2	492.5	444.7
7 and over	240.0	344.8	293.9	253.4	381.3	329.6
40–44 years						
0–3	333.3	654.2	561.7	481.4	649.2	597.1
4–6	337.8	534.5	479.2	355.4	554.2	499.7
7 and over	269.7	409.2	347.3	200.0	445.7	352.7
45–49 years						
0–3	417.8	646.6	600.4	448.1	656.8	599.3
4–6	302.5	495.0	442.0	358.5	499.7	458.1
7 and over	237.7	396.6	338.3	298.9	396.5	353.4

SOURCE OMUECE, CELADE; San Jose, Costa Rica, 1973, Mexico, 1970.

average (column 3), on the *between* 2-times-3 labour-force status–marital status fertility rates differences with respect to the average (column 2); and on the *between* 6-times-3 education–marital status fertility rates differences with respect to the average (column 4). Labour-force participation status and marital status differences explain more than one-half the observed fertility inequality in the age groups 15-19 and 20-4 in Mexico, and below one-half the observed inequality in the other age-groups. In Costa Rica, these differences do not explain more than one-half in all age-groups. Labour-force participation and educational differences do not explain much of the observed total inequality: below 30 per cent in all age-groups in Mexico and below 20 per cent in all age-groups in Costa Rica. Marital status and educational differences, however, account for more than one-half of the total observed fertility inequality in the younger age-groups in Mexico, though not so in Costa Rica.

The explained proportion differs in each country and according to age. Labour-force participation, educational attainment and marital status explain a much higher proportion of observed total fertility inequality in Mexico than in Costa Rica, and within each country for the young age-groups rather than the older ones.

The relative hierarchy in significance of the three characteristics is not unequivocal, at least between education and labour-force participation, and to a lesser extent between marital status and education. Remaining single and participation in economic activity together produce a different fertility rate than would be expected from marital status and labour-force participation status separately. At the same time, single women and higher education together also produce a different fertility rate than would be expected from the marital status and educational classifications alone. For this reason, Table 16.7 is prepared showing the tabulations on the contributions of specific characteristics under two different conditions. Firstly, letting the other characteristics vary (interactions included); secondly, holding all the other characteristics constant as they were (interactions excluded). In this treatment of the interaction, the relative hierarchy in significance of the specific characteristics is clarified. Education is enhanced, since it is by and large relatively more independent of marital status and labour-force status. It establishes marital status as the most important, followed by educational differences.

The hierarchy of these characteristics varies with the mode of calculation. The contribution to the observed fertility variation among women participating and not participating in the labour-force is reduced considerably when the other characteristics are controlled for. This happens even in the younger age-groups, where these differences proved to be important when the calculations were done with the interactions included. Yet, this is not to say that the promotion of job opportunities for women is unwarranted.

It most clearly reflects that job opportunities have been allocated by education and marital status, and therefore are not producing an effect on fertility different from that already attributed to these other character-

TABLE 16.5 Average number of live births per 100 women by age, marital status and labour-force participation

Age/Marital status	San Jose			Mexico City		
	Active	Non-active	Total	Active	Non-active	Total
15–19 years						
Single	4.6	2.3	3.0	2.1	3.2	2.8
Married or in stable union	72.0	72.5	72.4	88.4	107.7	106.0
Others	100.0	66.7	80.0	126.3	73.7	100.0
20–24 years						
Single	20.6	22.4	21.3	6.6	15.5	9.3
Married or in stable union	81.1	142.0	128.8	140.9	209.3	202.6
Others	151.4	297.1	176.2	158.6	177.4	166.7
25–29 years						
Single	56.6	64.0	58.3	18.6	35.1	22.7
Married or in stable union	171.1	258.0	234.9	197.0	323.8	305.0
Others	226.6	293.1	247.3	245.2	220.9	239.1
30–34 years						
Single	101.2	128.8	107.6	49.0	51.7	49.6
Married or in stable union	306.0	401.7	376.6	347.5	472.9	451.0
Others	283.6	316.7	291.1	280.7	346.7	298.8

35–39 years						
Single	135.3	132.9	134.6	46.9	24.2	– 39.5
Married or in stable union	364.1	494.0	462.5	486.5	569.6	553.8
Others	375.4	409.7	387.0	409.3	382.0	401.4
40–44 years						
Single	156.2	259.7	193.1	33.7	55.8	41.2
Married or in stable union	402.4	575.0	537.3	516.2	626.8	607.3
Others	374.1	550.0	460.4	416.6	438.8	425.3
45–49 years						
Single	135.9	160.0	146.3	87.5	60.4	75.9
Married or in stable union	433.0	572.1	548.9	468.0	600.9	574.7
Others	374.5	517.2	456.8	408.8	644.2	466.4

SOURCE OMUECE, CELADE; San Jose, Costa Rica, 1973; Mexico, 1970.

TABLE 16.6 *Percentage total inequality in the average number of live births explained by variations in labour-force participation, marital status and education*

Age-groups	Labour-force participation[a]		Labour-force participation and marital[b] status		Labour-force participation and education[c]		Marital status and education[d]	
	Costa Rica	Mexico	Costa Rica	Mexico	Costa Rica	Mexico	Costa Rica	Mexico
15–19	0.5	4.4	43.2	54.3	13.0	13.1	46.2	55.9
20–24	9.4	20.0	34.9	60.3	18.1	26.0	43.0	54.3
25–29	2.3	16.1	31.4	39.2	16.2	21.2	38.3	40.9
30–34	9.9	11.5	25.2	30.3	15.6	16.5	35.6	34.7
35–39	7.6	4.5	23.8	28.3	13.0	9.7	31.7	34.8
40–44	9.3	5.2	19.2	26.0	13.1	10.4	24.3	30.0
45–49	7.0	4.6	22.5	19.1	12.0	8.8	30.3	23.4

[a] We distinguish between economically-active and non-economically-active women.
[b] We distinguish six possible combinations to be formed among the economically-active and non-economically-active women by their three possible marital statuses: single, married or in stable unions, and others (separate, widowed or divorced).
[c] We distinguish twelve possible combinations to be formed among the economically-active and non-economically-active women by their six possible educational levels: none, 1–3 years of instruction, 4–6 years of instruction, 7–9 years of instruction, 10–12 years of instruction, 13 and more years of instruction.
[d] We distinguish eighteen possible combinations to be formed among the women according to their marital status and level of instruction.

SOURCE See text.

istics. What should be learned from these results is that job-opportunities should be more widely promoted, and not made available simply according to personal characteristics of women such as their education and marital status.

From Tables 16.6 to 16.8, we can highlight some similarities in both capital cities: (i) for all age-groups, marital status is by far the most important explanatory variable; (ii) labour-force participation and education-attainment level have similar statistical explanatory powers when interactions are included, i.e. when the other characteristics are allowed to vary; (iii) when the other characteristics are held constant, the importance of labour-force participation is substantially reduced, except for the

TABLE 16.7 *Percentage total inequality in the average number of live births explained by variations in labour-force participation, marital status and education; interactions included and excluded*

Age-groups	Labour-force participation		Marital status		Education	
	Costa Rica	Mexico	Costa Rica	Mexico	Costa Rica	Mexico
Interactions included[a]						
15–19	0.5	4.4	42.9	54.6	7.7	5.7
20–24	9.4	20.0	33.2	51.2	8.7	7.8
25–29	12.3	16.1	28.5	37.1	6.1	6.3
30–34	9.9	11.5	23.6	28.5	8.2	9.4
35–39	7.6	4.5	21.6	28.3	7.0	6.2
40–44	9.3	5.2	14.7	25.1	5.1	5.8
45–49	7.0	4.6	21.3	17.6	6.4	6.1
Interactions excluded[a]						
15–19	5.1	2.6	38.3	45.4	8.0	4.3
20–24	1.6	7.3	26.4	35.6	9.6	1.3
25–29	0.6	1.0	22.7	20.8	7.6	2.7
30–34	–	–	19.2	17.9	9.6	4.1
35–39	0.6	–	19.4	24.1	8.6	5.5
40–44	3.2	–	14.4	19.9	8.3	4.3
45–49	–	–	17.8	14.3	7.3	4.0

[a] We had information only on two-by-two variable interactions. So there is a mispecification in the figures under the title 'Interactions excluded'. We should have added the three-by-three interactions.

SOURCE See text.

age-groups 15–19 in San Jose and 20–24 in Mexico City; and (iv) when the population is divided into economically-active and non-economically-active, occupational status and education variables together explain a larger percentage of fertility differentials among the economically active than does education alone.

The most important differences between these two cities are the comparatively smaller importance of marital status and greater importance of education in San Jose than in Mexico City in the explanation of fertility differentials. It remains to be explained how the interaction between women's participation in economic activity and marital status is brought about. For this, we computed in Table 16.9 a measure for the concen-

TABLE 16.8 *Percentage total inequality in the average number of live births for active and non-active women explained by variations in marital status, education and occupation*

| | *Percentage explained by variations in the average number of live births per 100 women grouped by:* | | | | | |
| | *Marital status*[a] | | *Education*[b] | | *Education and occupation*[c] | |
	Costa Rica	*Mexico*	*Costa Rica*	*Mexico*	*Costa Rica*	*Mexico*
Economically-active						
15–19	21.0	46.2	1.1	4.0	8.0	13.8
20–24	18.0	53.0	6.5	10.9	9.6	15.5
25–29	20.0	42.7	4.3	9.6	5.1	15.5
30–34	21.5	35.6	5.6	6.8	9.0	11.6
35–39	20.4	35.7	4.8	6.1	7.8	11.4
40–44	18.9	38.2	1.4	10.5	3.3	13.1
45–49	18.9	18.8	3.5	3.8	10.1	7.0
Non-economically-active						
15–19	49.0	52.4	15.9	10.0	–	–
20–24	34.2	34.8	11.3	5.7	–	–
25–29	22.5	20.3	4.6	4.2	–	–
30–34	12.1	13.0	7.1	4.6	–	–
35–39	16.6	18.1	6.6	4.7	–	–
40–44	7.1	14.1	5.1	2.7	–	–
45–49	14.9	12.5	5.8	5.0	–	–

[a] The marital status categories are: single, married or in stable union, others (separated, widowed, divorced).
[b] The educational categories are: none, 1–3 years of instruction, 4–6 years of instruction, 7–9 years of instruction, 10–12 years of instruction, more than 13 years of instruction.
[c] The educational categories are the same as before, and the occupational categories are the corresponding census categories: managers or professionals, clerical workers, salesmen and transport equipment operators; artisans, operatives and manual workers; and others.

tration of female labour-force participation by marital status, education and number of live births. The Theil index was used for this purpose.

Among the younger age-groups, labour-force participation does not vary significantly by marital status (the value of the concentration index is low). This may be due to either delay of marriage or, given the proportion of women married, all women participating in labour activity at the same rate, regardless of marital status. What has been actually occurring

TABLE 16.9 *Concentration index of labour-force participation among women grouped by marital status, education and number of live births*

	San Jose			Mexico City		
	Marital status	*Education*	*Number of live births*	*Marital status*	*Education*	*Number of live births*
Total	0.074	0.015	0.045	0.168	0.016	0.066
15–19	0.025	0.204	0.003	0.091	0.074	0.025
20–24	0.096	0.003	0.064	0.251	0.012	0.180
25–29	0.129	0.033	0.101	0.314	0.024	0.218
30–34	0.143	0.056	0.098	0.257	0.034	0.165
35–39	0.125	0.061	0.101	0.197	0.020	0.077
40–44	0.122	0.041	0.137	0.196	0.027	0.091
45–49	0.159	0.045	0.146	0.141	0.023	0.078

Coefficient of correlation between concentration index for the corresponding column and the same index for the live births column

0.92	0.71	1.00	0.96	0.59	1.00

NOTE Let there be three classes of marital status ($i = 1, 2, 3$). If y_i is the proportion of women with marital status i among all economically-active women, and x_i is the proportion of women with marital status i among the total number of women, irrespective of their work status, then the concentration index is measured as:

$$\sum_{i=1}^{3} y_i \log \frac{y_i}{x_i} \, .$$

SOURCE OMUECE, CELADE; Mexico, 1970, Costa Rica, 1973. Calculations made by the author.

in the younger age-groups is the deferment of marriage. In the case of Costa Rica, this would appear to happen largely up to ages 20-4, where the proportion of single women still exceeds 50 per cent, and in Mexico up to the ages 15-19. Thus, in the younger age-groups, higher educational levels and greater desire to enter the labour-market would seem to be leading to postponement of marrriage. This deferment takes place on a considerably larger scale in Costa Rica than in Mexico.

In the younger age-groups, work participation by women could be expected to be influencing fertility. This influence would be exerted through women's aspirations for higher educational levels in order to secure better jobs which, in turn, with increasing role incompatibility, compels them to postpone marriage or childbearing. This phenomenon becomes more important with increase in women's educational level, and appears to be more marked in San Jose than in Mexico City, and, within Costa Rica, more in urban areas than rural.[7]

In those age-groups where the period measures of fertility are highest (20-34 years), labour-force participation is less common (concentration of participation by marital status is higher). In Mexico City, greater concentration is the result of a causal reversal in the labour-force participation–marital status relationship, with labour activity being determined by marital status. There is a marked concentration of work participation in the groups comprising single women and those who are widowed, separated and/or divorced, perhaps implying that it is by economic necessity that they engage in economic activity.

From these ages onwards, two different things happen with respect to women's labour-force participation: whereas in Mexico City it is largely concentrated by marital status and is not differentiated to any great extent by educational level, by contrast, in San Jose, concentration by marital status is less and education carries much more weight in the determination of female labour activity. Both these facts help to explain the fertility behaviour differentials between the two cities, highlighting not only the hypotheses relating to the socialising influence of work participation and the impact of industrial-urban culture on it (especially in the case of married women in Costa Rica), but also those linked to opportunity-costs as education gains increasing importance in the determination of work participation. The greater the extent to which married women are incorporated in the labour-force, the stronger will be the influence of women's economic participation on fertility, through its socialising influence and the impact of industrial-urban culture. An additional effect will also be produced, in so far as employment opportunities are more heterogeneous and education is used as a credential to give access to employment, with the resulting increase in the opportunity-cost of domestic work. This, perhaps, is the most marked feature of the differences between the two capitals as regards the effect of labour-force participation on fertility.

PROBABLE EFFECT OF THE PRINCIPAL CHANGES IN THE FEMALE POPULATION CHARACTERISTICS ON THE AVERAGE NUMBER OF LIVE BIRTHS

Up to now we have focused attention solely on the study of participation in economic activity and its interaction with marital status and education as structural factors in differential fertility behaviour. To highlight the importance of these factors and of their interaction in relation to changes in fertility, we have carried out two standardisation exercises. Firstly, the importance of labour-force participation and education-attainment level on changes in cumulative fertility during the intercensal period is explored by holding the age–labour-force participation–education specific cumulative fertility constant at the 1973 (Costa Rica) or 1970 (Mexico) values, and adjusting for the differences in population composition by age, labour-force participation and education. This is reported in Table 16.10A.

TABLE 16.10A *Effects of changes in age-structure, labour-force participation and education on the average number of live births*

	Mexico City	San Jose
Average number of live births per 100 women, 1970[a]	249.4	197.1
Standardised by age-structure, 1960[a]	259.8	215.9
Percentage change	−4.0	−8.7
Standardised by age and labour-force participation, 1960[a]	261.4	217.7
Additional percentage change	−0.6	−0.8
Total cumulative change	−4.6	−9.5
Standardised by age, labour-force participation and educational levels, 1960[a]	265.1	225.4
Additional percentage change	−1.4	−3.2
Total cumulative percentage change	−6.0	−12.6

[a] Figures for 1970 and 1960 correspond to 1973 and 1963 in the case of San Jose (Costa Rica).

Secondly, the importance of labour-force participation and marital status changes to changes in cumulative fertility during the intercensal period is also explored by a similar procedure, holding age–labour-force participation–marital status specific cumulative fertility constant at their 1973 (1970) values, and allowing the population composition by age, labour-force participation and marital status to vary at its 1963 (1960) structure. This is reported in Table 16.10B.

Table 16.10B indicates that in conjunction with the change in age-structure of the female population, the small increase in the rates of women's participation in economic activity had a minimal effect on fertility. Whereas, in Costa Rica, changes in marital status produced negligible effects and those in education important additional reductions in fertility, in Mexico the changes in marital status increased fertility and those in

TABLE 16.10B   *Effects of changes in age-structure, labour-force participation and marital status on the average number of live births*

	Mexico City	San Jose
Average number of live births per 100 women, 1970[a]	249.4	197.1
Standardised by age-structure, 1960[a]	259.8	215.9
Percentage change	−4.0	−8.7
Standardised by age and labour-force participation, 1960	261.4	217.7
Additional percentage change	−0.6	−0.8
Total cumulative change	−4.6	−9.5
Standardised by age, labour-force participation and marital status, 1960	251.5	217.6
Additional percentage change	+3.8	+0.1
Total cumulative percentage change	−0.8	−9.4

[a] Figures for 1970 and 1960 correspond to 1973 and 1963 in the case of San Jose (Costa Rica).

education had only minor effects in reducing fertility. Thus, the most important differences in the comparison between the countries are those of the effects on fertility of changes in the age-structure and education and the effect of changes in marital status.

Following the same approach, the next step is to analyse development with respect to average numbers of children among women in different age-groups, a distinction being made between the active and the non-active. It is hoped, by these means to clarify the effect of the above-mentioned interactions on our findings. This is not a cohort analysis, because the fertility measure used is not strictly comparable for different points in time.

The results of this exercise, presented in Tables 16.11 and 16.12, corroborate the views expressed before. The principal changes in the variables which interact with women's participation in economic activity in determining the average number of live births have operated in the direction of reducing fertility a good deal more intensively in Costa Rica than in Mexico. In both countries, changes in the marital distribution have raised the average level of cumulative fertility among the economically active women, as fewer are unmarried in 1973 (1970) as compared to 1963 (1960). In the case of Costa Rica, this is due to an increase in the labour-force participation of married women or women in stable unions, whereas in Mexico the cause is a general rise in nuptiality rates, particularly between the ages of 20 and 49 years (where there is a significant reduction in the proportion of single women).

As a result, in Costa Rica there is a trend towards similarity in the composition by marital status of the economically active and the non-active groups of women – average fertility is increasing among the former but decreasing among the latter. In Mexico, the reduction in the proportion of single women is common to both the active and the non-active groups, with the result that average fertility increases among all women except in the age-group 15–19 years, where the educational process seems to be deferring the age at first marriage.

To sum up, the rise in the educational level of women of childbearing ages and the slight increase in their participation in economic activity, observed both in San Jose and in Mexico City, suggest that a decline in fertility might be expected in both cases, although it would probably be greater in Costa Rica than in Mexico. We know, however, that in Mexico City, fertility levels remain high during the period under consideration. This phenomenon can be accounted for, at least in part, by what happens in respect to nuptiality: whereas in Costa Rica the proportion married declines in the younger age-groups – which would seem to reflect the fact that stable unions are being initiated at a later age – in Mexico the reverse takes place. In addition, in San Jose there is a considerable increase in the participation of married women in economic activity, which is not paralleled in Mexico City. Thus, in the latter case, the changes taking place in the nuptiality variable would seem to have more than offset the probable effect of the changes that occurred in education and participation in economic activity.

CONCLUSIONS

The exogeneous character which might be attributed to the female labour-force participation variable in the determination of changes in fertility levels is not so obvious. The effects of economic development on levels of fertility through changes in the scale of female work participation and in skills involved may prove insufficient to counteract the effects of other phenomena which cause, for example, change in nuptiality.

The lesson to be learned from developments in Mexico and Costa Rica during the 1960s is that significant changes in nuptiality may offset to a great extent the possible effects on fertility of changes in the scale of labour-force participation and the qualifications involved.

TABLE 16.11 *Effects of female population composition on the average number of live births by occupational status and age: Mexico (Mexico City)*

| | Observed in 1970 | Standardised by: | | | | | | | | | |
| | | Marital status | | Educational level | | Occupational category | | Occupational category and education | | Marital status and education | |
		1960	Percentage	1960	Percentage	1960	Percentage	1960	Percentage	1960	Percentage
Economically active											
15–19	6.5	7.0	− 7.1	7.5	−13.3	6.4	+ 1.6	7.3	−11.0	–	–
20–24	34.3	31.7	+ 8.2	40.4	−15.1	34.8	− 1.4	39.5	−13.2	–	–
25–29	107.9	99.5	+ 8.4	110.5	− 2.4	111.1	− 2.9	110.4	− 2.3	–	–
30–34	229.2	216.1	+ 6.1	235.4	− 2.6	231.6	− 1.0	229.3	–	–	–
35–39	365.1	319.9	+14.1	374.2	− 2.4	363.6	+ 0.4	377.4	− 3.3	–	–
40–44	376.3	334.0	+12.7	386.2	− 2.6	388.3	− 3.1	374.0	+ 0.6	–	–
45–49	382.0	358.0	+ 6.7	390.5	− 2.2	380.7	+ 0.3	390.2	− 2.1	–	–
Non-economically active											
15–19	21.3	25.5	−16.5	24.5	−13.1	–	–	–	–	–	–
20–24	159.2	152.6	+ 4.3	165.2	− 3.6	–	–	–	–	–	–
25–29	296.2	287.2	+ 3.1	302.1	− 2.0	–	–	–	–	–	–
30–34	450.0	436.6	+ 3.1	453.5	− 0.8	–	–	–	–	–	–
35–39	535.4	525.4	+ 1.9	531.1	+ 0.8	–	–	–	–	–	–
40–44	583.1	569.3	+ 2.4	579.8	+ 5.7	–	–	–	–	–	–
45–49	563.4	549.0	+ 2.6	565.8	− 0.4	–	–	–	–	–	–

All women

15–19	16.2	17.2	−18.4	18.3	−11.5	15.9	+ 2.5	18.2	− 9.3	18.0	−11.0
20–24	107.7	103.2	+ 4.4	114.2	− 5.7	108.3	− 0.6	113.8	− 5.4	107.1	− 0.6
25–29	234.1	230.3	+ 1.7	244.4	− 4.2	239.2	− 2.1	243.1	− 3.7	235.7	− 0.7
30–34	382.9	376.6	+ 1.7	394.2	− 2.9	390.6	− 2.0	392.5	− 2.4	378.8	+ 1.1
35–39	484.8	465.2	+ 4.2	483.2	+ 0.3	485.1	− 0.1	486.1	− 0.3	463.5	+ 4.6
40–44	522.5	498.3	+ 4.9	521.4	+ 0.2	524.3	− 0.3	517.6	+ 1.0	495.9	+ 5.4
45–49	507.2	487.9	+ 4.0	509.6	− 0.5	504.9	+ 0.5	509.6	− 0.5	493.7	+ 2.7

SOURCE: CELADE, Banco de Datos, OMUECE, Mexico City, 1960–70.

TABLE 16.12   *Effects of female population composition on the average number of live births by occupational status and age: Costa Rica (San Jose)*

	Observed in 1973	Standardised by:									
		Marital status		Educational level		Occupational category		Occupational category and education		Marital status and education	
	1973	1963	Percentage	1963	Percentage	1963	Percentage	1963	Percentage	1963	Percentage
Economically active											
15–19	5.9	5.8	+18.9	7.2	− 4.2	6.9	–	6.8	+ 1.5	–	–
20–24	35.7	34.3	+ 4.1	40.6	−12.1	38.4	− 7.0	41.4	−13.8	–	–
25–29	110.6	101.9	+ 8.5	122.8	− 9.9	113.0	− 2.1	117.6	− 6.0	–	–
30–34	210.8	197.2	+ 6.9	230.3	− 8.5	215.0	− 2.0	215.4	− 2.1	–	–
35–39	280.4	282.3	− 0.7	296.3	− 5.4	284.0	− 1.3	289.5	− 1.3	–	–
40–44	310.6	297.0	+ 4.5	316.7	− 1.9	315.8	− 1.6	311.8	− 0.4	–	–
45–49	305.5	312.4	− 2.2	322.9	− 5.4	318.6	− 4.1	316.6	− 3.5	–	–
Non-economically active											
15–19	10.0	13.0	−23.1	12.9	−22.5	–	–	–	–	–	–
20–24	92.6	101.1	− 8.4	107.7	−14.0	–	–	–	–	–	–
25–29	229.8	240.9	− 4.6	235.2	− 2.3	–	–	–	–	–	–
30–34	373.1	367.1	+ 1.6	378.3	− 1.4	–	–	–	–	–	–
35–39	454.9	464.9	− 2.2	456.6	− 0.4	–	–	–	–	–	–
40–44	543.5	539.5	+ 0.7	545.9	− 0.4	–	–	–	–	–	–
45–49	519.7	498.6	+ 4.2	540.5	− 3.8	–	–	–	–	–	–

All women

15–19	9.1	10.5	–13.3	10.7	–15.0	8.9	– 2.2	10.7	–15.0	10.9	–16.5
20–24	66.4	72.8	– 8.8	79.3	–16.3	69.6	– 4.6	79.6	–16.6	80.0	–17.0
25–29	175.0	186.0	– 5.9	190.8	– 8.3	188.7	– 4.7	188.7	– 7.3	192.5	– 9.1
30–34	305.3	300.4	+ 1.6	320.0	– 4.6	310.8	– 1.8	314.1	– 2.8	313.1	– 2.5
35–39	392.0	406.1	– 3.5	404.9	– 3.2	399.9	– 2.0	402.8	– 2.7	418.2	– 6.3
40–44	468.1	454.6	+ 3.0	465.4	+ 0.6	463.8	+ 0.9	463.4	+ 1.0	466.6	+ 0.3
45–49	460.5	448.2	+ 2.9	481.5	– 4.9	465.2	– 1.0	479.8	– 4.0	471.0	– 2.2

SOURCE   CELADE, Banco de Datos, OMUECE, San Jose, Costa Rica, 1963–73.

In Mexico, alongside the rising age at marriage and/or consensual unions and the rise in education-attainment levels and work participation, there was, whether independently of these factors or not (a point for future research), a significant upswing in the proportion of women married. In contrast to what occurred in Costa Rica, however, the economic activity rate among married women declined instead of increasing. Thus, as education-attainment level rose, labour-force participation and the occupational status of women improved, a pronounced downward movement in labour-force–marital status–age-specific fertility rates took place. The increase in the proportion married in Mexico, however, together with the reduction of married women's labour-force participation, brought about a recomposition of the female population with respect to the attributes which raise levels of fertility (marriage and non-participation in economic activity). The joint impact of the reduction in labour-force–marital status–age-specific fertility rates and the recomposition of the female population was responsible for the absence of change in the overall fertility level in Mexico.

In Costa Rica, while marriage rates were maintained, the labour-force participation rates of married women increased, particularly in the age-groups where reproduction is highest: a situation that follows up and accentuates the direction of the previous changes. The decline in fertility observed in Costa Rica and the absence of change in Mexico thus become more understandable.

The changes linked to socio-economic development must not only increase employment opportunities for women but must do so in such a way as to involve women independently of their marital status. This will be achieved only insofar as employment opportunities exist irrespective of a woman's social group of origin, so that through her job she can fulfil her aspirations and bring into line with them her own cultural values and those of her family. Otherwise, labour-force participation will result from the necessity of attaining subsistence levels, and will not so much condition fertility as reflect its result in the past. This latter situation seems to prevail in the more traditional societies and environments in Latin America.

In this chapter, the influence of labour-force participation in bringing about fertility change has been studied. No formal model has been used, and preference has been given to a method that gives us overall magnitudes of associations that may clear some *a priori* conceptions about the relationships between the variables involved. Since the relationship between fertility and economic activity is undoubtedly bidirectional, the specification of a formal model should consider the simultaneous determination of the variables included in the analysis in order to use estimation procedures that properly test hypotheses about the causal relationships involved.

NOTES

1. See Dirección General de Estadísticas (1975).
2. Recent statistics reported in UNFPA (1979b) show that from 1975 onwards, there has been a sharp decline in the birth rate in Mexico. The following figures are reported there:

1973 = 45.8	1976 = 37.1
1974 = 44.9	1977 = 35.3
1975 = 40.4	1978 = 38.4

3. The sample proportions were 1.5 per cent for Mexico, census 1960; 6 per cent for Costa Rica, census 1963; 1 per cent for Mexico, 1970; and 10 per cent for Costa Rica, 1973. See CELADE (1974).
4. In very few cases, women declared more than 9 children ever born.
5. We could anticipate at this stage some weak results due to the large aggregation with which we are classifying each one of our variables. A four-class decomposition for each variable has been shown to be the optimal minimum for the Theil index decomposition analysis. See Van Ginneken (1975).
6. For the fertility inequality decomposition, 2 labour-force participation, 6 educational and 3 marital status classes are considered. See notes to Table 16.6.
7. This last conclusion is based on results obtained by applying the same methodology as in this chapter for the analysis of fertility differentials in rural areas of Costa Rica (Uthoff and González, 1976).

17 Can Income Redistribution Reduce Fertility?

C. R. WINEGARDEN

INTRODUCTION

In recent years, the contention that developing countries could lower their birth rates by reducing internal income inequality has attracted much attention and achieved considerable acceptance (e.g. Colombo Declaration on Population and Development, 1979; McNamara, 1977). Within the community of population researchers, however, this has remained an open question (see G. B. Simmons, 1979, for a critical view). Systematic investigation has been confined to a few studies with varying, or inconclusive, results. Only the need for further research in this area may be deemed uncontroversial.

In this chapter, a multi-equation model is used to investigate the relationship between the size-distribution of income and fertility levels in developing countries. In place of the doctrine that decreased inequality lowers birth rates, an alternate set of interrelated hypotheses is proposed. According to these hypotheses, lessened income inequality acts directly to *raise* fertility, but there are indirect effects, which may be either positive or negative, depending on the complex interaction of income-distribution, fertility, and a third factor – mortality conditions. Therefore, the net result of an altered pattern of income-distribution depends on the strength of the direct, positive impact, relative to the strength and direction of the indirect processes.

These hypotheses are incorporated into an econometric model, which is then tested on cross-sectional data for a sample of developing countries. Estimation of the model's structure provides strong support for the predicted pattern of relationships. From the structural parameters, the reduced form of the model is derived. With this last step, it becomes

462

possible to gauge the net effect of income-redistribution on fertility, and to define the conditions that can change the direction of that effect. The reduced form also reveals the total impact – direct and indirect – of other policy variables, not only on fertility, but also on income distribution and expectation of life.

A brief and critical review of the relevant literature is presented in the next section of this chapter. The third section contains a statement of the theoretical issues, in the form of a set of testable hypotheses. The econometric model is described in some detail in the following section. The fifth section presents the results of testing the structure of the model. In the next section, the reduced-form parameters are derived, and the relationships among the key variables are re-examined in the light of this information. In the final section, the findings of this study are summarised, and their implications for theory and policy are briefly considered.

REVIEW OF THE LITERATURE

At the theoretical level, the thesis that income redistribution would reduce fertility has been best developed by Repetto (1974, 1978, 1979), although previously advanced by Kocher (1973) and Rich (1973).

Repetto's argument proceeds along these lines: fertility is a non-linear and non-monotonic function of household income, positive at very low income levels, but then becoming negative and remaining so until high income levels are attained. The negative stretch of this function dominates the relationship, and is characterised by an increasing slope coefficient, resulting in an eventual flattening out. Over this wide negative range Repetto believes, income gains reduce fertility by increasing the proportion of families able to participate in the 'process of modernisation'. Given the large concentration of families at the lower end of the income scale, and their characteristically high fertility, the redistribution of income, in an equalising direction, should result in an overall reduction in birth rates. Repetto sees the potential for decreasing fertility through redistribution policy as very substantial: in the typical developing country, the lower half of households receives perhaps 15 per cent of total income, but accounts for three-quarters of all births.

Income redistribution as a means of controlling population growth has been criticised at both the theoretical and policy levels. J. L. Simon (1977) distinguishes between direct, or short-run, effects and indirect, or longer-run, consequences. In the short run, the impact on fertility is positive because poor people can afford earlier marriage and the rearing of additional children. In the longer run, he believes, higher incomes at the bottom of the economic scale may indirectly reduce birth rates by operating through such variables as health and education. Simon also argues that income equalisation *per se* is not a valid policy option: it consists of a number of specific measures, such as land reform, for which fertility implications are not easily predictable. G. B. Simmons (1979) compares income redistribution and other roundabout interventions with government programmes aimed specifically at lowering fertility. From the available evidence, he concludes that the direct approach offers more likelihood of success and a far greater degree of cost-effectiveness.

Aside from some anecdotal comparisons of particular countries, the empirical evidence bearing on the thesis of Repetto *et al.* is primarily a product of cross-sectional regression analysis with international data. Systematic analysis of the historical experience of individual countries would be of undeniable value, but the scarcity of time-series data on income distribution and the relative stability of income shares over short periods combine to rule out this approach.

Repetto presents both single-equation and three-equation multivariate models relating fertility to the Gini coefficient. His single-equation model shows a statistically-significant, positive relationship between the Gini index and fertility when the regressions are based on his entire sample of countries. However, when the five communist nations in the original sample are deleted, significance drops to marginal levels. When he restricts his sample to 41 developing countries, the size of the error variance exceeds the coefficient for income distribution.

Conceptually, Repetto's three-equation model is far superior to his single-equation approach if, as contended in this chapter, income-distribution, fertility and mortality are interconnected variables. Fertility, the Gini coefficient and the infant-mortality rate are the endogenous variables of Repetto's system, although for an unspecified reason he does not include the Gini among the explanatory variables in the infant-mortality equation. The main defect of this system, however, appears *ex post*: it is not validated by his 3SLS regression results: only four of the eleven estimated coefficients show significance at the 0.05 (one-tailed) level. These regressions pertain to his full sample – including developed countries; he does not report separate 3SLS results for the developing countries. (For further discussion of Repetto's work, see Birdsall, 1977.)

Flegg (1979) objects to Repetto's use of the Gini coefficient as a measure of income-distribution, pointing to the sensitivity of that coefficient to redistributions affecting the middle income groups. He also presents his own single- and two-equation models. The endogenous variables of the two-equation model, which is of greater interest here, are the crude birth rate and the percentage of females in the labour-force. Income-distribution is measured by means of Atkinson's coefficient of inequality (Atkinson, 1973). Flegg's 3SLS regression results are much superior to Repetto's, with small error variances and greater evidence of robustness (e.g. significance is largely retained, even when the sample is limited to developing countries). He also derived reduced-form parameters from his structural estimates, showing that the total impact of inequality on fertility falls somewhat short of the direct effect, a result he ascribes to the negative influence of decreased inequality on the labour-force participation of women.

Several questions regarding Flegg's study should be raised. The model incorporates simultaneity in the birth-rate-labour-force relationship, but both income distribution and the infant-mortality rate, although contemporaneous, are treated as altogether exogenous. It is not clear that the female labour-force participation rate applies to the working ages; if not, some of the negative relationship with the birth rate is spurious (because higher birth rates raise the proportion of females too young to work).

A four-equation econometric model developed and tested by the present author (Winegarden, 1978) yielded evidence of a very small, but statistically-significant effect of income distribution on fertility: the income share of the lower four-fifths of households showed a negative effect on the gross reproduction rate. However, this study included both developed and developing countries in its cross-sectional data base, giving rise to the possibility that cluster effects were generated by the bimodal sample.

It should be emphasised that the main defect of all three studies is the omission of statistical controls for national family-planning effort.[1] Other studies (e.g. Maulden and Berelson, 1978) have documented a strong anti-natal influence attributable to such effort. This omission, together with other shortcomings, casts doubt on their findings with respect to the fertility–income-distribution relationship. Evidence contributing to this doubt is provided by a recent, related study by the present author (Winegarden, 1980), that incorporated a family-planning variable. In this study, which is limited to the developing countries, fertility was found to be positively (but not significantly) affected by both the income share of poorer households and the level of per capita income. Taken together, these results suggest that the partial effect of an egalitarian redistribution of income may be to raise fertility. Additional, and stronger, evidence supporting this inference, and also underscoring the need to control for family-planning programme variables, is presented below.

THE THEORETICAL ISSUES

The starting point of this investigation is the assumption that fertility, income-distribution and mortality are interrelated variables, linked both directly and indirectly in a set of causal processes. These processes can be stated in the form of five testable propositions that comprise the rationale of the econometric model.

The Direct Result of Lessened Income Inequality is to Raise Fertility

If the level of income per head is held constant, an increase in the relative share of the poorer households unequivocally represents an absolute gain in income for these households. The effect of household-income on child-bearing behaviour falls within a highly controversial area of economic and demographic literature. (For a review of this literature see Mueller and Short, forthcoming). The approach adopted in this paper is a modified version of one suggested by J. L. Simon (1977), who distinguishes between a 'short-run' pro-natal effect of higher incomes, and a 'long-run' impact in the opposite direction, reflecting changes in tastes, values and use of time caused by income variations. Two modifications are introduced here. Firstly, 'direct' and 'indirect' are substituted for the temporal dichotomy, since it is by no means clear how these processes operate in time. Secondly, the assumption that the indirect effects of higher income on fertility are, on balance, negative is replaced with a wider range of possibilities (as seen below).

In this framework, the income–fertility relationship becomes much more amenable to realistic modelling. In explaining fertility, a 'pure' (direct) income effect should emerge if associated influences are adequately controlled; this expectation is consistent with conventional micro theory, as applied to fertility (e.g. Becker, 1960). The indirect effects may then be separately specified as functions of income (and other variables). Accordingly, a pro-natal impact is predicted here as a direct consequence of lessened inequality. Although it represents the exact opposite of Repetto's thesis, there is an area of common ground, to the extent that both positions are based on the consequences of absolute income gains. It is also possible that relative income shares may influence fertility by operating on subjective perceptions of status, but this conjecture has not been developed into a formal theory.

Reduced Income Disparities Decrease Mortality

A favourable effect of higher levels of income on mortality conditions has been well documented (e.g. Preston, 1975). From this relationship, the hypothesis that lessened inequality should reduce mortality may be readily inferred. It is well known that income elasticities of demand for necessities, i.e. life-related goods and services such as simple food, shelter and health-care, show a strong inverse relationship to income levels. Thus, an equa-lising redistribution would improve survival probabilities in poor house-holds, without mortality effects on the more prosperous. Empirical evidence from cross-national studies clearly supports this inference (Rodgers, 1979; Winegarden, 1980).

Fertility is a Non-monotonic Function of Mortality Conditions

Theoretical and empirical studies of fertility commonly assign an important role to mortality conditions, as inversely measured by expectation of life or directly gauged by infant or child death rates (e.g. Schultz, 1969; Heer and Smith, 1968). In most of these studies, the hypothesised rela-tionship is straightforward (and often linear): the higher the probability of survival, the fewer births required to achieve some target level of survivors in the following generation. However, as Anker (1978) has shown, improve-ments in health conditions from very low levels may raise fertility by reducing the incidence of early widowhood, involuntary sterility, sub-fecundity and miscarriage. If this is true, the relationship of fertility to life-expectancy should be quadratic, as fertility rises with increased life-expectancy to the point where negative influences take hold and result in decreased fertility.

High Fertility Worsens Mortality Experience

Here, the causal link between fertility and mortality is reversed. The expectation is that high fertility tends to worsen mortality conditions by increasing the number of infants and young children relative to income, parental time and other scarce resources. It may also contribute to infant and child mortality through a process of more-or-less deliberate under-investment in less-wanted children (Scrimshaw, 1978). In addition, it tends to raise death rates of women in the childbearing ages, directly through the risks of pregnancy and parturition, and indirectly by harming the health of high-parity women (Wray, 1971).

High Fertility, Operating through the Rate of Population Growth, has a Disequalising Effect on Income-distribution

Economists appear to be in substantial agreement on the distributional effects of rapid population growth, although there are some differences regarding the process by which this occurs. (For a summary of this literature, see Boulier, 1975). A leading argument centres on the labour-supply effect: if labour-force growth – reflecting natural increase – outstrips rates of capital accumulation and/or the expansion of arable land, wage rates will tend to decline relative to other factor returns. This change in the functional distribution of income will, in turn, alter the size distribution in a disequalising direction, because of concentration in the ownership of capital and land. (For an application of this hypothesis to American experience, see Lindert, 1978.)

According to a parallel argument, an age-composition effect also intensifies inequality: rapidly-growing populations contain a large proportion of young workers, which multiplies the effect of existing age-differentials in income, and may tend to widen these differentials. Also, in larger families, income may be reduced because of limitations on female labour-force participation (Bilsborrow, 1977).

Taken together, these five hypotheses describe a complex set of direct and indirect causal linkages between income-redistribution and fertility change. The direct effects are to raise fertility, but the indirect effects may be positive or negative, depending on mortality conditions. Thus, the net result of an altered pattern of income distribution depends on the strength of the direct effect in relation to the strength and direction of the indirect processes. This information will be provided by the reduced-form analysis, but first it is necesssary to test the validity of these propositions through structural estimation of an econometric model.

THE ECONOMETRIC MODEL

An Overview

The hypotheses advanced in the preceding section may be succinctly stated as predicted relationships among the endogenous variables of the model. In functional form, these relationships are as follows:

$$F_{it} = f(\overset{+}{Q}_{it-k}, \overset{\pm}{E}_{it-k}), \tag{1}$$

$$Q_{it-k} = f(\overset{-}{\bar{P}}_{it-k}), \tag{2}$$

$$E_{it-k} = f(\bar{F}_{it-k}, \overset{+}{Q}_{it-k}), \tag{3}$$

$$\dot{P}_{it-k} = f(\overset{+}{F}_{it-k}, \overset{+}{E}_{it-k}), \tag{4}$$

where F is the general fertility rate, Q stands for the income share of the poorer segment of the population, E represents mean expectation of life at birth, and $\dot{P}$ is the rate of population growth. The signs above the arguments for each function indicate the expected direction of the relationship, based on the theoretical considerations previously delineated. The i subscript denotes individual countries in the international cross-section, t is a time subscript indicating the year 1975, and k is a lag period of five years, or somewhat longer.

The selection of time-periods was influenced by several factors. The year 1975 was chosen for the dependent fertility variable because it reflects the emergence, in the late 1960s and early 1970s, of highly disparate trends among developing countries, as some developing countries progressed (at varying speeds) toward a low-fertility pattern, while others maintained traditional fertility levels with little or no sign of change. Availability of data for a sufficiently large sample constituted another major consideration. Further, it was assumed that childbearing behaviour lags behind objective changes in the socio-economic environment. In the absence of established theoretical or empirical considerations determining the specific length of the lag period, an interval of five or so years was used.[2] This time-structure defines the model as block-recursive in form: equations (2)-(4) comprise a simultaneous system entering recursively into equation (1). Accordingly, OLS is appropriate for estimating the parameters of the first equation; the three-stage least squares method is employed for the simultaneous block.

Cross-sectional data are used to test the model. The observations comprising the cross-section are 36 developing countries for which the necessary data are available for the periods of reference. (These countries are listed in the Data Appendix, which also provides information on sources used for the regression variables.) A 31 country subsample is also employed in order to include a control variable representing qualitative aspects of national family-planning programmes. The principal constraint on sample-size is imposed by data on income-distribution, presently available for only a limited number of developing countries.

Specification of the Fertility Equation

The fertility equation is

$$F_{75} = a_0 + a_2 Q + a_3 E + a_4 E^2 + a_6 Y/Pw + a_7 S + a_8 A + a_9 Cd + \quad (5)$$
$$a_{10} Cmb + u_{F_{75}},$$

where

F_{75} = general fertility rate (births per 1000 women 15–49), 1975,

Q = income share of the poorest two-fifths of households (per cent), 1965–73,

E = mean expectation of life at birth, 1970 (years),

Y/Pw = GDP/population aged 15–64, 1969–70 (dollars),

S = combined primary and secondary school enrolment ratio, 1950, (per cent),

A = percentage of labour-force in agriculture, 1969–70,

Cd = government-sponsored family-planning programme in operation by 1965 (presence = 1; absence = 0),

Cmb = 'Mauldin–Berelson' index of governmental effort to reduce fertility, 1970–2 (points),

and the predictions are

$$a_2, a_3, a_6, a_8 > 0,$$
$$a_4, a_7, a_9, a_{10} < 0.$$

Use of the general fertility rate as the dependent variables is intended to minimise the influence of variation in population age structure.[3] As argued above, Q is expected to show a positive effect on fertility, i.e. fertility increasing as the relative income share of the poor increases. Income-distribution can, of course, be gauged in other ways, such as the Gini coefficient, but this would be less appropriate in the present context, which pertains to behavioural response to income change at the lower end of the economic scale, rather than to overall inequality.[4] The non-monotonic relationship between fertility and expectation of life is assumed to have an inverted U-shape: hence the quadratic form, with $a_3 > 0$ and $a_4 < 0$.

Most of the control variables are lagged for periods of about five years, for reasons paralleling those cited above. In some cases longer lags are appropriate. The enrolment ratios of 1950 are used in order to gauge the educational attainment of the adult population a quarter of a century later. The importance of schooling as an inhibiting influence on fertility is well established and need not be defended here. Similarly, the long-standing, positive association between the conditions of rural life and the large-family system requires no further elaboration (see the compilation of cross-national fertility studies in Mauldin and Berelson, 1978). The expectations regarding the income-level are more controversial. Firstly, it should be noted that the use of population per person of working age as a denominator is designed to minimise simultaneity bias. The usual total population denominator builds in a tendency toward a negative relationship with fertility, because high birth rates lower per capita income (as customarily calculated) by increasing the non-producing proportion of the population. Secondly, according to the micro-level postulates of the economic theory of fertility, the partial effect of higher income is to increase desired family-size. However, this effect may emerge, at the macro level, only when influences associated with income (such as urbanisation and schooling) are adequately controlled; if the associated influences are incompletely specified, then an inverse relationship may appear (as in the bivariate income–fertility relationship, which may be taken as the limiting case of inadequate control). It is evident that this expectation is a corollary of the argument previously advanced on behalf of a direct pro-natal impact of income redistribution.

The remaining control variables in the fertility equation may be the most important. Cd is a binary indicating presence or absence of an established family-planning programme. The inverse relationship with fertility can hardly be disputed, however intense the controversy over its strength or, indeed, the direction of the underlying causation. (On this question, see, for example, Mauldin and Berelson, 1978, or the opposing view of Demeny, 1979.) For this variable, the lag period has been set at 10 years. Family-planning programmes apparently require more time to 'take hold' than the five-year period assumed for most of the other variables (R. Freedman and Berelson, 1976). In the present study, the 10-year lag was shown, by statistical experimentation, to yield much more significant results than periods of five or eight years. It was also superior to a continuous variable based on the number of years of programme operation. There is, nonethless, an arbitrary element in this procedure, so that some supplementation may be needed. Accordingly, an additional family-planning variable, *Cmb*, is used in order to take into account the well-known differences among countries in the quality of their family-planning effort. However, these data on 'programme effort' are available for only 31 of the 36 countries comprising the main sample.

Specification of the Income-distribution Equation

The equation explaining intracountry differences in the size distribution of income is

$$Q = b_0 + b_5 \dot{P} + b_6 Y/Pw + b_7 S + b_8 A + b_{11} Ya + b_{12} Ig + \qquad (6)$$
$$b_{13} \dot{Y} + u_Q ,$$

where

$\dot{P}$ = average annual rate of population growth, 1965–73 (per cent),

Ig = public sector share of gross fixed investment, 1967–68 (per cent),

Ya = agriculture share of GDP, 1970 (per cent),

$\dot{Y}$ = average annual rate of growth in real GDP, 1965–73 (per cent),

$Q, Y/Pw, S$ and A are as previously defined,

and the predictions are

$b_7, b_{11}, b_{12}, b_{13} > 0,$

$b_5, b_6, b_8 < 0.$

The specification of this equation is based on other studies of the determinants of income-distribution (Ahluwahlia, 1976; Winegarden, 1978, 1980). The case for a disequalising effect of population growth on income-distribution was developed in the previous section of this chapter; hence the negative coefficients of the endogenous $\dot{P}$ variable. The other variables in this equation are exogenous, and differ with regard to the expected direction of their effects. Increases in Y/Pw and A, it is hypothesised, tend to decrease the share of the lower-income groups.

A number of cross-sectional studies have shown a U-shaped relationship between income per head and income distribution, with inequality tending to rise as income levels increase, up to a turning point around the dividing line between developing and developed countries. Beyond that point, the relationship is reversed. Thus, for the LDCs comprising the present sample, an inverse relationship between Q and Y/Pw is to be expected.

The relative size of the rural sector – measured in labour-force share – has an important link to income distribution arising from the relative poverty that usually characterises the countryside in developing countries. The larger this disadvantaged sector, the greater the departure from equality in the overall size distribution of income.

The remaining explanatory variables in the Q equation are expected to operate in the direction of greater equality. Increases in the general level of education of the working-age population, as gauged by the lagged school-enrolment rate, should tend to reduce income inequality, particularly if the gains in average attainment reflect a wider diffusion of schooling. However, this expectation is not above controversy. Jencks *et al.* (1972) argued that no substantial causal relationship between income-distribution and schooling could be shown; Chiswick (1974) contended that unequal educational attainment contributed to earnings inequality, but that raising the mean educational level also had a disequalising effect. On the other hand, Marin and Psacharopoulos (1976) suggested that raising average attainment has an income-equalising influence because of reduced rates of return to schooling, and Winegarden (1979) found substantial support for this hypothesis in an analysis of international data.[5]

The greater the relative size of the public sector, the smaller the income shares accruing to the holders of private property (all else equal), which works in an income-equalising direction because of the usual concentration in property-ownership. *Ig* is, of course, a proxy for public ownership of productive resources (for which data are not generally available). It has the virtue of distinguishing degrees of state intervention in economic life in contrast to the more-commonly employed, but often arbitrary, binary designating the socialist–capitalist dichotomy. The relative share of the rural sector influences the overall distribution of income by affecting the degree of intersectoral income inequality. In many developing countries, the income disparity between town and country is a major source of overall inequality. The relationship between the rate of economic growth, $\dot{Y}$ in this model, and income-distribution is a subject of longstanding controversy. In recent years, however, evidence has accumulated that the net effect of rapid growth is in the direction of greater equality (Ahluwalia, 1976; Winegarden, 1978).

Specification of the Life-expectation Equation

The regression equation designed to explain intercountry variation in mean expectation of life (at birth) is

$$E = c_0 + c_1 F_{70} + c_2 Q + c_6 Y/Pw + c_7 S + c_{14} P/N + u_E, \qquad (7)$$

where

P/N = population (thousands) per nursing person, 1969–70,

F_{70} = same as F_{75}, with a 1970 time-reference,

Q, Y/Pw and S are as previously defined,

and the predictions are

$c_2, c_6, c_7 > 0$,

$c_1, c_{14} < 0$.

In accordance with the theoretical arguments advanced above, life-expectancy should be related negatively to contemporaneous fertility rates, and positively to the relative income share of the poorer households.

With respect to the control variables, an opposing set of effects is anticipated. Higher levels of income per working-age person are expected to be conducive to lower mortality, on the assumption that there is a high income elasticity of demand, in developing countries, for goods and services that sustain life. Other studies of the income–mortality relationship support this view (e.g. Preston, 1975). The population/nurse ratio serves as an indirect measure of the availability of health services. Given the chronic scarcity of such services in most developing countries, a negative relationship is the normal expectation.

Specification of the Population-growth Equation

The population-growth equation is

$$\dot{P} = d_0 + d_1 F_{70} + d_3 E + u_{\dot{P}}, \qquad (8)$$

where the variables are as defined above, and it is predicted that

$d_1, d_3 > 0$.

This equation closes the model by expressing the observed rate of population growth as a function of the general fertility rate and the mean expectation of life. Given the time-structure of the model, E is an endogenous variable while F_{70} is exogenous. By means of this specification, population growth is explained in terms of its long-term determinants. Age-distribution and net migration are treated as transitory elements, assigned to the disturbance term. Without this stochastic equation, the use of 3SLS or other system methods of estimation would be precluded, with a probable loss of efficiency.

STATISTICAL RESULTS: STRUCTURAL ESTIMATES

Regression results for the fertility equation are shown in Table 17.1. The estimates in the first column pertain to the subsample. which includes the variable gauging the intensity of family-planning effort. It is evident that the results provide substantial support for the hypothesised explanations of intercountry variation in fertility levels. Significance levels of all coefficients exceed 0.01, based on a one-tailed t test (which is appropriate because all signs have been correctly predicted). An inverted-U function is strongly indicated for the life-expectancy relationship, with a computed turning point at 54.2 years ($\delta F/\delta E = 0$). This does not differ greatly from Anker's (1978) results, despite large differences in sample, specification, time-reference and estimating method. An anti-natal role for education and pro-natal influences associated with agriculture – both shown in numerous other studies – are again confirmed.

The measured impact of officially-sponsored family-planning programmes is particularly noteworthy. The intercept adjustment of -29, attributable to the establishment of such programmes 10 or more years earlier, equals about 18 per cent of the mean fertility rate for this sample. An equivalent reduction in the fertility rate also could be achieved, according to these results, by a 12 point rise in the rated quality of the family-planning effort (from the sample mean of approximately 10 points).

The outstanding result, however, is the positive and highly significant coefficient of the income distribution variable. Taken together with the positive and almost equally significant coefficient of the Y/Pw variable, the evidence thus far indicates that the partial effect of higher incomes, at the lower end of the economic scale, is to increase the demand for children.

At this point, it is useful to examine the consequences of certain changes in specification. In equation (5.1), the sample remains the same, but the

TABLE 17.1 *OLS regression results: fertility equations*
(dependent variable = F_{75})

	Equation number			
	(5.0)	*(5.1)*	*(5.2)*	*(5.3)*
Intercept	−510.501	−510.083	−525.479	−326.651
	(3.07)	(2.46)	(2.62)	(1.48)
Q	3.942	2.775	2.140	−0.529
	(3.25)	(1.90)	(1.46)	(0.38)
E	22.929	23.384	25.732	19.183
	(4.20)	(3.43)	(3.92)	(2.66)
E^2	−0.212	−0.226	−0.254	−0.197
	(4.28)	(3.67)	(4.37)	(3.07)
Y/Pw	0.037	0.046	0.042	0.034
	(2.60)	(2.60)	(2.43)	(1.74)
S	−0.642	0.786	−0.734	−0.490
	(2.76)	(2.75)	(2.60)	(1.56)
A	1.032	1.218	0.913	0.935
	(2.82)	(2.69)	(2.26)	(2.01)
Cd	−29.729	−34.783	−34.581	−
	(3.36)	(3.19)	(3.26)	
Cmb	−2.389	−	−	−
	(3.71)			
$\bar{R}^2$	0.84	0.75	0.79	0.72
(F)	(20.44)	(13.77)	(19.37)	(15.65)
N	31	31	36	36
$\delta F/\delta E = 0$	54.2	51.8	50.6	48.8

t ratios are shown (in parentheses) below the estimated parameters.

family-planning 'quality' variable is dropped. The coefficients of the other variables are virtually unaffected. It will be noted, however, that the coefficient of Q becomes somewhat smaller and its *t* ratio declines (although remaining in the significant range). A further variation appears in equation (5.2), where the specification is unchanged from the preceding equation, but where the sample now comprises the full set of 36 observations. Here, the coefficient shows a further small reduction in size, and the *t* ratio indicates a marginal level of statistical significance. Finally, both Cd and Cmb are omitted in a regression that uses the full sample (equation

(5.3)), with the result that the income-distribution coefficient has changed sign, but is now much smaller (in absolute magnitude) than its error variance. The point of this sequence should be clear: the more fully the national family-planning effort is controlled in the regressions, the stronger and more consistent the measured *positive* impact on fertility of an income-equalisation tendency. Without any such controls, a *negative*, but wholly insignificant, coefficient emerges. In this last case, the results closely parallel those obtained by Repetto, when he restricted his sample to developing countries. This supports the suggestion, made earlier in the present chapter, that the anti-natal influences of lessened inequality may be an artefact arising from failure to control for programme effort.[6]

Regression results for the three equations comprising the balance of the model are shown in Table 17.2. Three-stage least squares estimation was used for this overidentified block. The results support the relationships initially hypothesised. Of the 14 slope coefficients in the system, all have the predicted signs and exceed the absolute magnitude of their respective error variances; all but three are significant at the 0.05 level, based on one-tailed tests using the asymptotic t values generated by the 3SLS procedures.

Taken as a whole, the process of structural estimation has provided substantial evidence in support of the five hypotheses set forth in the third section of this chapter regarding the interconnection of fertility, mortality and income-distribution. Given the complexity of this structure, including the non-linear relationship of fertility to expectation of life, the ultimate fertility effect – direct plus indirect – of an alteration in income shares cannot be predicted from the information thus far developed. To do this, it is necessary to proceed to the next stage of the analysis.

THE REDUCED-FORM ANALYSIS

Structural estimation served to validate the model, but could reveal only first-order effects. In order to ascertain the outcome of the various causal forces, the reduced form must be derived. (This is the mathematical process of solving for the endogenous variables in terms of the exogenous variables, utilising the parameters supplied by the structural estimates; Goldberger, 1964.)[7] Two essential types of information can be obtained in this way.

(i) The inverse of the matrix of endogenous-variable coefficients shows the final impact of an autonomous change in each endogenous vari-

TABLE 17.2   *3SLS regression results: simultaneous system*

	Equation number		
	(6)	*(7)*	*(8)*
Dependent variable	Q	E	P
Intercept	13.645 (2.51)	47.519 (4.70)	−3.459 (3.01)
$\dot{P}$	−2.189 (2.10)	−	−
Q	−	0.642 (1.73)	−
E	−	−	0.045 (3.33)
F_{70}	−	−0.044 (1.44)	0.020 (8.25)
Y/P_w	−0.003 (1.27)	0.008 (3.55)	−
S	0.039 (1.05)	0.135 (2.89)	−
A	−0.123 (2.35)	−	−
Y_a	0.187 (2.07)	−	−
I_g	0.057 (1.74)	−	−
$\dot{Y}$	0.818 (3.55)	−	−
P/N	−	−0.554 (1.91)	−
$\bar{R}^2$	0.45	0.77	0.75
(F)	(5.07)	(24.94)	(53.22)

Asymptotic t ratios are shown (in parentheses) below the estimated parameters.
$\bar{R}^2$ and F values are based on OLS regressions.
$N = 36$.

able, after taking into account all the direct and indirect effects incorporated in the model.

(ii) The reduced-form coefficients of the exogenous variables measure the full impact of a change in each such variable on each endogenous variable. In this way, they illuminate the process by which the endogenous variables may be altered, within the framework of the model.

In order to focus more sharply on fertility, as a determinant as well as a consequence of income-distribution, the four equations of the model first were compressed into three by substituting the fertility and life-expectation equations for population growth in the income-distribution equation (using the parameters obtained by the estimation of equation (8)). In addition, lagged fertility in the life-expectation equation was treated as endogenous: contemporary and lagged fertility were combined into a timeless variable (on the assumption that the parameters determining fertility were invariant over this relatively short period). A third preparatory step was to select a value of E for the non-linear fertility–life-expectancy function. Three values were used for this purpose: the 36-country sample mean of 57.4 years, and this mean, plus and minus one standard deviation (8.9 years). Yet another choice entailed selection of the structural parameters of the fertility equation, which was estimated – it will be recalled – with varying samples and specifications. The choice made was conservative: equation (5.2) based on the full sample and lacking the qualitative family-planning variable; this meant incorporating a positive, but small, pro-natal effect of Q into the reduced form.

The result of the preceding operations was to create a system that shows – after inversion of the matrix of endogenous coefficients – the 'ultimate' interaction of fertility, life-expectancy and income-distribution, including both simultaneous and recursive processes. Table 17.3 presents the inverse matrices, with life-expectation set at the sample mean (top panel), at one sigma above the mean (middle panel), and at one sigma below the mean (bottom panel). In this way, the interaction of the endogenous variables is gauged under widely varying mortality conditions. Elasticities, computed at sample means, are also shown in the top panel. Thus, it can be seen that a unit increase (one year) in E would reduce F by 4.020, and would raise Q by 0.057 (with corresponding elasticities of -1.46 and 0.26, respectively).

It is immediately evident that mortality conditions determine both the magnitude and direction of the total impact of income redistribution on natality. In the situation represented by the sample mean of E (top panel), the positive and negative effects of change in Q net out to a near

TABLE 17.3 *Derived reduced-form coefficients: endogenous variables*

	Equation number and dependent variable		
Endogenous variable	(9)	(10)	(11)
	F	Q	E
	$(E = \bar{E})$		
F	1.179	−0.044	−0.080
	[1.18]	[−0.55]	[−0.22]
Q	−0.057	0.942	0.607
	[0.00]	[0.94]	[0.13]
E	−4.020	0.057	1.213
	[−1.46]	[0.26]	[1.21]
	$(E = \bar{E} + \sigma)$		
F	1.850	−0.069	−0.126
Q	−5.146	1.132	0.953
E	−14.183	0.436	1.904
	$(E = \bar{E} - \sigma)$		
F	0.866	−0.032	−0.059
Q	2.322	0.854	0.446
E	0.731	−0.120	0.891

Elasticities, where entered, were computed at variable means and appear under coefficients [in brackets].
$\bar{E}$ = 57.35.
σ_E = 8.91.

balance – an increase of one percentage point would result in a virtually imperceptible decline of −0.06 in the general fertility rate. (This represents an elasticity, taken at the variable means, that rounds to zero.) Underlying this outcome is the almost exact equivalence of the direct, pro-natal effect of income redistribution and its indirect anti-natal influence, operating through mortality conditions. In the typical developing country in this sample, life-expectancy was not sufficiently above the 'turning point' for this indirect effect to be dominant.

In the second panel, where mean expectation of life is assumed to have reached a relatively high level for a developing country – 66.3 years – the indirect influence of Q is strong enough to outweigh the direct pro-natal effect and to produce a net negative impact of some magnitude. A gain of one percentage point in the income share of the bottom two-fifths would reduce the fertility rate by more than five points per 1000.

The bottom panel portrays a third situation: lessened income inequality unequivocally increases fertility. In this case, the direct and indirect consequences of raising Q operate in the same positive direction on birth rates. This pattern reflects the situation in which improvement in mortality conditions, starting from an unfavourable level, has the initial effect of raising fertility. Here, the net result of a gain of one percentage point in Q is a rise of slightly over two points per 1000 in the general fertility rate.

In addition to revealing the widely varying role of income distribution, these matrices contain other pertinent information. Starting again in the situation portrayed in the top panel - with E at the sample mean - a gain of one year in mean expectation of life would have the net result of reducing the general fertility rate by only 4 per 1000. However, once the favourable mortality conditions of the middle panel had been achieved, the one-year gain in E would cause a substantial fertility decline - 14 per 1000. In both cases, it will be noted, the effect of an increase of a single year in mean expectation of life far outweighs the result that can be attributed to a rise of one percentage point in Q. In the third matrix, the expected pro-natal influence of an increase in E is evident, but it is small compared with the impact of Q, operating in the same direction.

The computed elasticities shown in the top panel of Table 17.3 provide information on the relative strength of the interactions among the variables. These data underscore the relative importance of mortality conditions as a determinant of fertility: the elasticity of F with respect to E is nearly 1.5. In contrast to the zero impact of income distribution on fertility, the reserve effect is substantial: the elasticity of Q with respect to F is -0.55.

Therefore, there is evidence of a very considerable asymmetry in the fertility–income equity relationship, as found in an earlier study (Winegarden, 1978). On the other hand, fertility reduction apparently has a greater relative effect in raising expectation of life than does income-redistribution, although in neither case is the effect very substantial.

The diagonal entries in the Table 17.3 matrices provide yet another kind of information. They show the total impact on an endogenous variable of an initial change in the value of that variable, after that change has 'worked through' all the relationships of the model. In the top panel, for example, an autonomous increase of one unit in the general fertility rate will ultimately raise that rate by 1.18 units. To the extent that this coefficient exceeds unity, the initial increase has been augmented by feedback effects; to the extent that it falls below unity, those effects have, on balance, had a dampening influence. Similarly, an autonomous one-year gain in mean expectation of life would be translated into an ultimate increase of 1.21 years. On the other hand, the processes affecting income distribution tend slightly to dampen change in that variable, according to the diagonal value of 0.94. In the latter case, a gain in Q raised fertility, which (via population growth) in turn exerts a disequalising influence on Q.

The importance of mortality conditions as a determinant of the strength and direction of the feedback effect can readily be seen by comparing the diagonal entries across matrices. In the second matrix, where E is assumed to be high, all three diagonal coefficients substantially exceed unity. Thus, an autonomous equalising change in Q would be strongly reinforced, mainly because it would increase E, which in this case would lower fertility, in turn acting in the direction of further equalisation. In the third panel, however, all such autonomous changes tend to be self-negating. For example, a gain in life-expectancy would raise fertility, which would cancel out some of the gain in E, because higher birth rates act both directly and indirectly (via Q) to raise mortality. In sum, it appears that a low level of E acts as a trap from which escape is impeded, whereas a high E level helps to generate a self-reinforcing advance.

Turning now to the role of the exogenous variables, Table 17.4 presents their reduced-form coefficients. Elasticities are also shown, in order to make it easier to compare the effects of variables measured in different units. These elasticities are taken at sample means, with the exception of the binary variable Cd, for which the value is arbitrarily set at unity (rather than at the sample mean of 0.33) in order to simulate more realistically the effect of a decade of family-planning efforts. If the elasticity thus computed is multiplied by 100, the amount of intercept adjustment associated with the binary is measured as a percentage of the mean of the dependent variable; it may be compared directly with the effect of a 100 per cent change in any other exogenous variable.

Both the coefficients and elasticities in Table 17.4 attest to the powerful impact on fertility of long-established family-planning programmes. The measured effect is a reduction of 40+ points in the general fertility rate, equal to 26 per cent of the sample mean. This result becomes even more impressive when one computes the amount of change in other exogenous variables required to achieve a comparable effect. Let us consider the expansion of school enrolments and the reduction of the relative size of the agricultural work-force as alternative approaches. The elasticities of fertility with respect to S and A are 0.34 and -0.34, respectively, the

TABLE 17.4   *Derived reduced-form coefficients: exogenous variables*

Exogenous variable	Equation number and dependent variable:		
	(12)	*(13)*	*(14)*
	F	Q	E
Y/Pw	0.018 [0.08]	−0.004 [−0.24]	0.005 [0.06]
S	−1.410 [−0.34]	0.077 [0.23]	0.246 [0.16]
A	1.084 [0.34]	−0.156 [−0.61]	−0.148 [−0.13]
Cd	−40.783 [−0.26]	1.520 [0.12]	2.77 [0.05]
Ya	−0.011 [0.00]	0.178 [0.33]	0.115 [0.05]
Ig	−0.003 [0.00]	0.054 [0.17]	0.035 [0.02]
$\dot{Y}$	−0.046 [0.00]	0.771 [0.36]	0.497 [0.05]
P/N	2.227 [0.04]	−0.031 [−0.01]	−0.672 [−0.04]

Coefficients in upper rows; elasticities in lower rows (in brackets). Elasticities computed at variable means, except for the binary *Cd* variable, which was set equal to unity for this purpose (see text for explanation).

largest magnitudes among the elasticities appearing in the fertility column. To achieve the fertility impact of −26 per cent indicated for *Cd*, the changes in *S* and *A* would have to equal +76 per cent and −76 per cent respectively. An expansion of school enrolments on that order, starting from the sample mean, implies a combined primary and secondary enrolment ratio of about 67 per cent, a level not attained by most developing countries, despite the recent rapid expansion of their educational systems. Also, there is a large difference in the time dimension: the model incorporates a 25-year lag in the enrolment rate to allow for the interval between schooling and the reproductive and working years, whereas the family-planning lag has been set at one decade. (There are also considerations of comparative cost, which lie beyond the scope of this paper. On this point, see G. B. Simmons (1979).

With regard to the connection between agricultural employment and the fertility rate, the foregoing argument takes on added weight. In the present example, a 76 per cent reduction in the agricultural proportion of the labour-force would reduce that share to less than 12 per cent, a level attained among the sample countries (as of 1970), only by the city-states of Hong Kong and Singapore. For most developing countries, this would be a slow and difficult process, tantamount to achieving full developed-country status.

The question of the consistency of policy instruments with diverse goals may also be explored by means of the data in Table 17.4. Family-planning stands out among the exogenous variables, not only for the size of its negative impact on fertility, but also for its substantial positive contribution to both income-equalisation and the improvement of mortality conditions. A decade of national family-planning programmes raises the income share of the bottom two-fifths by 1.5 percentage points (equal to about one-eighth of the income share of this group at the sample mean.) Similarly, it adds nearly three years (or about 5 per cent) to mean expectation of life. (These are both indirect effects, operating through the reduction of fertility, and its further consequences.)

Among the remaining exogenous variables, only S and A are at all comparable to family-planning in the sense of contributing substantially to the desired direction of change for all three policy goals. As stated above, a reduction in A cannot be separated from the development process as a whole. However, it does appear that an accelerated widening of educational opportunity would serve the useful purpose of outweighing the moderately pro-natal and disequalising effects that otherwise accompany higher levels of income. Finally, some attention should be given to variables that apparently contribute to the attainment of lessened income inequality and reduced mortality, but are at worst neutral with respect to fertility. In this category, we find both gains in the agricultural share of aggregate income (an important means of decreasing overall inequality) and the rate of growth in total output.

CONCLUSIONS

An alternative interpretation of the income-inequality–fertility relationship has been presented and tested. In place of the doctrine that reduced inequality lowers birth rates, it has been argued here that a much more complex model is required. The endogenous components of this model comprise fertility, income distribution, and mortality conditions (as gauged by mean expectation of life). It is on the interaction of these variables that the net effect on fertility of a change in income distribution depends for both its direction and strength. The econometric analysis of this model – tested with cross-sectional data – involved two major steps.

Firstly, the process of structural estimation validated the direct, or first-order, impacts that had been predicted. Among these direct effects, perhaps the most noteworthy is the positive influence of lessened income-inequality on fertility rates, when national family-planning effects are statistically controlled. Almost equally meaningful are the non-monotonic effects of life-expectation on birth rates: the functional relationship with fertility takes the form of an inverted-U, with its peak somewhat below the expectation attained in the developing country typical of the sample. Also important in this context are the disequalising effects of fertility on income-distribution, and the positive influence of greater income equality on expectation of life.

Secondly, the reduced-form parameters of the model were derived from the structural estimates. Given the complex pattern of interaction built into the model, the outcome of the various causal processes can be ascertained only by solving for the reduced form. The results of this operation reveal the crucial role of mortality conditions in determining the fertility effects of changes in income distribution. Where expectation of life is close to the sample mean, the direct (positive) and indirect (negative) impacts on fertility traceable to a lessening of income inequality are approximately balanced. Where relatively high levels of expectation of life have been attained, an equalising redistribution of income contributes to the reduction of fertility. However, where mortality conditions remain highly unfavourable, a narrowing of income disparities has the net effect of raising birth rates. The reduced-form analysis also underscores the importance of mortality experience as an independent influence on fertility, apart from its role in conjunction with income-distribution.

The reduced-form parameters serve the additional purpose of simulating the impact of alternate policy variables. Among these variables, long-established and officially-sponsored family-planning programmes are outstanding for their powerful, negative impact on fertility. They also contribute indirectly to greater income equity and to increases in expectation of life. Among the indirect approaches, the expansion of educational opportunities offers similar, but more modest, possibilities of multiple pay-off.

To sum up, the econometric evidence does not generally support income redistribution as a means of reducing birth rates, although it can have some anti-natal effect once low mortality rates have been achieved. A more cogent demographic argument for redistribution lies in its positive if modest, contribution to extending the average expectation of life.

DATA APPENDIX

The sample consists of, *inter alia*, the following countries: Bolivia, Brazil, Chile, Colombia, Costa Rica, Ecuador, Egypt, El Salvador, Hong Kong, Honduras, India, Ivory Coast, Kenya, Republic of Korea, Malawi, Malaysia, Mexico, Morocco, Pakistan, Panama, Peru, Philippines, Zimbabwe*, Sierra Leone, Singapore, South Africa*, Spain*, Sri Lanka, Tanzania, Trinidad and Tobago, Tunisia, Turkey, Uruguay*, Venezuela, Yugoslavia*. (The asterisks designate exclusions from the 31-country subsample because of unavailability of data on family-planning 'programme effort'.)

Income distribution data are primarily from S. Jain (1975), with supplementation from Adelman and Morris (1973), Pang (1975) and Webb (1977). All available observations for the period 1965–73 were averaged. Countries for which data for this period were not available were excluded from the sample.

Demographic data are from United Nations (1975), World Bank (1976), United Nations, *Demographic Yearbook* (various years) and United States Bureau of the Census, International Demographic Data Center. School-enrolment data are from the UNESCO *Statistical Yearbook* (various years).

The countries classed as having officially-supported family-planning programmes in effect since 1965 are as follows: Egypt, Hong Kong, India, Republic of Korea, Pakistan, Singapore, Sri Lanka, Tunisia. Turkey, Venezuela, Yugoslavia.

Sources used in classifying countries by year of initiation of family-planning effort are Nortman and Hofstatter (1976), International Planned Parenthood Federation (1974) and Watson (1977). Indices of such effort are taken from Mauldin and Berelson (1978). All other data are from World Bank (1971, 1976).

Means and standard deviations of the regression variables are shown below.

	$\bar{X}$	σ
F_{75}	158.2	49.9
Q	12.6	4.3
E	57.4	8.9
Y/Pw	744.4	480.9
S	37.9	19.3
A	49.4	21.9
Cd	0.33	0.48
Cmb	10.7	8.4
$\dot{P}$	2.6	0.7
Ig	38.8	19.0
Ya	23.5	12.1
$\dot{Y}$	5.9	2.3
P/N	3060.8	3331.7
F_{70}	169.4	44.6

(Cmb data pertain to 31 observations; all others to 36.)

NOTES

1. The Winegarden (1978) model includes a binary variable denoting liberalised abortion policy, which is shown to have a powerful effect on the gross reproduction rate.
2. A simultaneous relationship between F_{75} and the other endogenous variables was not supported by regression results.
3. As Ghazi Farooq points out, the gross reproduction rate is the most precise indicator of fertility change. However, for an international cross-section of the type comprising the present sample, the particular method used to gauge fertility makes little or no difference. Because of very high intercorrelation among the various fertility measures, regression results are quite insensitive to the measure used. For the 36-country sample, zero-order correlations among general fertility rates, total fertility rates, and crude birth rates are as follows.

	GFR	TFR	CBR
GFR	1.000	0.965	0.983
TFR		1.000	0.977
CBR			1.000

4. Regression results in which the Gini coefficient is substituted for Q are quite similar to those reported here (with signs reversed), although significance levels are lower. In another experiment, the income share of the lower 60 per cent was used, with outcomes closely resembling those shown. Various indices of income-dispersion tend to be highly correlated across the sample.

5. In a long-run sense, the enrolment rate may be viewed as endogenous, influenced by both population growth and income distribution. Here it is treated as exogenous, in order to simplify the model and to focus more directly on the fertility-inequality nexus.

6. With respect to Flegg's (1979) findings, it should be noted that an earlier version of the present model included an endogenous variable gauging female labour-force participation. This was found to be without statistical significance, possibly because of the confounding influence of unpaid or intermittent work by rural women that does not conflict with childbearing. A variable reflecting participation by women in full-time, paid employment would almost certainly show better results, but such data are not available for an LDC cross-section.

7. The derived reduced form used here should be distinguished from the 'direct' or 'unrestricted' reduced form, obtained by regressing each endogenous variable on all of the exogenous variables of the model. A principal advantage of the derived form is that it utilises information provided by the structural estimates (Goldberger, 1964). The derivation of the reduced form from the structural parameters is shown below.

In matrix notation, the general structural form (omitting the disturbance term) is

$$\mathbf{BY} = \mathbf{\Gamma X}, \tag{1}$$

where

$\mathbf{Y} = G \times 1$ vector of endogenous variables,

$\mathbf{X} = K \times 1$ vector of exogenous variables,

$\mathbf{B} = G \times G$ matrix of coefficients,

$\mathbf{\Gamma} = G \times K$ matrix of coefficients.

Then, after premultiplication of both sides by $\mathbf{B}^{-1}$, the reduced form may be rewritten as

$$\mathbf{Y} = \mathbf{B}^{-1} \mathbf{\Gamma X}. \tag{2}$$

The structural equations provide estimates of the $\mathbf{B}$ and $\mathbf{\Gamma}$ matrices. These values may then be used in equation (2) to solve for the reduced-form coefficients.

The same process may be more easily understood in the two-equation case, where simple algebra provides a ready solution. Assume the following structural model (again omitting error terms):

$$Y_1 = a_0 + a_2 Y_2 + a_3 X, \tag{3}$$

$$Y_2 = b_0 + b_1 Y_1 + b_4 Z, \tag{4}$$

where Y_1 and Y_2 are endogenous variables, and X and Z are exogenous. The corresponding reduced-form equations are:

$$Y_1 = \pi a_0 + \pi a_2 b_0 + \pi a_2 b_4 Z + \pi a_3 X, \tag{3.1}$$

$$Y_2 = \pi b_1 a_0 + \pi b_0 + \pi b_4 Z + \pi b_1 a_3 X, \tag{4.1}$$

where $\pi = \dfrac{1}{1 - a_2 b_1}$.

Firstly, we consider the effect of an autonomous change in an endogenous variable, say an increase of one unit in Y_1. An autonomous change is one not attributable to a change in an exogenous variable, X or Z, so that it must be expressed as a shift of an intercept. In equation (3.1), the impact of an autonomous gain in Y_1 is gauged by the coefficient of a_0, i.e. Y_1 changes by the amount π. In equation (4.1), the impact of an autonomous gain in Y_1 is also measured by the coefficient of a_0, i.e. Y_2 is altered by the amount πb_1. Thus these coefficients show the total effect – on Y_2 and on Y_1 itself – of a change in Y_1, after taking into account the feedback built into the model. In matrix form, π would be a diagonal element in $\mathbf{B}^{-1}$, and πb_1 an off-diagonal element.

Secondly, we examine the reduced-form coefficients of the exogenous variables. For example, the final impact of a unit increase in Z is a change of $\pi a_2 b_4$ in Y_1 and of πb_4 in Y_2. In matrix form, these coefficients are elements of $\mathbf{B}^{-1} \Gamma$.

For an application of this method, see Gregory *et al.* (1972).

Bibliography

Acsadi, Gyorgi, Adenola Igun and Gwendolyn Johnson (1972) *Surveys of Fertility, Family and Family Planning in Nigeria* (Ile-Ife, Nigeria: Institute of Population and Manpower Studies, no. 2, University of Ife).

Adegbola, O. (1977) 'New Estimates of Fertility and Child Mortality in Africa, South of the Sahara', *Population Studies*, vol. 31, no. 3 (Nov.) 467–86.

Adelman, Irma (1963) 'An Econometric Analysis of Population Growth', *American Economic Review*, vol. 53, no. 3 (June) 314–39.

Adelman, Irma, and Cynthia Taft Morris (1973) *Economic Growth and Social Equity in Developing Countries* (Stanford: Stanford University Press).

Adeokun, L. A., and F. A. Ilori (1976) 'Status of Women and the Knowledge, Attitude and Practice of Family Planning in South-West Nigeria', presented at the Conference of Nigerian Women and Development in Relation to Changing Family Structure (Ibadan, April) mimeograph.

Adlakha, Arjun (1973) 'Fertility and Infant Mortality: an Analysis of Turkish Data', *Demography India*, vol. 2, no. 1, 56–76.

Ahluwalia, Montek, S. (1976) 'Income Distribution and Development: Some Stylized Facts', *American Economic Review*, vol. 66, no. 2 (May) 128–35.

Aigner, D., and H. Simon, (1970) 'A Specification Bias Interpretation of Cross-Section vs. Time-Series Parameter Estimates', *Western Economic Journal*, vol. 8 (June) 144–61.

Amemiya, T. (1971) 'The Estimation of the Variances in a Variance-Components Model', *International Economic Review*, vol. 21 (Feb.) 1–13.

Anker, Richard (1977) 'The Effect of Group Level Variables on Fertility in a Rural Indian Sample', *Journal of Development Studies*, vol. 14, no. 1 (Oct.) 63–76.

Anker, Richard (1978) 'An Analysis of Fertility Differentials in Developing Countries', *Review of Economics and Statistics*, vol. 60, no. 1 (Feb.) 58–69.

Anker, Richard (1982) 'Demographic Change and the Role of Women: a Research Programme in Developing Countries', in Richard Anker, Mayra Buvinic and Nadia H. Youssef (eds), *Interactions Between Women's Roles and Demographic Trends* (London: Croom Helm).

Anker, Richard, and Martha Anker (1982) *Reproductive Behavior in Households of Rural Gujarat: Social, Economic and Community Factors* (New Delhi: Concept Publishing Co.).

Anker, Richard, Mayra Buvinic and Nadia H. Youssef (eds) (1982) *Women's Roles and Population Trends in the Third World* (London: Croom Helm).

Anker, Richard, and Ghazi M. Farooq (1978) 'Population and Socio-economic Development: the New Perspective', *International Labour Review*, vol. 117, no. 2 (March/April) 143–55.

Anker, Richard, and James C. Knowles (1978) 'A Micro Analysis of Female Labour Force Participation in Kenya', in G. Standing and G. Sheehan (eds), *Labour Force Participation in Low-Income Countries* (Geneva: International Labour Office).

Anker, Richard, and James C. Knowles (1982) *Determinants of Fertility in Developing Countries: a Case Study of Kenya* (Liege: Ordina Editions).

Anker, Richard, and James C. Knowles (1983) *Population Growth, Employment and Economic-Demographic Interactions in Kenya: Bachue-Kenya* (Aldershot, England and New York: Gower and St Martin's Press).

Aries, P. (1981) 'Two Successive Motivations for the Declining Birth Rate in the West: Notes and Commentary', *Population and Development Review*, vol. 6, no. 4, 645–56.

Arthur, W. Brian, and G. McNicoll (1975) 'Large Scale Simulation Models in Population and Development: What use to Planners?', *Population and Development Review*, vol. 1, no. 2 (Nov.) 251–66.

Arthur, W. Brian, and G. McNicoll (1978) 'An Analytical Survey of Population and Development in Bangladesh', *Population and Development Review*, vol. 4, no. 1 (March) 23–80.

Atkinson, A. B. (1973) 'On the Measurement of Inequality', in A. B. Atkinson (ed.), *Wealth, Income, and Inequality* (Harmondsworth: Penguin).

Atria, Raul (1979) 'Development Planning and Population in Latin America and the Caribbean: a Frame of Reference for Country Activities', in United Nations Fund for Population Activities, *Report on Latin American Conference on Population and Development Planning* (Cartagena, Columbia, 10–11 May) 22–34.

Bagozzi, R., and M. Van Loo (1978a) 'Towards a General Theory of Fertility: a Causal Modelling Approach', *Demography*, no. 15 (Aug.).

Bagozzi, R., and M. Van Loo (1978b) 'Fertility as Consumption: Theories from the Behavioral Sciences', *Journal of Consumer Research*, vol. 4, no. 4, 199–228.

Banks, J. (1954) *Prosperity and Parenthood* (London: Routledge and Kegan Paul).

Banskota, K., and R. E. Evenson (1978) 'Fertility, Schooling and Home Technology', *The Philippine Economic Journal*, vol. 17, nos 1–2, 32–61.

Barclay, George W. (1966) *Techniques of Population Analysis* (New York: John Wiley).

Barlow, Robin (ed.) (1982) *Case Studies in the Demographic Impact of Asian Development Projects* (Ann Arbor: Center for Research on Economic Development, University of Michigan).

Bauer, F. L. (1971) 'Elimination with Weighted Row Combinations for

Solving Linear Equations and Least Squares Problems', in J. H. Wilkinson and C. Reisch (eds), *Handbook for Automatic Computation, Volume II: Linear Algebra* (New York: Springer-Verlag) 119–33.

Beaujot, R., K. Krotki and P. Krishnan (1978) 'Socio-Cultural Variations in the Applicability of the Economic Model of Fertility', *Population Studies*, vol. 32, no. 1, 318–25.

Beaver, Steven E. (1975) *Demographic Transition Theory Reinterpreted: an Application to Recent Natality Trends in Latin America* (Lexington, Mass.: Lexington Books).

Becker, Gary S. (1960) 'An Economic Analysis of Fertility', in Ansley J. Coale (ed.), *Demographic and Economic Change in Developed Countries* (Universities National Bureau Conference, Series 11; Princeton: Princeton University Press) 209–31.

Becker, Gary S. (1965) 'A Theory of the Allocation of Time', *Economic Journal*, vol. 75, no. 229 (Sept.) 493–517.

Becker, Gary S. (1974) 'A Theory of Social Interactions', *Journal of Political Economy*, vol. 82, no. 6 (Nov./Dec.) 1063–93.

Becker, Gary S. (1981) *A Treatise on the Family* (Cambridge, Mass.: Harvard University Press).

Becker, Gary S., and Gregg H. Lewis (1973) 'On the Interaction Between the Quantity and Quality of Children', *Journal of Political Economy*, vol. 81, no. 2, pt II (March/April) 279–88.

Ben-Porath, Yoram (1975) 'Fertility and Economic Growth: Some Microeconomic Aspects', Discussion Paper no. 756, The Maurice Falk Institute for Economic Research (Israel, Jerusalem, Oct.).

Ben-Porath, Yoram (1980) *Transactional Elements in a Theory of Fertility*, paper presented at the Seminar on Determinants of Fertility Trends (Bad Hamburg: IUSSP).

Ben-Porath, Yoram, and Finis Welch (1972) 'Chance, Child Traits and Choice of Family Size' (Santa Monica, California: The Rand Corporation, Dec.) R-1117.

Berelson, Bernard (1976) 'Social Science Research on Population: a Review', *Population and Development Review*, vol. 2, no. 2 (June) 219–66, esp. 230.

Biddle, B. J. (1979) *Role Theory: Expectations, Identities and Behavior* (New York: Academic Press).

Bilsborrow, Richard E. (1977) 'Effects of Economic Dependency on Labour Force Participation Rates in Less Developed Countries', *Oxford Economic Papers*, vol. 29, 61–83.

Bilsborrow, Richard, E. (1981) 'Priority Areas for Future Research on Demographic-Economic Interrelationships', in *Population and Development Modelling*, Proceedings of the United Nations/UNFPA Expert Group Meeting (Geneva, 24–8 September 1979) 74–129.

Birdsall, Nancy (1976) 'Women and Population Studies', *Signs*, vol. 1, no. 3, pt 1, 713–20.

Birdsall, Nancy (1977) 'Analytical Approaches to the Relationship of Population Growth and Development', *Population and Development Review*, vol. 3, nos 1, 2 (March/June) 63–102.

Birdsall, Nancy, J. Fei, S. Kuznets, G. Ranis and T. P. Schultz (1979)

'Demography and Development in the 1980s', in P. Hauser (ed.), *World Population and Development: Challenges and Prospects* (Syracuse University Press).

Birks, J. S., and C. A. Sinclair (1980) *International Migration and Development in the Arab Region* (Geneva: International Labour Office).

Blake, Judith (1968) 'Are Babies Consumer Durables? A Critique of the Economic Theory of Reproductive Motivation', *Population Studies*, vol. 22, no. 1 (March) 5–25.

Blandy, Richard (1974) 'The Welfare Analysis of Fertility Reduction', *The Economic Journal*, vol. 84, no. 2 (March) 109–29.

Bleek, W. (1975) *Marriage Inheritance and Witchcraft: A Case Study of a Ghanian Family* (Leiden: Africa Studiecentrum).

Bogue, Donald J. and Amy Ong Tsui (1979) 'A Reply to Paul Demeny's "On the End of the Population Explosion"', *Population and Development Review*, vol. 5, no. 3 (Sept.) 479–94.

Böhning, W. R. (ed.) (1981) *Black Migration to South Africa* (Geneva: International Labour Office).

Bongaarts, John (1978) 'A Framework for Analyzing the Proximate Determinants of Fertility', *Population and Development Review*, vol. 4, no. 1 (March) 105–32.

Bongaarts, John (1982) 'The Fertility-inhibiting Effects of the Intermediate Fertility Variables', *Studies in Family Planning*, vol. 13, no. 67 (June/July) 179–89.

Boratov, K. (1972) 'Turkiye Tarimin 1960 lardaki Yapisi' ('The Structure of Turkish Agriculture in the 1960s'), *Siyasul Bilgiler Dergisis (Journal of Political Science)*, vol. 27, 771–816.

Boulier, Bryan L. (1975) 'The Effects of Demographic Variables on Income Distribution', Discussion Paper no. 61 (Princeton, New Jersey: Research Program in Economic Development, Woodrow Wilson School, Princeton University, May).

Boulier, Bryan L., and Mark R. Rosenzweig (1978) 'Age, Biological Factors, and Socio-economic Determinants of Fertility: a New Measure of Cumulative Fertility for Use in the Empirical Analysis of Family Size', *Demography*, vol. 15, no. 4 (Nov.) 487–97.

Brass, William (1975) *Methods for Estimating Fertility and Mortality from Limited and Defective Data* (Chapel Hill, North Carolina: Laboratories for Population Statistics, Occasional Publication, October).

Brodbeck, May (1968) *Readings in the Philosophy of Social Sciences* (New York: Macmillan).

Bulatao, Rodolfo A. (1980) *The Transition in the Value of Children and the Fertility Transition*, paper read at a seminar on Determinants of Fertility Trends: Major Themes and New Directions for Research (Bad Hamburg: IUSSP).

Bulatao, Rodolfo A., *et al.* (1980) *A Framework for Fertility Analysis*, based on a report from the working group of the panel on fertility determinants, Committee on Population and Demography of the National Research Council (Washington, DC: National Research Council).

Bulatao, Rodolfo A. (1981) 'Values and Disvalues of Children in Successive Childbearing Decisions', *Demography*, vol. 18, no. 1 (Feb.) 1–25.

Bulatao, Rodolfo A., and D. Lee with P. E. Hollerbach and J. Bongaarts (eds) (1983) *Determinants of Fertility in Developing Countries* (New York: Academic Press).

Burch, Thomas K. (1975) 'Theories of Fertility as Guides to Population Policy', *Social Forces*, vol. 54, no. 1 (Sept.) 126–38.

Burch, Thomas K. (1980) *Demographic Behavior: Interdisciplinary Perspectives on Decision-Making* (ASS Selected Symposium).

Burch, Thomas K. (ed.) (1981) *Demographic Behavior: Interdisciplinary Perspectives on Decision-Making*, AAAS Selected Symposium no. 45 (Boulder, Colorado: Westview Press [for] American Association for the Advancement of Science).

Cabañero, Teresa A. (1978) 'The Shadow Price of Children in Laguna Households', *The Philippine Economic Journal*, vol. 17, nos 1–2, 62–87.

Cain, M. T. (1977) 'The Economic Activities of Children in a Village in Bangladesh', *Population and Development Review*, vol. 3, no. 3 (Sept.).

Cain, M. T. (1978) 'The Household Life Cycle and Economic Mobility in Rural Bangladesh', *Population and Development Review*, vol. 4, no. 3 (Sept.) 421–38.

Cain, M. T. (1980) 'Risk, Fertility, and Family Planning in a Bangladesh Village', *Studies in Family Planning*, vol. 11, no. 6 (June) 219–23.

Cain, M. T., S. R. Khanam and S. Nahar (1979) 'Class, Patriarchy and Women's Work in Bangladesh', *Population and Development Review*, vol. 5, no. 3 (Sept.) 405–38.

Caldwell, John C. (1968a) 'The Control of Family Size in Tropical Africa', *Demography*, vol. 5, no. 2 (Jan.) 598–619.

Caldwell John C. (1968b) *Population Growth and Family Change in Africa* (Canberra: Australian National University Press).

Caldwell, John C. (1969) *African Rural–Urban Migration: The Movement to Ghana's Towns* (Canberra: Australian National University Press).

Caldwell, John C. (1976) 'Toward a Restatement of Demographic Transition Theory', *Population and Development Review*, vol. 2, nos 3, 4 (Sept./Dec.) 321–66.

Caldwell, John C. (1977a) 'The Economic Rationality of High Fertility: an Investigation Illustrated with Nigerian Data', *Population Studies*, vol. 31, no. 1 (March) 5–27.

Caldwell, John C. (1977b) 'Measuring Wealth Flows and the Rationality of Fertility: Thoughts and Plans Based in the First Place on African Work', in L. T. Ruzicka (ed.), *The Economic and Social Supports for High Fertility* (Canberra: Australian National University Press).

Caldwell, John C. (1979) 'Education as a Factor in Mortality Decline: an Examination of Nigerian Data', *Population Studies*, vol. 33, no. 3 (Nov.), 395–413.

Caldwell, John, C. (1980) 'Mass Education as a Determinant of the Timing of Fertility Decline', *Population and Development Review*, vol. 6, no. 2 (June) 225–55.

Caldwell, John C. (1982) *Theory of Fertility Decline* (London: Academic Press).

Caldwell, John C., and Pat Caldwell (1977) 'The Role of Marital Sexual Abstinence in Determining Fertility: a Study of the Yoruba in Nigeria', *Population Studies*, vol. 31, no. 2 (July) 193–217.

Campanario, Paulo (1976) 'Caracterización Demográfica de Costa Rica', *Proyecto*, Estralegias de Desarrollo y Políticas de Poblacion (Santiago, Chile: CELADE (Latin American Demographic Centre)).

Carnoy, Martin, and Hans H. Thias (1971) 'Rates of Return to Schooling in Kenya', *East African Economic Review*, vol. 3, no. 2, 63–103.

Carnoy, Martin, and Hans H. Thias (1972) 'Cost Benefit Analysis in Education: a Case of Kenya', *IBRD Occasional Papers*, no. 14 (Baltimore).

CELADE (Latin American Demographic Centre) (1974) *Boletin del Barrico de Datos* (Nov.).

Centar za Demografska Istrazivanja (1963) *Sema Stalnih Rejona za Demografska Istrazinvanje* (Beograd: Institut Drustvenih Nauka).

Chaudhury, Rafiqul H. (1979) 'Female Labour Force Status and Fertility Behaviour – Some Theoretical, Methodological, and Policy Issues', *Pakistan Development Review*, vol. 18, no. 4 (Winter) 341–57.

Chenery, Hollis, *et al.* (1974) *Redistribution with Growth* (Fair Lawn, New Jersey: Oxford University Press).

Chiang, Alpha C. (1974) *Fundamental Methods of Mathematical Economics*, 2nd edn (New York: McGraw-Hill).

Chipman, J. S. (1974) 'Homothetic Preferences and Aggregation', *Journal of Economic Theory*, vol. 8, 26–38.

Chiswick, Barry R. (1974) *Income Inequality: Regional Analyses Within a Human Capital Framework* (New York: National Bureau of Economic Research).

Chowdhury, A. K. M., A. R. Kahn and L. C. Chen (1976) 'The Effect of Child Mortality Experience on Subsequent Fertility: Pakistan and Bangladesh', *Population Studies*, vol. 30, no. 2 (July) 249–62.

Coale, Ansley J. (1967) 'Factors Associated with the Development of Low Fertility: an Historic Summary', in *Proceedings of the World Population Conference*, vol. II, Belgrade, 1965 (New York: United Nations) 205–9.

Coale, Ansley J. (1969) 'The Decline of Fertility in Europe from the French Revolution to World War II', in S. J. Behrman *et al.* (eds), *Fertility and Family Planning* (Ann Arbor: University of Michigan).

Coale, Ansley J. (1971) 'Age Patterns of Marriage', *Population Studies*, vol. 25, no. 2.

Coale, Ansley J. (1973) 'The Demographic Transition Reconsidered', *International Population Conference, Liege 1973*, vol. I (Liege: International Union for the Scientific Study of Population) 53–72.

Coale, Ansley J. (1977) 'The Development of New Models of Nuptiality and Fertility', *Population*, numéro spécial.

Coale, Ansley J., and E. M. Hoover (1958) *Population Growth and Economic Development in Low Income Countries: a Case Study of India's Prospects* (Princeton, New Jersey: Princeton University Press).

Coale, Ansley J., and T. James Trussell (1974) 'Model Fertility Schedules: Variations in the Age Structure of Childbearing in Human Populations', *Population Index*, vol. 40, no. 2 (April) 185–258.

Coale, Ansley, J., and T. James Trussell (1978) 'Technical Note: Finding the Two Parameters that Specify a Model Schedule of Marital Fertility', *Population Index*, vol. 44.

Cochrane, Susan Hill (1978) *Fertility and Education: What Do We Really Know?* (Baltimore: Johns Hopkins University Press).

Colegio de Mexico, El (1979) *Dinamica de la poblacion de Mexico* (Mexico).

'[The] Colombo Declaration on Population and Development' (1979) *Population and Development Review*, vol. 5, no. 4 (Dec.) 731–6.

Coombs, C. H. (1964) *Theory of Data* (New York: John Wiley and Sons).

Coombs, C. H., L. C. Coombs and G. M. McClelland (1975) 'Preference Scales for Number and Sex of Children', *Population Studies*, vol. 29, no. 2 (July) 275–98.

Coombs, Lolagene C. (1975) *Are Cross Cultural Preference Comparisons Possible? A Measurement-Theoretic Approach*, IUSSP Paper no. 5. (Liege: International Union for the Scientific Study of Population).

Coombs, Lolagene C. (1979a) 'Underlying Family Size Preferences and Reproductive Behavior', *Studies in Family Planning*, vol. 10, no. 1 (Jan.) 25–36.

Coombs, Lolagene C. (1979b) 'Prospective Fertility and Underlying Preferences', *Population Studies*, vol. 33, no. 3 (Nov.) 447–55.

Coombs, Lolagene C., and Ronald Freedman (1979) 'Some Roots of Preference: Roles, Activities, and Familial Values', *Demography*, vol. 16, no. 3 (Aug.) 359–76.

Cuca, C., and C. S. Pierce (1977) *Experiments in Family Planning: Lessons from the Developing World* (Baltimore: Johns Hopkins University Press).

DaVanzo, Julie (1972) *The Determinants of Family Formation in Chile, 1960: an Econometric Study of Female Labor Force Participation, Marriage and Fertility Decisions* (Santa Monica, California: The Rand Corporation) R-830-AID.

DaVanzo, Julie, and D. Lee (1978) *The Incomparability of Child-Care with Labour Force Participation and Non-Market Activities: Preliminary Evidence from Malaysian Time Budget Data*, paper presented at the International Center for Research on Women, Conference on Women and Poverty (Washington, DC).

Davis, Kingsley (1949) *Human Society* (New York: Macmillan).

Davis, Kingsley (1955) 'Malthus and the Theory of Population', in *The Language of Social Research* (New York: The Free Press).

Davis, Kingsley (1963) 'The Theory of Change and Response in Modern Demographic History', *Population Index*, vol. 29, no. 4 (Oct.) 345–66.

Davis, Kingsley and Judith Blake (1956) 'Social Structure and Fertility: an Analytical Framework', *Economic Development and Cultural Change*, vol. 4 (April) 211–35.

Demeny, Paul (1971) 'The Economics of Population Control', in Roger Revelle *et al.* (eds), *Rapid Population Growth* (National Academy of Sciences, Baltimore: Johns Hopkins Press) 192–221.

Demeny, Paul (1974) 'The Populations of the Underdeveloped Countries', *Scientific American*, vol. 231, no. 3 (Sept.) 149–59.

Demeny, Paul (1976) 'Discussion of the Paper by Professor Schultz', in

A. J. Coale (ed.), *Economic Factors in Population Growth* (New York: John Wiley and Sons) 125–35.

Demeny, Paul (1979a) 'On the End of the Population Explosion', *Population and Development Review*, vol. 5, no. 1 (March) 141–62.

Demeny, Paul (1979b) 'On the End of the Population Explosion: a Rejoinder', *Population and Development Review*, vol. 5, no. 3 (Sept.) 495–504.

DeTray, Dennis N. (1973) 'Child Quality and the Demand for Children', *Journal of Political Economy*, vol. 81, no. 2 (Mar./Apr. Supplement 2) S70–95.

DeTray, Dennis N. (1977) 'Age of Marriage and Fertility: a Policy Review', *Pakistan Development Review*, vol. 16, 89–100.

DeTray, Dennis N., and Z. Khan (1977) 'On the Care and Handling of Regression Specifications in Fertility Research', *Pakistan Development Review*, vol. 16, 309–24.

Dewdney, J. C. (1972) 'Turkey: Recent Population Trends', in J. I. Clarke and W. B. Fisher (eds), *Population of the Middle East and North Africa* (New York: Africana Publishing Corporation).

Diesing, Paul (1971) *Patterns of Discovery in the Social Sciences* (New York: Aldine Publishing Co.).

Dinan, C. (1983) 'Gold Diggers and Sugar Daddies', in C. Oppong (ed.), *Female and Male in West Africa* (London: Allen and Unwin).

Dirección General de Estadísticas (1975) *Estadísticas Vitales*, serie I, no. 1, cuadro 1.

Dixon, Ruth B. (1975) *Women's Rights and Fertility*, Reports on Population/Family Planning, no. 7 (New York: The Population Council).

Dixon, Ruth B. (1979) 'On Drawing Policy Conclusions from Multiple Regressions: Some Queries and Dilemmas', *Studies in Family Planning*, vol. 9, nos 10–11.

Dixon, Ruth B. (1982) 'Mobilizing Women for Rural Employment in South Asia: Issues of Class, Caste and Patronage', *Economic Development and Cultural Change*, vol. 30, no. 2 (Jan.) 373–90.

Douglas, M. (1966) 'Population Control in Primitive Groups', *British Journal of Sociology*, vol. 17, no. 3.

Duesenberry, James (1949) *Income, Saving and the Theory of Consumer Behavior* (Cambridge: Harvard University Press).

Dupaquier, Jacques (1980) 'Malthus Reconsidered', *Contemporary Sociology*, vol. 9, no. 4 (July) 462–5.

Dyke, B., and J. W. MacCluer (1973) *Computer Simulation in Human Population Studies* (New York: Academic Press).

Easterlin, Richard A. (1969) 'Towards a Socio-Economic Theory of Fertility: a Survey of Recent Research on Economic Factors in American Fertility', in S. J. Behrman, Leslie Corsa and Ronald Freedman (eds), *Fertility and Family Planning: A World View* (Ann Arbor: University of Michigan Press) 127–56.

Easterlin, Richard A. (1971) 'Does Human Fertility Adjust to Environment?', *American Economic Review*, vol. 61, no. 2 (May) 399–407.

Easterlin, Richard A. (1972) 'Relative Economic Status and the American Fertility Swing', in Eleanor Sheldon (ed.), *Social Structure, Family*

Life Styles and Economic Behavior (Philadelphia: J. P. Lippincott).

Easterlin, Richard A. (1975) 'An Economic Framework for Fertility Analysis', *Studies in Family Planning*, vol. 6, no. 3 (March) 54–63.

Easterlin, Richard A. (1976) 'Population Change and Farm Settlement in the Northern United States', *Journal of Economic History*, vol. 36, 45–75.

Easterlin, Richard A. (1978) 'The Economics and Sociology of Fertility: a Synthesis', in Charles Tilly (ed.), *Historical Studies of Changing Fertility* (Princeton, N.J.: Princeton University Press).

Easterlin, Richard A. (ed.) (1980) *Population and Economic Change in Developing Countries*, a Conference Report, Universities-National Bureau Committee for Economic Research, no. 30 (Chicago: University of Chicago Press).

Easterlin, Richard A., Robert A. Pollack and Michael L. Wachter (1980) 'Toward a More General Economic Model of Fertility Determination: Endogenous Preferences and Natural Fertility', in Richard A. Easterlin (ed.), *Population and Economic Change in Developing Countries* (Chicago: University of Chicago Press) 81–149.

Eberstadt, Nick (ed.) (1981) *Fertility Decline in the Less Developed Countries* (New York: Praeger Publishers).

Edlefsen, L. E. (1981) 'The Effect of Sample Truncation on Estimates of Fertility Relationships', *Research in Population Economics*, vol. 3, 41–66.

Ekanem, I. I. (1972) *The 1963 Nigerian Census: A Critical Appraisal* (Ethiopia).

Ekanem, I. I., and Ghazi M. Farooq (1977) 'The Dynamics of Population Change in Southern Nigeria', *Genus*, vol. 33, nos 1–2, 119–40.

Encarnacion, Jose, Jr (1974) 'Fertility and Labor Force Participation: Philippines', *The Philippines Review of Business and Economics*, vol. 11, no. 3 (Dec.) 113–44.

Enke, Stephen (1960) 'The Gains to India from Population Control: Some Money Measures and Incentive Schemes', *Review of Economics and Statistics*, vol. 42 (May) 175–81.

Epstein, T., and D. Jackson (eds) (1977) *The Feasibility of Fertility Planning: Micro Perspectives* (Oxford: Pergamon Press).

Evenson, R. E. (1978) 'Introduction to Symposium on Household Economics', *The Philippine Economic Journal*, vol. 12, nos 1–2, 1–31.

Farooq, Ghazi, M. (1980) *Household Fertility Decision-Making in Nigeria* (Geneva: International Labour Office) mimeographed World Employment Programme research working paper; restricted.

Farooq, Ghazi, M. (1981) 'Population, Human Resources and Development Planning: Towards an Integrated Approach', *International Labour Review*, vol. 120, no. 3 (May/June).

Farooq, Ghazi M., and L. A. Adeokun (1976) 'Impact of a Rural Family Planning Program, Ishan Division, Nigeria, 1969–1972', *Studies in Family Planning*, vol. 7, no. 6 (June) 158–69.

Farooq, Ghazi M., I. I. Ekanem and M. A. Ojelade (1977) *Family Size Preferences and Fertility in South Western Nigeria* (Geneva: International Labour Office) mimeographed World Employment Programme research working paper; restricted.

Farooq, Ghazi M., and B. Tuncer (1974) 'Fertility and Economic and Social Development in Turkey: a Cross-Sectional and Time-Series Study', *Population Studies*, vol. 28, no. 2 (July) 263–76.

Fawcett, James T., *et al.* (1974) *The Value of Children in Asia and The United States*, Institute Paper no. 32 (Honolulu: The East–West Population Institute).

Fishlow, A. (1972) 'Brazilian Size Distribution of Income', *American Economic Review* (March).

Flegg, A. T. (1979) 'The Role of Inequality of Income in the Determination of Birth Rates', *Population Studies*, vol. 33, no. 3 (Nov.) 457–77.

Flew, Anthony (ed.) (1973) *Malthus: an Essay on the Principle of Population* (Middlesex, England: Penguin Books).

Fortes, M. (1950) 'Kinship and Marriage Among the Ashanti', in A. Radcliffe-Brown and D. Forde (eds), *African Systems of Kinship and Marriage* (London: Oxford University Press).

Fortes, M. (1954) 'A Demographic Field Study in Ashanti', in L. Lorimer (ed.), *Culture and Human Fertility* (New York: United Nations).

Frederiksen, Harold (1969) 'Feedbacks in Economic and Demographic Trasition', *Science*, vol. 166 (Nov.) 837–47.

Freedman, Deborah (1964) 'The Relation of Economic Status to Fertility', *American Economic Review*, vol. 53, no. 3 (June) 414–26.

Freedman, Deborah (1975) 'Consumption of Modern Goods and Services and their Relationship to Fertility', *Journal of Development Studies*, vol. 12, no. 1.

Freedman, Ronald (1974) 'Community-level Data in Fertility Surveys', Occasional Paper no. 8 (London: World Fertility Survey, International Statistical Institute).

Freedman, Ronald (1975) *The Sociology of Human Fertility: an Annotated Bibliography* (New York: Irvington Publishers) 3–21.

Freedman, Ronald (1979) 'Theories of Fertility Decline: a Reappraisal', in Philip M. Hauser (ed.), *World Population and Development-Challenges and Prospects* (Syracuse, New York: Syracuse University Press; Copyright by the United Nations Fund for Population Activities) 63–79.

Freedman, Ronald, and Bernard Berelson (1976) 'The Record of Family Planning Porgrammes', *Studies in Family Planning*, vol. 7, no. 1 (Jan.) 1–40.

Friedlander, D. (1977) 'The Effects of Child Mortality on Fertility: Theoretical Framework of the Relationship', in *International Population Conference, Mexico 1977* (Liege: International Union for the Scientific Study of Population).

Friedman, Milton (1957) *A Theory of the Consumption Function* (Princeton: Princeton University Press).

Fry, C. L. (1929) 'Turkey', in F. A. Ross, C. L. Fry and E. Sibley (eds), *The Near East and American Philanthropy* (New York: Columbia University Press).

Fulop, Marcel (1977a) 'A Survey of the Literature on the Economic Theory of Fertility Behavior', *American Economist*, vol. 21, no. 1 (Spring).

Fulop, Marcel (1977b) 'The Empirical Evidence from the Fertility Demand Functions: a Review of the Literature', *American Economist*, vol. 21, no. 2 (Fall).

Gaisie, S. (1981) 'Child Spacing Patterns and Fertility Differentials in Ghana', in H. Page and R. Lesthaege (eds) *Child Spacing in Tropical Africa: Traditions and Change* (New York: Academic Press).

Galbriath, J. K. (1973) *Economics and the Public Purpose* (Boston, Mass.: Houghton Mifflin).

Germain, Adrienne (1975) 'Status and Roles of Women as Factors in Fertility Behavior: a Policy Analysis', *Studies in Family Planning*, vol. 6, no. 7 (July) 192–200.

Goldberg, D. (1960) *Some Recent Developments in Fertility Research* (Princeton: Princeton University Press).

Goldberger, Arthur S. (1964) *Econometric Theory* (New York: John Wiley and Sons).

Goldstein, Sidney (1972) 'The Influence of Labour Force Participation and Education on Fertility in Thailand', *Population Studies*, vol. 26, no. 3 (Nov.) 419–36.

Goodman, Leo A. (1953) 'Ecological Regressions and Behavior of Individuals', *American Sociological Review*, vol. 18, no. 6 (Dec.) 663–4.

Goodman, Leo A. (1959) 'Some Alternatives to Ecological Correlation', *American Journal of Sociology*, vol. 64, no. 6 (May) 610–25.

Goody, E. (1978) 'Some Theoretical and Empirical Aspects of Parenthood in West Africa', in C. Oppong *et al.* (eds), *Marriage, Fertility and Parenthood in West Africa* (Canberra: Australian National University Press).

Goody, J. (1972) *Domestic Groups* (Addison-Wesley Modules in Anthropology, Module 28).

Gorman, W. M. (1953) 'Community Preference Fields', *Econometrica*, vol. 21 (Jan.) 63–81.

Graff, H. J. (1979) 'Literacy, Education, and Fertility, Past and Present: a Critical Review', *Population and Development Review*, vol. 5, no. 1 (March) 105–40.

Gregory, Paul R. (1976) 'Fertility and Economic Development', in Michael C. Keeley (ed.), *Population, Public Policy and Economic Development* (New York: Praeger Publishers) 160–87.

Gregory, Paul R., and John M. Campbell, Jr (1976) 'Fertility Interactions and Modernization Turning Points', *Journal of Political Economy*, vol. 84, no. 4, pt I (Aug.) 835–47.

Gregory, Paul R., John M. Campbell, Jr and Benjamin Cheng (1972) 'A Cost-inclusive Simultaneous-equation Model of Birth Rates', *Econometrica*, vol. 40, 681–7.

Gronau, Reuben (1974) 'The Effect of Children on the Housewife's Value of Time', in T. W. Schultz (ed.) *Economics of the Family: Marriages, Children, and Human Capital* (Chicago: University of Chicago Press).

Guzevatyi, Yaropolk, N. (1975) 'Economic and Social Determinants of Contemporary Demographic Behavior', in *The Population Debate: Dimensions and Perspectives*, papers of the World Population Conference (Bucharest, 1974) vol. 1, 534–7.

Gwatkin, Davidson R. (1980) 'Indications of Change in Developing

Country Mortality Trends: the End of an Era?', *Population and Development Review*, vol. 6, no. 4 (Dec.) 615–44.

Hacettepe Institute of Population Studies (1980) *Turkish Fertility Survey 1978, First Report* (Ankara, Turkey: Hacettepe University).

Hammond, J. L. (1973) 'Two Sources of Error in Ecological Correlations', *American Sociological Review*, vol. 38 (Dec.) 764–77.

Hanushek, E. A., J. E. Jackson and J. F. Kain (1972) 'Model Specification, Use of Aggregate Data and the Ecological Correlation Fallacy', Discussion Paper no. 70, Program on Regional and Urban Economics (Harvard University, January).

Hardin, Garrett (1968) 'The Tragedy of the Commons', *Science*, vol. 162, 1243–8.

Harman, Alvin J. (1970) *Fertility and Economic Behavior of Families in the Philippines* (Santa Monica, California: The Rand Corporation).

Hass, Paula H. (1974) 'Wanted and Unwanted Pregnancies: a Fertility Decision-making model', *Journal of Social Issues*, vol. 30, no. 4, 125–65.

Hassan, Shafick S. (1973) 'Childhood Mortality Experience and Fertility Performance', in Abdel R. Omran (ed.), *Egypt: Population Problems and Prospects* (Chapel Hill, North Carolina: Carolina Population Center) 355–69.

Hausain, Iz (1970) 'Educational Status and Differential Fertility in India', *Social Biology*, vol. 17, no. 2 (June) 132–9.

Hauser, Philip M. (1973) 'Population Policies Affecting Fertility: a Sociological Perspective on Family Planning Programs', in *International Population Conference: Liege 1973*, vol. 3 (Liege: International Union for the Scientific Study of Population) 303–18.

Hauser, Philip M. (ed.) (1979) *World Population and Development: Challenges and Prospects* (Syracuse, New York: Syracuse University Press; Copyright by the United Nations Fund for Population Activities).

Hausman, J. A. (1978) 'Specification Test in Econometrics', *Econometrica*, vol. 46, no. 6 (Nov.) 1251–71.

Hausman, J. A., and W. E. Taylor (1979) 'Panel Data and Unobservable Individual Effects', Working Paper no. 255 (Massachusetts Institute of Technology).

Hausman, J. A., and W. E. Taylor (1981) 'Panel Data and Individual Effects', *Econometrica*, vol. 49, no. 6.

Hawthorn, Geoffrey (1978) 'Introduction', *Journal of Development Studies*, vol. 14, no. 4 (July) 1–21.

Hawthorn, Geoffrey (1980) *The Paradox of the Modern: Determinants of Fertility in Northern and Western Europe Since 1950*, paper read at a seminar on Determinants of Fertility Trends (Bad Hamburg: IUSSP, 14–17 April).

Heckman, James J. (1974) 'Shadow Prices, Market Wages and Labour Supply', *Econometrica*, vol. 42, no. 4 (July) 679–94.

Heckman, James J. (1976) 'The Common Structure of Statistical Models of Truncation, Sample Selection and Limited Dependent Variables and a Simple Estimator for Such Models', *Annals of Economic and Social Measurement*, vol. 5, no. 4, 475–92.

Heer, David M., and J. W. Boynton (1970) 'A Multivariate Regression

Analysis of Differences in Fertility of United States Counties', *Social Biology*, vol. 17, no. 3 (Sept.) 180–94.

Heer, David M. and Dean O. Smith (1968) 'Mortality Level, Desired Family Size, and Population Increase', *Demography*, vol. 5, no. 1, 104–21.

Heer, David M. and Hsin-ying Wu (1975) 'The Separate Effects of Individual Child Loss and Community Mortality Level upon Subsequent Fertility in Taiwan', in *Seminar on Infant Mortality in Relation to the Level of Fertility* (6–12, University Park, Los Angeles: Population Research Lab; Paris: *CICRED*) 203–24.

Hein, C. (1982) 'Factory Employment, Marriage and Fertility: the Case of Mauritian Women' (Geneva: International Labour Office) mimeographed World Employment Programme research working paper; restricted.

Henderson, James M., and Richard E. Quandt (1980) *Micro Economic Theory: A Mathematical Approach*, 3rd edn (New York: McGraw-Hill).

Hendershot, Gerry E. and Paul J. Placek (1981) *Predicting Fertility* (Lexington, Mass.: D. C. Heath).

Hermalin, Albert I. (1975) 'Regression Analysis of Areal Data', in C. Chaadrasekaran and A. Hermalin (eds), *Measuring the Effects of Family Planning Programs on Fertility* (Dolhain, Belgium: Ordina Editions).

Hermalin, Albert I., Ronald Freedman, Te-Hsiung Sun and Ming-Cheng Chang (1979) 'Do Intentions Predict Fertility? 1967–74', *Studies in Family Planning*, vol. 10, no. 3 (March) 75–95.

Hernandez, Donald J. (1981) 'A Note on Measuring Independent Impact of Family Planning Programs on Fertility Declines', *Demography*, vol. 18, no. 4, 627–34.

Herrin, Alejandro N. (1979) 'Rural Electrification and Fertility Change in the Southern Philippines', *Population and Development Review*, vol. 5, no. 1 (March) 61–86.

Hicks, John R. (1979) *Causality in Economics* (Oxford: Basil Blackwell).

Hill, C. R., and F. Stafford (1980) 'Parental Care of Children: Time Diary Estimates of Quantity Predictability and Variety', *Journal of Human Resources*, vol. 15, no. 2.

Hilton, Elizabeth T., and Arthur A. Lumsdaine (1975) 'Field Trial Designs in Gauging the Impact of Fertility Planning Programs', in Carl A. Bennett and Arthur A. Lumsdaine (eds), *Evaluation and Experiment: Some Critical Issues in Assessing Social Programs* (New York: Academic Press).

Hirschman, Charles (1981) 'The Uses of Demography in Development Planning', *Economic Development and Cultural Change*, vol. 29, no. 3 (April) 561–75.

Ho, T. (1979) 'Time Costs of Child Rearing in the Rural Philippines', *Population and Development Review*, vol. 5, no. 4 (Dec.).

Hoffman, Lois W. and Martin L. Hoffman (1973) 'The Value of Children to Parents', in J. T. Fawcett (ed.), *Psychological Aspects of Population* (New York: Basic Books).

Hoffman, Lois W. (1974) 'The Employment of Women, Education, and Fertility', *Merril-Palmer Quarterly of Behavior and Development*, vol.

20, no. 2, 99–119.

Hollerbach, P. (1980) *Power in Families, Communication and Fertility Decision-Making*, Working Paper no. 53 (New York: The Population Council).

Holsinger, D. B., and J. D. Kasarda (1976) 'Education and Human Fertility: a Sociological Perspective', in R. G. Ridker (ed.), *Population and Development* (Baltimore: Johns Hopkins University Press).

Hopkins, M. J. D., G. B. Rodgers and R. Wéry (1976) 'Evaluating a Basic-Needs Strategy and Population Policies: the BACHUE Approach', *International Labour Review*, vol. 114, no. 3.

Horner, M. S. (1972) 'Toward an Understanding of Achievement-Related Conflicts in Women', *Journal of Social Issues*, vol. 28, no. 2, 157–75.

Hotelling, H. (1932) 'Edgeworth's Taxation Paradox and the Nature of Demand and Supply Functions', *Journal of Political Economy*, vol. 40, 577–616.

Howell, S. (1979) 'The Chewong of Malaysia', *Populi*, vol. 6, no. 4.

Husain, I. (1970) 'Educational Status and Differential Fertility in India', *Social Biology*, vol. 17, no. 2 (June) 132–40.

Hutteroth, W. D. (1974) 'The Influence of Social Structure on Land Division and Settlement in Inner Anatolia', in P. Benedict, E. Tumertekin and F. Mansur (eds), *Turkey: Geographical and Social Perspectives* (Leiden: E. J. Brill).

Ilchman, W. F. (1975) 'Population Knowledge and Fertility Policies', in W. F. Ilchman *et al.* (eds), *Policy Sciences and Population* (Lexington, Mass.: Heath-Lexington Books).

International Labour Office (1982) *Population and Development: A Progress Report on ILO Research on Population, Labour, Employment and Income Distribution*, 4th edn, April (Geneva).

International Planned Parenthood Federation (1974) *Survey of World Needs in Family Planning* (London: IPPF).

Jaffe, A. J., and K. Azumi (1960) 'The Birth Rate and Cottage Industries in Underdeveloped Countries', *Economic Development and Cultural Change*, vol. 9, no. 1 (Oct.) 52–63.

Jagannadham, V. (ed.) (1973) *Family Planning in India: Policy and Administration* (New Delhi: Indian Institute of Public Administration).

Jain, Anrudh (1981) 'The Effect of Female Education on Fertility: a Simple Explanation', *Demography*, vol. 18, no. 4 (Nov.) 577–96.

Jain, Shail (1975) *Size Distribution of Income: a Compilation of Data* (Washington, DC: World Bank).

Jencks, Christopher, *et al.* (1972) *Inequality: a Reassessment of the Effect of Family and Schooling in America* (New York: Basic Books).

Johnson, J. Timothy, and Silvia Pedraza (1976) 'Stated Expectations of Use of Family Planning: How Good a Predictor of Subsequent Use?' Population Planning Working Paper no. 22 (Ann Arbor: Department of Population Planning, University of Michigan).

Johnston, J. (1972) *Econometric Methods*, 2nd edn (New York: McGraw-Hill).

Jones, Alan (1974) 'Measuring the Impact of the Kenyan Family Planning Programme', IDS Working Paper no. 148 (University of Nairobi, May).

Jones, G. (1977) 'Economic and Social Supports of High Fertility: Conceptual Framework', in L. T. Ruzicka (ed.), *The Economic and Social Supports for High Fertility* (Canberra: Australian National University Press).

Jordan, Bonnie Carlson (1976) 'The Status of Women and Fertility: Some Implications for Social Work Practice' (Ann Arbor: Social Work Education and Population Planning Project, University of Michigan).

Joreskog, K. (1973) 'A General Method for Estimating a Linear Structural Equation System', in A. S. Goldberger and O. D. Duncan (eds), *Structural Equation Models in the Social Sciences* (New York: Seminar Press).

Joreskog, K. (1979) *Advances in Factor Analysis and Structural Equation Models* (Cambridge, Mass.: Abbott Books).

Journal of Political Economy, vol. 81 (1973), supplement.

Kahan, James P. (1974) 'Rationality, The Prisoner's Dilemma and Population', *Journal of Social Issues*, vol. 30, no. 4, 189–210.

Kar, Snekendu B. (1978) 'Consistency between Fertility Attitudes and Behaviour: a Conceptual Model', *Population Studies*, vol. 32, no. 1 (Mar.) 173–87.

Keeley, Michael C. (1975) 'A Comment on "An Interpretation of the Economic Theory of Fertility" ', *The Journal of Economic Literature*, vol. 13, no. 2 (June) 461–8.

Kelly, Allen C., *et al.* (1982) *Population and Development in Rural Egypt*, Duke Press Policy Studies, Studies in Social and Economic Demography (Durham, NC: Duke University Press).

Keyfitz, Nathan (1980) 'Petersen on Malthus', *Contemporary Sociology*, vol. 9, no. 4 (July) 465–9.

Kintanar, Augustin, Jr, *et al.* (1974) *Studies in Philippines Economic-Demographic Relationships* (Quezon City: University of the Philippines).

Kmenta, Jan (1971) *Elements of Econometrics* (New York: Macmillan).

Knodel, John, and Visid Prachuabmoh (1973) 'Desired Family Size in Thailand: Are the Responses Meaningful?' *Demography*, vol. 10, no. 4 (June) 619–37.

Knodel, John, and Visid Prachuabmoh (1976) 'Preferences for Sex of Children in Thailand: a Comparison of Husbands' and Wives' Attitudes', *Studies in Family Planning*, vol. 7, no. 5 (May) 137–43.

Knodel, John, and Etienne van de Walle (1979) 'Lessons from the Past: Policy Implications of Historical Fertility Studies', *Population and Development Review*, vol. 5, no. 2 (June) 217–45.

Kocher, James E. (1973) *Rural Development, Income Distribution, and Fertility Decline*, an Occasional Paper of the Population Council (New York: The Population Council).

Kolars, J. (1974) 'Systems of Change in Turkish Village Agriculture', in P. Benedict, E. Tumertekin and F. Mansur (eds), *Turkey: Geographical and Social Perspectives* (Leiden: E. J. Brill).

Kuh, E. (1959) 'The Validity of Cross-Sectionally Estimated Behavior Equations in Time-Series Application', *Econometrica*, vol. 27 (April) 197–214.

Kumar, Josinder (1971) 'A Comparison between Indian Fertility, and Late

Nineteenth-Century Swedish and Finnish Fertility', *Population Studies*, vol. 25, no. 2 (July) 269–82.

Kunstadter, Peter (1978) 'Child Mortality and Maternal Parity: Some Policy Implications', *International Family Planning Perspectives and Digest*, vol. 4, no. 3 (Fall) 78–85.

Kupinsky, Stanley (ed.) (1977) *The Fertility of Working Women: A Synthesis of International Research* (New York: Praeger Publishers).

Kuznets, Simon (1976) 'Demographic Aspects of the Size and Distribution of Income: an Exploratory Essay', *Economic Development and Cultural Change*, vol. 25, no. 1 (Oct.) 1–94.

Kuznets, Simon (1978) 'Size and Age Structure of Family Households: Exploratory Comparisons', *Population and Development Review*, vol. 4, no. 2 (June).

Lahiri, K., and P. Schmidt (1978) 'On the Estimation of Triangular Structural Systems', *Econometrics*, vol. 46 (Sept.) 1217–21.

Laing, J. E. (1970) 'The Relationship Between Attitudes and Behavior: the Case of Family Planning', in D. J. Bogue (ed.), *Further Sociological Contributions to Family Planning Research* (Chicago: University of Chicago Press).

Lancaster, K. (1966) 'Economic Aggregation and Additivity', in Serman Krupp (ed.), *The Structure of Economic Science: Essays on Methodology* (New York: Prentice-Hall).

Lansing, John, and James Morgan (1973) *Economic Survey Methods* (Ann Arbor: University of Michigan Press).

Lau, L. J. (1977a) *Existence Conditions for Aggregate Demand Functions: the Case of a Single Index*, Technical Report no. 248, October (Stanford University).

Lau, L. J. (1977b) *Existence Conditions for Aggregate Demand Functions: the Case of Multiple Indexes*, Technical Report no. 249R, November (Stanford University).

Leamer, E. E. (1978) *Specification Searches: Ad Hoc Inference with Non-experimental Data* (New York: John Wiley and Sons).

Leasure, J. William (1963) 'Factors Involved in the Decline of Fertility in Spain 1900–1950', *Population Studies*, vol. 16, no. 3 (March) 271–85.

Lee, Ronald D. (1974) 'The Formal Dynamics of Controlled Populations and the Echo, the Boom and the Bust', *Demography*, vol. 11, no. 4 (Nov.) 563–85.

Lee, Ronald D. (1976a) 'Demographic Forecasting and the Easterlin Hypothesis', *Population and Development Review*, vol. 2, nos 3, 4 (Sept./Dec.) 459–68.

Lee, Ronald D. (1976b) 'An Historical Perspective on Economic Aspects of the Population Explosion', in *Conference on Population and Economic Change in Less Developed Countries* (Universities – NBER, 30 September–2 October).

Lee, S. B. (1977) *System Effects on Family Planning Behavior in Korean Villages*, PhD dissertation (Ann Arbor: University of Michigan).

Leibenstein, Harvey (1957) *Economic Backwardness and Economic Growth: Studies in the Theory of Economic Development* (New York: John Wiley and Sons).

Leibenstein, Harvey (1969) 'Pitfalls in Benefit–Cost Analysis of Birth Prevention', *Population Studies*, vol. 13, no. 2 (July) 161–70.

Leibenstein, Harvey (1974) 'An Interpretation of the Economic Theory of Fertility: Promising Path or Blind Alley?', *Journal of Economic Literature*, vol. 12, no. 2 (June) 457–79.

Leibenstein, Harvey (1975a) 'The Economic Theory of Fertility Decline', *The Quarterly Journal of Economics*, vol. 89 (February) 1–31.

Leibenstein, Harvey (1975b) 'On the Economic Theory of Fertility: a Reply to Keeley', *The Journal of Economic Literature*, vol. 13, no. 2 (June) 469–72.

Leibenstein, Harvey (1977) 'Beyond Economic Man: Economics, Politics, and the Population Problem', *Population and Development Review*, vol. 3, no. 3 (Sept.) 183–99.

Leibenstein, Harvey (1980) *Relaxing the Maximisation Assumption in the Economic Theory of Fertility*, paper presented at the seminar on Determinants of Fertility: Major Theories and New Directions for Research (Bad Hamburg: IUSSP).

Lesthaeghe, Ron (1980) 'On the Social Control of Human Reproduction', *Population and Development Review*, vol. 6, no. 4 (Dec.) 527–48.

Levine, R. (1980) *Influences of Women's Schooling on Maternal Behavior in the Third World* (Comparative and International Education Society).

Lieberman, Samuel S. (1980) 'A Community Approach to Aggregate Demographic Patterns in Rural Turkey', *Research in Economic Anthropology*, vol. 3, 349–83.

Lindbloom, Charles E., and David K. Cohen (1979) *Usable Knowledge: Social Science and Social Problem Solving* (New Haven: Yale University Press).

Lindert, Peter H. (1978) *Fertility and Scarcity in America* (Princeton: Princeton University Press).

Little, Dennis L. (1981) 'Global and Third World Population Patterns: an Overview', in O. M. Roth and D. L. Little (eds), *Rapid Population Growth in Third World Countries: an Overview of Social and Economic Effects and Their Relationship to US Multinational Corporations* (Washington, DC: Congressional Research Services, September).

Liu, W. (1977) 'The Myths of the Nuclear Family and Fertility in Central Philippines', in L. Lenero-Otero (ed.), *Beyond the Nuclear Family Model Cross-Cultural Perspectives*, Sage Studies in International Sociology no. 8 (Sage Publications Ltd).

MacFarlane, A. (1976) *Resources and Population: a Study of the Gurungs of Nepal* (Cambridge: Cambridge University Press).

MacFarlane, A. (1978a) 'Modes of Reproduction', *Journal of Development Studies*, vol. 14, no. 4 (July).

MacFarlane, A. (1978b) *The Origins of English Individualism* (Oxford: Blackwell).

McClelland, Gary H. (1979) 'Theoretical and Methodological Implications of the Influence of Sex Preferences on Fertility Attitudes–Behaviour Relationships', *Journal of Population*, vol. 2, 224–34.

McGreevy, William P., and Nancy Birdsall (1974) *The Policy Relevance of Recent Social Science Research on Fertility*, Smithsonian Institution,

Interdisciplinary Communications Program Occasional Monograph Series, no. 2 (Washington, DC).

McNamara, Robert S. (1977) *An Address on the Population Problem* (Cambridge: Massachusetts Institute of Technology).

McNicoll, Geoffrey (1975) 'Community-level Population Policy: an Exploration', *Population and Development Review*, vol. 1, no. 1 (Sept.) 1–22.

McNicoll, Geoffrey (1978) 'Population and Development: Outlines for a Structuralist Approach', *The Journal of Development Studies*, vol. 14, no. 4 (July) 79–99.

McNicoll, Geoffrey (1980) 'Institutional Determinants of Fertility Change', *Population and Development Review*, vol. 6, no. 3 (Sept.) 441–62.

Macura, M. (1974) 'Mortality', in H. Kisnisci (ed.), *The Population of Turkey* (Ankara, Turkey: Hacettepe University Press).

Macura, M. (1975) 'Estimates of Infant Mortality Trends in Turkey, 1944–1967', presented at the Second Conference on Turkish Demography (Cesme, Turkey).

Macura, M. (1979) *Indirect Estimation of Marital Fertility by Socio-Economic Group* (Belgrade: Ekonomski Institut) mimeographed.

Macura, M. (1980) 'Low Fertility in Yugoslavia: Analysis and Policy Implications', in G. S. Siampos (ed.), *Recent Population Change Calling for Policy Action* (Athens: National Statistical Service of Greece).

Macura, M. (1982) 'Pad Fertiliteta i Nastanak Niskog Fertiliteta u Jugoslaviji', u *Problem Obmavljanja Stanovsustva i Populaciona Politika* (Beograd: Ekonomski Institut).

Macura, M., B. Popovic and M. Rasevic (1977) *BACHUE-Yugoslavia: Regionalised Policy Simulation Economic-Demographic Model of Yugoslavia – Conceptual Basis* (Geneva: International Labour Office) mimeographed World Employment Programme research working paper restricted.

Maddala, G. S. (1971) 'The Use of Variance Components Models in Pooling Cross-Section and Time-Series Data', *Econometrica*, vol. 39 (March) 341–58.

Maddala, G. S., and T. D. Mount (1973) 'A Comparative Study of Alternative Estimators for Variance Components Models Used in Econometric Applications', *Journal of the American Statistical Association*, vol. 68 (June) 324–8.

Maddala, G. S. (1977) *Econometrics* (New York: McGraw-Hill).

Magnarella, P. (1979) *The Peasant Venture* (Boston: G. K. Hall and Co.).

Malinvaud, E. (1966) *Statistical Methods of Econometrics* (Chicago: Rand McNally and Co.).

Mamdani, Mahmoud (1972) *The Myth of Population Control: Family, Caste and Class in an Indian Village* (New York: Monthly Review Press).

Marin, Alan, and George Psacharopoulos (1976) 'Schooling and Income Distribution', *Review of Economics and Statistics*, vol. 48, 332–8.

Mason, Karen Oppenheimer, and V. T. Palan (1981) 'Female Employment and Fertility in Peninsular Malaysia: the Maternal Role Incompatibility Hypothesis Reconsidered', *Demography*, vol. 18, no. 4 (Nov.) 540–75.

Mauldin, W. Parker, Bernard Berelson and Zenas Sykes (1979) 'Conditions of Fertility Decline in Developing Countries, 1965–75', *Studies in Family Planning*, vol. 9, no. 5, 90–147.

Meek, Ronald K. (ed.) (1971) *Marx and Engels on the Population Bomb*, 2nd edn (New York: Ramparts Press).

Menken, J. (1975) 'Simulation Studies', in C. Chandrasekaran and A. I. Hermalin (eds), *Measuring the Effect of Family Planning Programmes on Fertility* (Dolhain, Belgium: Ordina Editions).

Merrick, T. W. (1978) 'Fertility and Land Availability in Rural Brazil', *Demography*, vol. 15, 321–36.

Mexico, Direccion General de Estadísticas (1975) 'Imagen Demográfica 1960–1973', *Estadísticas Vitales*, vol. I, no. 1.

Mexico, Secretaria de Industria y Comercio, Departamento de Estadísticas (1975) 'Imagen Demográfica 1960–1973', *Estadísticas Vitales*, vol. I, no. 1

Michael, Robert T., and R. J. Willis (1975) 'Contraception and Fertility', in N. E. Terleckyj (ed.), *Household Production and Consumption* (New York: National Bureau of Economic Research).

Miller, D., and I. Cetin (1974) 'Land and Man in Rural Turkey: a Concise View of Regional Land Tenure, Land Use, and Land Capability', Discussion Paper no. 20 (Ankara, Turkey: United States Agency for International Development).

Mincer, Jacob (1962) 'Labor Force Participation of Married Women', in H. Gregg Lewis (ed.), *Aspects of Labour Economics*, National Bureau of Economics Research, Universities National Bureau Conference Series, no. 14 (Princeton: Princeton University Press).

Mincer, Jacob (1963) 'Market Prices, Opportunity Costs, and Income Effects', in Carl Crist *et al.* (eds), *Measurement in Economics: Studies in Mathematical Economics and Econometrics in Memory of Yehuda Grunfeld* (Stanford: Stanford University Press) 67–82.

Miró, Carmen A., and Joseph E. Potter (1980a) *Population Policy: Research Priorities in the Developing World* (London: Frances Pinter).

Miró, Carmen A., and Joseph E. Potter (1980b) 'Social Science and Development Policy: the Potential Impact of Population Research', *Population and Development Review*, vol. 6, no. 3 (Sept.) 421–40.

Misra, B. D., A. Ashraf, R. Simmons and G. B. Simmons (1982) *Organizing for Change: a Systems Analysis of Fertility Planning in Rural India* (New Delhi: Radiant Publishers).

Misra, B. D., R. Simmons, A. Ashraf and G. B. Simmons (1976) 'The Dilemma of Family Planning in a North Indian State', *Studies in Family Planning*, vol. 7, no. 3 (March) 66–74.

Molnos, A. (1972) *Cultural Source Materials for Population Planning in East Africa* (Nairobi: East African Publishing House).

Morgan, R. W. (1975) 'Fertility Levels and Fertility Change', in J. C. Caldwell *et al.* (eds), *Population Growth and Socio-economic Change in West Africa* (New York: Columbia University Press).

Muellbaur, J. (1975) 'Aggregation Income Distribution and Consumer Demand', *Review of Economic Studies*, vol. 42, 525–43.

Muellbaur, J. (1976) 'Community Preferences and the Representative Consumer', *Econometrica*, vol. 44, 979–99.

Mueller, Eva (1972) 'Economic Motives for Family Limitation', *Population Studies*, vol. 26, no. 3 (Nov.) 383–403.

Mueller, Eva (1976) 'The Economic Value of Children in Peasant Agriculture', in Ronald G. Ridker (ed.), *Population and Development: the Search for Selective Interventions* (Baltimore: Johns Hopkins University Press for Resources for the Future) 98–153.

Mueller, Eva (1982) 'The Allocation of Women's Time and its Relationship to Fertility', in R. Anker *et al.* (eds), *Women's Roles and Population Trends in the Third World* (London: Croom Helm).

Mueller, Eva, and Richard Cohn (1977) 'The Relation of Income to Fertility Decisions', *Economic Development and Cultural Change*, vol. 25, no. 2 (Jan.) 325–47.

Mueller, Eva, and Kathleen Short (forthcoming) 'The Effect of Income and Wealth on the Demand for Children', in *Determinants of Fertility in Developing Countries: a Summary of Knowledge* (National Research Council).

Mundlak, Yair (1978) 'On the Pooling of Time Series and Cross-Section Data', *Econometrica*, vol. 46, no. 1 (Jan.) 69–85.

Nag, Moni (1980) 'How Modernization Can Also Increase Fertility', *Current Anthropology*, vol. 21, no. 5 (Oct.) 571–87.

Nag, Moni (1981) 'Economic Value and Costs of Children in Relation to Human Fertility', in Nick Eberstadt (ed.), *Fertility Decline in the Less Developed Countries* (New York: Praeger Publishers) pp. 274–94.

Nag, Moni, Benjamin N. F. White and Robert C. Peet (1978) 'An Anthropological Approach to the Study of Economic Value of Children in Java and Nepal', *Current Anthropology*, vol. 19, no. 2, 293–306.

Nag, Moni, R. Anker and M. E. Khan (1982) *A Guide to Anthropological Study of Women's Roles and Demographic Change in India* (Geneva: International Labour Office) mimeographed World Employment Programme research working paper; restricted.

Nakamura, M., A. Nakamura and D. Collen (1979) 'Job Opportunities, the Offered Wage, and the Labor Supply of Married Women', *American Economic Review*, vol. 69, no. 5 (Dec.) 787–805.

Namboodiri, N. K. (1972) 'Some Observations on the Economic Framework for Fertility Analysis', *Population Studies*, vol. 26, no. 2 (July) 185–206.

Naylor, Thomas H., *et al.* (1971) *Computer Simulation Experiments with Models of Economic Systems* (New York: John Wiley and Sons).

Nerlove, Marc (1971a) 'Further Evidence on the Estimation of Dynamic Relations from a Time Series of Cross Sections', *Econometrica*, vol. 39, no. 2 (March) 359–82.

Nerlove, Marc (1971b) 'A Note on Error-Components Models', *Econometrica*, vol. 39 (March) 383–96.

Nerlove, Marc, and T. Paul Schultz (1970) *Love and Life Between the Censuses: a Model of Family Decision Making in Puerto Rico, 1950–1960* (Santa Monica, California: Rand Corporation, September) RM-6322-AID.

Ness, Gayl D., and Hirofumi Ando (1984) *The Land is Shrinking: Population Planning in Asia* (Baltimore: Johns Hopkins University Press).

Nizamuddin, M. (1979) *The Impact of Community and Program Factors on the Fertility Behavior of Rural Pakistani Women,* PhD dissertation (Ann Arbor: University of Michigan).

Nortman, Dorothy L., and Ellen Hofstatter (1976) 'Population and Family Planning Programs: a Factbook', *Reports on Population/Family Planning,* no. 2, 8th edn.

Notestein, Frank W. (1944) 'Problems of Policy in Relation to Areas of Heavy Population Pressure', *Milbank Memorial Fund Quarterly,* vol. 22 (Oct.) 424–44.

Notestein, Frank W. (1945) 'Population – The Long View', in T. W. Schultz (ed.), *Food for the World* (Chicago: University of Chicago Press).

Notestein, Frank W. (1953 'Economic Problems of Population Change', in *Proceedings of the Eighth International Conference of Agri-Economists* (London: Oxford University Press).

Notestein, Frank W., Dudley Kirk and Sheldon Segal (1969) 'The Problem of Population Control', in P. Hauser (ed.), *The Population Dilemma* (New Jersey: Prentice Hall).

Nye, I. (1976) *Role Structure and the Analysis of the Family* (Sage Library of Social Research).

Olusanya, P. O. (1971a) 'The Problem of Multiple Causation in Population Analysis with Particular Reference to the Polygamy–Fertility Hypothesis', *The Sociological Review,* vol. 19, no. 2 (May) 165–78.

Olusanya, P. O. (1971b) 'Modernisation and the Level of Fertility in Western Nigeria', in *Proceedings of the International Population Conference, London, 1969* (Liege: International Union for the Scientific Study of Population).

Oppong, Christine (1973) *Growing Up in Dagbon* (Ghana Publishing Corporation).

Oppong, Christine (1974a) 'Attitudes to Family Type and Family Size: a study of Norms Among a Student Population', *International Journal of Sociology of the Family,* vol. 4, no. 2 (Autumn).

Oppong, Christine (1974b) 'Attitudes to Family Size Among Unmarried Junior Civil Servants in Accra', *Journal of African and Asian Studies,* vol. 9, nos 1–2 (Jan.–April).

Oppong, Christine (1975a) 'A Note on Attitudes to Jointness and Segregation and Family Size', *Human Relations,* vol. 28, no. 6.

Oppong, Christine (1975b) 'Norms and Variations: a Study of Ghanaian Students' Attitudes to Marriage and Family Living', in C. Oppong (ed.), *Changing Family Studies,* Family Research Paper no. 3 (Legon: Institute of African Studies).

Oppong, Christine (1976) 'Financial Constraints and Family Size', *Canadian Journal of African Studies,* vol. X, no. 3, 403–8.

Oppong, Christine (1977a) 'A Note on Chains of Change in Family Systems and Family Size', *Journal of Marriage and the Family* (Aug.) 615–21.

Oppong, Christine (1977b) 'The Crumbling of High Fertility Supports', in J. Caldwell (ed.), *The Persistence of High Fertility: Population Prospects in the Third World,* Family and Fertility Change Series no. 1 (Canberra: Australian National University Press) 331–60.

Oppong, Christine (1980) *A Synopsis of Seven Roles and Status of Women:*

An Outline of a Conceptual and Methodological Approach (Geneva: International Labour Office) mimeographed World Employment Programme research working paper; restricted.

Oppong, Christine (1982) *Middle Class African Marriage* (London: Allen and Unwin).

Oppong, Christine (ed.) (1983a) *Female and Male in West Africa* (London: Allen and Unwin).

Oppong, Christine (1983b) *Paternal Costs, Role Strain and Fertility Regulation: Some Ghanaian Evidence* (Geneva: International Labour Office) mimeographed World Employment Programme research working paper; restricted.

Oppong, Christine (1983c) 'Women's Roles, Opportunity Costs, and Fertility', in R. A. Bulatao and R. D. Lee with P. G. Hollerbach and J. Bongaarts (eds), *Determinants of Fertility in Developing Countries*, vol. 1: *Supply and Demand for Children* (New York: Academic Press).

Oppong, Christine, and K. Abu (1984) *The Changing Maternal Role of Ghanaian Women: Education, Migration and Employment* (Geneva: International Labour Office) mimeographed World Employment Programme research working paper; restricted.

Oppong, Christine, and W. Bleek (1982) 'Economic Models and Having Children: Some Kwahu Evidence from Ghana', *Africa*, vol. 52, no. 3.

Orcutt, M. H., M. Greenberg, J. Korbel and A. Rivlin (1961) *Micro-Analysis of Socio-economic Systems* (New York: Harper).

Orubuloye, I. O. (1979) 'The Significance of Breastfeeding for Fertility and Mortality in Africa', *Expert Group Meeting on Fertility and Mortality Levels, Patterns and Trends in Africa and Their Policy Implications* (Monrovia, Liberia, November; ECA, September).

Ozbay, Ferhunde (1979) 'Education and Fertility in Rural Turkey', *Middle East Technical University Studies in Development*, vol. 6, 51–68.

Ozbay, Ferhunde, F. Shorter and S. Yener (1977) 'Accounting for the Trend of Fertility in Turkey', *Demographic Transitions and Socio-economic Development*, Proceedings of the UN/UNFPA Expert Group Meeting (Istanbul, 27 April–4 May).

Page, H., and R. Lesthaege (eds) (1981) *Child Spacing in Tropical Africa: Traditions and Change* (New York: Academic Press).

Pakistan, Government of, Planning Commission (1978) *Fifth Five Year Plan* (Islamabad).

Palmore, James A., Jr (1975) *Measuring Fertility and Natural Increase: a Self-Teaching Guide to Elementary Measures* (Honolulu: East–West Population Institute).

Pang, Eng Fong (1975) 'Growth, Inequality and Race in Singapore', *International Labour Review*, vol. 111, 15–28.

Pelto, J., and G. Pelto (1978) *Anthropological Research: the Structure of Inquiry*, 2nd edn (Cambridge: Cambridge University Press).

Petersen, William (1960) 'The Demographic Transition in the Netherlands', *American Sociological Review*, vol. 25, 334–47.

Petersen, William (1971) 'The Malthus–Godwin Debate, Then and Now', *Demography*, vol. 8, no. 1 (Feb.) 13–26.

Petersen, William (1979) *Malthus* (Cambridge, Mass.: Harvard University

Press).

Petersen, William (1980) 'Further Comments on Malthus and *Malthus*', *Contemporary Sociology*, vol. 9, no. 4 (July) 469–71.

Phillips, James F., *et al.* (1982) 'The Demographic Impact of the Family Planning–Health Services Project in Matlab, Bangladesh', *Studies in Family Planning*, vol. 13, no. 5 (May) 131–40.

Piepmeier, K. B., and T. S. Adkins (1973) 'The Status of Women and Fertility', *Journal of Biosocial Science*, vol. 5, no. 4 (Oct.) 507–20.

Pollack, Robert A., and Michael L. Wachter (1975) 'The Relevance of the Household Production Function and Its Implication for the Allocation of Time', *Journal of Political Economy*, vol. 83, no. 2 (April) 255–77.

Population Council, International Research Program on the Determinants of Fertility (1981) 'Research on the Determinants of Fertility: a note on Priorities', *Population and Development Review*, vol. 7, no. 2 (June) 311–24.

Population Information Program (1979) *Age at Marriage and Fertility*, Population Reports, Special Topic Monograph, Series M, no. 4 (Baltimore: Johns Hopkins University).

Prais, S. J., and H. S. Houthakker (1955) *The Analysis of Family Budgets* (Cambridge: Cambridge University Press).

Pressat, R. (1967) *Pratique de la Demographie* (Paris: Dunod).

Preston, Samuel H. (1975) 'The Changing Relation Between Mortality and Level of Economic Development', *Population Studies*, vol. 29, no. 2 (July) 231–48.

Preston, Samuel H. (ed.) (1978) *The Effects of Infant and Child Mortality on Fertility* (New York: Academic Press).

Preston, Samuel H. (1980) 'Causes and Consequences of Mortality Declines in Less Developed Countries During the Twentieth Century', in Richard A. Easterlin (ed.), *Population and Economic Change in Developing Countries* (Chicago: University of Chicago Press).

Quandt, R. E. (1965) 'On Certain Small Sample Properties of k-Class Estimators', *International Economic Review*, vol. 6 (Jan.) 92–104.

Rainwater, L. (1965) *Family Design, Marital Sexuality, Family Size and Family Planning* (Chicago: Aldine Atherton).

Reining, P. (1981) *Anthropology of Fertility*, paper presented for the panel on Fertility Determinants, Committee on Population and Demography (Washington: Academy of Sciences) mimeographed.

Reining, P., *et al.* (1977) *Village Women, Their Changing Lives and Fertility: Studies in Kenya, Mexico and the Philippines* (AAAS).

Repetto, Robert G. (1974) 'The Interaction of Fertility and the Size Distribution of Income', Research Paper no. 8 (Cambridge, Mass.: Center for Population Studies, Harvard University).

Repetto, Robert G. (1977) 'Income Distribution and Fertility Change: a Comment', *Population and Development Review*, vol. 3, no. 4 (Dec.) 486–9, and reply by Birdsall.

Repetto, Robert G. (1978) 'The Interaction of Fertility and the Size Distribution of Income', *Journal of Development Studies*, vol. 14, no. 4, 22–38.

Repetto, Robert G. (1979) *Economic Equality and Fertility in Developing*

Countries (Baltimore: Johns Hopkins University Press for Resources for the Future).

Research Triangle Institute (1971) *Social and Economic Correlates of Family Fertility: a Survey of the Evidence* (North Carolina).

Retherford, R. D. (1979) 'A Theory of Rapid Fertility Decline in Homogeneous Populations', *Studies in Family Planning*, vol. 10, 61–7.

Rich, William (1973) *Smaller Families Through Social and Economic Progress*, Monograph no. 7 (Washington, DC: Overseas Development Council).

Robinson, Joan (1979) *Aspects of Development and Underdevelopment* (Cambridge: Cambridge University Press).

Robinson, W. S. (1950) 'Ecological Correlations and the Behavior of Individuals', *American Sociological Review*, vol. 15 (June) 351–7.

Rodgers, G. B. (1976) 'Fertility and Desired Fertility: Longitudinal Evidence from Thailand', *Population Studies*, vol. 30, no. 3 (Nov.) 511–26.

Rodgers, G. B. (1979) 'Income and Inequality as Determinants of Mortality: an International Cross-Section Analysis', *Population Studies*, vol. 33, no. 2 (July) 343–51.

Rodgers, G. B., M. J. D. Hopkins and R. Wéry (1978) *Population, Employment and Inequality: BACHUE-Philippines* (Farnborough: Saxon House, for the International Labour Office).

Rodgers, G. B., R. Wéry and M. J. D. Hopkins (1976) 'The Myth of the Cavern Revisited: Are Large Scale Behavior Models Useful?', *Population and Development Review*, vol. 2, nos 3–4 (Sept./Dec.) 395–409.

Rodgers, G. B., and R. Wéry (1977) *The Effects of Economic Policy on Fertility* (Geneva: International Labour Office) mimeographed World Employment Programme research working paper; restricted.

Rodríguez, Germán, and John Cleland (1980) *Socio-Economic Determinants of Marital Fertility in Twenty Countries: a Multivariate Analysis*, World Fertility Survey Conference, Substantive Findings Session no. 5 (July).

Rosenzweig, Mark R. (1977) 'The Demand for Children in Farm Households', *Journal of Political Economy*, vol. 85, no. 1 (Feb.) 123–46.

Rosenzweig, Mark R. and R. E. Evenson (1977) 'Fertility, Schooling and the Economic Contribution of Children in Rural India: an Econometric Analysis', *Econometrica*, vol. 45, no. 5 (July) 1065–79.

Rosenzweig, Mark R., and K. I. Wolpin (1980) 'Life Cycle Labor Supply and Fertility: Causal Inferences from Household Models', *Journal of Political Economy*, vol. 88, no. 2 (April) 328–48.

Rosenzweig, Mark R. and T. Paul Schultz (1982) 'Market Opportunities, Genetic Endowments, and Intrafamily Resource Distribution: Child Survival in Rural India', *American Economic Review*, vol. 72, no. 4 (Sept.) 803–15.

Roth, O. M., and D. L. Little (eds) (1981) *Rapid Population Growth in Third World Countries: an Overview of Social and Economic Effects and Their Relationship to US Multinational Corporations* (Washington, DC: Congressional Research Services, Sept.).

Russett, Bruce, Steven Jackson, Duncan Snidal and David Sylvan (1981)

'Health and Population Patterns as Indicators of Income Inequality', *Economic Development and Cultural Change*, vol. 29, no. 4 (July) 759–79.

Rutstein, Shea O. (1974) 'The Influence of Child Mortality on Fertility in Taiwan', *Studies in Family Planning*, vol. 5, no. 6 (June) 182–8.

Ryder, Norman B. (1959) 'Fertility', in P. M. Hauser and O. D. Duncan (eds), *The Study of Population* (Chicago: University of Chicago Press).

Ryder, Norman B. (1969) 'The Emergence of a Modern Fertility Pattern: United States, 1917–66', in S. J. Behrmann *et al.* (eds), *Fertility and Family Planning* (Ann Arbor: University of Michigan Press) 99–123.

Ryder, Norman B. (1972) 'Notes on the Concept of a Population', in M. W. Riley, M. Johnson and A. Foner (eds), *Aging and Society*, vol. 3: *A Sociology of Age Stratification* (New York: Russell Sage Foundation).

Ryder, Norman B. (1973) 'A Critique of the National Fertility Study', *Demography*, vol. 10, no. 4 (Nov.) 495–506.

Safilios-Rothschild, Constantia (1977) 'The Relationship Between Women's Work and Fertility: Some Methodological Issues', in S. Kupinsky (ed.), *The Fertility of Working Women: a Synthesis of International Research* (New York: Praeger Publishers) 355–68.

Samuelson, P. A. (1956) 'Social Indifference Curves', *Quarterly Journal of Economics*, vol. LXX, 1–22.

Sarma, M. T. R. *et al.* (1975) *Changes in Rural Income in India* (New Delhi: National Council of Applied Economic Research).

Sarma, M. T. R. (1976) *Effects of Household Structure, Size and Household Income on Expenditure Patterns* (Geneva: International Labour Office) mimeographed World Employment Programme research working paper; restricted.

Scanzoni, J. H. (1975) *Sex Roles, Life Style and Child Bearing* (New York: Free Press).

Scanzoni, J. H. (1976a) 'Gender Roles and the Process of Fertility Control', *Journal of Marriage and the Family*, vol. 38, 43–60.

Scanzoni, J. H. (1976b) 'Sex Role Change and Influences on Birth Intentions', *Journal of Marriage and the Family*, vol. 38, 43–60.

Scanzoni, J. H. (1980) 'Contemporary Marriage Types', *Journal of Family Issue*, vol. 1, no. 1 (March) 125–40.

Scanzoni, J. H., and M. Szinovacz (1980) *Family Decision-making, A Developmental Sex Role Model* (Sage Library of Social Research no. 111).

Schmidt, P. (1976) *Econometrics* (New York: Marcel Dekker).

Schultz, T. Paul (1969a) 'An Economic Model of Family Planning and Fertility', *Journal of Political Economy*, vol. 77, no. 2 (March/April) 153–80.

Schultz, T. Paul (1969b) *Population Growth and Internal Migration in Colombia* (Santa Monica, California: The Rand Corporation).

Schultz, T. Paul (1972) 'Fertility Patterns and Their Determinants in the Arab Middle East', in Charles A. Cooper and Sidney S. Alexander (eds), *Economic Development and Population Growth in the Middle East* (New York: American Elsevier) 339–500.

Schultz, T. Paul (1974a) 'Birth Rate Changes Over Space and Time', in

T. W. Schultz (ed.), *Economics of the Family: Marriages, Children, and Human Capital* (Chicago: University of Chicago Press) 255–91.

Schultz, T. Paul (1974b) *Fertility Determinants: a Theory, Evidence and an Application to Policy Evaluation* (Santa Monica, California: The Rand Corporation, Jan.) R-1016/RF/AID.

Schultz, T. Paul (1976a) 'Determinants of Fertility: a Micro-economic Model of Choice', in A. J. Coale (ed.), *Economic Factors in Population Growth* (New York: Halsted Press) 89–124.

Schultz, T. Paul (1976b) 'Interrelationships Between Mortality and Fertility', in Ronald Ridker (ed.), *Population and Development – The Search for Selective Interventions* (Baltimore: Johns Hopkins University Press) 239–89.

Schultz, T. Paul (1978a) 'Fertility and Child Mortality Over the Life Cycle: Aggregate and Individual Evidence', *American Economic Review*, vol. 68, no. 2 (May) 208–15.

Schultz, T. Paul (1978b) 'The Influence of Fertility on the Labour Force Behavior of Married Women: Simultaneous Equation Estimates', in Ronald G. Ehrenberg (ed.), *Research in Labor Economics: an Annual Compilation of Research*, vol. 2 (Greenwich, Conn.: JAI Press) 273–351.

Schultz, T. Paul (1980) 'An Economic Interpretation of the Decline in Fertility in a Rapidly Developing Country: Consequences of Development and Family Planning', in Richard A. Easterlin (ed.), *Population and Economic Change in Developing Countries* (Chicago: University of Chicago Press).

Schultz, T. Paul (1981) *Economics of Population* (Readings, Mass.: Addison-Wesley).

Schultz, Theodore W. (1974) 'Fertility and Economic Values', in T. W. Schultz (ed.), *Economics of the Family: Marriages, Children, and Human Capital* (Chicago: University of Chicago Press).

Scrimshaw, Susan C. M. (1978) 'Infant Mortality and Behavior in the Regulation of Family Size', *Population and Development Review*, vol. 4, no. 3 (Sept.) 383–403.

Shafer, W. and H. Sonnenschein (1981) 'Market Demand and Excess Demand Functions', in K. J. Arrow and M. Intriligator (eds), *Handbook of Mathematical Economics* (New York: Elsevier).

Shorter, F. C. (1968) *Estimating Turkish Mortality, Fertility and Age Structures: Application of Some New Techniques*, Reprint no. 53 (Ann Arbor: Population Studies Center, University of Michigan).

Shorter, F. C. (1969) 'Information on Fertility, Mortality and Population Growth in Turkey', in F. C. Shorter and B. Guvenc (eds), *Turkish Demography: Proceedings of a Conference* (Ankara, Turkey: Hacettepe University Press).

Shorter, F. C. (1971) 'Estimates of Crude Birth Rates from Place of Birth Data, 67 Provinces, 1955–1965', *Hacettepe Population Publications*, bull. 3, 1–7.

Shorter, F. C., and B. Tekce (1974) 'The Demographic Determinants of Urbanization in Turkey, 1935–1970', in P. Benedict, E. Tumertekin and F. Mansur (eds), *Turkey: Geographical and Social Perspectives*

(Leiden: E. J. Brill).

Shryock, Henry S., Jacob S. Siegel and associates (1973) *The Methods and Materials of Demography* (Washington, DC: US Government Printing Office).

Simmons, George B. (1979) 'Family Planning or Development: How Persuasive is the New Wisdom?', *International Family Planning Perspectives*, vol. 5, no. 3 (Sept.) 101–10.

Simmons, George B., Celeste Smucker, Stan Bernstein and Eric Jensen (1982) 'Postneonatal Mortality in Rural India: Implications of an Economic Model', *Demography*, vol. 19, no. 3 (Aug.) 371–89.

Simmons, George B., Celeste Smucker, Stan Bernstein and B. D. Misra (1979) 'Some Aspects of Infant and Child Mortality in Rural North India', *Social Issues*, vol. 29, 249–67.

Simmons, George B. *et al.* (1978) *Organisation for Change: A System Analysis of Family Planning in Rural India* (Ann Arbor: Center for Population Planning, University of Michigan).

Simmons, Ruth S., George B. Simmons, B. D. Misra and A. Ashraf (1975) 'Organizing for Government Intervention in Family Planning', *World Politics*, vol. 27, 569–96.

Simmons, Ruth, Gayl D. Ness and George B. Simmons (1983) 'On the Institutional Analysis of Population Programs, *Population and Development Review*, vol. 9, no. 3 (Sept.) 457–74.

Simon, H. B. (1968) 'Causation', in *International Encyclopedia of the Social Sciences* (New York: Macmillan).

Simon, Julian L. (1974) *The Effects of Income on Fertility*, Carolina Population Center Monograph 19 (Chapel Hill, North Carolina: University of North Carolina).

Simon, Julian L. (1977) *The Economics of Population Growth* (Princeton: Princeton University Press).

Smith, Stanley K. (1981) 'Determinants of Female Labor Force Participation and Family Size in Mexico City', *Economic Development and Cultural Change*, vol. 30, no. 1 (Oct.) 129–52.

Snyder, Donald W. (1974) 'Economic Determinants of Family Size in West Africa', *Demography*, vol. 11, no. 4 (Nov.) 613–27.

Sonnenschein, H. (1974) 'Market Excess Demand Functions', *Econometrica*, vol. 40, 549–63.

Srikantan, W. S. (1977) *The Family Planning Program in the Socioeconomic Context* (New York: The Population Council).

Standing, Guy (1978) *Labour Force Participation and Development* (Geneva: International Labour Office).

Standing, Guy, and G. Sheehan (eds) (1978) *Labour Force Participation in Low-Income Countries* (Geneva: International Labour Office).

Stark, O. (1978) 'Desired Fertility and Rural-to-Urban Migration in LDC's: the Positive Connection', Paper no. 6178 (The David Horwitz Institute for Research on Developing Countries, Sept.).

Steiner, S. (1977) *The Female Factor: a Study of Women in Five Western European Societies* (New York: G. P. Putnam and Sons).

Stinson, Wayne S., *et al.* (1982) 'The Demographic Impact of the Contraceptive Distribution Project in Matlab, Bangladesh', *Studies in Family*

Planning, vol. 13, no. 5 (May) 141-8.

Stirling, P. (1965) *Turkish Village* (London: Weidenfeld and Nicolson).

Stone, L. (1977) *The Family, Sex and Marriage in England, 1500-1800* (New York: Harper and Row).

Studies in Family Planning (1981) Special Issue: 'Focus Group Research', vol. 12, no. 12 (Dec.) pt I.

Stycos, Mayone J., *et al.* (1982) 'Contraception and Community in Egypt: a Preliminary Evaluation of the Population/Development Mix', *Studies in Family Planning*, vol. 13, no. 12 (Dec.) pt I, 365-72.

Sullivan, J. M. (1972) 'Models for the Estimation of the Probability of Dying between Birth and Exact Ages of Early Childhood', *Population Studies*, vol. 26, no. 1.

Summers, R. (1965) 'A Capital Intensive Approach to the Small Sample Properties of Various Simultaneous Equation Estimators', *Econometrica*, vol. 33 (Jan.) 1-41.

Swamy, P. A. V. B. (1971) *Statistical Inference in Random Coefficient Regression Models* (Berlin: Springer Verlag).

Tabbarah, Riad B. (1971) 'Toward a Theory of Demographic Development', *Economic Development and Cultural Change*, vol. 19, no. 2 (Jan.) 257-76.

Taylor, Carl E., J. S. Newman and Narindar U. Kelly (1976) 'The Child Survival Hypothesis', *Population Studies*, vol. 30, no. 2 (July) 263-78.

Thadani, Veena N. (1978) 'The Logic of Sentiment: the Family and Social Change', *Population and Development Review*, vol. 4, no. 3 (Sept.) 457-99.

Theil, Henri (1954) *Linear Aggregation of Economic Relations* (Amsterdam: North Holland).

Theil, Henri (1967) *Economics and Information Theory* (Chicago: Rand MacNally and Co.).

Theil, Henri (1971) *Principles of Econometrics* (New York: John Wiley and Sons).

Timur, Serim (1977) 'Demographic Correlates of Women's Education: Fertility, Age at Marriage and the Family', International Population Conference, Mexico 1977, vol. 3 (Liege: International Union for the Scientific Study of Population) 463-95.

Tobin, P. (1976) 'Conjugal Role Definitions, Value of Children and Contraception Practice', *Sociological Quarterly*, vol. 17, 314-22.

Toros, A. (1978) '1973 Arastirmasinda Dogurganlik' ('Fertility in the 1973 Survey'), in *Turkiye'de Nufus Yapisi ve Nufus Sorunlari 1973 Arastirmasi (Turkey's Population Structure and Population Problems: The 1973 Survey)* (Ankara, Turkey: Hacettepe University Publications).

Trussell, T. James (1975) 'A Re-estimation of the Multiplying Factors for the Brass Technique for Determining Childhood Survivorship Rates', *Population Studies*, vol. 29, no. 1 (March) 97-108.

Tsui, Amy Ong and Donald J. Bogue (1978) 'Declining World Fertility: Trends, Causes, Implications', *Population Bulletin*, vol. 33, no. 4 (Oct.).

Tuncer, Baran (1977) 'A Survey of Economic and Social Correlates of Turkish Fertility', in *Demographic Transition and Socio-economic Development*, Proceedings of the UN/UNFPA Expert Group Meeting

(Istanbul, 27 April–4 May).

Turchi, Boone (1975a) 'Microeconomic Theories of Fertility: a Critique', *Social Forces*, vol. 54, no. 1 (Sept.) 107–25.

Turchi, Boone (1975b) *The Demand for Children: the Economics of Fertility in the United States* (Cambridge: Ballinger Publishing Co.).

Turchi, Boone, and E. Bryant (1979) *Rural Development Activities, Fertility and the Cost and Value of Children* (Washington, DC: USAID).

Uner, S. (1978) 'Methodologi', ('Methodology'), *Turkiye'de Nufus Yapisi ve Nufus Sorunlari 1973 Arastirmasi (Turkey's Population Structure and Population Problems: The 1973 Survey)* (Ankara, Turkey: Hacettepe University Publications).

United Kingdom, Office of Health Economics (1972) *Medical Care in Developing Countries* (London: Office of Health Economics).

United Nations (published annually) *Demographic Yearbook* (New York).

United Nations (1975) *Poverty, Unemployment and Development Policy: a Case Study of Selected Issues with Reference to Kerala*, UN Publication, Sales no. E. 75. IV. 11. (New York).

United Nations (1979) *Prospects of Population: Methodology and Assumptions*, papers of the *Ad Hoc* Group of Experts on Demographic Projections, ch. IV (Nov. 1977, ST/ESA/SER.A/67, New York).

United Nations (1980) *World Population Trends and Policies: 1979 Monitoring Report*, vol. II, *Population Policies* (New York).

United Nations (1982) *Demographic Indicators of Countries: Estimates and Projections as Assessed in 1980* (New York).

United Nations, Department of Economic and Social Affairs (1975a) *Selected World Demographic Indicators by Countries 1950–2000* (New York: Population Division, Department of Economic and Social Affairs, United Nations Secretariat, ESA/P/WP.55).

United Nations, Department of Economic and Social Affairs (1975b) *Status of Women and Family Planning* (New York) 38–50.

UNESCO [United Nations Educational, Scientific and Cultural Organization] (published annually) *Statistical Yearbook* (Paris).

United Nations Fund for Population Activities [UNFPA] (1979a) *Report of a Conference on Population and Development Planning* (New York).

United Nations Fund for Population Activities (1979b) *Mexico, Documento de Antecedentes en Materia de Poblacion en Mexico* (Oct.).

United Nations Secretariat (1979) 'Measuring the Impact of Socio-Economic Factors on Fertility in the Context of Declining Fertility: Problems and Issues', in *Demographic Transition and Socio-Economic Development: Proceedings of the United Nations/UNFPA Expert Group Meeting* (Istanbul, 1977; New York) 38–55.

United States Bureau of the Census (1980) *World Population 1979 – Recent Demographic Estimates for the Countries and Regions of the World* (Washington, DC).

Uthoff, Andras, and Gerardo González (1976) *Women's Participation in Economic Activity as a Strategic Factor of Change in Fertility: the Case of Mexico and Costa Rica*, WEP 2-21/WP.42 (Nov.) (Geneva: International Labour Office).

Van Ginneken, Jeroen K. (1974) 'Prolonged Breastfeeding as a Birth Spacing Method', *Studies in Family Planning*, vol. 5, no. 6 (June) 201–6.

Van Ginneken, W. (1975) *Characteristics of the Head of the Household and Income Inequality in Mexico*, WEP 2-23/WP.16 (Geneva: International Labour Office).

Varian, Hal R. (1978) *Micro Economic Analysis* (New York: W.W. Norton).

Varian, Hal R. (1981) 'Social Indifference Curves and Aggregate Demand', Working Paper C-35 (Ann Arbor: University of Michigan).

Venkatacharya, K. (1978) 'Influence of Variations in Child Mortality on Fertility: a Simulation Model Study', in S. Preston (ed.), *The Effects of Infant and Child Mortality on Fertility* (New York: Academic Press) 235–57.

Wallace, T. D. and A. Hussain (1969) 'The Use of Error Components Models in Combining Cross Section with Time Series Data', *Econometrica*, vol. 37, no. 1 (Jan.) 55–72.

Ware, Helen (1974) *Ideal Family Size*, World Fertility Survey Occasional Papers, no. 13 (Oct.).

Ware, Helen (1975) 'The Relevance of Change in Women's Roles to Fertility Behavior: the African Evidence', presented at the Population Association of America' (Seattle).

Watson, Walter, B. (ed.) (1977) *Family Planning in the Developing World: a Review of Programs* (New York: The Population Council).

Webb, Richard C. (1977) *Government Policy and the Distribution of Income in Peru, 1963–1973*, Economic Studies no. 147 (Cambridge: Harvard University Press).

Weller, Robert H. (1968a) 'The Employerment of Wives, Dominance and Fertility', *Journal of Marriage and the Family*, vol. 30, no. 3 (Aug.) 437–42.

Weller, Robert H. (1968b) 'The Employment of Wives, Role Incompatibility and Fertility: a Study Among Lower- and Middle-Class Residents of San Juan, Puerto Rico', *Milbank Memorial Fund Quarterly*, vol. 46, no. 4 (Oct.) 507–26.

Wéry, R., G. B. Rodgers and M. J. D. Hopkins (1978) 'Population, Employment and Poverty in the Philippines', *World Development*, vol. 6, 519–22.

Wilkinson, M. (1973) 'An Econometric Analysis of Fertility in Sweden, 1870–1965', *Econometrica*, vol. 41, no. 4 (July) 633–42.

Williams, Anne D. (1976) 'Review and Evaluation of the Literature', in Michael C. Keeley (ed.), *Population, Public Policy and Economic Development* (New York: Praeger Publishers) 119–59.

Williams, Anne D. (1977) 'Measuring the Impact of Child Mortality on Fertility: a Methodological Note', *Demography*, vol. 14, no. 4 (Nov.) 581–90.

Williamson, Nancy E. (1982) 'An Attempt to Reduce Infant and Child Mortality in Bohol, Philippines', *Studies in Family Planning*, vol. 13, no. 4 (April) 106–17.

Willis, Robert J. (1973) 'A New Approach to the Economic Theory of Fertility Behavior', *Journal of Political Economy*, vol. 81, no. 2, pt II (March/April) S14–69.

Winegarden, C. R. (1978) 'A Simultaneous-equations Model of Population

Growth and Income Distribution', *Applied Economics*, vol. 10, 319–30.

Winegarden, C. R. (1979) 'Schooling and Income Distribution: Evidence from International Data', *Economica*, vol. 46, 83–7.

Winegarden, C. R. (1980) 'Socioeconomic Equity and Fertility in Developing Countries: a Block-Recursive Model', *De Economist*, vol. 128, 530–57.

Wold, H. (1954) 'Causality and Econometrics', *Econometrica*, vol. 22, 162–77.

World Bank (1971) *World Tables* (Washington, DC).

World Bank (1974) *Population Policies and Economic Development* (Baltimore: Johns Hopkins University Press).

World Bank (1976) *World Tables 1976* (Baltimore: Johns Hopkins University Press, for the World Bank).

World Health Organisation [WHO] (1974) 'Health Trends and Prospects in Relation to Population and Development', in *The Population Debate: Dimensions and Perspectives*, papers of the World Population Conference (Bucharest) vol. 1, pp. 573–97.

Wray, Joe D. (1971) 'Population Pressure on Families: Family Size and Child Spacing', in Roger Revelle *et al.* (eds), *Rapid Population Growth: Consequences and Policy Implications*, vol. II, prepared by a Study Committee of the Foreign Secretary, National Academy of Sciences (Baltimore: Johns Hopkins University Press) 403–60.

Wyon, John B. and John E. Gordon (1971) *The Khanna Study: Population Problems in the Rural Punjab* (Cambridge, Mass.: Harvard University Press).

Zachariah, K. C. (1973) 'Fertility, Mortality, and Population Growth Interrelations and Policy Implications', Bank Staff Working Paper no. 163 (Washington, DC: World Bank).

Index